MIND/BODY HEALTH

The Effects of Attitudes, Emotions, and Relationships

Brent Q. Hafen
Brigham Young University

Keith J. Karren
Brigham Young University

Kathryn J. Frandsen
Novell, Inc.

N. Lee Smith, M.D.
University of Utah, School of Medicine

Allyn and Bacon
Boston • London • Toronto • Sydney • Tokyo • Singapore

Senior Series Editor: Suzy Spivey
Editor-in-Chief, Social Sciences: Susan Badger
Editorial Assistant: Lisa Davidson
Executive Marketing Manager: Anne Harvey
Senior Production Administrator: Susan McIntyre
Editorial-Production Service: Ruttle, Shaw & Wetherill, Inc.
Cover Administrator: Suzanne Harbison
Composition Buyer: Linda Cox
Manufacturing Buyer: Megan Cochran

Copyright © 1996 by Allyn & Bacon
A Simon & Schuster Company
Needham Heights, Massachusetts 02194

Library of Congress Cataloging-in-Publication Data

Mind/body health: the effects of attitudes, emotions, and relationships / Brent
    Q. Hafen . . . [et al.].
        p.   cm.
    Includes bibliographical references and index.
    ISBN 0-205-17211-3
        1. Medicine, Psychosomatic.   2. Emotions—Health aspects.
    3. Psychoneuroimmunology.   I. Hafen, Brent Q.
    RC49.M522   1996
    616'.001'9--dc20
                                                                    95-13437
                                                                    CIP

Printed in the United States of America

10 9 8 7 6   00 99 98

CONTENTS

PART IV *Spirituality and Health*

PART V *Perception and Health*

Jan 01 (handwritten)

PREFACE

In the pages that follow you'll learn what we know about how emotions and attitudes affect health. Drawing on landmark scientific studies by distinguished researchers, we build a solid foundation of evidence that shows the undeniable connection between the mind and the body. You'll see how "negative" emotions such as worry, anxiety, depression, hostility, and anger, when nurtured, can increase susceptibility to disease, and how "positive" emotions such as optimism, humor, and a fighting spirit can protect your health and help to heal. We hope you will be able to see a little bit of yourself in these pages and will be able to make some affirmations about what you will do with the emotions you experience in the course of everyday living. In exploring the powerful connection between your mind and body, we discuss:

- how your body responds to the way you see yourself and your circumstances;
- why social support, friendship, and strong, stable relationships protect your health;
- how different personalities are either prone to, or able to resist, disease;
- the scientifically-proven changes in your body chemistry, heart rate, and hormones that accompany various attitudes and emotions; and
- how attitudes and emotions actually affect your immunity from disease.

Above all, what is written here may help you learn to appreciate the tremendous healing power of your mind and your heart, and may help you focus both on an appreciation of life itself. Perhaps former *Saturday Review* editor Norman Cousins said it best in these words:*

An appreciation of life can be a prime tonic for mind and body. Being able to respond to the majesty of the way nature fashions its art—the mysterious designs in the barks of trees, suggesting cave paintings or verdant meadows interrupted

*Norman Cousins, *Head First, The Biology of Hope* (New York: E. P. Dutton, 1989).

by silvery streams; the rich and luminous coloring of carp fish with blues and yellows and crimsons seemingly lit up from within; the bird of paradise flower, an explosion of colors ascending to a triumphant and jaunty crest of orange and purple; the skin of an apple, so thin it defies measurement but supremely protective of its precious substance; they say the climbing trunk of a tree will steer its growth around solid objects coming between itself and the sun; the curling white foam of an ocean wave advancing on the shore, and the way sand repairs and smooths itself by the receding water; the purring of a kitten perched on your shoulder, or the head of a dog snuggling under your hand; the measured power of Beethoven's Emperor Concerto, *the joyous quality of a Chopin nocturne, the serene and stately progression of a Bach fugue, the lyrical designs in a Mozart composition for clarinet and strings; the sound of delight in a young boy's voice on catching his first baseball; and, most of all, the expression in the face of someone who loves you—all these are but a small part of a list of wondrous satisfactions that come with the gift of awareness and that nourish even as they heal.*

The Tomato Effect?

Take your mind back several hundred years to a simple, rough-hewn dinner table somewhere in colonial North America. No one was eating tomatoes because they were "poisonous." Everyone knew they were poisonous. After all, they were a member of the nightshade family, and members of the nightshade family were poisonous.

The fact "that the French and Italians were eating tomatoes in increasing quantities without seeming harm did not encourage colonial Americans to try them. It simply did not make sense to eat poisonous food. Not until 1820, when Robert Gibbon Johnson ate a tomato on the steps of the courthouse in Salem, New Jersey, and survived, did the people of America begin, grudgingly, we suspect, to consume tomatoes."*

"The tomato effect," as scientists call it, happens in medicine when "an efficacious treatment for a certain disease is ignored or rejected because it does not 'make sense' in light of accepted theories of disease mechanism and drug action. The tomato was ignored because it was clearly poisonous; it would have been foolish to eat one. In analogous fashion, there have been many therapies in the history of medicine that, while later proved highly efficacious, were at one time rejected because they did not make sense."*

You've undoubtedly savored the rich pungency of a juicy tomato—either fresh from the garden, sliced and lightly sprinkled with salt, or ladled over a steaming plate of firm spaghetti noodles and dusted with parmesan cheese.

*James S. Goodwin and Jean M. Goodwin, "The Tomato Effect: Rejection of Highly Efficacious Therapies," *Journal of the American Medical Association*, May 11, 1984.

There's nothing poisonous there. So we ask you to savor the evidence presented in this book. Nothing here will hurt you. On the contrary, you may find information that will change your life, enhance your health, and help you live a richer, fuller existence in return.

1

THE MIND–BODY CONNECTION

Great men are they who see that spiritual force is stronger than any material force, that thoughts rule the world.
—RALPH WALDO EMERSON

In a pronouncement that at first surprised the medical community, if not the lay public, one practitioner proclaimed that an estimated 90 percent of all physical problems have emotional roots. He followed up by saying that his estimate was, at best, conservative. A growing body of evidence indicates that virtually every illness known to modern humanity—from arthritis to migraine headaches, from the common cold to cancer—is influenced, for good or bad, by our emotions.

The very words we use to describe our emotions are revealing. Arthur J. Barsky, author of *Worried Sick: Our Troubled Quest for Wellness*, put it this way:

> *We feel emotions in our bodies. We "burn" with anger, "tremble" with fear, feel "choked up" with sadness; our "stomachs turn" with revulsion. Everyone tends to experience unpleasant emotions as unpleasant bodily symptoms and thus to feel physically distressed when emotionally distressed.[1]*

What we have learned from the most recent research in the exciting new field of psychoneuroimmunology is this: Illnesses don't just happen to us. Many are caused by bacteria, viruses, fungi, or other microbes. But what factors work together to determine whether we will fall ill when exposed to these microscopic troublemakers? What determines our immunity?

Part of it could be emotional. In a thirty-year study of initially healthy young men, those with the most mature emotions and psychological style—including a sense of humor, an altruistic bent, and so on—were the healthiest thirty years later.[2] And the health differences at middle age were striking. After thirty-five years, only 3 percent of those who dealt with the stresses of life in a mature, adaptive way had any chronic illness, as compared with 38 percent who were either dead or chronically ill in the other, less mature, groups (who coped by using denial, blaming, repression, and intellectualization). This says something important is going on with regard to where our most important preventive medicine may lie. Much will be said in later chapters about that mature, adaptive coping style, and also about what happens to health when we consciously develop it.

Internist Roger Hill said that, based on his twelve years of practice, "The mental status of a patient definitely does affect the rate of recovery from disease." Gastroenterologist Joseph Duva pointed out that he does "a lot of psychological counseling in my practice. I've told patients to change jobs, seek marriage counseling, or spend more time with their spouses. In each of these instances, I felt that emotions were affecting the patient's physical health." Duva concluded his comments with the observation that "medical school never taught us to treat emotions. I remember being instructed on how to measure the muscle contractions of the colon, but I never learned what psychological factors bring on these contractions."

While the controversy continues, a growing number of respected physicians and researchers are taking a hard new look at the burgeoning body of evidence that points to an almost revolutionary concept: What is going on inside our minds, our hearts, and our spirits may have tremendous impact on what happens to our bodies.

The Role Emotions Play in Disease

Can emotions—the way we think, the way we feel—really be responsible, at least in part, for disease? A growing body of evidence indicates that they can. Some researchers in the field believe that as many as half of all patients who visit physicians have physical symptoms that are directly caused by emotions; others believe that the figure is as high as 90 to 95 percent. That's not to say that the symptoms are imaginary; it's just to say that their root is primarily mental more than organically physical.

In reality, it may be too simplistic to say that emotional stress *causes* disease. More accurately, it is only one important factor that appears to create a vulnerability in the body's resistance mechanisms when it is exposed to other causative factors. Normal "homeostasis," the optimal balance of hormones, immunity, and nervous system functioning, protects us from the many threats to health we encounter daily. Disrupted emotional responses, feeling "out of control," leads to disrupted homeostasis. Physiological processes then get out of control. Interestingly, the same part of the midbrain that controls most automatic homeostasis and keeps physiology balanced also controls emotional response, allowing responses to be "enough, but not too much."

There's a physiological reason why emotions can impact health. According to research, different parts of the brain are associated with specific emotions, and they are also associated with specific hormone patterns. The release of certain hormones, then, is associated with different emotional responses, and those hormones affect health.[3] We know, for example, that emotionally induced shifts in hormones can lead to chronic disease, such as high blood pressure. When a person is aggressive and anxious, for example, too much norepinephrine and epinephrine are secreted, even at rest. The arteries thicken, and the excess hormones

Focus on Research

In one unique study, psychosomatic disease experts W. J. Grace and D. T. Graham conducted in-depth interviews with patients suffering from the symptoms of one of twelve different diseases. The researchers tried to identify what life situations were associated with attacks of the patients' syndromes.

The results showed a pattern that was at once revealing and meaningful. Patients had diarrhea when they wanted to end a particular situation or to get rid of something or somebody; they had constipation when they were grimly determined to persevere through a seemingly insurmountable problem. They felt nauseated or vomited when they wished something had never occurred; they developed ulcers when they had the desire for revenge or getting even.

Patients suffered from hives that eventually blistered and became inflamed when they felt interfered with or were prevented from doing something they wanted to do. These patients felt they couldn't find a way to deal effectively with their problem.

Those with hay fever and asthma faced a situation they would rather not have had to confront—or that they wished would disappear. The hay fever and asthma victims had circumstances they wanted to hide from, avoid, or divest themselves of responsibility for.

People with migraine headaches felt provoked after making an intense effort to complete a task. And people with low back pain wanted to do something involving the entire body—usually running away. Finally, people with hypertension continually worried about meeting all possible threats.

Source: Dennis T. Jaffe, *Healing From Within* (New York: Bantam Books, 1980).

cause blood vessel muscles to constrict. The gradual rise in blood pressure can then result in hypertension, stroke, or heart failure.[4]

Obviously, these were results from an isolated study that involved just more than a hundred people, so they shouldn't be generalized. Not everyone with diarrhea is trying to end an unpleasant situation, for example. But what we can learn from this study (and from the trends it established) is that emotions can and do play a vitally important role in physical illness.

In a national survey of adult black Americans, those who had many and intense emotional problems were more likely to have physical illnesses too, even after controlling for socioeconomic level and other factors. Those who had emotional upsets were much more likely to have ulcers, hypertension, diabetes, kidney problems, nervous system malfunctions, and circulatory system difficulties.[5]

Other studies have borne similar results. It has long been believed, for instance, that as many as 70 percent of all people who go to a gastrointestinal specialist have irritable bowel syndrome, a mixture of pain, diarrhea, constipation, nausea, and, sometimes, vomiting. Most are women, and most have some kind of an emotional problem. One-fourth of gastroenterology patients have major depression.

One scientific study reported in the *Medical Journal of Australia* tested what would happen when irritable bowel syndrome patients received psychotherapy instead of conventional medical treatment for their condition. The result was that symptoms among the treated patients improved dramatically.[6] After receiving counseling for their emotional upsets, 89 percent of the patients reported less pain as a result; 96 percent had less diarrhea, 90 percent less constipation, 92 percent were less nauseated, and 81 percent had less vomiting. Researchers who conducted the study concluded that "the symptoms of irritable bowel syndrome were seen as a physical expression of emotions caused by recent loss or ongoing stressful life situations."

Feeling these emotions is only one factor in the subsequent development of disease. Many researchers believe that the inability to express emotions is an even greater cause of disease. Studies have confirmed that the failure to perceive and express emotions can lead to various disease states.[7]

Loyola University Medical Center professor of psychiatry Domeena Renshaw maintains that "emotions have to be expressed somewhere, somehow. If they're repeatedly suppressed, and there is conflict about controlling them, they then often show themselves through physical symptoms." Renshaw thinks women have been culturally taught to keep negative emotions within the family, and to keep anger suppressed.

Others agree with Renshaw about the deleterious effects of suppressing emotion. Yale surgeon Bernie S. Siegel, well known for his humanistic work with cancer patients, put it this way:

> *Patients must be encouraged to express all their angers, resentments, hatred, and fears. These emotions are signs that we care to the utmost when our lives are threatened. Time after time, research has shown that people who give vent to their negative emotions survive adversity better than those who are emotionally constricted. Among patients with spinal-cord injuries, those who express strong grief and anger make more progress in rehabilitation than those with a more stoical attitude. Mothers who show great distress after giving birth to a deformed infant give the child better care than those who seem to take the misfortune calmly. In a study of people living near Three Mile Island, Dr. Andrew Baum found that those who showed their rage and fear suffered far less from stress and psychological problems than those who took a "rational" approach. Unexpressed feelings depress your immune response.[8]*

In a battery of tests conducted by Leonard Derogatis, it was found that breast cancer patients who showed little emotion were the ones who died early on. The "survivors" were the ones who felt and openly expressed a lot of anger, fear, depression, and guilt.[9] Apparently the process of suppressing emotion contributed to the tenacity of the disease.

Another physician believes, "Physical problems are often an expression of emotions we can't experience or display—to ourselves or others. In the case of those who are overweight, the extra pounds may be emotional armor, a fleshy cage that keeps feelings they don't like—loneliness, anxiety, sadness—penned up where they can't see them."[10]

Sometimes, because of complex emotional situations, we may even "create" illness or turn to it as a solution. According to Siegel,

[Sickness] gives people "permission" to do things they would otherwise be inhibited from doing. It can make it easier to say no to unwelcome burdens, duties, jobs, or the demands of other people. It can serve as permission to do what one has always wanted but has always been "too busy" to start. It can allow a person to take time off to reflect, meditate, and chart a new course. It can serve as an excuse for failure. It can make it easier to request and accept love, speak your feelings, or otherwise be more honest. Even a cold has a meaning. Often, its message is, "You've been working too hard. Go home and nurture yourself." Remember we are brought up on "sick days," not "health days." Take days to meet your needs and you won't need an illness.[11]

Siegel also points out that getting sick can provide needed balm for emotional woes. Throughout our lives, he says, "We're trained to associate sickness with rewards. We get to stay in bed and relax. People send us cards and flowers. Friends visit us and tell us they love us. Parents and spouses bring us chicken soup and read to us."[12]

As mentioned earlier, emotions can even play a role in the development of infectious diseases. Infectious diseases such as infectious hepatitis or gonorrhea are caused by identifiable microorganisms such as bacteria or viruses. But emotions can determine in part how susceptible we are to these infectious agents, and whether they will actually make us sick.

An excellent example is the herpes simplex virus, the culprit that causes fever blisters and cold sores. Most adults harbor this virus in a quiescent state at all times. It often resides around the nostrils and the mouth but remains dormant and does not cause sores. Sometimes, in response to lowered resistance, it flares up, especially when the person is ill with something else (such as the common cold). Many times, it flares up in response to emotional upset. In fact, mental stress is the most common precipitant of herpes skin lesions.

A number of studies have demonstrated the power of emotions in bringing on an attack of herpes virus infection. In one, University of Vienna researchers Robert Heilig and Hans Hoff placed three patients under hypnosis and then reminded them of unpleasant situations (such as the death of a loved one). All three patients developed active herpes breakouts in response to the *suggestion* of a situation that evoked powerful negative emotions.[13]

Medical officer Jerome M. Schneck at California's Fort MacArthur recalls a soldier who could accurately predict when his herpes simplex infection would become active. He knew that as soon as he felt hostile emotions, he could anticipate a breakout. He also learned that if he channeled his hostility into something else (such as reading), he was able to prevent the lesions from erupting.[14]

One of the reasons strong negative emotions can cause illness, even infectious disease, is that they may, over time, disrupt the immune system. When we experience strong emotions, the internal organs respond by preparing to flee or strike out (the classic "flight or fight response" characteristic of stress). Glandular activity sends hormones coursing through the bloodstream, which in turn send messages back to the nervous system. Sometimes immediately, but more often gradually, these messages wear down the immune system. In a sense, our immunity against disease is affected by the emotions we feel.[15] The mechanisms of this are discussed further in Chapter 2.

A growing body of evidence suggests that emotions send chemical messages to the brain; in response, the brain alters involuntary physiologic responses. The resulting alteration may affect the way the immune system responds to messages from the brain in the presence of disease.[16]

According to William L. Mundy, clinical professor of medicine at the University of Missouri School of Medicine, immune cells "might actually have a mind of their own." In discussing how people react to stress, Mundy points out that the immune system does exactly the same thing by responding to stressors with a fight-or-flight response of their own.[17]

New research indicates that the immune system may be affected by *any* kind of emotion, negative or positive. In an interesting study, Margaret Kemeny, an assistant professor of psychiatry and behavioral sciences at UCLA, had actors participate in monologues that elicited either happy or sad emotions. Throughout the experience, researchers tested the actors' blood to measure immune function. When Kemeny and her colleagues analyzed their findings, there were several surprises. First, the immune system was affected significantly by both happiness and sadness—in other words, by both positive and negative emotions. Second, Kemeny and her colleagues were surprised by how quickly the immune system responded. "We saw an increase in killer cells within twenty minutes," she said. "And then, once the actor got out of the negative state or the positive state and was sitting quietly for half an hour, the immune system returned to normal." The third surprise may have been the greatest: during intense sadness, the immune system actually *rallied.* The researchers working with Kemeny discovered that during intense short-term sadness there was an increase in the actual number of natural killer cells as well as an efficiency in the way the natural killer cells worked.[18] The response to *long-term* sadness and stress is a different story.

The Emotion Connection to Various Conditions

Research into the impact of emotions is gradually changing the way we look at disease, and it has prompted even more research by scientists eager to see if there really is a connection. Emrika Padus edited a book called *The Complete Guide to Your Emotions and Your Health*, a comprehensive volume that outlines what has been established about the disease–emotion connection. Its conclusions show that emotions have a strong influence on a wide variety of conditions—everything from automobile accidents to skin disease.[19]

Accidents

Problems at home, on the job, in a marriage, or with children, render us unlikely to give 100 percent attention to whatever we're doing, and the odds of having an accident increase, sometimes dramatically. Researcher Abraham Bergman and his colleagues at the University of Washington in Seattle conducted a study of 103 junior high school boys. During the five months of the study, the boys reported any life changes (characteristic of evoking strong emotion) and any accidents. At the end of the five-month research period, Bergman and his colleagues tallied the score. The results were revealing. The boys who were under little stress and emotion from life changes suffered a total of 395 accidents. Those who were under high levels of stress (and therefore experiencing strong emotion) had 946 accidents.

In another study, researchers tested thirty-one nurses. They tallied all positive and negative "challenging events" in the nurses' lives (ranging from illness or injury to the birth of a grandchild). From the data collected, they used emotional vulnerability to predict which nurses were most likely to have accidents in the following weeks. The link between emotions and accident-proneness was so strong that the researchers were successful in predicting which nurses would be involved in a rash of accidents or job-related errors.

Emotions also correlated to the likelihood of having car accidents. Researchers from the University of Michigan gave a questionnaire to 500 men; in the survey, they were asked to list the number of automobile accidents they had been involved in during the previous year as well as any stressful or emotional events during that same year. The accidents and the emotional events matched up. The researchers concluded that the events most likely to "predict" an automobile accident were physical stress responses (smoking, insomnia, headaches, and ulcers, for example); problems with parents or in-laws; problems or pressure in school or on the job; and financial problems.

Allergies and Asthma

The process involved in allergy is fairly basic: The white blood cells, part of the body's defense system, mistake a harmless substance (such as wheat or pollen) for an enemy agent. In response, the white cells produce antibodies that latch onto cells in the nose, throat, lungs, stomach, intestines, or skin in readiness for battle. The result is a full-blown allergy attack.

The most common antibody produced in allergy is Immunoglobulin E (IgE). Research has shown that stress and emotional strain cause the level of IgE in the blood of animals to increase. In one study, guinea pigs were subjected first to stress and then to a chemical irritant. They showed greater skin sensitivity to the irritant than did a similar group of mice that had not first been stressed. Studies of humans show similar results.

Physiologically, asthma is much the same as allergies. Repeated studies have shown that bronchial asthma is closely tied to emotional factors; feelings of frustration and conflict are often what trigger an attack. Psychiatrist Iris R. Bell concludes that, based on scientific evidence, any period of stress or intense emotion can weaken the immune system so that you react more easily to food or chemicals, which can increase susceptibility to either asthma or allergies.

A study of people said to be "allergic to everything" (i.e., those who have multiple chemical, pollen, and food reactions) found that 62 percent had major depression or anxiety disorders[20] (and perhaps more had a milder form of mental distress). Clinical experience has shown that effectively treating such patients for these mental components reduces the allergic reactions, allowing safe exposure to substances that were previously intolerable.

Angina and Heart Disease

Angina—chest pain that occurs when the heart muscle is temporarily deprived of oxygen—can be caused by physical exertion. It can be aggravated by emotional stress as well. "Excessive stress can trigger an angina attack," points out James L. Levenson, assistant professor of psychiatry at the Medical College of Virginia. "In some forms of stress the adrenal glands secrete epinephrine—the hormone associated with the 'fight or flight' response. This, in turn, increases heart rate and blood pressure and hence the workload on the heart. . . . Some patients may be more vulnerable to artery spasms at these times."

Heart disease, too, has long been associated with emotional stress.[21] As early as the seventeenth-century, physician William Harvey, credited with discovering the circulatory system, noted, "Every affliction of the mind that is attended with pain, pleasure, hope, or fear is the cause of an agitation whose influence extends to the heart."

According to comprehensive research, the most common feature of sudden cardiac death is "marked emotional perturbation," a flood of strong emotion. The most provocative emotional circumstances that lead to sudden death include the death of or threat of injury to a close person, the early grief period following any loss, and the threat of personal injury.

Extreme emotional stress in people with otherwise structurally normal hearts can lead to primary arrhythmias (disturbance in heart rhythm that causes it to beat unusually fast or slow). In people who have coronary artery disease, the effects of emotional stress are even more severe and can result in angina, silent ischemia, or fatal arrhythmias.

In one study of twenty-five persons who suffered life-threatening arrhythmias following acute emotional stress, eleven had no heart disease. Two follow-up studies showed that people can suffer life-threatening disruptions of the heart rhythm in response to emotional stress, even if they have no underlying heart disease.

Arthritis

A wide variety of studies have focused on the causes of arthritis, and emotional upheaval or stress keeps surfacing as a significant factor in the disease. In one study, researchers found that arthritis sufferers "try overly hard to be nice to other people, to not lean on others for emotional support, and to stow things away down inside, especially anger." Researchers who conducted the study pointed out that those traits antedated the arthritis, not the other way around.

The situation is similar for sufferers of rheumatoid arthritis. Many have a history of long-term tension or emotional upheaval in their lives. In addition, says clinical psychologist Robert Fathman, they are generally full of inner turmoil, likely to be excessively conscientious, fearful of criticism, frequently depressed, and battling a poor self-image. The end result, according to Fathman, is that "these people have so much repressed anger that it 'eats them up.' The anger gets turned against the person herself." Fathman also pointed out that perhaps one reason women are afflicted with rheumatoid arthritis as much as four times more frequently than men is "because of what we do to little girls in our society. We teach them that it's wrong to get angry."

Renowned rheumatologist Loring T. Swaim concluded, after years in private practice, that emotional factors are crucial in the development, and perhaps even the causation, of rheumatoid arthritis. Based on results of the studies being done today, a growing number of researchers are agreeing with that assessment.

In one study conducted by physician John Baum and his colleagues at the University of Rochester, researchers studied the medical records of eighty-eight children who had been treated for juvenile rheumatoid arthritis at a Rochester hospital. They found that 28 percent of the children had come from broken homes—a much higher percentage from broken homes than among the general population. For half of the children, the divorce or death of a parent had occurred within two years of the onset of the disease.

A landmark study conducted by George Solomon and Rudolph Moos, at the Stanford University School of Medicine, suggested that emotions can overcome genetics. Their results indicated that even those who are genetically predisposed to arthritis can avoid the disease by staying emotionally healthy. Genetic disposition to rheumatoid arthritis is indicated by a blood factor present in arthritis patients as well as in about 20 percent of their healthy relatives. The common thread in the healthy relatives that may have protected them against the arthritis, according to researchers, is emotional resiliency and buoyancy. "We assume from this that if you have the rheumatoid factor in your blood but stay in good condition psychologically, you won't get arthritis," say Solomon and Moos. "On the other hand, if you're genetically predisposed, and endure long periods of anxiety and/or depression or suffer some major emotional upset, you are at high risk for arthritis."

Back Pain

Based on current studies, researchers estimate that as many as 95 percent of all backaches are triggered by the psyche, not by physical abnormalities or by heavy lifting. According to New York psychiatrist Hans Draus, back muscles tense up in response to emotional stress. If the muscles remain tensed too long, they start to hurt. The same mechanism causes tension headaches. Tense muscles are more prone to injury. So if you're emotionally upset and your back muscles are tense, you're more likely to injure it with even minor exertion.

One physician who believes that back pain is an emotional response to a difficult circumstance, Dr. Leon Root, says that "an individual develops pain in his back as a defense mechanism in a situation in which he finds he can no longer cope with emotional difficulties." Root is quick to add that the pain the person feels is as real as if he had suffered a back injury and it must be treated just as earnestly.

Cancer

Cancer is a far-reaching malady. Statistics tell us that it affects three of four families. About a third of all Americans living today will contract cancer in their lifetime, and cancer kills more children between ages three and fourteen years than any other disease. Someone dies from cancer in the United States approximately every minute.

According to the most widely accepted theory, cancer cells are constantly being formed from normal cells in the body, but "as long as the individual's natural immune system holds up, these cells are detected and destroyed before they can begin to multiply. When a person's body defenses break down, the cells grow and reproduce and cancer develops. It may be that psychological factors affect the strength of the immune system, and thereby play a part in the occurrence of cancer."[22]

Some studies at the University of Pennsylvania involved injecting cancer cells into animals under much mental stress, then comparing their responses with those of nonstressed animals similarly injected. The stressed animals were further divided into two groups: one was truly victimized, the stressor being out of their control, whereas animals in the other group were given warnings that allowed them to abort the stressor. Their ability to reject the cells and remain cancer-free revealed some striking differences in the groups. Those in the stressed group that had control over the stressor immunologically rejected the cancer 63 percent of the time, as compared with only 28 percent in the "victim" group. Animals that were not stressed rejected the cells 60 percent of the time, revealing a trend seen repeatedly in many such studies: it's not being stressed that is most important, but rather the ability to deal well with stress, to gain a sense of control.

Researchers struggling to identify the causes of cancer have repeatedly come face to face with the factor of emotions. Lawrence LeShan, one of the primary authorities on the psychological aspects of cancer, extensively reviewed nineteen standard medical textbooks written between 1800 and 1900, a period that, though less scientifically sophisticated, produced physicians who were keen observers. All but one contained a statement similar to this one: "Of course, the [emotional history] plays a major role in the tendency of the person to get cancer and in the progress of the cancer."[23]

Many studies conducted by researchers throughout the world have shown that cancer-prone persons tend to deny or repress unpleasant emotions, especially anger, hostility, and depression. As one researcher put it, "They seem to be out of touch with their own wants and needs, choosing to effect a permanent pleasant attitude and personality, regardless of the bleakness of their inner lives."[24]

The connection between repressed emotions and the development of cancer was recognized in a research setting as early as two decades ago. Dr. Caroline B. Thomas of Johns Hopkins Medical School did an exhaustive thirty-year study to determine how well psychological factors predicted five different disease states. Hers was one of the first prospective studies (i.e., it detailed the psychological characteristics of people *before* they were diagnosed with disease).

Dr. Thomas and her team found that the disease most correlated with psychological traits was cancer. They also determined that three specific characteristics predispose a person to developing cancer: a perceived lack of closeness with one or both parents; responding to stress with a sense of hopelessness; and bottling up emotions or having impaired emotional outlets.[25]

The emergence of specific emotional patterns among many cancer patients led researchers to identify what they call "the cancer personality" (a spin-off from the kind of research that led to identification of the Type A personality). According to researchers, those who have a cancer-prone personality often equate close personal relationships with suffering and rejection—possibly because of negative emotional experiences in childhood—and they conceal their true feelings of isolation behind a mask of cheerful self-confidence.[26] This personality pattern is discussed in greater detail in Chapter 5.

In commenting on the trademarks of a cancer-prone personality, psychologist Eugene Blumberg noted that "we were impressed by the polite, apologetic, almost painful acquiescence of the patients with rapidly progressing disease, as contrasted with the more expressive and sometimes bizarre personalities of those who responded brilliantly to therapy with remissions and long survival."[27] The patients in Blumberg's study who had the fastest-growing tumors tended to be "consistently serious, overcooperative, over-nice, overanxious, painfully sensitive, passive, apologetic personalities," and had been all their lives. Another specialist in catastrophic illness, Lawrence LeShan, pointed out that "the big thing the majority of cancer victims have in common is that they have lost their major outlet for creative energy. The death of a spouse, retirement, whatever, has closed off their channel of expression, their uniqueness."

Repression of emotions has been linked so closely with cancer proneness that many researchers are now considering it a valid risk factor for cancer. Several long-term studies have stressed the link between cancer and emotions. One of the best-known was conducted on medical students who attended Johns Hopkins University between 1948 and 1964. Students were shown a series of ten Rorschach inkblots and were asked to describe what they saw. Twenty years after the last students were given the inkblot tests, psychologist Pirkko L. Graves and her colleagues rated the responses on an eleven-point scale that pinpointed varying degrees of positive and negative emotions.[28]

Graves and her colleagues had not set out to do a cancer study; initially they had wanted to see what kinds of emotions led to later mental illness. They found that those whose pattern of scores indicated distant, withdrawn approaches to relationships and poorly balanced emotions were more likely to have developed a severe mental disorder by 1984. And, much to their surprise, the researchers found that the same pattern of scores was linked to the later appearance of cancer, particularly cancers of the stomach, pancreas, rectum, large intestine, and lymph nodes; Hodgkin's disease; leukemia; and multiple myeloma.

Refining the original study, Graves and her colleagues chose 972 medical students from the study and divided them into five groups based on fourteen psychological measures. They then kept track of the students for thirty years. Those who suppressed their emotions were *sixteen times* more likely to develop cancer than those who expressed their emotions freely and took active measures to relieve their frustrations or anger.

Similar findings emerged from a controversial long-term study conducted in Yugoslavia by University of South Florida psychologist Charles D. Spielberger and his Dutch colleague Henk M. van der Ploeg. Although some believe their study was flawed, it did show that repression and denial of emotions on a regular basis were related to increased risk for both cancer and heart disease.

Some studies show that emotions can be even more powerful as a predictor of cancer than factors such as cigarette smoking.[29] Cigarette smoking is a direct cause of lung cancer. Although the majority of those who develop lung cancer are cigarette smokers, most cigarette smokers do not develop lung cancer. Researchers hoping to find the difference between the smokers who develop cancer and those who don't studied more than a thousand industrial workers in Glasgow, Scotland who came to a health clinic with respiratory complaints. Dr. David Kissen and his colleagues tested all of the men psychologically before performing a physical examination and rendering a diagnosis.

He found that those who had cancer when they came to the clinic displayed what he and his colleagues called "a striking inability to express emotions." The inability was significant enough that they were vastly different from the men who did not have cancer.

Researchers who saw the results of Kissen's study were eager to perform a similar test. Two of them, Dr. R. L. Horne of the Shreveport Veterans Administration Hospital and Dr. R. S. Picard of the Washington University School of Medicine, believed that, if Kissen's findings were correct, they could actually *predict* which patients had cancer based on psychological findings alone. The group headed by Horne and Picard used a variety of studies on lung cancer, including Kissen's, to develop a composite scale of psychological variables. They then began testing patients who came to the hospital complaining of respiratory complaints, and, based on the results of the psychological testing, they made predictions about which patients had lung cancer. They made these predictions without the benefit of any physical examination. The result was that they were able to predict which men had cancer and which had benign lung disease with 73 percent accuracy, a rate researchers regard as "highly significant."

In discussing the results of their study, Horne and Picard maintain that "emotional repression is part of a personality pattern that led to grave difficulties in coping with life's challenges and sorrows. After the loss of a central relationship—with a person or a valued job—those with cancer often reported profound depression which had predated the cancer by six to eighteen months."

And emotions can play a role in the outcome of cancer: The way cancer patients react to the diagnosis apparently affects the course of the disease. Those with the bleakest prognosis are the ones who expect the worst, feel helpless, and give up. On the other hand, those who expect to survive and feel a sense of control over making that happen, who exhibit a powerful "fighting spirit," are most likely to beat the odds and survive the longest.

Dental Cavities

Emotions have been shown to play a role even in the development of dental cavities. Based on the results of a handful of studies, researchers at the Temple University School of Dentistry say that stressful thoughts and emotions can actually contribute to the mechanisms that cause dental caries. In one test, researchers analyzed the saliva of a group of twelve dental students both before and after a twenty-minute meditation session. The saliva was opaque and contained moderate to high levels of bacteria before the meditation session. After the students had become deeply relaxed, their saliva became watery and translucent and bacteria levels decreased. "Considering the salivary changes that occur during stress," the researchers noted, "it could be hypothesized that chronic stress would be a causative factor in the development of dental caries."

The same factors are apparently at play in gum disease as well. Researchers at the University of Alabama found that trench mouth victims have higher levels of stress hormones in their urine. These stress hormones, secreted in response to emotional difficulties, have also been shown to affect the immune system. In several studies, patients with gum disease had experienced more negative, unsettling life events in the preceding year and demonstrated high levels of anxiety, depression, and emotional disturbances. Whether the stress itself is the cause or whether it is co-associated with socioeconomic situations associated with trench mouth is not entirely clear.

Diabetes

The link between emotions and diabetes was made as early as the seventeenth century, when British physician Thomas Willis noted that diabetes first appeared in many cases among patients who had experienced significant life stresses.[30] Nearly two hundred years later, Claude Bernard, considered the father of modern physiology, found that he could produce diabetes in a normal animal by making a lesion in the area of the hypothalamus. That finding helps explain why there could be a link between stress, anxiety, and diabetes, which may be linked to an upset in the central nervous system.

Recent research shows that there may very well be a "diabetic personality": those most prone to diabetes are characterized by decreased alertness, apathy, and depression. Some researchers also believe that diabetics are more prone to immaturity, passivity, masochism, and perhaps even sexual identity problems. Children with diabetes have a greater tendency for anxiety, aggressiveness, and problems with self-perception. Interpretation of this association needs to be tempered, however, by the fact that some of these behaviors could be affected by erratic blood sugar control.

Stomach Ulcers

In a series of tests designed to determine the most likely causes of gastric ulcers, gastroenterologists Charles Richardson and Mark Feldman found that ulcer patients had a much higher prevalence of emotional distress than volunteers who did not have ulcers. The physicians and their colleagues at the University of Texas Health Sciences Center at Dallas found that certain emotions, especially hostility, resentment, guilt, and frustration, are associated with increased acid in the stomach, which contributes to ulcers. More recently, however, stress appears to be less important than is an infection with a bacterium called *H. pylori.*

Hair and Scalp Problems

A variety of studies have shown that emotions can literally go to your head, causing whitening of the hair, dandruff, and hair loss (alopecia areata). In one study, researchers questioned thirty people who were losing their hair to common inherited baldness and thirty who were losing their hair to fungal infection. More than 80 percent of those with inherited baldness had suffered recent emotional problems, as also had more than half of the people losing hair due to fungal infection. A team of Italian doctors studied a group of alopecia areata patients who were losing their hair because antibodies were attacking their hair follicles. An overwhelming number, 87.5 percent, had experienced an emotionally stressful period during the six months before the hair loss began. Two thirds of the people in the study had also suffered a serious depressing setback such as the death or departure of a friend or family member.

Hypertension

An emotional upheaval can drive up blood pressure; getting extremely angry can "make your blood boil." According to a report in the *Journal of Nervous and Mental Disease*, data from forty-eight studies over a ten-year period show that the primary *psychological* characteristics of many people with high blood pressure are anger and hostility, difficulty with interpersonal contacts, and frequent denial and self-repression.[31] But the reason why strong emotions could almost be measured with a blood pressure cuff is physiological. A number of studies have proven that strong emotion causes the body to pump epinephrine (popularly called adrenaline) into the system. Adrenaline has two effects on the cardiovascular system: (1) it speeds up the heart, and, (2) it constricts the blood vessels. The result is high blood pressure.

Hundreds of studies have been completed on emotions and high blood pressure, but one is particularly interesting to anyone in the workplace. Researchers wanted to test the emotional impact of noise and its effects on health, so for nine months they exposed monkeys in a laboratory to the typical sounds of a worker's life. The monkeys' blood pressure increased by an average of 27 percent, and when the experiment was over, blood pressure levels did not return to normal for more than a month.

Insomnia

It is widely accepted that emotional upset causes insomnia, but there are also physiological reasons why strong emotions can interfere with sleep or make sleep less restful. Studies have shown that emotional stress raises body temperature, raises skin resistance, narrows blood vessels, and causes increased body movement, all of which make sleep more difficult and less comfortable. A majority of persons with insomnia have anxiety and depression disorders the neurochemistry of which is the principal cause of most sleep disturbance.

Irritable Bowel Syndrome

Emotions are linked to irritable bowel syndrome, a painful combination of cramping, diarrhea, and occasional vomiting. According to Johns Hopkins Medical School associate professor of behavioral biology William E. Whitehead, the gastrointestinal tract is particularly susceptible to emotional stress and "very readily comes under the influence of external factors and events." He says that irritable bowel syndrome tends to occur among people who overreact to everyday worries; sufferers tend to be both more anxious and more depressed than others. They may have nagging concerns about family problems, work problems, or finances, and studies show that they usually have a number of other stress-related problems, such as headaches or insomnia.

Whitehead makes the interesting observation that many irritable bowel syndrome patients have learned to be especially attentive to what's going on in their bodies and to overreact to symptoms. He also believes that many have subconsciously learned that irritable bowel syndrome is one way of getting emotional needs met. When he compared irritable bowel syndrome patients with persons who did not have the syndrome, those with irritable bowel syndrome reported that parents had given them gifts, toys, or "treat" foods (such as ice cream) when they were ill as children. Such treatment, he says, may reinforce a child's health complaints. As adults, irritable bowel syndrome may also be a means of getting nurturing and may serve as an excuse not to do some things. Whitehead is quick to point out that such reactions are not intentional but completely subconscious and that most people with the disorder are simply responding to stress, not trying to manipulate others.

Pregnancy-Related Problems

Major emotional setbacks in a woman's life during pregnancy can determine the course of the pregnancy and can even result in premature delivery and low birth weight. Researchers who studied more than 200 women at St. Mercy's Hospital in Manchester, England, showed that low birth weight and prematurity were associated with major life events. Stressful events had the greatest impact, the researchers said, when they occurred during the final three months of pregnancy.

Other research indicates that the effects of emotional stress may be cumulative. Researchers completing studies on pregnancy noted that emotional stress during pregnancy was inversely related to birth weight.

Sexual Dysfunction

Recent findings that give credence to folklore show that emotions and emotional stress cause real physiological changes that result in sexual dysfunction. Strong emotions and emotional stress affect the central nervous system, causing it to curtail sharply the body's testosterone supply. Testosterone is essential in both men and women for normal sexual desire and performance.

In one study, researchers chose a population under incredible emotional stress: American soldiers in Vietnam preparing to go to the battlefront. Blood tests showed that their adrenaline levels had soared and their testosterone levels had plummeted. Few of the soldiers had any interest in sex at all. When they returned from the front, blood tests were repeated, and researchers found that adrenaline and testosterone levels had returned to normal. So had the soldiers' sexual desire.

Helen Singer Kaplan, head of the sex therapy and education program at Payne Whitney Clinic of New York Hospital, says, "depression, stress, and fatigue can damage sexuality profoundly. When a patient is severely depressed, sex is the furthest [sic] thing from his mind. Even moderately depressed patients lose interest in pursuing sexual activity and are very difficult to seduce and arouse."

Even people with "normal sexual appetites can psychologically turn themselves off with overwhelming problems," maintains Wanda Sadoughi, director of the sexual dysfunction clinic at Chicago's Cook County Hospital. "By the time some patients come to the clinic, they are having major dysfunctional problems, . . . but before all that occurred, the first symptom some of these people had was a loss of desire."

Protection from the Common Cold

Exciting new research shows that, while negative emotions can give the immune system a beating, even small pleasures can give it a big boost. In a study reported at the annual meeting of the Society for Behavioral Medicine, psychologist Arthur Stone of the State University of New York Medical School tracked one hundred men for three months. He found that both stress and pleasure had an effect on the immune system, but here's the real news: Stone and his colleagues found that stress weakened the immune system for one day whereas pleasurable events enhanced the immune system for *two days*. "Having a good time on Monday still had a positive effect on the immune system on Wednesday," he reported, "but the negative immune effect from undesirable events on Monday lasts for just that day."

Stone's recent study follows up on a similar one he did earlier involving seventy-nine men. The big surprise in that study? A drop in the usual number of pleasant events made the research volunteers more susceptible to the common cold than did a jump in the usual number of stressful events. The mind clearly is a healing tool like no other, and connecting the power of the mind and the heart with the body can unlock tremendous healing powers that can change the course of disease and that may be able to prevent it in the first place.

Does all this mean we should never have negative emotions? Does that mean we must banish anger and resentment and hostility, and fill our lives only with love and happiness? No. Such an existence is impossible. The key lies not in which emotions seize us but in how we react to them.

Rachel Naomi Remen is an accomplished physician who herself has battled a chronic illness for thirty-five years. Her private practice has focused on behavioral medicine, and she concentrates on working with patients and their families who are facing chronic illness. She is medical director of the Commonweal Cancer Help Program and a member of the adjunct faculty of the Saybrook Institute.

"I must confess that I find the notion of 'positive' emotions a disturbing concept, and perhaps even a dangerous one," she told her colleagues during a conference sponsored by the Institute for the Advancement of Health. "At best, it implies that there is a way to live, a certain set of attitudes, that may guarantee survival. At worst, the concept of positive emotions can degenerate into self-tyranny and may lead the individual into some kind of mind control. Many people now seem to fear harboring 'negative' or 'wrong' thoughts in the same way people used to fear having evil thoughts."

According to Remen, the issue is deeper than simply experiencing a negative emotion. Her advice is profound when she told the group assembled at the conference that "perhaps there is a positive way to feel *all* emotions. It seems to me that all emotions serve a purpose and are potentially life affirming. Perhaps it is not so much the emotions themselves as the way we deal with them that either is or is not life affirming."[32]

In another revealing statement, Remen said, "I asked fifteen or twenty clinical colleagues if they could identify positive emotions in their patients—that is to say, emotions that they felt were directly associated with survival. There was no question that all these physicians and psychologists liked certain emotions better than others, but the correlation between survival and emotional attitude was not clear to any of them, including the oncologists. All had worked with loving, cheerful people who died, grieving people who lived, angry people who never became ill, and humorous people who were unable to heal themselves. And yet all had the clinical hunch that emotions indeed affect healing. So we have a mystery. Perhaps we need more sensitive tools for studying emotional and psychological states. The sensitivity of our emotional assessment needs to equal the sophistication of our immunological knowledge, and we are not there yet." [33]

Indeed, there is still far to go. The body of knowledge we have so far is exciting, full of promise for the prospect of a whole new horizon on how we look at and treat disease—and, most important, how we might prevent it. But, as Stanford University psychologist David Spiegel wrote in the *Journal of the National Cancer Institute,* "We are entering the twenty-first century with twentieth-century science and technology and a nineteenth-century understanding of what it tells us about mind–body relationships."

Notes

1. Arthur J. Barsky, *Worried Sick: Our Troubled Quest for Wellness* (Boston, Massachusetts: Little, Brown, and Company, 1988).

2. George E. Vaillant, "Natural History of Male Psychological Health," *Archives of General Psychology,* 33: 1976, 535–545.

3. James P. Henry, "The Arousal of Emotions: Hormones, Behavior, and Health," *Advances,* 6: 2, 59–62.

4. James P. Henry, "Neuroendocrine Patterns of Response," in R. Plutchik, editor, *Biological Foundations of Emotions* (New York: Academic Press, 1986), pp. 37–60.

5. Ernest H. Johnson, "Psychiatric Symptoms and Health Problems Among Black Americans: A National Survey," *Journal of the American Medical Association,* 81(12): 1989, 1217–1223.

6. William Gottlieb, "Your Emotions and Your Health: A Woman's Guide," *Complete Woman,* n.d., pp. 8–10, 67.

7. J. P. Henry and P. M. Stephens, *Stress, Health, and the Social Environment: A Sociobiologic Approach to Medicine* (New York: Springer, 1977).

8. Bernie S. Siegel, *Love, Medicine, and Miracles* (New York: Harper and Row Publishers, Inc., 1986).

9. Siegel.

10. Gottlieb.

11. Siegel.

12. Siegel.

13. Reported in Herbert Benson, *The Mind/Body Effect* (New York: Simon and Schuster, 1979).

14. Benson.

15. Marc Pilisuk and Susan Hillier Parks, *The Healing Web* (Hanover, New Hampshire: The University Press of New England, 1986).

16. "Emotions: Linked to the Immune System," *Better Health,* 4(12): 1987, 1–2.

17. William L. Mundy, "Curing Allergy with Visual Imagery," *The Psychology of Health, Immunity, and Disease,* vol. A, p. 417, in Proceedings of the Sixth International Conference of the National Institute for the Clinical Application of Behavioral Medicine.

18. Margaret Kemeny, "Emotions and the Immune System," in Bill Moyers, editor, *Healing and the Mind* (New York: Doubleday, 1993), p. 197.

19. Emrika Padus, William Gottlieb, and Mark Brickin, editors, *The Complete Guide to Your Emotions and Your Health* (Emmaus, Pennsylvania: Rodale Press, 1986).

20. Terr, et al., *Archives of Internal Medicine* 146: 1986, 145–149.

21. Michael J. Shea, "Mental Stress and the Heart," *CVR&R,* April: 1988, 51–58.

22. Jerome D. Frank, "The Medical Power of Faith," *Human Nature,* August: 1978, 40–47.

23. Simonton and Henson, p. 6.

24. Steven Locke and Douglas Colligan, *The Healer Within* (New York: E.P. Dutton, 1986).

25. Simonton and Henson, p. 708.

26. Frank.

27. Locke and Colligan.

28. Bruce Bower, "The Character of Cancer," *Science News,* 131: 1987, 120–121.

29. Joan Borysenko and Myrin Borysenko, "On Psychoneuroimmunology: How the Mind

Influences Health and Disease ... and How to Make the Influence Beneficial," *Executive Health,* 19(10): 1983.

30. Mark N. Feinglos and Richard S. Surwit, *Behavior and Diabetes Mellitus* (Kalamazoo, Michigan: The Upjohn Company, 1988).

31. "Mind/Hypertension Link Certain, Researchers Say," *Brain/Mind Bulletin,* July: 1989, 2.

32. Rachel Naomi Remen, "Feeling Well: A Clinician's Casebook," *Advances* 6: 2, 43–49.

33. Larry Dossey, *Healing Words* (San Francisco: Harper San Francisco, 1993), pp. 33–34.

2

PSYCHONEUROIMMUNOLOGY

The arrival of a good clown exercises a more beneficial influence upon the health of a town than the arrival of twenty asses laden with drugs.
—*THOMAS SYDENHAM, SEVENTEENTH-CENTURY PHYSICIAN*

Dr. Thomas Sydenham, considered by historians to be the "British Hippocrates," was referring to the medicine of his day when he ascribed greater healing powers to a good clown than to all available pharmaceuticals. But some of the most sophisticated research being carried out today by some of the nation's most skilled scientists is revealing that Sydenham may have been right after all: A good, hearty laugh—and the other positive emotions that accompany it—may do more to promote health and prevent disease than all the drugs lining the shelves at your local pharmacy.

That's not to say that drugs aren't necessary, nor does it imply that modern medicine is useless or that the mind controls the body. It *is* to say that what we think and how we feel appear to have powerful effects on the biological functions of our bodies. It *is* also to say that there is a complex, dynamic interaction between the mind and the body. It opens the revolutionary possibility that we can work with our physicians by virtue of our attitudes and our emotions.

A Definition

The scientific investigation of how the brain affects the body's immune cells and how the immune system can be affected by behavior is called *psychoneuroimmunology*, a term coined in 1964 by Dr. Robert Ader, director of the division of behavioral and psychosocial medicine at New York's University of Rochester. In their landmark study, Ader and his colleagues showed that immune function could be classically conditioned.[1] The science of psychoneuroimmunology (PNI) focuses on the links between the mind, the brain, and the immune system, with an intricate interaction of consciousness, brain and central nervous system, and the immune system.[2] As a science, it has received the endorsement of the National Institutes of Health.

Though some are still skeptical about the concepts behind it, researchers in psychoneuroimmunology are proving that the way persons think and feel influences the immune system. Immunologists, physiologists, psychiatrists, psychologists, and neurobiologists "who have explored the murky boundary between mind and body now suspect that certain negative psychological states, brought on by adversity or a chemical imbalance, actually cause the immune system to falter."[3] Some even go so far as to claim that positive attitudes, such as a feeling of control, may in some way "inoculate against disease and act as a valuable supplement to conventional medical care."[4]

Psychoneuroimmunologists focus on the link between the mind, the brain, and the immune system. People involved in the research believe that these links are solid, but, because "evidence buttressing such claims has been hard to come by, most researchers warn against overenthusiastic interpretations of the findings. Nonetheless, they view the new field—whether it goes by the name of psychoneuroimmunology or simply behavioral medicine—as the hottest and most promising area of medical research today."[5]

The evidence for a link between the mind, the emotions, and the body has accelerated remarkably in the past few years. An article in *Time* cited some examples[6]: A ten-year follow-up study at Stanford University showed that women who were ill and received psychotherapy in groups survived nearly twice as long as similar women who didn't. Dr. Dean Ornish, of the Preventive Medicine Research Institute in California, showed that a mind-body program can reverse even severe coronary artery blockage after only a year, and he says it may prevent it as well. Other studies have enabled researchers to predict which people in a group will become ill—based on nothing more than psychological profiles.

The late Norman Cousins, formerly the editor of the *Saturday Review* and a member of the UCLA medical faculty, twice intrigued both the medical community and the public by overcoming usually fatal conditions—once a massive heart attack and once an advanced case of ankylosing spondylitis (a degenerative spinal disease). Cousins followed his physicians' regimen each time, but also infused himself with vast doses of positive emotions and laughter. According to Cousins himself, he was healed not only by the miracle of modern medicine but also by the healing emotions of love, hope, faith, confidence, and a tremendous will to live. Because of his experiences, both with his own illness and with the hundreds of patients he saw, he became an acknowledged authority on the power of emotion. Cousins said emotions play a profound part in bringing on disease and in helping to combat it, and he isn't alone in that belief. Specialists in psychophysiological medicine estimate that possibly as many as 90 percent of all health problems can be traced, at least in part, to the influence of emotions.

The field is not without controversy. It has inspired some of the most heated medical debates of our time. In a 1985 editorial published in the prestigious *New England Journal of Medicine*, executive editor Marcia Angell labelled the fledgling science of psychoneuroimmunology "folklore," and she stands by that assessment today. Her editorial claimed that no one has "shown unequivocally that someone's state of mind can cause or cure a specific disease."[7] Her musings raised the hackles of physicians and researchers across the nation and set off a debate that still rages.

A Brief History

The stormy controversy over how emotions affect health is not a new one.[8] More than 4000 years ago, Chinese physicians noted that physical illness often followed episodes of frustration. Egyptian physicians of the same period prescribed good cheer and an optimistic attitude as ways to avoid poor health. Half a millennium before the birth of Christ, Hippocrates, the father of medicine, cautioned physicians that, to cure a patient, they needed a knowledge of the "whole of things," of mind as well as body. That philosophy persisted for hundreds of years. In one of the best-known examples, the Greek physician Galen observed during the second century that melancholic women were much more prone to breast cancer than women who were cheerful.

The "holistic" attitude and philosophy of medicine changed dramatically in the seventeenth century as a result of the musings of philosopher–scientist Rene Descartes. He preached that there were two separate substances in the world: matter, which behaved according to physical laws, and spirit, which was dimensionless and immaterial. The body was material and the mind spiritual. His notion of a fundamental, unbridgeable chasm between the body and the spirit—between the brain and the mind—came to dominate not only medical philosophy but religious philosophy as well.

Descartes's theory gained even more momentum just a century ago, when a young German country doctor made one of the most significant medical discoveries of his time. Robert Koch found that germs cause anthrax in sheep. In crude experiments, he recovered the anthrax germs from dying sheep, injected them into healthy sheep, and then watched those healthy sheep sicken and die of anthrax.

Since anthrax germs caused only anthrax disease, and no other disease, Koch theorized that every disease had a simple, specific cause: germs. The most respected medical authority of the time, Rudolf Virchow, disagreed; he told Koch that diseases are complex and that they involve factors like environment, heredity, nutrition, psychological state, preexisting health, and stress. He told Koch that germs undoubtedly played a role but that many other factors were involved, too. But Koch held stubbornly to his view, and so did most other practitioners of his day.

Until recently, most practitioners shared the theory that pathogens—and nothing else—cause disease, but then things slowly started to change again. Around the turn of the century, anatomists discovered that rich networks of nerve fibers were laced through the tissues of the immune system.[9] The researchers who grasped that information and used it in a variety of experiments on animal brains found that, by stimulating parts of the brain, they could help increase an animal's resistance to disease. Conversely, they found that by damaging or destroying part of an animal's brain, they could compromise the immune system and make the animal more susceptible to infection and disease.

One of the pioneers, American physiologist Walter Cannon, conducted a series of experiments early in this century that provided physical proof that glands in the body respond to stress. His early experiments demonstrated the relationship between the hypothalamus, pituitary, and adrenal glands and stress. Several decades later, Austrian-born physician Hans Selye conducted brilliant and sophisticated experiments that gave us what we now know as the fight-or-flight response to stress.[10]

It was not until the 1960s that researchers began studying the immune system in earnest. The immune defense system proved to be so complex that researchers were overwhelmed with the task of unraveling its parts and functions. We now know that no body system, including the complex immune system, works entirely on its own and independently of the other body systems. All body systems' functions are coordinated by the brain. George Washington University immunologist Nicholas Hall points out that the immune system must have links with other body systems, even though its cells can function in a test tube. "You can take the heart out of a frog and drip the appropriate groceries on it, and it will continue to beat," he says. "That doesn't mean the heart functions in isolation in the body."[11]

Not until the 1980s did immunologists finally start looking at the evidence, growing to overwhelming proportions, that there might be anatomical links between the brain, the nervous system, and the immune system. They found, in essence, that the brain was literally "talking" to the cells of the immune system. It was telling the immune system about the emotions. And the broad spectrum of scientists who are devoting their time to the study of the brain–immune system link are now concentrating on how the emotions work to either enhance or cripple the immune response.

Current Status

In his book *Psychoneuroimmunology*, psychologist Robert Ader, whose key experiments laid a foundation for the field, gives the following evidence for connections between the mind, the immune system, and the nervous system:

- The central nervous system is linked to both the bone marrow and the thymus (where immune system cells are produced) and to the spleen and lymph nodes, where such cells are stored.
- Scientists have found nerve endings in the tissues of the immune system.
- Changes in the brain and spinal cord affect how the immune system responds. That's not all: when researchers trigger an immune response in the body there are changes in the way the brain and spinal cord function.
- Researchers have discovered that lymphocytes (important immune system cells) respond chemically to hormones and neurotransmitters, and that they can actually *produce* hormones and neurotransmitters.

- Cells that are actively involved in an immune response produce substances that send signals to the central nervous system.
- The body's immune response can be influenced by stress; stress and other psychosocial factors can make the body more susceptible to infectious diseases (such as the common cold), autoimmune diseases (such as arthritis), or cancer.
- The body's immune response can be "trained," modified by the same kind of classical conditioning used in psychological experiments to train dogs.
- Immune function can be influenced and changed by psychoactive drugs, including alcohol, marijuana, cocaine, heroin, and nicotine.[12]

Physicians and surgeons on the cutting edge of technology are coming to realize that emotions play an extremely powerful role in both sickness and health. Dr. Theodore Miller of the renowned cancer institution, Memorial Hospital in New York, urged his fellow cancer surgeons to follow his example and not operate on patients who are convinced they will not survive surgery. In an address to the Society of Surgical Oncology, Miller told the surgeons that these patients usually do die, despite a technically successful operation.[13]

Part of the power of emotions on health is undoubtedly related to their effect on the immune system. An entire cadre of studies demonstrates clearly that positive emotions help improve immune responses (and therefore help protect health), whereas negative emotions can compromise the immune system (and therefore lead to disease). This phenomenon is at least partly responsible for the increased rates of illness and death among widows and widowers. Mount Sinai medical school researchers did blood tests of men whose wives had died. They found that immune function was depressed and that there was a significant decline in the number of white blood cells, which defend the body against disease. It took a full year before the men's immune systems functioned normally again.[14] Other experts believe that the effect of losing a spouse may be even more prolonged. A report released by the National Academy of Sciences notes that, for a "sizeable fraction" of widow(er)s, immune system depression may persist as long as three years.

Jonas Salk, developer of the first polio vaccine, concluded years of his own scientific research by saying that "the mind, in addition to medicine, has powers to turn the immune system around." That power is so great, says Salk, that he advocates a major clinical study of the effects of emotions on the body, requiring dozens of years, millions of dollars, and an enormous number of scientists and children. It would be worth the investment, he says, if the study showed us conclusively that children who were positive and in control thrived and stayed healthier than their peers. "The people who do such a study," he concludes, "will be the poets of biology."[15]

Some impressive studies have compared animals under relentless, uncontrollable stress to those not stressed when both were exposed to agents that cause disease but that are usually prevented from doing harm by a healthy immune response. The stressed groups showed several effects:

- Greater susceptibility to viral illnesses when exposed (the viruses included, among others, herpes simplex, coxsackievirus B, poliovirus and polyoma virus)
- Decreased immune rejection of injected cancer cells of many types
- More severe, accelerated, and crippling arthritis when a substance that stimulates an autoimmune response is injected into the joint.

Note that the immune response can be too weak or too strong; mental distress causes a disturbance in the regulation of the immune response. For example, chronically stressed or depressed people frequently have high blood concentrations of antibodies to viruses like Epstein-Barr virus, herpesviruses, or cytomegalovirus—a fact that can be misleading when measurements are taken. When *stronger* or *improved* immunity is reported in these pages, it does not necessarily denote *more* immunity but rather better regulation of immune responses. In humans, the commonest precipitator of cold sores attacks (herpesvirus lesions) is mental stress. Recurrences are associated with either depression or passive, avoidant coping.

Psychoneuroimmunology is considered to be in its infancy, but already a number of medical schools are integrating it into their curricula, and a host of federal grants are underwriting increased research. Most important, conferences on immunology now include at least one seminar on the relationship between the brain and the immune system.[16] An increasing number of physicians are acknowledging that how a patient thinks and feels can be a powerful determinant of physical health.

The Brain

Five hundred years before the birth of Christ, the Greeks knew the brain as a three-pound organ inside the head.[17] Hippocrates believed that its role was to cool the blood and secrete mucus, which then flowed down through the nose. Through crude clinical observation over the ensuing years, beliefs about the brain and its function changed. In the Middle Ages, scientists regarded the brain as the seat of the soul. And during our own century, our ability to measure and analyze electrical activity of the brain has generated major advances in understanding its function.

What It Is

The brain is a very privileged organ. It has a heart to supply it with blood, lungs to supply it with oxygen, intestines to supply it with nutrients, and kidneys to remove poisons from its environment. The most important part of our nervous system, it is the focal point of organization. For the body to survive, the nervous system, and particularly the brain, must be maintained; all other organs will sacrifice to keep the brain alive and functioning when the entire body is under severe stress.

By weight, 90 percent of the central nervous system is located inside the head in the form of the brain. A long extension of the brain, the spinal cord, descends down the back, inside the spinal column. From both the brain and the spinal cord, nerves go out to the sensory organs, like the eyes, ears, and nose. Nerves also branch out to the muscles, the skin, and all the organs of the body.

A series of tough membranes cover and protect the brain; just beneath these membranes, cushioning the brain itself, is a layer of clear cerebrospinal fluid, which also circulates down the length of the spinal cord. Beneath the cerebrospinal fluid is the brain, which is grayish and looks like the inside of a huge walnut covered with blood vessels.

The brain itself is made up of nerve cells and nerve fibers. If you cut a section through the brain, you would see mostly gray matter (containing cells) and white matter (containing fibers surrounded by a fatty insulation called *myelin*). The fibers and nerves of the spinal cord, as well as those that branch out through the body, are also insulated with myelin; this insulation serves to isolate the nerve fibers so that electrical nerve impulses can't "short out."

What It Does

Simply stated, the brain masterminds nerve impulses that are carried throughout the body; it sends information to various parts of the body. It controls voluntary processes such as the direction, strength, and coordination of muscle movements; the processes involved in smelling, touching, and seeing; and other processes over which you have conscious control. The brain also controls many automatic, vital functions in the body, such as breathing, the rate of the heartbeat, digestion, bowels and bladder, blood pressure, and release of hormones.

Finally, the brain is the cognitive center of the body, where ideas are generated, memory is stored, and emotions are experienced. Thus it is that the emotions that so affect the body originate in the brain, and this process explains the brain's powerful influence over the body as well as its link to the emotions and the immune system.

We are still learning about how the brain functions. For example, for years researchers have believed that memories exist in the brain as fixed traces, carefully filed and stored. They have taught that memory exists in a small seahorse-shaped section of the hippocampus and that other functions are centered in other localized areas of the brain. New research and a group of pioneering experts are now challenging that assumption.

In his book *The Invention of Memory: A New View of the Brain*, physician Israel Rosenfield presents the view that our brain is not "neatly and permanently wired up by our genes. Rather, whatever connections between nerve cells (neurons) we started with are continually reshaped by our experiences. It's a Darwinian struggle up there, and only the fittest connections—the ones that help us survive in our particular environment—get strengthened. Because experiences and contexts differ for each person, so do the connections. And since the demands of our own life vary over time, so do the patterns of connections, as some win and some lose."[18]

The philosophy of these pioneering scientists is "a radical departure from the past: Instead of having fixed memories, we invent what we remember. That is, we recategorize what we've learned, depending on the situation. We're creative magicians: The rabbit we pull out of memory's hat is different from the rabbit that went in—and so is the hat."[19]

According to Rosenfield's theory, we constantly reshape what enters our brain and we constantly assign new meaning to it. Our memory, he says, is inexact and fragmentary. "One reason why the search for memory molecules and specific information storage zones in the brain has so far been fruitless may be that they are just not there."[20]

Rosenfield's theory has begun to gain support in the scientific community, and even those who cannot wholeheartedly endorse it still admit that previous, rigid philosophies about the brain may not be entirely correct. Even if the theory is only partly valid, it may help explain how the brain so readily interacts with the emotions it produces and how its effect works on the body. According to Rosenfield, "a mental life cannot be reduced to molecules. Human intelligence is not just knowing more, but reworking, recategorizing, and thus generalizing information in new and surprising ways."[21]

Indeed, the experience of emotion "has less to do with specific locations in the brain and more to do with the complicated circuitry that interconnects them and the patterns of nerve impulses that travel along them," according to new research. California neuroscientist Floyd Bloom sums it up when he compares the manufacture of emotion to a television set. "There are individual tubes," he points out, "and you can say what they do, but if you take even one tube out, the television doesn't work."[22]

The Emotions It Produces

The emotions produced by the brain are, in a very real sense, a mixture of feelings and physical responses—and every time the brain manufactures an emotion throughout its loose network of lower brain structures and nerve pathways known as the limbic system, physical responses accompany those emotions. A report published in *U. S. News and World Report* presents a vivid picture of what happens as feelings and physical responses are combined:

> *Seeing a shadow flit across your path in a dimly lit parking lot will trigger a complex series of events. First, sensory receptors in the retina of your eye detect the shadow and instantly translate it into chemical signals that race to your brain. Different parts of the limbic system and higher brain centers debate the shadow's importance. What is it? Have we encountered something like this before? Is it dangerous? Meanwhile, signals sent by the hypothalamus to the pituitary gland trigger a flood of hormones alerting various parts of your body to the possibility of danger, and producing the response called "fight or flight":*

Rapid pulse, rising blood pressure, dilated pupils, and other physiological shifts that prepare you for action. Hormone signals are carried through the blood, a much slower route than nerve pathways. So even after the danger is past—when your brain decides that the shadow is a cat's, not a mugger's—it takes a few minutes for everything to return to normal.[23]

This description tracks what happens with fear, a relatively uncomplicated emotion. According to brain researchers, the pathways of more complicated sensations, such as sadness or joy, are much more difficult to trace, but they are just as responsible for physical effects in the body.

Endorphins

The body manufactures natural, morphine-like brain chemicals called endorphins. The word *endorphin* itself is a derivative or combination of the words *endogenous morphines.* Early researchers discovered that endorphins work as the

---

Focus on Research

The "pleasure center" of the brain and its products, the endorphins, were discovered completely by accident. The story of that discovery is a potent reminder of how powerful the endorphins are. McGill University researcher James Olds wanted to condition an ordinary white rat to avoid a corner of its cage. To do so, he decided to sink an electrode into the rat's hypothalamus and stimulate the electrode whenever the rat ventured into the corner of the cage. Since stimulation of the hypothalamus is unpleasant, Olds believed that the rat would soon begin avoiding the corner of the cage.

Much to Old's surprise, the opposite thing happened: The rat began showing a "compulsive fondness for the corner, returning to it like an obsessed lover." Olds was puzzled; he couldn't understand why stimulation of the hypothalamus, which was supposed to be unpleasant, was causing the rat to develop behavior that actually sought what presumably was unpleasant.

On further investigation, Olds discovered that he had missed the targeted hypothalamus by a fraction of an inch and had, instead, sunk the electrode into the septal region of the brain. Based on his studies and those of others, the septal region would soon become known as the pleasure center of the brain.

Building on his accidental discovery, Olds invited colleague Peter Milner to work with him on an experiment that allowed the rats to stimulate the "pleasure center" themselves. Electrodes were sunk into the septal region of the brain, and were activated when the rats pressed a bar.

The rats gave up everything—food, water, and even sex—in their pursuit of the bar. Some rats pressed the bar thousands of times, around the clock, until they dropped dead from starvation, thirst, or sheer exhaustion. In summing up the results of the research, one writer penned the sentiment that "the implication was clear: The brain—not the genitals, the stomach, or anything else—is the Grand Central Station of pleasure."

Description of the experiment is found in Judith Hooper, "The Brain's River of Rewards," *American Health,* December 1987, p. 38

brain's natural pain killer, sometimes exerting analgesic effects more powerful than those of narcotic drugs, and that they produce a sense of calm and well-being (responsible for the well-known runner's high). What started as a mere trickle of interest in the scientific community a few decades ago has become a cascade, as researchers eagerly try to determine what role endorphins play. Even with all the research, we still don't have all the answers.

We do know that the role of endorphins is apparently much more complex than was originally thought. According to a report published in *Psychology Today*, endorphins play a role in "crying, laughing, thrills from music, acupuncture, placebos, stress, depression, chili peppers, compulsive gambling, aerobics, trauma, masochism, massage, labor and delivery, appetite, immunity, near-death experiences, and playing with pets."[24]

Scientists are also now proving what most of us already suspected: Certain foods give people a "sensory hit" and stimulate the release of endorphins. The result is a "feel good all over" experience that causes us to relate pleasure with food. And the main culprit, researchers have found, is sugary sweets. Johns Hopkins psychologist Elliott Blass has found that giving a sugar solution to rats under stress calms them in the same way that administering morphine does. But when the rats are given a drug that blocks the release of endorphins, the sugary solution no longer has a calming effect.[25]

Can there be a downside to all this ecstasy? Apparently so. In moderate amounts, endorphins can produce calm, kill pain, and give us the thrill of anticipation over a warm-from-the-oven slice of spicy apple pie. But when too many endorphins are released by the brain, the effect can be devastating to the immune system.

According to research being conducted at UCLA, a flood of endorphins that are released in response to pain or stress can bind to the natural killer cells, those that search out and destroy tumor cells. When endorphins bind to the natural killer cells, they falter and become less effective in their role as the body's "surveillance system."

Peptides

Some of the most exciting brain–body research currently being conducted focuses on peptides, the body's natural chemical messengers. Pioneered by neuropharmacologist Candace Pert, formerly with the National Institute of Mental Health, peptide research studies the hormones that govern communication between the brain and the body cells. "There's probably a peptide solution to every medical problem," she says. "An overstatement? I don't think so."[26] A band of researchers agrees with her—and believes peptide research may even hold the cure for acquired immunodeficiency syndrome (AIDS).

Peptides are intercellular messengers that are widely distributed throughout the nervous system, the gastrointestinal tract, and the pancreas.[27] "We have currently identified sixty to seventy, a number that may change rapidly as research advances, and they act like a sophisticated game of telephone played by the brain, the immune system, and the other organs and systems."[28]

The research continues, and the potential solutions are complex and difficult to grasp. Putting it simply, Pert says, "There's so much emphasis on molecular biology—on getting the genes for things—but the genes are only the blueprints. What can you do with blueprints? If you wanted to have a house, would you beg someone to give you the blueprints or would you want the house? The peptides are the house because the peptides are the *products* of genes."[29]

The Immune System

The immune system patrols and guards the body against attackers, both from without and from within. It is a complex system consisting of about a trillion cells called *lymphocytes* and about a hundred million trillion molecules called *antibodies*. According to Dr. Steven Locke, the associate director of Psychiatry Consultation Services at Beth Israel Hospital in Boston, the immune system does not operate within a biological vacuum but is sensitive to a number of outside influences. Locke sums up the role of the immune system as "a surveillance mechanism that protects the host from disease-causing microorganisms. It regulates susceptibility to cancers, infectious diseases, allergies, and autoimmune disorders."[30]

Dr. Barton F. Haynes, chief of the Division of Rheumatology and Immunology at Duke University Medical Center, points out that, like the brain:

> *The immune system is one of the body's most complex organizations. It must respond quickly to all external stimuli and be exquisitely precise in recognizing and killing foreign and abnormal cells, while not destroying the body's normal tissues. To operate in such a selective manner, it has evolved an intricate network of regulatory cells that turn the immune response on and off as needed.*[31]

When something goes awry in the immune system, Haynes says, infection results; when the entire immune system is compromised, as in AIDS, victims "eventually die from overwhelming infections."[32]

Lymphoid Organs

The organs of the immune system are spread throughout the body.[33] They are generally referred to as *lymphoid* organs because they are concerned with the growth, development, and deployment of lymphocytes, the white blood cells that are the key operatives of the immune system. Lymphoid organs include the bone marrow, the thymus, the lymph nodes, and the spleen, as well as the tonsils, the appendix, and clumps of lymphoid tissue in the small intestine known as Peyer's patches.

Cells that are destined to become lymphocytes are produced in the bone marrow cells in the hollow shafts of the long bones. Some of these cells, known as *stem cells*, migrate to the thymus, a multilobed organ that lies high behind the breastbone. There they multiply and mature into cells capable of producing an immune response.

Stem cells that develop in the thymus are called *T cells;* other lymphocytes, which appear to mature either in the bone marrow itself or in lymphoid organs other than the thymus, are called *B cells.* Lymph nodes are small bean-shaped structures distributed throughout the body in strings in the neck, armpits, abdomen, and groins, for instance.

Each lymph node contains a variety of specialized compartments. Some house T cells; others, B cells. Still others are filled with another type of immuno-competent cell, macrophages. Lymph nodes also contain webbed areas that enmesh antigens. The lymph node brings together the various components that are needed to produce the body's immune response.

Lymph nodes are linked by a network of lymphatic vessels similar to the blood vessels; they carry lymph, a clear fluid that bathes all of the body's tissues and that contains a variety of cells, most of them lymphocytes. Like a system of small creeks and streams that empty into progressively larger rivers, the vessels of the lymphatic network merge into increasingly larger tributaries. At the base of the neck, the large lymphatic ducts empty into the bloodstream.

Lymph and the cells and particles it carries, including antigens (cell-surface glycoproteins that the body recognizes as foreign) that have entered the body, drain out of the body's tissues, seeping through the thin walls of the smallest lymph vessels. As the lymph passes through lymph nodes, antigens are filtered out and more lymphocytes are picked up. The lymphocytes, along with other assorted cells of the immune system, are carried to the bloodstream, which delivers them to tissues throughout the body. The lymphocytes patrol everywhere for foreign antigens, then gradually drift back into the lymphatic system to begin the cycle all over again.

During their travels, circulating lymphocytes may spend several hours in the spleen, an organ in the abdomen that contains a high concentration of lymphocytes. Anyone whose spleen has been damaged by trauma or disease is very susceptible to infection.

The Immune System in Action

The immune system stockpiles a tremendous arsenal of immunocompetent cells. By storing just a few cells specific for each potential invader, it has room for the entire array. When an antigen appears, these few specifically matched cells are stimulated to multiply into a full-scale army. Later, to prevent this army from proliferating wildly, like a cancer, powerful suppressor mechanisms come into play.

Lymphocytes are the white cells that bear the major responsibility for carrying out the activities of the immune system; the immune system contains about a trillion of them. The two major classes of lymphocytes are the T cells, processed in the thymus, and B cells, which grow to maturity outside the thymus. B cells secrete antibodies; each specific antibody exactly matches a specific invading antigen, much as a key fits a lock. These antibodies inactivate the antigens, rendering them incapable of causing disease. The body is capable of making antibodies to millions of antigens.

T cells do not secrete antibodies, but their help is essential for antibody production. The T cells act as both messengers and destroyers in the fight against pathogens. T cells ravage healthy cells from another person's body, which is why organ transplant recipients have problems with rejection. Some T cells become *helper* cells that *turn on* B cells or other T cells; others become *suppressor* cells that turn these cells off. Scientists believe there are as many as 100 million different varieties of T cells and another 100 million antibodies.[34]

Natural killer cells are granular lymphocytes. As their name suggests, they attack and destroy other cells. They are called *natural* because they go into action without prior stimulation by a specific antigen. Most normal cells are resistant to natural killer cell activity. Most tumor cells, as well as normal cells infected with a virus, however, are susceptible. Thus, the natural killer cell may play a key role in immune surveillance against cancer, hunting down cells that develop abnormal changes.

Macrophages and monocytes are large cells that act as scavengers, or phagocytes: They can engulf and digest marauding microorganisms and other antigenic particles. Monocytes circulate in the blood, whereas macrophages are seeded through body tissues in a variety of guises.

Macrophages play a crucial role in initiating the immune response by "presenting" antigens to T cells in a special way that allows the T cells to recognize them. In addition, macrophages and monocytes secrete an amazing array of powerful chemical substances called monokines that help to direct and regulate the immune response.

Granulocytes, like macrophages and monocytes, are phagocytes and thus are capable of enveloping and destroying invaders. They contain granules filled with potent chemicals that enable them to digest microorganisms. These chemicals also contribute to inflammatory reactions and are responsible for the symptoms of allergy.

Approximately twenty proteins circulate in the blood in inactive form and make up the immune system's *complement system.* The complement substances are triggered by antibodies that lock onto antigens; the result is often the redness, warmth, and swelling that occur with inflammation. They can also rapidly kill bacteria and other pathogens by puncturing their cell membranes.

Immunity

As long ago as the fifth century B.C., Greek physicians noted that people who had recovered from the plague never got it again. They had acquired immunity, although that is not the name the Greeks attached to it. Acquired immunity results when T cells and B cells are activated and some of their subsets become "memory" cells. Then, the next time an individual encounters the same antigen, the immune system is primed to destroy it.

The degree of immunity depends on the kind of antigen, its amount, and how it enters the body. Infants are born with relatively weak immune responses, but they do get natural immunity during the first few months of life from antibodies they receive from their mothers. Children who are nursed receive even more antibodies through breast milk. In addition to acquiring immunity naturally, it is possible to be immunized with a vaccine. Vaccines contain microorganisms that have been altered so they produce an immune response but not full-blown disease.

Malfunctions

Fortunately, the immune system usually functions according to plan. Unfortunately, there are factors that can cause breakdown or failure of the immune system.[35] For example, studies have shown that the immune system weakens as we age.[36] As we age, the thymus shrinks; at age twenty it has lost approximately 75 percent of its size and function, and it is virtually gone by age sixty. The result is a significant change in the number and activity of T cells. Aging also upsets the ratio of helper to suppressor cells, resulting in turning off of the immune response. Still another effect of aging is the production of antibodies by B cells.

The immune system can also be suppressed by cancer; and it can be damaged by the drugs and radiation therapy used to treat cancer. These treatments kill the rapidly growing cancer cells in the body, but can also destroy normal cells, especially those of the immune system.

The body can also develop a serious overreaction to substances that are usually harmless. In this malfunction of the immune system, there is a severe allergic reaction; the result can be a condition like asthma or anaphylactic shock.

A similar malfunction of the immune system is what researchers have termed *autoimmune disease*. The fine mechanisms of the immune system become unbalanced, and the immune system reacts to normal body tissues as though it were allergic to them. Simply stated, the body becomes allergic to itself. Many of these diseases are serious, progressive ones, such as rheumatoid arthritis and systemic lupus erythematosus.

Cells of the immune system themselves may undergo malignant transformation, resulting in diseases such as lymphoma or leukemia. Finally, the immune system may be damaged or even destroyed by viral infections (such as AIDS) or congenital diseases that cause abnormalities in the immune system. Such immune system failures are called *immunodeficiency diseases*. When the immune system breaks down as a result of these diseases, the body is overwhelmed by infections and cancers because it can't destroy invading organisms.

We've known for years that disease can affect the immune system, but a more recent series of studies gives ample evidence that thoughts and emotions can also. A study of more than 4000 Vietnam-era army veterans showed that the immune system is affected by emotions such as depression and psychiatric conditions such as schizophrenia.[37]

Guided Imagery

Scientists expanding on Ader's research have since shown that people can consciously control the immune response by what they think. One experiment that uses guided imagery[38] has been conducted by G. Richard Smith, a psychiatrist at the University of Arkansas for Medical Sciences. A woman injected with chickenpox virus on the underside of her arm, had already had chickenpox; researchers knew then that her system would "recognize" the virus and cause a small bump to rise at the injection site within forty-eight hours. They also knew that, because she had already had chickenpox, she would not develop the disease itself.

Within a few hours, a nickel-sized bump appeared at the injection site. The bump slowly shrank and disappeared over the ensuing four to five days. Researchers confirmed the woman's immune response by taking blood samples that show increased size and activity among her white blood cells as they responded to the challenge by the virus. Researchers repeated the test twice, with the same results.

Researchers then determined whether the woman could indeed "turn down the volume" of her immune response. They injected the virus three more times over a period of three weeks. Each time, the woman used visualization techniques to visualize the reaction bump as being smaller; each time, the bump was actually smaller. Blood tests confirmed that there was less of a white blood cell response to each.

Finally, the woman was instructed to let her immune system response return to normal. Several more injections then resulted in nickel-sized bumps and a return to increased white blood cell activity. According to Smith, the researchers who conducted the study were "startled by the outcome," but further experiments have yielded the same results.

Focus on Research

One of the most startling examples of how the mind can alter the immune response was discovered by accident. In 1975, psychologist Robert Ader wanted to condition mice to avoid saccharin. He accomplished this by feeding mice saccharin while simultaneously injecting them with a drug that caused upset stomach, and that, incidentally, also suppressed the immune system. Associating the saccharin with the stomach pains, the mice soon learned to avoid the sweetener.

Ader then decided to try to reverse the taste aversion to saccharin. This time, Ader gave the same mice saccharin again, but without the drug that caused upset stomach. He was startled to find that the mice who had received the highest amounts of sweeteners during the initial conditioning died when they received saccharin alone.

Ader speculated that he had so successfully conditioned the mice that saccharin alone now served to weaken their immune systems enough to kill them.[39]

Source: Bernard Dixon, "Dangerous Thoughts," *Science,* April 1986, 63–66.

In another experiment, Dr. Howard Hall of Pennsylvania State University showed that humans can generate a more active immune response through imagery. In his experiments, volunteers imagined their white blood cells to be "strong and powerful sharks," and immune system activity soared. In their work with 126 cancer patients, psychologists G. Frank Lawlis and psychophysiologist Jeanne Achterberg asked the patients to use imagery in their fight against cancer. The pair found that how well the cancer responded—whether the tumors grew or shrunk—was directly related to how specific, vivid, strong, and clear the mental imagery of the patients was.[40]

Mental imagery is so powerful that it can even be used to zoom in on specific cells without affecting others, researchers say. Jeanne Achterberg paired up in a separate study with Dr. Mark S. Rider to examine just that. For the study, they chose thirty people and randomly assigned them to one of two groups. One group was asked to concentrate on their neutrophils; the other, on their lymphocytes. (Together, the neutrophils and the lymphocytes make up 85 to 90 percent of the white cells in the bloodstream.)

The people in the study underwent a six-week training program in which they were taught to focus on images of the location, shape, and movement patterns of either the neutrophils or the lymphocytes. The researchers used music to enhance the imagery. When blood counts were taken both before and after the final twenty-minute imagery session, the results were undeniable: the specific cell that each person had concentrated on was decreased significantly. The other cells were not. In commenting on the study, Achterberg and Rider said, "The directed image was cell specific: that is, it affected the cells toward which it was intended or directed, and not others.[41]

Imagery can be combined with traditional medical treatment to boost the immune system and enhance traditional treatment, researchers say. In one study, researchers looked at 225 patients who had advanced cancer of the breast, bowel, or lung; the patients used imagery in combination with the traditional medical treatment usually prescribed for their individual cancers.

At the end of the study, researchers found that the patients had an average survival time of eight to nineteen months longer than the national average for persons with those cancers. Two years after the study was completed, eighty-two of the patients were still alive. Of those, 19 percent had tumor regression; 22 percent showed no evidence at all of the cancer.

Researchers conducting the study were interested in determining whether personality affects how well people are able to use imagery. They gave the study participants five different psychological tests, then subjected them to medical and social interviews. As the study drew to a close, the researchers chose twelve patients who had already outlived their predicted survival time and compared them with ten patients with matching diagnoses who had died. Researchers found that the survivors were more creative, more receptive to new ideas, more flexible, and more argumentative. They also had strong egos and expressed feelings of adequacy and vitality. They turned to their own inner resources when things started going downhill.

Other research shows that imagery specifically impacts the immune system cells responsible for fighting cancer. In one study, cancer patients practiced both relaxation and guided imagery. After one year, the patients had improved T-cell activity and increased natural killer–cell activity. (T cells recognize the presence of an antigen and initiate specific mechanisms to destroy it; they are the cells responsible for cancer surveillance in the body. The natural killer cells, of course, zero in on cancer cells and destroy them.)

Janice Kiecolt-Glaser studied the impact of imagery on the immune system's powerful killer cells, but here subjects were healthy. Kiecolt-Glaser found that imagery not only improved T-cell functioning but also produced a slower resting heart rate, a slower breathing rate, and less perspiration.[41]

The Brain–Immune System Connection

Various studies have shown a real connection between the central nervous system and the immune system, a connection that allows the mind to influence either susceptibility or resistance to disease. For example, the thymus gland plays an essential role in the maturation of immune system cells, and researchers have discovered extensive networks of nerve endings laced throughout the thymus gland.[42] Rich supplies of nerve also serve the spleen, bone marrow, and lymph nodes, giving further evidence of a link between the brain and the immune system.

Further, the cells of the immune system seem to be equipped to respond to chemical signals from the central nervous system. For example, the surface of the lymphocytes has been found to contain receptors for a variety of central nervous system chemical messengers,[43] such as catecholamines, prostaglandins, serotonin, endorphins, sex hormones, thyroid hormone, and growth hormone.[44] National Institute of Mental Health researchers discovered that "certain white blood cells were equipped with the molecular equivalent of antennas tuned specifically to receive messages from the brain."[45]

Because of these receptors on the lymphocytes, physical and psychological stress alter the immune system. Stress causes the body to release several powerful neurohormones, including catecholamines, corticosteroids, and endorphins, which bind with the receptors on the lymphocytes and alter immune function. Corticosteroids, in fact, have been found to have such a powerful influence in suppressing the immune system that they are widely used to treat allergic conditions (such as asthma and hay fever) and autoimmune disorders (such as rheumatoid arthritis and rejection of transplanted organs).[46] These corticosteroids and other brain chemicals are unleashed by the hypothalamus, a section of the brain that is a virtual drug factory.[47] The chemicals released by the hypothalamus have the most profound effects on the immune system.

More than three decades ago, Soviet researcher Elena Korneva discovered at the Institute of Experimental Medicine in Leningrad that she could produce changes in the immune system by selectively damaging different parts of the hypothalamus. Expanding on that theory, French researcher Gerard Renoux showed that not only does the brain influence immunity, but that different sides of the brain exercise different kinds of immunity. Renoux's brain experiments on mice show the profound influence of the brain—and the differing influences as well. When Renoux removed a third of the left side of the mouse's brain, the mouse could no longer respond with vigor to foreign material. When part of the right brain was removed, the number of T cells in the mouse's spleen was decreased.

While we do understand many of the connections between the brain and the immune system, some remain a mystery. For example, when the thymus secretes its hormones, two things happen: (1) thymosin is secreted, causing the T cells to mature, and (2) the brain is signaled. Researchers still don't know the function and purpose of the signals to the brain.

Indiana University researcher David Felten and his colleagues did some of the pioneering neurological research showing that the brain and the nervous system are related to the immune system. Their research showed that many of the areas near nerve endings where impulses are sent out are situated near the thymus and spleen, and whole groups of nerve fibers are situated near these cells, suggesting a direct connection between the immune system and the central nervous system.[48]

According to the latest scientific studies, the link between the mind and the immune system "has gained a new dimension with the growing evidence that psychosocial factors directly affect immune function," and thus, say researchers, have the potential of influencing a wide range of disorders, including allergies, infections, autoimmune diseases, and even cancer.[49] As one practitioner put it, "The human body can be conceived of as a five million-year-old healer, with an internal pharmacopoeia of neuropeptides, neuroendocrine secretions, and immunological restoratives that maintain and enhance health."[50]

More research is needed in the infant science of psychoneuroimmunology; fortunately, federal agencies and private foundations alike are pledging increasing amounts. But too few researchers have interdisciplinary training and experience. For example, few psychologists also are trained as immunologists, and few immunologists really understand psychology.[51] So the most challenging issue presented by psychoneuroimmunology, some researchers believe, is whether thought, emotion, and behavior can directly enhance immune function and thereby prevent the onset or alter the course of diseases involving immunity.

Notes

1. Janice K. Kiecolt-Glaser and Ronald Glaser, "Psychoneuroimmunology: Past, Present, and Future," *Health Psychology*, 8(6): 1989, 677–682.

2. Kenneth R. Pelletier and Denise L. Herzing, "Psychoneuroimmunology: Toward a Mind–Body Model," *Advances*, 5: 1, 27–56.

3. Gina Maranto, "Emotions: How They Affect Your Body," *Discover*, November: 1984, 35.

4. Maranto.

5. Maranto.

6. Melissa Ludtke, "Can the Mind Help Cure Disease?" *Time*, March 12: 1990, 76.

7. Angell, Marcia, "Disease as a Reflection of the Psyche," *New England Journal of Medicine*, 312: 1985, 1570–1572.

8. The historical data are summarized from "Emotions and the Body," *Executive Health Report*,

11: 10, July:1985, 1–4; and Gina Maranto, "The Mind Within the Brain," *Discover,* May: 1984, 34–43.

9. From Bob Wechsler, "A New Prescription: Mind Over Malady," *Discover,* February: 1987, 52– 53.

10. Maranto, "Emotions: How They Affect Your Body," p. 36.

11. Wechsler, p. 53.

12. Daniel Goleman and Joel Gurin, editors, *Mind/Body Medicine: How to Use Your Mind for Better Health* (New York: Consumer Reports Books, 1993), pp. 58–59.

13. "Emotions and the Body," pp. 2–3.

14. "Emotions and the Body," p. 3.

15. Maranto, "Emotions," p. 38.

16. Wechsler, p. 52.

17. Donald B. Calne, *The Brain* (Bethesda, Maryland: U. S. Department of Health, Education, and Welfare, Public Health Service, National Institutes of Health, NIH Publication #79-1813, July 1979), pp. 7–10.

18. Anne H. Rosenfeld, "Brain Attack," *Psychology Today* May: 1988, 68.

19. Anne Rosenfeld.

20. Israel Rosenfeld, *The Invention of Memory: A New View of the Brain* (New York: Basic Books, 1988).

21. Israel Rosenfeld, p. 69.

22. Erica E. Goode, "Accounting for Emotion," *U. S. News and World Report,* June 27: 1988, 53.

23. Erica Goode.

24. Janet L. Hopson, "A Pleasurable Chemistry," *Psychology Today,* July/August: 1988, 29.

25. Paul Raeburn, "Eater's High," *American Health,* December: 1987, 42.

26. Joan Goldberg, "Peptide Power," *American Health,* June: 1990, 35–41.

27. Marvin R. Brown and Laurel A. Fisher, "Brian Peptides and Intercellular Messengers," *Journal of the American Medical Association,* 251(10): 1984, 1310–1314.

28. Goldberg.

29. Goldberg.

30. Signe Hammer, "The Mind As Healer," *Science Digest,* April: 1984, 49.

31. Barton F. Haynes, "The Body's Defense Strategy," *Executive Health Report,* 23(11): 1987, 1.

32. Haynes.

33. National Institute of Allergy and Infectious Diseases, *Understanding the Immune System* (Bethesda, Maryland: National Institutes of Health, July 1985, NIH Publication #85–529), pp. 2–10.

34. Shannon Brownlee, "The Body at War," *U. S. News and World Report,* July 2: 1990, 48–54.

35. These factors are summarized in Haynes, p. 3.

36. Jeff Gates, "Aging and the Immune System," *Vibrant Life,* September/October: 1989, 16–19.

37. Drue H. Barrett and W. Dana Flanders, "Immune System Function and Its Relationship to Psychiatric Conditions," Presented at the Annual Meeting of the Society of Behavioral Medicine, April 1, 1989, San Francisco, CA.

38. Sally Squires, "Visions to Boost Immunity," *American Health,* July: 1987, 56–61.

39. Stephen S. Hall, "A Molecular Code Links Emotions, Mind, and Health," *Smithsonian,* June 1989.

40. Dossey, p. 105.

41. Rebecca Stephens, "Imagery: A Strategic Intervention to Empower Clients," *Clinical Nurse Specialist,* 7(4): 1993, 172–173.

42. Dossey, pp. 105–106.

43. Hall.

44. Ornstein and Sobel.

45. Brownlee.

46. Brownlee.

47. Information on the hypothalamus is from Steven Locke and Douglas Colligan, *The Healer Within* (New York: E.P. Dutton, 1986).

48. Locke and Colligan.

49. Jorge H. Daruna and Jane E. Morgan, "Psychosocial Effects on Immune Function: Neuroendocrine Pathways," *Psychosomatics,* 31(1): 1990, 4.

50. Maureen Groër, "Psychoneuroimmunology," *American Journal of Nursing,* August: 1991, 33.

51. Groër.

3

THE IMPACT OF STRESS ON HEALTH

The only difference between a diamond and a lump of coal is that
the diamond had a little more pressure put on it.—ANONYMOUS

Early in the nineteenth century, English author Thomas Lovell Beddoes penned a poetic sentiment that could serve as an eloquent description of the battle that, today, we wage daily against an opponent we call *stress*. Lacking today's sophisticated medical technology, Beddoes still managed to capture the essence of stress in a few brief lines:

If a man could see
The perils and diseases that he elbows
Each day he walks a mile; which catch at him,
Which fall behind him as he passes;
Then would he know that Life's a single pilgrim,
Fighting unarmed among a thousand soldiers.

Almost a century later, practitioners gathered at the 1949 Conference on Life and Stress and Heart Disease provided the first formal recognition that stress could precipitate chronic disease and gave stress one of its earliest formal definitions: "A force which induces distress or strain upon both the emotional and physical makeup."[1]

Definitions of Stress

Our understanding of stress has come a long way in the last four or five decades. Stress researcher Hans Selye, whose work in the early half of the twentieth century was recognized as some of the first to identify stress and its effects on the

Focus on Research

Early observations of the relationship between stress and health included the phenomenon of "voodoo death," or otherwise unexplained death that follows extreme fear. In 1942 Dr. Walter Cannon described a case in which a tribeswoman ate some fruit that she later learned to be spiritually forbidden. Although no one directly threatened her, she expected evil spirits to attack and harm her. Wound up by this expectation, she literally scared herself to death. Cannon postulated that the battering of her body by continual stress was what led to her death.

Source: Howard S. Friedman, *The Self-Healing Personality* (New York: Henry Holt and Company, 1991), p. 31.

body, defined stress as a nonspecific response of the body to any demand. The pioneers of stress research categorized all stress as negative or bad; today, we understand that stress is anything in the environment that causes us to adapt and that a "stressful" situation can be either happy (like the birth of a baby) or sad (like the death of a loved one).

We also understand that stress isn't limited to what goes on in our thoughts. We know that stress is "a nonspecific automatic biological response to demands made upon an individual."[2] Scientifically speaking, stress is "any challenge to homeostasis," or the body's internal sense of balance. Stress is a biological and biochemical process that begins in the brain and that spreads through the autonomic nervous system, causing hormone release and eventually exerting an effect on the immune system. Simply stated, the stress response starts in two major systems: (1) the nervous system, which reacts almost simultaneously, and (2) the endocrine (or hormone) system, which takes longer to react but which persists much longer. Stress sets off a complex domino effect in the body, involving an entire series of body systems and a whole range of powerful hormones.

We know that stress does not do the same thing to all people. One researcher defined stress as the point at which the organism's ability to perform easily is exceeded by the demands put upon it and that the result, psychophysiological strain, can be tempered by a person's coping ability and by moderating factors.[3]

A good example of how stressful situations can be altered by perception and outlook was witnessed by Colorado cardiovascular researcher Dr. Robert Eliot while he was traveling in the Middle East.[4] In downtown Riyadh, Saudi Arabia, Eliot saw two Arabs, both driving Mercedes, crash into each other. The two men, uninjured, jumped out of their cars and began hugging and laughing instead of yelling at each other, as Eliot would have expected. Curious about their odd exchange, Eliot asked his interpreter what the two men were saying. The interpreter explained that the two men were thanking Allah for the chance to meet this way.

Plenty of evidence confirms that the way you perceive stress has a lot to do with how stress affects you. American Institute of Stress president Paul J. Rosch likens stress to a ride on a roller coaster. "There are those at the front of the car, hands over head, clapping, who can't wait to get on again," he points out, "and those at the back cringing, wondering how they got into this and how soon it's going to be over."[5] Or, to put it another way, one roller coaster passenger "has his back stiffened, his knuckles are white, his eyes shut, jaws clenched, just waiting for it to be over. The wide-eyed thrill-seeker relishes every plunge, can't wait to do it again."[6]

Another difference depends on the timing of the stress.[7] We are all more vulnerable to the effects of stress at certain times—especially when we're already weakened by some circumstance in our lives. Most researchers agree that the time to make major changes in life is *not* the period following an already stressful event; for example, it's probably not the best idea to move to a new town and begin a new job just after going through a divorce. And since everyone is vulnerable to different stresses at different times, it's wise to reduce unnecessary challenges when you're particularly vulnerable, say the researchers.

Rosch points out, too, that differences in perception can cause some stress to be good stress (*eustress*) rather than bad stress (*distress*), and he uses as an example symphony conductors. "They work long hours, travel frequently, deal with prima donnas and sensitive artists, yet they live long and productive lives. They've got positive vibes going. They enjoy what they're doing, have pride of accomplishment, the approbation of their peers, and the applause of the audience, all positive stresses."[8]

In essence, some things that are stressful also promote curiosity and exploration; they are challenging, stimulating, and rewarding. Competitive sports are an excellent example. It's extremely stressful, both physically and emotionally, to gear up for a football game, worry about winning, and then pound across the field for three hours in an attempt to do it. But many believe the rewards and the thrill are well worth the stress, and millions of fans couldn't agree more. On the other hand, boredom and understimulation can also be distressful.

Effects on the Body

No one is free of stress. According to figures from New York's American Institute of Stress published in *Time* magazine, 90 percent of all American adults experience high stress levels one or two times a week; a fourth of all American adults are subject to crushing levels of stress nearly every day. A survey of American women revealed that 57 percent felt excessively *di*stressed much or most of the time.

Eustress promotes productivity and facilitates our efforts; distress leads to a loss of productivity and causes health problems.[9] As one writer describes it, eustress is exhilarating: You're under control but excited, like riding a canoe in a swiftly flowing stream. The opposite things happen with distress: Out of control, you feel like a victim in a runaway train.[10] The key to good health, the researchers say, is learning how to turn bad stress (distress) into good stress (eustress).

Stress occurs whenever there is change and whenever we are forced to adapt to that change. The process that happens in the body in response to stress is called the *general adaptation syndrome*, because it occurs as we adapt. The very process of living entails change, so people of all ages, both sexes, every occupational group, and every socioeconomic group are susceptible to stress. Unremitting stress, the kind that requires constant adaptation to chronic change, can become a threat to health, because it is very difficult to maintain lifelong wellness when a large percentage of body energy is channeled into coping with stress.[11]

Stress has been shown to affect almost all body systems, resulting in cardiovascular disease, neuromuscular disorders (including migraine headache and chronic back pain), respiratory and allergic disorders, immunologic disorders, gastrointestinal disturbances (including peptic ulcer disease, irritable bowel syndrome, nausea, vomiting, and diarrhea), skin diseases, dental problems, and a host of other disorders. Since most diseases are caused by a variety of different factors instead of a single cause, stress probably does not *cause* illness, but various studies have demonstrated a strong link between distress and the onset of disease. In preventing disease, the best strategy is to eliminate as much distress as you can, and to change your attitude toward the things you can't prevent.

Today, brain research is booming; scientists from a wide range of disciplines have entered the field, and great strides are being made toward finding out exactly how emotions impact health.

Types of Stress

Basically, there are three types of stress: physical, psychological, and psychosocial.

Physical stress involves stressors in the environment—factors such as extremes in temperature, environmental pollution, constant noise, or electric shock. Researchers also categorize physiological factors as physical stress; examples include injury, surgery, hypoglycemia, prolonged exercise, or an inadequate supply of oxygen.

Psychological stress stems from the way we feel, the attitudes we have, and the way we react toward anything that is threatening us, whether the threat is real or imagined. As in the example of the roller coaster, one person may react calmly, while another may become extremely stressed.

Psychosocial stress involves stressors from interpersonal relationships, arguments or conflicts with family members, neighbors, employers, friends, or other people around us. Psychosocial stress may result from intense social interactions, but it can also occur when there is isolation as a result of inadequate social interactions.[12]

The Stress Response

When the body becomes stressed, regardless of the source of the stress, it undergoes what scientists now recognize as the stress response. The stress response is, simply stated, the fight-or-flight response used by primitive people as they faced the various threats in their environment. When facing one of their enemies, a saber-toothed tiger, let's say—their bodies reacted in a very specific way that prepared them to either fight the tiger or run for their life.

Unfortunately, our bodies still react the same way to threats—real or imagined—even though, in a vast majority of cases, the stressor does not require us to fight or flee. As Harvard cardiologist Herbert Benson remarked, "The fight-or-flight emergency response is inappropriate to today's social stresses."[13] And Boston University psychiatrist Peter Knapp pointed out that "when you get a Wall Street broker using the responses a cave man used to fight the elements, you've got a problem."[14]

With stress as an enemy, the body has powerful and intricate weapons to use in response. "The problem is that many of our battleship's weapons are beautifully designed," one writer commented, "but for the wrong war. The enemy has greatly changed. Our stress responses were programmed for life in the primitive state, thousands of years before we became 'civilized.' No longer are our stresses a simple matter of life and death threats; they now involve much more intricate and complex challenges."[15]

Each phase of the stress response carried with it benefits for the primitive man or woman who faced physical dangers, and those same benefits have become drawbacks for the modern man or woman who faces the social stresses of our day. Let's look at a dozen phases of the stress response and examine why yesterday's benefits are today's drawbacks.[16]

1. The adrenal glands start pumping out a group of hormones called the glucocorticoids, which are essential to the metabolism of glucose in the body; they are, in the right amounts, critical to life (if the adrenal glands are removed, death follows within a few days). But secreted in excessive amounts, they can impair the immune system and render the body susceptible to illness and disease.[17] The hormones pumped out by the adrenal glands include cortisol, cortisone, and catecholamines (the body's chemical messengers of stress); they provided primitive people with the protection of an instant allergy reaction from a dust-off with an attacking foe. Today, we're not so lucky: Too much cortisone and catecholamines destroy the body's resistance to cancer, infections, illness, and the complications of surgery; the immune response weakens. It becomes difficult to fight off even a minor cold. Too much cortisone over a prolonged time causes lymph glands to shrivel, bones to become brittle, blood pressure to soar, and the stomach to lose its resistance to gastric acid.

2. The thyroid pumps out thyroid hormones, which accelerate metabolism and helped primitive people burn fuel faster to give them energy for fight or flight. It does the same thing to us today, but because we're not engaged in life-or-death battles, it produces a different set of symptoms: insomnia, shaky nerves, heat intolerance, and exhaustion. It's the reason why some people lose weight under stress.

3. The hypothalamus releases endorphins, powerful natural pain killers that enabled primitive people to fight or flee even when injured. But chronic, relentless stress depletes endorphins and can in turn aggravate migraine headaches, backaches, and even arthritis pain. The hypothalamus, located at the place in the brain that connects thinking to peripheral body processes, also releases the brain's key initiator of the stress response; corticotropin-releasing hormone (CRH). CRH, injected into the midbrain, causes anxiety and the physical stress response.

   4.   Sex hormones (progesterone in females and testosterone in males) are reduced. That served an important function in primitive times: The decreased libido and fertility came in handy during times of drought, overcrowding, and decreased food supply by giving the community fewer mouths to feed. Sadly, the same thing happens to you under stress: You may lose your sex drive, become infertile, or suffer from sexual dysfunction (such as premature ejaculation or failure to reach orgasm). Women under acute stress may precipitate a menstrual period early. With unrelenting, chronic stress, they may be more likely to bleed irregularly or not at all (amennorrhea).

   5.   Coordination of the digestive tract shuts down. In primitive people, all blood was diverted to the muscles, rendering them capable of extraordinary feats of power; the mouth went dry, too. The same things happen today. Eating while under stress can result in stomach bloating, nausea, abdominal discomfort or cramping, and even diarrhea. The dry mouth problems persist, too. Ask any public speaker whose mouth is so dry he or she can't speak. Dry mouth is such an acute symptom of stress, in fact, that in China it's used as a lie detector test.

   6.   Release of sugar (glucose) into the bloodstream is followed by a boost in insulin to metabolize it, something that provided primitive people with "fuel for the sprint," or a burst of short-lived energy. That same scenario today can cause hypoglycemia; in some cases, increased insulin demand on the pancreas can aggravate diabetes.

   7.   Cholesterol is released into the bloodstream, mostly from the liver; it took over where blood sugar left off in supplying sustained energy to the muscles. But today's man or woman under chronic stress doesn't generally need more cholesterol to sustain energy, so the cholesterol is deposited in the blood vessels. The result is well-publicized and well-documented by our nation's rate of heart disease fatalities.

   8.   The heartbeat begins racing, a physiological response that pumps more blood to the muscles and lungs, enabling fuel and oxygen to be carried more efficiently to the muscles, something primitive people needed. Blood flow to the muscles of the arms and legs increases 300 to 400 percent.[18] The result today is high blood pressure; left unchecked, it can lead to stroke, bursting of an aneurysm, or many less dire problems.

   9.   Breathing rate increases, and in turn air supply. Deeper breathing enabled primitive people to have a greater supply of oxygen for the increased blood supply coursing through the lungs. That's okay unless you're a smoker (or live with one); the lung damage from cigarette smoke is much amplified during stress because the elements in the smoke penetrate the lungs more easily.

   10.   The blood thickens and coagulates more readily. Thickening of the blood enabled primitive people to fight infection, stop bleeding from a wound, and increase the capacity of the blood to carry oxygen to the muscles. When the blood

turns thick under stress today, the result can be heart attack, stroke, or embolus.

11. The skin "crawls," blanches, and sweats. This was a tremendous benefit to primitive people, who found themselves in a dire struggle for life: All of the hairs stood on end, increasing the appearance of overall size. It gave them a sort of "radar" that helped detect the elements of the environment. It heightened the sense of touch. It provided a cooling mechanism for overheated muscles. It diverted blood away from wounds. Today, it decreases the resistance of skin to electricity (the principle behind most lie detector tests).

12. All five senses become acute. In primitive people, pupils dilated to enhance night vision; overall mental performance was sharpened; the senses of hearing and touch were improved; and the entire body was brought to peak function. The same thing happens today, but without the burst of physical energy that brings an end to a sporadic stressful situation, we are more likely to suffer from chronic stress. Thus, the senses are constantly on red alert, and sensory burnout can result. As a result, your sight, hearing, taste, smell, and sense of touch actually become less efficient over time.

The combination of all the things that happen during the twelve phases of the stress response adds up to a real assault on the body. That assault may be even greater if stress is prolonged, a condition that causes what Robert S. Eliot calls the *vigilance reaction*. According to Eliot, the vigilance reaction, too, was helpful to our ancestors. It gave them "staying power" they needed to survive with scant supplies of food, salt, and water, during both summer droughts and long, harsh winters.

But like the stress response, the vigilance reaction that served our ancestors so well today wreaks havoc on our bodies. The response originates in the hypothalamus, stimulating the pituitary gland, which then stimulates the cortex of the adrenal gland to produce cortisol. The effect? Over the long haul, as when stress is long unabated, the cortisol causes fat storage, salt retention, and increased fats and cholesterol in the bloodstream. Other effects include erratic heart rhythms, increased blood pressure, increased stomach acid, irritability, suppression of the sex hormones, and loss of essential minerals, including potassium and magnesium.[19]

Outcomes of Stress

Stress is costly. Obviously, no one can put a precise price tag on the various health costs of stress, but figures from a variety of sources give us a fairly good idea of its devastating impact. For example, researchers at the American Institute of Stress estimate that 75 to 90 percent of all visits to health-care providers result from stress-related disorders. The American Heart Association says that more than half of all Americans who die succumb to heart disease and that more than 50 million work days a year, adding up to a whopping $8 billion, are lost annually to heart-related diseases. Just among the nation's executives, an estimated $10 to $20 billion is lost each year through absence, hospitalization, and early death, much of it as a result of stress.[20] The National Council on Compensation Insurance says that stress-related claims account for almost one fifth of all occupational disease.[21] Fully one-fourth of all Workman's Compensation claims are for stress-related injuries, and researchers estimate that 60 to 80 percent of all industrial accidents are related to stress.

Stress-related symptoms and illnesses are costing industry a conservatively estimated $150 billion a year in absenteeism, company medical expenses, and lost productivity.[22] The results of a study at New Mexico State University suggest a strong relationship between stress and absenteeism. Other studies show that stress accounts for more than 20 percent of the costs associated with high job turnover, strikes, work stoppages, absenteeism, and decline in productivity.[23]

What happens when people under stress turn to drugs and alcohol to ease the pain? This nation loses an estimated $20 billion in worker productivity as a result of alcoholism. And for years the two most frequently prescribed drugs in this country are Valium and Librium, both tranquilizers.[24] The four best-selling drugs in the nation are ulcer medications, hypertension drugs, tranquilizers, and antidepressants. The American Academy of Family Physicians estimates that two thirds of all office visits to family doctors are prompted by stress-related symptoms.

"We live in a world of uncertainties," summed up cardiologist Herbert Benson, "everything from the nuclear threat to job insecurity to the near assassination of the President to the lacing of medicines with poisons."[25] Those stressors, say the experts, can accumulate enough to result in chronic stress, and, if the human organism isn't resilient enough, the final product is illness.

Left unchecked, unremitting stress can also shorten your life. In one long-term study that gives a particularly good measure of the effects of stress, researchers studied more than 600 people over twelve years. Researchers tested each study subject at the beginning of the period, asking if they suffered from distress; at the end of the twelve years, they discovered that the existence of distress at the study's outset was a good predictor of who would die during the period of the study. Even when researchers tried to "juggle" the results—by controlling for factors such as smoking, cholesterol levels, obesity, or high blood pressure, or by excluding people with chronic heart disease—the figures remained the same.[26]

A similar study in Sweden followed 752 men for seven years. Researchers found what they expected: The men who were under stress were more likely to die prematurely than those who weren't under stress. But the researchers also found something a little unexpected: the *type* of stress matters, too. In the Swedish study, certain kinds of stress had more pronounced effects than others. For example, those who felt insecure at work had a 2.4-fold increased risk of dying. Those who had been divorced or separated from their wives or who were in serious financial trouble during the year before the evaluation had triple the risk of dying. And those who had been sued had 7.7 times the risk of dying prematurely than those who had not. Overall, say the researchers, suffering three or more stressful life events more than tripled the risk of dying for the men involved in the study.[27] One might wonder, of course, whether the greater culprit for health risk was the external act of being sued or divorced, or perhaps some personality characteristic that made them more likely to get divorced or sued.

The good news is that stress doesn't have to knock you out. Research shows that some people manage to be resilient to stress; others exhibit what scientists call "hardiness," an ability to resist the ill effects of stress. Research has also indicated that there are things that help you cope better with stressors. To figure out where you stand, it's important to know the factors that lead to stress, the physiological reactions of the body when under stress, and the way that stress can compromise the immune system and lead to illness.

Factors Leading to Stress

While researchers recognized the presence of stress decades earlier and had specifically linked it to disease several years earlier, it was not until early in the 1950s that anyone was able to identify a list of specific events that contributed to stress. During the early 1950s, University of Washington psychiatrist Thomas Holmes noted that tuberculosis had occurred among patients after a cluster of disruptive events, such as a death in the family, a new job, or a marriage. Based partly on that observation and partly on his extensive research, Holmes pronounced that the single common denominator for stress is ". . . significant change in the life pattern of an individual." Holmes emphasized that stress did not *cause* the tuberculosis—tuberculosis bacteria had to be present—but that stress somehow weakened the body or made it more vulnerable to the disease.[28]

Branching out in his research, Holmes began to search for specific links between disease and what he called *life events,* those things in life that call for the greatest adjustment. He found that the more life events a person was subjected to within a brief period of time, the more likely he or she was to become ill. Holmes developed a social-readjustment rating scale along with his colleague Richard Rahe; commonly known as the Holmes-Rahe Scale, it assigns a numerical score to the almost four dozen stressors, or life changes, that increase the risk of disease. Subsequent research by hosts of independent scientists has verified the accuracy of the Holmes-Rahe scale.

The Holmes-Rahe Scale

The testee scans the list of life changes, pinpoints the ones experienced within the last year, and adds up the numerical scores to get a total. The items in the Holmes-Rahe scale, along with their numerical scores, are:

100	Death of spouse
73	Divorce
65	Marital separation
63	Jail term
63	Death of close family member
53	Personal injury or illness

50	Marriage
47	Fired at work
45	Marital reconciliation
45	Retirement
44	Change in health of family member
40	Pregnancy
39	Sexual difficulties
39	Gain of new family member
39	Business readjustment
38	Change in financial status
37	Death of close friend
36	Change to different line of work
35	Change in number of arguments with spouse
31	Mortgage or loan over $10,000
30	Foreclosure of mortgage or loan
29	Change in responsibilities at work
29	Son or daughter leaving home
29	Trouble with in-laws
28	Outstanding personal achievement
26	Wife begins or quits work
25	Change in living conditions
24	Change in personal habits
23	Trouble with boss
20	Change in work hours or conditions
20	Change in residence
19	Change in recreation
19	Change in number or type of church activities
18	Change in number or type of social activities
17	Mortgage or loan under $10,000
16	Change in sleeping habits
15	Change in number of family get-togethers
15	Change in eating habits
13	Vacation
12	Christmas
11	Minor violations of the law

According to Holmes and Rahe, if you score between 150 and 199 in one year, you have a 37 percent chance of getting sick during the following year. If you score between 200 and 299, your chances of getting sick jump to 51 percent. And if you score over 300, you have a 79 percent chance of getting sick during the following year.

Note that not all the items on the scale are "bad" things. Few of us would consider things like marriage, an outstanding personal achievement, a vacation, or Christmas to be negatives. Also, some items could be either negative or positive.

A change in the number of arguments with your spouse, for instance, might mean that you are having fewer arguments and getting along better than ever.

The key word is *change*. Each item on the Holmes-Rahe scale describes something that causes us to change our routine, to adapt. The thing that requires change or adaptation can be positive or negative. "In contrast to what most people think, a stressor is not necessarily an unpleasant stimulus," wrote one researcher. "Many stressors are unpleasant, such as a rude clerk in a store or stepping from an air-conditioned room to the hot and humid out-of-doors or being exposed to pollution, or having a stomach ache. A kiss from a pretty girl or a handsome man can be a source of stress, too."[29]

The mind is extremely powerful. Research has shown that merely *thinking about* one of the stressors on the list can evoke emotions so strong that they can induce the stress response. Isolating one of the items on the list, Holmes said that "a person often catches cold when a mother-in-law comes to visit. Patients mentioned mothers-in-law so often that we came to consider them a common cause of disease in the United States."[30]

Major Life Events

Your attitudes, your perceptions, and the way you look at stressful events in your life can help you resist the ill effects of stress. A perfect example of resilience to stress was uncovered by University of Michigan researcher Louis Ferman. He found a "hard-luck victim" who had been laid off three times: first in 1962 when the Studebaker Corporation folded, next in the 1970s by a truck manufacturer that went under, and finally during cutbacks at a Chrysler plant. Ferman said that by all accounts, "He should have been a basket case, but he was one of the best-adjusted fellows I've run into." Asked his secret, the man replied, "I've got a loving wife and go to church every Sunday."[31]

Without that kind of attitude or perception, major life events can weaken the system enough to bring on serious illness or disease. Yale oncologist and surgeon Bernie S. Siegel attributes some of the cancers of his patients to traumatic loss or crisis in their lives. One study of children with leukemia showed that thirty-one of the thirty-three in the study had experienced a traumatic loss or move within the two years prior to their diagnosis. A separate study at Albert Einstein College of Medicine found that children with cancer had twice as many recent crises as similar, cancer-free children. Even career reversals may play a role, says Siegel; "The defeats of Napoleon Bonaparte, Ulysses S. Grant, William Howard Taft, and Hubert Humphrey have often been implicated in their fatal cancers."[32]

Still another study involved more than 3000 women who came to the Heidelberg University Gynecological Clinic for breast examination. The women who were not diagnosed with cancer were compared to those who did have cancer as diagnosed through various tests. Researchers determined that three life events had significant relationship to the development of cancer. One was the death of the mother before the woman was sixteen. The second was divorce, separation, or widowhood at any time during the woman's life. And the third was at least one traumatic event during World War II that caused considerable disturbance (researchers noted events like air raids, the death of close relatives, becoming a refugee, transfer of population, encampment, being buried alive, or injury to relatives as among the most disturbing).[33]

A study of 8000 cancer patients with various types of tumors concluded that "in most of the cases, the cancer appeared during a period of severe and intense life stress often involving loss, separation, and other bereavements."[34] To sort out genetic factors from those attributable to stress, W. H. Green at the University of Rochester studied identical twins, one of whom had developed leukemia, and found that one twin in each pair usually developed leukemia shortly after a major psychological upheaval, while the stress-free twin did not.

Various studies have shown that children, too, respond to stressful life events by becoming ill. In essence, children who suffer frequent stressful life events within a short time (such as a year) usually report more physical illness, ranging from streptococcal infections to cancer, and more visits to the doctor, higher rates of psychiatric illness or maladaptive behavior, more accidents, and more injuries. While much more research needs to be done involving children, evidence from the studies that have been completed indicate that there may be an association between life stresses among children and episodes of chronic illnesses such as asthma, diabetes, and hemophilia.[35]

Hassles

Another factor involved in stress is what researchers call *hassles.* The theory is aptly illustrated in an excerpt from a poem by Charles Bukowski:

> *. . . It's not the large things that*
> *send a man to the*
> *madhouse . . . no, it's the*
> *continuing series of*
> *small tragedies*
> *that send a man to the madhouse . . .*
> *not the death of his love*
> *but a shoelace that snaps*
> *with no time left. . . .*

"In a survey of 210 Florida police officers, psychologists Charles Spielberger and Kenneth Grier of the University of South Florida found that far more stressful than responding to a felony in progress or making arrests while alone was the day-to-day friction of dealing with what the officers saw as an 'ineffective' judicial system and 'distorted' press accounts about their work."[36] The same report said that other stress surveys showed that police sergeants in other areas of the country as well as teachers and air traffic controllers—whose jobs are usually considered as very stressful—were bothered more by the mundane matters than the major stressors.

Research into stress shows that it's not always the major events, but sometimes the minor hassles, that can accumulate and cause problems—things like running out of gas on the way to work, having unexpected company drop in, or getting delayed at a busy intersection. Various studies show that hassles are strongly related to episodes of illness, even when there are no major life events to consider.

As an example, psychiatrist and behavioral scientist Ian Wickramasekera points out that men "who experience such important life changes as divorce or the death of a wife may then be exposed to a wave of minor hassles (paying bills, dressing children, cooking, or doing the laundry) as they encounter new responsibilities (moving from father and husband, for example, to father and housekeeper)." Wickramasekera, director of the Eastern Virginia Medical School's Behavioral Medicine Clinic and Stress Disorders Laboratory, adds that a person in this kind of situation often develops back pain, headaches, stomach distress, or chest pain. "Sometimes it is not the mountain in front of you," he says, "but the grain of sand in your shoe that brings you to your knees."[37]

One group of researchers found that hassles have a greater impact on health than do major life changes events—and that the influence of major life changes may actually be indirect. Major life changes may influence health because they cause an increased number of minor hassles.[38]

Job Stress

Still another factor leading to stress is one that affects a growing number of people in the work population: job stress, sometimes called organizational stress (Chapter 4). It's not the high-powered executives at the top of the career ladder who suffer the most acutely. Studies show that the highest levels of stress are often borne by the people in the organization who feel little control or challenge, such as assembly line workers and clerks.

Research shows that four kinds of organizational demands cause stress in the workplace:

1. *Physical demands:* inadequate lighting, poor working conditions, uncomfortable seating, temperatures that are too hot or too cold.
2. *Task demands:* repetition, too few or too many changes, job insecurity, or work overload, for example.
3 *Role demands:* conflict or ambiguity about the employee's role.
4. *Interpersonal demands:* working for an abrasive boss or having to function under passive leadership.[39]

Apparently, the boss—and the boss' style—has a lot to do with mediating the effects of a stressful situation on the job. Researchers studied nearly 200 AT&T employees during the tumultuous breakup period. Those with supportive bosses suffered only half the illness of those with unsupportive bosses. Those with unsupportive bosses, in fact, suffered two times the illness, obesity, sexual problems, and depression that their colleagues with supportive bosses did.[40]

In addition to the four major stresses listed, research reported in *Health Promotion in the Workplace* shows that other major occupational stresses include task ambiguity or task rigidity; too much or too little responsibility; negative competition or no competition; constant change or boring stability; contact with stress carriers or social isolation; a corporate climate of suppressed hostility; lack of upward mobility; and daily stressors at work such as meetings and phone calls.[41]

Some of the most "relentless physical and psychological pressures in the workplace" are suffered by video display terminal operators. "Their jobs are paced by machines that impose inflexibility, lack of privacy, and production quotas. Workers sit all day at a keyboard and process checks, insurance claims, address changes, and customer orders under the watchful eyes of supervisors who can verify, on *their* video display terminals, exactly how much work is done. It is the electronic counterpart of the nineteenth century sweatshop."[42]

Researchers point out that this kind of relentless stress is often endured by people who have little control over the pace and style of their work. Evidence is strong, and growing, that people whose jobs are demanding but allow little decision making have higher rates of many diseases. That finding holds true independently of all other risk factors: People with demanding jobs that allow little control run two to four times the risk of disease.[43] And people without job control run four to five times the risk of heart attack. According to research, those at the bottom 10 percent of the job ladder are at the top 10 percent for incidence of illness.

Other factors that can cause occupational stress include boredom, burnout (a particular problem among people in the "helping" professions and among people responsible for the lives of others), powerlessness, overwork, power conflicts, lack of rewards, fear of failure, intense competition, underutilization, and when people are poorly fitted to their jobs.[44]

Age-Related Stressors

Prenatal

People are susceptible to different stressors at different stages of their lives. The impact of stress begins before we are even born: Stress experienced by a pregnant woman has definite physiological effects on her unborn baby. In one study of more than 500 rural women, those who experienced increasing stress levels between the second and third trimester had a significantly higher rate of complications, including neonatal death, neonatal illness, and low birth weight. These findings held true even when the researchers figured in all the standard risk factors.[45]

A variety of studies have shown that chronic stress during pregnancy contributes to preterm labor. Studies conducted in Germany showed that stress hormones directly affect the uterus. For instance, norepinephrine secreted during stress causes uterine contractions. And although epinephrine reduces contractions in the short run, it increases them in the long run. And the oxytocin associated with stress has been linked in the German study and others to premature birth.[46]

Major studies on prenatal stress have shown that psychosocial stress in the life of the mother—most specifically critical life events—can cause a number of problems in the baby, including obstetrical complications, physical illness, and behavioral problems later in childhood. Even nonspecific psychosocial stress can cause problems in the fetus and complications at and immediately following birth.[47] Specifically, one group of researchers found that stress during the pregnancy was associated with "deviant behavior" during the first five days of life. Babies born to stressed mothers cried more, slept less, were more irritable, and did not eat or have bowel movements with normal frequency.[48]

There is some evidence the neurochemical abnormalities of major stress, depression, or anxiety disorders may influence the fetal brain development in ways that affect personality and behavior long after delivery. For example, during a study of pregnant animals, when the mother to be was stressed for a protracted period, the male offspring were much more reserved, withdrawn, and nesting than those of nonstressed mothers. Speculation has been raised about whether the depression seen in children of depressed mothers is all genetic or could be influenced by in utero programming of the developing brain by the mother's neurohormones. This raises some very practical dilemmas for the physician and mother when, while pregnant, she for example, gets moderately depressed or has panic disorder. If these problems cannot be controlled without medication, is the risk to the baby greater if the mother goes untreated or takes medication that may or may not be safe during pregnancy? With the more recent data documenting risks to the baby of the mother's mental stress disorders, more physicians are opting to treat with medication when it's really needed. The improved results at and after birth tend to support that decision, but long-term effects on the baby are uncertain.

Children and Adolescents

The most tremendous stress an infant faces, of course, is its own birth.[49] Suddenly newborns must obtain their own oxygen, regulate their own temperature, and cope with bright lights and loud noises not filtered through amniotic fluid. In addition, major physiological changes are involved, such as the shift from fetal to infant blood circulation.

Evaluating exactly how an infant may respond to stress is difficult simply because an infant can't articulate. As a result, research has been limited. Results of some preliminary studies do show, however, that infant stress is related to the syndrome known as "failure to thrive" (a child simply does not grow, despite the fact that there is no known biological problem). Researchers also believe that, while some amount of stress is healthy for an adult, infants do not benefit from any stress at all.[50] The first year of life is, in some very important ways, critical to the global world view a person carries. "Is the world a safe and nurturing place, or it is hostile and dangerous? Can I express my needs and feelings safely and will they be honored, or am I likely to get zapped if I do so?" Things as simple as how a cry is responded to can establish longstanding attitudes and expectations in the baby and can later affect the person's ability to express feelings and needs or propensity to look at the world in a hostile, competitive way. Much mental programming occurs in these early years, even if there is no conscious memory of whence it arose.

One stressor that seems almost universal among both children and adolescents is parental divorce. More than a million children in the United States alone are involved in a parental divorce each year, and the Select Panel for Promotion of Child Health projects that approximately a third of all U.S. children will experience divorce. As many as half will spend part of their childhood with only one parent.[51] There are other stressors that can cause illness, psychological problems, and behavioral problems among children and adolescents. Research has found that children are susceptible to different stressors at different stages in their lives.

During the preschool years, a number of stressors are part of a child's normal development as he or she becomes aware of self in relation to others, struggles for independence, and forms meaningful attachments to others. Some common stressors for preschoolers that occur as part of normal development include having both parents work outside the home, having inferior quality day care, and adjusting to the birth of a sibling. (Interestingly, none of these is necessarily *stressful* to the child under many circumstances.) Preschool children normally react to these stresses in behavioral ways, such as regression, attention seeking, social withdrawal, and changes in play patterns.[52]

There are, of course, stressors on preschoolers that occur outside normal development. These include divorce of parents, loss of a parent, the violent loss of a parent, child abuse or neglect, witnessing violence (including the abuse of another person), and hospitalization.

A number of factors help determine how profoundly a child will react to stressors: the child's sex, age, intelligence level, and temperament. Children tend to suffer fewer effects of stress if they have an environment that is stable and well-structured, adults who act as strong "attachment figures," and secure relationships with one or both parents.[53]

School-aged children are understandably stressed by many of the same things that stress preschoolers—divorce of parents, serious illness that requires hospitalization, witnessing violence. But when school enters the picture, so does a whole new host of stressors. According to researchers, the most common stressors of school-aged children include anxiety about going to school, bullies, changing schools, conflicts with the teacher, forced competitiveness, difficulty with classmates, fads, dares with classmates, failing exams or getting failing grades, failing to make an athletic team, having to give oral reports in front of the class, learning disorders, being unable to complete homework assignments, lack of parental interest in achievements, parental pressure to achieve, dealing with the reputation of older siblings (bad or good), worry about taking tests, and even special recognition (for making the honor roll, winning a debate match, and so on). A significant amount of stress stems from peer teasing—about being overweight, being of a different race, wearing glasses, having red hair, wearing dental braces, and so on.[54]

School-aged kids suffer all kinds of stressors that have nothing to do with school, too. These include fear of going to the doctor or dentist, watching too much television, seeing violence on television, pressure to take sides in a parental conflict or divorce, and embarrassment about a parent's unemployment, alcoholism, or illness.[55]

Characteristically, school-aged children react to stress in a number of behavioral ways. They may regress (start wetting the bed or sucking their thumbs, for example), have problems getting along with classmates, lose motivation or concentration, become irritable, or withdraw. But, according to researchers, there are a number of physical signs and symptoms as well: School-aged kids under stress may suffer headaches, stomach aches, poor appetite, and sleeplessness.[56]

Parental reaction to the stress-induced illness can also be important. If illness becomes a safe haven because much nurturing and attention are given, it can become an unconsciously automatic response when safety and nurturing are needed. It may be kinder in the long run, to make it a not so pleasant time, perhaps with bed rest, isolation, and not much that's fun to do, given kindly. This, of course, is a tricky call, because serious organic disease may heal faster with loving support.

Typical stressors in adolescence, according to researchers, include the growth changes that occur as part of puberty, including hormonal changes; heightened sexuality and the problems associated with new sexual relationships, including issues related to gender roles; changing relationships with parents, siblings, and friends; pressures at school, including changing schools; and cultural and societal expectations. In addition, some adolescents have the pressures of encounters with the law, sexual mistreatment, abuse, divorce of parents, and serious illness in the family. Add to that the stressor of adolescence being a time of genetic vulnerability to illness.[57]

Adolescents, just like people of all other ages, react to stress differently, depending on a host of factors in their homes, environments, and histories. Researchers have found that adolescents who react poorly to the stressors of adolescence are vulnerable to some specific stress-related disorders: depression, drug or alcohol abuse, eating disorders (such as anorexia or bulimia), and suicide.[58]

Parents are wise to understand that this is a time when the need for independence and acceptance is foremost. A teenager knows he must become his own person, autonomous and "okay." The problem, often, is that a teen lacks the experience to make wise decisions, and parents may undermine the very empowering of their children by offering what they call "constructive criticism" in ways that imply they are not capable or acceptable and that they need to depend on the parent to make the right decision for them.

Adults

College students are generally stressed by academic pressure, course overload, career decisions, self-doubt, changing roles in the family, and the pressures associated with developing intimate relationships with sexual partners. Young and middle-aged adults often suffer from family stressors, such as changing roles within the family; the stresses associated with marriage, divorce, and remarriage; the stresses associated with parenthood, including single parenthood and step-parenting; financial problems; family planning; and the challenges of dual-career marriages. People in this age group also face the stressors associated with gender roles, including sexual harassment on the job, defining gender roles within the family, women entering the workplace, and men and women sharing the tasks associated with domestic engineering.

The elderly face the unique stresses associated with adjusting to retirement, failing health, deteriorating sight and hearing, the loss of friends and family members, and the stress of facing their own death.[59] A major source of distress for those who are aging is Western society's notion that one's worth as a person depends on productivity and on looking young. In societies where wisdom and understanding are venerated, elders tend to thrive and to look forward to old age. It is, of course, possible for one to come to that conclusion on his or her own, regardless of the notions of others.

Miscellaneous Stressors

Plenty of miscellaneous stressors can sap energy and contribute to physical illness, regardless of age. These include poor diet, inadequate nutrition, cigarette smoking (or even living with someone who smokes), drinking alcohol, insomnia, irregular sleep patterns, or the overuse of over-the-counter or prescription drugs (as well as any use of illegal drugs).

Coping with Stress

Researchers have found that, just as various factors lead to stress, various factors enable people to cope better with it. Basic factors that reduce the ability to cope with stress include genetic susceptibility to overreacting or to depression, insomnia, poor diet, obesity, unrealistic goal setting, smoking, financial distress, unstable home circumstances, working at a job for which one is ill-suited, and consumption of drugs (including caffeine). Genetic susceptibility to distress may be indicated by parents or grandparents who die before age sixty-five years.[60]

The genetics of being stressed are also interesting. The Wisconsin Primate Laboratory, studying mother monkeys for their stress resilience to separation from their family, found that the animals could be bred in stress-resistant and stress-vulnerable strains.[61] One way this happens may relate to the similar genetic inheritance observed for depression and for alcoholism. For example, a person may inherit the tendency to produce much of an enzyme (monoamine oxidase, or MAO) that removes brain neurotransmitters (such as serotonin and dopamine) involved in maintaining control and pleasurable mood. Animals prone to alcoholism by genetics have lower than normal levels of these neurotransmitters; treating them with medication that restores serotonin to normal causes a reduction in their voluntary consumption of alcohol.

If these neurotransmitters are removed too rapidly by MAO, a person tends to be shy, "on guard," more antisocial, and more prone to seeing the negatives in life—and, as a result, more distressed. If the MAO is low, on the other hand, the neurotransmitters increase and a person is more likely to be a risk taker who fails to see dangers.

Factors that increase the ability of children to cope with stress include gender (girls are generally more resilient under stress, though researchers are not sure why), high intelligence, easygoing temperament, a strong internal locus of control, the availability of adults who exhibit warmth and structure, and families with a high socioeconomic status.[62] Attitudes and perceptions are a major factor in the ability to cope with stress. Other factors include good genetics, a good sense of humor, a well-balanced and nutritious diet, realistic goal setting, plenty of sleep, thorough job preparation, financial security, stability at home, an understanding of stress, and use of relaxation skills.[63] More documented protective factors include high self-esteem, learning to be flexible and innovative in solutions, close personal relationships, having success/mastery experiences, self-discipline (including good control of time), positive expectancy (hope), and humor.

The Physiological Reactions to Stress

When something sets off the complicated series of physiological responses in the body, the resulting "stress response" involves a series of more than 1400 known physiochemical reactions. Some of the most common signs and symptoms of stress include headache, backache, insomnia, tightness in the neck and shoulders, indigestion, loss of appetite or excessive eating, and a pounding heartbeat.

The aches and pains we feel in response to stress can be the result of a complex physical reaction. As one reporter put it, when you are "originally confronted with a stressor, the whole body responds. If the stressor continues, effects gradually become focused on the smallest part of our body that can deal with the stress. If the stress continues, eventually that body part will wear out and we will respond with our whole body again."[64]

The basics of the physiological reaction to stress were first discovered in 1936 by stress pioneer Hans Selye, who observed three sets of responses whenever he injected an animal with a toxin: the animal's adrenal glands enlarged; the animal's lymph nodes (and other lymphocyte-producing structures) shrank; and severe bleeding ulcers developed in the animal's stomach and intestines.[65] He had noticed the same types of responses ten years earlier, as a medical student. Selye theorized that the same pattern of changes occurs in the body in reaction to any kind of stress and that the pattern is what eventually leads to disease conditions, such as ulcers, arthritis, hypertension, arteriosclerosis, or diabetes. Selye called the pattern the *general adaptation syndrome.*

For decades, researchers have studied the syndrome, and Selye's theories have held up to all levels of scientific scrutiny. The general adaptation syndrome is an excellent summary of the physiological changes that follow stress; its major stages are these:

1. *Alarm reaction.* In the first stage, the alarm reaction, the body immediately responds to stress; various physiological changes occur that enable the body to combat stress (the fight-or-flight reactions discussed earlier). One of the changes that occurs almost immediately during the alarm reaction is depression of the immune system; normal resistance is lowered, and the victim becomes more susceptible to infection and disease. If the stress is brief, the body's response is limited to that of the alarm reaction. When the stress ends, so does the reaction. The body tends to bounce back and recover quickly.

2.   *Resistance.* In stage two, resistance, the body makes physiological changes that enable it to adapt to prolonged stress. The body actually works overtime to bring immune response and resistance up to par. During this second stage, the body's immunocompetence is actually stronger than it normally is, an attempt by the body to keep itself in fighting form. There would be no problem if the body could maintain this level of resistance indefinitely; stress could go on forever, and no one would be the worse. But that's not how it works.

3.   *Exhaustion.* The body eventually loses the ability to keep up with the demands that stress puts on it and it enters the third stage, exhaustion. Simply stated, the body has its limits. They're different in every person, but when the body reaches its limit, it collapses. Immunity plummets. During stage three, immunity breaks down. The organ systems of the body malfunction. The life-preserving reactions are shut down. This results in *diseases of adaptation,* the diseases we know as stress related.[66]

Note that there is significant difference between the acute and chronic stress responses. The immune response in many ways parallels the emotional one. Studies of stress must always take this difference into account. It's much easier to test the effects of short-term, acute stress than to test the effects of chronic stress, which has many more unknown variables.

How quickly a person bounces back from short-term stress depends on that individual body. How well one withstands long-term stress is an individual thing, too. So is the determination of how long you can go on without breaking down and becoming exhausted. The reactions to stress differ with age, with life circumstance, and with the conditions that surround us at the time we become stressed. A particularly important factor is the way we regard, or think about, the stress. Different modes of thinking produce significantly different responses. For example, the comment, You're looking good! could be received by an older person as a compliment, as patronization, or as an implication that the person looks good for such an old person. In each case, the stress response would be very different.

There apparently is even a difference between the way men and women respond to stress. New research shows that, though women complain more about the minor symptoms of stress such as headaches and backaches, they actually suffer fewer long-term stress-related problems such as cardiovascular disease. Researchers aren't sure why, but they think the key may lie in female hormones. In one study, women asked to perform stressful tasks registered higher blood pressure and higher heart rates after menopause than before.[67] Other reasons may well involve a woman's greater propensity to express feelings and seek support.

What exactly is the stress response? There is no simple answer, but you can begin to understand some of the profound effects of stress by understanding how it affects major body systems.

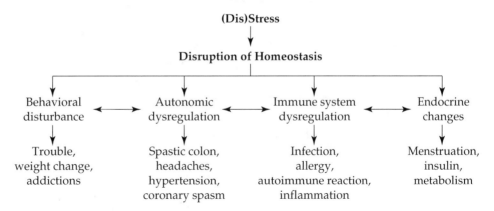

FIGURE 3.1   Effect of Distress on Homeostasis

Stress and the Brain

The brain is usually the first body system to recognize a stressor. It reacts with split-second timing to instruct the rest of the body in how to adjust to the stressor. The latest research shows that the brain continues to stimulate the "stress reaction" for as long as seventy-two hours after a traumatic incident. Thus, if a person is suffering from repeated stress, the brain might be directing a chronic stress response throughout the body.

The brain is not a discriminator of stressors. It reacts the same whether the stress is physical (you are almost hit by a car that comes careening around the corner when you step off the curb) or emotional (your boss calls you in for another of his "talks"), or even immune-mediated (confronted, for example, with a threatening infection). What that reaction entails, basically, is the release of a cascade of hormones and brain chemicals that course through the bloodstream, instructing other organs, such as the pituitary, the thyroid, and the adrenals, to release their respective hormones. Just as the brain is the organ that turns on the stress response, it is also the organ that finally turns it off.

Unfortunately, all this hormonal brain activity takes its toll. The latest research reveals that elevated levels of stress hormones kill off significant numbers of vitally important brain cells.[68] According to Stanford University biologist Robert Sapolsky, the stress hormones, the glucocorticoids, trigger the fight-or-flight response that is intended to save us human beings when we are confronted by danger, "but these all-important glucocorticoids also trigger a curious cascading death of the very brain cells that those hormones are meant to protect."

New research has shown that stress does, simply, destroy brain cells. University of Kentucky researchers under the direction of Philip Landfield exposed rats to prolonged stress—five days a week for six months. After only three weeks, the rats showed reduced electrical activity in the hippocampus (the crucial area of the brain most affected by Alzheimer's disease). When examined in autopsies at the end of six months, the rats that were exposed to stress had lost twice as many brain cells—50 percent of all their brain cells—as same-age rats that had been spared the stress.[69]

It's the delicate hippocampus, centrally involved in learning and memory, that is most profoundly affected by stress hormones. Sapolsky's experiments with rats also demonstrated that the hippocampus, which is supposed to shut off the flow of glucocorticoids after a stressful event is over, becomes worn down by prolonged exposure to the hormones. It can no longer do its job, and the body suffers from the chronic presence of stress hormones. Sapolsky is quick to point out, too, that even a "mildly stressful" situation (like doing math for thirty minutes) can double or even triple the stress hormones pumped out by the brain.

Sapolsky emphasizes that it's not the stressor that's important but the perception of it: "The exact same external event can happen to two different people, and, depending on the psychological baggage of the individual experiencing it, the outcome will be different, the disease will be different."

Stress and the Endocrine System

The function of the endocrine system, with its network of glands, is to secrete hormones, and when the body is under stress, the pineal, pituitary, thyroid, parathyroids, thymus, adrenals, pancreas, ovaries, and testes all respond with "hostile" hormones. As discussed in Chapter 2, hormones released by the brain travel rapidly through the bloodstream, stimulating the release of other hormones throughout the body. Even organs that are not considered part of the endocrine system (such as the stomach and the kidneys) pour out hormones to accomplish the vast response to stress.

When the body is under stress, two main hormone groups are galvanized to combat: the catecholamines and the corticosteroids. The two catecholamines, adrenalin (or epinephrine) and norepinephrine, can cause the heart to beat faster, the blood vessels to constrict, the muscles to tense up, the respiratory system to work more rapidly, and the blood to thicken and clot in case of injury.

When catecholamine levels are too high, as in chronic stress, the effects can range from minor problems (such as tics and muscle tremors) to more serious, potentially long-range problems, such as ulcers, gout, diabetes, heart attack, and stroke. Ultimately, elevated catecholamine levels can significantly suppress the immune system, resulting in susceptibility to infection and disease.

The other major hormone group secreted in response to stress is the group of corticosteroids, including cortisone and cortisol. What happens when there is too much cortisol in the body? Too much cortisol can cause the previously mentioned stress-induced, progressive nerve loss in the hippocampus, as proved by a study on rats conducted by biologists at Stanford University.[70]

In a separate study at the Rockefeller University Laboratory of Neuroendocrinology, researchers found that cortisol makes the cells of the hippocampus smaller. In addition, it causes fewer nerve branches throughout the hippocampus.

Excessive cortisol changes the nerve cells and branches of the hippocampus in as little as three weeks.[71]

The changes that occur in the hippocampus as a result of excessive cortisol mimic the loss of cells that result from aging. There are several reasons why the nerve cells are affected. A major reason, say researchers, is that cortisol prevents the brain cells from absorbing and utilizing glucose, the fuel needed as energy.

Stress may actually intensify any brain cell loss that normally occurs among the aging. Studies done at New York University Medical Center point out that aged people are less able to regulate their stress response, and, as a result, levels of cortisol produced during stress don't return to normal for long periods of time. Under these conditions the aged can suffer rapid destruction of brain cells. The New York researchers believe as a result that stress can actually play a role in the development and progression of Alzheimer's disease.[72]

Apparently, stress can also interfere with the hormones that influence fertility. Alice Domar, director of the Behavioral Medicine Program for Infertility at the New England Deaconess Hospital, conducted a small study that, despite its size and restrictions, may provide the impetus for further research. She found that women whose infertility was caused by some hormonal problem *also* had fewer sources of emotional support. Domar theorizes, then, that stress, in this case, from a lack of emotional support, may have an adverse effect on the hormones that influence fertility. Again, Domar warns that her study involved only a small number of patients, and she's hesitant to draw "definitive conclusions," but urges more study of stress and infertility.[73] Clearly, stress can contribute to some infertility; even worrying about not being able to get pregnant can become a self-fulfilling prophecy. A common scenario is an "infertile" mother who, when she quits "trying" and adopts a baby, then becomes pregnant. There may be more than just stress involved here, such as the power of pictured expectations. (Worry is picturing the negative happening: i.e. being unable to conceive.) The brain has a way of creating in the body what is being pictured.

The effect of chronic high levels of cortisone is devastating: cortisone stimulates the kidneys to produce renin, a hormone that increases blood pressure. The cells lining the heart and blood vessels can be damaged; the body responds by secreting cholesterol to repair the arterial tears. The build-up of plaque and cholesterol leads to atherosclerosis, eventual heart disease, and possibly heart attack. Further, cortisone inhibits vitamin D activity, resulting in loss of calcium and eventual development of osteoporosis. It causes the liver to overproduce glucose, which, over the long term, can increase the risk of diabetes. It slows down the digestive system, which can lead to ulceration of the lining of the stomach and intestines if chronic.

But perhaps the most serious complication of chronic high cortisone levels is suppression of the immune system. High cortisol levels can cause shrinkage of the spleen and thymus, which are vital for the production of white blood cells. Known as powerful immunosuppressants, the corticosteroids, especially cortisol, "breaks down lymphoid tissues in the thymus and lymph nodes, reduces the level of T helper cells and increases T suppressors, and inhibits the production of natural killer cells. Cortisol also reduces virus-fighting interferon."[74] (Nevertheless, cortisol is not the whole story in stress-induced immunosuppression.)

According to research investigating the link between stress hormones and the immune system, a wide range of diseases is associated with elevated cortisol levels including cancer, hypertension, ulcers, heart attack, diabetes, arthritis, stroke, Parkinson's disease, multiple sclerosis, myasthenia gravis, and a variety of infections. Researchers believe that elevated cortisol levels associated with stress may contribute to psychoses of the aged, depression, "and even perhaps Alzheimer's disease. . . . Elevated cortisol levels are even reported to be a useful predictor of suicide."[75]

Stress and the Gastrointestinal System

Anyone who is familiar with basic biology knows how the gastrointestinal system works. Food is chewed, and the saliva begins the essential breakdown process. Chewed food travels through the muscular esophagus to the stomach, moved along by powerful muscular contractions. In the stomach, enzymes begin the major breakdown of the food; from there, it passes through the small intestines, where breakdown is completed. Nutrients are absorbed into the bloodstream through the walls of the small intestine, and are circulated throughout the body. Whatever the body can't use—the waste matter—travels through the large intestine (the colon) and is eliminated through the rectum and anus.

That's how it's supposed to work, and does—until stress enters the picture. Stress affects the gastrointestinal system at every step of the way.

1. *The mouth.* Under stress, a person stops producing saliva. It's the body's attempt to prevent any added fluids from reaching the stomach. A dry mouth is considered such a reliable sign of stress that it is used as a lie detector test in China; suspected criminals are given a mouthful of rice to chew.

2. *The esophagus.* Stress can either halt the regular rhythmic contractions of the esophagus or can cause uncontrollable, irregular contractions. Either way, it becomes extremely difficult to swallow. That accounts for the well-known lump in the throat of many a nervous person, the body's primitive way of keeping a stressed person primed and ready for action.

3. *The stomach.* The stomach, along with the rest of the digestive system, slows down; as a result, acids are in contact with the stomach lining for a prolonged period, and ulcers can develop. Stress also causes an increase in the stomach's manufacture of hydrochloric acid, a second factor that leads to the elevated risk of gastric ulcer. Finally, stress can cause the stomach lining to become engorged with blood, which makes it more fragile and susceptible to ulceration. The usual companions of stress are decreased appetite, nausea, and heartburn.

4. *The small and the large intestine.* An increase in the production of hydrochloric acid increases the risk of duodenal ulcers (ulcers that occur in the top portion of the small intestine). Stress also disrupts normal peristaltic action of the entire intestinal tract; the food mass is either rushed through too quickly, resulting in diarrhea, or moved through much too slowly, resulting in constipation.

Researchers have noted other stress-related effects on the gastrointestinal system as well. Stress causes the liver to overproduce glucose, disturbing the normal blood sugar level and increasing the risk of diabetes. Recent research indicates that stress may also cause chronic inflammation of the pancreas and blockage of the pancreatic and bile ducts, leading to a variety of disease conditions.[76]

How the gastrointestinal system reacts to the challenges of stress, however, depends in a large part on personality traits, say researchers. A study that called on men to solve arithmetic problems and anagrams while under stress showed that some had an increase in gastric acid while others actually had a decrease. The difference, say the researchers, was due to personality traits—in other words, the way people coped with stress.[77]

One study showed that the important factor seems to be *perceived* stress. More than 4500 people took part in the National Health and Nutrition Examination Survey Epidemiologic Follow-Up Study. At the beginning of the study, participants did not have peptic ulcer disease; during the thirteen years of the study, researchers followed the participants to see who developed it. Interestingly, during that time, those who *perceived* themselves as stressed were 1.8 times more likely to develop ulcers than those who did not perceive themselves to be stressed, regardless of how many stressors actually existed.[78]

Stress and the Cardiovascular System

As early as 1628, physician William Harvey maintained that "every affection of the mind that is attended either with pain or pleasure, hope or fear, is the cause of an agitation whose influence extends to the heart."[79] Today, stress is recognized as a major contributor to heart disease, and researchers recognize that one of the most profound influences of stress affects the cardiovascular system. In his book *From Stress to Strength,* cardiologist Robert S. Eliot describes exactly how stress causes coronary artery disease:

- First, stress causes the blood pressure to spike. The increased pressure of the blood pounding through the vessels pummels and weakens the delicate, protective inner lining of the arteries.
- When the lining is damaged, the body starts its first attempt at repair: fats are deposited in the arteries. The result? Blood vessels are narrowed, blood circulation is slowed, and the likelihood of clotting becomes high.
- The body continues its arsenal of healing: Platelets are mobilized to the damaged arteries. Clots start to form. More fatty material is deposited, and the arteries finally become rigid and inflexible.

That would be bad enough, but when stress continues, or recurs, blood pressure spikes again in response to the stress. Now, look at what happens to the arteries already rendered inflexible by earlier stress:

- The inflexible border on the underside of the fatty deposit is distorted and torn by surges in blood pressure.
- The underside of the fatty deposit (the plaque) is filled with tiny blood vessels, attempting to send nutrients to the damaged artery. When surges in blood pressure cause them to tear, they bleed into the softer surrounding tissues under the plaque. In time, this bleeding dislodges the plaque.
- Once it's dislodged, this rigid, fatty plaque is pushed outward, causing instant obstruction of an already narrowed vessel.
- As the brain recognizes the injury, it instructs the remaining flexible sections of the artery wall to constrict. The result? A sizable length of the artery itself is narrowed.
- Finally, the heart is deprived of oxygen, because oxygenated blood can't circulate through the diseased and narrowed arteries. The result? Heart tissue dies because of cardiac infarction.[80]

Researchers have noted that in parts of the world where stress is uncommon so is heart disease.[81] And stress can be life threatening to a person who already has coronary heart disease: stress causes the heart to speed up, the blood to circulate more quickly and with greater force, and the blood pressure to escalate. It's a deadly combination to someone whose arteries are already narrowed by disease, as one can imagine from the scenario Eliot describes above. The result is coronary occlusion, damaged heart tissue, and, sometimes, cardiac arrest.[82]

Interestingly, Eliot's research shows that stress-induced heart attack can occur even when plenty of oxygen is circulated to the heart. How? Stress causes tiny tears in the heart muscle fiber itself; these tears, which weaken the heart, are called *contraction band lesions.* When they happen, heart attack can occur even if the arteries are well and the heart is getting enough oxygen.[83]

And research reported in 1994 to the Society of Behavioral Medicine by James Muller of Harvard Medical School shows that happy stress can be just as harmful to the heart as negative stress. When he studied more than 500 survivors of heart attack, Muller found that almost half had experienced an "extremely meaningful" psychological event in the twenty-six hours before the heart attack. Of the events that patients considered to be "extremely meaningful," some were negative and some were positive. As Muller told *USA Today,* "It seems like a son returning safely from a combat mission can be just as stressful as an IRS audit." Does Muller, then, advocate avoiding excitement? Absolutely not. As he told *USA Today,* "If a person did everything he could to avoid triggering a heart attack, he'd probably die of boredom."

Increased Heart Rate

Simply stated, the heart beats, or pumps, in an effort to circulate blood carrying oxygen and other nutrients to all the body's cells. The fewer times the heart has to pump to accomplish this task, the longer it will last; conversely, the harder it has to work, the more prone it will become to being overworked.

When the human body is stressed, hormones signal the heart to start pounding. It is the way the body prepared primitive people for fight or flight. But today, an executive sitting in a boardroom or a commuter stuck in rush-hour traffic, or a customer dealing with a rude salesclerk does not need the physiological response required by a primitive person facing a saber-toothed tiger. So, today we sit without moving much while our hearts pound. If stress becomes frequent or chronic, the result is a chronically overworked heart—and, in essence, a heart with a seriously shortened life span.

Higher Blood Pressure

In the second change, the hormones released in response to stress cause a sharp increase in blood pressure, another response that prepared primitive peoples for the physical demands of fleeing or fighting for their life. Changes in the autonomic nervous system in response to stress cause constriction of the blood vessels; further constriction occurs in response to the stress hormones. A temporary increase in blood pressure usually isn't dangerous, but when stress becomes frequent or chronic, the ensuing chronic high blood pressure can become life-threatening, as shown in Eliot's scenario.

Stress is believed to be the major factor in triggering the onset of at least 20 percent of all cases of high blood pressure. Stress-induced high blood pressure is even greater among men whose arteries are already clogged by atherosclerosis (characterized by fatty deposits).[84] According to North Carolina A&T researcher Andrew Goliszek:

> *The stress of factory noise, for example, has been closely linked to high blood pressure in factory workers exposed to prolonged, daily noise; flood victims experiencing devastating property and financial loss have developed permanent high blood pressure during their recovery periods; and executives in their early thirties, who were chronically angry and hostile but who suppressed their anger and hostility because they couldn't express themselves, developed high blood pressure before they reached their fifties. Even school children are susceptible to high blood pressure when placed in stressful situations.*[85]

Added to this scenario is the problem with some people whom researchers have dubbed *hot reactors,* people whose blood pressure seems normal at rest but shoots up to dangerously high levels during stress.[86] Eliot estimates that as many as one in five persons exhibits undetected daily blood pressure changes that place them at high risk for stroke or sudden cardiac death.

"I call those with the most extreme heart and blood pressure responses *hot reactors,* Eliot maintains. "They burn a dollar's worth of energy for a dime's worth of trouble." And, according to Eliot, they "are pressure cookers without safety valves, literally stewing in their own juices." The worst part of it all, according to Eliot, is that "these people do not suspect that their bodies are paying a high price for overreacting to stress."[87]

What kind of price do hot reactors pay? Eliot has identified ten possible complications of hot reacting: permanent high blood pressure, damaged blood vessel linings, atherosclerosis, accelerated blood clotting, ruptured heart muscle fibers, heart rhythm disturbances, kidney and heart failure, heart attack, stroke, and sudden death.[88]

Eliot's research, along with the research of many other scientists, shows that there are three different kinds of hot reactors. The first has increased output: The heart pumps extra hard under stress. In the second, the heart pumps harder and the small blood vessels constrict, combining to drive up blood pressure. In the third and most serious type, most of the blood vessels tighten while the heart pumps so hard that it begins to falter; no matter how hard the heart works, it cannot force the blood through the narrowing arteries. Regardless of which mechanism is at work, hot reactors face a number of serious cardiovascular insults, including sudden death. Studies with pigs have found that those under stress are far more apt to drop dead suddenly than those that are not stressed.

At the opposite end of the spectrum is the finding that humans who reduce stress enjoy the benefit of lower blood pressure. Research by psychologists at Harvard University followed residents of eight Massachusetts nursing homes for three years. Researchers randomly selected some of the patients in each nursing home and taught each to meditate as a way of reducing stress. At the end of three years, the survival rate among the meditators was 100 percent: Not a single one of the patients who meditated had died, and most had significant drops in systolic blood pressure. Among the patients who did not meditate, survival rate was only 62.6 percent.[89]

Damaged Blood Vessels

Traditional risk factors fail to account for half the cases of clinical coronary artery disease worldwide,[90] yet more than a half million deaths in the United States every year are attributed to arteriosclerosis. Stress delivers a double whammy to people who already have coronary artery disease: Stress causes vessels already choked by plaque to narrow even more, boosting the chance for heart attack. In studies at Harvard Medical School, researchers put subjects under stress to determine the multiplied effect of stress on already damaged arteries. While under stress, the damaged arteries constricted 24 percent more and blood flow declined by 27 percent in the damaged vessels, though it didn't decline in the smooth vessels.[91]

Serum Cholesterol

Researchers have also shown that stress can elevate levels of serum cholesterol. In one of the first studies showing a link, researchers followed forty accountants who, because of their work, were forced to meet stressful deadlines at specific times of year. The researchers found that the most strenuous work periods coincided with the highest levels of cholesterol, even though the diets and activity levels of the accountants remained unchanged.[92] Freidman, Rosenman, and Carroll reported that, during the period from January 1 to April 15, the cholesterol levels of the accountants rose as much as 100 points over their normal levels.[93]

A number of studies duplicate these findings.[94] One group of researchers measured serum cholesterol levels of medical students a few hours before final examinations and again forty-eight hours later. In all but one student, the serum cholesterol value was an average of 20 percent higher in the stress period before the exam. A similar study showed that the highest cholesterol levels among military pilots in training occurred during examination periods. And studies among college students showed an increase of 11 to 17 percent in cholesterol levels during testing periods.

Almost any kind of stress can cause significantly increased amounts of cholesterol to be released into the bloodstream. A number of studies show that shift work is extremely stressful and that people who work on the night shift are under the most stress. One study found that night labor was associated with significantly elevated cholesterol levels.[95]

Cardiovascular Disease

Research efforts have shown a strong link between stress and all kinds of cardiovascular disease, including deaths due to cardiovascular disease. A variety of studies have shown that stress can cause sudden cardiac death. In one study, researchers examined a hundred cases of sudden cardiac death drawn from a coroner's records. The researchers found that almost two-thirds of the victims were under moderate to severe stress on the final day of life, and more than one in five were experiencing acute stress during the last thirty minutes of life. The coroners' reports revealed stressors such as receipt of divorce papers, a fight over a game, an automobile accident, and an attack by dogs as some examples.[96] The sudden deaths were probably due to an irregular heart rhythm caused by catecholamines and increased nervous input to the heart as a result of stress.

Research has also linked stress to transient myocardial ischemia, a condition in which blood does not circulate adequately to the heart. In a majority of the cases, the ischemia is silent; it does not cause pain or other symptoms. And, though it can be the result of exposure to cold, cigarette smoking, or strenuous physical exercise, researchers have often linked it to stress.

In one study, researchers monitored patients hospitalized in London who were being evaluated for possible coronary bypass surgery. The researchers carefully studied heart function but also measured the levels of stress hormones in the urine and asked patients themselves to record their feelings at various times during the day. The findings showed that the higher the levels of stress hormones in the urine, the more frequent the episodes of silent ischemia.[97]

A growing body of research has shown that, among heart disease patients, mental stress is as dangerous to the heart as physical stress.[98] In a study conducted at the UCLA School of Medicine, subjects were given both mental and physical stress tests; all had been diagnosed as having heart disease. The mental stress caused ischemia in more than half the patients. Researchers found that asking patients to discuss their own shortcomings caused almost the same intensity of heart reactions as did strenuous riding of a stationary bicycle.[99]

While early research on cardiovascular disease centered on diet and exercise, it has taken a dramatic swing toward the examination of stress as a leading factor. Maryland psychologist David Krantz summarizes heart disease as "some interaction of mind, body, and behavior. Your coronary risk probably depends on how your mind interprets situations, how your body reacts, and how often your behavior leads you into stressful situations."[100]

Stress and Nutrition

Stress not only influences the way various body systems operate; it can also change the way the body absorbs nutrients from food. Research shows that "almost any form of stress may upset nutritional balance,"[101] and stress can cause increases in the metabolic rate, hyperglycemia from the liver's overproduction of glucose, and a breakdown of proteins and other nutrients in the body.[102] While more research is needed into the specific nutritional demands put on the body during stress, researchers do know that the body requires increased levels of vitamin A, vitamin C, thiamine, riboflavin, and protein (to repair tissue), as well as efforts to maintain a moderate, nutritionally balanced diet.

Interestingly, stress can even affect how much you eat. In laboratory studies, rats whose tails were constantly pinched, overate. Research has shown that, among overweight persons, stress leads to overeating whereas among thin people it tends to lead to loss of appetite.[103]

Stress and the Immune System

As research continues into the link between stress and the immune system, scientists have come up with a veritable shopping list of conditions caused or aggravated by stress: coronary heart disease, arteriosclerosis, atherosclerosis, high blood pressure, coronary thrombosis, stroke, angina pectoris, respiratory ailments, ulcers, irritable bowel syndrome, ulcerative colitis, gastritis, pancreatitis, diabetes, hyperthyroidism, migraine headache, myasthenia gravis, epileptic attacks, chronic backache, kidney disease, chronic tuberculosis, allergies, rheumatoid arthritis, systemic lupus erythematosus, impotence, infertility, psoriasis, eczema, cold sores, shingles, hives, asthma, Raynaud's disease, multiple sclerosis, cancer, and an entire spectrum of endocrine and autoimmune problems, to name just a few. Physicians caution that "few of these diseases are caused or triggered solely by stress." Other factors must also be considered,[104] but findings of continuing research is clear: Stress plays a moderate to major role in a whole Pandora's box of diseases.

New research shows that stress can even cause susceptibility to the common "cold." Psychologist Sheldon Cohen and his colleagues at Carnegie Mellon University assessed stress levels for more than four hundred healthy adults. They were then given nasal drops that contained a small dose of respiratory-disease viruses. Those with the highest amount of stress ran twice the risk of getting a cold, and more than five times the risk of becoming infected with a cold virus. The study, says Cohen, "clearly suggests that stress helps produce a susceptibility to colds."[105]

In a similar study done in England, a hundred people were asked to keep a diary of things that happened, how they felt about them, and their health. "Uplifts"—experiences that brought pleasure or happiness—were found to decrease significantly in the four days before people developed a cold. Interestingly, the number of "uplifts" seemed more important than the number of hassles, which wasn't as strongly associated with colds. People also reported that they had been feeling more angry, tense, and skeptical during the four days before getting a cold.[106]

Stress is a leading factor in disease because, many researchers feel, it compromises the immune system, rendering the body less capable of fighting disease and infection. Psychiatrist Steven Locke of Harvard Medical School and Boston's Beth Israel Hospital defines the immune system as "a surveillance mechanism that protects the host from disease-causing microorganisms. It regulates susceptibility to cancers, infectious diseases, allergies, and autoimmune disorders."[107]

Stress enters the picture because it can significantly slow the immune response.[108] According to George Washington University biochemist Nicholas Hall, "The net effect of stress is a depression of immunity."[109] Very simply stated, stress suppresses the immune system's ability to produce and maintain lymphocytes (the white blood cells necessary for killing infection) and natural killer cells (the specialized cells that seek out and destroy foreign invaders), both vital in the fight against infection and disease.[110] Research shows that stress causes an increase in the number of circulating white blood cells but a decrease in the number of circulating B cells, T cells, helper T cells, suppressor or cytotoxic T cells, and large granular lymphocytes. Interestingly, some research shows that short-term stress (lasting between several days and a month) decreases the number of helper T cells more than stress that lasts more than a month.[111]

Human development consultant Rosalind Forbes, author of *Life Stress*, writes;

> *When stresses pile up and too many things happen at once, your coping ability fails and the resulting effects take their toll on your health. If too many changes take place in a short period of time, a person's resistance to disease can be lowered and physical illness may result.*[112]

While it's not possible in all cases to measure the precise effect of stress on immunity, we do know that it packs quite a punch. There is a complex relationship between the immune system and the central nervous system, as outlined earlier; we know that the long-loop regulatory feedback system is influenced by catecholamines released during stress, by pituitary hormones, and by others. The exact impact on the immune system depends on the type of immune response, the physical and psychological characteristics of the stressor, the timing, and other factors.[113]

It should be noted that stress itself does not always lower immunity. According to research, stressful events that are interpersonal in nature (such as losing a spouse) are more likely to depress the immune system. According to research by Tracy Bennett Herbert and Sheldon Cohen, the fact that persons under stress have a compromised immune response might be due to other factors associated with stress. "Distressed people sleep less, exercise less, have poorer diets, smoke more, and use alcohol and other drugs more often than nondistressed people," they point out. "These behaviors have all been shown to alter immune response."[114]

At least part of the reason why stress lowers resistance is that its overall impact on the immune system appears to be substantial. Stress and the hormones involved in the stress response affect all the "key players" in the immune response: Stress causes a decrease in the number of natural killer cells and of T lymphocytes, an increase in the number of T suppressors, a decrease in the level of interferon, and even shrinkage of the organs vital to immune system functioning (such as the thymus). As a result, points out Mount Sinai School of Medicine psychiatrist Marvin Stein, stressful incidents in life—bereavement, depression, divorce, job loss, the task of caring for a seriously ill person—all have been proven to lower resistance to disease.[115]

In a study of women with rheumatoid arthritis, researchers assessed each woman's life stresses and did blood tests to measure immune function. Interestingly, stress did not seem to cause a flare-up of rheumatoid arthritis, but it did cause significant immune system changes. Major stresses resulted in fewer circulating T cells and lower ratios of helper and suppressor T cells. Minor stresses affected the proportions of B cells in the bloodstream.[116]

For years researchers thought that the immune system regulates itself. Now they know that the brain is closely involved in the control of this disease-fighting system. The relationship is complex, but, in simple terms, the brain sends out specific hormones when under stress. The lymphocytes, the main players in the immune system scenario, have surface receptors to which these hormones attach. The hormones secreted as part of the stress response cause all the trouble.[117]

The cells of the immune system that seem to be particularly compromised by stress are the natural killer cells, or those white blood cells that destroy viruses, cancer cells, and other foreign invaders. The number of studies that prove the compromise of natural killer cells are far too many to cite here, but a few examples can show the devastating effect of stress on the body's surveillance system.

In one study, more than a hundred people were given swine flu vaccine; researchers measured how well their bodies produced antibodies afterward. The researchers found that people who coped poorly with stress had an impaired immune response and diminished activity of natural killer cells. Interestingly, people who were under stress *but who coped well with their stress* did much better in terms of immune response.[118]

Researchers who wanted to measure the immune system effects of stress injected a group of mice with cancer cells. Half the mice were then put in a specially designed protective environment that kept them pretty much free of stress. The other mice were put in a traditional laboratory setting filled with stressors—crowded conditions, harsh lighting, human voices and odors, and so on. The mice subjected to stress were much more likely to develop tumors than those kept free of stress. Pacific Northwest Research Foundation scientist Darrel Spackman, who participated in the study, says it's because the stressed mice had significantly fewer lymphocytes circulating in their blood.[119]

The same thing has been shown to be a factor among humans. A study of first-year medical students under the stress of final exams showed that the number of white blood cells dropped significantly during that exam stress.[120] Steven Keller and his colleagues at the Mount Sinai School of Medicine studied men whose wives had died. Their lymphocyte functioning was significantly impaired for at least two months after the death of their wife; for some, the immune system did not return to normal for more than a year.

In another study, researchers at Brown and Yale Universities tracked the immune function and disease rate of people they knew to be under stress. One group was made up of men who knew they were about to lose their jobs. They developed accelerated arteriosclerosis, ulcers, swollen joints, diabetes, gout, and patchy bald spots. Workers at Cape Kennedy who knew that their jobs would end immediately following a successful moon landing suffered a 50 percent higher than normal death rate from sudden cardiac death.[121] A number of other studies show a direct link between stress and sudden cardiac death.[122]

The physical effects of stress were also apparent in a study of prisoners of war. In a broad-scale study, researchers studied 25,000 World War II prisoners of war, and followed their medical records for six years after the prisoners were liberated or escaped. Mortality rates were much higher among the prisoners of war than among the general population. But researchers found another interesting thing: Prisoners who endured the greatest stress during their imprisonment later had seven times as many hospital admissions for a variety of ailments and diseases. In fact, the number of doctor visits and the degree of illness were almost entirely dependent on the extent of stress the prisoners suffered during their imprisonment.[123]

In still another study, healthy men were twice shown a graphic film of doctors performing surgery. They were then asked twice during the following half hour to recall the details of the film. Researchers compared their blood tests to those of healthy men who did not observe the surgery. The men who saw the film and then had to talk about it had fewer lymphocytes in their blood.[124]

Apparently, stress doesn't have to be chronic to compromise the immune system. In one study conducted by researchers at the University of Rochester, mice were separated into three groups. One group was not stressed at all. A second group was stressed just once. And a third group was subjected to stress every other day for about two weeks. Researchers found that the mice who were exposed to stress just once showed a drop in natural killer cells.[125]

Though stress doesn't have to be chronic to compromise the immune system, chronic stress has been shown in numerous studies to deal a particularly bad blow to immunity. In one, researchers studied caregivers who were taking care of Alzheimer's patients. During the thirteen months of the study, the caregivers were ill for more days with respiratory tract infections and showed a decrease in three measures of immune system function when compared to people of the same gender, age, and income level. The recent study, say researchers, provides "good evidence that chronic stress leads to chronically lower immune system activity—which may in turn lead to a higher rate of illness."[126]

And the immune changes associated with stress don't necessarily mean you'll get sick, either. Ohio State University psychologist Janice Kiecolt-Glaser, known for her work in immune studies, says;

> Just because your immune function goes down during a stressful period doesn't mean you are going to get sick. Where stress seems to have the greatest impact on health is on individuals who already have poor immune function due to age or diseases that impair the immune system, or on individuals who have already been chronically stressed for reasons other than health.[127]

Interesting new research shows that the response to stress may even vary with gender. William McIntosh and his colleagues at Texas A & M University evaluated 192 people aged fifty-eight years or older. The researchers found significant differences in the way men and women responded to stress. The only event that reduced immune response for the men was recent sexual difficulty. For women, the only events that caused changes in the immune response were family or legal problems, and, interestingly, those caused the women's immune response to *improve* rather than worsen. The differences, say researchers, may be due to the different expectations associated with gender (men may feel more pressure than women to perform sexually, for example).[128]

Stress and Cancer

The established effect of stress on the immune system has led researchers to explore the notion that stress may also lead to an increased incidence of cancer, a theory that has been around for a number of years. Several cancers have been tentatively linked with stress, among them those of the lung and cervix and leukemia. And while the findings are still tentative, the most prevalent theory is that stress may contribute to cancer because it alters the immune system, providing an advantage for the development of cancer.[129]

While researchers are careful to note that there is no direct evidence that stress *causes* cancer,[130] some studies indicate that it may be a factor in the *development* of cancer. In one study,[131] researchers did personality profiles of women who did not have symptoms but who had reported to clinics for Pap smears. The researchers wondered if they could predict which women would test positive for cancer of the cervix on the basis of personality traits. They found that cancer of the cervix occurred most often in women who were hopelessly frustrated over a stressful situation. In another study, researchers evaluated sets of twins one of whom had died of leukemia while the other remained healthy. They found that the twin who developed leukemia usually had experienced a psychological upheaval, whereas the healthy one had not.[132] In still another study, researchers found that certain elements of the classic Type A personality, among them, proneness to stress, seemed to be associated with the development of breast cancer.[133]

Despite the results of these and other studies like them, researchers are still hesitant to declare a direct link between stress and the development of cancer. Dr. Guy R. Newell of the Department of Cancer Prevention and Control at the University of Texas M. D. Anderson Cancer Center theorizes that it may be the inability to cope with stress, rather than the stress itself, that leads to development of cancer. While clinical studies suggest "an association" between cancer and stress, he says, there is still no "direct evidence that stress is a predisposing risk factor for the development of cancer."[134]

Self-Perceptions of Stress

Obviously, stress can be very detrimental. And, just as obviously, no one can live without some stress. Are we all, then, destined to become victims of stress? Fortunately not.

The researchers who have pinpointed the effects of stress also know that the way a person perceives stress and the way he copes with it can keep it from making him sick. Attitudes, beliefs, and perceptions can help keep humans well. Ample evidence, cited throughout this book, shows how factors like optimism, faith, hope, and a good explanatory style can help overcome the devastating effects of stress.

Yale oncologist and surgeon Bernie S. Siegel, one of the nation's better-known explorers of the link between behavior and disease, points out that "stresses that we *choose* evoke a response totally different from those we'd like to avoid but cannot. Helplessness is worse than the stress itself. That is probably why the rate of cancer is higher for blacks in America than for whites, and why cancer is associated with grief and depression."[135]

Epidemiologist Leonard Sagan remarked that "whether altered conditions are viewed as threatening or challenging, and whether the consequences contribute to personal growth or apathy and despair, is the result of the interaction of two factors: the magnitude and quality of the external stressor and the capacity of the individual to cope."[136]

How to Protect Yourself from Stress

If everyone is a victim of stress, are there ways we can protect ourselves from the effects of stress? Absolutely! One of the first ways, says Baylor College of Medicine psychologist Michael Cox, is to face the stress head-on. Recognize it, and get ready to deal with it. "Avoiding and denying that stress exists won't make it go away," he says. "Look at different ways you can change the situation to lessen the stress, make your decision, and face the stress head on. Action is the fastest way to reduce the level of stress."[137]

Following are some ideas from cardiologist Robert S. Eliot and others as to how you can reduce the effects of stress:

- Develop what Eliot calls a game plan for your personal aspirations, both short-term and long-term ones. Take a personal inventory and reestablish important priorities. You need to balance your talents and goals, similar to the way in which you'd balance your financial portfolio. Work to get things back into balance, and figure out where your long-term goals may be losing out to short-term pressures, Eliot says.
- Be nice to yourself. Do something nice for yourself every day. Take the time to read something you love, soak in a warm bath, take a brisk walk, or call an old friend.
- Develop a system of time management that will help you plan your day *without* becoming a stressor itself. When you're scheduling your time, remember to leave time for play, time for hobbies and friends, and time for simple relaxation. If you have to, schedule in time for breaks.
- Just as you need to develop a game plan for your personal aspirations, Eliot advises developing a game plan for your career or work. Especially important in today's economy is the ability to adapt, continually assess where you are, look ahead, and prepare for change.
- If you commute to work, make sure you plan enough time to arrive without feeling stressed. If you can, turn your commute into something pleasant: Ride the bus instead of driving, and take the chance to catch up on some favorite books or magazines. If you have to drive, try out some entertaining tapes instead of the usual radio fare.
- Once at work, try the following strategies: Pair up with people you like. Instead of letting the telephone control you, control the telephone; have someone take messages, and block out several periods during the day in which to return calls. Delegate as much work as you can. Do what you can to reduce environmental stresses at work (noise, temperature extremes, and so on). And, at least once a day, concentrate on doing at least one task—no matter how small—that brings you satisfaction.
- Save a little money each month.
- Take frequent nonbusiness weekends away from home, preferably with your spouse.
- Get married if you're not. Marriage has been shown to protect against illness.
- Be realistic in your expectations of your children. According to Eliot, it's crucial to accept *who they are* and let children express their own ideas. Eliot also advocates giving children at least one adult they can look up to and letting them stay closer to home until they have the skills and resources to make it on their own in an increasingly complex world.
- Take a look at your neighborhood. What's going on? Do as much as you can to create a calm, controlled, quiet, comfortable neighborhood.

- Pay attention to your physical health. Have regular checkups, and take care of health problems promptly. If you notice unusual symptoms, have a doctor check them out as soon as possible. Above all, *believe* that you are well.
- Get plenty of sleep. British researchers concluded that flexibility, spontaneity, and originality of thought can be seriously undermined by as little as one sleepless night.
- Eat a balanced diet; avoid alcohol, tobacco, and caffeine. During periods of particular stress, go for a small, high-protein meal featuring something like chicken breast, turkey breast, tuna, or Swiss cheese.
- Get plenty of exercise.
- Stay socially connected. According to Eliot, "Friends are not just nice, they are a necessity." If you have problems, talk them out with a trusted friend; if you're facing something difficult, rehearse it with a friend first. Share your feelings often.
- Develop at least one confidant, someone with whom you can share your deepest thoughts and feelings. And write your thoughts down on a regular basis. Keeping a journal is good, but so is jotting your thoughts on scraps of paper.
- Find and trust in a higher power; develop a sense of spiritual support. Attend your church or synagogue on a regular basis, affiliate with the religious community there, and practice forgiveness on a daily basis. Fill your life with faith; let go of guilt and shame.
- Get a pet!
- Learn to laugh at yourself, and fill your life with humor.
- When things get tough, take a warm bath or shower, or sip a cup of warm herbal tea. And, above all, stay flexible. There may be more ways to cope with any situation than at first are apparent.[138]

Notes

1. Marc K. Lewen and Harold L. Kennedy, "The Role of Stress in Heart Disease," *Hospital Medicine*, August: 1986, 125–138.

2. Ari Kiev, "Managing Stress to Achieve Success," *Executive Health*, 24(1): 1987, 1–4.

3. Dharma Singh Khalsa, "Stress-Related Illness," *Postgraduate Medicine*, 78(6): 1985, 217–221.

4. Susan Jenks, "Further Clues to CAD-Stress Link," *Medical World News*, June 13: 1988, 108.

5. Lorraine Daigneault, "Stress Self-Defense," *Self*, January: 1984, 112.

6. Paul Rosch, "Good Stress: Why You Need It to Stay Young," *Prevention*, April: 1986, 29.

7. Howard S. Friedman, *The Self-Healing Personality* (New York: Henry Holt and Company, 1991), p. 40.

8. Rosch, pp. 28–29.

9. Ruthan Brodsky, "Identifying Stressors Is Necessary to Combat Potential Health Problems," *Occupational Health and Safety*, pp. 30–32.

10. Emrika Padus, *Positive Living and Health: The Complete Guide to Brain/Body Healing and Mental Empowerment* (Emmaus, Pennsylvania: Rodale Press, 1990).

11. Paul Pearsall, *Super Immunity* (New York: McGraw-Hill, 1987).

12. From Mary F. Asterita, *The Physiology of Stress* (New York: Human Sciences Press, 1985), pp. 4–5.

13. Claudia Wallis, "Stress: Can We Cope?" *Time*, June 6: 1983, 48–54.

14. Wallis.

15. Peter G. Hanson, *The Joy of Stress* (Kansas City: Andrews, McMeel, and Parker, 1986).

16. Hanson.

17. Lawrence E. Lamb, "Your Vital Adrenal Steroids (Corticosteroids)," *The Health Letter*, 34(4): 1989, 1–8.

18. "The Anti-Stress Power of Exercise," *Self*, November: 1989, 166.

19: Robert S. Eliot, *From Stress to Strength* (New York: Bantam Books, 1994), p. 24.

20. Kiev.

21. Brodsky.

22. Brodsky.

23. Brodsky.

24. Wallis.

25. Wallis.

26. P. D. Somervell, B. H. Kaplan, and G. Heiss, "Psychologic Distress as a Predictor of Mortality," *American Journal of Epidemiology*, 130(5): 1989, 1013–1023.

27. *British Medical Journal,* October 30: 1993, 1102–1105.

28. Hanson.

29. Clifford J. Sherry, "What Should You Know About Stress?" *Bestways*, July: 1985, 38–39.

30. Wallis.

31. Wallis.

32. Bernie S. Siegel, *Love, Medicine, and Miracles* (New York: Harper and Row Publishers, 1986).

33. Horst Scherg and Maria Blohmke, "Associations Between Selected Life Events and Cancer," *Behavioral Medicine*, Fall: 1988, 119–124.

34. H. J. F. Baltrush, reported at the Third International Symposium on Detection and Prevention of Cancer.

35. Ann S. Masten, "Stress, Coping, and Children's Health," *Pediatric Annals*, 14(8): 1985, 544–547.

36. Wallis.

37. Ian Wickramasekera, "Risk Factors Leading to Chronic Stress-Related Symptoms," *Advances* 4(1): 1987, 21.

38. M. Weinberger, S. L. Heiner, and W. M. Tierney, "In Support of Hassles as a Measure of Stress in Predicting Health Outcomes," *Journal of Behavioral Medicine*, 10(1): 1987, 19–32.

39. Susan Kripke Byers, "Organizational Stress: Implications for Health Promotion Managers," *American Journal of Health Promotion*, Summer: 1987, 21–26.

40. "Good Boss, Good Health," *Your Personal Best*, September: 1990, 3.

41. Michael P. O'Donnell and Thomas H. Ainsworth, *Health Promotion in the Workplace* (New York, John Wiley & Sons, 1984), p. 185.

42. Donald S. Jewell and Maureen Mylander, "The Psychology of Stress: Run Silent, Run Deep," in George P. Chrousos, D. Lynn Loriaux, and Phillip W. Gold, editors, *Mechanisms of Physical and Emotional Stress* (New York, Plenum Press, 1988), pp. 489–505.

43. "Healthy Lives: A New View of Stress," *University of California Berkeley Wellness Letter*, June: 1990, 4.

44. Byers; and Jewell and Mylander.

45. Harold A. Williamson, Jr., Michael LeFevre, and Melvin Hector, Jr., "Association Between Life Stress and Serious Perinatal Complications," *The Journal of Family Practice*, 29(5): 1989, 489–496.

46. Haim Omer and George S. Everly, Jr., "Psychological Factors in Preterm Labor: Critical Review and Theoretical Synthesis," *Advances* 7(1): 1990, 11–13, adapted from *American Journal of Psychiatry*, 145(72): 1988, 1507–1513.

47. Lynne C. Huffman and Rebecca del Carmen, "Prenatal Stress," in L. Eugene Arnold, editor, *Childhood Stress* (New York: John Wiley and Sons, Inc., 1990), pp. 144–172.

48. Huffman and del Carmen.

49. Marie L. Lobo, "Stress in Infancy," in Arnold, editor, *Childhood Stress*, pp. 173–192.

50. Lobo.

51. W. Thomas Boyce, "Stress and Child Health: An Overview," *Pediatric Annals*, 14(8): 1985, 539–542.

52. Marianne L. Barton and Charles H. Zeanah, "Stress in the Preschool Years," in Arnold, editor, *Childhood Stress*, pp. 193–222.

53. Barton and Zeanah.

54. Susan Jones Sears and Joanne Milburn,

"School-Age Stress," in Arnold, editor, *Childhood Stress*, pp. 223–246.

55. Sears and Milburn.

56. Sears and Milburn.

57. Robert L. Hendren, "Stress in Adolescence," in Arnold, editor, *Childhood Stress*, pp. 247–266.

58. Hendren.

59. Age-related stressors summarized from Jerrold S. Greenberg, *Comprehensive Stress Management*, 3d ed. (Dubuque, Iowa: Wm. C. Brown Publishers, 1990), pp. 299–393.

60. Hanson.

61. G. P. Sackett, "Genotype Determines Social Isolation Rearing Effects on Monkeys," *Developmental Psychology* 17: 1981, 313–318.

62. Masten, p. 546.

63. Hanson.

64. Sherry.

65. Andrew G. Goliszek, *Breaking the Stress Habit* (Winston-Salem, North Carolina: Carolina Press, 1987).

66. Goliszek.

67. Kelly Costigan, "What Is a Woman's Most Stressful Occupation?" *Complete Woman*, April: 1988, 32–33.

68. From Jerry Lazar, "New Proof That Stress Ages the Brain," *Longevity*, 2(3): 1988, 25.

69. "Workplace Warning: Stress May Speed Brain Aging," *New Sense Bulletin*, 16(11): 1991, 1.

70. Bruce S. McEwen, "Hormones and the Nervous System," *Advances* 7(1): 1990, 50–54.

71. McEwen.

72. McEwen.

73. "The Stress-Infertility Link," *Longevity*, September: 1993, 26.

74. Michael A. Weiner, *Maximum Immunity* (Boston: Houghton Mifflin Company, 1986).

75. Weiner.

76. Greenberg, p. 31.

77. G. Holtmann, R. Kriebel, and M. V. Singer, "Mental Stress and Gastric Acid Secretion: Do Personality Traits Influence the Response?" *Editor's Citation Abstract*, 35(8): 1990, 998–1007.

78. R. F. Anda, D. F. Williamson, L. G. Escobedo, P. L. Remington, E. E. Mast, and J. H. Madans, "Self-perceived Stress and the Risk of Peptic Ulcer Disease: A Longitudinal Study of U.S. Adults," *Archives of Internal Medicine* 152: 1992, 829–833.

79. Goliszek.

80. Eliot, *From Stress to Strength*, pp. 30–31.

81. Goliszek.

82. "Stress Can Make You Sick," *Consumer Reports Health Letter*, 2(1): 1990, 1, 3.

83. Eliot, *From Stress to Strength*, p. 34.

84. "Can Stress Clog Arteries?" *Consumer Reports on Health*, December: 1993, 133.

85. Goliszek.

86. Jenks.

87. Robert S. Eliot and Dennis L. Breo, "Are You a Hot Reactor? Is It Worth Dying For?" *Executive Health*, 20(10): 1984, 1–4.

88. Eliot, *From Stress to Strength*, p. 18.

89. Stephen Brewer, "Anti-Old-Age Stress," *Longevity*, June: 1990, 82.

90. John E. Sutherland, "The Link Between Stress and Illness," *Postgraduate Medicine*, 89(1): 1991, 162.

91. K. A. Fackelmann, "Stress Puts Squeeze on Clogged Vessels," *Science News*, November 16: 1991, 309.

92. Larry A. Tucker, Galen E. Cole, and Glenn M. Friedman, "Stress and Serum Cholesterol: A Study of 7,000 Adult Males," *Health Values*, 2(3): 1987, 34–39.

93. Eliot, *From Stress to Strength*, p. 40.

94. Tucker, Cole, and Friedman.

95. Tucker, Cole, and Friedman.

96. Peter Riech, "How Much Does Stress Contribute to Cardiovascular Disease?" *Journal of Cardiovascular Medicine*, July: 1983, 825–831.

97. Marjory Roberts, "Stress and the Silent Heart Attack," *Psychology Today*, August: 1987, 7.

98. C. Noel Bairey, et al., "Mental Stress as an Acute Trigger of Left Ventricular Dysfunction and Blood Pressure Elevation in Coronary Patients," *American Journal of Cardiology* 66: 1991, 28G.

99. Editors of *Prevention Magazine*.

100. Cited in John Tierney, "Stress, Success, and Samoa," *Hippocrates*, May/June: 1987, 84.

101. R. Dubos, *American Journal of Clinical Nutrition*, 32: 1979, 2623–2626.

102. Deborah Kipp, "Stress and Nutrition," *Contemporary Nutrition*, 9(7): 1984.

103. Glenn D. Wilson, "Eating Styles and Stress," *Healthline*, November: 1989, 12.

104. S. I. McMillen, *None of These Diseases*, Revised Edition (Old Tappan, New Jersey: Fleming H. Revell Company, 1984).

105. S. Cohen, D. A. Tyrrell, and A. P. Smith, "Psychological Stress and Susceptibility to the Common Cold," *New England Journal of Medicine*, 325: 1991, 606–612.

106. P. D. Evans and N. Edgerton, "Life-Events and Mood as Predictors of the Common Cold," *British Journal of Medical Psychology*, 64(1): 1991, 35–44.

107. Signe Hammer, "The Mind As Healer," *Science Digest*, April: 1984, 47–49, 100.

108. Goliszek.

109. Goliszek.

110. Goliszek.

111. Tracy Bennett Herbert and Sheldon Cohen, "Stress and Immunity in Humans: A Meta-Analytic Review," *Psychosomatic Medicine* 55: 1993, 364–379.

112. Netta Kanoho, "Predicting Stress," *Bestways*, July: 1985, 42–43.

113. R. Dantzer and K. W. Kelley, "Stress and Immunity: An Integrated View of Relationships Between the Brain and the Immune System," *Life Sciences*, 44: 1989, 1995–2008.

114. Herbert and Cohen.

115. "Can Undue Stress Lower Resistance to Disease?" *Medical Times*, April:1988, 99–100.

116. Alex J. Zautra, Morris A. Okun, Sharon E. Robinson, Douglas Lee, Sanford H. Roth, and Jansen Emmanual, "Life Stress and Lymphocyte Alterations Among Patients with Rheumatoid Arthritis," *Health Psychology*, 8(1): 1989, 1–14.

117. "Can Undue Stress Lower Resistance to Disease?"

118. Blair Justice, "Those Who Stay Healthy," *New Realities*, July/August: 1988, 35–39, 69–71.

119. Daigneault.

120. "Stress Can Make You Sick."

121. Goliszek.

122. Cathrine Frank and Stephen Smith, "Stress and the Heart: Biobehavioral Aspects of Sudden Cardiac Death," *Psychosomatics*, 31(3): 1990, 255–262.

123. Goliszek.

124. Sandra G. Zakowski, Cathy G. McAllister, Marlene Deal, and Andrew Baum, "Stress, Reactivity, and Immune Function in Healthy Men," *Health Psychology*, 11(4): 1992, 223–232.

125. Nan Silver, "Long-Term Stress: Does Your Body Fight Back?" *American Health*, May: 1986, 20.

126. Daniel Goleman and Joel Gurin, editors, *Mind/Body Medicine: How to Use Your Mind for Better Health* (New York: Consumer Reports Books, 1993), p. 52.

127. Betty Weider, "The Stress-Free Personality," *Shape*, July: 1990, 18.

128. *International Journal of Aging and Human Development*, 37(1): 1993.

129. Guy R. Newell, "Stress and Cancer," *Primary Care and Cancer*, May: 1991, 30.

130. Guy R. Newell, "Stress and Cancer," *Primary Care and Cancer*, May: 1991, 29–30

131. A. H. Schmale and H. D. Iker, "Hopelessness as a Predictor of Cervical Cancer," *Social Science and Medicine*, 5: 1971, 95–100.

132. W. A. Green and S. N. Swisher, "Psychological and Somatic Variables Associated with the Development and Course of Monozygotic Twins Discordant for Leukemia," *Annals of the New York Academy of Sciences*, 164: 1969, 394–408.

133. E. B. Faragher and C. L. Cooper, "Type A Stress Prone Behaviour and Breast Cancer," *Psychological Medicine*, 20(3): 1990, 663–670.

134. Newell.

135. Siegel.

136. Leonard A. Sagan, *The Health of Nations* (New York: Basic Books, Inc., Publishers, 1987).

137. "Learn to Manage the Stress in Your Life," *Healthline*, September 1993.

138. Eliot, *From Stress to Strength*, pp. 107–144.

4

JOB STRESS AND HEALTH

No one dies just from working too hard. But when people don't get any recognition in their work, the stress of that lack of control can kill them.
—*BARRIE S. GREIFF*

"This job's killing me!" The often heard complaint contains more than a kernel of truth. The stress connected with certain kinds of jobs can, indeed, hurt your health, and if stress on the job gets too intense, it *can* kill you.

High-powered executives who cope with the stress of running corporations, humoring clients, balancing budgets, and solving personnel problems are not those most likely in danger. They're under stress, but research indicates that the people most likely to be negatively affected by job stress are the ones who have little control or decision-making power: assembly line workers, factory workers, computer operators who are constantly scrutinized by supervisors.

All kinds of factors—from the hours worked, to the boss, to general attitude about the job—come into play, but researchers do know for certain that job stress is costing America a tremendous price.

The Cost of Job Stress

How many Americans suffer work-related stress? It's difficult to come up with an exact number, but there are some pretty good estimates. Stress on the job led 34 percent of all American employees to consider quitting their jobs in 1990, as reported in a study conducted by Northwestern National Life Insurance Company. According to the study, 46 percent of American workers find their jobs highly stressful.[1]

A recent Gallup poll conducted for the National Occupational Information Coordinating Committee came up with similar figures. It determined that about half of all Americans say that job stress affects their health, personal relationships, or ability to do their job.[2]

Of the employed adults who responded to the poll, a fourth said that job stress had interfered with off-the-job relationships. One in five said that the stress had interfered with their ability to do their job. The same number, 20 percent, said that job stress had affected their physical health. The poll also found that fewer than half of all employed Americans were on the career or job path they had planned. The rest were influenced by family or friends, got their jobs by "chance," or grabbed the only job they could find. Well over half (65 percent) said that, given a chance to start over, they would look more carefully at their career options. And almost a third of the work force hoped to change jobs within the next three years.[3]

What price does industry pay for all this worker stress and dissatisfaction? Recent estimates are that job stress costs American industry more than $150 billion a year in absenteeism, lost productivity, accidents, and medical insurance.[4]

There's no question that job stress causes underproductivity, absenteeism, illness (resulting in health insurance payouts and workers' compensation claims), employee turnover, and even theft and sabotage. That presents a hefty bill to American companies—estimated by one researcher to be about $1700 per employee per year for a medium-sized manufacturing firm. It can add up to more than the company's profits.[5]

The costs are due to a number of different factors. Some estimate that 60 percent of all absence from work is caused by stress-related disorders[6] (and that anywhere from 60 to 90 percent of all visits to health care professionals are for stress-related disorders[7]). One study estimates that, in the United Kingdom alone, 100 million working days are lost each year because "people cannot face going to work."[8] And American employers spend some $700 million per year replacing men below retirement age owing to coronary heart disease incapacity.[9]

In an attempt to dull the effects of job stress, many of the nation's workers are turning to drugs and alcohol on the job, and the results are staggering. According to a report in *Time* magazine, "Illegal drugs have become so pervasive in the U.S. workplace that they are used in almost every industry, the daily companions of blue- and white-collar workers alike. Their presence on the job is sapping the energy, honesty, and reliability of the American labor force, even as competition from foreign companies is growing ever tougher."[10]

Job stress-related employee claims are skyrocketing; analysts say they escalated more than 300 percent in a single year in California.[11] During the last decade in that same state, more than half of all worker compensation cases were for disorders that stemmed from stress on the job.[12] To sum it up, says New York Medical College psychiatrist Paul J. Rosch, who heads the American Institute of Stress, "Work stress may be America's number-one health problem."

Job Characteristics

No job is completely free from stress, and we wouldn't want that kind of job anyway. Just as some stress is critical to life, some stress is essential on the job. It's what keeps us motivated, inspired, and productive—as long as it's kept to a healthy level. In their book *Healthy Work*, authors Robert Karasek of the University of Southern California and Dr. Tores Theorell of Sweden's National Institute for Psychosocial Factors and Health, say that the following are characteristics of healthy jobs:

- *Skill discretion.* Your job allows you to make maximum use of your skills and provides the opportunity for you to increase or broaden your skills.
- *Autonomy.* Your job allows you some sense of control. You don't feel as though you are a child being disciplined. You get to participate in long-term planning, and your employer allows flexible hours. You control the machines at your workplace, not the other way around.
- *Psychological demands.* You have some say over the magnitude of the demands placed on you, and the routine demands you are faced with are mixed with new, unpredictable challenges that help keep the job exciting.
- *Social relations.* You're encouraged to collaborate with your coworkers. There's a sense of teamwork and support.
- *Social rights.* When problems arise, democratic procedures are used to solve them. If you have some kind of a grievance, you know there's an accepted way for you to solve it.
- *Meaningfulness.* Your job has some meaning for you. You know what you're producing, and who it's for. You have ready access to feedback from your customers (the people you work for all day).
- *Integration of family and community life with work.* The people on the job share the responsibilities of running the business so there's time—and energy—left over for activities other than work.[13]

Some jobs are known for being "active" or "low-stress" occupations; others, by virtue of the work they encompass, are passive and high in stress. According to *Healthy Work*, the categories are these:

   1.   *Low-stress jobs.* These are occupations that afford low demands with plenty of decision-making power; essentially, workers are self-paced. There can be certain stresses (such as the pressure to perform or the stress of deadlines), but that stress seems to be offset by a sense of control and latitude. Examples of such occupations include tenured professors, carpenters, repairmen, and successful artists and performers.

   2.   *Active jobs.* While there is heavy pressure to perform in these occupations, there is plenty of leeway for problem solving. There are also solid opportunities for developing new skills or advancing job-related education. The hours can be long but are at least partly at the employee's discretion. Workers are valued for their initiative. These occupations include jobs such as physicians, farmers, engineers, executives, and other professionals.

   3.   *Passive jobs.* Few demands are placed on either skills or thinking ability, but there is also little leeway for personal decision-making or for developing skill levels in passive jobs. Some people in these occupations actually find that their skills atrophy. There is almost no reward for initiative. They include jobs like billing clerks, keypunchers, janitors, dispatchers, and night security personnel.

4.   *High-stress jobs.* There is heavy pressure to perform but almost no decision-making power. The hours and procedures are rigid; there is little or no flexibility that allows workers to take a break or time off for personal needs. No new skills are learned as part of the job. The threat of layoff usually looms. These occupations include assembly-line workers, waiters, waitresses, nurse's aides, and telephone operators, to name a few.[14]

Sources of Stress on the Job

A stressor is any demand that upsets your sense of balance and makes it necessary to regain that balance.[15] Stressors on the job, then, can be the boss, coworkers, the noise, deadlines. Virtually anything at all can, under the right conditions, become a source of stress at work. Through decades of research, however, certain factors have continually reared their heads as particular sources of stress on the job.[16]

Physical Environment Stressors

Plenty of things in the physical environment of the workplace can cause stress. Some of them include noise, poor temperature control (too hot or too cold), crowding, poor arrangement of space, lack of privacy, and problems with lighting (lights are too bright, too dim, too glaring, or flickering). In some jobs there are even safety hazards—work with dangerous machinery, the threat of being hurt by dangerous people, the presence of toxic chemicals, exposure to air pollution, and so on. These kinds of problems tend to be concentrated in blue-collar professions, but that's not always true. White-collar executives, engineers, nuclear scientists, and others are exposed to constant danger in nuclear power plants, for example.

Physical stressors on the job are different than other kinds of job stressors because they can cause direct physical trauma. A worker's lungs can be seared by exposure to toxic fumes, for example, or an employee can go deaf from dangerous levels of unremitting noise.

Organizational Stressors

The very culture in a company can produce high levels of stress for employees. Several years ago *Dun's Review* published a list of what it considered to be the ten most stressful companies in America. On the list was ITT (its chairman, Harold Geneen, decided to fire a hundred executives, turning the company on its ear). Also on the list was Gallo Winery (co-owner Ernest Gallo is famed for his hard-driving style, his unrelenting insistence on superior performance, and his low tolerance for failure). One of the top sources of organizational culture stress is the *power struggle* and related heightened competition, power games, and political alliances.

Another organizational stressor is the organization's *structure* itself. Merely by the way a company is structured, it may afford little opportunity for advancement or growth and little chance for decision making. The company may be so specialized that division of labor is stringent and inflexible. The mere size of the company can lead to excessive formalization, rigid expectations, and inflexible conditions.

Organizational *policies* can be another source of stress. Workers may be faced with pay inequities, rotating work shifts, unfair performance evaluations, or ambiguous policies. Frequent forced relocation can be a potent stressor, as can the underlying threat of layoff. Finally, workers may be given a rosy picture when they interview then find their job expectations shattered by reality.

Processes in the organization itself can cause stress. Employees may struggle because of inadequate training programs, poor or inadequate feedback on job performance, ambiguous or conflicting goals, ineffective delegation, or poor communication with coworkers and supervisors alike.

Job Demands

Demands of certain jobs can pose real stress. Some jobs, for example, have low skill requirements; employees end up feeling that what they are doing has no value, makes no difference in the world. At the opposite end of the spectrum are jobs that demand almost superhuman skills; employees feel that nothing they ever do is quite good enough.

Some jobs are fraught with time pressures and deadlines; the fear of missing a deadline, having to answer to disgruntled customers, or failing to perform within time parameters can translate into crushing stress. In others, employees are responsible for people, often in life-and-death scenarios: A nurse must put the right fluid in an intravenous bag, a policeman must be calm and say the right thing in a hostage situation, and a ski-lift operator must be on constant alert for possible malfunctions in the machinery that could plunge riders to their death.

Some jobs cause stress because they are so repetitive. There's a unique kind of stress in sitting at a station and inserting the same screw into the same hole all day, just as there is numbing boredom in sewing the same side seam on parkas all day.

Job stress can also result from overemployment or underemployment. The first means a job that you are not qualified to do (because it demands skills, knowledge, or experience that you don't have), and the latter refers to a job that you are too qualified to do (the job doesn't challenge or use your skills, knowledge, or experience).

Interpersonal Relationships on the Job

In almost every job, employees are forced to deal with coworkers and a boss. The quality of those relationships can be a source of overwhelming stress. Some leaders actually reduce the stress on the job. Their technical knowledge is needed by others, they work smoothly within the political system of the organization, and they value and work smoothly with subordinates. On the other hand, some leaders exert unnecessary power over their subordinates. Some use punishment when things start going wrong. Others discipline their employees as they would children.

In essence, the greatest amount of stress in interpersonal relationships occurs when employees are subject to inconsiderate or unfair supervisors, feel a lack of trust, do not feel accepted or recognized, or are subjected to conflicts between people or groups. Other interpersonal stress can arise when an employee has trouble delegating work or responsibilities or when an employee is subjected to intense competition with others in the company.

Role Characteristics

One of the most intense stressors on the job is *role ambiguity*: The employee is not clear about what he or she is supposed to be doing. The worker may not understand the responsibilities of the position, what the job is all about, or his or her place in the larger scheme of things.

Everybody occasionally feels some kind of role ambiguity. It's common on a first job, right after a promotion or a transfer, just after the organizational structure changes, after a new boss takes over, or the first time an employee is in a supervisory position. In a healthy situation, however, people bounce back quickly. The problems start when role ambiguity lingers—because management is uncooperative, or the employee isn't getting questions answered, or isn't able to get fair or timely feedback, or is simply in too deep. Ongoing role ambiguity is a major stressor in the workplace. Its results are job dissatisfaction, job-related tension, low levels of work motivation, anxiety, depression, and turnover.

Job Stresses outside the Organization

There are also job stresses away from the job. One is the *family*. It's difficult to concentrate on work if a marriage is failing or a child is in trouble with the law. Employees worry, too, about adequate child care. And job stress is generated when an employee cannot arrange time to deal with the problems and crises that erupt in any family (such as death of a relative, illness of a child, or broken water pipes at home).

The family itself may be a source of stress, because men, in particular, may feel trapped in their jobs because of the necessity of providing for a family. According to New York psychologist and career counselor Maynard Johnson, "Sure, initially you have some choice in a career. But once you've been at a company for five years and have picked up a spouse, a mortgage, and a child, you have very little choice about jumping ship if things aren't turning out the way you planned. A steady paycheck can be the biggest manacle of all."[17]

Another stress is *relocation*. It's becoming increasingly more common for people to move, whether for job-related or for personal reasons. The average homeowner stays in a house only about seven years; the average American switches jobs about every three years; and every year one in five Americans changes addresses.

Even if relocation results in better pay and working conditions, it can still create considerable stress. Dual-career couples can end up sacrificing one job. People lose friends and familiar surroundings. Their familiar sources of support are disrupted. They may lose affiliation with groups that were important to them, or may no longer be able to participate in activities they enjoy (such as hunting ducks along the marshy shores of a local lake). They can also lose credentials they have worked hard to establish (such as credit relationships with local banks and stores). They have to get used to a new job, a new routine, a new set of working relationships, a new house, a new neighborhood, new grocery stores, a new bank, new schools, and so on. Add to that the various stresses that relocation customarily creates in both preschoolers and school-aged children.

Another stress outside the workplace that can affect job performance is what researchers have called *residential stress*. People work better and with less stress if they feel safe, happy, and secure in their general surroundings. Residential stresses include things like inadequate police protection, rising crime rates, lack of public transportation, poor public schools, harsh climate conditions, inadequate garbage collection, high local taxes, inconvenience of services and shopping, lack of parks and playgrounds, racial tension, poor housing conditions, feelings of estrangement from neighbors, and environmental pollution.

Finally, one of the greatest stresses off the job that spills over to the job is *financial pressure*. A person may worry about having too little money to provide the basics for the family—a place to live, food, clothes, trips to the doctor and dentist, electricity to run the lights. If there is a threat (or perceived threat) of being laid off or being asked to retire early, the stress from financial pressure may greatly intensify.

Stress as Part of the Job

Some stress comes along with the job, not because of anything the employee does but because certain stressors are part and parcel of certain jobs.[18] Blue-collar workers, for example, have inherent stresses that are generally categorized into three groups. First, they tend to perform heavy work in difficult conditions that usually include heat, noise, dust, or toxic substances. Second, they often perform monotonous or repetitive work that requires no skill or over which they have no control. Finally, they tend to perform somewhat complex jobs under time constraints.

Managers and professionals have a different set of characteristic stressors. For them, some of the greatest conflict arises from their role in the organization: how much decision making they do, how committed they are to the organization, how well they tolerate conflict, and how cohesive they perceive their group to be. They also tend to experience stress as a result of trying to start, to develop, or to maintain a career, weathering the transitions in careers, and working out relationships with others in the organization (supervisors as well as coworkers and subordinates). Rapid changes in technology, in applications, and even on the world political scene subject many professionals and managers to uncertainty about the future of their jobs, a certain source of stress.

Even people who operate computers are subject to certain characteristic stresses.[19] They have to cope with varying hardware characteristics, difficulties in different video display and keyboard designs, and sometimes uncomfortable or inefficient work station layout. Computer operators are also likely to have the stress of solving problems with the computer, lack of adequate training and support, few opportunities for control or discretion, and figuring out how to implement what they need.

How Much Stress Is Enough?

Every job is going to include some stress. It might be thunderous noise and wilting heat from the blast furnace of a steel plant, or it might be the inescapable deadlines of reporting for a newspaper. It might be the monotonous repetition of working on an assembly line, or the crushing stress of running a multi–million-dollar corporation. No one would want a job that is totally devoid of stress. *Some* stress is what makes life (not to mention a job) interesting. But what are the signs that enough is enough, when you've inched over the line toward stress that is debilitating?

Basketball great Bill Russell of the Boston Celtics described the rush that can come from the right level of job stress when he told how the pressures of a pro game begin to percolate: "It usually began when three or four of the ten guys on the floor would heat up," he explained. "The feeling would spread to other guys, and we'd all levitate. . . . The game would be in the white heat of competition, and yet somehow I wouldn't feel competitive. . . . I'd be putting out the maximum effort. . . . and yet I never felt the pain. My premonitions would be consistently correct. . . . There have been many times in my career when I felt moved or joyful, but these were moments when I had chills pulsing up and down my spine."[20] It's a level of stress that provides a sense of cohesion, intense satisfaction, great challenge, supreme accomplishment, and personal control.

When there's enough stress to stimulate challenge and satisfaction and control, you'll feel certain emotions and you'll find that your job performance meets certain standards. An optimum level of stress is characterized by high energy, mental alertness, high motivation, calmness under pressure, thorough analysis of problems, improved memory and recall, sharp perception, and an overall optimistic outlook.[21] The signs of too little or too much stress on the job are much the same. Whether absence of job stress has created a monotonous environment devoid of challenge and excitement, or you're in over your head at a job you can't perform to anyone's liking, the signs generally include boredom, apathy, a high accident rate, frequent grievances, absenteeism, a negative outlook toward the employer, widespread fatigue, insomnia, changes in appetite, increased errors, indecisiveness, and increased use of tobacco, drugs, or alcohol.[22]

How Job Stress Affects Health

Stress on the job affects the body in many of the same ways as stress in general: The body prepares for a fight-or-flight situation by revving up, most markedly by boosting respiration and heart rate and by pumping out certain hormones. How these changes affect the physiological functioning of the body is covered in detail in Chapter 3, but a growing body of research shows that there are even greater odds of being knocked out by stress on the job. There is even a good possibility that work is the *source* of a great deal of "ordinary" stress.

In one British study, researchers for the National Survey of Health and Development questioned more than 1400 twenty-six-year-old men. Those who were under stress were asked to pinpoint the source of their stress. Surprisingly, only 8 percent of the men reported stress at home or in some other arena of their personal lives. A staggering 38 percent reported work as the source of severe stress in their lives, and almost half of those said they were physically ill as well.[23]

Researchers use several methods to sort out and pinpoint job stress as a culprit. They compare various factors within groups until they can establish cause. For example, according to the Framingham Heart Study, *the* authority on the prevalence of heart disease, only about 9 percent of the general population suffer from coronary heart disease, and that figure includes both myocardial infarction and angina. But in one study of civil servants, rates were as high as 22 percent. In another study of factory workers, almost one in four had coronary heart disease.[24]

Another technique is to compare people in high-stress jobs with those in low-stress jobs in the same occupation. One group of researchers chose to study physicians. The doctors in high-stress jobs (general practitioners and anesthesiologists)

Focus on Research

International researchers decided to take a close look at blue-collar workers as part of the International Collaborative Study. They zeroed in on men over thirty years of age in a Zurich factory. Ninety-four percent of the workers in the factory were blue-collar workers.

At first glance, it appeared that the men were, or *should have been*, healthy. Few had elevated levels of blood cholesterol, and even fewer had any history of coronary heart disease. A look at the employees' health records told a different story, though. Almost one in ten had some kind of cardiovascular disease. The same number suffered from chronic high blood pressure or had had a stroke or myocardial infarction. And a whopping 36.6 percent had a severe illness or accident.

Source: Cooper and Payne; Schafer; Matteson and Ivancevich; and Arthur P. Brief, Randall S. Schuler, and Mary Van Sell, *Managing Job Stress* (Boston: Little, Brown, 1980), pp. 66–67.

had almost three times the rate of heart disease as the doctors in low-stress jobs (dermatologists and pathologists).[25] Researchers have also found that people under much job stress are prone to certain diseases.[26] Studies indicate that the higher the level of stress on the job, the greater the incidence of certain maladies.

Consider as an example purine uric acid, which crystallizes in the urinary tract or joints and causes kidney stones or gout. Researchers found in one study that excess purine uric acid was a problem for only 12 percent of craftsmen, who are normally considered to have very little job stress. But it affected 43 percent of the executives, who were considered to be under greater job stress. Researchers couldn't blame their findings on the traditional risk factors for purine uric acid, such as obesity, diet, and aspirin consumption. The only difference in the two groups was the amount of job stress.

Similar findings held true for cholesterol levels. In one study of nearly 15,000 middle-aged men in Oslo, those with the highest cholesterol level were the ones in high-stress jobs that underutilized their abilities and allowed little flexibility—tram drivers, metal foundry workers, construction machinery operators, and taxi drivers.

In still another study, forty-three different occupational groups were assessed for coronary risk. The executives, who *seem* to be under all kinds of stress, fared well. It was the blue-collar workers, who are in actuality under the greatest job stress, who had the highest blood pressure, highest cholesterol levels, and highest triglyceride levels.

In a series of studies done at Cornell University Medical College, researchers evaluated a total of 260 men who worked at various jobs in New York City. Men who worked in high-stress jobs—those characterized by plenty of pressure but little power to make decisions—were more than three times as likely to have high blood pressure as the men who worked in low-stress jobs.[27]

Risk factors from job stress may be greater than even researchers first realized. In a 1972 study done in Massachusetts for the Department of Health, Education, and Welfare, scientists found that the best predictor for heart disease was *job dissatisfaction,* not the major risk factors traditionally associated with heart disease, such as cigarette smoking, high blood cholesterol, high blood pressure, and diabetes.[28]

Some studies show that "burnout" resulting from excess stress on the job is a clear risk factor for coronary heart disease. Burnout is characterized by fatigue, irritability, inability to concentrate, insomnia, and a temporary inability to do one's job. In one study that assessed almost 4000 middle-aged men, burnout significantly increased the chances of suffering a heart attack (myocardial infarction).[29]

Risk also applies to people who are under stress on the job but who don't recognize it or deal with it. Driving a bus in a big city is recognized as a job that causes a high level of stress, pairing high demands with a sense of little control. Big-city drivers have to cope with much noise, heavy traffic, physical discomfort, and rude or hostile passengers, all while they're under extreme pressure to meet a schedule (one that is sometimes unrealistic) and the possibility of an accident or breakdown. When researchers studied nearly 1500 San Francisco bus drivers, they found that those who scored low on the stress scale—in other words, those

---

Focus on Research

Unemployment affects not only workers but also their families, and it can cause not only physical illness but psychological illness as well. One study conducted by psychiatrist Lili Penkower and her colleagues at the University of Pittsburgh involved 149 Pennsylvania women. Half of the women had husbands who were continually employed. The other half had husbands who were recurrently or persistently unemployed during the two years of the study.

As expected, the women whose husbands were unemployed had significantly more psychological distress than did the women whose husbands were employed. Their distress intensified over time, and was worse at the end of the two years than at the one-year mark. Several factors drove their rate of psychological distress even higher: a family history of psychiatric illness, preexisting financial problems, and lack of social support from relatives.

Source: "Long-term Effects of Husbands' Layoffs on Spouses' Mental Health," *Family Practice Recertification,* 11:11 (November 1989), p. 50.

who didn't admit how stressful things were—tended to have high blood pressure *more often* than those who recognized the stress they worked under.[30]

Studies show that job stress can even continue to affect people after they retire. One Swedish study followed more than 600 men who had retired. The Swedish researchers found that those who had job stress while working had nearly twice the relative mortality risk after retirement. Researchers also found that if job stress during work had been coupled with weak social support, the risk of early death jumped by more than 400 percent.[31]

Unemployment can be devastating to health. One of the most conclusive studies was conducted in Scotland and reported in the *British Heart Journal.*[32] Researchers were puzzled by coronary heart disease rates in the country: Scotland has one of the highest death rates in the world from coronary heart disease, but there is a vast difference from one region to another. They studied men in fifty-six local regions, and they looked at all kinds of factors, ranging from typical socioeconomic factors to amount of annual rainfall and hardness of drinking water. The strongest predictor of coronary heart disease among the men in the study was found to be unemployment.

Reports recently released by Johns Hopkins University economist M. Harvey Brenner and University of Utah economists Mary Merva and Richard Fowles show that every percentage point in the unemployment rate results in a 3.1 percent increase in deaths due to a stroke and a 5.6 percent increase in deaths due to heart disease.

"Directed outward, stress from unemployment may lead to an increase in criminal activities," report Merva and Fowles. "Directed toward oneself, stress may result in higher rates of morbidity and mortality, as depression, poor diet, and consumption of alcohol and cigarettes increase." The Utah pair conclude that the problems associated with unemployment "extend beyond those who are experiencing unemployment and poverty to those Americans who fear the possibility of job loss and declining economic status." According to Brenner, the debates on economic and social welfare policy "would become more pointed if it were clearly understood that the general health, life expectancy, and mental health of the nation are the final outcomes."[33]

Workaholics

Workaholism is a compulsive disorder, described by one writer as being "as ravaging and insidious as alcoholism or eating disorders."[34] Another called it "the only lifeboat guaranteed to sink." Diane Fassel, author of *Working Ourselves to Death*, calls it "a killer stalking our society."[35]

Workaholics are hard to spot.[36] They are not always working; the problem is the way they approach work. They are addicted. Their identity, their sense of self-worth, and their self-concept are all tied up in their work. They don't "have it all together"; as a matter of fact, their personal and professional lives are usually in shambles. Their families are filled with anger and resentment. They are driven by compulsion and rarely feel a peaceful sense of well-being.

Most important, it can strike anybody; it's not the domain of the high-powered executive. Factory workers can get it. So can housewives (who dedicate sixteen hours a day to being the perfect wife and mother) and children (who are driven to excellence and a host of extracurricular activities at school).

Plenty of people have tried to dismiss the notion of workaholism. After all, isn't work good for you? How can addiction to something that's good for you be *bad* for you? The key is the term *addiction*. Addiction is never good. And addiction to work can ruin health or even kill.

Workaholics are stricken with a disease "that affects them not only physically but also emotionally, mentally, and spiritually." Fassel says that characteristic health problems of workaholics include severe headaches, backaches, high blood pressure, and ulcers. An inordinate number have heart attacks or strokes. "Some die," she adds. "Some who survive are scared enough to get help. Others continue working from their hospital beds, until the next attack occurs."[37]

The Special Case of Women

In the workplace a woman's average level of decision-making latitude is still much lower than a man's. Women still fill more than their fair share of high-stress jobs, and they have less than their fair share of active jobs. Many women are employed in newly created clerical jobs that, by their nature, are killers when it comes to stress. Some experts believe that the future scope of women's health may be altered as a result.[38] Further, a woman who works outside the home is still usually the person primarily responsible for rearing the children and maintaining the home—doing the laundry, scrubbing the floors, cooking.

According to studies completed by University of Pennsylvania biologist Ingrid Waldron and sociologist Jerry Jacobs, working outside the home doesn't necessarily hurt health, and it may actually be *good* for some women. Reporting in the journal *Women and Health*, researchers concluded that women may actually have better health if they work outside. Overall, women who fill more than one role tend to develop fewer new illnesses than those who have only one role. As the number of roles increases, the number of new illnesses decreases.[39]

Researchers did present a few cautions in reporting on the study. First, the women in the study were between the ages of forty and fifty-nine; findings may not hold true for younger women (many of whom still have very young children at home). They also pointed out that the study results varied by race: Both marriage and jobs seem to boost the health of white women, regardless of whether they had children, but jobs protected the health only of those black women who had children at home. Why? Having a job might "buffer the stresses of child rearing by providing social support and time away from children's demands" and an "alternative, more structured, and perhaps more readily controllable course of gratification."

According to researchers, job stress may have a particularly hazardous effect on pregnant women. According to a study conducted by Dr. Vern L. Katz at the University of North Carolina, job stress causes the body to produce increased levels of catecholamines. The result? Catecholamines have been shown to contribute to premature labor, early delivery of very small babies, and babies who have breathing problems and other serious health problems at birth.

Katz and his colleagues stress that the study was small and should be considered only a pilot study. "I certainly wouldn't want anyone to think we've found the link between work and poor pregnancy outcome," said study coauthor Watson A. Bowes, Jr. However, he adds, stress on the job could be one of many factors that could boost the risk of premature labor and other pregnancy problems.[40]

The Key to Handling Job Stress

The same researchers who found that job stress is a killer have also identified a buffer: social support on the job. It might be a boss who treats you with respect. It might be a great feeling of camaraderie with coworkers. It might be regular feedback from customers who appreciate the job you're doing. It might be professional networking with others. Or it might be membership in a labor or professional union. In fact, say researchers Karasek and Theorell, social support on the job "may be one of the most important factors in improving health and well-being in the work environment."[41] As in all other facets of life, the people around us can be the key to good health and long life.

In addition to increasing your social support on the job, try the following measures to alleviate job-related stress:

- Take a hard look at the meetings you have to attend. Start by avoiding unnecessary meetings. Could you accomplish the same thing by memo or a few phone calls? When you do find yourself scheduled for a meeting, go in with a clear objective, then stick to task.

- Set your priorities every morning. Make sure you accomplish at least one thing every day that has value.
- Fridays tend to be "down days," so save the last hour or so on Friday for housekeeping tasks, such as straightening your desk, sorting your mail, returning phone calls, or listing your tasks for Monday. Then save something you really *like* to do for Monday morning, to get your week started off on a pleasant note.
- Take frequent breaks. You know you need a break when you find yourself daydreaming, you start procrastinating, you have a mental block, or you're feeling tense. Remember that you should take more frequent breaks if you are doing work that requires a lot of concentration.

According to *Prevention* magazine, here are some ways of coping with unemployment:

- First and foremost, try not to panic. Don't hide.
- Take care of yourself physically; eat a well-balanced diet, get plenty of sleep, and exercise regularly. Avoid alcohol, caffeine, and tobacco.
- Realize that grieving is normal. You have lost a job, and it's normal to grieve over any significant loss in your life. Be prepared for ups and downs as you work through the grieving process.
- Keep a diary, and find a few good friends you can rely on as confidants.
- Do something fun or something nice for yourself. Even if you don't have any money, you can always soak in a warm bath, read a good book from the library, or go for an early morning walk.
- If you catch yourself "catastrophizing" (imaging the worst that could possibly happen), replace that thought pattern with more positive, rational thoughts. Say some affirmations in front of a mirror. Convince yourself how valuable you are.
- Save money as you can, but don't be a miser.
- Stick to a schedule. Avoid the temptation to stay up half the night watching television, then sleep until noon. It's a good idea to keep the same kind of schedule you had when you were working.
- Avoid the late news; the last thing you see before going to bed should be uplifting.
- If you can, take advantage of career counselling. You can get valuable tips on how to brush up your resume, how to prepare for a successful job interview, and even networking tips on how to find the best available jobs.

If you're still working but scared you're going to lose your job in an upcoming layoff, Prevention experts suggest getting accurate information; doing whatever you can to make your current job better; building your skills now; sticking with hobbies and volunteer work; and assessing your finances so you can prepare for possible unemployment.[42]

Notes

1. "Stress in Workplace Is Rising, Survey Says," *Deseret News,* May 8: 1991, 3A.

2. "About Half Suffer From Stress Due to Job, Gallup Poll Says," *Deseret News*, January 11: 1990.

3. "About Half Suffer."

4. Donald Robinson, "Stressbusters," *Parade Magazine,* July 22: 1990, 12.

5. Walt Schafer, *Stress Management for Wellness* (New York: Holt, Rinehart & Winston, Inc., 1987), p. 310.

6. Cary L. Cooper and Roy Payne, editors, *Causes, Coping, and Consequences of Stress at Work* (New York: John Wiley & Sons Ltd., 1988), p. 9.

7. K. Pelletier and R. Lutz, "Healthy People—Healthy Business: A Critical Review of Stress Management in the Workplace," *American Journal of Health Promotion,* 2(3): 1988, 5–12.

8. Cooper and Payne, p. 10.

9. Cooper and Payne.

10. "Battling the Enemy Within," *Time,* March 17: 1986, 52.

11. Ronald B. Goodspeed and Ann G. De-Lucia, "Stress Reduction at the Worksite: An Evaluation of Two Methods," *American Journal of Health Promotion,* 4(5): 1990, 333.

12. "Healthy Lives: A New View of Stress," *University of California Berkeley Wellness Letter,* June: 1990, 5.

13. Robert Karasek and Tores Theorell, *Healthy Work.*

14. *Healthy Work.*

15. Michael T. Matteson and John M. Ivancevich, *Controlling Work Stress: Effective Human Resource and Management Strategies* (San Francisco: Jossey-Bass Publishers, 1987), p. 33.

16. Cooper and Payne; Schafer; Matteson and Ivancevich; and Arthur P. Brief, Randall S. Schuler, and Mary Van Sell, *Managing Job Stress* (Boston: Little, Brown, 1980), pp. 66–67.

17. David Diamond and Mark Golin, "Dare to Love Your Job," *Men's Health,* June: 1991, 85.

18. Cooper and Payne.

19. Cooper and Payne, p. 116.

20. "Healthy Lives," p. 4.

21. Rosalind Forbes, *Corporate Stress* (Garden City: Doubleday, 1979), p. 43.

22. Forbes, p. 44.

23. Cooper and Payne, pp. 13–14.

24. Cooper and Payne, p. 16.

25. Cooper and Payne, p. 16.

26. Cooper and Payne.

27. "Does Tension Cause Hypertension?" *Consumer Reports on Health,* June: 1994, 67.

28. Larry Dossey, *Meaning and Medicine: A Doctor's Tales of Breakthroughs and Healing* (New York: Bantam Books, 1991), p. 63.

29. A. Appels and E. Schouten, "Burnout as a Risk Factor for Coronary Heart Disease," *Behavioral Medicine* 17(2): 1991, 50–53

30. "How Anger Affects Your Health," *Wellness Letter,* January: 1992, 5.

31. "Anders Falk, Bertil S. Hanson, Sven-Olof Isacsson, and Per-Olof Ostergren, "Job Strain and Mortality in Elderly Men: Social Network, Support, and Influence as Buffers," *American Journal of Public Health,* 82(8): 1992, 1136–1138.

32. I. K. Crombie, M. B. Kenicer, W. C. S. Smith, and H. D. Tunstall-Pedoe, "Unemployment, Socioenvironmental Factors, and Coronary Heart Disease in Scotland," *British Heart Journal,* 61(2): 1989, 172–177.

33. *Deseret News,* October 16, 1992.

34. Bryan E. Robinson, "Are You a Work Addict?" *East/West,* August 1990, 50.

35. Diane Fassel, "Work- and Rushaholics: Spotting a Lethal Disease," *Longevity,* September: 1990, 78.

36. Fassel.

37. Fassel.

38. "Healthy Lives," p. 5.

39. Rob Stein, "Many Roles May Keep 'Supermoms' Healthy," *Deseret News,* January 28: 1990.

40. "Job Stress: A Risk for Pregnant Workers?" *Science News,* March 16: 1991, 165.

41. Karasek and Theorell.

42. "Stress Relief," *Prevention,* May: 1992, 47–50.

5

THE DISEASE-PRONE PERSONALITY

The tragedy of life is what dies inside a man while he lives.
—ALBERT SCHWEITZER

Psychologist and clinical professor of community medicine at the University of California Howard S. Friedman wrote, "I have never seen a death certificate marked 'Death due to unhealthy personality.' But maybe pathologists and coroners should be instructed to take into account the latest scientific findings on the role of personality in health."[1]

Definitions and Foundation

Personality is the whole of your personal characteristics, the group of behavioral and emotional tendencies that make up *you*. It is the way your habits, attitudes, and traits combine to make the person that is uniquely you. Because of your personality, you act in a similar way from one day to the next, and when you are placed in various situations, you still tend to act in a generally consistent way. Your personality, in essence, is the pattern of behavior that distinguishes you from everybody else.[2] Personality depends partly on genetics and biology—on the unique set of genes you inherited from your parents—but it is also shaped powerfully by the family you grow up in, the environment that surrounds you, and the culture and subcultures that influence you.[3]

The theory that personality affects health is, as world-renowned psychologist Hans J. Eysenck put it, a theory "based on centuries of observations made by keen-eyed physicians."[4] The notion that a certain personality type leads to heart disease dates back more than 2000 years, to Hippocrates, and the belief that a certain personality type is associated with cancer goes back several centuries. What is new is the flood of scientific data that now seem to be substantiating those notions.

Contemporary research on personality and health has been embroiled in controversy—for many reasons.[5] First, many, if not most, physicians are simply not trained to think that way. They want a simple or tangible reason for a disorder so they can "fix it." The notion of a disease-prone personality simply doesn't fit the traditional training most physicians receive. Second, many physicians still think of the mind and the body as two separate entities that do not affect each other. Third, many physicians (and patients) are skeptical about unusual approaches, including the notion that personality affects health. Frightened off by quacks and hucksters offering "miracle cures," they shy away from anything that deviates from traditional medicine. Finally, applying the notion that personality affects health is simply not as financially rewarding for a practitioner. We have set up a medical delivery system that pays far more for mechanical procedures than for knowledgeable patient teaching and "healing." A surgeon who removes a diseased gallbladder makes hundreds of dollars for an hour's work; not so for a doctor who spends an hour talking to a depressed patient troubled by headaches.

One of the first recorded suspicions of a link between personality and disease occurred in the 1940s, when Dr. Franz Alexander, a leading proponent of psychosomatic medicine, treated two women for breast cancer.[6] The two were similar in almost every way, but two years after their mastectomies, one was dying while the other was well. What could explain the differences? After plenty of searching, Alexander turned to personality. The woman who was dying told everyone she was getting well, but, underneath her brave facade, she couldn't confront either the disease or its possible outcome. The woman who was well, on the other hand, faced her problems head-on. She acknowledged that her situation was tough and then went about finding ways of making adjustments, workable solutions.

Subsequent research on personality and health was pioneered by Yugoslav psychologist Ronald Grossarth-Maticek, who began his studies in his native country and eventually moved to West Germany. Theories had been formulated prior to Grossarth-Maticek's work, when researchers had noted that people with certain illnesses (most commonly heart disease and cancer) had certain personality traits in common. But there was a flaw in those early theories: All of the studies involved people who were already ill. Who was to say that the illness itself had not engendered the personality traits, rather than the other way around?

What was needed was a study involving healthy people. Someone needed to study and characterize their personality traits and then watch them for a number of years to see which ones got ill. They needed to then determine whether there was any correlation between personality traits and the tendency to develop certain diseases.

Grossarth-Maticek took on the challenge. He started by identifying large random samples of subjects.[7] He recorded each person's current physical health, smoking and drinking habits, and other health behaviors. Then he devised several ways to measure personality, one with a series of short questionnaires, another with lengthy interviews. At the end, Grossarth-Maticek categorized people according to four categories: One was prone to develop cancer; one was prone to develop heart disease; and two who were prone to remain healthy.

He followed each group closely for at least ten years and monitored the people in some groups for thirteen years. The results were remarkable. He was able to predict death from cancer with six times greater accuracy than it was possible to predict based on cigarette smoking.

Among the groups he said were prone to develop cancer (those with a helpless, victimized personality style), almost half *did* die from cancer, but fewer than one in ten died from heart disease. Among those he predicted to be prone to heart disease (those with a hostile, aggressive personality style), more than a third *did* die of heart disease, but only one in five died from cancer. Among the two groups he predicted to be prone to good health, there were, indeed, relatively few deaths.[8] To his credit, points out Eysenck, Grossarth-Maticek's ideas "in the early 1960s agree almost perfectly with the most recent results of American and British research in this field."[9]

Grossarth-Maticek then set out to determine whether the outcome of disease could be affected by *changing* some personality traits. In one study, he identified people with disease-prone personalities. Then he split that group randomly in half: One half received counselling that included modelling, suggestion, relaxation, visualization, desensitization, and other standard behavioral techniques used to modify personality. The other half received no counselling at all. The group that received counselling had lower death rates from cancer and heart disease. He later repeated the studies with Eysenck.[10] Together, they found they could reduce by half the death rates from cancer and heart disease with as few as six hours of group therapy.

The pair then provided one group of twenty-four cancer patients with counselling designed to increase a sense of personal control and empowerment. They then compared survival rates among the group that got counselling to survival rates among a matched group of twenty-four other cancer patients. The median survival rate for the group that had counselling was five years, as compared to only three years for the group that didn't receive counselling.

In still another study, the pair followed a hundred women diagnosed with "terminal" breast cancer: Fifty women who had chosen to have chemotherapy were matched with fifty women who chose not to have chemotherapy. At random, some in the study received counselling; the others did not. Study results pointed out what many practitioners have felt about combining mind–body techniques with traditional medical care: those who received no therapy at all (counselling or chemotherapy) survived an average of eleven months. Those who received chemotherapy but no counselling survived an average of fourteen months. Those who received counselling but no chemotherapy fared slightly better: average survival was fifteen months. The clear winners were the ones who had both chemotherapy and counselling: their median survival time was twenty-two months.[11]

Grossarth-Maticek's work is the subject of considerable controversy. One report on his work maintains that his claims have "raised eyebrows, skeptical inquiries, and even some charges of scientific fraud."[12] Others charge that the work of Grossarth-Maticek was riddled with technical and statistical problems that can cast doubt on his "too good to be true" data. In defense of the work, however, one editor opined,

> *Many great scientific discoveries, of course, have had uncertain and spotty histories. Physicist Niels Bohr won a Nobel Prize for his model of the atom, which turned out to be inaccurate but inspired the research that got it right. Gregor Mendel made serious mistakes in his genetics experiments, but his research led to our modern understanding of human genetics and biology. And despite the criticism, no one, since Grossarth-Maticek began publishing his findings in 1980, has been able to knock down his numbers.[13]*

Even though critical reviews since that time *have* challenged Grossarth-Maticek's numbers,[14] University of South Florida psychologist Charles Spielberger, who traveled to West Germany to discuss the findings personally with Grossarth-Maticek, says that therapies aimed at changing personality traits may have some validity after all. "Even if the benefits of these therapies were reduced by one-half, or two-thirds, one could not reasonably allow the information to be suppressed," Spielberger says. "In the five or ten years needed to replicate these findings, thousands of men and women will die from cancer and heart attacks." As Spielberger points out, preventive psychotherapy isn't going to hurt anyone, and if it helps some, "more power to it."[15]

Regardless of the controversies surrounding Grossarth-Maticek's findings, say the experts, they endow us with hope and encourage further research to pinpoint what influence personality may have on health. There have not yet been any studies as broad and detailed (either in terms of numbers or years) as Grossarth-Maticek's, but there have been smaller studies that addressed the link between personality and health. Their results have been promising and, to a surprising extent, have substantiated Grossarth-Maticek's findings.

In a nutshell, we don't know everything about the link between personality and health, but we do know a great deal about how personality influences health and which personality traits seem particularly connected to certain diseases. A warning is in order, however. With all of our research into the impact of personality on disease, we must carefully avoid blaming any person for his illness. Any person can get almost any illness. Personality styles or mental stress do not *cause* disease so much as they act as a risk factor that, when combined with other risk factors, increases vulnerability.

> *If you breathe high levels of cigarette smoke or certain other pollutants, there is a good chance that you will develop lung cancer. If you are a woman whose mother and aunts and sisters developed breast cancer, there is a good chance that you will develop breast cancer. In all of these cases, there is little about the victim's emotional responses that can prevent the cancer. Disease is influenced not only by psychological factors but also by the genes we are born with and the environment in which we live. In fact, most instances of disease are caused*

by a convergence of factors. As the case of the comic Gilda Radner recently demonstrated, it is a sad fact of life that some people contract cancer and die of it at a young age, regardless of personality or heroic struggle.[16]

There are two important issues to be addressed, and, at first glance, they may seem at odds. Even when people accept blame for an illness, it may be a mistake to assume that they brought it on themselves. Such a viewpoint may lead to inhumanity and a lack of compassion for people who most need it. On the other hand, we must study the links that we know exist between personality and disease—because we know that there is a great deal we can do to protect and preserve our own health. It won't work all of the time for all of the people in all circumstances, but a fair share—a majority, in fact—can help themselves stay healthy, and a fair share of those who become ill can help themselves recover.

Disease and Personality: Exploring the Connection

Most people, whether they know it or not, associate certain personality types with particular illnesses. Workaholics have heart attacks. Worriers get ulcers. People who get too uptight have asthma attacks. In reality, can they be so neatly categorized?

Not yet, but researchers have made tremendous strides in proving that personality does have an impact on health, and they have found that the way we look at things, as determined by our personality, may actually contribute to illness (or help keep us well).

A variety of studies dating back more than four decades have exposed the "tip of the iceberg" as far as personality and health connections are concerned. In 1948, a group of medical students at Johns Hopkins University wrote descriptions of what they saw when presented with ten Rorschach inkblots. Psychologist Pirkko L. Graves says she prefers Rorschach inkblot tests to the more popular questionnaires because, "people bring stuff from their guts to the Rorschach test because of its projective nature."[17]

What the medical students saw when gazing at the images of the inkblots tells a great deal about their outlook, which is reflected in their personalities. The varying responses of the students as they looked at the same inkblot demonstrates the great differences in personality: Some saw the inkblot as a young couple kissing, two people shaking hands, or two dancers; others saw in the same pattern two dogs snarling at each other or two cannibals boiling Macbeth in a kettle.[18]

More than three decades later, Graves and her colleagues rated the responses of the students who took that early Rorschach test, and combined them with the responses of other groups of students who had also been tested (some as recently as 1964). Graves rated the students according to an eleven-point scale, and categorized them according to their general personality style and their personal interaction style.

No one was surprised to learn that the distant, withdrawn students who had a generally "negative" approach to interactions were much more likely to have developed a severe mental disorder in the three decades following the first study. What *was* a surprise was a separate finding: The students with the distant, withdrawn personalities were also much more likely to have developed cancer—especially cancers of the stomach, pancreas, rectum, large intestine, and lymph nodes, as well as Hodgkin's disease, leukemia, and multiple myeloma.[19]

The Generic View

Other studies have also shown a link between personality and health. In one, University of California psychologists Howard S. Friedman and Stephanie Booth-Kewley analyzed 101 studies that had been conducted over four decades (from 1945 to 1984). They concluded that there are "strong links" between personality and health.[20] After analyzing the host of studies, however, Friedman and Booth-Kewley weren't ready to attach a single personality trait to a single disease. They did conclude that there was a strong connection between certain personality traits and "all diseases except ulcers," the most damaging personality traits being depression, anxiety, anger, and hostility.[21]

Based on their analysis of the studies, the two say, they are not sure there is a specific "personality" for an individual disease, but they are convinced there may well be "a generic 'disease-prone personality.' Personality may function as diet does: Imbalances can predispose one to all sorts of diseases."[22]

One viewpoint, then, holds that certain personality traits (or, in essence, a certain personality type) causes disease. Researchers who support this point of view believe that there may be a generic "disease-prone personality," but not individual "disease personalities" (such as cancer personality or ulcer personality, for example).

The Disease Personalities View

Other researchers disagree, saying that certain "personalities" or personality traits can be specifically linked to certain diseases. Most prominent in research has been the "coronary-prone personality," the hard-driving and competitive Type A personality who is also hostile, angry, and suspicious. Also prominent in current research is the "cancer-prone personality," characterized by people who demonstrate little emotion, are ambivalent toward self and others, and were not close to their parents (this personality is discussed in greater depth later in this chapter).

Researchers have even been able to ascribe certain personality traits to very specific illnesses. Dr. Arnold Levy, vice-president of the American Digestive Disease Society, says that young women who are characteristically self-demanding and high achievers are the most likely candidates for irritable bowel syndrome.[23] Psychologist Ross R. Vickers, Jr., of the Naval Health Research Center in San Diego, says that people who are neurotic, especially if neurosis is coupled with depression, are particularly prone to upper respiratory tract infection.[24]

The Disease Cluster View

A third group of researchers believe that a specific personality may make a person susceptible to a "cluster" of conditions, not just a specific disease. Some of the longest-standing research in this area has been conducted by Caroline Bedell Thomas and her coworkers at the Johns Hopkins School of Medicine. Based on her extensive research beginning in 1947, she believes that people can be categorized into three broad personality types: alphas, betas, and gammas. Those broadly defined personality types, then, can determine whether a person is more prone to become ill or stay healthy.[25]

   1. *Alphas.* Alphas are slow and solid, wary in new situations, gradually adaptable, and undemanding. Only about one-fourth of the alphas Thomas has studied became seriously ill in the thirty years studied.
   2. *Betas.* Betas are cool and clever, quick to respond to new situations, articulate, and understanding. Only about one-fourth of the betas became seriously ill within thirty years. This group was most prone to be healthiest.
   3. *Gammas.* The group with the greatest health problems are the gammas: either too careful or devil-may-care; often brilliant, but also moody and confused in new situations; and either too demanding or not demanding enough. In one of Thomas's studies involving forty-five people, 77 percent of the gammas developed cancer, mental illness, high blood pressure, or heart disease or committed suicide. In another study, half of all the sick students were in the gamma group.

The Personality Cluster View

Rather than grouping people by personality traits or types, other researchers have identified what they call *clusters* or *cluster groups,* groups who have similar specific personality types. Researchers then identify diseases that seem most closely related to that cluster type.

   Georgia State University researchers Douglas J. Stanwyck and Carol A. Anson studied 194 different groups of people who had been given the Minnesota Multiphasic Personality Inventory, a well-respected and widely used measure of personality. Those groups of people were discussed in sixty-eight published reports, which Stanwyck and Anson analyzed in an attempt to see what relationship personality might have to health. They identified five clusters of illnesses and determined which patterns of personality were strongly associated with each cluster.[26] In a nutshell, their results looked like this:

   Cluster 1: A personality pattern characterized by depression, indecision, hopelessness, chronic fatigue, physical weakness, and severely low self-esteem. This personality pattern is one of the most frequent types among psychiatric patients and is only rarely found among people considered to be "normal." People in Cluster 1 are at high risk of suffering from alcoholism or eating disorders (anorexia and bulimia).

Cluster 2: The "sick" cluster, made up of people who are mildly neurotic. They tend to convert psychological distress into physical symptoms, though not in as pronounced a way as members of another cluster. Cluster 2 contains a real mix: Its members are prone to heart disease, asthma, general medical disorders, arthritis, cancer, and intestinal disorders. Eleven of the fifteen heart disorder groups, including angina, coronary heart disease, and coronary artery disease, fall into Cluster 2. That's not surprising, says one researcher, because "the heart has symbolic meaning and may be used to communicate psychological conflicts and distress."[27]

Cluster 3: Persons whose personality patterns tend to be angry and moody, unpredictable, nonconforming, emotionally shallow, and plagued with problems

---

Focus on Research

In trying to determine exactly how personality influences health, regardless of which theory they held fast to, researchers turned to the thing that determines whether anyone is healthy: the immune system. To test what impact personality has on the immune system, a team of psychologists and psychiatrists led by J. Stephen Keisel of Charles River Hospital in Massachusetts studied 111 physically healthy Harvard University students.

In the first phase of the study, Keisel and his colleagues gave each student the Minnesota Multiphasic Personality Inventory; the 566-item questionnaire has become a standard tool for measuring personality. In general, it spots trouble such as hypochondria, depression, paranoia, social isolation, and maladjustment, as well as positives such as tolerance, self-esteem, and confidence. Each student was scored according to standard scoring methods and was given a numbered rating based on the test score.

In the second phase of the study, the researchers took blood samples from each student and studied the natural killer cells, cells that seek out and spontaneously kill cancer cells "like bloodhounds on a scent. They may also play an important role in fighting illnesses such as multiple sclerosis and AIDS.

Some scientists believe the killer cells may be the most important defense early in the development of a disease." *

Once the blood was drawn, Keisel and his colleagues took natural killer cells from the blood of each student and exposed them to cancer cells. Researchers then measured how many tumor cells were killed within a four-hour period.

The results were fascinating. The cells from all 111 Harvard students who took part killed some cancer cells. But some of the students' cells in the study killed forty times more cancer cells than other students' cells.

When the number of tumor cells killed was compared with the personality test scores for each student, a "startlingly consistent pattern" emerged. The healthier the student's personality, the more cancer cells were killed by the natural killer cells. The unhealthier the student's personality, the weaker the immune system. Students with the weakest immune response were those who, according to the personality test, were unhappy, socially withdrawn, fatigued, pessimistic, felt guilty, and had low self-esteem. Students with the strongest immune systems were those who had the ability to adapt to various situations.†

---

* Peter Jaret, "The Immune Personality," *Hippocrates,* July/August: 1987, 88.
†B. Bower, "Personality Linked to Immunity, " *Science News,* 130: 1986, 310.

in social communication fall into Cluster 3. Their illnesses are most likely to be drug addiction, rheumatic fever, and complications of parturition.

Cluster 4: These people have serious neuroses (whereas Cluster 2 people are mildly neurotic). They convert psychological stress into physical complaints and then deny any psychological involvement. They tend to be bitter and pessimistic about vague and general physical complaints. Illnesses most associated with Cluster 4 include nonorganic back pain, nonspecific pain, peptic ulcers, colitis, enteritis, and multiple sclerosis.

Cluster 5: People who, according to the Minnesota Multiphasic Personality Inventory, are closest to "normal." Not surprisingly, say the researchers, they are the people most likely to stay well.[23]

The Controversy

The link between personality and health has become the subject of a number of aggressive studies, and researchers are beginning to attempt to duplicate long-term studies (such as the ones done by Grossarth-Maticek and others). Most now accept the notion of an "immune-prone personality," one whose hardiness enables them to tolerate the ravages of stress without becoming ill. There is not such widespread acceptance of the notion that certain personality traits are linked to illness.

The controversy was fueled a few years ago in response to the report of a study by Barrie R. Cassileth and her colleagues at the University of Pennsylvania. After studying more than 350 people with advanced cancer, her research team declared that neither positive attitudes nor feelings of depression or hopelessness had any effect on the cancer victims' survival rates. Cassileth's study was printed in *The New England Journal of Medicine*, which prompted pathologist and senior deputy editor of the journal Marcia Angell to editorialize, "Our belief in disease as a direct reflection of mental state is largely folklore."[28]

In her editorial, Angell criticized the medical community and the media for giving too much credit to personality and emotions as factors in physical health. "We are told," she wrote, that "type A people are vulnerable to heart attacks, repressed people (especially those who have suffered losses) are at risk of cancer, worry causes peptic ulcers, and so on."[29] Further, Angell said that studies relating personality to health were flawed in their design, analysis, or interpretation and that it was dangerous for patients to believe their emotional attitude can save them from serious illness because it could cause patients to forego necessary medical control in favor of some "method of mind control." Finally, Angell argued, saying that a patient can "control" an illness is fine if all goes well, but it can be detrimental if the illness progresses. "In our desire to pay tribute to gallantry and grace in the face of hardship," she wrote, "we sometimes credit these qualities with cures, not realizing that we may also be implying blame when there are reverses."[30]

Angell's editorial was incendiary. The journal was flooded with letters from physicians and former cancer patients disputing the editorial's claims. The 60,000-member American Psychological Association issued a statement attacking

Angell's piece as "inaccurate and unfortunate." In the years that have followed, the debate has raged.

Shortly after the editorial appeared in the journal *MD* conducted a poll of its physician readers, asking, "Does emotional state affect disease?"[31] The doctors could not have been more unequivocal in their answers: Of the 126 who responded, 124 said yes; only two said no. Some of the physicians who responded did not believe that emotions or personality "cause" illness, but almost all conceded that personality has a profound effect on the outcome of an illness.

"I'm not convinced of the cause-effect of the onset of a disease," wrote Illinois internist Roger Hill, "but, from twelve years of practice, I've found that the mental status of a patient definitely does affect the rate of recovery from disease." A New Hampshire internist agreed, pointing out that the emotional state regulates the release of hormones "that influence the course of disease."

Florida cardiologist Maurice Laszlo wrote that he has seen the influence of personality and emotions on his patients every day for the past twenty-seven years. "Marcia Angell is trying to disprove something that doctors have known for 5000 years," he scoffed. "Consider the hypertensive patient. If a doctor looks stern and wears a white 'authoritative' coat while taking a patient's blood pressure, it will certainly rise. When the patient goes home, his blood pressure will return to normal." In summing up his remarks, Laszlo pointed out that the influence of emotions and personality on health is controversial because it's very difficult to prove to members of a profession that is used to scientific documentation. "You can't weigh or measure emotions," he wrote, "yet 75 percent of my patients . . . have nothing organically wrong with them."

Another reason the personality–health theory may be difficult for physicians to accept is that it challenges traditional methods of treatment. "Medical school never taught us to treat emotions," points out New York gastroenterologist Joseph Duva. "I remember being instructed on how to measure the muscle contractions of the colon, but I never learned what psychologic factors bring on these contractions."

Explaining the Differences in People

Regardless of where you stand on the controversy over personality and health, there's one clear fact: We all respond differently to the stresses and problems that confront us in life. Whether it's a bad day or a chronic emotional crisis, some of us sail through valiantly and others of us get sick. Even among those who get sick, there are differences; some suffer from insomnia, others from crippling headaches, still others from indigestion.

We know that stress can cause physical illness. What we have not known until recently is why it has such a different effect on different people. Researchers think they have the answer, and while part of it is physiological, part of it also falls back onto personality.

It begins with hormones: The brain directs the various glands in the body to secrete them, and the hormones circulate through the bloodstream, giving "orders" to various tissues and organs. They may direct the blood vessels to constrict, for example, or instruct the body to metabolize sugar. Once the specific task has been completed, a feedback system signals the brain, and the hormone subsides. Everyone has the same network, the same sets of hormonal switches and cycles. They control how we respond in all kinds of situations, including stressful ones.

If everyone has the same physiological makeup, why do we react so differently? Researchers believe that personality may play a key role—as do diet, accidents, early childhood experiences, and our genetic makeup. These factors create what researchers call *weak links,* and those weak links determine where stress is apt to strike a given person.[32] Psychoanalyst Herbert J. Freudenberger points out that these weak links, part of our personality, are for the most part "learned and reinforced behaviors."[33] It explains why one person under stress gets a backache while another gets an ulcer. In essence, it's another explanation of how personality can affect health.

Regardless of differences, there are certain things we do that render us vulnerable to illness, and many of them reflect certain personality traits. In his landmark work *Peace, Love, and Healing,* Yale oncologist and surgeon Bernie Siegel offers a tongue-in-cheek analysis of how to get sick:

- Don't pay attention to your body. Eat plenty of junk food, drink too much, take drugs, have lots of unsafe sex with lots of different partners—and, above all, feel guilty about it. If you are overstressed and tired, ignore it and keep pushing yourself.
- Cultivate the experience of your life as meaningless and of little value.
- Do the things you don't like and avoid doing what you really want.
- Be resentful and hypercritical, especially toward yourself.
- Fill your mind with dreadful pictures, and then obsess over them. Worry most, if not all, of the time.
- Avoid deep, lasting, intimate relationships.
- Blame other people for all your problems.
- Do not express your feelings and views openly and honestly. Other people wouldn't appreciate it. If at all possible, do not even know what your feelings are.
- Shun anything that resembles a sense of humor. Life is not a laughing matter!
- Avoid making any changes that would bring you greater satisfaction and joy.[34]

Keeping in mind that there is controversy among researchers and the medical profession about the personality–health link, it's also important to realize that a host of new research is slowly unraveling the mystery behind the effects of personality. The bulk of the research centers on the existence of a generic disease-prone personality, one that creates a tendency toward illness. Other research is focusing on the possible existence of a cancer-prone personality, which some researchers have called *Type C.* Others have looked at personality traits that predispose to either arthritis or ulcers.

The Cancer-Prone Personality

One of the most controversial notions being explored by medical researchers today is that of a cancer prone personality, a set of traits that predisposes a person to cancer. The exact effect of personality on cancer is difficult to assess: People can be exposed unwittingly to carcinogens that may play a role, and there can also be a vast difference in a number of factors between the time of prognosis and the time of diagnosis. Nonetheless, an increasing number of physicians believe that the trends definitely point to a link between personality and cancer and that these notions give a new and pressing direction to medical research.[35]

The notion of a cancer-prone personality isn't new. The second-century physician Galen noted that "melancholic" women had a greater tendency toward breast cancer than their more "sanguine" counterparts. Medical writers in the eighteenth century described in detail the personality traits and experiences shared by cancer patients. And eminent British physician Sir James Paget noted in 1870, "The cases are so frequent in which deep anxiety, deferred hope, and disappointment are quickly followed by the growth or increase of cancer that we can hardly doubt that mental depression is a weighty addition to the other influences that favor the development of the cancerous constitution."[36]

Blumberg's Research

Closer to our own time, researchers became keenly interested in the possibility of a cancer-prone personality during the 1950s, when psychologist Eugene Blumberg began noticing a "trademark" personality among cancer patients in a Long Beach veterans' hospital. He wrote: "We were impressed by the polite, apologetic, almost painful acquiescence of the patients with rapidly progressing disease as contrasted with the more expressive and sometimes bizarre personalities of those who responded brilliantly to therapy with remissions and long survival."[37]

To figure out whether there was any connection, Blumberg administered psychological tests to the cancer patients. The tests measured whether they could release pent-up emotions, how anxious they were, and whether they were depressed. Then he matched test results with patients at intervals and checked to see how rapidly their disease was progressing.

He found that the patients with the fastest-growing tumors were the ones who were "consistently serious, overcooperative, overly nice, overly anxious, painfully sensitive, passive, and apologetic."[38] And they had been that way all their lives. The patients with the slow-growing tumors, on the other hand, were the ones who had developed a way of coping with life's stresses.

Temoshok's Studies

At about the same time, physicians at San Francisco's Malignant Melanoma Clinic were becoming interested in the same questions. They had noticed a "disturbing pattern" in the personalities of patients with melanoma (a particularly virulent form of skin cancer). The patients were "nice," *too nice.* In fact, they were passive about everything, including their cancer. Could it be a coincidence? The doctors didn't think it was, so they asked University of California School of Medicine psychologist Lydia Temoshok to talk to the patients and determine whether a personality pattern did indeed emerge.

The doctors were right. After talking in detail to 150 of the clinic's melanoma patients, Temoshok declared that there was a distinct pattern. The cancer patients were, indeed, very, very nice. They never seemed to express any negative emotion—not fear, or sadness, or anger, or denial, or any of the other emotions common to a patient struggling with a terminal disease. The patients couldn't express negative emotion, assert themselves, acknowledge or attend to physical pain, or admit their own needs. In fact, say the researchers, these patients "were the rock of stability for their families. Even in the face of cancer, they maintained this composure. When one of them was diagnosed, they might say, 'I'm doing fine. But I'm really worried about my husband. He takes things so hard,'" explained Temoshok.[39] These cancer patients, in the face of a painful, devastating, and almost certainly terminal disease, seemed always happy, always in control.

The idea of a shared personality pattern among cancer victims fascinated Temoshok, so she probed more deeply. The result of her research was what she called the Type C personality, essentially the complete opposite of the hard-driving Type A (who was usually considered to be at high risk for coronary disease). Type Cs, said Temoshok, are overwhelmed by emotions they have not been able to express or resolve. The Type C, she reasoned, was at high risk for cancer. Here's what she found when she studied the 150 melanoma patients in light of her definition of a Type C personality:

- The melanoma patients who demonstrated more Type C behavior had thicker, more aggressive tumors, both signs of a bleaker prognosis.
- Temoshok was able to predict survival based on the way the patients initially reacted when they heard their diagnosis: Those most likely to die were women who reacted with stoicism and men who reacted with helplessness and hopelessness.
- When Temoshok did an experiment designed to provoke emotion, she found that the melanoma patients were significantly more likely than either healthy people or people with heart disease to repress their emotions (a Type C strategy).
- The melanoma patients who were more able to openly express their emotions (such as sadness or anger) also had more lymphocytes (key cells in fighting cancer) around their tumors. The patients who repressed their emotions had fewer lymphocytes at tumor sites.
- Among the patients she followed, Temoshok found significant associations between every single negative emotional state and recurrence of the disease or death several years later. What happened? Temoshok believes that the data show "powerful evidence" that people who died of cancer had suffered a collapse of their usual Type C coping style and were then overwhelmed by emotions they couldn't express or resolve.[40]

To test the validity of her theory, Temoshok videotaped detailed interviews with each of the 150 melanoma patients she had originally talked to in the clinic. She then invited a group of her colleagues to look at the videotapes and to help her categorize the patients by what they judged to be each one's personality type: Type A, Type B (relaxed and easygoing), or Type C (passive, overly compliant, and unable to express negative emotions—what Temoshok called "a fragile accommodation to the world"). Temoshok followed the patients' progress for the next year and a half. Most of the Type Cs were concentrated in what doctors called the relapser's group, the patients whose conditions worsened or who died.

Temoshok then analyzed similar cancer–personality studies that had been conducted during the previous thirty years and continued with her own research. Her conclusion was this: Behavior and personality may not cause cancer, but certain personality traits affect how an individual copes with stress, and those personality traits may very well affect at least the outcome of the disease. She even went so far as to say that people with a Type C personality are likely to have "a worse outcome than might be expected on medical grounds."[41] In discussing the Type C personality, Temoshok points out that it is not actually a personality, but a "behavior pattern." At its origins, she says, is a defense mechanism, useful in moderation, that later gets out of control.

The findings of the melanoma study and of various follow-up studies have convinced Temoshok of two things. First, she says, changing Type C behavior can both improve the health of persons who are already sick and actually help prevent cancer among healthy ones. Some of the most important skills, she says, are developing an awareness of needs, reframing ideas about feelings (*feelings* aren't bad, but *blocking feelings* is), learning how to express emotion, taking charge, getting social support, working through hopelessness, and cultivating a fighting spirit.[42] Second, Temoshok "learned that *people did not bring cancer on themselves.* No one can be blamed for mind–body factors in cancer, because no one *intentionally* develops the cancer-prone behavior pattern. . . . When brought about with compassion and self-care, awareness of Type C behavior offers the person opportunities for growth and empowerment, not self-blame."[43]

LeShan's Analysis

Since Temoshok's pioneering work in looking for personality links to cancer, interest has soared among researchers who have hoped to determine whether certain personality traits may either bring on cancer or contribute to its progression. One of the researchers most prominent in the study of a cancer personality is psychologist Lawrence LeShan, who began his research at about the same time Blumberg was puzzling over his "nice" cancer patients in the veterans' hospital.

LeShan interviewed 250 patients who had been hospitalized for cancer, and compared their response to those of patients who had been hospitalized for other diseases. Even before he began analyzing personality factors, LeShan was fascinated by a striking similarity in the life history of the cancer patients. He found three specific "life events" that seemed to be common to the cancer patients:

1. Cancer patients described a "bleak" childhood; they had a tense, hostile relationship with one or both parents, and they felt lonely and isolated. They began to feel that a satisfying, "safe" relationship with another person was not possible.

2. As young adults they finally found something to which they were able to make a strong emotional commitment; it may have been another person, a cause, a job, or something else. The emotional investment was strong, and that object of emotional investment became the centerpiece of their lives.

3. Something happened to take away the object of emotional investment: The spouse died, they were fired from their job, a beloved child took up with unsavory companions and forsook the family. There was nothing to replace the great void, and six to eight months later these people were diagnosed with cancer.[44]

Other Research

Another psychologist who noticed a striking similarity in the histories of cancer patients was Claus Bahnson, then at Jefferson Medical College in Philadelphia. In interviewing cancer patients, he, too, found that they had very similar backgrounds, and most pronounced was a cold, strict, aloof relationship with their parents. Scottish researcher David Kissen, who has spent the bulk of his career studying the personality traits of lung cancer victims, has also noted the common thread among this particular group—the loss of someone close during childhood and the apparent lack of emotional involvement over the loss.

Expression of Emotion

The hallmark of the cancer personality, according to Temoshok, is the "nonexpression of emotion."[45] Other researchers agreed wholeheartedly. Kissen says that whatever emotions they feel they keep bottled up inside. Many have unresolved tension, usually concerning a parent or other family member, but they refuse to express or resolve it.[46] Even when they are experiencing tremendous despair, it is characteristically "bottled up"; while cancer patients are often described by other people as kind, sweet, and benign, this sweetness is "really a mask they wear to conceal their feelings of anger, hurt, and hostility."[47]

"I remember smiling my way through a divorce," remembers Connecticut school teacher Marie Mosbach, who was diagnosed with breast cancer and underwent a mastectomy. Two years later, the cancer spread to her bone, and her prognosis was poor. Once she became more assertive and expressive—and, coincidentally, survived her cancer—she mused, "I feel the cancer is related to the repression of my feelings and to chronic stress."[48]

While stress may play a role, researchers believe that stress alone is probably not the cause of cancer. As one put it, "The stress of life changes alone does not induce the development of cancer. There must also be an underlying personality structure that handles such life changes in an unhealthy way. Feelings of loneliness and hopelessness, of being helpless or trapped, often characterize people who develop this dread disease."[49]

Most other researchers agree. After analyzing groups of cancer personality studies, one commented that cancer patients are more commonly lonely, angry, rigid, self-sacrificing, repressed, depressed, and hopeless.[50] Others say that cancer patients characteristically react to stress, loss, or change with a feeling of helplessness, hopelessness, or an overwhelming inability to cope. Still others say that repressed anger and negative emotions in general contribute to the progression of cancer.

Depression

Until recently, researchers believed that the personality trait of depression had a strong link to the development of cancer. But new research shows that depression apparently is not a factor in development of cancer.

According to research conducted by National Institute on Aging psychologist Alan Zonderman and published in the *Journal of the American Medical Association*, depressed people have no greater risk of developing cancer than the general population.[51] Zonderman and his colleagues studied a group of more than 6000 people, 1000 of whom showed signs of depression (such as crying spells, insomnia, loss of appetite, poor concentration). They followed the medical histories of all 6000 people for the next ten years. At the end of ten years, 11 percent of the depressed people had developed cancer, but so had 10 percent of the nondepressed ones. The number in each group who had died from cancer during the ten-year period was exactly the same: 4 percent.[52]

According to the investigators, earlier studies that showed a link between depression and cancer were probably flawed for a variety of reasons (too small a sample group, failure to control for other factors, and so on). In concluding his study, Zonderman stated that "we found that depressive systems didn't predict who was going to get cancer or who was going to die from cancer ten years later."[53]

Other Factors

While depression does not contribute to cancer, people who develop cancer do tend to be what researchers call loners, people who feel lonely and who face the world with bland, unemotional exteriors. To test that notion, psychologists Pirkko Graves and John Shaffer, along with their colleagues at the Johns Hopkins University School of Medicine, analyzed psychological data collected between 1948 and 1964 on nearly 1000 male medical students at the school. They used personality traits to divide the men into five groups. Then they scrutinized the students' medical records, which had been collected each year through 1987.

Graves and Shaffer found that the people most likely to develop cancer were the loners, the people who were lonely and unemotional. They developed cancer, in fact, sixteen times more often than members of the healthiest group. The ones least likely to develop cancer were members of what Graves and Shaffer called the acting out–emotional group, people who were anxious, easily upset, and depression prone but who expressed their feelings freely. Fewer than 1 percent of the people in the acting out–emotional group developed cancer during the 40 years of follow-up.[54]

Helplessness and hopelessness have also been associated with cancer in a wide range of studies, and they appear to influence not only who *develops* cancer, but who is able to *survive* it. "It is well-known, if quietly admitted, that the best medicine may be to no avail when given to someone who has already given up the struggle for life," stated one researcher. "Even if there is no strong relationship between the origins of cancer and some personality type, the evidence does suggest that the way in which a person responds to the threat may have a lot to do with surviving the physical insult of cancer."[55]

Other researchers agree. British psychiatrist H. Steven Greer and his colleague Dr. Tina Morris have been following the health of breast cancer patients at Kings College Hospital in London. They have discovered an interesting phenomenon, according to Greer: The breast cancer patients seem to be constantly holding their emotions in check (much like the "nice" cancer patients described by Temoshok), and the helpless or hopeless patients are the ones who fare the worst.[56]

In fifteen years of following breast cancer patients, Greer maintains, the ones who survive the longest with no recurrence of disease are also the ones who reacted to their cancer diagnosis in one of two ways: Either they denied that there was anything seriously wrong with them, or they rallied with a "fighting spirit," or a determination to do everything possible to beat the cancer. Fighting spirit also involved a positive expectation, a feeling that they could control their lives, regardless of the cancer. At seven years after appropriate treatment, the survival of the deniers and the fighters was about the same (about 80 percent), but then the protection provided by denial faded. At twelve years, 80 percent of those with "fighting spirit" were still alive, as compared with only 50 percent of those who used denial to cope. Those who succumbed most easily were the ones who kept a stiff upper lip (the stoics, as Greer called them) and the ones who collapsed in a hopeless, helpless, all-is-lost response; only 20 percent of the helpless–hopeless survived at five years (see Figure 5.1 on page 114).[57] Other studies have confirmed that a strong will to live prolongs survival of breast cancer patients, as does better coping ability in dealing with problems.[58]

With all the research findings that are emerging, most agree that there does seem to be a particular cancer-prone personality—if not one that actually causes cancer, then at least one that contributes to its development, spread, and tendency to claim its victim. But there may still be cautions regarding cancer personality research and theory. In the first place, says one researcher, there is a danger in delving into the personalities of people already diagnosed with cancer: To become a person with cancer is to cease to be a "normal" person, and a cancer victim may look back and interpret everything that happened in life in light of the cancer.[59] Second, asking a cancer patient to recount details from the past makes a researcher reliant on the person's memory. There's also the natural tendency for recent events

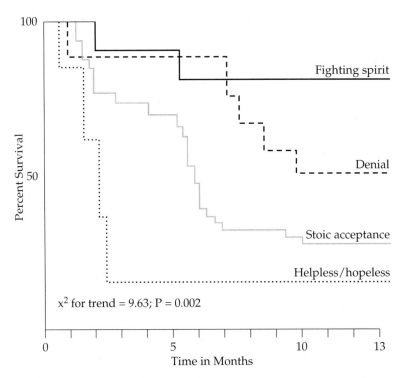

FIGURE 5.1   **The Effects of Attitudes on Survival of Patients with Breast Cancer**

to eclipse earlier ones. All in all, it's difficult for anyone to look back at a time in life and weigh the particular stresses or events that may have occurred then. (These weaknesses are precisely why researchers lean more heavily on studies that test an entire population before cancer is ever diagnosed.)

In a long-term follow-up study of physicians, certain psychological factors displayed when they were students and healthy were associated with a four times greater risk of developing cancer twenty-five years later. Those factors included feeling less close to parents as a child, having less satisfactory personal relationships, ambivalence, and avoidance of dealing directly with stress.[60] A research summary of attitudes and coping style factors found to affect cancer prognosis or incidence is found in Table 5.1.

It's important to note that in this, as in almost all other areas of medical research, there are inconsistencies in research findings.[61] Not every study finds a link between cancer and personality, and a few have found no relationship at all between the two. Others find that personality may play a role in either (but not both) the development of cancer or its progression once it is established. Even with these inconsistencies in mind, however, leading researchers believe there is enough evidence for a link between cancer and personality that researchers need to look at the possibility with confidence.

TABLE 5.1 Attitudes Related to Cancer Prognosis

Good Prognosis	Poor Prognosis
A sense of personal control	Helplessness; lack of assertiveness
Faith, hope of survival	Hopelessness
Determination to live, sense of purpose	Apathy, lack of meaning
A sense of connectedness	Unsatisfactory personal relationships
Good coping skills	Ineffectiveness with practical problems
Ability to express feelings	Stoicism, inability to discuss concerns

Above all, we need to be cautious in how we apply any findings. Henry Dreher, speaking to the fourth national conference on the Psychology of Health, Immunity, and Disease, said, "People do not give themselves cancer. Patients who believe that, by dint of their personality, behavior, inadequacy, or some kind of death wish, they have brought cancer upon themselves should be disabused of this idea." Cancer, he pointed out to conference attendees, can result from "an immunologic breakdown caused, only in part, by psychological factors operating below the level of consciousness."[62]

Finally, warns Dr. Joan Borysenko, the very presence of cancer can create physiological changes that could affect personality, such as "attacking the central nervous system or by skewing the delicate internal balance of hormones. Certain tumors are known to secrete hormones, some of which alter behavior or moods."[63]

The Personality of Rheumatoid Arthritis

Of all the forms of arthritis, rheumatoid arthritis is among the most crippling and most devastating. It's an autoimmune disease, which means the immune system actually turns against the body and begins attacking the collagen in the connective tissue in joints. Also, whereas other kinds of arthritis are largely the result of wear and tear over the years, and so are limited to the elderly, rheumatoid arthritis can and does attack people of all ages, including children.

Could there be a set of personality traits that is characteristic of people with rheumatoid arthritis? Researchers think so. Even in the midst of controversy regarding a certain personality type for arthritis, the disease has long been considered to have a powerful psychological component. As early as 1909, in fact, one doctor said, "That mental shocks, continuous anxiety, and worry may determine the onset or provoke an exacerbation of rheumatoid arthritis is, I think, beyond question."[64] It was not until the early 1970s, however, that research findings began to demonstrate the relationship between the onset of rheumatoid arthritis and distress in a certain subgroup of, though not in all, patients.[65] Some researchers are so convinced of the arthritis–personality connection that they have described rheumatoid arthritis as the "expression of a personality conflict."[66]

Identical Twin Study

Study of the link between personality and rheumatoid arthritis began in earnest in the early 1960s, when a team of researchers from the University of Rochester studied eight pairs of identical twins—one of whom had rheumatoid arthritis while the other did not. The fact that researchers chose to study identical twins and the fact that only one twin in each set had the disease eliminated for researchers the possibility of a genetic factor.

Researchers interviewed each of the twins—all women—in great detail to determine not only personality traits but also life events that may have led to the diagnosis of rheumatoid arthritis. They found some strikingly similar patterns among the women afflicted with arthritis. In each pair of twins, the one with arthritis seemed to put herself under a great deal of stress; in fact, these women actually seemed to seek out stress. And the disease seemed to manifest itself only after each woman had decided to dedicate her energies to a particularly stressful or distasteful situation.[67] For example, one woman took a job she really didn't want, just to impress her in-laws. Another gave up personal pursuits to spend her life caring for her psychotic stepfather.

Striking similarities also emerged. The healthy twins felt free to express criticism and to argue but described their marriages as happy ones. The arthritic twins spoke ill of their husbands and apparently put up with considerable abuse in their marriages. The arthritic twins said they never argued with their husbands.[68] In summing up that peculiar dichotomy, one researcher remarked that people with rheumatoid arthritis "will endure stressful situations longer than their siblings. The arthritic patients' inability to express anger may make some situations more stressful to them than these same situations would be to other people."[69]

When the results of the interviews were in, the team of researchers were fascinated to learn how the women described themselves. The healthy women described themselves as people who liked people. They said they were easy to get acquainted with, were active, were constantly busy, were productive workers, and enjoyed life in general. The self-image of the arthritic twins was just the opposite. They described themselves as moody and easily upset. They claimed they were nervous, tense, worried, depressed, and high strung. While the healthy sisters enjoyed life, the arthritic ones said, simply, that they were struggling.

The results of the identical twin study seem to be consistent with what other researchers have found. One researcher who examined more than 5000 rheumatoid arthritis patients found "that in a high percentage of cases the patients suffered from worry, work pressures, marital disharmony, and concerns about relatives immediately prior to the onset of disease."[70]

Others characterize rheumatoid arthritis patients as people who, on the outside, appear to be calm, composed, and optimistic and who rarely, if ever, express anger. Some believe these patients don't even *feel* anger. On the rare occasions when these patients express anger or rage, they feel overcome with remorse and guilt and feel a strong need to punish themselves. Research has established that people with rheumatoid arthritis are more likely to suffer from emotional disturbance and that they tend to suffer from perfectionism, chronic anxiety, depression, hostility, and introversion.[71]

Solomon and Moos's Study

At about the same time the University of Rochester team of researchers was studying the identical twins, Stanford University School of Medicine psychiatrist George Solomon and his colleague Rudolf Moos had become fascinated with the medical "myth" that there might be personality traits associated with rheumatoid arthritis. They decided to try out a theory on a group of people who were suspected to have arthritis that had not yet been diagnosed.

Solomon and Moos went to the emergency room of San Francisco General Hospital, and asked to be able to examine each patient who came into the emergency room complaining of a tender, inflamed, or "hot" joint. Emergency room personnel administered laboratory tests to each patient; a simple blood test indicates the presence of rheumatoid factor (an antibody in the blood of rheumatoid arthritis sufferers). While patients were waiting for the results of the test, Solomon and Moos asked them to participate in a psychodrama.

Solomon and Moos knew that rheumatoid arthritis patients were characteristically unassertive and inhibited. So they constructed a psychodrama that would put that trait to its most severe test: They asked the emergency room patients to return an item (an iron for women, a shaver for men) to someone playing a hostile department store clerk. It was a role that required great assertiveness, and the researchers watched carefully as each suspected—but yet undiagnosed—patient play-acted.

Based on how each patient interacted with the "hostile clerk," Solomon made his own diagnosis, predicting which patients would eventually be proven to have rheumatoid arthritis and which would not. He guessed right 100 percent of the time. He was able to predict exactly which patients had rheumatoid arthritis, simply by watching how they asserted themselves in an unpleasant situation.

Following their initial experiment, Moos compiled everything he could find on the link between personality and arthritis and he became familiar with the case studies of more than 5000 people with rheumatoid arthritis. He concluded, based on his exhaustive studies, that there was a distinct psychology involved in the rheumatoid arthritis process.[72]

Since arthritis is an immune-mediated disorder, researchers have looked at dysregulation of the immune system by personality among arthritis sufferers.[73-75] In both animals and humans, emotional distress has significant effects on both the immune dysfunction and the inflammatory response characteristic of arthritis.[76] Rheumatoid arthritis patients have been shown to have an imbalance in the white blood cells (lymphocytes) that regulate much of the immune response. In their blood and joint fluid, rheumatoid patients have a disturbed "immunoregulatory ratio" of helper T lymphocytes (which enhance the immune response) to suppressor T lymphocytes (which decrease the response).[77] At the University of Pennsylvania, Martin Seligman has shown this same ratio of helper to suppressor cells to be significantly affected by a person's expectational style; that is, optimistic people have a significantly better ratio than do pessimistic people.

Other neurochemicals that modulate immune function and inflammation are endorphins, the body's natural pain killers.[78] These are well-known to be affected by mental state; for example, getting happily excited turns them on, and being depressed turns them off. Less well-known is the fact that endorphins are deficient in both the blood and the brain in many kinds of arthritis.[79] Endorphins not only reduce pain perception in the brain but also block the release in tissues of inflammation-producing neurochemicals, such as substance P and prostaglandins. Substance P has also been thought to be a mechanism by which the nervous system might be involved in rheumatoid arthritis.[80] Low endorphin levels, then, lead to more inflammation. And endorphins run low not only in persons with rheumatoid arthritis, but even more so in chronically distressed persons. Stress, however, does not always suppress endorphins. Patients who respond to stress adaptively, with a sense of control, show increased endorphin levels under pressure.

Two of the traits common to arthritis victims, chronic anxiety and repressed hostility, have been shown in repeated studies to compromise the immune system.

In one recent study, researchers carefully studied thirty-three women who suffered from rheumatoid arthritis. They looked at the number of daily "hassles" each went through, the major challenges they faced, and the amount of psychological distress each one had. They then measured the immune function of each woman. As expected, the researchers found major effects on the immune system, and those effects were stronger among the women who suffered greater psychological distress, major challenges, and minor hassles.[81]

Based on several decades of research into the connection between personality and rheumatoid arthritis, Solomon constructed what he believes to be an accurate picture of the arthritis patient's personality. According to Solomon,[82] rheumatoid arthritics are likely to be dependent and feel inadequate, but they deny their dependency by overcompensating with an outward facade of independence, self-assurance, and self-control. They are aware of strong, unexpressed feelings of anger, but they are severely blocked in their ability to express anger or other emotions. They tend to court others' favor, but they avoid closeness in interpersonal relationships. They tend to become overactive—a way of dealing defensively with their tensions—and they overreact to even the slightest criticism or rejection. The single most powerful precipitating factor in rheumatoid arthritis, says Solomon, "was the loss of, or separation from, important key figures upon whom these patients depended for support."[83]

Personality and Ulcers

Physicians have long acknowledged that the physiology behind gastric ulcer is simple: The ulcer sufferer secretes too much gastric acid. That acid eats away at the lining of the stomach, causing erosion; in severe cases, the ulcer becomes "perforated" (eating a hole through the wall of the stomach). Interestingly, ulcers were rare until the last hundred years or so.

Physicians have also recognized for years some of the factors that increase secretion of gastric acid. Use of tobacco, alcohol, caffeine (especially coffee), and aspirin have all been shown to increase gastric acid production. (Cigarette smoking is a two-edged sword, since it also delays healing.) Certain emotions can also bring on increased acidity; most powerful seem to be frustration, hostility, and resentment. Some people even experience an increase in gastric acid when they see food, smell food, taste or chew food, or even think about it.

Antiinflammatory medications like aspirin (which are more commonly used by stressed patients) can compound the problem by breaking down the mucus barrier that protects the stomach and intestinal lining from the acid. More recently, most ulcers have been shown to be caused by infection with a bacterium (*Helicobacter pylori*) that interacts with the acid. Whether mental stress in a susceptible person increases the likelihood of persistent *Helicobacter* infection, as it does with other infections, has not yet been studied.

The link between specific personality traits and gastric ulcers has not been as well defined, but recent research has indicated the presence of an "ulcer personality." Much like the so-called cancer personality or arthritis personality, the ulcer personality may actually cause ulcers, or it may figure in determining how severe ulcers become.

Pioneering Research

One of the first recorded observations of the emotional link to ulcers occurred in the mid-nineteenth century:[84-94] Dr. William Beaumont had a patient whose abdominal wall had an opening clear into his stomach. It, of course, afforded the perfect window through which to view the rate of stomach secretion. What Beaumont noticed was that the secretion of stomach juices changed when the man became emotionally stressed.

The pioneering research in the ulcer–personality link has been conducted by Dr. Charles Richardson and Dr. Mark Feldman, professors of internal medicine at the University of Texas Health Science Center in Dallas. The two conducted a series of studies, both independently and together with doctors at the Veterans Administration medical center in Dallas.[95] They found that ulcer patients seem to have the same number of stressful situations as people who don't have ulcers, but that ulcer patients perceive the situations as being far more negative than do other people. When they were faced with a job change, for example, or relocation, these people did not regard it as an adventure or a positive change; they perceived disaster and upset. In addition, ulcer patients seemed much more likely than others to be neurotic—people preoccupied with their own aches and pain, who are too concerned with their bodily functions. They expected the worst, and felt threatened by a wide variety of situations, even situations that did not pose much of a real risk.

Characteristic Traits

Emotions do appear to have a role in the development of ulcers, a fact that has been confirmed repeatedly in laboratory studies. Medical research shows that negative emotions break down the normal chemical balance between stomach acid and the protective lining of the stomach. While stress was once thought to be the dominant cause of ulcers, today biological factors such as *Helicobacter* infection and constitutionally poor intestinal mucus protection seem to be more important. The commonest cause of abdominal pain and nausea mimicking ulcers, however, continues to be stomach and bowel spasm aggravated by mental distress. Of patients attending gastroenterology clinics, more than a third have major anxiety disorders, a third have major depression, and far more than a third have somatization disorders (a form of anxiety that is manifested predominantly in physical symptoms). For ulcer disease itself, the pattern is changing. In late nineteenth century western Europe, young women had a much higher prevalence of ulcers than men. In the twentieth century, the situation reversed, and men had much higher rates.[96]

The ulcer personality is characterized by excessive dependency on others and a tendency to rely on other people in ways that are not healthy. Even though such persons are very dependent, they enjoy far less social support than most healthy people do. Many ulcer patients express the feeling that they have few friends or relatives on whom they could depend in times of crisis. They tend to suffer from excessive worry, annoyance, and fear of common situations or circumstances. And, unfortunately, ulcer patients seem to have more times of crisis than others, possibly because the ulcer personality is also marked by deep pessimism or the tendency always to expect the worst. Finally, ulcer patients who have been given psychological tests show a fairly consistent quality: While other people are able to bend with stress, an ulcer patient tends to break. This tendency leads to higher rates of emotional distress, anxiety, and depression among those with ulcers. The situation is aggravated by doing other things to damage the lining of the stomach, such as drinking too much coffee or alcohol.

Researchers are, however, quick to point out the bright side of ulcer personality research: With help and determination, ulcer patients can learn to change the way they look at things, and with a change in personality traits, the tendency toward ulcers can diminish considerably.

An Asthma Personality?

Researchers have been extremely reluctant to suggest the existence of an asthma personality owing mostly to a set of outlandish suppositions regarding the role of sexual fantasy in asthma that caused psychosomatic medicine to fall into disrepute thirty years ago.[97] Since then, research shows that several factors may be at work in the personality traits of an asthmatic. Initially, many asthma episodes are caused by bronchial infection or an allergic reaction; air passages narrow, the victim can't get enough air, and that feeling is profoundly distressful. Any attending emotional reaction, of course, just makes the asthma worse. Asthma is usually maintained by an inflammatory process in the airways that may have some of the same underlying mechanisms involving the central nervous system as those described above for rheumatoid arthritis. It is not uncommon to see the airway disease of anxious or depressed asthmatics improve significantly when those mental conditions are treated appropriately.

It is now believed that some people later develop an almost Pavlovian response to whatever triggers their asthma. Simply thinking, "I feel a cold coming on; it's going to cause an asthma attack" or, the pollen count is going to be high today" can be enough to trigger a full-fledged asthma attack *without* an actual physical insult.

There's also a vicious cycle among asthmatics, especially childhood asthmatics, that is very difficult to break. An asthma episode tends to engender sympathy, attention, compassion, and to keep the child home from school. If that's what asthmatic persons need in their life—more sympathy, attention, and compassion—attacks may become more frequent. Although the biology of the attack is very real, it is precipitated by emotional need.

A few traits seem more common among those with asthma. Many are anxious and feel powerless. Even though they are angry and hostile, they feel weak and out of control of their lives. Finally, many feel ready to strike out at those around them.

Regardless of the illness involved, researchers reporting their findings in the *British Journal of Medical Psychology* pointed out perhaps one of the most telling traits of a disease-prone personality. What is it?

Researchers at the University of Helsinki studied almost 200 people with various diseases and found an amazing difference: Unlike their normal counterparts, those with disease-prone personalities felt more emotionally stable when they were *ill*.[98] More than anything else, that finding may help us distinguish those who, as Friedman wrote, may suffer "death due to unhealthy personality."

Is it possible to overcome a disease-prone personality? Some researchers think it is. In an address before the National Institute for the Clinical Application of Behavioral Medicine, Henry Dreher suggested the following ideas for change:

- Develop an awareness of your own needs. You can start on a small scale—maybe you need a few minutes alone when you get home from work before you plunge into family life, for example.
- Discover what Dreher calls an "inner guide," essentially, an awareness of your innermost thoughts and feelings. If you're used to suppressing emotion or ignoring your needs, it can take some real concentration.
- Reframe your ideas about your feelings. If you're troubled by the thought that you are angry toward an abusive parent, stop feeling guilty for your anger. Find appropriate ways to express your anger, work through it, and then build on what is left, even eventually forgiving your abuser.

- Learn the skills of emotional expression. Everyone occasionally feels angry, hostile, disappointed, depressed, or resentful. The key is to acknowledge your emotion, express it appropriately, and then move on.
- Take charge of your medical care; find a physician who will take the time to talk to you, who will explore options, and who will answer questions. Find out all you can, and make your own decisions.
- Get as much social support as you can. A broad network of family and friends is ideal, but you should cultivate at least a few close friends in whom you can confide.
- Work through your feelings of hopelessness. Getting information is the first step; next, figure out what your challenges might be, then work out a game plan for each. As soon as you realize that you have viable options, you'll find that you feel in charge instead of hopeless.
- Cultivate a fighting spirit; be willing to face challenges head-on and to fight to the finish.[99]

Notes

1. Howard S. Friedman, *The Self-Healing Personality* (New York: Henry Holt and Company, 1991), p. 1.

2. Clive Wood, "Type-Casting: Is Disease Linked with Personality?" *Nursing Times,* 84(48): 1988, 26.

3. Friedman, p. 22.

4. Hans J. Eysenck, "Health's Character," *Psychology Today,* December 1988, p. 28; and Hans J. Eysenck, "Personality, Stress, and Cancer: Prediction and Prophylaxis," *British Journal of Medical Psychology* (part 1), 61: 1988, 57–75.

5. Friedman, p. 15.

6. Friedman, p. 57.

7. Grossarth-Maticek's studies are described in Eysenck, pp. 30–31.

8. R. Grossarth-Maticek, D. T. Kanazir, P. Schmidt, and H. Vetter, "Psychosomatic Factors in the Process of Carcinogenesis: Theoretical Models and Empirical Results," *Psychotherapy and Psychosomatics* 38: 1982, 284–302; and R. Grossarth-Maticek, D. T. Kanazir, P. Schmidt, and H. Vetter, "Psychosomatic Factors Involved in the Process of Carcinogenesis: Preliminary Results in the Yugoslavian Prospective Study," *Psychotherapy and Psychosomatics* 40: 1983, 191–210.

9. Eysenck, p. 30.

10. Eysenck.

11. Eysenck.

12. Joshua Fischman, "Fighting Cancer and Heart Disease: The Character of Controversy," *Psychology Today,* December: 1988, 27.

13. Fischman.

14. See the Nineteen Critical Commentaries in *Psychological Inquiry: An International Journal of Peer Commentary and Review,* 2(3): 1991.

15. Fischman.

16. Friedman, pp. 94–96.

17. Bruce Bower, "The Character of Cancer," *Science News,* 131: 1987, 120.

18. Bower.

19. Bower.

20. Judy Berlfein, "An Ill Nature," *Psychology Today,* n.d., p. 16.

21. Berlfein.

22. Berlfein.

23. "How Your Personality Affects Your Health," *Good Housekeeping,* June 1983.

24. Clive Wood, "The Cold Character," *Psychology Today,* April: 1988, 13.

25. Joann Rodgers, "Longevity Predictors: The Personality Link," *Omni,* February: 1989, 25.

26. Douglas J. Stanwyck and Carol A. Anson, "Is Personality Related to Illness? Cluster

Profiles of Aggregated Data," *Advances*, 3(2): 1986, 4–15.

27. Stanwyck and Anson, p. 11.

28. Marcia Angell, "Disease as a Reflection of the Psyche," *New England Journal of Medicine*, 312: 1985, 1570–1572.

29. Angell.

30. Angell.

31. The analysis of the Angell editorial is found in June Zimmerman, "Does Emotional State Affect Disease?" *MD*, April: 1986, 30, 41.

32. Joel Davis, "Anxiety Aches," *Self*, January: 1985, 100.

33. Steven Locke and Douglas Colligan, *The Healer Within: The New Medicine of Mind and Body* (New York: E. P. Dutton, 1986), p. 140.

34. Bernie S. Siegel, *Peace, Love, and Healing: Bodymind Communication and the Path to Self-Healing* (New York: Harper and Row, 1990).

35. William H. Redd, "Cancer and Emotions: Is There a Connection?" *Executive Health Report*, 26(3): 1989, 1, 4–6.

36. Locke and Colligan.

37. Locke and Colligan.

38. Locke and Colligan.

39. Locke and Colligan.

40. Lydia Temoshok and Henry Dreher, *The Type C Connection: The Behavioral Links to Cancer and Your Health* (New York: Random House, 1992).

41. Locke and Colligan, pp. 133–134.

42. Henry Dreher, "The Type C Connection: A Powerful New Tool in the Fight Against Cancer," in Proceedings of the Fourth National Conference on the Psychology of Health, Immunity, and Disease, published by the National Institute for the Clinical Application of Behavioral Medicine.

43. Temoshok and Dreher.

44. Locke and Colligan, p. 134.

45. Locke and Colligan, p. 134.

46. Barbara A. Schindler, "Stress, Affective Disorders, and Immune Function," *Medical Clinics of North America*, 69(3): 1985, 585–597.

47. Michael A. Weiner, *Maximum Immunity* (Boston: Houghton-Mifflin Company, 1986).

48. Eleanor Smith, "Fighting Cancerous Feelings," *Psychology Today*, May: 1988, 22.

49. Smith.

50. Schindler.

51. Alan Zonderman, "Depression Not Linked to Cancer," *Executive Health Report*, 26(3): 1989, 5.

52. "Is There a Cancer Personality?" *The Johns Hopkins Medical Letter*, 2(1): 1990, 1.

53. Zonderman.

54. Smith, pp. 22–23.

55. Phillip L. Rice, *Stress and Health* (Monterey, California: Brooks/Cole Publishing Company, 1987), pp. 103–104.

56. Locke and Colligan.

57. S. Greer, et al, "Psychological Response to Breast Cancer and Fifteen-Year Outcome," *Lancet* 1: 1990, 49–50; and Greer, Morrison, and Pettingale, *Journal of Psychosomatic Research* 19: 147–153.

58. A. D. Wiseman, *Cancer—The Behavioral Dimensions*, p. 331.

59. Locke and Colligan.

60. Caroline B. Thomas, *Johns Hopkins Medical* 151: 1982, 193.

61. Friedman, p. 62

62. Dreher, "The Type C Connection."

63. Locke and Colligan.

64. Locke and Colligan, p. 106.

65. H. Weiner, "Rheumatoid Arthritis," in *Psychobiology and Human Disease* (1977), pp. 416–494; J. S. Heisel, "Life Changes as Etiologic Factors in Juvenile Rheumatoid Arthritis," *Journal of Psychosomatic Research* 17: 1972, 411–420; and K. O. Anderson, L. A. Bradley, L. D. Young, L. K. McDaniel, and C. M. Wise, "Rheumatoid Arthritis: Review of Psychological Factors Related to Etiology, Effects, and Treatment," *Psychological Bulletin* 98: 1985, 358–387.

66. Barbara Powell, *Good Relationships Are Good Medicine* (Emmaus, Pennsylvania: Rodale Press).

67. Locke and Colligan, p. 107.

68. Powell.

69. Powell.

70. Powell.

71. Friedman, p. 85.

72. Locke and Colligan, p. 108.

73. G. F. Solomon and A. A. Amkraut, "Psychoneuroendocrinological Effects on the Immune

System," *Annual Review of Microbiology* 35: 1981, 155–184.

74. G. F. Solomon, N. Kay, and J. E. Morley, "Endorphins: A Link Between Personality, Stress, Emotions, Immunity, and Substance P," in N. P. Plotnikoff, R. E. Faith, A. J. Murgo, and R. A. Good, editors, *Enkephalins and Endorphins, Stress and the Immune System* (New York: Plenum Press, 1986), pp. 129–144.

75. C. D. Anderson, J. M. Soyva, and L. J. Vaughn, "A Test of Delayed Recovery Following Stressful Stimulation in Four Psychosomatic Disorders," *Journal of Psychosomatic Research* 26: 1982, 571–580.

76. E. M. Sternberg, G. P. Chrousis, R. L. Wilder, and P. W. Gold, "The Stress Response and the Regulation of Inflammatory Disease," *Annals of Internal Medicine,* 117(10): 1992, 854–866.

77. E. M. Veys, P. Hermanns, G. Verbruggen, J. Schindler, and G. Goldstein, "Evaluation of T Cell Subsets with Monoclonal Antibodies in Synovial Fluid in Rheumatoid Arthritis," *The Journal of Rheumatology,* 9(6): 1982, 821–826.

78. R. A. Good, N. P. Plotnikoff, R. E. Faith, A. J. Murgo, and R. A. Good, *Enkephalins and Endorphins, Stress and the Immune System* (New York: Plenum Press, 1986), pp v–vi; and G. F. Solomon, et al., in Plotnikoff, et al., pp. 129–144.

79. C. Denko, "Serum Beta Endorphins in Rheumatic Disorders," *Journal of Rheumatology,* 9(6): 1982, 827–833.

80. J. D. Levine, D. H. Collier, A. L. Basbaum, M. A. Moskowitz, and C. A. Helms, "Hypothesis: The Nervous System May Contribute to the Pathophysiology of Rheumatoid Arthritis," *Journal of Rheumatology* 12: 1985, 406–422.

81. Friedman.

82. Weiner.

83. Weiner.

84. Friedman, p. 89.

85. A. R. Rimon, "A Psychosomatic Approach to Rheumatoid Arthritis: A Clinical Study of 100 Patients," *Acta Rheumatologica Scandinavica,* Supplement 13: 1969, 1–154.

86. R. Rimon and L. Riika-Liisa, "Life Stress and Rheumatoid Arthritis: A 15-Year Follow-Up Study," *Psychotherapy and Psychosomatics* 43: 38–43.

87. T. W. Smith, J. R. Peck, and J. R. Ward, "Helplessness and Depression in Rheumatoid Arthritis," *Health Psychology,* 9(4): 1990, 377–389.

88. A. O' Leary, S. Shoor, K. Lorig, and H. R. Holman, "A Cognitive-Behavioral Treatment for Rheumatoid Arthritis," *Health Psychology* 7: 1988, 527–544.

89. K. Lorig, *Arthritis and Rheumatism* 28: 1985, 680–685.

90. S. Crown, J. Crown, and A. Fleming, "Aspects of the Psychology and Epidemiology of Rheumatoid Disease," *Psychological Medicine* 5: 1975, 291–299.

91. M. Gringas, *Journal of International Medical Research* 4 (Supplement 2): p. 41.

92. M. Scott, *Practitioner* 202: 1969, 802.

93. I. Oreskes, et al., *Annals of Rheumatic Disease* 27: 1968, 60.

94. G. G. Haydn, *Annals of Rheumatic Disease* 33: 1974, 274.

95. "Is There an Ulcer Personality?" *The Wellness Newsletter,* July: 1987, 2; and Sharon Faelten, David Diamond, and the Editors of *Prevention Magazine,* "Take Control of Your Life: A Complete Guide to Stress Relief" *Prevention* (Emmaus, Pennsylvania: Rodale Press, 1988), pp. 206–207.

96. Friedman, p. 90.

97. Friedman, pp. 86–88.

98. L. Keltikangas-Jarvinen, "'Psychosomatic Personality'—A Personality Constellation or an Illness-Related Reaction?" *British Journal of Medical Psychology,* 62(4): 1989, 325–331.

99. Dreher, "The Type C Connection."

6

THE CORONARY/ARTERY DISEASE–PRONE PERSONALITY

Live always, my friend, as if there is world enough and time.
—MEYER FRIEDMAN

Our technologically advanced society has come a long way in the battle against disease. While some maladies such as the common cold elude our most persistent efforts at cure, we have made giant strides in many areas. Diseases that signaled death and horror just a few generations ago—polio, smallpox, diphtheria, tetanus—today are scarcely known. Children once paid a devastating price for childhood diseases such as measles, mumps, and rubella; today, immunizations during infancy protect against these and other maladies.

We've conquered most bacteria, including the "killers" that were so commonly associated with bacterial infection, such as pneumonia. Streptococcal-pharyngitis, once so feared, claimed the life of George Washington, our first president. Today, strep throat is cured with a ten-day course of antibiotics. Although we have conquered pneumonia and smallpox and polio, they have been replaced by other threats, among them diabetes and this nation's number one-killer, heart disease.

With heart disease, we're not fighting bacteria. We can't prevent coronary artery disease with antibiotics and we've enjoyed only small success with pharmacotherapy. Recent research suggests that we must look to ourselves—to the way we think, the way we behave, the way we react to stress, the way we express anger. In large part it is personality—that solid, consistent core of character and temperament that dictates how we react to the world around us—that determines our health and our susceptibility to disease. If recent breakthroughs in research are any indication, personality and behavior may play a major role in heart disease.

In a summary of research printed in *Psychology Today* a writer editorialized:

> *By treating the heart as an unfeeling pump, surgeons have been able to create pacemakers and work their way up to the ultimate in high-tech medicine: the artificial heart. But even as Barney Clark and other courageous patients were testing the electronic pumps, scientists were using chemistry, psychology, and hard data to discover that trouble in the heart may come in part from sickness of the soul.*[1]

That sickness of the soul has evolved over the past three decades from a notion called the *Type A personality* to a broader-based concept that some still prefer to call the Type A behavior pattern. Two bits of good news have emerged from the most recent research: The behavior pattern (whatever you choose to call it) isn't set in stone. It's not a character flaw. It can be changed. As Yale-trained clinical psychologist Dennis Jaffe put it, "When you call something a personality, you make it seem unnecessarily rigid. Unchangeable. But when you think of Type A as a series of behavior patterns, you see that each one of those patterns is nothing more than a bad habit. You can work on changing a habit. It's difficult and it takes time, but you can do it. You can change."[2] The second piece of good news is that some of the more desirable parts of the Type A behavior pattern (such as increased productivity) are not the toxic parts. One can safely retain some of the positive characteristics and change the harmful parts.

Personality traits that increase your risk for coronary artery disease, then, are not inherent flaws. They are, more accurately, patterns of behavior that have been shown through scientific research to boost the chances of developing (or intensifying) heart disease. For ease of discussion throughout this chapter, we will refer to this collection of personality traits by the name most researchers have preferred, the Type A personality.

The Type A Personality

Definitions

One thing Type A is *not* is a reaction to stress. Cardiologist Ray Rosenman, who with colleague Meyer Friedman originated the theory of Type A personality three decades ago, points out,

> *[We should] not equate Type A behavior pattern with a stressful situation or distressed response. Type A does not mean stress and is not the same as anxiety, depression, worry, fear, or neurosis. It merely refers to the behaviors of an individual who reacts to the environment with characteristic gestures, facial expressions, fast pace of activities, and the perception of daily events and stresses as challenges, all leading to an aggressive, time-urgent, impatient, and more hostile style of living."*[3]

Soon after they began to shift emphasis from physical risk factors to psychological risk factors for heart disease, Rosenman and Friedman defined the Type A personality as "an action–emotion complex that can be observed in any person who is aggressively involved in a chronic, incessant struggle to achieve more and more in less and less time, and if required to do so, against the opposing efforts of other things or other persons."[4]

As Friedman points out, the way Type A personalities view the world causes them to "create a chronic struggle against time, and against other people." That struggle, Friedman contends, is what causes physical damage (a process that will be detailed more completely later in this chapter). In essence, as one researcher put it, Type A personalities "are not only more hostile, competitive, and impatient" but are also guided by the central view that they "are indeed responsible for everything, control everything, and are not only the captains of their own ship but the crew and cargo as well."[5]

How Common Is Type A Personality?

What percentage of the American population can be classified as Type A? No one knows for sure. Researchers have been able to come up with some estimates, based largely on the results of studies that involved thousands of people selected randomly from general populations.

A conservative estimate advanced by one researcher is 40 percent of the American population.[6] Another researcher believes that as many as half of all men can be classified as Type A and that the personality type is becoming increasingly common among women in the work force.[7] Meyer Friedman, the San Francisco cardiologist who was part of the team that originally developed the Type A personality theory, believes that three-fourths of all urban men are Type A. He adds that an increasing number of women can also be classified as Type A.[8]

Ethel Roskies, who has spent more than a decade on studies of Type A behavior, says,

> [It is] possible that there has been an actual increase in type As. But any classification that grows to include most of the population of North America is not very useful, either for epidemiological or for treatment purposes. Unless it is possible to sift out the specific coronary-prone characteristics from the general type A classification, we shall soon find ourselves in the ridiculous situation of seeking to treat just about everybody.[9]

Roskies adds that if the coronary-prone traits are not identified and segregated, "most of these treatments will be directed to modifying characteristics that are largely irrelevant to coronary risk."[10]

Thus, those on the cutting edge of Type A research are beginning to concentrate their efforts, not on estimating how many Americans might be afflicted, but on segregating the most harmful traits of Type A from the traits that don't cause health problems. From this, researchers hope to learn which traits are the most detrimental to health so they can concentrate on helping people alter the most harmful ones.

Impact on Men, Women, and Children

While much of the early research centered on men, scientists are now looking more closely at the impact of Type A behavior on women and children. Today's stereotype of the average Type A as a harried male executive does not tell the whole story. Women can pay an even greater price for Type A behavior than men do.

Many early studies showed that men are approximately three times more likely to develop heart disease if they are Type A, but the picture for women is even bleaker. The prestigious Framingham Heart Study showed that a Type A woman runs four times the risk of heart disease as compared with her Type B sister.[11] Other studies portray the gap as even wider: Statistics from the Western Collaborative Group Study show that Type A women are three times as likely as Type B women to develop angina.[12] Friedman found that Type A women are seven times more likely than Type Bs to develop heart disease.[13]

There are some basic differences, too, in the way women manifest Type A personality. The hallmarks of Type A personality in men, researchers say, are time urgency, relentless drive for achievement, free-floating hostility, and inability to relax. Women have many of the same traits, but they often can't express their hostility as directly.[14] The result is an increasing feeling of isolation and alienation that may be an even more dangerous manifestation for women than busyness or anger.

Meyer Friedman and colleague Diane Ulmer give a graphic portrayal of the Type A woman's dilemma:

> *Fired up to beat men at their own game, many Type A women work 50- to 60-hour weeks. In addition, they shop and cook for themselves, their children, husbands, or boyfriends, do their housekeeping, laundry, and ironing, attend exercise classes, see friends, and try to appear attractive and feminine at all times.*[15]

It's that double pressure—to succeed both professionally and at a woman's traditional role—that causes anger and frustration. But that's where trouble creeps in. As one writer put it, "Throughout their lives, women are taught that it's 'not feminine' to express anger, so they suppress it."[16] Heart disease can result.

Ulmer says it's time to explode the myth that women are more comfortable with their emotions than are men. That statement is "true for every emotion except anger. Men are usually quick to let you know they're angry, but women tend to keep their anger under wraps. They let it smolder. When you ask them what's wrong, they say they're annoyed, or frustrated, or upset, or depressed, but never angry." Ulmer points out that it "took quite a while" for the Type A women she counseled with to admit their anger, but once they did, "it turned out that 90 percent were angry at their fathers, husbands, and employers for undervaluing their contributions to their families and jobs."[17] There's even a difference between men and women in the manifestation of heart disease, points out Friedman. Men are more likely to suffer heart attacks (myocardial infarction). Women, on the other hand, more commonly suffer angina (severe, chronic chest pain) or congestive heart failure.

Obviously, then, Type A personality can affect both men and women, but researchers have learned it's not exclusively the domain of adults. Children, too, can exhibit Type A personality and can pay the price in terms of susceptibility to heart disease. As is the case with adults, no one knows what percentage of the nation's children exhibit characteristics similar to those of the Type A personality, but the process of coronary heart disease begins early in childhood. "Although present research does not show a direct link between coronary-prone behavior in children and coronary heart disease in adults, there is evidence that children assessed as Type A exhibit behavior patterns similar to those of adults assessed as Type A."[18]

Do children who exhibit Type A traits as youngsters carry that attitude into adulthood? Many of them do, studies show. New research reported in *Science News* indicates that "the Type A pattern of aggression and competitiveness shows up early in life and can persist, perhaps putting the individual at risk of heart disease as an adult."[19]

According to research, about half of all children tend to remain in the personality category they exhibit during childhood. Researchers at the Louisiana State University Medical Center in New Orleans studied 1744 children and young adults aged eight to twenty-four years. Those participating in the study were tested for Type A behavior traits during the 1981–1982 school year and again three years later. Of the children who scored highest on the Type A test, 43 percent were also among the highest scorers three years later. Of those who scored lowest (and, therefore, were the most easygoing of the students), 45 percent were among the lowest scorers three years later.

The researchers also used sophisticated testing procedures to measure the students on hostility, one of the Type A traits that seems to be most toxic in terms of predicting heart disease. Of the children who initially scored the highest on hostility, 40 percent remained among the highest hostility scorers three years later.[20]

While research on Type A among children is still relatively new, scientists who are examining these characteristically hard-driving children are finding out a great deal about how they behave and what factors may drive them toward aggression and competitiveness. One group of researchers working in the Department of Psychiatry at the University of Pittsburgh found that young Type A boys (but, interestingly, not girls) had Type A mothers and fathers, suggesting "early modeling of Type A behaviors by boys."[21] The same researchers, along with other scientists engaged in independent research, found that parents and teachers tended to reinforce (and therefore encourage) the behavior most often associated with Type A personality, high achievement, striving for achievement, and speedy task completion.[22]

Type A personality manifests itself among children much as it does among adults. Researchers who have done various long-term studies on selected groups of children and adolescents have identified some typical behaviors common among Type A children. Almost all score high on hostility and anger; many are suspicious.[23] Most had higher achievement test scores and classroom grades, independent of IQ test scores, most likely because of their competitive nature.[24] Type A children also tend to be more outgoing, talkative, and physically active; more aggressive in their interactions with others; and more likely to experience a greater number of aversive significant life events than are Type B children.[25]

What Influences "Cause" Type A Personality?

Many influences are at work on each of us: A certain gene pool determines the color of our eyes; the way our parents treat each other can influence the way we act in relationships. Some researchers believe that environmental factors are the sole cause of Type A personality; others cite data in an attempt to prove that we inherit Type A behavior as surely as we inherit the color of our hair. In actuality, there is research, carefully done, scientifically interpreted, that supports both sides.

Environmental Factors

Ray Rosenman, one of the two cardiologists who originated the Type A theory, stands firmly on the environmental side; he maintains, that there is little evidence of a genetic component for Type A behavior, although some genetic influence may exist for traits such as drive, competitiveness, compulsiveness, dominance, sociability, and impulsiveness.[26] The greatest influence, according to Rosenman, is adult modeling and conditioning, which, he says, explains why children tend to behave the same way within family units. It's not the gene pool; it's the way the parents act.[27]

Partly as a result of that modeling, Rosenman says, Type A behavior pattern is more common among children who have parents with higher educational level and higher occupational status, and children who live in urban rather than rural areas. It is more common among boys than girls. It is also more common among children whose mothers work full-time outside the home.

Studies conducted by Dr. Karen Matthews and her colleagues at the University of Pittsburgh make a convincing case for environment and parenting styles in determining Type A behavior. In a series of studies, parents of Type A children were more likely to make critical remarks and were more apt to encourage their children to try harder, even when the children were already doing very well on a specific task. Mothers of the Type A children made fewer positive remarks about their children's performance on the achievement task. Even discipline seems to play a role. Type B children tend to have parents who explain the reasons behind discipline. Type A children, on the other hand, tend to have parents who use more physical and restrictive disciplinary techniques.[28]

When the University of Pittsburgh researchers zeroed in on family environments, they found that hostile and angry children—those most prone to be Type A—tended to come from very similar backgrounds. According to the research, the families were "less supportive, less open with their feelings, less positively involved with their children, and more likely to use physical and restrictive techniques in disciplining their children."[29]

Meyer Friedman, who worked with Rosenman to originate the Type A theory, claims that various aspects of Type A behavior stem from "the failure of the Type A person in his infancy and very early childhood to receive *unconditional* love, affection, and encouragement from one or both of his parents."[30] They learn their worth as a person is determined in quantified terms: doing more, the highest score, winning the competition, having the most. There develops a need to continually prove themselves, usually by doing the most or being the best. They often come to feel acceptable only if they get approval from others, never making a mistake. Motivation begins to come more from fear of failure than from love of what they are doing.

Genetics

Just as much evidence exists to point the finger at genetics. Scientists have learned over the past few years that numerous personality traits, even social attitudes and political beliefs, are at least half determined by genetics. Duke University's Redford Williams says,

> While the notion that behavioral tendencies can be inherited in humans flies in the face of many egalitarian ideals and raises fears of biological determinism, it cannot be ignored that, just as with eye color, body build, tendencies toward baldness, and a host of other "physical" characteristics, one's psychological makeup is also very much a product of one's genes.[31]

According to Williams, the traits applicable to Type A personality "have all been found to show strong, clear-cut genetic influences."[32] The results of animal studies have shown at least some evidence that attitudes and behavior may be controlled by neurotransmitters in the brain.

Researchers who have attempted to determine the role of genetics in personality formation have generally used twins as study subjects. One such study involved more than a hundred pairs of twins, aged six to eleven, living in the Philadelphia area. Most of the twins in the study were identical (they shared exactly the same genetic makeup); approximately a third of the twins in the study were same-sex twins who were not identical. After studying a number of traits as well as a variety of physical characteristics (such as blood lipid levels), it was concluded that some of the characteristics were due to environmental influence, but some of the physical characteristics, the Type A behavior pattern, and some of the traits that accompany the Type A personality were determined by genetics.[33]

A long-term study of identical twins conducted by the University of Minnesota confirmed that genetics influenced at least half of the personality traits essential to the Type A personality. The study examined identical twins who were separated at birth and reared in different environments. (The true diversity of the environments can be demonstrated by one pair of male twins in their late forties: One was reared as a Jew in Trinidad, the other as a Catholic in Germany.)

Numerous personality traits were found to be "about 50 percent explainable by the genetic similarity."[34] Since the shared traits were almost as strong in twins who were reared apart as in those who were reared together, "researchers have been forced to conclude that the environment shared by twins raised in the same family had little or no role in producing whatever personality similarities they had,"[35] concludes Williams. The twins' genetic makeup was more crucial to personality than the fact that they were raised in the same home.

What exactly is inherited? Part of the answer seems to be related to the same neurochemical inheritance (such as deficient serotonin neurotransmitter function in the brain) that characterizes depression and anxiety. The more toxic Type A characteristics are more common in families with inherited vulnerability to these anxiety and depression disorders, and treatment with medication (or exercise) that corrects the serotonin neurotransmitter deficiency reduces Type A behavior.

The Controversy

The one thing that is certain about coronary-prone personality is that nothing is certain. Or, to put it more precisely, no aspect of coronary-prone personality (or Type A behavior) is without controversy. One possible reason is that Type A behavior isn't all bad. Recent research has shown that some aspects of Type A personality—anger, hostility—wreak havoc on health, but can it really be so dreadful to be ambitious, hard working, time oriented, and energetic?

Psychologist Ethel Roskies has some other ideas about why controversy has surrounded the notion of a coronary-prone personality. Her theory is that behavior is much more difficult to pinpoint as a risk factor than are other, more specific risk factors that can be measured in a laboratory (such as high blood pressure or elevated cholesterol levels). "Behavior comes from the soft, fuzzy science of psychology, rather than from the hard, precise, biomedical sciences," she points out, a fact that may make it difficult for medical researchers to accept the coronary-prone personality. Medical personnel may have even more difficulty with the concept, she adds, "if behavioral modification, rather than conventional medical and surgical techniques, is seen as the treatment of choice for this new type of risk factor."[36]

Still another reason for controversy, says Roskies, is the "personal involvement of most health professionals and scientists with Type A behavior." The competitive selection process itself guarantees that a large majority of professional health care workers are more likely to be Type A, and may thus feel threatened when behavioral issues are brought up. "When we speak of diabetes mellitus or smoking, we are speaking of other people, 'them,' 'out there'; but when we talk about Type A, in contrast, we are talking about ourselves."[37]

British researchers add still another reason for the controversy that brews over the Type A personality: The researchers themselves have different concepts of exactly what a Type A personality is. There have been broad differences and inconsistencies in some of the research into Type A behavior. Researchers differ in their own standards; they use different criteria to assess what they believe to be Type A personalities; they rely on people to judge themselves as Type A, a judgment that isn't always accurate; and many researchers have problems judging Type A behavior in anyone except male executives.[38] Self-assessment tests for qualities like hostility are notoriously unreliable because of a well-demonstrated self-delusion. It is, after all, not very socially acceptable to be trying to prove oneself in a hostile way.[39]

Still, a growing body of evidence links Type A behavior—or at least some components of it—to the development of heart disease, the likelihood of suffering recurrent heart attacks, and death from heart disease. Many researchers believe it is still the most, or one of the most, important risk factors, especially in the development of angina-related coronary artery disease. Many researchers also believe that other risk factors may be amplified by the presence of a Type A personality.[40] Important new data also link some of the components of Type A behavior with other illnesses as well and with the increased likelihood of premature death.

The Story behind the "Coronary Personality"

The link between the emotions and the heart has been recognized for thousands of years—and is, in fact, referred to in the most ancient medical records. Physicians recording their thoughts in the oldest surviving medical "textbooks," the Egyptian papyri, stated that, in examining a patient's limbs, they were examining the heart, "because all his limbs possess its vessels, that is: the heart speaks out of the vessels of every limb." Medical historians believe from this passage that the Egyptians were keenly aware of the influence of emotions on the heart.[41]

Hippocrates and Others

Early written history is replete with examples of the mind's influence over the heart; even the Bible speaks of people who were struck dead after some great emotional upheaval. More than 2000 years ago, the ancient physician Hippocrates opined "this is the great error of our day in the treatment of the human body, that physicians separate the soul from the body."[42]

In 1628, William Harvey, recognized as a founder of modern physiology and medicine, published a landmark book in which he provided the first documented description of the human circulation. After accurately describing the pathway of the blood through the heart and lungs and via the arteries to the tissues of the body, Harvey echoed the sentiments of the Egyptian physicians in linking the heart to the mind. He wrote, "Every affection of the mind that is attended with either pain or pleasure, hope or fear, is the cause of an agitation whose influence extends to the heart."[43]

A little more than 200 years later, physicians gave even more credence to the effect of the mind on the heart. Researchers of the day noted that soldiers in the American Civil War had something in common with those in Europe's Crimean War: Both had a particular type of heart murmur and certain types of irregular heart rhythms.[44]

At about the same time, German physician T. von Deusch made a definite link between behavior and heart disease. In 1868, he described the coronary-prone person as one who often worked through the night and who spoke with a loud voice.[45]

The first description of the Type A personality, though it was not given that name, was set forth at the turn of this century by Sir William Osler, the American physician who became professor of medicine at Oxford University. He attributed heart disease to "the high pressure at which men live and the habit of working the machine to its maximum capacity." In debunking myths popular at the time, Osler described the typical coronary patient not as "the delicate, neurotic person" but as "the robust, the vigorous in mind and body, the keen and ambitious man, the indicator of whose engine is always at 'full speed ahead.'" Osler went a step farther in describing the circumstances likely to bring on angina chest pain: "mental worry, severe grief, or a sudden shock."[46]

Other researchers followed, adding their own evidence to the heart–behavior link. In the 1930s, the Menningers noted that coronary artery disease patients often exhibited a "strongly aggressive personality." A decade later, one psychosomatic medicine pioneer described a "coronary personality," whose pattern consisted of the hard-driving, goal-directed behavior he often saw among coronary heart disease patients. Other researchers followed in the ensuing fifteen years who noted specific behavior patterns and "personalities" of their patients with heart disease.[47]

Friedman and Rosenman's Research

The most significant and far-reaching work on coronary personality came in the mid-1950s, as a result of research done by cardiologists Meyer Friedman and Ray Rosenman. According to Friedman and Rosenman, their discovery of the Type A behavior pattern came as somewhat of an accident. As the story goes, an upholsterer who came to their office to repair some furniture pointed out that the fabric was worn only on the very edge of the couches and chairs. It was a sign, he mused, that the patients were, literally, "on edge." Armed with hard-core evidence that their patients were literally perched on the edge of their seats, Friedman and Rosenman launched the landmark series of studies that led to identification of the Type A behavior pattern,[48] a pattern they initially dubbed *the hurry sickness.*

With the idea that coronary heart disease patients might have a peculiar behavior in common, Friedman and Rosenman embarked on a series of exhaustive studies that looked in detail at the emotional and behavioral characteristics of their patients. Friedman and Rosenman found that their coronary heart disease patients *did* share a set of peculiar and specific behaviors, which they initially described as "an action-emotion complex that can be observed in any person who is aggressively involved in a chronic, incessant struggle to achieve more and more in less and less time, and if required to do so, against the opposing efforts of other things or other persons."[49] They named their discovery the *Type A behavior pattern.*

Why the name *Type A*? This time the advice came from a scientist, not an upholsterer. Once they had a pretty good idea that personality or behavior was behind heart disease, Friedman and Rosenman began applying for federal funding to conduct their studies; they requested funds to research a "coronary-prone personality." Their repeated requests were denied, apparently because the scientists who were reviewing the funding applications did not believe that personality could increase the risk of heart disease. Finally, a scientist at the National Institutes of Health advised the pair to come up with a more generic name for their research project—something that wouldn't stir the emotions and the biases of the decisionmakers. Friedman and Rosenman came up with the harmless label *Type A behavior;* they called the opposite personality simply *Type B*. With the new name, funding was approved.[50]

Friedman and Rosenman ventured where no man had dared in making two bold proclamations:

1. There are literal biochemical reasons why behavior can increase the risk for coronary heart disease.
2. Certain behavior patterns can be used as a tool for predicting who will get heart disease—not just as a detail to be confirmed at a postmortem exam.

The two cardiologists worked out several ways of measuring Type A behavior and set about conducting a series of preliminary studies that confirmed their theories. The results were as Friedman and Rosenman had hoped, but they were ruled to be scientifically circumstantial.

In 1960 the two began what was to become the definitive study on Type A behavior pattern: The Western Collaborative Group Study. Working out of San Francisco's Mt. Zion Hospital, Friedman and Rosenman found 3154 men, aged thirty-nine to fifty-nine years who did not show any signs of existing coronary heart disease. Most of the men chosen for the study were white, middle- and upper-level executives. They were tested at the beginning of the study and classified as either Type A or Type B, and any traditional risk factors (such as cigarette smoking or obesity) were recorded.

The men were then observed carefully for eight and a half years. Researchers noted which of the men showed any manifestations of coronary heart disease— angina pectoris (chest pain resulting from arteriosclerosis), "silent" heart attack (changes in the electrocardiogram without physical symptoms), a heart attack requiring hospitalization, or death due to coronary artery disease.[51]

About half of the men were classified as Type A at the beginning of the study, and the other half as Type B. By the end of the eight and a half years, those with existing risk factors were significantly more likely to have developed coronary artery disease. The more risk factors an individual manifested, the greater his chances of developing heart disease. The Type A theory held up under scrutiny: Those who had been classified as Type A at the beginning of the study were more than twice as likely to get heart disease as those who had been classified as Type B. The Type As ran into problems in every category: They developed more angina, had more silent heart attacks, suffered more overt heart attacks, and fell victim to more coronary deaths. They even had more second heart attacks if they survived an initial one.[52]

There were skeptics. Some claimed that Type A behavior simply resulted from other risk factors (if you had heart disease, for example, you might be more in a hurry to accomplish your goals because your life span was shorter). Others said that Type A led to other risk factors (a Type A personality is probably more likely to smoke and drink, for example). But, despite criticism, the Western Collaborative Group Study succeeded in establishing Type A behavior as an *independent* risk factor for heart disease.[53]

It seemed that Friedman and Rosenman had eloquently proven their hypothesis. Type A behavior was added to the list of heart disease risks, and was accepted as such for nearly two decades.

The MRFIT Study

Then the ax fell—and the confusion began. Data flooded in from a second study, one even larger than the Western Collaborative Group Study, that cast doubt on the relationship between Type A personality and coronary heart disease. The National Heart, Lung, and Blood Institute figured that if people reduced their risk factors, their chances of developing heart disease would also be reduced. They hoped to launch a study that would prove exactly that and then fund a massive public education campaign that would help people identify and reduce their risks.

The study, begun in 1973 and concluded in 1982, was called the Multiple Risk Factor Intervention Trial (MRFIT). At a cost of more than $100 million, researchers studied more than 12,000 men who did not yet have signs of heart disease but who did have specific factors that placed them at high risk for a heart attack. The risk factors included high blood pressure, high cholesterol levels, and a cigarette smoking habit. Each man was also classified as Type A or Type B; to make sure that classifications were accurate, Rosenman himself made the final determination of status.

The more than 12,000 men enrolled in the study were then put in programs to reduce their heart attack risk. Medical treatment reduced blood pressure, diet and medication brought down cholesterol levels, and men stopped smoking. Researchers found exactly what they had expected, with one important exception: *They found no relationship between Type A behavior and any kind of coronary heart disease event.* Of ten subsequent studies conducted during the late 1970s and early 1980s, eight also failed to confirm the Type A hypothesis.[54]

"Second-Generation" Studies

As if that weren't confusing and disheartening enough to the Type A proponents, more study results surfaced in 1988: Those in the Western Collaborative Group Study who had suffered heart attacks during the eight and a half years of the study were followed for a total of twenty-two years. The researchers learned that if the men survived the first twenty-four hours after a heart attack, the Type A men actually had a significantly *better* long-term survival rate. In fact, they died at only about half the rate of the Type Bs who had heart attacks.

Armed with these statistics, critics of the Type A theory scoffed. But advocates of the theory were not about to give up. They began what pioneer researcher Redford Williams calls the second generation of Type A research. They learned that Type A is more of a risk factor for those under age fifty years and that it varies as a risk factor depending on the level of cholesterol in the blood.

In the meantime, a growing number of scientists were investigating the relation between personality and heart disease. Leading researchers in the coronary heart disease field found that not all cholesterol was "bad": low-density lipoprotein, one kind of cholesterol, did indeed increase the risk of coronary disease, but another kind of cholesterol, high-density lipoprotein, actually seemed to offer *protection* against heart disease. And so, the researchers wondered, could there also be a "good" and a "bad" component of Type A behavior? Could Type A behavior—or at least part of it—still hold up as a viable risk factor for coronary heart disease?

Several years of research and a great deal of hard work on the part of leading researchers like Friedman, Rosenman, and Williams proved that the hunch was true: There was a "good" and a "bad" part of Type A behavior—or at least components of Type A behavior that were relatively harmless and others that formed what researchers now call the "toxic core" of the personality type. With that discovery, both sides of the controversy have been placated. Some components of Type A behavior (the good ones) can indeed increase the chances of survival after a heart attack. But other components of Type A behavior (the bad ones, the toxic core) can significantly increase the risk of suffering the heart attack in the first place.

Characteristics of the Coronary-Prone Personality

In the decades since the Type A, or coronary-prone, personality was first identified by researchers, it has been perhaps one of the most scrutinized areas of medical research—and certainly one of those most studied by scientists interested in behavioral influences on health. While these researchers may disagree on its precise influence on health, one finding has continued to emerge: The general consensus among researchers is that Type A is not so much a specific personality style as it is a set of behaviors. Those behaviors, say the researchers, are related to exaggerated neuroendocrine responses that then produce the characteristic behaviors (such as time urgency, hostility, and anger).[55]

When Type A behavior was first described by Friedman and Rosenman, it was called "the hurry sickness," partly because its victims seemed to be in such a hurry. An entire shopping list of characteristics were attributed to the Type A personality, and Americans intent on reducing their cardiac risk started sizing themselves up against the identified traits.

The Probably Harmless Behaviors

Whoever named Type A the hurry sickness had probably watched plenty of these people dash around. Type As never slow down; they eat, walk, and talk quickly. Type As are extremely time conscious: They hate to be late, and they hate to be kept waiting. Standing in line is extremely annoying to a Type A personality. In research, Type A personalities have expressed the notion that success comes from doing things quickly. They feel guilty when they are relaxing. In fact, they can't even relax when they are *supposed* to relax. Type As simply don't know how to relax. Even on vacation, they feel a pressing need to be in motion, to be doing something they believe to be useful, instead of just "lying around."[56]

Nor do typical Type A personalities do only one thing at a time. They almost always try two or three things simultaneously. A Type A executive, for example, eats a sandwich at his desk while talking on the phone to a colleague and filling out a monthly sales report. Another Type A washes dishes while she watches a television program and talks on the phone to a friend.

Type A personalities are extremely competitive and tend to "keep score" of even insignificant and trivial situations. Almost everyone is competitive when it comes to professional sports or a highly sought-after promotion, but a Type A personality acts that way even in a game of checkers with a child. Extreme Type As compete when there's nothing to compete for and no one to compete against. They simply have to be the fastest, the smartest, the brightest, and the best.

A key characteristic of Type A behavior pattern is aggression—and an aggressive style of speech. Other Type A characteristics include an insatiable drive for success, high ambition, impatience, insecurity, and a constant drive to control others and the environment. Type A personalities tend to set unrealistic goals, and they tend to use other people to achieve their goals. Many are selfish, easily bored, compulsive, and unobservant. Many Type A personalities live dangerously, and with time and fatigue, may develop a tendency toward self-destructive behavior.

A Type A personality often can be spotted just by casual observation. Type A personalities have some telltale ways of moving, talking and gesturing. They may glare or look disgusted. You're likely to see facial tautness; rapid and jerky movements; rapid eye blinking; tic-like lifting of the eyebrows; tongue clicking; head nodding; repetitive hand, arm, and leg movements; rapid speech, often explosive or staccato; and overforceful gestures, such as a clenched fist or a pointed finger.[57]

Friedman, who originated the concept, says that there are five basic characteristics of the Type A personality. One is free-floating hostility, part of the toxic core that will be discussed in greater detail later. The other four characteristics still hold up after almost three decades of extensive research: insecurity of status, hyperaggressiveness, sense of time urgency, and the drive to self-destruction.

Insecurity of Status

Occasionally, persons who exhibit Type A behavior are truly caught in a position that demands superhuman efforts; much more frequently, however, their careers or family demands are no different than those of others. According to Friedman, Type As struggle ceaselessly and senselessly to accomplish more and to involve themselves in more, not because demands are being placed on them but because they are placing the demands on themselves. Friedman theorizes that the typical Type A struggles because of a hidden lack of self-esteem and a need to prove himself.

Friedman, who has studied a number of famed Type A personalities, found that most of them—including the presidents of huge corporations, bank executives, distinguished military officials, presidents of universities, film stars, and even presidents of the United States—had hidden insecurities. To make up for those insecurities, to soothe their fears about themselves, they dived in with both feet, working furiously to immerse themselves in important and prestigious activities.

Type As are not generally reacting to what others say or think about them. Most are reacting to what they think of themselves. History is replete with Type A personalities who drove themselves because of their own estimation of themselves. William James pointed out almost a century ago that self-esteem depends on the balance between what we expect to achieve and what we do in actuality achieve. If our own expectations far outweigh our achievements, we will suffer from inadequate self-esteem, even though the world may consider our achievements to be spectacular. A world-renowned heart surgeon who pioneers life-saving methods may not think his accomplishments are worthy enough if he expects to save every patient he encounters.

Hyperaggressiveness

Plenty of people are aggressive, and they are not necessarily Type A personalities. Ordinary aggression denotes a desire to compete and win, a wish to achieve. Aggression is often coupled with ordinary ambition and is often manifested by those who set goals and work to achieve them. Some use aggression as a form of self-assertion; however, aggression is different from assertiveness, which couples a courageous honesty about one's opinion with a type of kindness in the expression of that position.

Hyperaggression—excessive aggression—is different: It is marked by a ruthless, driving desire to prevail and to dominate. That desire to dominate is at all costs, totally disregarding the feelings or fundamental rights of others. In some cases, it even involves an attempt to destroy the self-esteem of others—an emotional drive that aims to strip others of their security.

Type As at risk play games not for the enjoyment or the leisure, but to win. They are not merely satisfied with winning, either; they must prove all other players to be worthless and stupid. Someone once said that an aggressive Type A personality couldn't even play a game of Scrabble with a group of children without soundly defeating all of them.

Hyperaggression is often evident early in the life of a Type A person. Friedman remembers one psychologist claiming that he could pinpoint the Type A babies in a hospital nursery at the age of a few days.

Sense of Time Urgency

The sense of time urgency manifest in Type A personalities comes from the desire to accomplish too much in too short a time. The Type A is forever setting unrealistic deadlines, vowing to accomplish too much or an unrealistic number of things, and constantly volunteering to take on even more tasks in the face of near-total exhaustion. The Type A personality copes with the incredible pressure of hurry sickness in two ways: (1) by speeding up all activities; and (2) trying to think of or do more than one thing at a time.

In an effort to speed up, Type A personalities walk faster, talk faster, drive faster, eat faster, read faster, and move faster than their more easygoing counterparts. They are always in a hurry. They will do almost anything to avoid waiting in a line, even a short line at a restaurant, a bank, or a ticket counter. They often abandon a project altogether if it involves waiting in a line. They become hostile and irritated if they have to wait for five minutes at the dentist's office; they bristle with anger if a business associate does not arrive for their lunch appointment at precisely the prearranged time.

(Friedman described the epitome of a man possessed by hurry sickness: He shaved with two electric razors so he could save time by shaving both sides of his face at the same time. Another researcher, reporting on Friedman's patients, recalls one who liquefied his food in a blender so he wouldn't have to waste time chewing—and still another who saved time spent going to the bathroom by keeping a bottle at his desk.[58])

When they can no longer speed up, Type A personalities often cram their waking hours with accelerated thoughts, plans, and activities. Still not convinced that they are making the most of their time, they try to think about or do two or more things at a time. Such "polyphasic" activity, involving mental time sharing (the flitting back and forth between subjects) has been shown to induce distress. (Many stress-reduction programs involve primarily training the mind to focus completely on one thing at a time.)[59]

In our hurry-sick society, some of these polyphasic practices have become so common that we take them for granted. The Type A may attempt to watch television, read the evening newspaper, and eat dinner simultaneously. Friedman said that some even watch two football games on two different television sets at the same time. A woman executive may leaf through her morning mail, compose an agenda for the afternoon staff meeting, read her phone messages, and breeze through a trade journal while she talks to a client on the telephone. Many Type A personalities jot down notes on index cards—ideas, memoranda, or plans while attending church, sitting in a staff meeting, riding the bus, at a symphony concert, even at a funeral.

Researchers have even studied the issue of time urgency in relationship to entire cities or regions, and the evidence holds up. Cities and regions with the fastest pace of life are also populated with people who have the highest incidence of coronary heart disease. The "speed of the environment" seems to predict the likelihood of coronary heart disease as well as Type A predicts it, no matter how the research findings are corrected for age and other risk factors.

One reason for these findings, say some researchers, may be that Type A personalities are drawn to areas where there is a fast pace of life. They may, in a sense, help to create it. University of Utah social psychologist Timothy Smith says that Type As both seek *and* create time-urgent surroundings, so the entire scenario may feed on itself.[60]

The Drive to Self-Destruction

After studying Type A personalities for more than a decade, Friedman and Rosenman were forced to admit the difficult reality that many Type As, even the good-natured, optimistic ones, seem to harbor an unconscious drive to self-destruct. Friedman uses the example of a powerful head of an international corporation who failed to file income tax returns year after year, was finally caught, pleaded no contest, and was forced to resign from his position. His excuse was that he had no time to fill out the forms. Those who worked with him, however, suspected that the stress and strain of the position caused the executive to do something that would give him a release. Another example is President Richard Nixon. Henry Kissinger, who served in Nixon's cabinet and became one of his closest advisors, commented, "It was hard to avoid the impression that Nixon, who thrived on crisis, also craved disasters."

Troubled by the evidence, Friedman began to interview heart attack victims during recovery and convalescence. He was startled to learn that more than half had expected the heart attack before it ever occurred—and that they had, in fact, yearned for it. For some, it was the chance to finally be released from the cycle of stress and pressure; for others, it was a chance to at last lay quietly in a hospital bed and concentrate on only one thing, getting better.

What these key characteristics add up to, according to Friedman and Rosenman, is "joyless striving." Type A personalities are hard-driving, achievement-oriented people who seem to yearn for the approval of others but who secretly castigate and criticize themselves. As Rosenman puts it, they conduct a constant "postmortem" on themselves, magnifying even minor errors and constantly demanding more of themselves. Rosenman believes that most are terrified by underlying feelings of insecurity and inadequacy, and that their constant upward striving is merely an attempt to allay feelings of fear, depression, and loss of prestige. Where most find great joy in accomplishment, these people find no joy; they are plagued instead by an even deeper torment.

The "Toxic Core" of Type A Behavior

The hurry-sickness attributes of a Type A personality are probably the best known, but they are also the least detrimental to health. The second generation studies, which exploded the coronary risk of specific components of Type A behavior, found some behavior elements far more dangerous than others. Rather than the hurry tendency, the toxic core of Type A personality (the set of traits that creates major health risks) consists instead of hostility, anger, cynicism, suspiciousness, and excessive self-involvement.

Free-Floating Hostility

Free-floating hostility is a permanent, deep-seated anger that hovers quietly until some trivial incident causes it to rupture to the surface in a burst of hostility. Researchers Margaret Chesney, Nanette Frautschi, and Ray H. Rosenman believe that Type A persons often have an "enhanced potential for hostility." This potential can be created by either the genetic or learned causes discussed earlier. Because the enhanced potential is chronic, or ever present, even minor irritations or upsets can trigger a hostile rage. Type As who have free-floating hostility react with seething anger and dwell on the objects of their despising. They become irritated and explosive and find it difficult not to become physically abusive. Sometimes the anger that accompanies free-floating hostility is displaced: A woman who gets angry and hostile in a traffic jam may lash out at a child in the back seat, for example.

The kind of free-floating hostility manifested by a Type A personality is always there, waiting to latch onto something—no matter how trivial or silly or illogical. A driver explodes if the car in front of him does not pull out of the intersection quickly enough. A shopper becomes loudly profane at the prospect of having to wait in line at the grocery store. He launches into an abusive tirade when a teenaged boy walks by with a loud radio.

Important and still-controversial studies have made a startling conclusion about the hostility factor: Apparently you can have many of the characteristics typically associated with the Type A personality—such as competitive drive, an aggressive personality, and impatience—without running the risks of a heart attack *as long as you are not hostile.*

Chapter 8 details the physiological process of hostility and cites myriad studies that have shown hostility to be the most health-harming Type A trait. Renowned experts, such as Duke University's Redford Williams, point to hostility as one of the most crucial elements in heart disease. "We have strong evidence that hostility alone damages the heart," Williams emphasizes. In one study, hostility was shown to increase the risk of heart disease by a staggering seven times. "The kind of person at risk is someone who generally feels that other people are not to be trusted," Williams adds, "that they'll lie and cheat if they can get away with it."

In a report published in *Psychology Today*, the kind of personality Williams describes as being at highest risk is "deeply suspicious. They feel that they must remain constantly on guard against others, whom they believe are dishonest, antisocial, and immoral." The Duke University team of researchers claims that this kind of hostility predicts not only blockages in the coronary arteries, as measured by x-ray studies of patients suffering chest pains,[61] but also death from heart disease and other causes.[62]

Hostility, whether it is directed inward or outward, appears to be the key in determining which Type A personalities are most at risk for coronary disease. One study conducted by University of Maryland psychologist Aron Siegman shows that, in young patients, outward aggression and hostility are key to determining how much coronary artery blockage occurs.

"Hostility, anger, and their biological consequences are the toxic part of Type A behavior," Williams explains. "Hostility and anger not only account for the increased risk of developing coronary heart disease among Type A persons, but may also increase the risk of suffering other life-threatening illnesses as well." The other aspects of Type A behavior—such as being in a hurry and being competitive—appear to be harmful only to the extent that they activate one's hostility and anger."[63] Because hostility and its associated cynical mistrust are at the heart of Type A toxicity, references to Type A through the rest of the chapter will be to the hostile kind of Type A behavior.

Part of the reason hostile Type A personalities run a greater risk of heart disease is that they have a psychological short fuse. They more frequently trigger the cascade of potentially damaging hormones that are released as part of the fight-or-flight response. (See a detailed discussion of these hormones and their effects in Chapter 8.) As Williams puts it, "Trusting hearts may live longer because for them the biologic cost of situations that anger or irritate is lower."[64]

Another reason hostility may be correlated so strongly with heart disease is that people who are hostile tend to drive others away, and social support, social networking, and social integration have been repeatedly proven to be strong protectors of health. A ten-year study of 150 middle-aged Swedish men investigated the difference between Type As who had good social support and those who did not. Published in *Psychosomatic Medicine*, the results of the research were dramatic: The Type As who were socially isolated had three times the death rate from heart disease as did the Type As who were socially integrated.[65]

In summing up the importance of hostility as a toxic component of Type A personality, Williams says that the coronary-prone hostile personality has three parts: cynical mistrust of other people's motives, frequent feelings of anger, and aggressive expression of hostility toward others without regard for their feelings. "These are the people who, if they are waiting for an elevator and it's stopped on a higher floor, will immediately begin thinking that someone is purposely delaying the elevator and being inconsiderate," Williams explains. They are also the people who will, while standing in an express checkout line, count the items in the basket of the person in front of them and cast hostile glances if the limit is exceeded.[66]

Anger

Another part of the toxic core of the Type A behavior pattern is anger—defined by researchers as "an emotional state incorporating feelings ranging from irritation and aggravation to rage and fury."[67] (Anger is often confused with hostility, which is an habitual way of evaluating people or events in a negative, cynical, paranoid way.) Researchers now believe that it is the powerful combination of hostility and unexpressed anger that carries the greatest risk of heart disease.

The particular combination is deadly, say researchers, and it appears to have a much greater impact on health than any single factor. "It isn't the impatience, the ambition, or the work drive," says Redford Williams, explaining the health risk of Type A personality. "It's the anger: it sends your blood pressure skyrocketing. It provokes the body to create unhealthy chemicals. For hostile people, anger is poison."[68]

The greatest risks, researchers believe, are from hostility paired with unexpressed anger, or "anger-in," a specific way of reacting to the people or situations that make a person angry. People who harbor unexpressed anger are not able to express their angry feelings, even when those feelings are appropriate or justified.

Studies conducted by researchers at Duke University and Eckerd College show that people who tend to hold in their anger are at much higher coronary risk than people who vent anger. Researchers who have done extensive studies on the effects of anger have conclusively shown that repressed anger leads to a higher risk of developing a number of diseases, including rheumatoid arthritis and cancer. (Detailed discussions of this research are contained in Chapter 7.) The habit of suppressing anger is extremely common among Type A personalities.

There is some disagreement among researchers about the dangers of suppressing anger. Social psychologist Carol Tavris cites statistics from the Western Collaborative Group Study in her argument against expressing anger: The men most likely to have a heart attack were the ones who became angry more than once a week and who "blew up" more than once a week.

Some other researchers agree with Tavris that keeping cool is better than "blowing up." One study conducted at the University of Michigan School of Public Health measured the way that "cool reflection," suppression of anger, and expression of anger affected blood pressure. Research team director Ernest Harburg said that the healthiest approach was "cool reflection," acknowledging the anger but not expressing it with verbal or physical hostility.

Still other studies point the finger at "anger-out," a style of expressing anger by verbal or physical expression. In one study, eighty-five healthy patients screened at a preventive cardiology clinic were given a complete medical evaluation by a cardiologist, and a psychological evaluation. Each patient was rated on coronary disease risk using the Framingham Risk Factor Score, which evaluates classic risk factors for coronary disease. Researchers then studied various other behavior traits to see which correlated most closely with the Framingham Risk Scores (i.e., to see which were most likely to provide accurate risk information). Only "anger-out" was judged to be a significant risk factor for coronary heart disease.[69] Anger expressed in a hostile way can perpetuate both the causes and self-justification of the anger.

It appears that just the presence of ongoing anger may be more important than how it is expressed; thus, the value of cognitive therapy approaches that simply allow the anger to dissolve so it no longer needs to be expressed.

Cynicism

Cynicism, anger, and hostility are closely related emotions: As Redford Williams describes it, cynical mistrust of others is the driving force behind hostility. It almost starts a chain reaction, he explains:

> *Expecting that others will mistreat us, we are on the lookout for their bad behavior—and we can usually find it. This generates the frequent anger to which the hostile person is prone, and that anger, combined with a lack of empathy for others—a natural consequence of the poor opinion we hold of others in general—leads us to express our hostility overtly, in the form of aggressive acts towards others.[70]*

When cynicism is paired with hostility, the effects can be devastating to health. In one experiment, Duke University Medical Center psychologist Edward Suarez was able to measure the physiological responses of people who were hostile—and he was able to compare those people to people who were also cynical. Researchers asked a group of college students (some of whom were hostile and some of whom were not) to solve a difficult series of scrambled word puzzles. Physiological responses, such as blood pressure, were measured during the experiment.

At the end of the first part of the experiment, researchers found that there was no difference between the two groups as they were doing the puzzles. Then they added another factor designed to separate the students who were cynical: Researchers stood over the students while they were doing the puzzles and made snide remarks, things like, "Stop mumbling; I can't understand what you are saying"; "Remember, you're getting paid to do this."

Once the element of harassment was added, the students who were cynical showed sharp differences in physiological responses. The students who scored high on cynicism had higher blood pressure, higher blood flow, and more anger while they were doing the puzzles and being harassed. And their blood pressure remained high for fifteen minutes after they did the puzzle. Suarez attributes the changes in the cynical students to the fact that hostile people "view other people's actions and motives very cynically. They thought the researchers were 'out to get them,' felt threatened, and reacted, while low hostiles did not perceive the researchers' actions as a personal attack."[71]

Cynicism is detrimental to health and longevity, even when it's not paired with hostility. Scientists at the Center for the Study of Aging and Human Development at Duke University studied 500 people (half men, half women) with an average age of fifty-nine years. Each of the people in the study was given a personality test and then watched carefully for fifteen years to detect any major changes in health. According to the research results, men who are cynical are 48 percent more likely to die an early death than are men who are not cynical; cynical women are 29 percent more likely to suffer premature death. These percentages hold up even after classical risk factors (such as smoking, drinking, and cholesterol levels) were taken into consideration.

Data from the study show that certain diseases are also more likely to afflict cynical people. Almost half of the premature deaths among them were a result of heart disease; an additional one-fifth were due to other cardiovascular disorders. An additional fifth were attributable to cancer.[72]

One reason behind increased illness and premature death among cynical people may be the lack of social ties—a phenomenon that has been solidly linked to disease and mortality. According to John C. Barefoot, the study director, "Other research suggests that people with strong social ties may enjoy strengthened immunity, so obviously someone who is mistrusting to the point of costing himself such a supportive network is sacrificing this sort of advantage."[73]

Suspiciousness

Suspiciousness is a trait closely allied to cynicism. In the study conducted by John C. Barefoot at Duke University's Center for the Study of Aging and Human Development, he noted that "people who are suspicious are constantly on guard, and there's evidence to suggest that this may raise levels of potentially harmful stress-induced hormones in the blood."[74] In the same study, incidentally, the suspicious people fared no better than the cynical ones. Those who scored high on a test of suspiciousness were significantly more likely to become ill and die during the fifteen years the study was conducted. The greater risk for illness and death due to suspiciousness held up even after researchers took into account other risk factors, such as age, sex, physician rating of functional health, smoking, cholesterol, and alcohol intake.[75]

In a separate study, Friedman and Rosenman studied 1990 middle-aged men who had not yet developed coronary heart disease. Each man was given the Minnesota Multiphasic Personality Inventory as well as a questionnaire that evaluated sixteen personality factors. The study subjects were then monitored for five years to determine which ones became ill or died. Those most likely to develop coronary heart disease were the suspicious ones. The other two factors leading to a greater risk for coronary heart disease were greater independence in social relationships and greater feelings of inner tension.[76]

Excessive Self-Involvement

One of the most interesting of the new theories about Type A behavior and the potential link to heart disease points to a personality trait that researchers think is a killer: excessive self-involvement. A person whose language is excessively peppered with references to *I, me, mine,* and other self-references seems to be at the greatest risk of all for coronary heart disease.

A trio of researchers working under the auspices of the National Heart, Lung, and Blood Institute and the California Affiliate of the American Heart Association studied a group of students whom they had determined to be Type A personalities. Two findings were significant: (1) Blood pressures increased when these students made self-references; and (2) those with Type A personalities made twice as many references to themselves as did those with Type B personalities.

The original study involved only fifty-nine participants, so the trio of researchers, Larry Scherwitz, Lewis Graham II, and Dean Ornish, decided on a more extensive study. They followed almost 13,000 middle-aged men for six to eight years, noting which were Type A and which Type B, and which had the tendency to excessive self-involvement. The longer-term, more involved study bore out the findings of the first study: Those who developed coronary heart disease (especially those who died from it) were those who tended to be excessively self-involved. Based on study results, the researchers believed that the degree of self-involvement helped dictate the severity of heart disease: The more self-involved, the more likely the patient was to develop fatal heart disease.

Studying a group of 156 men who had confirmed coronary heart disease, researchers stated, "We found that the most self-involved patients had more severe coronary artery disease . . . and were more likely to have suffered a heart attack already, had poorer heart muscle contraction and could not exercise as long on the treadmill as the less self-involved ones."

Self-involvement seems to be such an important factor because people who are self-involved tend to be "hot reactors"; the excessive self-involvement may be what actually *causes* the hostility and anger that have been so strongly linked to Type A heart disease. Researchers quoted in Rodale Press's newsletter *Men's Health* pointed out that self-involved Type A personalities who are "ambitious, competitive, or time urgent for purely selfish reasons" may be "at greater risk than if they are ambitious to serve others or higher ideals." These researchers point out the relative good health of what they have dubbed the *Ghandi Type A* personalities, those who may not be at particular risk for heart disease, despite their hard work and exacting standards, because they are involved in serving others.

The facts are that self-involvement may be related to, and often accompanied by, other dangerous Type A traits such as hostility. In his research on the impact of hostility, Ted Dembroski of Eckerd College found that people who are hostile also tend to be heavily self-involved. Using structured interviews to measure the amount of hostility, Dembroski also noticed that those scoring highest—the most hostile ones—used the most references to self (*I, me,* and *mine,* for example).

In a different study, cited in the *Advances,* researchers used seventy-five structured interviews of middle-aged men. Those who practiced "self-aggrandizement" (behavior that exaggerated their own importance or called attention to their status) were also the ones found to be the most hostile. In fact, the level of self-aggrandizement correlated more strongly with hostility than did any other factor.

Researchers are not yet sure why hostility and self-involvement seem so closely linked. Scherwitz, Graham, and Ornish hypothesize that it may be due to the fact that people who are highly self-involved become threatened by any-one claiming to be comparably important. They may react to that "threat" with hostility, and the subject of hostility may be either the threatening person or the self-involved victim. The need to prove oneself important underlies both the self-involvement and the competitive hostility.

Workaholics

The characteristics of the Type A personality lead many to confuse Type A with the contemporary affliction of "workaholism," but a workaholic isn't necessarily a Type A. Yale researcher Marilyn Machlowitz, who wrote a dissertation on workaholics, defines them as people "whose desire to work hard and long is in-trinsic, and whose work habits almost always exceed the prescriptions of the job and the expectations of those with whom or for whom they work."[77] Machlowitz further defines the workaholic as "that blur of a person rushing by with an over-flowing briefcase, dictating into a tape recorder, checking the time, and munch-ing on a sandwich."[78]

John M. Rhoads, a professor of psychiatry at Duke University Medical Cen-ter, says that workaholics are "people who just don't know when to stop work-ing. Some people seem to lack an inner monitoring device for regulating the work–rest–recreation balance. Plagued by a compulsive need to work, they deny the existence of fatigue and push themselves beyond reason."[79] And, he adds, anyone, from a housewife to a school kid to a corporate executive, can become a workaholic.

Not all workaholics are Type As; in fact, most are Type B personalities. But there are some common characteristics of Type As and workaholics. For one, most workaholics tend to be intense, a characteristic also common to Type A per-sonalities. Other Type A traits common to workaholics include the tendency to work hard at making the most of their time, often eating while they work, and difficulty in taking a vacation. (Type A personalities find it extremely difficult to relax; workaholics don't like time away from the work routine.)

There are some important distinctions between the two, however. Type As tend to have a hard-driving, competitive approach to work because they crave the recognition and approval of others; most workaholics do it because they truly love to work. Type As play with the same feverish pitch they bring to the office; a workaholic simply prefers work over play and, given the choice, will work in-stead of play. Type As are driven and unhappy; many workaholics are satisfied, happy people who genuinely enjoy what they are doing. The difference lies in the motivation behind the hard-working busyness—one person driven by fear of fail-ure and the need to prove oneself worthy, the other by love of work and a sense of mission.

In a nutshell, Type As seek power, prestige, and impact. They are driven, ag-gressive, and high achievers who set almost impossible goals for themselves.

They are inflexible in meeting their self-imposed standards, and they batter their self-image if they begin to fail at them. They feel guilty when they sit back and relax. They are aggressively hostile, and have a low threshold for anger and frustration; they are usually impulsive.

Workaholics are characterized by intense and energetic activity; they sleep less than most people and have difficulty doing anything but working during their waking hours. They prefer work to play and often blur the distinction between work and play. They can and do work anywhere and everywhere and frequently eat while they work.

The real difference between workaholics and Type A personalities seems to lie with hostility. The workaholic seldom is hostile. The Type A is almost always hostile.

While Type A personalities are hostile and often unhappy, most workaholics, says Machlowitz, are happy. Four basic elements contribute to a workaholic's degree of happiness:

1. The acceptance of their work habits by their families.
2. The amount of autonomy and variety in their work.
3. The good match between their personal skills and those required by their job.
4. Their general state of health.[80]

If all four elements exist, happiness and workaholics almost always go hand in hand.

Richard G. Lonsdorf, a psychiatrist and professor of law at the University of Pennsylvania, agrees that workaholics are there for the sheer joy of it. "People whose life is their work are doing that because they like what they are doing," he explains. "Although there are some compulsive people who are compulsive about anything, it's true that workaholics often are very healthy people. And you usually don't find workaholics in jobs that don't interest them."[81]

When does workaholism become a health problem? According to Robert Rosen, director of the Institute on Organizational Health at the Washington Business Group on Health, an *inflexible* addiction to work is what is unhealthy: "If you're avoiding something or if the need for manipulation and power becomes the overriding fuel for the commitment to work, you're placing yourself at risk of affecting your health."[82] Researchers point out that most health problems occur when workaholics are mixed with nonworkaholics, either at home or in the office. And then, ironically, it's the *non*workaholic who usually pays the price in terms of health risks.

It's obvious, then, that workaholics aren't necessarily Type A personalities. In terms of achievement and occupational advancement, how do the Type A personalities fare? Is their time-urgency, goal-setting, hard-working way of doing things paying off? Some rationalize that their hard-charging, hostile, and unhealthy Type A behavior is worth it because of the future career success it ensures. Type As do work hard. One study of more than 2500 employed men and women in the Minneapolis-St. Paul area showed that among both sexes, Type A behavior was related to long work hours, high occupational mobility, and other attributes that would seem to guarantee career success,[83] but that's not usually what happens.

In one study that looked at the career advancement of the Type A personality, Dr. Muhammad Jamal, a professor of management at Concordia University in Montreal, studied 325 white-collar employees of a large Canadian manufacturing firm. In terms of quality of job performance, the Type B men and women actually did better than the Type A employees. Jamal then measured career progress by considering all the promotions obtained over the preceding five years. He found no difference between Type As and Type Bs, even though the male (but not female) Type As exerted "more effort on the job."[84] There may be a plausible explanation as to why the Type As lagged behind, says Jamal. Some of the characteristics of the Type A personality, "such as time urgency and outright hostility toward others, might have backfired, especially if their immediate boss happened to be a Type A."[85]

There could be another reason why the Type A personality gets passed over for promotions. According to Larry Pace, professor of management at the University of Tennessee, Type A personalities have the qualities often sought after in middle management (such as impatience, anger, aggression, and irritation). But, he says, the traits that make Type As effective midlevel plant managers don't always work well at the top.

According to Pace, upper-level personnel "need to be able to put out fires, not create excitement. That's where the laid-back Type Bs tend to shine."[86] Those at the top need the qualities most often associated with Type B behavior: the ability to take a global perspective, to encourage teamwork, and to defer judgment until all the facts are in. Type As, he says, excel at speed and solitary activity; Type Bs are best at tasks "requiring long-term decision-making and complexity of judgment." Type Bs are better able to lift and inspire others to work for them, usually creating a team effort that is more productive than the rugged individualist's.

Effects of Coronary-Prone Behavior on the Body

There's a reason why coronary-prone behavior causes health problems: It literally wreaks havoc on the body. In his book *Superimmunity*, psychologist Paul Pearsall gives a vivid description:

> *The supersystem sizzles with neurochemical changes, we roast in our hormonal stew, and, as if by some universal wisdom, the body can be stopped in its tracks by adopting an "enough is enough" strategy. We overload, our heads start pounding for attention, our hearts get attacked for our lack of intimacy, and our vessels cause the doctor's mercury gauge to warn us that things are getting too high. Even our bowels can get irritated with us and show their displeasure in their own unique language. Somewhere in our bodies, through our overuse and abuse of our supersystems, something is burning out.*[87]

What happens, essentially, is that the body responds to what it believes is a threat, an actual or threatened loss of control. Type A behavior, essentially, is an exaggerated stress response, and, as when stressed, the body begins pumping out hormones needed to fight or flee. It's the classic fight-or-flight reaction we all have in response to stress, whether mental or physical. As part of the reaction, physical changes take place.

People who are under stress have the fight-or-flight response temporarily, and then they return to normal until they are again presented with a stressful situation. The hostile Type A personality, however, lives in a chronic state of what Redford Williams calls vigilant observation.[88] The body is on constant alert. It never relaxes. And the body—especially the cardiovascular system—pays the price. Apparently, humans long ago evolved a fight-or-flight response system to protect us when confronted with threats such as being chased by wolves. But seldom are we chased by wolves today, except for the wolves we create in our heads, the *have tos, shoulds,* and *forced tos.* When thus stressed today, however, both fighting and fleeing are usually inappropriate.

Chapter 8 gives a detailed discussion of the hormones released in response to the Type A personality; they are hormones that boost a number of responses. The result is increases in circulation, blood cholesterol level, blood triglyceride levels, and blood sugar level. In brief, the physical effects of the Type A behavior pattern begin in the hypothalamus, a complex portion of the brain that lies at its base, directly over the pituitary gland. The hypothalamus is like a coding device, sending out signals to various parts of the body in response to emotion. The anger and hostility that are chronically experienced by a Type A personality are processed by the hypothalamus as it would process an intense physical struggle. As a result, the system is bathed with excessive catecholamines, epinephrine (adrenaline), testosterone, estrogen, thyroxine, and insulin.

Unfortunately, the Type A's body is not engaged in a temporary fight or flight phenomenon; instead, the anger and hostility and struggle become chronic, so the body is always pumped full of excess hormones. Even during supposedly "low-voltage" periods of the day, Type As expose their bodies to "high-voltage" chemicals that can damage and even eventually destroy it. Some of the most profound effects of chronic overload of stress hormones are increased levels of cholesterol and fat, blood platelet changes, alterations in the heart and arteries, excess insulin secretion, magnesium deficiency, and defective immune system function.

Increased Cholesterol and Fat Levels

Stress hormones pumped into the blood cause the serum cholesterol and blood fat levels to increase. The higher levels of hostility among Type A personalities have been linked specifically to higher levels of total blood cholesterol as well as increased levels of low-density lipoproteins ("bad" cholesterol). The link between Type A hostility and increased cholesterol levels gets stronger with age; the older the person, the higher the cholesterol level is apt to be driven by Type A behaviors.[89]

Not only does Type A behavior drive up cholesterol levels, but it makes it more difficult for the body to compensate. The additional hormones associated with Type A behavior cause the Type A personality to take three to four times longer to rid the blood of serum cholesterol following each meal, as compared with the Type B personality. Therefore, the linings of the arteries are constantly exposed to serum cholesterol in its most damaging form. Particularly in the presence of increased norepinephrine, an adrenaline-like hormone that damages the vessel lining, cholesterol works its way through the inner lining of the artery walls, plaque builds up, arteries narrow and clog, cell damage occurs, and coronary heart disease is born.

Some of the earliest research conducted by Friedman and Rosenman at Mt. Zion Hospital in San Francisco gave evidence of the link between Type A behavior and increased cholesterol levels.[90] A group of accountants reported to the hospital on a regular basis and gave blood samples, which were analyzed for cholesterol level. Friedman and Rosenman noticed that the cholesterol levels were quite low and fairly stable throughout the year, with a few exceptions: When the accountants were required to do more and more work in less and less time (a hallmark of Type A personality), the cholesterol levels increased dramatically. For the accountants, it was the weeks leading up to the January 1 and April 15 tax deadlines. Similarly, studies of medical students showed that cholesterol levels rose at test times, then fell when the stress had passed. There is a destructive synergy between hostility, harassing situations, and high cholesterol levels. Any one of the three in the absence of the other two is less toxic. Type A behavior provokes all three.

Blood Platelet Adhesiveness

Some of the neurotransmitter hormones released in response to either hostile Type A behavior or mental depression cause the blood platelets (the blood-clotting elements) to stick to each other. The platelets then attach to the plaque that is already narrowing the coronary artery walls. The buildup of platelets on the plaque speeds its growth and causes thickening of the plaque.

As tiny capillaries become starved of blood by arterial plaque buildup, tissues fed by the capillaries die and coronary heart disease sets in. Another hazard is associated with the adherence of blood platelets. Clots that form in the narrowed arteries cut off the blood supply to a portion of the heart muscle, precipitating a heart attack, or myocardial infarction.[91]

Overworking the Heart and Arteries

Increases in adrenaline among Type A personalities cause the heart to work harder, at the same time causing spasm of the blood vessels that feed the heart. Other hormonal changes accelerate hardening of the arteries. Still others drive up blood pressure.[92]

Scientists have long recognized that Type A behavior leads to a dramatically higher risk of coronary artery disease, but they weren't sure why or how the process took place. Recent research has provided the clues scientists were looking for and has helped unlock the mystery of the mechanisms surrounding Type A behavior and heart disease.

One phase of research that provided answers was conducted by Duke University researchers Redford Williams and James Blumenthal. They concentrated their efforts on patients who were undergoing coronary arteriography procedure in which a dye is injected into the coronary arteries (the vessels that feed blood to the heart muscle) so that researchers can "see" the inside of the arteries.[93]

Williams and Blumenthal suspected that patients who are Type A personalities would have a higher tendency toward coronary blockages, and they put their theory to the test. Over the span of a year, Blumenthal interviewed patients who were at the hospital for coronary arteriogramphy. Based on the results of the interview, each patient was categorized as either Type A or Type B. He then compared the interview records with the coronary arteriogram results.

The results were, in Williams's words, "as predicted and quite striking." Of the patients who had few or no blockages in their coronary arteries, about half were Type A and half Type B. Among those with more extensive blockage, more than 70 percent were Type A. And among those with very severe blockage (at least two major arteries totally shut down), more than 90 percent were Type A.[94]

A sophisticated test conducted by Jeffrey P. Kahn and his colleagues at Columbia University sheds light on exactly how Type A behavior may damage the arteries. The process has to do with microscopic receptors on the outside of the muscle cells lining the coronary arteries; these receptors control arterial blood flow by constricting and dilating the coronary arteries.[95] One set of receptors, the alpha receptors, cause the muscle cells to constrict the coronary arteries; this reduces the volume of arterial blood flow. The other set of receptors, the beta receptors, cause the muscle cells to relax the coronary arteries, increasing blood flow. In the experiments, Kahn and colleagues found that the more pronounced were the Type A personality traits, the greater was the stimulation of the alpha receptors and the less the stimulation of the beta receptors. Translated, Type A behavior causes chronic constriction of the coronary arteries, hampering blood flow and leading to the risk of disease.

Excess Insulin Secretion

Excessive secretion of insulin usually signals a breakdown in the body's ability to utilize fats and sugars. In Type A personality, constant prompting from the system causes a chronic overabundance of insulin that is pumped from the pancreas. This causes rapid deterioration of the structure of the arteries. Combined with the tendency of Type A personalities to secrete other hormones detrimental to the intricate network of blood vessels, the excess insulin can lead to severe coronary artery disease.

Magnesium Deficiency

Magnesium deficiency can complicate heart disease. Hormones secreted in excessive amounts by Type As include the catecholamines and the steroid cortisol. These cause the body to excrete excessive amounts of magnesium, leading to magnesium deficiency. During any kind of stress, magnesium is released from the cells into the bloodstream. If that's as far as it goes, the body recovers; the magnesium is eventually reabsorbed into the cells. But when too many catecholamines and steroids are circulating in the blood, as with the Type A personality, the magnesium is chased out of the bloodstream and into the urine, in which it is excreted from the body.

In one study, researchers exposed a group of healthy Type As and Type Bs to a stress-provoking situation. The Type A personalities reacted to the stressful situation much more dramatically than the Type Bs: Their urine contained significantly higher levels of both catecholamines and magnesium, and 80 percent of the Type As (as compared with only 44 percent of the Type Bs) experienced a drop in the level of magnesium in the red blood cells. The magnesium depletion can lead to muscle spasm, increased heart rhythm, irregularity, and sudden death.

Immune System Function

Studies have borne out the fact that Type A personalities have fewer defensive antibodies in their saliva. As a result, they can't fight off bacteria and viruses as easily and are more likely to develop serious upper respiratory tract infections. Further studies show that Type As are less able to cope with psychological stress that afffects overall immune function. When the immune system is compromised, the risk for many kinds of diseases increases significantly.

The Emotional Effects of Type A Behavior

The anger and hostility that accompany Type A behavior are apt to have emotional effects. Researchers looking into the emotions and lifestyles of Type A personalities are finding some interesting trends. Significant links exist between Type A hostility (with its attendant insecurity) and the neurochemical changes that cause depression, which has also now been shown to be a significant coronary risk factor (see Chapter 10). Many of the same neuroendocrine problems described above for Type A are also features of depression. Overt mental depression occurs more frequently in Type A people,[96] and hostility improves with antidepressant medication.[97]

Type A hostility can especially affect relationships and social support networks. According to a pair of researchers in St. Louis, a woman's personality can have tremendous effect on whether a relationship lasts. Psychologists Michael Strube and Lisa Rosenberger claim that "whether a woman is a Type A or B may make the crucial difference in whether a new romance lasts," and the woman's personality seems to be much more crucial than the man's.[98]

In studying dating couples at Washington University in St. Louis, Strube and Rosenberger found that Type A traits, including competitiveness, desire to control others, and time urgency, actually gave some women a head start on lasting relationships. The women with Type A traits were able to react twice as quickly as the women with Type B traits. But that's where the advantage ended. Six months later, Type B women were twice as likely to be in a satisfying, stable, and ongoing relationship, no matter what the man's personality type. Apparently, a woman's personality is most important during dating, whereas a man's personality grows in importance once the relationship becomes permanent. Studies have shown, for example, that, among married people, both partners are less happy if the man is a Type A.

In recent research published in the *Journal of Applied Social Psychology*, it was shown that Type As fail to display the sensitivity and understanding that a long-term relationship requires. Psychologist Don Byrne of the State University of New York at Albany says that this not only limits the Type A's chances of tying the marriage knot, but also greatly increases the likelihood of divorce. According to Byrne, "Type A behavior creates a 'vicious cycle' within the marital structure. Type As inadvertently create a stressful home environment with their self-centered need for achievement, then respond to the stress by withdrawing farther into their work, alienating their spouses even more."[99]

Marriage and the kind of spouse you have can have a significant effect on your risk for heart disease. Researchers at SRI International in Menlo Park, California, studied partners in 130 marriages to find out what kind of an effect wives had on their husbands. A Type A man who is married to a well-educated woman with at least one year of college under her belt is significantly more likely to have coronary heart disease than a Type B man who is married to the same kind of woman. As reported in the *American Journal of Epidemiology*, women who think it's important to get ahead but who are frustrated in the attempt or don't believe they will, tend to be married to men with heart disease, regardless of whether the men are Type A or Type B personalities. Such a woman probably puts stress on the marriage and home life, which could be the answer.

According to the study results, if the wife is not frustrated—but is merely educated, active, and dominant, her husband's risk of developing coronary artery disease increases if he is a Type A personality. If he is a Type B personality, on the other hand, having an educated, active, and dominant wife actually seems to protect the husband from developing heart disease.

There can be considerable impact on women in marriage, too, say researchers Debra Weaver and Darlene Shaw of the Medical University of South Carolina. After studying a number of marriages, the psychologists found that, on average, Type A women had worse marriages than Type B women. There could be a number of reasons, they say. A highly ambitious, hard-driving Type A woman could find the confines of home and family too restrictive, for example. The researchers did find that Type A women did better when married to less competitive, more relaxed Type B men who were uninterested in competing with them than if they were married to Type A men.

Type A personalities have also been shown to have a weaker network of social support than more easygoing Type Bs. Psychiatrist Karen A. Matthews of the University of Pittsburgh points out that some of the "abrasive" interpersonal traits of the Type A personality (such as hostility) may interfere with social relationships, leading to increased social isolation.[100] Cynicism has been shown to be highly predictive of marital difficulties. Myriad studies over a number of years have shown that lack of strong social support increases the risk of not only heart disease but many other diseases as well and may be one of the reasons, according to Matthews, why Type A personalities have an increased risk for heart disease.

Others agree with Matthews. Researchers at Duke University Medical Center say that, based on their findings, "Type As with low levels of social support had more severe coronary artery disease than Type As with high levels of social support. . . . These results are consistent with the hypothesis that social support moderates the long-term health consequences of the Type A behavior pattern."[101] An example of this was a study of 10,000 Israeli men at high coronary risk. Those with loving support from their wives had half the angina incidence of those who lacked such support.[102]

Type A Behavior and Heart Disease Risk

According to some researchers, "the most important trait in the coronary-prone person is the existence of the hostile Type A pattern."[103] The Type A who seems most at risk is the minimally educated and trained assembly line worker who has the least amount of control over his environment.[104] Close behind is the demanding person who has been placed in a position for which he is not competent or the middle manager given much responsibility but little control. The factors of social support, lack of control, and other situational elements all affect the Type A personality. While various research results may show different rates of risk, they all show one thing: A Type A personality (or coronary-prone personality) definitely increases the risk of heart disease.

The reasons are many. Among them, the stress associated with Type A behavior causes these effects:

- An increase in adrenaline-like hormones (norepinephrine) that cause microvascular drainage in blood vessel walls allows cholesterol in the blood to seep into the wall, creating atherosclerotic plaques.[105]
- An increase in coronary artery spasm further narrows the vessels supplying oxygen to the heart muscle.
- An increase in blood pressure increases the heart's workload and oxygen requirement. Type A behavior typically results in an increase in norepineph-

rine, which constricts the blood vessels, resulting in high blood pressure.[106] Several studies have found that high blood pressure is much more common among people with unexpressed anger, especially among those with an "anger-in" style of coping, a very specific Type A trait.[107]

- Blood platelets become more "sticky," part of the process that leads to atherosclerosis and clotting to complete the obstruction of the narrowed arteries. This is a definite risk factor for coronary heart disease.[108]
- All of the above phenomena lead to oxygen imbalance in the heart, resulting in myocardial infarction (heart attack).

In Friedman and Rosenman's Western Collaborative Group Study, which watched for the development of coronary heart disease in more than 3000 men over a period of eight and a half years, men classified as Type A developed heart disease at 2.2 times the rate of those classified as Type B.[109] The greater risk of the Type A men in the study held up even when researchers figured in the classic risk factors, including blood pressure, blood cholesterol, cigarette smoking, obesity, and family history.

Other studies, including the Framingham Heart Study, the Belgian-French Collaborative Study, and the Japanese-American Study, also placed the heart disease risk of the Type A personality at more than twice the risk in the population at large.

Other studies have shown that hostile Type A personality increases the risk of heart disease as much as or more than the "standard" risk factors of cigarette smoking, high serum cholesterol, and high blood pressure and is synergistic with them. If Type A coexists with another risk factor, the risk of developing coronary heart disease is four times greater. If Type A personality exists alongside two additional risk factors, the risk of developing coronary heart disease is eight times greater.[110]

The risk from Type A may be even more important at younger ages. In the normal population, approximately one of every 162 Americans will suffer a heart attack. In the age bracket of thirty-nine to forty-nine years, Type A men are 6.5 times more likely to have a heart attack.[111]

While most studies begin with disease-free subjects and monitor them to determine which ones will develop disease, a study in China adopted the opposite approach but came up with the same results. Type A personality also apparently increases the risk of angina pectoris (chest pain), according to findings from the Framingham study. Some researchers believe that the prevalence of angina, as compared with myocardial infarction, is greater among Type As. Many Type As have coronary spasm alone, they point out, whereas others have it in conjunction with full-blown coronary artery disease.[112] Recently released data from the study show that 570 men and 719 women were categorized as Type A or Type B personality in the 1960s. Both groups had similar risk factors for heart disease, such as systolic blood pressure, total– and high-density lipoprotein cholesterol levels, body-mass index, alcohol intake, cigarette smoking, and the prevalence of diabetes.

Focus on Research

Researchers with the Department of Psychology at Peking University in Beijing identified 714 coronary heart disease patients, 424 disease-free patients, and 220 relatives of people with coronary heart disease. The people who participated in the study were scattered among eighteen provinces and municipalities in China; those who participated in the study had at least a high school education, and ranged in age from forty to sixty-five years.

The researchers, headed by Dr. Zhang Bo-yuan, gave each participant a questionnaire designed to detect traits common to the Type A personality, such as time hurry, time urgency, impatience, rapid work, competitiveness, hostility, and irritability. The questionnaire included a ten-item category designed to determine whether the respondents were being truthful in their responses to the questionnaire. To guarantee some stability, approximately one hundred of the participants were tested again on a second occasion. The coronary heart disease patients were more than twice as likely to have Type A personality than the disease-free patients.

Source: Zhang Bo-yuan, "Behavior Patterns of Coronary Heart Disease Patients and Healthy Controls in China," *Behavioral Medicine,* (Winter 1988), pp. 156–159.

According to the figures reported in the *American Journal of Cardiology,* the Type As developed angina at twice the rate of the Type Bs. And, say the researchers who did the study, those with angina have a more than fourfold greater risk of dying from heart disease than the subjects without angina.[113]

There's an interesting twist to the Type A personality story: Even though Type A personalities are much more likely to have a heart attack if not depressed, they are more likely to survive the heart attack,[114] even after severe heart damage, and they are much *less* likely than Type B personalities to suffer a second heart attack.

Two researchers from the University of California at Berkeley—epidemiologist David Ragland and biostatistician Richard Brand—followed up on the sample of men from the Western Collaborative Group Study who had suffered heart attacks in the eight and a half years of the study. Ragland and Brand, who reported their findings in the *New England Journal of Medicine,* followed the heart attack victims for an additional thirteen years. They found that an equal proportion of Type As and Type Bs died suddenly of their first heart attack.[115] Friedman, the cardiologist who originated the Type A concept, says that the condition of the heart, and not behavior, is the greatest predictor of who survives an initial heart attack. "If you have a patient whose left ventricle is half knocked out by a heart attack," Friedman says, "his chances of survival are much worse than if only a small portion of heart muscle stopped functioning, regardless of behavior type."[116] Other researchers believe that, though Type A behavior may cause a heart attack, other factors such as high cholesterol levels and high blood pressure predict whether the heart attack will be fatal.[117]

But what about a second heart attack? Ragland and Brand found that those with Type A personality were only about half as likely to die of a second heart attack than the Type Bs. Ragland and Brand were as surprised as the rest of the scientific community when the statistics became apparent. While no one knows exactly why, "Type A behavior in coronary patients is not dangerous," concludes Ragland. "It may be slightly protective."[118] Ragland also argues that "a take-charge attitude may be the As secret. Perhaps they're quicker to drop unhealthy habits."[119] It was not clear from the study whether the heart attack caused the Type As to modify their hostile and aggressive behavior. Not infrequently, such a critical event helps a person to reassess what is most important, resulting in greater emphasis on improving relationships and focusing with more humility on their deeper values.

Besides the the Western Collaborative Group Study, another far-reaching study brought researchers to the same conclusions. In a twenty-year study of several thousand men, the Type A personalities were at significantly higher risk for an initial heart attack but the Type B personalities were 60 percent more likely to have a second heart attack, and die from it, than were the Type As.

In commenting on the study, a report in the *New York Times* speculated that "these findings show a protective effect far greater than that achieved by any other coronary intervention study to date."[120] Friedman added that, when people changed their Type A habits, "they gave themselves a fuller, more productive life. They granted themselves the freedom to listen, to play, to take pleasure in

---

Focus on Research

Friedman and Rosenman, who originated the Type A theory, decided to determine whether Type A behavior could be modified—and whether those changes might alter the chances of having a second heart attack. To find the answers, they organized the Recurrent Coronary Prevention Project at San Francisco's Mt. Zion Hospital and Medical Center.

The study, which began in 1978, compared three different treatments: (l) regular individual medical care; (2) group treatment focusing on diet, exercise, medications, and awareness of the way the heart works; and (3) group counseling combining the components of the first group's counseling along with helps on how to change Type A behavior.

All of the 1013 participants in the study had had at least one heart attack; 151 were assigned to the control group (which received only individual medical care), while the re-maining 862 were randomly assigned to the other two groups. Approximately one-fourth of the participants had already undergone coronary bypass surgery; many were also taking medication to control high blood pressure. All participants were required to stop smoking in order to take part in the study. The groups were followed for three years.

The results of the study pointed out the dramatic impact of Type A behavior on the heart. According to Friedman, "There was a significant decrease in Type A behavior in the people who got counseling. But more important, this group had *half* as many heart attacks as those in the other group. No other therapy—not diet, drugs, surgery, or exercise—has ever achieved such remarkable results. We had demonstrated that Type A behavior isn't just associated with heart disease, but helps cause it."

Source: Lewis Vaughn, "Smile Your Way to a Longer Life," *Prevention*, August 1987.

friends and family, to mature, to regain self-esteem, to give and receive love. These advantages alone make altering Type A behavior worthwhile, even for persons who don't yet have heart disease."[121]

Eight controlled behavior modification programs designed to help heart attack victims reduce hostility and develop Type B characteristics have shown an average reduction in recurrent attacks of 39 percent and a 33 percent reduction in deaths, as compared with the usual cardiac rehabilitation program that doesn't focus on Type A issues. These improvements are greater than those achieved with any other risk-reduction strategy except stopping smoking and using aspirin to thin the blood. (Other strategies include treating blood pressure, lowering cholesterol, using drugs to block catecholamine effects, and exercising.[122])

Psychosocial Coronary Risk in Women

Most Type A study subjects have been men. The story may be quite different for women, who account for about half of the coronary deaths each year; on average the women die at an age ten years older than the men's. Though global Type A behavior has been associated with a *first* myocardial infarction in women (in the large-scale Framingham study[123]), it was not predictive of *recurrent* coronary events or of cardiac death.[124] Hostility also seems somewhat less important in women. According to the results of two other studies, what does create significant risk for coronary death in women, however, was being divorced and disempowered,[125] feeling socially isolated,[126] and being depressed.[127] Sudden death in women, presumably from heart rhythm abnormalities, has also been linked to bereavement and to being childless. Interestingly, behavior nearly opposite of the angry, hard-driving Type A man was more predictive of cardiac mortality in women—suppressed (but real) anger, slowness, and low level of arousal (as is seen in depression).

Studies of female monkeys showed that isolating a female from her social group increased the severity of atherosclerotic coronary artery narrowing four times.[128] The same held true of "subdominant," disempowered females who remained in the social group but who tended to be more withdrawn and were touched less than the more dominant, sociable females.[129] All of this raises some fascinating questions about whether, even in men, the real toxic factor is social isolation fostered by anger, hostility, and cynicism.[130]

The Role of Type A Personality in Other Illnesses

The role of Type A personality in heart disease has been acknowledged and widely known for decades, but the health-harming aspects of Type A personality aren't limited to heart disease. Type A personality can increase risk for a number of other diseases as well. In one study reported in the *British Journal of Medical Psychology*, researchers got a glimpse of how broad the impact of Type A personality may be on health. The Type A subjects had not only more coronary heart disease but also significantly more peptic ulcers, asthma, rhuematoid arthritis, and thyroid problems. The reported number of diseases per person was dramatically higher among Type As, even though the Type A subjects in the study were markedly younger than the others. Globally, the Type As had much more illness. Study leaders concluded that Type A behavior is a general disease-prone condition.[131]

One broad-range study showed that people with Type A personality ran a significantly higher risk of having accidents, dying from accidents, and dying from violence.[132] In another study that involved a group of more than 2000 men who had survived the Western Collaborative Group Study follow-up period, men aged sixty-one to eighty-one years filled out detailed health status questionnaires. Those who had the most pronounced Type A characteristics during the original study were the most ill (with a variety of diseases); those who had the fewest Type A characteristics had the best health twenty-two years later.[133]

Conditions that seem particularly related to the presence of Type A personality include ulcers, headache, cancer, genital herpes, and vision problems.

Ulcers. A number of studies have shown that people with Type A personality are significantly more prone to peptic ulcers than those with the less intense Type B personality. According to Dr. Arnold Levy, vice-president of the American Digestive Disease Society, Type A seems to be a particular culprit in peptic ulcers and a related disorder: irritable bowel syndrome. Those most likely to develop irritable bowel syndrome, says Levy, are "young women who are high achievers and are characteristically self-demanding."[134]

Headache. Doctors' general impressions, batteries of psychological tests, and detailed studies of patients have led physicians and researchers to believe that there is a "migraine personality" and that it is, in essence, a clone of the Type A personality. Those most likely to suffer from chronic migraine headaches are "ambitious, hard-working, hard-driving, demanding of themselves and others, eager to please, and sensitive to criticism."[135] Those who suffer from cluster headaches have virtually the same personality, with the addition of another classic Type A trait: heavy goal orientation.

Cancer. Apparently, Type A behavior increases the risk of cancer. Researchers at Boston University School of Medicine classified more than 3000 men as Type A or Type B personality. Twenty-two months later, they collected data on the entire group to determine how many had died of cancer. After accounting for age, education level, and smoking habits, the researchers concluded that "the incidence of death in Type As from cancers other than lung cancer was more than one and a half times that of the Type Bs."[136]

Researchers who conducted the study theorized that Type A personalities often feel frustrated and out of control, which may weaken the immune system and give cancer an opportunity to develop (see Chapter 26).

Genital herpes. According to the results of several studies, Type A personality seems to determine the severity of genital herpes outbreaks. In one, 105 members of a herpes self-help group participated in a study to determine the impact of personality type on outbreaks. Most of the participants were young women who were single, highly educated, and living in rental accommodations. The participants were given a variety of tests to enable researchers to categorize them as to Type A or Type B personalities.

Researchers found that personality type did not determine rate of infection or frequency of outbreaks. It did, however, determine severity of outbreaks. According to the researchers, those with Type A personality were significantly more likely to have severe outbreaks and were much more likely to seek treatment for the outbreaks.[137]

Vision problems. Researchers have long made the connection between emotional factors and eyesight. In one recent study, a disturbing psychological experience preceded vision loss in 30 of 33 patients, from an eye disorder called central serous chorioretinopathy. In this condition, the retina becomes detached at the area of most acute vision, leading to the loss of sight in one or both eyes. According to psychiatrist Gary S. Gelber and ophthalmologist Howard Schatz,[138] classic Type A personality traits—hostility, competitiveness, perfectionism, and time urgency—predispose people to central serous chorioretinopathy.

Gelber and Schatz believe that chronic high blood pressure and other physiological reactions typical of Type A cause fluid to leak from the capillaries near the retina. This serous fluid puts pressure on the retina, causing it to detach from the subretinal tissues and resulting in loss of vision. If the physiological reactions don't ease up, the condition deteriorates and vision continues to get worse.[139]

Gelber likens the source of trauma, whether a personality type or a singular traumatic event, to what he calls the *Captain Ahab complex*. In *Moby Dick*, Captain Ahab is tied to his persecutor, the white whale Moby Dick, and is drowned. These people lose their vision if they stay tied to their white whale, the source of their distress or misery."[140]

Type A behavior does increase the risk of developing certain diseases, and the hostile Type A personality does cause heart disease. But there may be a silver lining to the Type A cloud: Internist Brian Miller believes that Type A personality, often described as a liability to good health, can actually become an asset when a person is fighting disease. "Interestingly," he points out, "I see patients with very driven personalities get better faster than other patients. Apparently, these patients feel there is more to live for."[141] The key appears to be transforming the hostility and cynicism while preserving some of the assertive, active-living characteristics.

As Duke University researcher Redford Williams points out, not all components of the Type A personality are harmful to health. It's not essential to get everyone to slow down, he says—as long as they are not driven by hostility. Those who have many of the Type A traits without the toxic core that harms health, he reminds us, are "driven by a positive, enthusiastic approach to the world," a characteristic that can be protective, not harmful.[142]

An important question is whether Type A characteristics are so ingrained that they cannot be changed. Eighteen controlled studies have now shown that the toxic, hostile parts of Type A (and even the excessive busyness) can indeed be transformed into safer behaviors.[143]

To stress components that are more positive and productive, Dr. Meyer Friedman uses the following drills to help people change the negative components of a Type A personality into the health-protective characteristics of an effective Type B:

- Smile at yourself in the mirror for a minute or two.
- Don't interfere with someone who is doing a job more slowly than you would do the same job.
- Eliminate two phrases from your vocabulary at work: *How much?* and *How many?*
- Take regular breaks from work; try daydreaming, meditating, or even playing with your pet.

Other effective practices to modify Type A behaviors can include:

- Practice *mindfulness:* Do one thing at a time, being completely present with full attention. Give yourself with caring creativity to whatever is chosen to be done in the present moment.[144]
- While waiting in lines, practice the enjoyment that comes with socializing or doing relaxation exercises.
- Smile at the competitive antics of yourself or others.
- Drive around the block when you try to beat someone out in traffic.
- Read books that have nothing to do with your vocation.
- Take restful breaks during the day, perhaps using relaxation exercises.
- Eat slowly and mindfully.
- Ask, "What did I do well today, and what's worth remembering?"
- Practice conditioning a relaxation response after exercise and other arousal.[145]

In making the transition, it's more important to envision what you want (valued Type B traits) than to try *not* to be hostile. (The brain doesn't do well with *not* commands, because it needs to picture clearly the desired outcome before change can occur. Picturing what *not to do* is very difficult.) Remember that Type B behavior patterns are desirable. Type B people are often peak performers and hold many top positions.

As you try to envision the effective Type B traits, work toward these habits:

1. Having less time urgency:

   Give more attention to the central task at hand.
   Be less eager to move on to something else.
   Be on time, but without frenzy or rage.

Be patient.

Contemplate, especially beauty and metaphor.

Tend to see the whole more than the parts.

Value and enjoy the things you've already done (or you're doing now) as much as the things you will do in the future.

2. Relinquishing control:

Delegate.

Be tolerant of—or even *enjoy*—differences.

Inspire creative involvement with others.

3. Valuing yourself:

Appreciate yourself for what you *are* as much as for what you *do*.

Accept and value yourself as you are.

Understand that self-identity is far more than numbers.

Feel valued and of worth, regardless of your achievements.

Work hard, but don't let failure collapse your self-esteem.

Learn to love growth and the process of getting better through mistakes.

Compete with yourself, not with others.

4. Getting rid of free-floating hostility:

Don't find fault with others to bolster your own ego.

Accept with equanimity the trivial errors of subordinates.

Enjoy empowering and lifting others.

Don't feel tense or induce tension in others.

Be self-confident enough to be objective, to see through another's eyes.

Be capable of both feeling and expressing affection; enjoy intimate relationships.[146]

The behavior change methods that develop these characteristics are beginning to be proven one of medicine's most valuable preventive approaches!

Notes

1. T. George Harris, "Heart and Soul," *Psychology Today*, n.d., p. 50.

2. Emrika Padus, *The Complete Guide to Your Emotions and Your Health* (Emmaus, Pennsylvania: Rodale Press, 1986), p. 243.

3. Ray Rosenman, "Do You Have Type 'A' Behavior?" *Health and Fitness '87*, Supplement, pp. S-12–S-13.

4. Ethel Roskies, *Stress Management for the Healthy Type A* (New York: The Guilford Press, 1987), p. 8.

5. In Paul Pearsall, *Superimmunity*, pp. 45–46.

6. S. I. McMillen, *None of These Diseases*, revised edition (Old Tappan, New Jersey: Fleming H. Revell Company, 1984).

7. Peter G. Hanson, *The Joy of Stress* (Kansas City, Missouri: Andrews, McMeel, and Parker, 1986).

8. Lewis Vaughn, "Smile Your Way to a Longer Life," *Prevention*, August: 1987, 87–94.

9. Roskies, p. 16.

10. Roskies, p. 16.

11. S. Haynes et al., *American Journal of Epidemiology,* 3: 1980, 37–58.

12. Roskies, p. 14.

13. Meyer Friedman and Diane Ulmer, *Treating Type-A Behavior and Your Heart* (New York: Knopf, 1984), pp. 83–102.

14. Michael Castleman, "Are You a Type-A Woman?" *Medical Self-Care,* n.d., pp. 30–33.

15. Friedman and Ulmer.

16. Friedman and Ulmer.

17. Friedman and Ulmer.

18. Tandy J. McClung, "A Profile of Low, Moderate, and High Type A Female Children," paper presented at the 10th Anniversary Meeting, Society of Behavioral Medicine, April 1, 1989.

19. Kathy A. Fackelmann, "Child's Aggression May Foretell Heart Risk," *Science News,* July 1: 1989, 15.

20. Fackelmann.

21. Karen A. Matthews, Catherine M. Stoney, Charles J. Rakaczky, and Wesley Jamison, "Family Characteristics and School Achievements of Type A Children," *Health Psychology,* 5(5): 1986, 453–467.

22. Matthews, et al., and McClung.

23. Carl E. Thoresen, Jean R. Eagleston, Kathleen Kirmil-Gray, Sue Wiedenfeld, "Examining Anger in Low and High Type A Children and Adolescents," paper presented at the 10th Anniversary Meeting, Society of Behavioral Medicine, March 31, 1989.

24. Matthews, et al.

25. David M. Murray, Karen A. Matthews, Susan M. Blake, Ronald J. Prineas, and Richard F. Gillum, "Type A Behavior in Children: Demographic, Behavioral, and Physiological Correlates," *Health Psychology,* 5(2): 1986, 159–169.

26. Ray H. Rosenman and Margaret A. Chesney, "Stress, Type A Behavior, and Coronary Disease," in *Common Psychiatric and Somatic Conditions,* pp. 547–565.

27. Rosenman and Chesney.

28. Redford Williams, *The Trusting Heart: Great News About Type A Behavior* (New York: Times Books, Division of Random House, Inc., 1989), p. 120.

29. Williams, p. 120.

30. Williams, p. 121.

31. Williams, p. 122.

32. Williams, p. 122.

33. J. C. Meininger, L. L. Hayman, P. M. Coates, and P. Gallagher, "Genetics or Environment? Type A Behavior and Cardiovascular Risk Factors in Twin Children," *Nursing Research,* 37(5): 1988, 341–346.

34. Williams, p. 122.

35. Williams, p. 122.

36. Roskies, p. 5.

37. Roskies, pp. 5–6.

38. Paul Bennett and Douglas Carroll, "The Assessment of Type A Behavior: A Critique," *Psychology and Health,* 3: 1989, 183–194.

39. Friedman and Ulmer, p. 62.

40. Melvin J. Steinhart, *Emotional Aspects of Coronary Artery Disease* (Kalamazoo, Michigan: The Upjohn Company, 1984).

41. Williams, p. 17.

42. Ray H. Rosenman, "Do You Have Type 'A' Behavior?" p. S-12.

43. Williams, p. 19.

44. Rosenman, p. S-12.

45. Williams, p. 19.

46. Williams, p. 19.

47. Roskies, p. 6.

48. Phillip L. Rice, *Stress and Health: Principles and Practice for Coping and Wellness* (Monterey, California: Brooks/Cole Publishing Company, 1987), p. 95.

49. Roskies, p. 8.

50. Williams, p. 22.

51. Williams, pp. 24–25.

52. Williams, pp. 25–26.

53. Williams, p. 27.

54. Williams, p. 37.

55. Steinhart.

56. Steinhart.

57. Information on characteristics is largely from M. Friedman and L. H. Powell, "The Diagnosis and Quantitative Assessment of Type-A Behavior: Introduction and Description of the Videotaped Structured Interview," *Integrative Psychiatry,* 12(9): 1984; and Bill Lawren, "Type-A Giveaways: The Telltale Glare," *Longevity,* November: 1990, 82.

58. Jeffrey Pepper Rodgers, "Type A: Healing the Spirit," *Psychology Today,* April 1989.

59. Jon Kabat-Zinn, *Full Catastrophe Living* (Boston: Delacorte Press, 1990).

60. Robert Levine, "The Pace of Life," *Psychology Today*, October 1989, 42–46.

61. R. B. Williams, T. L. Haney, et al., "Type A Behavior, Hostility, and Coronary Atherosclerosis," *Psychosomatic Medicine* 42: 1980, 539–549.

62. R. B. Shekelle, M. Gale, A. Ostfeld, and D. Paul, "Hostility, Risk of Coronary Artery Disease and Mortality," *Psychosomatic Medicine* 45: 1983, 109–114; and J. C. Barefoot, W. G. Dahlstrom, and R. B. Williams, "Hostility, CHD Incidence, and Total Mortality: A 25-Year Follow-Up Study of 255 Physicians," *Psychosomatic Medicine* 45: 1983, 59–63.

63. Redford Williams, "The Trusting Heart," *New Age Journal,* May/June: 1989, 26.

64. Chris Raymond, "Distrust, Rage May Be 'Toxic Core' That Puts 'Type A' Person at Risk," *Journal of the American Medical Association,* 261(16): 1989, 813.

65. Kristina Orth-Gomer and Anna-Lena Unden, "Type A Behavior, Social Support, and Coronary Risk: Interaction and Significance for Mortality in Cardiac Patients," *Psychosomatic Medicine,* 52: 1990, 59–72.

66. Orth-Gomer and Unden.

67. Roskies, p. 17.

68. Earl Ubell, "The Deadly Emotions," *Parade,* February 11: 1990, 4–6.

69. Sanford Slater, Nadine Grissett, Nancy Norvell, Gail Brenner, and Marian Limacher, "The Relationship of Psychological Factors and Risk for Coronary Heart Disease in Healthy Adults," paper presented at the 10th Anniversary Meeting, Society of Behavioral Medicine, March 31, 1989.

70. Redford Williams, "The Trusting Heart," *New Age Journal,* p. 26.

71. Joshua Fischman, "Type A Situations," *Psychology Today,* August: 1988, 22.

72. "Cynics Die Young," *Men's Health,* February: 1988, 4.

73. John C. Barefoot, Ilene C. Siegler, John B. Nowlin, Bercedis L. Peterson, Thomas L. Haney, and Redford B. Williams, "Suspiciousness, Health, and Mortality: A Follow-up Study of 500 Older Adults," *Psychosomatic Medicine,* 49: 1987, 450–457.

74. Barefoot.

75. Barefoot.

76. Donald E. Girard, Ransom J. Arthur, and James B. Reuler, "Psychosocial Events and Subsequent Illness—A Review," *Western Journal of Medicine,* 142(3): 1985, 358–363.

77. Tom Ferguson, "Contented Workaholics," *Medical Self-Care,* Summer: 1981, 20–24.

78. Ferguson.

79. Padus.

80. Ferguson.

81. Sharon Faelton, David Diamon, and the Editors of *Prevention* Magazine, *Take Control of Your Life* (Emmaus, Pennsylvania: Rodale Press, 1988).

82. Faelton, et al.

83. G. Sorensen, D. R. Jacobs, P. Pirie, et al., "Relationships Among Type A Behavior, Employment Experiences, and Gender: The Minnesota Heart Survey," *Journal of Behavioral Medicine,* 10(4): 1987, 323.

84. Muhammed Jamal, "Are Type A's Really High Achievers?" *Men's Health,* January: 1986, 7.

85. Jamal.

86. Larry Pace, "When Do Type A's Succeed?" *Health,* December: 1988, 9.

87. Pearsall, p. 52.

88. Williams, *New Age Journal,* May/June: 1989, 26.

89. "Taming Your Inner Type A," *Executive Fitness,* 18(8): 1987, 1.

90. Williams, "The Trusting Heart," p. 5.

91. Marvin Moser, "Relaxing Your 'Type A' Responses," *RX Being Well,* September/October: 1985, 5; F. DeClerck, "Effects of Serotonin on Platelets and Blood Vessels," pp. 51–55, P. M. Vanhoutte, "Platelet-Derived Serotonin, the Endothelium, and Cardiovascular Disease," pp. 56–512, and J. T. Willerson, "Serotonin and Thrombotic Complications," pp. 513–520, *Journal of Cardiovascular Pharmacology* 17: 1991, Supplement 5; and J. I. Haft and Y. S. Arkel, "Effect of Mental Stress on Platelet Aggregation in Humans," *Chest* 70: 1979, 501–525.

92. Moser.

93. Williams, "The Trusting Heart," p. 31.

94. Williams.

95. S. Eisenberg, "Type A and Coronary Artery Disease," *Science News,* 132: 1987, 293.

96. S. J. Schleifler, et al., "The Nature and Course of Depression Following Myocardial Infarction," *Archives of Internal Medicine* 149: 1989, 1785–1789.

97. P. Berzanyi, E. Galateo, and L. Valzeli, "Fluoxetine Activity on Muricidal Aggression Induced in Rats by *p*-chlorophenylalanine," *Aggressive Behavior* 9: 1983, 333–338.

98. Vince Bozzi, "Type A's Make the A-Team," *American Health,* April: 1987, 98.

99. "SWM, Type A, Seeks SWF, Type B," *Men's Health,* November: 1987, 4.

100. Denis J. Lynch and Kay Schaffer, "Type A and Social Support," *Behavioral Medicine,* Summer: 1989, 72.

101. *Psychosomatic Medicine,* Vol. 4 (1987), as quoted in "Friendship: Heart Saver For Type A's," *Men's Health,* November: 1987, 4.

102. J. H. Medalie and U. Goldburt, "Angina Pectoris Among 10,000 [Israeli] Men: Psychosocial and Other Risk Factors," *American Journal of Medicine* 60: 1976, 910–921.

103. Rice, p. 97.

104. Steinhart.

105. Eileen M. Mikat, Jorge V. Bartolome, Jay M. Weiss, Saul M. Schanberg, Cynthia M. Kuhn, and Redford B. Williams, "Chronic Norepinephrine Infusion Accelerates Atherosclerotic Lesion Development in Sand Rats Maintained on a High-Cholesterol Diet," *Psychosomatic Medicine* 53: 1991, 211.

106. Robert S. Eliot, *Behavior and Cardiovascular Disease* (Kalamazoo, Michigan: The Upjohn Company, 1989).

107. Neil Schneiderman, Margaret Chesney, and David S. Krantz, "Biobehavioral Aspects of Cardiovascular Disease: Progress and Prospects," *Health Psychology,* 8(6): 1989, 649–676.

108. Eliot.

109. Allan V. Abbott and Ruth K. Peters, "Type A Behavior and Coronary Heart Disease: An Update," *AFP,* November: 1988, 106.

110. Marcia Angell, "Disease As a Reflection of the Psyche," *New England Journal of Medicine,* 312(24): 1985, 1570–1572.

111. R. M. Suinn, "The Cardiac Stress Management Program for Type A Patients," *Cardiac Rehabilitation,* 5: 1975, 13–15.

112. E. D. Eaker, R. D. Abbott, and W. B. Kannel, "Frequency of Uncomplicated Angina Pectoris in Type A Compared with Type B Persons (The Framingham Study)," *American Journal of Cardiology,* 63: 1989, 1042–1045.

113. Eaker et al.

114. "Heart Disease: Encouragement for Type-A Patients," *Medical Abstracts Newsletter,* November 1989, as cited in *American Journal of Cardiology,* 64: 1989, 427.

115. I. Shoham-Yakubovich, D. R. Ragland, R. J. Brand, and S. L. Syme, "Type A Behavior Pattern and Health Status After 22 Years of Follow-up in the Western Collaborative Group Study," *American Journal of Epidemiology,* 128(3): 1988, 579–588.

116. Marjory Roberts, "Can What Harms Also Heal?" *Psychology Today,* n.d., pp. 8–10.

117. Roberts.

118. "Uptight A's Do Better Than Laid-Back B's," *Newsweek,* January 25: 1988, 56.

119. Vaughn.

120. Castleman.

121. Vaughn.

122. M. W. Ketterer, "Secondary Prevention of Ischemic Heart Disease: The Case for Aggressive Behavioral Monitoring and Intervention," *Psychosomatics* 34: 1993, 478–484.

123. S. G. Haynes, M. Feinleib, and W. B. Kannel, "The Relationship of Psychosocial Factors to Coronary Heart Disease in the Framingham Study: Eight-Year Incidence of Coronary Heart Disease," *American Journal of Epidemiology* 111: 1980, 37–58.

124. R. B. Shekelle, M. Gale, and M. Norusis for the Aspirin Myocardial Infarction Study Group, "Type A Score (Jenkins Activity Survey) and Risk of Recurrent Coronary Heart Disease in the Aspirin Myocardial Infarction Study," *American Journal of Cardiology* 56: 1985, 221–225.

125. L. H. Powell, L. A. Shaker, et al., "Psychosocial Predictors of Mortality in 83 Women with Premature Myocardial Infarction," *Psychosomatic Medicine* 55: 1993, 426–433.

126. L. F. Berkman, V. Vaccarino, and T. Seeman, "Gender Differences in Cardiovascular Morbidity and Mortality: The Contribution of Social Networks and Support," *Annals of Behavioral Medicine* 15: 1993, 112–118.

127. Margaret A. Chesney, "Social Isolation,

Depression and Heart Disease: Research on Women Broadens the Agenda," *Psychosomatic Medicine* 55: 1993, 434–435.

128. C. A. Shively, T. B. Clarkson, and J. R. Kaplan, "Social Deprivation and Coronary Artery Atherosclerosis in Female Cynomolgus Monkeys," *Atherosclerosis* 77: 1989, 69–76.

129. J. R. Kaplan, M. R. Adams, et al., "Psychosocial Influences on Female 'Protection' Among Cynomolgus Macaques," *Atherosclerosis* 53: 1984, 283.

130. Kaplan, et al.

131. B. Rime, C. G. Ucros, Y. Bestgen, and M. Jeanjean, "Type A Behavior Pattern: Specific Coronary Risk Factor or General Disease-Prone Condition?" *British Journal of Medical Psychology*, 62(3): 1989, 229–240.

132. J. Suls and G. S. Sanders, "Type A Behavior as a General Risk Factor for Physical Disorder," *Journal of Behavioral Medicine*, 11(30): 1988, 201–226.

133. Shoham-Yakubovich.

134. "How Your Personality Affects Your Health," *Good Housekeeping*, June: 1983, 217.

135. Padus, p . 591.

136. *Internal Medicine News*, June 15–30:1987.

137. J. Michael LaCroix and Candace Offutt, "Type A and Genital Herpes," *Journal of Psychosomatic Research*, 32(2): 1988, pp. 207–212.

138. Findings reported in the *American Journal of Psychiatry*, 144: 1987, 46–50.

139. "Visions of Stress," *Mind/Body/Health Digest*, 1(2): 1987, 3.

140. "Visions of Stress."

141. "Does Emotional State Affect Disease?" *MD*, April: 1986, 30, 41, 43.

142. Williams, "The Trusting Heart," p. 74.

143. E. V. Nunes, K. A. S. Frank, and D. S. Kornfield, "Psychological Treatment for the Type A Behavior Pattern and for Coronary Artery Disease: A Meta-analysis of the Literature," *Psychosomatic Medicine* 48: 1987, 159–173.

144. John Kabat-Zinn and Trich Nhat Han, *The Miracle of Mindfulness: A Manual of Meditation* (Boston: Beacon Press, 1976).

145. Hal Straus, *Men's Health*, June: 1992, 72.

146. See the discussion of the characteristics of coronary-protected individuals in Meyer Friedman and Diane Ulmer, *Treating Type A Behavior and Your Heart* (New York: Fawcett, 1984), Chapter 3.

7

ANGER AND HEALTH

> *Of the seven deadly sins, anger is possibly the most fun.*
> *To lick your wounds, to smack your lips over grievances long past,*
> *to roll over your tongue the prospect*
> *of bitter confrontations still to come,*
> *to savor to the last toothsome morsel both the pain you are given*
> *and the pain you are giving back—*
> *in many ways it is a feast fit for a king.*
> *The chief drawback is that what you are wolfing down*
> *is yourself.*
> *The skeleton at the feast is you.*
> *—FREDERICK BUECHNER*

Anger has assumed a whole new importance in the scenario of heart disease. What used to be blamed on "the hurry disease," as researchers called it, has now been more accurately identified. You can be a heart-healthy Type A as long as, among other things, you're not angry. The impact of anger on health doesn't stop there. The exploding rage you feel when you get really angry brings with it actual physical changes in your body, surging hormones and chemicals, for starters, that affect many organs and systems other than the heart. The health consequences of anger certainly can include high blood pressure and other coronary problems, but the consequences are much more widespread than that. When you are chronically angry, as Buechner so graphically stated, "what you are wolfing down is yourself. The skeleton at the feast is you."

"Anger kills," says famed Duke University researcher Redford Williams. "We're speaking here not about the anger that drives people to shoot, stab, or otherwise wreak havoc on their fellow humans. We mean instead the everyday sort of anger, annoyance, and irritation that courses through the minds and bodies of many perfectly normal people."[1]

The Definition of Anger

What, exactly, is anger? First of all, everyone experiences it. Just watch two toddlers fighting over a favorite set of blocks, a teenager challenging an unreasonable curfew, an executive whose car gets rear-ended on the way to an important business presentation.

Anger is an emotion. It's temporary. It combines physiological arousal with emotional arousal. It can range in severity all the way from intense rage to "cool" anger that doesn't really involve arousal at all (and might more accurately be described as an *attitude,* such as resentment).[2] People express anger in all sorts of ways, such as hurling verbal insults, using profanity, slamming doors, or smashing a fist into the nearest available object.

The words we use to describe our anger strongly hint at the turmoil that is going on inside our bodies when we're angry. Some of the most common ones were pointed out by social psychologist and anger expert Carol Tavris:

> You make my *blood boil.*
> His pent-up anger *welled up* inside him.
> He was *bursting with anger.*
> I *blew my stack.*
> She *flipped her lid.*
> He *hit the ceiling.*[3]

Our blood "boils," our muscles tense up, our stomach feels like it's tied up in knots, and our cheeks feel like they're burning up. The more angry we become, the stronger and more powerful we feel—and the more pressed to "strike out."[4]

The terms *anger* and *hostility* are often used interchangeably to describe a set of negative emotions, but they are not the same. Anger has been defined as a temporary emotion that may or may not be accompanied by outward expressions (physical or verbal). Hostility, on the other hand, is not a temporary emotion, but rather an attitude. It is anger that is expressed in aggressive behavior motivated by animosity and hatefulness

"Anger is generally considered to be a simpler concept than hostility or aggression," explain researchers Margaret A. Chesney and Ray H. Rosenman. "The concept of anger usually refers to an emotional state that consists of feelings that vary in intensity, from mild irritation or annoyance to fury and rage. Although hostility usually involves angry feelings, it has the connotation of a complex set of attitudes that motivate aggressive behaviors directed toward destroying objects or injuring other people."[5] We'll examine the effects of hostility more closely in Chapter 8. In this chapter, we look at the significance of anger, the need to express anger in healthy ways, the physiological reactions that accompany anger, and the ways that anger can affect health.

Manifestations of Anger

Anger has as many different causes as there are situations and people in them. A common one is physical or psychological restraint—being held back from something we intensely want or want to do.[6] Others include being forced to do something against our will, being taken advantage of, being frustrated, being insulted, being ridiculed, or having plans defeated. Sometimes other emotions (such as distress, sorrow, or fear) can lead to anger.

Besides individual differences in the way we feel and express anger, there are also some important cultural differences. In a number of Latin and Arab cultures the free expression of anger is heartily endorsed; two who are angry at each other may fight because they figure that a strong third party (such as a neighbor or family member) will intervene before things go too far.[7] The Utku Eskimos fall at the opposite end of the spectrum: They ostracize anyone who loses his temper, regardless of the reason. Tavris tells of an anthropologist who was shunned for several months by the Utkus when she became angry at some Caucasian fishermen who broke an Eskimo canoe.[8]

Between these two extremes are all kinds of middle ground. The Japanese don't display anger as their traditional Western counterparts do; instead of lashing out verbally, the Japanese assume a neutral expression and a polite demeanor when angry. The Mbuti gatherer-hunters of northeast Zaire take it a step farther; when angry, they laugh. Some individual disputes have become "full-scale tribal laugh fests."[9]

There are also profoundly different "rules" from one culture to another for the way anger is choreographed. People of one background move through the "stages" of anger in quite a different order than people of another background. As Tavris describes it, members of Anglo societies follow a fairly predictable set of steps: hints, indirect efforts, involvement of a third party, direct confrontation, escalating anger, lawsuits, and, when all else fails, violence.[10] The steps are quite different, however, in Iran, Latin America, and some American Indian cultures: There, you might observe silent brooding (for five years or even five hundred years) while the tribe decides what to do; an act of violent revenge; then more resolute measures, such as discussion, direct negotiation, or the involvement of a third party.[11]

The Significance of Anger

Back when people needed the fight-or-flight response to defend themselves against aggressors, they needed anger. It was important to survival. That surge of energy helped early people defend themselves. Anger enabled them to fight with vigor and great strength.

Our culture evolved much more rapidly than our bodies. We are now a society and a civilization who are expected to deal calmly and rationally with each other. We don't need to fight saber-toothed tigers; our battles are waged in boardrooms and bedrooms. We no longer need the fight-or-flight response, but our bodies still respond that way. We call it stress. We no longer need the physical stimulus of anger, either, but we still get angry. Instead of being a benefit, most regard it as a liability.

In rare cases, anger may play a valuable role in self-defense or in the physical defense of a loved one. Any other time, an angry assault is considered today, a violation of both legal and moral ethics, and while the victim may suffer physical harm, the aggressor almost always gets in serious trouble.[12]

According to researchers, anger rarely exists in isolation. When researchers at the University of Tennessee studied eighty-seven middle-aged women to determine their anger levels, they found that the women who were angry also tended to be pessimistic, to lack social support, to be overweight, to sleep poorly, and to lead sedentary lives. The angriest women were also more likely to have existing health problems and to feel they could do nothing to control their problems.[13]

The Need to Express Anger

Research has shown that, to be healthy, people need to express anger. It is a mandate to confront the things that are making us angry and to work through the anger. According to University of Arizona psychologist Roger J. Daldrup, there are two classic ways of expressing anger in an unhealthy way: misdirecting it or suppressing it completely.[14]

Unhealthy Expression of Anger

Misdirected anger, Daldrup says, "is the classic kicking the cat because you're angry at your spouse maneuver. Though people who misdirect their anger seem to be expressing it, they are just burying the real problem and creating more problems along the way."

The other classic response, complete suppression of anger, doesn't work either, because, says Daldrup, it creates what he calls "the keyboard effect." Once a person starts repressing one emotion, he begins repressing them all, something he likens to pressing down the soft pedal on the piano: "That pedal will soften all the notes on a piano, just as dulling one emotion will dull them all. Sadly, people become used to that feeling of dullness, but the anger is still there, destroying your relationships, sabotaging creativity, or interfering with your sex life."[15]

There are many other unhealthy ways of expressing anger, according to researcher Carol Tavris. Some of the most common ones are miscommunication, emotional distancing, escalation of the conflict, endless rehearsals of grievances, assuming a hostile disposition, acquiring angry habits, making a bad situation worse, loss of self-esteem, and loss of the respect of others.[16]

What is needed, researchers agree, is the ability to confront the source of anger and express feelings without getting overwhelmed by the anger. As Carol Tavris put it, "The purpose of anger is to make a grievance known, and if the grievance is not confronted, it will not matter whether the anger is kept in, let out, or wrapped in red ribbons and dropped in the Erie Canal."[17]

According to Daldrup, anger becomes frightening (to you and to others) only when it is repressed for a long time and is then expressed—with the "force to turn silverware into metal filings."[18] "If you were discharging anger as it came up for you," he says, "there wouldn't be any extra energy attached to it. You'd be able to say 'I disagree with you' or 'I don't like what you are saying' in a straightforward manner without any extra energy attached to it." Instead of doing that, says Daldrup, most people store up—or "stuff"—their anger. "Stuffing is the only way you'll have enough energy for an explosion."[19]

Preliminary research has shown that bottling up anger can lead to many health consequences, among them heart disease, cancer, rheumatoid arthritis, hives, acne, psoriasis, peptic ulcer, epilepsy, migraine, Raynaud's disease, and high blood pressure.[20] And most researchers agree that expressing anger is essential to good health as long as the expression itself is healthy. The classic idea about expressing anger in screaming and pounding hysteria doesn't stand up under experimental scrutiny, says Tavris. Instead of helping, this kind of reaction "makes you angrier, solidifies an angry attitude, and establishes a hostile habit. If you keep quiet about momentary irritations and distract yourself with pleasant activity until your fury simmers down, chances are that you will feel better, and feel better faster, than if you let yourself go in a shouting match."[21] In her book *Anger: The Misunderstood Emotion*, Tavris adds, "Ventilating is cathartic only when it restores our sense of control, reducing both the rush of adrenaline that accompanies an unfamiliar and threatening situation and the belief that you are helpless and powerless."[22]

The way you deal with anger will have considerable impact on your health, say the researchers. If you get momentarily irritated at something, the best approach might be to distract yourself—to concentrate on more pleasant thoughts. But if you start feeling chronic or continual anger at someone or something, more aggressive action is needed to confront your feelings and work through the anger. "If you're angry at something that is trivial but still infuriating, you can choose to distract yourself," says Tavris, "but if you're continuously angry at someone, you have a problem. You need to look at that problem and work on solving it."[23]

Healthy Expression of Anger

Tactics that can work to distract you from trivial irritations, ironically, are the traits that are often considered to be "feminine." One researcher describes these as "leaving an angry situation, staying in the situation but thinking about more pleasant things, attempting to understand why the other person is angry at us and reacting with kindness. . . even crying has been shown to remove a buildup of bodily stress chemicals; it's good for us."[24]

One of the keys to the healthy expression of anger is to face the situation early, before it has a chance to accumulate and fester. Dr. Lenore Walker, one of the nation's top experts on domestic violence, points out that "you can either talk yourself into getting angrier, or you can talk yourself out of it. You have a choice.

When you learn to recognize anger and work through it early on, it tends to go instead of grow."

The goal of expressing anger in healthy ways, then, is to get rid of it. "Research data and all my experience with clients show that when anger is properly expressed, it is completed and processed out of the system," says Daldrup. And, he adds,

> [Properly expressing anger] is liberating, not destructive. Don't be afraid. You won't get stuck in your rage. You won't put your relationship at risk. You will, however, free up the energy you were using to stuff your anger down. That's more energy for enjoying sunsets, listening to music, appreciating our children, our relationships, study, exciting work, helping others, spiritual growth, travel, making love. The options are endless, and they are ours. This is freedom.[25]

How the Body Reacts to Anger

According to one researcher, "Medical research shows that no matter how many times you work out at the gym or how careful you are to eat correctly, you're putting yourself at risk if you don't manage your anger effectively."[26] And the most recent research shows that the effects of anger are diverse and widespread.

To understand the broad consequences of anger, consider the wide range of physiological reactions that go with it:[27] changes in muscle tension, scowling, grinding of teeth, glaring, clenching of fists, flushing (redness of the face), goosebumps, chills and shudders, prickly sensations, numbness, choking, twitching, sweating, losing self-control, or feeling hot or cold. Common reactions associated with chronic anger include fatigue, teeth clenching, pain in the neck or jaw, ringing in the ears, lowered skin temperature, excessive sweating, redness, hives, acne, itching, severe headache, migraine headache, belching, hiccupping, peptic ulcers, chronic indigestion, diarrhea, constipation, intestinal cramping, loss of appetite (without accompanying weight loss), and frequent colds.[28]

Psychologist G. Stanley Hall wanted to get a clear picture of how people feel when they are angry, so he gave several thousand people questionnaires that helped examine their responses to anger. The responses were remarkably similar among the 2184 people who completed the questionnaires. Anger, they said, produced "cardiac sensations, headaches, nosebleed, mottling of the face, dizziness, tears, snarls, or a complete inability to vocalize."[29] Those reactions are probably due in part to the immediate physical changes that accompany anger: Blood rushes to the face, the heartbeat speeds up, and the body undergoes a physical reaction much like that of stress, or the classic fight-or-flight response. Respiration speeds up, blood pressure rises, the digestive process slows down, and the muscles tense up, all in readiness for action.

The chronic repression of anger, then, has physical effects very similar to those of chronic stress. According to Carnegie-Mellon historian Peter Stearns, author of *Anger: The Struggle for Emotional Control in America's History*, chronic anger "is an insidious thing, because we aren't even aware that we are repressing. We think we are free to express anger, but we're not as free as we might believe."[30]

One of the major physiological effects of anger is on the release of chemicals and hormones, principally adrenaline and noradrenaline. According to Tavris, "Adrenaline and noradrenaline are what provide the *feeling* of a feeling: that tingle, arousal, excitement, energy. The adrenal hormones act on all organs of the body reached by the sympathetic nervous system, stimulating the heart, dilating coronary vessels, constricting blood vessels in the intestines, and shutting off digestion. That is why, when you are excited, scared, furious, or wildly in love, you don't want to eat."[31] When the release of adrenaline and noradrenaline is chronic or prolonged, resulting in chronic or prolonged anger, some of the most serious effects are high blood pressure, headache, heart attack, stroke, and kidney problems.

Famed cardiac researcher Meyer Friedman confirms that anger causes a flood of adrenaline and noradrenaline, which alter the functioning of the heart and the degree of constriction or dilation, of the body's large and small arteries. That situation, says Friedman, is "chiefly responsible for the development of arterial diseases."[32]

The results of repressed, chronic, or prolonged anger can be devastating. And, say researchers, if there's enough anger, almost any part of the body can be harmed. The effects can be as serious as cancer and heart disease or as minor (but annoying) as the common cold or skin disorders.

Psychologist Ted Grossbart points out that one of the two most "common human agonies that provide the underlying fuel for skin diseases" is anger.[33] In his research, Grossbart has traced a number of disfiguring skin disorders and rashes—among them eczema, hives, warts, and genital herpes—to anger. When patients are helped to work out their anger, Grossbart says, the skin disorders improve dramatically.

Anger also apparently predisposes its victims to the common cold. Some of the most comprehensive research connecting the two has been conducted at Cornell Medical School and at the Great Lakes Naval Medical Research Unit. Researchers exposed a group of men of similar medical status to the cold virus. Only the ones who were depressed, angry, and frustrated got sick; the rest stayed healthy. Even more important, say the researchers who conducted the studies, was the powerful effect of simply recalling episodes of anger. While simply talking about anger, the researchers say, the patients were more likely to develop nasal congestion, mucoid discharge, and even asthma attacks.[34]

Anger has been shown to be a major cause of migraine headaches. In detailed research, a large percentage of migraine sufferers have been those who are unable to express anger verbally. Mismanaged anger, anger that is either suppressed or misdirected, has also been shown to be a major factor in bulimia and anorexia.[35]

Anger that is not expressed apparently can affect the heart as well. Lynda H. Powell, psychologist at Rush–Presbyterian–St. Luke's Medical Center in Chicago, found that women who survived one heart attack but who kept a lid on their anger and had a pattern of reacting slowly to outside events were the ones most likely to suffer fatal heart problems. In commenting on the study, University of California psychologist Margaret A. Chesney said that it challenges traditional thinking: For men, expressing anger and hostility can lead to heart problems. Apparently, the opposite can be true for women: Repressing anger and hostility leads to heart disease.[36]

Anger: The Cancer Connection

Studies conducted as early as the 1950s show a link between anger and cancer. Most often implicated is either chronic anger or an inability to express anger appropriately. Researchers who were interested in exploring the link between anger and cancer studied the life patterns of approximately 400 cancer patients during the 1950s. There was a common thread among them: Many seemed unable to express anger or hostility in defense of themselves. The same patients were able to get angry in the defense of others, or even in the defense of a cause, but not in defense of themselves.[37]

Other studies of cancer patients, especially women with breast cancer, indicate that the style of expressing anger (or the ability to express it at all) seems to have considerable impact on the development and spread of cancer. In one study, researchers interviewed a group of women with breast disease; some had benign breast disease and others were later diagnosed with breast cancer. Before the diagnoses were made, interviewers made notes on the anger style of each woman. The women who were later diagnosed as having breast cancer had an entirely different anger style than those who had benign breast disease. The cancer victims were much more likely to suppress their anger and then finally explode with anger when they could no longer hold it in. Many didn't express anger at all, and those who did let it go all at once.[38]

In a separate study, Marjorie Brooks, an assistant professor at Jefferson Medical College, surveyed 1100 women who did not have breast cancer and compared the results of the surveys to those of fifteen women with benign tumors and fifteen women with malignancies. The results represented a strong case against anger. Both the women with benign tumors and the women with malignant tumors had experienced much more anger during the previous year than had the 1100 women who had no breast disease. According to Brooks and her colleagues, "A larger percentage of women with malignancies had felt angry more often than the women who had benign tumors. And a larger percentage of women with benign tumors had felt angrier the year before than women in normal health."[39]

There was also, according to Brooks, a big difference in the way the women expressed anger. Women in normal health tended to get angry and then forget about it. They were able to confront the situation that made them angry, work quickly through their angry feelings, and move on without anger. The women who had benign breast disease tended to get angry and stay angry. Interestingly, the women with malignant tumors got angry, but they either didn't express it or they apologized for it, even when they were in the right.[40]

A number of other studies have linked suppression of anger with cancer. In Lydia Temoshok's study of malignant melanoma patients, those who suppressed anger had fewer lymphocytes at their tumor sites. When Temoshok and her colleagues taught some of the patients ways to express their anger, tumor growth in those patients stopped.

The ability to express anger may even affect survival rates among cancer patients. In one prospective study, researchers found that patients who were able to express negative emotions—anger, hostility, guilt, depression, aggression—survived longer than the patients who said they had fewer negative emotions.[41]

An Angry Heart, an Ill Heart

Perhaps one of the most devastating effects of anger is on the heart and the circulatory system. According to research data published in *New England Journal of Medicine*, mismanaged anger is perhaps the principal factor in predicting cardiovascular disease. In fact, "The Type A personality is increasingly being defined as a person who can't manage anger."[42]

According to Dr. Redford B. Williams, Jr., director of the Behavioral Medicine Research Center at Duke University Medical Center, not all the aspects of a Type A personality are harmful to the heart, but one of the aspects that is definitely a risk is anger. As an example of his concept, Williams points out the person who is stuck in a long line of traffic when he needs to get to an appointment on time. "Anyone will be stressed if he really has to keep an appointment," Dr. Williams explains. The person who is at risk, though,

> . . . *may not even have a real deadline or an important appointment to keep, and still becomes angry and hostile in a short period of time. And he'll immediately think that the whole thing is someone's fault—that the police are incompetent because they aren't directing traffic properly, for instance.*
>
> *He'll get annoyed at the motorists in the other lane, because he thinks they're staring at him. His breathing will become deeper and faster. He may start honking the horn. The anger and resentment just keep building up. He may even try to drive up on the shoulder to get around the other cars.*[43]

It's that kind of person, Williams says, who is at risk of a heart attack or other major illness. In fact, a recent study released by the American Heart Association says that people who can't keep their tempers under control and who tend to explode in anger during arguments *double* their risk of heart attack. The study, conducted by Dr. Murray Mittleman of Harvard University Medical School, involved more than 1500 men and women. Mittleman and his colleagues found that people who felt moderate or severe anger were 2.3 times more likely to have a heart attack, even when researchers figured in the traditionally established risk factors such as cigarette smoking, high blood pressure, high blood cholesterol, and inactivity.

A number of major studies have now definitely linked anger and heart disease, and the evidence continues to mount. In addition to heart attack, anger leads to a much higher risk of high blood pressure. Studies linking high blood pressure and anger have been going on for a number of years and have been conducted by a variety of groups, and all have produced the same result: Anger that is prolonged or chronic leads to high blood pressure.

In one study, University of Michigan research scientist Mara Julius studied 696 married and single adults for twelve years. As one part of her study, she gave every subject a questionnaire to determine whether they were angry and, if so, how they expressed their anger. Of the questionnaire respondents, the ones with the highest blood pressure were those who suppressed anger, expressed anger but then felt guilty, or never protested an unjustified attack. Even more fascinating was Julius's findings on death from high blood pressure: A person with high blood pressure who suppresses anger, is five times more likely to die than is a high blood pressure victim without suppressed anger.[44]

A separate study at the University of Michigan School of Public Health measured the effects of anger expression, suppression, and "cool reflection" on blood pressure. The men who agreed to be studied had their blood pressure measured and were given psychological tests and interviews to determine their "anger style." The men with the lowest blood pressure were those who kept their cool, who acknowledged their anger but were not openly hostile, either verbally or physically. Those with the highest blood pressure were the ones who either bottled up their anger or became openly hostile.[45]

Focus on Research

One of the most prestigious studies, the Western Collaborative Group Study, followed 3154 California men aged thirty-nine to fifty-nine for several years to gather accurate information on heart attack–prone behavior. The men most likely to suffer a heart attack were the ones who got angry more than once a week—and who lashed out at others when they did get angry.

Researchers who analyzed the data provided by the study found that seven particular characteristics were related to coronary heart disease: the potential for hostility, getting angry more than once a week, directing anger toward others (rather than toward oneself), irritability at having to wait in lines, competitiveness in games with peers, explosive voice patterns, and vigorous responses to interview questions (rather than calm, deliberate answers).

According to researchers, "a single thread wove through the seven deadly specifics: anger, hostility, irritability, impatience, explosive behavior and other symptoms added up to plain and fancy versions of the hothead."

Source: Charles Spielberger and Perry London, "Rage Boomerangs," *American Health*, March/April 1982, p. 55.

In still another study, blood pressure screening was done at the offices of the Massachusetts Division of Employment Security among people who had previously been working but who had involuntarily lost their jobs. Researchers posted an announcement in the hall saying that free blood pressure screening would be performed; volunteers were weighed and asked to be seated for five minutes before blood pressure was taken. While the volunteers waited, they filled out brief questionnaires that sought information on health history and de-mographics. Questions also determined the style of anger of each respondent.

Three blood pressure readings were taken for each volunteer, and re-searchers adjusted their data according to age, social class, and obesity. When survey data were controlled for these factors, researchers found a surprisingly consistent result: There was a significant relationship between suppressed anger and systolic blood pressure. The more anger was suppressed, the higher was the blood pressure.[46]

According to studies, suppressed anger is especially dangerous for women. Researchers at the University of Michigan conducted an eighteen-year study of 700 persons. They found that women who suppress their anger are three times likelier to die early of any cause than those who expressed it. Men, they found, were at higher risk from suppressed anger only if they already had high blood pressure or chronic bronchitis.

In commenting on the study, Estelle Ramey, professor emeritus of physiology at Georgetown University Medical School, said that women suffer more "when they hold their anger in because they don't have a choice. A man can decide to keep his temper because it's the gentlemanly thing to do. But a woman may have to suppress her anger because she'll trigger male violence if she lets go."[47]

And what about the people who sometimes express anger, sometimes repress it? New research has found that people who have it both ways—who both express *and* suppress anger—are most prone of all to coronary heart disease.[48]

Recent research also gives us some important clues as to why anger causes heart disease. Research reported to the American Psychosomatic Society by Brown University psychologist Catherine Stoney shows that people who seethe with anger and try to repress it are slowest at ridding their bodies of dietary fat. As Stoney reported to *USA Today*, researchers haven't known why anger and hos-tility translate to high cholesterol. "This metabolism finding," she says, "is a pos-sible explanation."

There's more: Anger might affect the heart muscle itself. A study by re-searchers at Stanford University and the University of California at San Francisco evaluated eighteen people with known coronary disease and nine healthy peo-ple. For each, researchers studied the pumping ability of the heart under a vari-ety of conditions; in particular, they measured the percentage of blood that was squeezed out of the left ventricle with each contraction, a measure known as the *ejection fraction*. Among subjects with heart disease, anger caused a 5 percent drop in the ejection fraction, decreasing the heart's pumping ability.[49]

And anger suppression might even spill over into lifestyle decisions that af-fect the heart. Studies show that people who suppress anger tend to exercise less and have poorer cardiovascular capacity than those who let it out.[50]

Reactions to anger aren't limited to the body. A host of studies show that anger is linked to an array of psychological symptoms and behaviors, too. In one, reported in the *American Journal of Health Promotion,* anger was assessed in middle-aged women. Those who were angry generally got inadequate sleep and too little exercise and used a greater than average number of over-the-counter drugs. The angry women in the study also showed lower optimism and a greater number of (and more severe) daily hassles, had less social support, and had lost an important relationship during the previous year.[51]

What does all this boil down to? Anger can compromise health and shave years off life. Redford Williams sums up the situation thus, "Trusting hearts may live longer. For them the biological 'cost' of situations that anger or irritate is lower . . . . So *that's* what they mean when they say that nice guys finish last. It's because most of the angry, hostile, nasty ones aren't in the race anymore!"[52]

Does that mean you can never feel anger? No. Yale oncologist and surgeon Bernie Siegel tells us, "Anger has its place, so long as it is freely and safely expressed rather than held inside where it can have a destructive effect and lead to resentment and hatred."

So how can you get a handle on anger? Try these suggestions:

- Next time you start feeling angry, or when you encounter a situation that you know causes anger, distract yourself. Meditate, listen to a favorite concerto through a pair of headphones, close your eyes and imagine something you really love (like that border of yellow tulips that breaks through the sodden ground at the edge of your road every spring).
- It sounds trite, but it works: When you feel like you're really going to explode, take two or three *very* deep breaths and count to ten, slowly. Just taking a pause will help you get your perspective so you can express your feelings in a more appropriate way.
- One of the best ways to get a handle on anger is to practice forgiveness. If you need some ideas on how to start forgiving others, see the suggestions in Chapter 17.
- Social connectedness goes a long way toward getting rid of anger. Do what you can to get connected: Find a confidant, get a pet.
- Finally, when you start to feel angry, step back. Take a critical look at your negative thoughts. Reason with yourself. Then laugh![53]

Notes

1. Redford Williams and Virginia Williams, *Anger Kills* (New York: Random House/Times Books, 1993), p. xiii.

2. Carol Tavris, "On the Wisdom of Counting to Ten," in P. Shaver, editor, *Review of Personality and Social Psychology,* 5 (Sage, 1984), pp. 170–191.

3. Tavris, pp. 173–174.

4. C. E. Izard, *Human Emotions* (New York: Plenum Press, 1977), p. 331.

5. Margaret A. Chesney and Ray H. Rosenman, *Anger and Hostility in Cardiovascular and Behavioral Disorders* (Washington: Hemisphere Publishing Corporation, 1985).

6. Izard, pp. 329–330.

7. Tavris, p. 175.

8. Tavris.

9. Sharon Faelten, David Diamond, and the Editors of *Prevention* Magazine, *Take Control of Your Life: A Complete Guide to Stress Relief* (Emmaus, Pennsylvania: Rodale Press, 1988), p. 84.

10. Tavris, p. 175.

11. Tavris, pp. 175–176.

12. Izard, pp. 333–334.

13. "How Anger Affects Your Health," *Wellness Letter*, January: 1992, 5

14. Roger Daldrup, "How a Good Dose of Anger Therapy Can Restore Peace of Mind," *Your Personal Best*, April: 1989, 8.

15. Daldrup.

16. Tavris.

17. Tavris.

18. Daldrup.

19. Daldrup.

20. Izard, p. 351.

21. Tavris.

22. Carol Tavris, *Anger: The Misunderstood Emotion* (New York: Touchstone, 1982).

23. Tavris, *Anger.*

24. Tavris, *Anger.*

25. Daldrup, p. 8.

26. Hendrie Weisinger, "Mad? How to Work Out Your Anger," *Shape*, January: 1988, 86–93.

27. Tavris, *Anger.*

28. Elizabeth Weiss, "How Anger Affects Our Bodies," *New Woman*, December: 1984, 98–103.

29. Tavris, *Anger.*

30. Karen Judson, "Anger: The Shapes of Wrath," *BH&L*, February: 1988, 57–58.

31. Tavris, *Anger.*

32. Barbara Powell, *Good Relationships Are Good Medicine* (Emmaus, Pennsylvania: Rodale Press, 1987), pp. 158–159.

33. Steven Locke and Douglas Colligan, *The Healer Within: The New Medicine of Mind and Body* (New York: E. P. Dutton, 1986), p. 183.

34. Weiss.

35. Weisinger.

36. Bruce Bower, "Women Take Un-Type A Behaviors to Heart," *Science News*, 144:244.

37. Emrika Padus, *The Complete Guide to Your Health and Your Emotions* (Emmaus, Pennsylvania: Rodale Press, 1986).

38. Padus.

39. Padus.

40. Padus.

41. James W. Pennebaker and Harald C. Traue, "Inhibition and Psychosomatic Processes," in Harald C. Traue and James W. Pennebaker, editors, *Emotion Inhibition and Health* (Seattle, Washington: Hogrefe and Huber Publishers, 1993), pp. 152–153.

42. Weisinger.

43. "The A is for Anger," *Men's Health*, July: 1989, 10.

44. Judson.

45. Padus.

46. Joel E. Dimsdale, Chester Pierce, David Schoenfeld, Anne Brown, Randall Zusman, and Robert Graham, "Suppressed Anger and Blood Pressure: The Effects of Race, Sex, Social Class, Obesity, and Age," *Psychosomatic Medicine*, 48(6): 1986, 430–435.

47. "Women Who Suppress Anger Die Sooner," *American Health*, July/August: 1991.

48. Pennebaker and Traue, p. 151.

49. "Depression, Anger, and the Heart," *Harvard Health Letter*, February: 1993, 7.

50. *Journal of Psychosomatic Research* 35: 197–208.

51. Sandra P. Thomas and Madge M. Donnellan, "Correlates of Anger Symptoms in Women in Middle Adulthood," *American Journal of Health Promotion*, 5(4): 1991, 267–272.

52. Redford Williams, cited in "The A is for Anger," p. 11.

53. Bernie Siegel, *Peace, Love and Healing: Bodymind Communication and the Path to Self-Healing* (New York: Harper and Row, 1989), p. 28.

8

HOSTILITY
AND HEALTH

If we lose affection and kindliness
from our life;
we lose all that gives it charm.
—CICERO

Hostility comes from the Latin word *hostis*, which means *enemy*. For the hostile, enemies seem to abound. They are everywhere: at the office, in the elevator, in the grocery store checkout line, on the freeway, in the house on the corner. And, because of the health-damaging effects of hostility, hostile people become their own enemy.

Pioneering researchers like Redford Williams now suspect that the notorious Type A personality may not play the major role once believed in heart disease. Instead, a handful of traits—hostility among them—may be the actual culprits. According to Williams, about 20 percent of the general population have a level of hostility high enough to be dangerous to health.

Definitions of Hostility

Hostility is an ongoing accumulation of anger and irritation. As psychologist Robert Ornstein and physician David Sobel put it, hostility is "a permanent resident kind of anger that shows itself with ever greater frequency in response to increasingly trivial happenings."[1] Psychologist Carol Tavris says that "into each life come real problems that people should be angry about. But hostile personality types get equally angry about cold soup and racial injustice. They're walking around in a state of wrath." And, the researchers warn, hostility may go undetected for a long time.

Redford Williams, whose research on hostility is making medical history, claims that it "is a basic lack of trust in human nature, in human motives. It's a belief that people are more bad than good, and that they will mistreat you."[2]

Though hostility involves an accumulation of anger, it is not the same as anger. According to Diane Ulmer, clinical director of Berkeley's Clinical Institute of Behavioral Medicine, anger is an "intense emotion that usually springs from some sort of fear, a defense reaction." Hostility, on the other hand, is "anger projected outward and at something or someone," anger that is manifested "in an aggressive or antagonistic way."[3]

According to Williams, hostility has three components:

- Attitude: Hostile persons are generally cynical toward others.
- Emotion: Hostile persons express frequent anger, especially over petty incidents or issues.
- Behavior: Hostile people display threatening or aggressive behavior.[4]

Hostility is more than a simple emotion. It is more than an isolated angry outburst in a moment of frustration. And for some reason, hostility rarely stands alone; it is often intertwined with cynicism, suspiciousness, and self-centeredness. Unfortunately, in the puzzle surrounding hostility and health no single clear-cut definition is agreed upon by those who study it.

Current research has, however, managed to home in on a *concept* that encompasses most aspects of hostility: the desire to hurt or punish somebody.[5] A hostile person has an orientation toward hurting other people, either physically or verbally.[6] Researchers have found that the most health-harming kind is free-floating hostility, an attitude characterized by anger. Hostile people are angry, or on the verge of anger, most of the time, with or without cause. At the best, hostile people are grouchy; at the worst, they are constantly consumed by hatred. Occasional hostility is not the problem; the problem is the constant, slow-burning anger and the willingness to see almost everyone as the enemy.[7]

The famed researcher Dr. Meyer Friedman, whose work led to the original concept of a Type A personality, believes hostility can best be defined by considering its manifestations: irritation or anger at the relatively minor mistakes of others; looking for whatever might go wrong; inability to laugh at what other people laugh at; inability to trust others; suspicion that other people have selfish motives; frequent use of obscenities; difficulty in complimenting or congratulating others; and a preoccupation with the "errors" of the government, large corporations, or the younger generation. People who are hostile are often overly proud (and boastful) of their ideals—and become preoccupied with their status, income, possessions, investments, pension, and anything else that gives them "worth."[8]

Other researchers have come up with their own "shopping list" to define hostility. In one description of traits, the hostile person is characterized by emphatic gestures, loud voice, excitability, and dominance. The forceful, hostile person generally has a stiff posture, tight lips, and is quick to argue with anyone who has a different point of view.

Noted Harvard psychiatrist James Gill has compiled a somewhat different list of traits that indicate hostility, but, while the individual traits may be different, the overall attitude is strikingly similar. A hostile person, says Gill, notices with irritation the perceived faults of others, has an intense need to win at games and sports and gets extremely angry (with self and others) at losing, turns most conversations into a debate, and argues tenaciously until winning the point, is extremely demanding and critical, not only of others, but also of self, and is extremely sensitive to any kind of criticism or uncomplimentary remark. Even when smiling, the hostile person appears tight and tense, as though ready to quarrel on a second's notice.[9] The key in relating them to hostility, says Gill, is consistency: These aren't occasional attitudes but habitual and characteristic ways of reacting.

Still another definition of hostility might be obtained from the psychological tests that researchers use to pinpoint it. One of the most standard—and most reliable—is the Hostility Scale, administered as part of the Minnesota Multiphasic Personality Inventory. Various researchers have studied the various components of the test (called *the HO scale*), and have pinpointed various "traits" that they believe describe a hostile personality.

University of Utah researcher Dr. Timothy Smith used what Redford Williams calls a time-honored way of isolating personality traits from the test. He administered the test, along with a wide array of other tests, to a large group. Then he studied how the other tests related to the scores on the hostility test. Based on his results, he concluded that the traits most related to hostility were suspiciousness, resentment, frequent anger, and a cynical mistrust of other people. He also noted that people who tested most hostile were less hardy or resilient, experienced more frequent and severe hassles every day, and derived little satisfaction from their daily social contacts.[10]

Vanderbilt University psychologist Kenneth Dodge is another researcher who attempted to categorize "hostility traits" based on a study of test scores. His traits, grouped into six categories, give a good overall definition of what it means to be hostile. Redford Williams reported Dodge's categories are:[11]

Cynicism. Hostile people have a generally negative view of humankind; they tend to depict others as selfish, deceptive, and unworthy. They tend to have the same kind of attitude toward the world in general, even when their sense of mistrust is not directed at anyone specifically. Redford Williams claims that those with cynical hostility and cynical mistrust are at the greatest health risk of all.[12] Others say that mistrust and dependency on others to confirm self-worth put a person at highest risk.[13]

Hostile attributions. Hostile people tend to have an attitude of paranoia. They believe that other people are intentionally out to get them, purposely trying to hurt them. They tend to be suspicious and paranoid, and they feel constantly threatened.

"A common belief among hostile patients is that nobody gives a damn about them," says Pasadena psychologist Paul Clement. "That's a setup for hostile response. If no one cares about you, then you don't care about yourself or anyone else. You're off and running through life with a chip on your shoulder."[14]

Hostile affect. Generally, hostile people have negative, not positive, emotions about their relationships with other people. Although they might not overtly act like it, they regard other people with anger, impatience, and loathing.

Aggressive responding. Hostile people tend to use anger and aggression as a way of solving problems, and they feel reasonable and justified in doing so.

Social avoidance. Hostile people often (but not always) avoid other people.

In addition to these five categories, Dodge created a sixth, miscellaneous, category for a variety of traits that did not fit into the others.

It's also possible, says Williams, to get a good mental picture of hostility by looking at its opposite, the trusting heart. According to Williams,

> *[The] trusting heart believes in the basic goodness of humankind, that most people will be fair and kind in relationships with others. Having such beliefs, the trusting heart is slow to anger. Not seeking out evil in others, not expecting the worst of them, the trusting heart expects mainly good from others and, more often then not, finds it. As a result, the trusting heart spends little time feeling resentful, irritable, and angry. From this it follows that the trusting heart treats others well, with consideration and kindness; the trusting heart almost never wishes or visits harm upon others.*[15]

The Characteristics of Hostility

If what current research indicates is true, hostility may have a powerful influence over, not only the central nervous system, but the body's arsenal of hormones as well. As such, it may play a significant role not only in health and illness but in premature death. Hostility has such an impact on health, in fact, that University of Maryland's Theodore M. Dembroski claims it's easy to spot an intensive-care patient in the making: "He's the fellow who mutters and curses to himself if the line at the video store is too long; the one who leans on his horn if you hesitate even a millisecond when the light turns green. He's the hostile man, the one who gets angry over everyday frustrations and expresses those feelings in rude, antagonistic ways."[16]

According to Diane Ulmer, signs of hostility include tics of the eyes and mouth; an angry, hostile face; clenched fists; a hostile laugh; frequent use of obscenity; an angry, explosive, or unpleasant voice; and a challenging, aggressive, abrasive manner. Those who are hostile, she says, admit to being easily irritated or angry over the trivial errors of others, become angry or irritated when talking about something that caused them anger, react with aggression or unpleasant behavior to verbal challenges, are highly competitive, and are often critical of others.[17]

Sophisticated research has shown that hostility is bad for health and can even shorten life. Redford Williams, who has spent his professional career as a physician trying to determine the role hostility plays in disease, believes that not all components of hostility are equally risky; the answer isn't as simple as just getting rid of hostility. Through his research, he's isolated what he believes are the three most "toxic" traits associated with hostility:

1. Cynical beliefs that others are inherently bad, selfish, mean, and not to be trusted.
2. Frequent angry feelings when these negative expectations are fulfilled.
3. Overtly expressing those angry feelings in aggressive acts directed toward others.[18]

Those aggressive acts toward others may not always be obvious; they may be extremely subtle. In fact, one researcher says, some people use illness as a way to express hostile and aggressive feelings in a very subtle but effective way. "They transform reproach toward others into complaints to others,"[18] According to Arthur Barsky:

> *First, by displaying their suffering and misery, they arouse the other person's sympathy and elicit a desire to help. But then they thwart the person's assistance, dismissing it as ineffective and inadequate. They complain that their suffering is no better or has actually worsened, subtly implying that the Good Samaritan is a bungler who has only made matters worse. Those around the sufferer, including physicians and family, end up feeling impotent and guilty, wondering if they were responsible for the misery in the first place.[20]*

Hostility can also play a role in other illnesses, Barsky points out. It may be expressed unconsciously as bodily distress "when people in our current life don't seem loyal enough or helpful enough, when they don't live up to our expectations, when they disappoint us by being too absorbed in their own problems and uninterested in ours."[21]

A final characteristic of hostility that bears discussion is its apparent link to self-centeredness. It seems linked to narcissism, love of oneself, the excitement and gratification that come from admiring oneself and one's physical and mental attributes. The concept of narcissism is derived from Narcissus, the mythological figure who fell in love with his own reflected image.

According to researchers, narcissism is normal in children. It persists in a diluted form, as self-esteem, in psychologically healthy adults. Researchers tell us that, in proper perspective, it is a valuable element of a mature personality, necessary for a sense of security and well-being, a sense of self-respect, and the ability to be at peace with ourselves.[22]

But taken beyond that well-balanced ideal, narcissism can cause disturbing, even incapacitating, problems. And, it seems it's a problem closely related to hostility. Psychologist Paul Pearsall has termed the combination "running hot," and says it can be lethal. "At those times in our lives when we are running hot," he explains, "we are not only more hostile, competitive, and impatient, we are also guided by the central view that we, ourselves, are indeed responsible for everything, control everything, and are not only the captains of our own ship but the crew and cargo as well. Our supersystem becomes totally consumed by this self-focus."[23] As a result of this kind of thinking, the body becomes "quick on the draw and easily set out of balance. The result can be diseases related to an impulsive type of immune system, or one that is too quick to identify *other* as 'enemy.'"

Self-centeredness is the mind set that accompanies hostility. As Ornstein and Sobel put it, "There is a strong sense of self-involvement underlying hostility. A person who thinks of himself or herself as better than others in many ways is vulnerable to anyone who confronts such claims. Hostility may be a strategy for coping with such challenges by saying, 'Who do you think you are to challenge me like this!'"[24]

When people become that self-involved, Ornstein and Sobel say, "almost any event can be viewed as a personal threat: the turn of the stock market, the prospects for one's company, and the daily difficulty in marriage. Individuals who think that everything is theirs—*my* wife, *my* kids, *my* company, *my* car, *my* neighborhood, *my* church—have a lot of territory to defend."[25]

People who are hostile tend to use many more self-references in conversation; their conversations are peppered with words like *me, mine, my,* and *I* much more than the conversations of people who aren't hostile. And looking at the world through those eyes, the researchers tell us, causes trouble in the body. "Self-centered, hostile people set themselves apart from the world rather than see themselves as a part of it," Ornstein and Sobel explain. "They have seceded from the social union, and cut themselves off from the life-sustaining give and take of social intercourse. The result may literally break their hearts."[26]

And break their hearts it does—in a very real way. According to Pearsall, the immune system as a result undergoes inappropriate, impaired responses. In essence, it gets confused. It overheats, and things begin to "bulge, stretch, clog up, and block, especially around the heart."[27]

University of California social psychologist Larry Scherwitz says that people who show hostile self-centeredness, especially those who use the word *my* repeatedly in their conversations, are at high risk for heart disease. He and his colleagues studied interviews with male volunteers that had been audiotaped as part of a preexisting study on coronary heart disease. They compared the speech samples of 193 men who later suffered coronary disorders that killed some of them with speech samples from 384 other men who developed no heart symptoms at all. As part of the study, the researchers counted the number of times that all subjects used the words "I," "me," and "my."

Overall, those who used self-references eventually had more heart problems. Interestingly, the number of self-references wasn't useful in predicting who would *have* a heart attack, but it did serve as an accurate predictor of who would *die* from a heart attack. Most troublesome were the words *I* and *my*; people who used those terms frequently in their conversation were more than twice as likely to die of the attack than those who used the terms less frequently.[28]

In a similar study, Martin J. Stern and his colleagues at the University of Washington asked a group of men to respond to the question, "What's it like to be black (or white) in America today?" Researchers tape-recorded the men and measured their blood pressure while they were talking. They then counted the number of self-references (such as *I, me,* and *my*) in each man's answer. The men who referred to themselves most often during their response had the sharpest increase in blood pressure during the interview.[29]

Causes of Hostility

Where does hostility come from? What in our makeup may predispose us toward a hostile attitude? Researchers aren't sure, but they're beginning to get clues by studying the lives and backgrounds of people who are hostile. In one study conducted by University of Kansas researchers Christine Vavak and Kent Houston, 134 college students were given the Cook-Medley Hostility Scale. They were then asked to complete detailed questionnaires about their self-esteem, their health behaviors, their parents' child-rearing practices, and other background factors.

The students who were most hostile seemed to have had an "oppositional orientation" toward people that was developed during childhood. They came from homes where both parents were strict and coercive, used frequent physical punishment or hostile control, and frequently communicated dissatisfaction with the child. Those who scored high on the hostility scale described parents who were less warm and accepting, less likely to have treated the child as an equal, and less likely to have encouraged independent thinking.[30] Those who were the most hostile (as determined by test scores) were also those who had the lowest self-esteem and the greatest levels of anger. They were also those who did not seek social support and those who felt the least amount of acceptance from others.

A team of researchers studying the hostility levels of more than 200 young adults found that hostile people tend to take poorer care of themselves. Those with the highest scores on the Hostility Scale had poorer health habits overall, had poorer physical fitness, did not seem to take care of themselves, and used more drugs and alcohol. These results, "suggest that the poor health habits of individuals with high hostility scores may be an additional explanation of the link between hostility and subsequent disease."[31]

Finally, the results of at least one sophisticated study indicate that hostility is a learned, not an inherited, trait. Researchers came to that conclusion by studying identical twins who had been separated at birth and raised in different families.[32]

Psychologist Michael J. Strube has seen a pattern of hostility in children as young as age three. One of the main culprits, he says, is "parents urging them to excel, while presenting them with ill-defined goals and little, or ambiguous, feedback."[33]

The Effects of Hostility

How can an attitude, such as hostility, have such a tremendous impact on health? Hundreds of studies over the past two decades, by psychologists, immunologists, and neuroscientists, have shown beyond doubt that emotions and attitudes can have a significant impact on health. And researchers who have zeroed in on hostility have learned that the emotions related to it have very specific physical effects on the body, effects far more pronounced than those associated with other emotions.[34]

The effects of hostility are so devastating because hostility does two things to the body:

1. Hostility causes the constant, unending release of stress hormones, especially norepinephrine, which work to destroy health in a variety of ways.
2. Hostility weakens the branch of the nervous system designed to calm the body down after an emergency.

To understand why hostility is so harmful to health, it's important to understand what happens in both these scenarios.

Hostility and Hormones

In essence, chronic hostility causes a reaction in the body much like that of stress. Basically, the body has two different kinds of stress reactions: (1) the fight-or-flight response (the body prepares to confront or flee from an enemy), and (2) vigilant observation (the body stays constantly "on guard" in case it should be threatened). Hostility causes both reactions simultaneously—a "double whammy" for the body to deal with.

While stress or a perceived danger may cause occasional or short-term reactions of this kind in the body, hostility is a constant, chronic condition. A hostile person goes throughout the entire day in this condition. (Many hostile people don't even get relief at night while sleeping; researchers have shown that stress hormones are secreted throughout the night and eliminated in the urine around the clock.)

To begin with, hostility causes the body to release corticotropin-releasing-hormone (CRH), which mobilizes the whole sequence of stress hormones. CRH instructs the pituitary gland and the adrenal glands to secrete special stress hormones. The result is a classic stress response: Blood pressure increases, the heart beats harder and faster, blood volume is increased, blood moves from the skin and organs to the brain and muscles, the liver releases stored sugar, and breathing speeds up.

Those reactions in themselves wouldn't be so bad if they happened only occasionally, and if there were a physical way for the body to overcome the reaction. With hostility, neither is the case. And there's a possibly lethal reaction connected with hostility as well: The constant on-off of stress hormones that accompanies hostility can trigger a coronary artery spasm, resulting in heart attack.[35]

But it's the stress hormones themselves, released in response to chronic hostility, that create the greatest havoc. The five principal stress hormones released in response to hostility have definite hazardous effects, mostly on the circulatory system.

Epinephrine and Norepinephrine

Epinephrine, sometimes called adrenaline, constricts the blood vessels, especially the minute ones in the extremities. At the same time, it causes the heart to work harder and stimulates the heart muscle. As a result, the heart pumps rapidly in high-pressure spurts, driving blood pressure dangerously high.

Sometimes called noradrenaline, norepinephrine also causes the blood vessels to constrict; it is generally released when blood pressure is too low. In addition, it disturbs the platelets and the red blood cells, and damages endothelium (the lining of the heart and blood vessels). Finally, norepinephrine converts testosterone to estradiol, the most potent naturally occurring estrogen; while researchers are not sure of all its effects, they do know that estradiol is significantly elevated in men who have heart attacks.

Studies have shown that people who are hostile (people traditionally labeled Type A) release much more epinephrine and norepinephrine into their systems, and they release much more norepinephrine if confronted with a challenge. In an early study by Friedman and Rosenman (the researchers who pioneered the Type A theory), a group of men were seated at a table. In the middle was an expensive bottle of French wine. Each man was given a pile of puzzle pieces and told that whoever solved the puzzle first would win the bottle of wine.

The men eagerly began trying to put together the puzzle. Soon, loud rock music began to blare out of concealed speakers in the room. The men worked for several minutes, the music blasting, until researchers told them to stop. (No one completed his puzzle, because some of the pieces had not been provided.)

Researchers had drawn blood samples from the men at the beginning of the experiment, and they drew samples again after they told the men to stop working on the puzzle. All the men in the study had similar levels of epinephrine and norepinephrine before they started competing for the bottle of wine, but the Type A men—the hostile ones—had much higher levels of norepinephrine after trying to win the contest.[36]

In a similar experiment, New York City researcher David Glass asked firemen and policemen to volunteer for a study in which they played Pong, a computer game. Each man had the same opponent; a man who was introduced as a fireman or policeman but who was in reality a colleague of Dr. Glass and an expert Pong player. The expert won every game. But it didn't stop there: As he played, he disparaged the opponents—for their lack of skill and their clumsiness, and even impugned their manhood. As in the first experiment, blood samples were taken before the game began and again after it was finished. The Type A men (those who were most hostile) had significantly higher levels of epinephrine in their blood than the calmer, more easygoing men.[37]

Cortisol

A corticosteroid, cortisol is the most potent hormone released by the body in an effort to defend itself. Cortisol inhibits the breakdown of epinephrine and norepinephrine, in essence making it very difficult for the body to calm down after a perceived emergency or threat. To make matters worse, it increases the body's responsiveness to epinephrine and norepinephrine, rendering those hormones more potent.

Cortisol appears to be responsible for heart disease in several different ways. The cortisol itself may be a contributing factor; people with Cushing's disease (a syndrome characterized by unusually high cortisol release) have a high rate of arteriosclerosis. Patients with rheumatoid arthritis are often given corticosteroids to reduce inflammation; in many, atherosclerosis is accelerated.

Second, cortisol releases chemicals that damage the endothelium (the cells lining the heart and blood vessels). Endothelium damage has been shown to cause arteriosclerosis, and it is one of the main causes of atherosclerosis. Sophisticated research has shown that blood vessel blockage begins with damage to the endothelium. Finally, in addition to damaging the vessels, cortisol causes an increase in the level of fats in the blood, a known contributor to heart disease.

Prolactin

Prolactin has a dual effect on the cardiovascular system: It releases calcium into the bloodstream, and it makes the blood vessels more vulnerable to the effects of epinephrine and norepinephrine. In addition, prolactin has some role in regulating blood pressure.

Testosterone

Released into the bloodstream in large amounts in response to hostility, testosterone increases arteriosclerosis and speeds the development of fat deposits in the blood vessels. In addition, it reduces the number of high-density lipoproteins in the blood (high-density lipoproteins—HDL or "good cholesterol"—are considered beneficial in protecting the body against heart disease).

In addition to the specific effects of each individual stress hormone released in response to hostility, the hormones working together have six effects:

1. The hormones together have effects on the cardiovascular system that greatly increase the risk of acute cardiac events.[38] The fluctuation of the hormones released during hostility can trigger spasms of the coronary arteries, resulting in heart attack.

2. The hostility hormones (especially epinephrine, norepinephrine, and cortisol) contribute to premature development of arteriosclerosis,[39] a leading cause of heart disease. Blair Justice, a psychologist who has specialized in the mind's influence on the body, points out that "excessive stress hormones—found in hostile people even when not actively angry—trigger an outpouring of cholesterol and triglycerides, which are associated with heart disease."[40]

3. The hormones compromise the immune system, making the individual less resistant to disease. According to researchers at the University of Texas Cancer Center, norepinephrine and other stress hormones completely block the ability of macrophages (scavenger cells that provide resistance against disease) to kill tumor cells.

4. Hormones released in response to hostility interfere with the body's DNA repair system. As a result, the body loses its first line of defense against a number of diseases, including cancer.

5. The combination of hormones secreted during hostility interferes with the body's natural messengers that reduce blood pressure. Under normal conditions, tiny "thermostats" in the walls of the blood vessels send messages to the brain to restore blood pressure to normal. Stress and hostility hormones inactivate these thermostats (called *baroreceptors*), leaving them unable to signal a reduction in blood pressure. As a result, blood pressure stays elevated and can be driven even higher by epinephrine.

6. The hostility hormones block entry of sugar into brain cells. Hostility mimics stress, and when the body perceives stress, it prepares to fight or flee. The body believes that the muscles need sugar to fuel them for an attack or a getaway, so sugar that would normally fuel the brain is shunted to the muscles instead. If this condition persists long enough, brain cells are deprived of sugar for an extended time and may seriously malfunction.

In disproportionate amounts, the hormones released in response to hostility are "dangerous drugs."[41] According to work done as part of the Western Collaborative Group Study, people who are hostile secrete significantly more of these hormones in their urine day and night.

Difficulty with Calming Down

The first thing hostility does to the body is to stimulate constant release of stress hormones, which, over the long term, have hazardous effects on the body. The second thing it does is interfere with the body's ability to calm itself after a perceived threat.

Research conducted by Williams and others has shown that there are two main branches of the autonomic nervous system: (1) the emergency (sympathetic) branch, which pumps out the hormones discussed and prepares the body to respond in case of an emergency or threat, and (2) the parasympathetic branch, which Williams has nicknamed the *calming branch*, designed to calm the body down after a confrontational situation. The sympathetic branch kicks in, in an emergency, and the parasympathetic branch switches it back off when the emergency is past.

The parasympathetic, or calming system, literally calms and soothes the body when things are working as they should. It keeps things on an even keel. It prevents the body from remaining too long in an aroused state, which can result in disease. It blunts the potentially harmful effects of stress.

When the heart speeds up during stress, the liver releases sugar to the muscles, breathing quickens, digestion slows down or stops, and the pupils of the eyes dilate. The body is in a state of readiness. As soon as the perceived threat is over, the parasympathetic branch (the calming system) secretes acetylcholine, a substance that slows down the heart, stops release of sugar from the liver, returns the breathing rate to normal, activates digestion, and constricts the pupils. It returns things to normal.

That's when things are working as they should. When hostility enters the picture, all that changes. The parasympathetic branch of the nervous system becomes weak; it can't effectively do its job any more. It can't secrete acetylcholine. The body cannot bounce back from the surge of stress hormones. No calming takes

Focus on Research

In a study demonstrating the impact of hostility on the calming system, Williams and his colleagues sought to test a reflex they knew was related to the calming branch: the "dive reflex." The dive reflex is what enables most mammals (including humans) to dive beneath the surface of water and stay there for long periods. What happens is that the calming branch of the autonomic nervous system slows the heart rate and the breathing, reducing the body's need for oxygen while under the water. Williams knew that he could stimulate the dive reflex in humans by immersing their faces in cold water—or, more simply, by placing a plastic bag filled with ice and water on a person's forehead.

Williams chose the ice bag method, since it didn't require people to hold their breath. For the study, he selected ten Type A men (characterized by their hostility) and ten Type B men. He measured their heart rates before placing the ice bag on their foreheads; in the initial measurement, their heart rates were identical.

Researchers then placed ice bags on their foreheads, waited one minute, and measured heart rate again. After one minute, all the men had shown identical decreases in heart rate. The calming system had kicked into gear and was slowing the heart rate.

After two minutes, however, the difference between the hostile men and their non-hostile counterparts became pronounced: The heart rates of the men who were not hostile continued to drop. Their calming system continued doing its job. Not so with the hostile men: Two minutes after the ice bags were placed on their foreheads, their heart rates had not returned to normal. Their calming system was no longer working—after two short minutes. Williams concluded from the study that two elements are at work in the hostile person: The emergency system, which kicks the body into gear, is much more exaggerated—and the calming system, which is supposed to return it to normal, is extremely weakened.

Source: Redford Williams, *The Trusting Heart: Great News About Type A Behavior* (New York: Times Books Division of Random House, Inc., 1989), pp. 101–102.

place, and the body remains in a state of prolonged arousal. Repeated research has shown that people who are not hostile recover physically much more quickly from stimulation that mimics stress.[42]

Hostility and Heart Disease

Ornstein and Sobel note that the concept of hostility has long been associated with coronary artery disease and death. They tell of Dr. John Hunter, an influential British physician, whose biographer described his temper as "very warm and impatient, readily provoked, and when irritated not easily soothed. . . . He hated deceit, and he was above every kind of artifice, he detested it in others and too openly vowed his sentiments. . . . In conversation, he spoke too freely, and sometimes harshly of his contemporaries." But Hunter was obviously far ahead of his eighteenth-century contemporaries, at least inadvertently. He must have at least subconsciously made some connection between his own hostility and the health of his heart when he hissed to an acquaintance, "My life is in the hands of any rascal who chooses to annoy me." His statement was prophetic. It did seem to be annoyance, after all, that did him in: Dr. Hunter died after taking part in a heated argument at a board meeting of London's St. George's Hospital.[43]

According to Redford Williams, "Hostile men get angry more often and with greater intensity than others, and each and every time, it hits the heart." Indeed, according to the latest research, the traits most common to coronary artery disease include aggressive tendencies, anger and hostility, and a striving for power and achievement.[44]

Hostility, one of the components of Type A behavior, is now known to be an independent risk factor for coronary heart disease. Williams says that "we have strong evidence now that hostility alone damages the heart." The hostility that causes heart disease is, as researchers put it, a multifaceted trait: Heart-harming hostility is characterized by anger-proneness, resentment, suspicion, and the tendency to view photographs of strangers as unfriendly or dangerous.[45] It is also hallmarked by explosive and vigorous vocal mannerisms, competitiveness, impatience, and irritability. According to University of Texas Medical School cardiologist K. Lance Gould, hostility worsens other heart disease risk factors, too, by driving up both blood pressure and cholesterol levels.[46]

There is still some controversy over the notion of Type A personality as it relates to heart disease risk. The most recent research conducted by scientists on the cutting edge of technology presents a convincing case that hostility is the real culprit instead of any specific personality type."[47] According to the researchers, all Type As are not at increased risk of coronary heart disease—only those who are hostile. The most toxic mix is hostility, anger, cynicism, antagonism, and mistrust.

A number of studies have focused on hostility as a leading factor in heart disease risk. In one, researchers studied more than 400 patients at Duke Medical Center to determine coronary artery health and personality traits. More than 80 percent of the men who were classified as Type A and who also measured high in hostility had seriously diseased coronary arteries; only half of the other men did.

For women, the risk was even more significant: 50 percent of the hostile Type A women had seriously diseased arteries, while only 12 percent of the others did.[48]

In a similar study by Redford Williams and Ilene C. Siegler in the mid 1960s, students at the University of North Carolina were given personality tests. Twenty years later, Williams and Siegler followed up on the students. They found that hostility had an effect on serum cholesterol: The students who had scored high on the hostility scale in college had high levels of blood cholesterol and low levels of HDL twenty years later. One explanation for the findings, Williams told the Associated Press, is "the effect of hormones that mobilize lipids from fat stores."

A separate study also hints at another possible reason, this one connected to lifestyle: Women who are hostile eat more animal fat and less dietary fiber, a combination that has been proven to increase cholesterol. And men who are hostile smoke more cigarettes, eat more sugar, and eat less calcium.[49]

Are there other explanations for why hostility causes coronary heart disease? Researchers think there are several:

1. An excess of the hormones produced in response to hostility leads to heart disease, especially atherosclerosis. Former president of the American Heart Association, Donald C. Harrison, agrees that the hormones released in connection with hostility lead to heart disease as well as death from cardiac arrhythmia.[50] Evidence from a host of studies supports the belief that hormones are at least partially responsible for increases in heart disease among hostile persons. An editorial in *Psychosomatic Medicine* states,

> It is conceivable that the overly competitive and active Type A individuals who also have a basic mistrust in others spend a substantial amount of time in a high arousal . . . state. This could be associated with increased sympathetic nervous system activity and discharge of catecholamines, such as norepinephrine . . . , which may contribute to the atherosclerotic process.[52]

The response of hostile people to hormones may also be at fault. According to Williams, hostile men with high cholesterol are more likely to have *larger* adrenaline responses to stress, and that combination increases their likelihood of developing plaque build-up in the coronary arteries.[53]

2. Hostility increases levels of cholesterol and fats in the bloodstream. In one study, researchers from the Oregon Health Sciences University and the State University of New York at Stony Brook measured the hostility levels of 352 men and women in Portland, Oregon. The highest total levels of cholesterol and LDL were found among people who scored high on both hostility and Type A behavior.[54] Researchers at Harvard showed that hostile Type A people have lower levels of HDL, the "good cholesterol" that protects against heart disease.

3. A lack of social support is linked to disease in general and premature death, and we also suspect that, because of their personality traits (particularly cynical suspicion of others), hostile people do not build or maintain strong networks of social support. This has been termed psychosocial vulnerability.

According to Williams, "Their cynical mistrust and aggressive behaviors often isolate hostile persons from sources of social support that could help to ameliorate the harmful consequences of hostility."[55] In a series of studies, cynically hostile people have reported less satisfactory—and sometimes fewer—social supports, as well as more frequent and severe negative life events and daily irritants. Hostile people have also had less family support, greater conflict among family members, greater conflict and less satisfaction with marriage, and less social support on the job.[56]

4. Hostility is associated with high-risk behavior. Researchers at Louisiana State University who studied more than 3000 people for six years found that those who were hostile drank and smoked more than everyone else in the study. No link between smoking or drinking and other Type A traits was found.[57] Other research by Redford Williams found that people with much hostility were more likely to be smokers and tended to eat more (on average, 600 calories more per day).[58] Researchers have also found that hostility alone has as much detrimental effect on health as does smoking and drinking.

Hostility has been shown to cause coronary heart disease and coronary death, to cause coronary blockage, to contribute significantly to a second heart attack, and to lead to the premature death of people with existing heart disease. A physiological contributor to that premature death, says Redford Williams, is that the fatal combination of hostility and anger sends blood pressure skyrocketing. "It provokes your body to create unhealthy chemicals," he points out. "For hostile people, anger is a poison."[59]

Several large-scale and long-term studies have linked hostility to coronary heart disease. In one spearheaded by Redford Williams and his colleagues, more than 2280 Duke University Medical Center patients were studied for signs of Type A behavior and for the trait of hostility. The patients had been referred to the medical center for coronary angiography, a diagnostic procedure for determining the extent of coronary artery disease. Researchers found that they could predict which patients would be found to have coronary artery disease by pinpointing which ones were hostile and that hostility served as well as or better than Type A as a predictor.[60]

This study and several follow-up studies involving middle-aged men who had taken the MMPI twenty-five years earlier showed that the effect of hostility on both coronary disease and mortality was much stronger among younger men than among the middle-aged ones. For younger hostile men, the risk of disease was four to six times greater; for hostile middle-aged men, the risk dropped to one-and-a-half times. As a result, researchers now theorize that early hostility may most accurately predict premature health problems. As Williams pointed out, "Once middle age is reached, the surviving men with hostility traits may represent a group of biologically hardy survivors."[61]

In another study, more than 3000 healthy men between ages forty-five and fifty-five years were studied more than eight years in the San Francisco area; all

---

Focus on Research

One of the most touted studies involving hostility was the Western Electric coronary heart disease study, performed by Dr. Richard B. Shekelle and his colleagues at the University of Texas School of Public Health in Houston. For the study in the late 1950s, 1877 middle-aged, employed men who were free of heart disease were enrolled; all were tested for hostility.

The men were followed for two and a half decades, and researchers kept track of their health records. The men who scored high on hostility were later linked with a 50 percent higher risk of heart attack and sudden cardiac death. And high hostility also seemed to make the men more vulnerable to death from all causes, including cancer.

Source: Redford B. Williams, Jr ., "Neurocardiology," issue in series of *Current Concepts* (Kalamazoo, Michigan: The Upjohn Company, 1989).

the men were free of apparent coronary artery disease when the study began, and researchers watched them carefully over the years for signs of disease. When the study began, researchers taped interviews with each man and used the interviews to rate each person's potential for hostility. The hostile patients developed heart disease at a much higher rate than those who did not show signs of hostility. Furthermore, the men who reported getting quite angry at least once a week and expressing it outwardly were much more likely to develop heart disease than the hostile men who did not feel or express anger as often.[62]

In still another study of more than 1800 factory workers in Illinois, study subjects were carefully followed for more than twenty years. Researchers found that the factory workers who were high in hostility had one-and-one-half times more heart disease than those who weren't and that hostility was significantly associated with death from all causes over the twenty-year period.[63] Interestingly, there was also an increased rate of cancer among the men with high hostility scores, suggesting that hostility might contribute to the risk of cancer as well.[64]

In a smaller but still convincing study, more than 250 young physicians were tested for personality traits and then followed for twenty-five years. The death rate from heart disease and from all causes in general was six times greater for the physicians who measured high in hostility.[65]

Hostility also appears to contribute to coronary artery blockage. As part of his work at Duke University, Redford Williams selected 400 patients admitted to the medical center for coronary arteriography (a study to determine blockage of coronary arteries). Cardiologists let Williams test patients before their arteriogram; each patient was interviewed and given the MMPI. Based on interviews and psychological test scores, Williams determined which of the patients were hostile; then, cardiologists performed the arteriograms.

Williams was fascinated by his findings. In previous studies, Type A personality had always been a predictor of heart disease. It still was, but Williams found that hostility was an even more accurate and powerful predictor. In his study, 70 percent of the patients who were hostile had at least one major blockage of a coronary artery (as compared to 48 percent who were not hostile). Type

A people were 1.3 times more likely to have a blockage than non-Type As, but hostile people were 1.5 times more likely to have blockages than the non-hostile people.[66] Overall, hostility seemed to be the most influential factor. According to Williams, "Not only did people with higher [hostility] counts have more severe arteriosclerosis, but the [hostility] scores were also associated with arteriosclerosis even more strongly than were Type A scores."[67]

Williams followed up that research with a recent study linking hostility to high blood cholesterol, a leading risk factor in heart disease, and his results showed that hostile teenagers are likely as adults to have high cholesterol. "People with high hostility at nineteen tend to have high cholesterol levels at forty," Williams said in summing up the study, which was presented to the American Heart Association.[68] For the study, Williams and his colleague, Dr. Ilene C. Siegler, studied 830 subjects who took personality tests at the University of North Carolina. They followed the men and women for twenty years. Those who scored high on a hostility scale while in college tended, twenty years later, to have high levels of total cholesterol in their blood but low levels of HDL cholesterol.

Williams believes that one reason for the finding is that anger and hostility cause the body to pump out stress hormones, such as adrenaline, which provide energy to the body by releasing fat into the bloodstream. The effect of hostility, says Williams, is stress hormones, and "stress hormones give you a Hershey bar when they fire off." [69]

Researchers with the Recurrent Coronary Prevention Project in San Francisco found that hostility is a significant factor in determining which heart attack patients will have a second attack. In addition, people who are more "retributional"

Focus on Research

In one landmark study, researchers studied 3750 Finnish men between the ages of forty and fifty-nine. The researchers were most concerned with finding the factors that lead to ischemic heart disease. Study subjects were rated on traits such as irritability, ease of anger arousal, and argumentativeness, to allow researchers to determine the severity of their hostility. Researchers then made adjustments for classic risk factors of ischemic heart disease, such as cigarette smoking, obesity, heavy alcohol use, and snoring.

The men—selected from a registry of twins—were first rated on hostility; then they were divided into four groups, depending on their degree of hostility. Angina, the chest pain caused by ischemic heart disease, was almost three times more common among people with the highest hostility as compared to people with the lowest hostility. Researchers also found that high hostility was associated with high blood pressure, heavy smoking, and heavy drinking.

Hostility did not always predict which men would develop ischemic heart disease. But it did play a major role in the worsening of the disease among men who already had it—and was a significant factor in determining which of the men with the disease would die prematurely from it.

Source: M. Koskenvuo, J. Kaprio, R. J. Rose, A. Kesaniemi, S. Sarna, K. Heikkila, and H. Langinvainio, "Hostility as a Risk Factor for Mortality and Ischemic Heart Disease in Men," *Psychosomatic Medicine*, 50:5 (September/October 1988), p. 554.

in their hostility (people who want to get back at others) are much more likely to have another myocardial infarction than are hostile people who are less retributional.[70] Finally, hostility has been shown to accurately determine which people with preexisting heart disease will die prematurely from the disease.

Hostility and Mortality

A number of researchers who have attempted to pinpoint the health effects of hostility have found that it contributes to premature death from many causes, including cancer. In one study, students in law school were given a battery of psychological tests intended to measure hostility. In a twenty-five-year follow-up, researchers found that only 4 percent of the nonhostile lawyers died from any cause but 20 percent of the hostile attorneys died during the same period.[71]

In his many studies involving hostility, Redford Williams has pronounced that hostility and anger are much more accurate predictors of premature death than the once sacred Type A personality. But, he adds, hostility has been shown positively to predispose a person to premature death from all causes, not just heart disease.[72]

Duke psychologist John Barefoot agrees that hostile or cynical attitudes can lead to premature death. Barefoot and his colleagues followed 500 middle-aged participants for fifteen years. All had similar health and lifestyle patterns. Those who scored high on hostility tests had more than six times the death rate of those with low scores. When the researchers followed up on death records at the end of the study, about one-fifth of the participants had died; the survivors were generally the ones with low hostility and less suspiciousness.[73]

Hostility is hazardous: hazardous to outlook on life, hazardous to health, and hazardous to life. Redford Williams and his colleagues who pioneered the studies of hostility believe that people who are hostile can change—and that a change of outlook is critical to good health and long life.

Williams and others suggest trying the following techniques to reduce your level of hostility:

- Admit to someone that you're too hostile and that you're trying to do something about it. Just admitting it makes you more accountable to yourself.
- Monitor your cynical thoughts, and when you find yourself becoming cynical, yell "Stop!"
- Have a silent conversation in which you reason with yourself. If you can't distract yourself from your anger, try to talk yourself out of your anger. Figure out an alternative way of approaching the situation.
- When you find yourself getting hostile, begin to meditate. Learn effective ways to relax, and practice them when you feel hostility and anger starting to build.
- Try to be more empathetic to the plight of others; as Williams says, try to put yourself in the other person's shoes. If you find that someone is truly mis-

treating you, learn to be effectively assertive in protecting your interests instead of getting aggressive. When people wrong you, forgive them.

- Increase your social connectedness; cultivate friends where you work and where you worship. Learn to trust; learn to listen. Get a pet.
- Try some of Diane Ulmer's recommended drills:[74] Practice smiling at others, compliment others, practice giving yourself permission to stay calm when things don't go the way you want, practice laughing at yourself, play fun games, stop using obscenities, and look for opportunities to say, "Maybe I'm wrong."
- Volunteer to help people who are less fortunate than you are.
- Learn more about the teachings of your chosen religion.
- And, something mentioned by several researchers, including Williams, pretend that today is your last day.[75]

Ellen Goodman, a writer for the *Washington Post*, summed up the sentiment eloquently in a piece about New Year's resolutions. In calling for the resolution to be a civil, social creature, she wrote:

This may be a peak period for the battle against the spread of a waistline and creeping cholesterol. But it is also within our willpower to fight the spread of urban rudeness and creeping hostility. Civility doesn't stop nuclear holocaust and doesn't put a roof over the head of the homeless. But it makes a difference in the shape of a community, as surely as lifting weights can make a difference in the shape of a human torso.[76]

Notes

1. Robert Ornstein and David Sobel, *The Healing Brain* (New York: Simon and Schuster, 1987), p. 181.

2. Emrika Padus, *The Complete Guide to Your Emotions and Your Health* (Emmaus, Pennsylvania: Rodale Press, 1986), p. 595.

3. Diane K. Ulmer, "Helping the Coronary Patient Reduce Hostility and Hurry Sickness: A Structured Behavioral Group Approach," *The Psychology of Health, Immunity, and Disease,* vol. A, p. 580 in Proceedings of the Sixth International Conference of the National Institute for the Clinical Application of Behavioral Medicine.

4. "Anger: How a Toxic Emotion Can Harm Your Health," *UT Lifetime Health Letter,* May: 1994, 7.

5. Earl Ubell, "The Deadly Emotions," *Parade Magazine,* February 11: 1990, 4–5.

6. Howard S. Friedman, *The Self-Healing Personality* (New York: Henry Holt and Company, 1991), p. 47.

7. Paul Bagne, "Rude Awakening," *Men's Health,* October: 1990, 34–35.

8. Ornstein and Sobel.

9. Carl E. Thoresen, "The Hostility Habit: A Serious Health Problem?" *Healthline,* April: 1984, 5.

10. Redford Williams, *The Trusting Heart: Great News About Type A Behavior* (New York: Times Books Division of Random House, Inc., 1989), p. 66.

11. Williams, p. 67.

12. Ubell.

13. *Journal of Psychosomatic Research*, 33, pp. 449–456, as summarized in *Brain/Mind Bulletin*, May: 1990, 3.

14. Bagne.

15. Williams, p. 71.

16. Bagne.

17. Ulmer, p. 587.

18. "Is Yours a Hostile Heart?" *Men's Health*, 5(7/8): 1989, 1.

19. Arthur J. Barsky, *Worried Sick: Our Troubled Quest for Wellness* (Boston: Little, Brown, and Company, 1988).

20. Barsky.

21. Barsky.

22. Barsky.

23. Paul Pearsall, *Super Immunity* (New York: McGraw-Hill Book Company, 1987).

24. Robert Ornstein and David Sobel, *Healthy Pleasures* (Reading, Massachusetts: Addison-Wesley Publishing Company, Inc., 1989), p. 232.

25. Ornstein and Sobel, *Healthy Pleasures*, p. 232.

26. Ornstein and Sobel, *Healthy Pleasures*, p. 233.

27. Pearsall.

28. Gurney Williams III, "The Selfish Heart," *Longevity*, November 1988, p. 24.

29. Joshua Fischman, "Blood Pressure Woes: The 'I's' Have It," *Psychology Today*, August: 1988, 22–23.

30. Brent K. Houston and Christine R. Vavak, "Cynical Hostility: Developmental Factors, Psychosocial Correlates, and Health Behaviors," *Health Psychology*, 10(1): 1991, 9–17.

31. Mark Leiker and B. Jo Hailey, "A Link Between Hostility and Disease: Poor Health Habits?" *Behavioral Medicine*, Fall: 1988, 129–133.

32. D. Carmelli, R. H. Rosenman, and G. E. Swan, "The Cook and Medley HO Scale: A Heritability Analysis in Adult Male Twins," *Psychosomatic Medicine*, 50(2): 1988, 165–174.

33. Bagne.

34. Information on effects of hostility was taken from Williams, *The Trusting Heart*; Redford Williams, "Lifestyles of the Healthy and Hearty," *Psychology Today*, January/February: 1989, 35–42; "Trusting Hearts Last Longer: Hostility May Be Type A Toxin," *Brain/Mind Bulletin*, March: 1989, 3; and "How Hostile Thinking Makes You Heart-Sick," *Your Personal Best*, April: 1989, 5.

35. J. L. Marx, "Coronary Artery Spasms and Heart Disease," *Science* 208 (4448): 1127–1130; and E. Braunwald, "Coronary Artery Spasm," *Journal of the American Medical Association*, 244(17), 1957–1959.

36. Williams, *The Trusting Heart*, p. 83.

37. Williams, *The Trusting Heart*, pp. 83–84.

38. Williams, "Lifestyles," p. 40.

39. Williams, "Lifestyles," p. 40.

40. "How Hostile Thinking," p . 5 .

41. "How Hostile Thinking."

42. Williams, "Lifestyles," p. 40.

43. Ornstein and Sobel, p. 181.

44. Redford B. Williams, Jr., "Neurocardiology."

45. John Droubay Hardy and Timothy W. Smith, "Cynical Hostility and Vulnerability to Disease: Social Support, Life Stress, and Physiological Response to Conflict," *Health Psychology*, 7(5): 1988, 448.

46. "Warning: Hostility Can Be Dangerous to Your Health," *University of Texas Lifetime Health Letter*, 1(9): 1989, 3.

47. R. B. Williams, Jr., T. L. Haney, K. L. Lee, Y-H. Kong, J. A. Blumenthal, and R. E. Whalen, "Type A Behavior, Hostility, and Coronary Atherosclerosis," *Psychosomatic Medicine*, 42(6): 1980, 539–549; and Paul Bagne, "Rude Awakening," *Men's Health*, October: 1990, 34–35.

48. Thoresen.

49. L. Musante, F. A. Treiber, H. Davis, W. B. Strong, and M. Levy, "Hostility: Relationship to Lifestyle Behaviors and Physical Risk Factors," *Behavioral Medicine*, 18(1): 21–26, 1992.

50. Harrison.

51. "Hostility: Heart-Harming Type-A Trait?" *Medical World News*, February 14: 1983, 14.

52. "Hostility: Poison to the Heart," *Men's Health*, August: 1987, 4.

53. Redford Williams and Virginia Williams, *Anger Kills* (New York: Random House/Times Books, 1993), p. 49.

54. "Hostility: Poison to the Heart."

55. Williams and Williams, p. 43.

56. Hardy and Smith, p. 449.

57. *Internal Medicine News*, 23(1): 1990, 5.

58. Williams and Williams, p. 53.

59. Ubell.

60. Redford B. Williams, Jr., "Hostility, An-

ger, and Heart Disease," *Drug Therapy*, August: 1986, 43.

61. Williams, "Hostility, Anger, and Heart Disease."

62. Thoresen.

63. Thoresen.

64. Williams and Williams, p. 36.

65. Thoresen; and Williams, "Neurocardiology."

66. Williams, *The Trusting Heart*, pp. 50–52.

67. Williams and Williams, p. 35.

68. Ilene C. Siegler, Bercedis L. Peterson, John C. Barefoot, and Redford B. Williams, "Hostility During Late Adolescence Predicts Coronary Risk Factors at Mid-Life," *American Journal of Epidemiology*, 136(2): 146–152.

69. "High Hostility May Lead to High Cholesterol, Researchers Say," *Deseret News*, November 16: 1990, A20.

70. Thoresen.

71. Kathy A. Fackelmann, "Hostility Boosts Risk of Heart Trouble," *Science News*, 135: 1989, 60.

72. Linda C. Higgins, "Hostility Theory Rekindles Debate Over Type A Behavior," *Medical World News*, February 27: 1989, 21.

73. The Editors of *Prevention* and the Center for Positive Living, *Positive Living and Health: The Complete Guide to Brain/Body Healing and Mental Empowerment* (Emmaus, Pennsylvania: Rodale Press, 1990), p. 155.

74. Ulmer, p. 592.

75. Daniel Goleman and Joel Gurin, editors, *Mind/Body Medicine: How to Use Your Mind for Better Health* (New York: Consumer Reports Books, 1993), p. 80.

76. Ellen Goodman, "Thoughts for a New Year," *Reader's Digest*, January: 1989, 118.

9

WORRY, ANXIETY, FEAR, AND HEALTH

I have had many troubles in my life,
but the worst of them
never came.
—JAMES A. GARFIELD

Worriers slide into the seat of an airplane, snap the seatbelt closed, and worry that the plane might crash. They worry that a fussy toddler might have contracted chickenpox. They worry that their term paper wasn't good enough or that they'll be fired because they called in sick one too many times.

Worry is something most Americans are familiar with. According to statistics from a variety of studies, only about a third classify themselves as nonworriers, people who worry less than an hour and a half each day. More than half classify themselves as moderate worriers, people who worry between 10 and 50 percent of the day and may or may not be troubled by worrying. The rest are chronic worriers, people who worry more than eight hours a day.[1]

Andrew Matthews of Louisiana State University says that worry might be a form of increased vigilance against threats, a form of problem solving or a way to rehearse potentially unpleasant events. If you use it to prepare for and deal with a bad situation, it can be beneficial. If it becomes excessive, it can harm health.[2]

Definitions of Worry

According to clinical psychologist Thomas Pruzinsky of the University of Virginia,

[Worry is] a state in which we dwell on something so much it causes us to become apprehensive. It differs from the far stronger emotion we call fear, which

205

*causes physical changes such as a racing pulse and fast breathing in our bodies.
Worry is the thinking part of anxiety.[3]*

And, says Pruzinsky, most people who report to a doctor that they are worried say they worry anywhere from 80 to 95 percent of the day.

Worrying reflects our attempts to cope mentally with our concerns and fears. It's not always bad; worry can be useful if it helps us become more vigilant or helps us take steps that will keep something negative from happening. Worry becomes harmful when there's no way to keep our worries from becoming reality or when worrying becomes so pervasive that we are immobilized by it.[4]

Surveys show that the most common sources of worry for Americans are family and relationships, job or school, health, and finances. According to Jennifer L. Abel, associate director of the Stress and Anxiety Disorders Institute at Pennsylvania State University, most people worry about 5 percent of the time. Chronic worriers, on the other hand, spend an average of about 50 percent of their time worrying. And for some, says Abel, it's 100 percent of the time.[5]

And for those chronic worriers, most worry elaborately. In one study that demonstrates that point, psychologists compared twenty-four chronic worriers with twenty-four people who say they don't worry. The psychologists then gave both groups a scenario: What if you got bad grades? The nonworriers fashioned simple responses: They might get into trouble with their parents, or might feel embarrassed for a few days. The chronic worriers, however, were characterized by responses that progressed quickly from bad grades to the more catastrophic possibilities of loss of control, mental illness, pain, deterioration, and even death and hell.[6]

Generalized Anxiety Disorder

Some people have what has been termed *generalized anxiety disorder,* a problem disabling enough to require medication.[7] Generalized anxiety disorder occurs only in the absence of some other condition that may cause the anxiety, such as panic attacks, underlying depression, or of some physical disease that may cause anxiety, such as heart or respiratory disease, hyperthyroidism, or diabetes. The diagnosis is made only if the person has excessive anxiety almost daily over two or more life circumstances for a period of at least six months.

According to the National Institute of Mental Health in Bethesda, Maryland, the anxiety disorders that stem from worry are America's most commonly reported mental health problems.[8] And what starts in the mind as worry can have a profound effect on the body.

Somaticizing

People afflicted with the phenomenon of somaticizing, those whom experts have come to call *the worried well,* are extremely anxious or worried. Because they feel unable or unwilling to face emotional difficulties, they subconsciously somatize them or convert them into physical complaints.[9] As many as two-thirds of all patient visits to the doctor may be made by the worried well, and because physicians don't recognize the emotional basis of the physical complaints these patients are often sent from one physician to another without being helped.[10]

Hosts of studies compiled over the past three decades have shown that addressing the emotional problems that underlie somatized physical problems can cut health care costs by an estimated 5 to 80 percent per year.[11]

Psychologist Nicholas Cummings, who founded the Biodyne Institute, a mental health facility in Hawaii, says that "some patients spend as much as $28,000 a year in a fruitless attempt to isolate a physical cause for what is basically an emotional problem. . . . On some days these patients saw four different physicians." Cummings says the emotional problems of anxiety and worry have to be addressed if there is to be an improvement in the patient's condition and says he never disputes the reality of patients' difficulties: "I can say with all honesty: 'I know you hurt. But as long as you're here, tell us a bit more about you.'" Cummings adds that addressing the emotional problems often helps when other treatments have failed.[12]

Effects on the Body

Physician Marty Rossman explains, worry "creates negative images about some future event like a deadline or a test. The down side is that chronic worry can overwork and wear down the immune system, leading to chronic stress, a state that has been associated with numerous ailments, from headaches to heart disease."[13]

When people somatize an emotion like worry into a physical complaint, they literally feel something physically. But worry can actually cause physical changes that can compromise the immune system and result in physical illness.

Worry and the Circulatory System

Worry has been shown to have effects on the heart and circulatory system as a whole. Researchers interested in the effects of worry tested 125 patients for a year following their heart attacks. A real distinction developed between the ones who worried about their condition and the ones who didn't: Those who worried were significantly more likely to have arrhythmias (abnormal heart rhythms that can lead to sudden, fatal heart attacks).[14]

Worry has been related to high blood pressure in a number of studies. Some of the most convincing ones involved animals in the laboratory. In one, researchers confined monkeys in a cage in which they had to press a bar once every twenty seconds for twelve hours a day to avoid electrical shocks. After a few months, the monkeys developed high blood pressure. Researchers removed the

Focus on Research

One experience in particular powerfully demonstrates the influence of mind over body and the way that worry can bring about literal physical changes. A fifty-three-year-old man's father and brother had both died of heart attacks at the age of fifty-four. Just before his own fifty-fourth birthday, the man went to the health clinic experiencing severe angina. Doctors ran the routine tests, including an electrocardiogram and a measure of his blood pressure.

Everything was normal. There was no physical reason why he should have been developing symptoms of angina. Still, the pain persisted.

At the man's insistence, doctors delved deeper. They found an amazing thing: In worrying about a potential heart attack, the man had involuntarily shut down the circulation of blood to his left arm and hand. The result was angina pain—as a result of worry.

Source: Emrika Padus, *The Complete Guide to Your Emotions and Your Health* (Emmaus, Pennsylvania: Rodale Press, 1986).

bar from the cage, and stopped delivering electrical shocks. What happened then was the real surprise: The monkeys' blood pressure skyrocketed!

Apparently the monkeys worried constantly about not being able to avoid the shocks, even though none was delivered. Examinations of the monkeys showed that the arteries to the skin, kidneys, intestines, and muscles were tightly contracted, causing tremendous increases in blood pressure.[15–17]

A similar thing happened when researchers placed mice in a room with a cat that was confined in a cage. The cat was never let out of the cage, and was never allowed or enabled to chase the mice. Within six to twelve months, the mice all developed high blood pressure. They apparently were worried about the cat, and their constant worrying caused high blood pressure.[18]

Worry and Asthma

From scientific tests, we know that the emotion of worry causes the body to produce the chemical acetylcholine, which causes the airways to contract. When enough acetylcholine is secreted, the result is asthma. The muscles around the bronchioles constrict so tightly that air can no longer flow freely through them.

Obviously, then, worry can have a significant impact on victims of asthma. In one study, researchers simply *told* a group of asthmatics that they were being exposed to pollens and other aggravating agents. Then the researchers stood back and watched what happened. More than half of the asthmatics developed a full-blown asthma attack, even though no pollens or other irritants were actually present. Worry that it would happen triggered the attack.[19]

In a similar study, children with asthma were observed to determine the effect of various emotions on their illness. Most saw their parents as overbearing or rejecting, and these children constantly worried that they might not measure up or be accepted. To test a theory, researchers sent the parents on a paid vacation. They left the children with trained observers and watched what happened in the parents' absence. Half of the children improved dramatically without any other treatment. They stopped worrying, and their blood levels of acetylcholine diminished.[20]

If you're a worrier, can you stop? Researchers suggest the following techniques:[21]

- Learn to solve problems. According to Dr. Timothy A. Brown, associate director of the Center for Stress and Anxiety Disorders at the State University of New York, most worriers jump from one topic to another without reaching any solutions.
- Work on improving your thoughts. Pennsylvania State University's Jennifer L. Abel says that doesn't mean seeing the world through rose-colored glasses. Worriers, she points out, see the world through cracked glasses: "Our goal is to give people clear glasses, so they see things more accurately."
- Use visualization and deep breathing to get you through the worry.
- Focus on what's going on right now. According to Abel, worry is almost always future oriented, "so if we can focus on what we're doing right now—the sentence we're reading, the voice of the person speaking—rather than thinking about what someone might say next, we're better off."
- It seems odd, but it works. Dr. Michael Vasey, assistant professor of psychology and Ohio State University, has joined a number of other researchers in advising people to set aside a worry period, a specific period of time every day (researchers suggest thirty minutes). During that entire period, focus completely on your worry and try to think of solutions to your problems. "If you practice focusing on worries and thinking of solutions for 30 minutes each day for several weeks, your anxiety starts to taper off. You'll get better at generalizing solutions or realize it's not worth worrying about."

The Effects of Uncertainty

One specific kind of worry, uncertainty, has been shown to create a particularly devastating kind of stress. Uncertainty is *not knowing*. It's being confronted with a complex situation that the person can't figure out. It's confusion over what is meant by a person or situation. It's a situation that is not predictable and, therefore, a situation in which the individual can't determine how to act. If it gets confusing enough or unpredictable enough, it can cause feelings of futility or helplessness and can lead to most devastating stress.[22]

Mounting evidence shows that "worry over life's uncertainties—those future *what-ifs* and past *if-onlys* that can drive us crazy with speculation—creates a particularly devastating kind of stress response. . . . It's what we don't know (and can't do anything about) that can really hurt us."[23]

Studies involving uncertainty prove the point. One researcher studied a group of 100 patients in a Veterans Administration Hospital. Each had rated an upcoming event—treatment, surgery, or the like—as being extremely stressful. When the researcher probed into each patient's situation, however, he found an amazing thing: The patients were not really stressed over the event itself. They were stressed because of uncertainty. They did not have enough information about the event. They didn't feel they knew exactly what was going to happen to them. They didn't really understand the outcome. It was the uncertainty, not the event itself, that caused all the upset.[24]

Uncertainty keeps a person in a constant state of semiarousal, putting "an extreme burden on the body's adaptive resources and resistance systems." It's the same reason that predictable pain is so much less stressful: The person is capable of "learning when it is safe to 'lower its guard' and relax."[25] Not knowing when a pain or a shock is coming means having to stay on guard—tensed and stressed—all the time.

A series of studies demonstrate the effect of uncertainty. A report by the British Health Service monitored the prevalence of peptic ulcers during World War II, when England was being bombed frequently by enemy troops. People living in the center of London, where the bombings were regular and predictable, suffered a 50 percent increase in the rate of gastric ulcers. In contrast, the increase in ulcer rate among residents on the outskirts of the city, where the bombings were extremely unpredictable, was six times greater than among the residents of London's central district.[26]

In an experiment in New Jersey, two psychologists divided a group of laboratory rats into two groups. Rats in the first group were given electrical shocks at random and without warning. Rats in the second group were also given electrical shocks, but rats in the second group were warned of the impending shock shortly before each one was delivered. The rats that were given unpredictable shocks developed gastric complications at a significantly greater rate than the rats whose shocks were predictable.

It works likewise with people. A psychologist in New York interviewed college students and kept track of their health histories during the year. He noted not only when the students reported being sick but the circumstances that preceded and surrounded the episodes of illness. He found that they reported being sick most often following events in their lives that were undesirable. Furthermore, most of the sickness followed events that were not only undesirable but also left the students uncertain about how much control they had.

Other studies show that undesirable life events and uncertainty are a deadly combination. Undesirable life events alone don't usually result in illness, nor do uncontrollable life events about which we are uncertain. But when the two are paired up—when events are both undesirable and unpredictable—there is a "significant impact" on health that usually results in illness.[27]

The Health Consequences of Fear

When worry escalates, the result is fear. Everyone has experienced fear. A swimmer of only moderate skill might be afraid of swift waters; a child might be afraid of the dark. A hiker will probably experience fear on hearing the distinctive warning of a rattlesnake; a jogger might feel fear when confronted with the bared fangs of a Doberman pinscher. According to Norman Cousins, "Fear and panic create negative expectations." Then, he says, "One tends to move in the direction of one's expectations."[28] Fear causes the heart to race, the head to spin, the palms to sweat, the knees to buckle, and breathing to become labored. The level of arousal that results is similar to the effects of stress, and the human body can't withstand it indefinitely.

Fear causes the body to secrete epinephrine, or adrenaline, a hormone also secreted in response to stress. Fear floods the system with epinephrine. Its most powerful effect is on the heart: Both the rate and strength of contractions increase. Blood pressure soars. The body is stimulated to release other hormones, which act on various other organs and systems. In essence, the body is put on alert. If the fear is intense enough, all systems can fatally overload.

Medical history is replete with examples of people who were literally frightened to death.[29] Take, for instance, Pearl Pizzamiglio. Fifteen minutes after she started the 11 P.M. shift at the In-Town Motor Hotel in Chevy Chase, Maryland, Michael Stewart walked in with another man. Stewart handed her a paper bag with a note that said, "Don't say a word. Put all the money in this bag and no one will get hurt." Pizzamiglio put $160 in the paper bag, the men fled, and she called the police. Two hours later, Pearl Pizzamiglio, aged sixty, free of any history of heart problems, was dead of heart failure. Stewart was arrested and charged with murder; the jury decided that, indeed, a simple paper bag and a piece of paper could be considered instruments of death. Stewart had, literally, scared Pizzamiglio to death.

In another incident, Barbara Reyes was spending her Memorial Day weekend floating on a raft on Georgia's peaceful Lake Lanier. The calm of the peaceful, warm afternoon was shattered when a man riding a motorized jet ski roared within a foot of the forty-year-old Reyes. In a panic, Reyes paddled to shore, collapsed, and died. Randolph Simpson, the Gwinnett County coroner who examined Reyes, said "There's no question she was literally scared to death." The man who roared by on the jet ski was arrested and charged with involuntary manslaughter.

One forty-five-year-old man died of fright as he stepped to a podium to give a speech. An elderly man sitting on his lawn collapsed and died when a car jumped the curb and appeared to be headed straight for him. Panamanian dictator Omar Torrijos reportedly amused himself by killing a prisoner with an unloaded gun; the sound of the blanks firing was enough to scare the man to death. And in the year 840, Bavarian Emperor Louis died of fright when he saw a solar eclipse.

The physical effects of fear are the same whether the fear is perfectly understandable or illogical. "The messages from the brain to the body are the same," one researcher pointed out, "whether you're teetering on the edge of a cliff, about to fall, or standing safely at the foot of a mountain, fearful of climbing to the top." [30] Another explained,

If demand on the heart exceeds its reserve capacity, the muscle can starve, developing "dead zones" that short-circuit electrical impulses. A heart damaged by a previous heart attack or constricted by clogged arteries is especially vulnerable. When the signals misfire, the heart forsakes its deliberate pumping and begins quivering randomly, its surface undulating like a mass of frenzied worms. Blood supply to the brain and other tissues falters, and death can follow in minutes.[31]

When dogs are injected with catecholamines, the hormones released in response to fear, they die. Autopsies reveal certain characteristic lesions on the surface of the heart, presumably an effect of the catecholamines. The same lesions are visible under microscopic examination on the hearts of 80 percent of all victims of sudden cardiac death. While much of the evidence on being scared to death is anecdotal, some is very scientific. Consider, for example, the monitoring of Air Force test pilots. Robert Eliot, a cardiologist who is an expert on sudden death, studied scientific documentation from five separate incidents. In each, Air Force test pilots lost control of their aircraft and were not able to eject. "Their electrocardiograms were being monitored from the ground," Eliot points out. "These people died before they hit the ground, and they died of fright."[32]

One of the most dramatic examples was provided by Bernard Lown, a renowned Harvard cardiologist who witnessed an incredible incident involving a middle-aged woman who had been hospitalized with tricuspid stenosis, a non–life-threatening narrowing of a heart valve. As they were making their rounds one morning, they entered this woman's room. Her physician turned to Lown and the other doctors who were gathered around her bedside and announced, "This woman has TS." The doctors then left the room. The woman for some reason decided that *TS* meant *terminal situation.* She began to hyperventilate, and sweat profusely, and her pulse shot up to 150. Upon learning of her fear, her doctor tried to explain and calm her, but in vain. She died later the same day of heart failure.[33]

Strongest of all fears are phobias, fears that are irrational and inappropriate. A phobia is an intense fear of an object or situation that would not frighten most people. Victims of phobia become almost immobilized, rearranging their entire life to avoid the feared object or place. One of the most common phobias is agoraphobia, or fear of going out into open spaces (stores, restaurants, theaters—anywhere outside a "safe" place, like home). Other phobias include fear of being trapped in a cramped space, fear of speaking in public, fear of dogs, fear of eating in public, fear of heights, fear of blood. An estimated 13 million Americans have a phobia of some kind.[34]

When a phobic encounters the feared object or situation, the result is a panic attack or phobia attack, and the effect on the body is the same as the well-known fight-or-flight response. In this case, the emphasis is on flight. Typical physical reactions include shortness of breath, palpitations, chest pain or discomfort, choking or smothering sensations, dizziness, vertigo, unsteady feelings, feelings of unreality, hot and cold flashes, sweating, faintness, trembling, and shaking.[35]

And, again, fear enters the picture. The most severe physical reactions occur *before* an encounter with the dreaded object or situation. The mere anticipation of what might happen is enough to cause pain and disability on its own. Hormones surge into the bloodstream, and the body is intensely stressed. It can't endure the state of arousal for long. If the fear is prolonged or intense, the body can literally short-circuit or gradually become devastated by the physical effects of stress.

Notes

1. Sharon Faelten, David Diamond, and the editors of *Prevention, Take Control of Your Life: A Complete Guide to Stress Relief* (Emmaus, Pennsylvania: Rodale Press, 1988).

2. "Worrying Well," *Berkeley Wellness Letter* (June: 1993).

3. Amy H. Berger, "Are You a Chronic Worrier?" *Complete Woman,* October: 1987, 58.

4. Faelten et al.

5. Cathy Perlmutter, "Conquer Chronic Worry," *Prevention,* November: 1993, 75.

6. "Worrying Well."

7. Susan Ince, "People Who Worry Too Much," *Weight Watchers Women's Health and Fitness News,* September: 1990, 3.

8. Berger.

9. Winifred Gallagher, "Treating the Worried Well," *American Health,* January/February: 1988, 36.

10. Carol Turkington, "Help for the Worried Well," *Psychology Today,* August: 1987, 46.

11. Turkington.

12. Turkington.

13. Will Stapp, "Imagine Yourself Well," *Medical Self-Care,* January/February: 1988, 27–30.

14. "Heart Attack: Can You Worry Yourself to Death?" *Medical Abstracts Newsletter,* November: 1988, 3.

15. J. P. Henry, J. P. Meehan, and P. M. Stephens, "The Use of Psychosocial Stimuli To Induce Prolonged Systolic Hypertension in Mice," *Psychosomatic Medicine,* 29: 1967, 408.

16. R. P. Forsyth, "Blood Pressure Responses to Long-Term Avoidance Schedules in the Restrained Rhesus Monkey," *Psychosomatic Medicine,* 31: 1969, 300.

17. R. P. Forsyth, "Regional Blood Flow Changes During 72-Hour Avoidance Schedules in the Monkey," *Science,* 173: 1971, 546.

18. Henry et al.

19. T. J. Luparello et al., "The Interaction of Psychologic Stimuli and Pharmacologic Agents in Airway Reactivity in Asthmatic Subjects," *Psychosomatic Medicine,* 5: 1970, 500.

20. K. Purcell et al., "Effect on Asthma in Children of Experimental Separation from the Family," *Psychosomatic Medicine,* 31: 1969, 144.

21. Perlmutter, pp. 76–80.

22. Phillip L. Rice, *Stress and Health: Principles and Practice for Coping with Wellness* (Monterey, California: Brooks/Cole Publishing, 1987), pp. 80–81.

23. Emrika Padus, *The Complete Guide to Your Emotions and Your Health* (Emmaus, Pennsylvania: Rodale Press, 1986).

24. Rice, p. 81.

25. Padus.

26. Studies of uncertainty are from Padus.

27. Rice, p. 81.

28. Norman Cousins, *The Healing Heart,* (New York: W. W. Norton, 1983).

29. Examples are from Edward Dolnick, "Scared to Death," *Hippocrates,* March/April: 1989, 106–108.

30. Padus.

31. Dolnick, p. 108.

32. Dolnick.

33. Dolnick.

34. Faelten et al., p. 97.

35. Faelten et al., p. 98.

10

DEPRESSION, DESPAIR, AND HEALTH

One who expects completely to escape low moods is asking the impossible. Like the weather, life is essentially variable, and a healthy person believes in the validity of his high hours even when he is having a low one.
—*HARRY EMERSON FOSDICK*

Life is a series of natural ups and downs. Everyone who lives feels intermittent sadness and grief. While those intermittent sad moods can be depressing, they don't really constitute depression.

A Definition

The word *depression* has several meanings:

1. As a *normal human affect,* it's caused by the disruption of normal life balance, loss, conflict, or trauma.
2. Depression can be a *symptom* of an illness or a medication side effect.
3. Depression is also a *clinical syndrome* based on neurochemicals; that's the definition used through most of this chapter.
4. Finally, depression can be a combination of all three. And any of these can follow a crisis.

Depression as an illness is not a normal reaction but can occur even without a clear reason. It is much more than an occasional sad mood. It generally involves quitting or just plain giving up. A person who is depressed feels that the present conditions and the future possibilities are intolerable. A depressed person"goes on strike" from life, doing less and less, losing interest in people, abandoning hobbies, and giving up at work.[1]

One reason depression is difficult to define is its elusiveness. Steven Paul, chief of clinical neuroscience at the National Institute of Mental Health, says that depression is "like a fever, in that it's often an unspecific response to an internal or external insult. Like fever, it has a number of origins and treatments."[2]

Frederick Goodwin, the scientific director of the National Institute of Mental Health, says that depression is the richest, most striking example in psychiatry, and possibly in all of medicine, of the relationship between the mind and the body.[3] Rather than being a single illness or condition, many experts believe it is a group of mood disorders that strike with varying intensity. No one yet has all the answers, but one thing is certain: Depression, together with its neurochemical cousin, anxiety, has some profound effects on who gets sick and, in particular, who comes to see the physician.

Prevalence and Manifestations

If you survey the U.S. population at any given time, about 7 percent of all women and 3 percent of all men have major depression; probably another 4 to 5 percent have minor depression (not quite enough of the criteria for a diagnosis of major depression), and 8 percent have major anxiety disorders. The percentages go even higher in winter. During their lifetime, nearly one-fourth of all women suffer clinical depression.[4] The percentage of teenagers with diagnosed clinical depression has increased more than fivefold over the past forty years.[5]

Medically, depression is a huge problem. Approximately one-fourth of all primary care medical patients come from the 15 percent of the population with major depression and anxiety disorders. That climbs to almost half of all patients if you include minor depression and anxiety. Almost half of the top users of medical care are those with major depression.[6] Only about one-third of the depressed are recognized and treated, and fewer than one-fourth of the anxious are recognized and treated,[7] largely because depression and anxiety cause so many medical symptoms, and often because patients don't want to recognize a "mental" component to their medical illness. (Depression and anxiety are combined here because they so often overlap and because they appear to be caused by some of the same neurochemical abnormalities. Nearly a third of all depressed people have generalized anxiety disorder[8] (i.e., nearly continuous background anxiousness). In essence, huge numbers of people whose underlying mental problems go untreated repeatedly return complaining of medical problems. Treating the depression has proven to greatly reduce not only suffering and disability but medical illness and costs as well (see Chapter 28).

People in all walks of life and of all ages suffer from depression. Depression seems particularly rampant among downtrodden persons and women. According to Martin E. P. Seligman, "Women are twice as likely to suffer depression as men are, because, on the average, they think about problems in ways that amplify depression. . . . Women tend to contemplate their depression, mulling it over and over, trying to analyze it and determine its source."[9] Studies show that depression is prevalent among people with poor social support and a dearth of supportive relationships.[10] Well-known people, have also struggled with the "black dog of depression."—Abraham Lincoln, Ernest Hemingway, Winston Churchill, Sylvia Plath, Thomas Eagleton, and even Biblical figures, including Saul and Nebuchadnezzar.[11]

Depression can lead to suicide. Some experts estimate that as many as 15 percent of those who are depressed eventually resort to self-destruction.[12] The problem may be even more pronounced among the adolescent victims of depression. Elliot S. Gershon, chief of the clinical psychogenetics branch of the National Institute of Mental Health states,

> *The chilling fact is that we may be on the verge of an epidemic-like increase of mania, depression, and suicide. The trend is rising almost exponentially and shows no signs of letting up. I would go so far as to say this is going to be the public health problem of the 1990s and beyond if the trend continues.[13]*

According to one study of the elderly, depression is often associated with illness, disability, isolation, bereavement, and poverty.[14] A variety of studies confirm that finding. And according to a study of more than 11,000 people published in *The Journal of the American Medical Association*, people with depression had worse physical, social, and role functioning; were in worse physical health; and suffered more bodily pain than did people with a chronic medical disease such as arthritis, back problems, gastrointestinal disease, or diabetes.[15] Depressed people have five times the normal disability rates.[16] If you compare the most common chronic medical diseases, only severe heart or pulmonary failure comes close to depression in causing disability. Overall, costs of depression in the United States are estimated at $43 billion per year, and only about 10 percent of that is out-patient treatment costs.[17] (This figure doesn't include the costs of treating medical illness caused by undetected depression.) People with depression have two and a half times more poor physical health, more physical illnesses, and four times the normal mortality rate,[18] 63 percent of it due to cardiovascular conditions.

Causes

Most researchers today think that certain brain circuits are fragile and that this renders some people vulnerable to depression. That fragility is determined primarily by the deficient function of the neurotransmitter chemicals, such as serotonin and dopamine, that enable brain signals to be transmitted from one cell to the next. That deficiency of brain neurochemicals can often be genetic and it may explain why depression sometimes runs in families. The familial tendency is real. One early but well-known study of the Amish in Pennsylvania showed that all twenty-six suicides between 1880 and 1980 were members of only four extended families.[19]

In commenting on the studies and the tendency of depression to run in families, John Mann, director of the laboratory of psychopharmacology at Cornell Medical College, explains, "Serotonin levels are under some genetic control to begin with, and this suicidal tendency appears to be an inherited biochemical trait."[20] To separate the genetic causes from depressed behavior learned from families, studies of identical twins adopted to different families have shown a very clear inheritance pattern, even among those raised by very upbeat families. Nevertheless, the cause is not entirely predetermined by genes, though heredity is an important factor in creating vulnerability to stress.

Still other theories (which have been criticized) say that depression occurs as a result of a severe adverse life event or a series of less serious difficulties that gradually erode self-esteem. One scientist who believes that theory is Dr. George W. Brown of the Department of Social Policy and Social Science at the University of London's Royal Holloway and Bedford New College. Brown compiled the results of ten different studies. They show, he says, that 88 percent of depressed women had experienced some recent severe life event or a "major difficulty" in their lives.[21]

Later, Brown studied that group of results, paying more attention to the details of the adverse life events suffered by the women. He reported a fifteen-fold difference in the predicted risk of depression between women who had the worst assortment of life events and those who reported no adverse life events at all during the period in which the study took place.[22]

So which is the cause of depression, inherited neurochemistry or repeated negative experiences that cause a depressed habit pattern? Episodes of depression coming out of the blue, for no reason, certainly make a case for a neurochemical cause. Nevertheless, some fascinating experiments in mental conditioning suggest it may be both, that neurochemical dysregulation stems from either genetics or learning, or both.

Under unrelenting stress they cannot control, people and animals show depletion of brain serotonin activity. If the pattern is repeated several times in association with a certain place or situation, subsequent exposure to the same place or situation will cause a drop in serotonin function, even in the absence of the stressor: Serotonin suppression becomes a conditioned response. (The body has an immense capacity to produce physiological responses the brain "expects," clear down to the cellular level, as has been proven repeatedly by the placebo response.) In the case of learned, conditioned neurochemical changes likely to cause depression, the effect can combine with genetic predisposition to sustain even the biological depression. There is some evidence that repeated depressive episodes can condition the enzymes which allow genes to express themselves physically to respond so as to lay down "hard-wired" neurological circuits that automatically create a depressed response that is more resistant to treatment, the so-called kindling phenomenon.[23]

One theory about the cause of depression, then, combines a variety of perspectives. As reported in *Psychology Today* and proposed by psychiatrists Hagop

Akiskal of the University of Tennessee and William McKinney, Jr., of the University of Wisconsin:

> *Assume, first, that a person is genetically susceptible to depression, meaning that certain circuits in the brain areas particularly concerned with pleasure and rewarding experiences are chemically fragile and somewhat easily upset. Give that person some early traumatic experiences and undermine confidence and self-esteem, such as the loss of or separation from a parent at a critical stage of development. Add the kind of psychological stress later in life that echoes the early loss and places unusual demands on the already vulnerable reward system. (Events are particularly likely to affect people with few social supports—family, friends or lovers.) The brain's response to this is felt as a diminished ability to experience emotion, including pleasure. Paradoxically, this lack of emotion, this emptiness, is deeply felt and incredibly painful. At the same time, activity decreases, as do sociability and the opportunity for pleasure and rewards: One tries less, gets less and feels worse.[24]*

Characteristics

Depression has been called the common cold of mental illness,[25] and, like the common cold, it can have a variety of symptoms that reflect the entire spectrum of severity. In some cases of depression, the few symptoms are quite mild; in others, a host of symptoms are quite severe. Medical symptoms that cannot be clearly attributed to organic disease are especially likely to be due to depression and anxiety disorders (Table 10.1).

These symptoms are not imagined; rather, they arise from a very real physiological upset that occurs when the midbrain no longer controls those operations, as happens in persons with depression or anxiety disorders. Normal function

TABLE 10.1   Prevalence of Depression and Anxiety Disorders in Medical Patients with Unexplained Symptoms

Symptom	Unexplained (%)	Depression (%)	Anxiety (%)
Headache	48	53	44
Chest pain	36	66	66
Back pain	30	53	40
Joint pain	26	58	48
Shortness of breath	25	64	44
"Stomach" problems	46	46	50

gets out of balance as do mood and arousal, when the part of the midbrain that exerts control is not working properly. The chemical neurotransmitter that largely governs function of that part of the brain is serotonin, the same chemical that is deficient in persons who suffer depression or anxiety.

The midbrain harbors both pleasure and punishment centers. When the pleasure center is stimulated electrically a great euphoria is felt. Animals can become addicted to self-stimulating the pleasure center, even to the point of starving to death while they continue the stimulation. The same effect can be obtained by injecting serotonin and dopamine; the release of both is the normal way the pleasure centers are stimulated when pleasurable thoughts occur. When either is deficient, you can't feel pleasure, even in situations that are normally very pleasurable. This *anhedonia*, the inability to experience pleasure, is the hallmark of a neurobiological depression.

On the other hand, if the punishment center in the midbrain is stimulated, a feeling of great dysphoria (unpleasantness, fear, loss of control) occurs. When the punishment center in an animal is stimulated, the animal cowers, looks everywhere for danger, and, if the stimulus persists long enough, simply gives up. Because these centers are operated by a different set of neurotransmitters, they continue to work well during depression.

What happens, then, for a depressed person? A normally pleasant event feels punishing rather than pleasurable, creating the perception error that makes everything look grim. It's a vicious cycle, because the distress that results compounds the neurochemical problem, intensifying the situation. The neurochemical imbalance negatively distorts thought, and the stressful thoughts exacerbate the neurochemical imbalance.

Simply stated, then, the illness called depression reflects a disturbance of mood that occurs when the pleasure centers of the brain are not working (or when the punishment centers are working overtime). This illness called *depression* can be much more, however, and occasionally depressed mood can be absent, since it is only one component of the syndrome. In depression, the other automatic "vegetative" functions of the midbrain—appetite, sex drive, sleep, metabolism, energy regulation, modulation of hormone and immune function—are also obtunded.[26]

This mental state can color the way a person feels and thinks until it affects virtually all the activities that are normally considered a part of daily life. The classic mood associated with depression is a combination of *helplessness and hopelessness*. Often, there is a disturbance in sleep patterns: A person may sleep much more than normal, may sleep at unusual times, may not be able to fall asleep, or may fall asleep easily but then awaken, unable to fall back to sleep. Partly because of these sleep problems and partly as a result of the depression itself, the person may feel fatigued and lacking energy all the time. Insomnia itself can trigger depression.

Many times, victims of depression also have eating problems. Some overeat, but many lose their appetite and suffer severe weight loss. In many cases, depression leads to complete loss in the pleasure of eating. Many who are depressed sharply increase their alcohol consumption.

A variety of physical complaints can accompany depression. Most depressed people experience a number of vague physical pains and complaints; some become frantically obsessed with their health and convinced that they are suffering from serious physical diseases. Many lose interest in sex; others suffer from sexual dysfunction.

Many who are depressed struggle with feelings of personal worthlessness; others have vague guilt feelings. A classic sign is indifference to things that normally held importance in a person's life—family, friends, hobbies, leisure activities, work. Many contemplate suicide, and, unfortunately, unable to see any good, some complete the act. (Depression and panic disorder are the commonest causes of suicide. It may even be possible to predict who is at higher risk of suicide by measuring some of the neurochemical abnormalities associated with depression.[27]) Some of the more meaningful parts of life are lost, along with the ability to savor the things that normally brought great enjoyment—a stroll along a shady street on a Sunday afternoon, a baby's smile, the companionship of good friends.

Researcher Richard Sword has identified what he calls a depression-prone personality, a person who is more likely than others to become depressed. According to Sword, a depression-prone person is ambitious, conscientious, responsible, and hard working; has a high standard of personal honesty and integrity; sets high standards for others, but even higher standards for self. This person is generally pleasant and seems to be happy, even when inwardly sad. Finally, says Sword, the depression-prone person rarely shows anger.[28] National Institute of Mental Health psychiatrist Phillip Gold says that a person with "melancholic depression" has low self-esteem, a sense of hopelessness, intense anxiety about the future, a loss of sleep and appetite, and decreased sexual desire.[29]

In its earlier and most minor forms, inherited neurochemical depression, with its sense of punishment and negative expectations, can tend to put a person more on guard, looking for danger or possible exploitation and disregard by others. This may be manifested as shyness; a feeling of being unaccepted and the need to prove oneself; or hostile cynicism (particularly in men).

Depression and Premenstrual Syndrome

Women with premenstrual syndrome (PMS) much more often have a history of treated depression than normal healthy women—31 percent, as compared with 6 percent of normal controls, 9 percent of women with heavy menstrual bleeding, and 22 percent of women with significant menstrual cramps.[30] A drop in estrogen in the late cycle appears to be associated with a drop in brain serotonin (and endorphin) levels in women who are genetically vulnerable to depression. These women are also more vulnerable to postpartum depression, when estrogen levels fall at delivery, and are probably more susceptible to depression at menopause.

If PMS sufferers are followed long enough, the symptoms may begin to extend back through the entire cycle, worsening at ovulation or before the period.

For many, PMS appears to be an early, mild form of depression unmasked by the hormone changes. If the PMS is more severe, many of the physical symptoms associated with depression can appear before the menstrual period, then disappear afterward. Many women find significant relief from PMS with some of the same treatments used for depression—medications that improve serotonin function, exercise, a high-carbohydrate and low-protein diet, stress management and relaxation techniques, and avoidance of stimulants (such as caffeine).

Many women with either PMS or depression crave sweets as the symptoms worsen, the brain's attempt to boost serotonin levels. In fact, craving sweets is often a signal that serotonin function is deficient. Why? Serotonin is manufactured in the brain from tryptophan, an amino acid in the diet. To get into the brain, tryptophan has to cross the blood–brain barrier, which protects the brain from potentially dangerous substances in the bloodstream. To do that, it has to compete with the other amino acids in dietary proteins. If there are too many other amino acids, tryptophan has trouble getting into the brain and serotonin production falls. The solution? Eating carbohydrates (either sugars or starches) suppresses competing amino acids and makes it easier for tryptophan to enter the brain. (Starches are better than sugars, because an excessive rebound in adrenaline often occurs in anxiously depressed people as the sugar level falls a few hours after eating; starches reduce that rebound effect.)

Seasonal Affective Disorder

Depression can strike anyone, and it has been known to affect people of all ages and from all walks of life. We do know that certain people are at increased risk for depression. One of the most significant factors is sunlight. Recent experiments at the National Institute of Mental Health have concluded that the ability to deal with stress—and thus to avoid depression—can be significantly influenced by the amount of sunlight received each day. Data from the studies indicate that a number of people seem better able to cope with stress, change, and challenge during the spring, summer, and early autumn months. As winter approaches and the days grow shorter and darker, many persons become lethargic, anxious, and depressed.[31]

Investigators at the National Institute of Mental Health wanted to see exactly what was the effect of light. One of them, Dr. Thomas Wehr, commented, "Most people say that they slow down a little in the winter. They sleep more, they gain a little weight. The number of people who have an extreme problem is larger than we thought at first. These are people who know that something is wrong, but they've never known what to call it."[32]

Researchers at the Institute kept seeing patients who were seriously ill, who had something more than just a mild case of the blues. According to Wehr, "They're almost incapacitated by it. They stop cooking meals, they don't see their friends. They are experiencing a great deal of stress and they may even become suicidal."[33]

To test their theory, investigators exposed persons predisposed to suffer from "light deprivation" to strong artificial, broad-spectrum light for at least five hours a day. For those exposed to light, symptoms of depression and distress were significantly reduced or even completely eliminated.[34] The therapeutic light is broad-spectrum white light; yellow incandescent bulbs do not work. Since those early studies, the daily regimen has been much simplified and has produced nearly the same benefits. The usual regimen, today, is exposure to bright lights for 30 to 60 minutes in the early morning.

Researchers who have studied the phenomenon of light have noticed that its effects seem to be influenced by geography. The propensity toward depression is more pronounced in northern climates such as the Scandinavian countries and Canada, where sunlight is limited. By contrast, sunny areas of the world, as on the Mediterranean coast, people are much less likely to suffer from depression. This winter effect is not uncommon: The seasonal depression effect is seen in nearly 10 percent of the population in New Hampshire and 6 percent in New York, but in only 2 percent of those who live in Florida.[35]

What is the effect of the sunlight? While we're not completely sure, we have been able to glean information by studying animals that hibernate in winter. The seasonal behavior changes in animals—migration, hibernation—seem to be related to a light-sensitive area of the brain, the *pineal gland.* As days grow shorter, less light is transmitted through the eyes to the brain's pineal gland. In response, the pineal gland releases more of the hormone melatonin, which, among other things, suppresses reproduction and heightens survival adjustments.[36] Melatonin, secreted in response to darkness, is also involved in day–night biorhythms of such things as hormone secretion and sleep cycles. Taken orally, melatonin induces fatigue and sleepiness (like that of hibernating animals). Injected, melatonin induces depression (possibly by interfering with serotonin function) and may therefore be the culprit in the darkness-aggravated depression and sluggishness seen in what researchers have now dubbed *seasonal affective disorder* (SAD). Symptoms can include pain that is worse in the winter (as with fibromyalgia) and even the increased prevalence of infections seen during the winter; and anecdotes indicate light therapy may be effective, though that has not been rigorously studied. Immune function becomes somewhat dysregulated during the winter in victims of SAD, and it improves with light treatment.[37] Scientists working on the projects say "the sunlight influence seems to be mediated via the retina, in the eye. It is by looking at the light, not just being generally exposed to it, that one obtains the beneficial results."[38]

Some researchers believe that strong artificial light can even benefit those who suffer from depression year round. Physician Daniel Kripke of the University of California at San Diego believes that depression may occur when the body's circadian rhythm goes awry, causing the body's inner clock to speed up or slow down, and that light could correct the problem in many people. To test his theory, Kripke found twelve depressed patients who agreed to be awakened at odd hours of the night for one hour at a time on three consecutive nights. Patients were awakened at various times, sometimes a few hours before their usual

wake-up time, and sometimes a few hours after they first fell asleep. On some occasions the patients were exposed to a bright white light, and on others they were
exposed to a dim red light. The dim red light had no effect. But the bright white
light, used in the early morning, significantly reduced patient depression.[39]

In another experiment, Wehr and his colleague Dr. Norman Rosenthal
treated a manic-depressive man in his mid-sixties who suffered from SAD. The
man's depression usually began in midsummer and peaked near year's end.
Treatment with drugs had been unsuccessful because of side effects, so the researchers decided to try artificial light. During the first week of December and for
ten days, the researchers created the conditions of a spring day: They used extremely bright artificial light to "lengthen" his days. The light was used from 6:00
to 9:00 in the morning, and again from 4:00 to 7:00 in the afternoon. Within four
days, the man's depression lifted.[40]

The Physiological Changes of Depression

Depression obviously has a profound influence on the mind and the emotions,
but researchers have found that depression has an equally profound influence on
the body as well. Some of those changes can be obvious. When a person gets depressed, for example, "he or she may not have the energy to get out of bed," points
out internist Dr. Brian Miller. "Physiologic changes occur, cardiovascular tone decreases, muscles begin to atrophy."[41]

Other changes aren't so obvious, but they can have even more profound effects. Researchers have learned that during depression the body undergoes hormonal and chemical changes similar to those imposed by stress, mostly, says National Institute of Mental Health psychiatrist Phillip Gold, because in depressed
people, the mechanisms that normally regulate the stress response fail. "Although
depressed people often seem to think and react slowly," he says, "they are actually
in a highly aroused state, focusing obsessively on their own sense of inadequacy.
This state of mind parallels the heightened sense of awareness and focus that plays
a positive role in a short-term response to stress, but in depression that intense
awareness and focus is turned inward, with psychologically crippling results."[42]

Gold and a host of other researchers have been able to identify the physiological changes that occur during depression, and those changes are almost identical to the ones that occur in response to stress. After carefully comparing the
physiological results of both stress and depression, some researchers have concluded there may be a close relationship among the changes that occur in the
body:

> Stress induces physiological responses that accompany emotional and intellec-
> tual ones. One such response is the activation of hormones such as cortisol.
> When we are challenged, the pituitary gland, located near the brain and respon-
> sive to signals from it, excretes larger than usual amounts of a compound called
> the adrenocortical-stimulating hormone, or ACTH. As a result, the adrenal

gland, located near the kidney, increases its production of cortisol, a compound that, along with adrenalin, heightens the alerting and protecting systems in the body. When stress passes, or as we adapt effectively to longer term stresses, hormone production diminishes, returning again to normal levels.

However, researchers have shown that in certain people subject to serious chronic depression, this endocrine system, once activated, does not seem able to turn itself off. Cortisol levels remain elevated. The suppression of hormone activity that should occur after the administration of a compound called dexamethasone fails to occur. . . . Consequently, it may take an unduly extended period of time for the individual to recover from the impact of stress; or, in some instances, he may not recover at all without medical intervention.[43]

As serotonin and dopamine function in the brain fall, in parallel the endorphin levels drop.[44] Endorphins are the brain's own chemicals, designed to relieve pain and help us feel good.[45] (Morphine works to relieve pain largely by stimulating the natural endorphin receptors in the brain.) Depression is a state of endorphin deficiency; other conditions characterized by low endorphin (and sometimes serotonin) levels include chronic pain disorders, migraine, premenstrual syndrome, and some arthritis. This fall in endorphins may explain why so many people with depression—approximately 60 percent—have recurrent, multiple pain problems. People with more than one pain complaint are six to eight times more likely to have clinical depression than others, and treatment of the depression usually solves the pain problem.[46]

One painful condition that deserves attention is fibromyalgia, a common problem that causes multiple painful or tender points at sites of muscle insertion, fatigue, sleep disturbance, and headache. The pain is often exacerbated by mental stress; for many, it's also worse in wintertime. Since the pattern of fibromyalgia is so similar to that of depression, some experts have wondered if the same neurochemical link causes both. That point of view is strengthened by the high incidence of major depression (71 percent) and the strong family history of depression in fibromyalgia patients.[47] Antidepressants, stress management, and relaxation techniques are helpful in treatment, as are a strong physician-patient relationship and a positive expectation about treatment.

High rates of underlying depression and panic disorder are also seen in persons who have other, more specific, medical problems that combine pain with muscle spasm. Examples include irritable bowel syndrome ("spastic colon") patients (23 percent are depressed); esophageal motility disorder patients (40 percent are depressed, and 38 percent have panic disorder); and patients with chest pain but normal coronary arteriograms (who have nine times more depression and seven times more panic disorder than normal).

There are a number of medical conditions that can mimic depression—so closely, in fact, that a physician may miss the underlying medical condition altogether. According to Gregory Manov and William Guy of the Department of Psychiatry at Vanderbilt School of Medicine and the Tennessee Neuropsychiatric Institute in Nashville, at least seven major categories of medical disease can charade as depression. The following can appear—even with careful scrutiny—to be depression:

- *A number of disorders of the central nervous system.* Tumors of the brain—especially slow-growing ones that affect the left hemisphere in general or the frontal or temporal lobes—often cause depressive symptoms. So do multiple sclerosis (especially in its early stages), brain injuries, cerebrovascular accidents (strokes), and chronic bleeding in the brain. Depression is also the earliest symptom of a developing irreversible dementia, such as Alzheimer's disease, Huntington's chorea, Jakob-Creutzfeldt disease, and Wilson's disease.
- *Some endocrine disorders.* These include hypothyroidism, slowly-developing hyperthyroidism, and other disorders of the thyroid gland. Severe depressive symptoms are also characteristic of Addison's disease and Cushing's syndrome.
- *Chronic and debilitating disorders of the gastrointestinal tract.* Some gastrointestinal diseases do not result in localized gastric symptoms; at times depression is the only symptom. A classic case is cancer of the pancreas; patients feel no local pain from the cancer, but almost all suffer from serious depression, making it difficult for a physician to find the real illness. Depression very frequently occurs with Crohn's disease (regional enteritis), ulcerative colitis, and amyloidosis, and may be the only symptom in the early stages of these diseases.
- *Chronic systemic illnesses.* Lupus erythematosus is one of the most classic. Chronic infections and infectious diseases, too, may have direct effects on brain chemistry, leading to serious depression, most often diseases such as malaria, tuberculosis, syphilis, viral encephalitis, and meningoencephalitis.
- *Simple nutritional deficiencies.* Most commonly at fault are vitamin deficiencies, such as niacin, folate acid, and vitamin B_{12}. Simple electrolyte imbalances can cause all the classic symptoms of depression, too, most often in persons who take diuretics and those who eat a strict low-sodium diet.[48]

Depression and Longevity

Depression can increase mortality in some obvious ways. As mentioned, severe depression can lead to suicide; estimates are that approximately 15 percent of all depressed people take their own lives, the vast majority being those whose depression goes untreated. And even though treatments are highly effective, the large number of medical problems in depressed persons can mask the underlying depression.

Depression can also worsen the plight of people who already have a medical problem. Research shows that, when sick people become depressed, they tend to become sicker, need more medication, and spend more days in the hospital. Worst of all, it can actually curtail survival.[49] Mortality rates are four times normal in depressed persons, mostly from medical illness (63 percent of it cardiovascular disease), not just from suicide. The severity of any disease and the likelihood that it will cause death are substantially worse if the patient is also depressed. This is particularly true for stroke, coronary artery disease, myocardial infarction, heart rhythm disturbances, sudden death, rheumatoid arthritis, certain cancers, multiple sclerosis, Parkinson's disease, epilepsy, kidney disease, psoriasis, acne, and diabetes.[50]

Another recent study also shows that depression shortens life. One group of researchers studied 454 patients that were newly admitted to eight nursing homes in the Baltimore area. Depression at the time of admission raised the risk of death within a year by 59 percent, regardless of physical health. Why? Researchers think several factors may be at work, including poor nutrition, inadequate rest, or impaired immune function among depressed persons.[51]

Just how depression shortens the survival time of patients who are already ill is not exactly known, although we do have some important clues. One came from a study of children who died from asthma attacks; twelve who died were compared with twelve who survived their attacks. According to researchers, "Family and personal characteristics of those who died suggested that depression may have played a role."[52]

In addition, seven of the children who died—but only two of the ones who survived—came from families marked by marital discord, lack of emotional support, alcoholism, and drug abuse. According to family members, ten of the children who died—but only two of the survivors—were unusually sensitive to separation and loss. And eight of the children who died—as compared with three who survived—had talked about death or suicide within a month of the fatal attack.

Researchers who conducted the study and analyzed its results wanted to find out *why* depression may have been indicated in the asthma deaths, so they probed more deeply into the chemistry of depression. According to investigator Bruce Miller, director of the pediatric psychophysiological treatment unit at the National Jewish Center for Immunology and Respiratory Medicine in Denver, depression creates a chemical imbalance in the body that boosts the parasympathetic nervous system. The result can be deadly for an asthmatic: The parasympathetic nervous system closes the airways.[53] The increased smooth muscle spasm in the airways is much like the increased spasm of the coronary arteries and bowel seen in depression.

Even among people who are not ill, depression can cut life short. Epidemiologic studies of depressed people (bereaved and divorced adults and psychiatric patients) show that they have significantly higher mortality rates than people who are not depressed. Some studies have shown that depressed persons also have a greater incidence of deaths from cancer than the general population.[54]

In one study, researchers followed up on 1593 men and women who had been hospitalized for depression at a care facility in Iowa; for a control group, the researchers used randomly selected people of the same age and sex who also lived in Iowa. Follow-up studies began two years after the patients were released from the hospital and continued for fourteen years. Death rates among the depressed patients soared for the first two years following hospitalization and remained higher than average throughout the fourteen years of the study.[55]

Depression itself can become a potent risk factor in determining whether a person will die sooner than expected, whether of "natural causes" or of disease. In one important large-scale study, Dr. Richard Shekelle of the University of Chicago examined the health of about 2000 men who were employed by Chicago's Western Electric Company. The men's personalities were first measured in 1958; then researchers tracked their health for the next two decades. During the next twenty years, those who had scored high on depression in 1958 were more likely than other men to die of cancer. (Depression was also associated with noncancer deaths, making it a general risk factor for early death.) It's important to note that this increased risk remained even after the researchers took into account the men's age, occupation, cigarette smoking, and family history of cancer. Researchers found one interesting footnote to the study: The more time that elapsed since the measurement of depression, the weaker was its association with illness and death.[56]

According to research, depression becomes a significant risk factor for mortality among the elderly, people with health impairments, people who have preexisting immune system problems (including people with immunodeficiency diseases such as acquired immunodeficiency syndrome [AIDS]), and people who have been exposed to an infectious agent or a carcinogen.[57]

Depression has also been linked to sudden death in a number of studies. In one of the best-known, psychiatrist William Greene and colleagues at the University of Rochester studied twenty-six employees at Eastman Kodak Company who died suddenly and unexpectedly. Almost all of the employees who died had been depressed before their death—some for only a week, some for several months. Researchers found that the depressed employees suddenly underwent definite arousal; in other words, people who had been living in slow motion or depression became suddenly lurched into third gear. The "arousal" that occurred was in the form of an increased workload and the accompanying stress, a conflict in the workplace, or marital stress or other conflict at home. The sudden shift from depression to arousal could have produced an incompatible variety of reactions, leading to arrhythmia or myocardial infarction, or both.[58]

Depression and the Immune System

Several years ago the first phases of an unusually severe Asian influenza epidemic began to creep around the world. In a midwestern college community, people in an enterprising college health center wondered what effect preexisting mental distress would have on those exposed to the flu. Before the epidemic arrived, a large number of college students whose health care was provided by the clinic were screened with the Minnesota Multiphasic Personality Inventory (MMPI), a test that has become a standard for defining mental state. Then they waited for the flu to hit. Those who got influenza returned after three and six weeks to see who was still sick (most people recover well by three weeks). Those depressed before the epidemic were significantly more likely to still be sick at six weeks.[59]

Other physicians have noted that depressed (or sometimes chronically stressed) patients not infrequently complain of "getting everything that's going around," or of having trouble getting rid of their respiratory or intestinal infection. How could that be? What is it about depression that might affect the immunity that protects from such common infections? Are some of the same mechanisms discussed in Chapter 2 the culprit?

Depression appears to have a significant impact on the immune system in a variety of ways. One of the most significant impacts of depression on immune function is on the activity of natural killer cells, the immune cells that assist the body in its surveillance against tumors and in its resistance to viral disease. A number of studies show that natural killer cell activity is reduced among people who are depressed. Researchers at Boston University School of Medicine, for example, reported lower natural killer cell activity in depressed persons.[60]

Dr. Michael Irwin and his colleagues at the University of California at San Diego measured the natural killer cell activity of women whose husbands had recently died. The widows had significantly reduced levels of natural killer cell activity than did women who were not bereaved. Among the bereaved women, the ones who were depressed had the greatest impairment in natural killer cell activity.[61]

It wasn't just the bereavement that curtailed immune function, then, because the more severely depressed the woman, the more reduced her natural killer cell activity. In reporting on his findings, Irwin commented,

Depression is qualitatively different from grief. People who are depressed feel down, blue, and gloomy persistently. Those who are grieving move in and out of those feelings.

In summing up the study results, Irwin confirmed that it was "the severity of their depression," not merely their husbands' death, that seemed to be related to their weakened immune system.[62]

Other components of the immune system are crippled by depression as well. Psychiatrists at the Mount Sinai School of Medicine in New York have been doing long-term studies in which they observe men whose wives have breast cancer. As early as two weeks after the wives die, the men show a "striking" drop in the white blood cell response when the immune system is challenged.[63]

A similar study looked at forty-nine men who were judged to be at risk because of the severe illness or recent death of a close family member. The researchers—Bernard S. Linn, professor of surgery at the University of Miami School of Medicine, and Margaret Linn, professor of psychiatry at the University of Miami—once again found a diminished white blood cell response to immune challenge.[64]

Researchers working in the laboratory with animals have had similar results. Psychiatrist Martin Reite, University of Colorado, and his colleagues created depression in monkeys by separating them from their mothers at the age of six months. The baby monkeys, who were put into cages separate from their mothers, showed all the classic signs of depression. To test immune response, Reite took blood samples from the baby monkeys both before and after the separation; as part of the tests he ran, he checked the ability of white blood cells to proliferate. Following separation from their mothers, the baby monkeys showed a "significant reduction" in white blood cell activity.[65]

Researchers also suspect that depression interferes with the ratio of helper and suppressor cells. Helper and suppressor cells are two classes of lymphocytes; the helper cells turn on the immune response, and the suppressor cells turn off the immune response. If the immune system is to function normally, the two kinds of cells have to have a proper ratio. The higher the ratio of helpers to suppressors, the stronger the immune response; the lower the ratio, the weaker the response. When suppressors severely outnumber helpers, the immune system is considered to be suppressed (which is what happens in AIDS).

The results of a large number of studies show that depression definitely has an influence on the ratio, although the precise results vary. Test results differed somewhat for various reasons: Some of the studies involved patients who were hospitalized, though most did not; in some of the studies, patients were on antidepressant drugs; and so on. In some studies, depressed people had a normal number of suppressor cells but a small proportion of helper cells. In other studies, the people who were depressed had lower numbers of both kinds of cells.[66]

One study involving the helper-suppressor ratio was conducted by psychologist Margaret Kemeny and her colleagues at the University of California School of Medicine in San Francisco. To test the effect of depression on the immune system, they studied thirty-six subjects with genital herpes. Kemeny took regular blood samples over a six-month period and monitored outbreaks and recurrences. The people in the study who were depressed showed a drop in both helper and suppressor cells; they had significantly lower levels of suppressor cytotoxic T cells, which are thought to help keep outbreaks from occurring. The depressed people had more recurrences of symptoms and more outbreaks than did others in the study. Kemeny and her colleagues discovered that they could accurately predict which study subjects would have outbreaks based on how depressed they were.[67]

The hormones and chemicals produced in depression may also affect the immune system. One is cortisol. In depression, the adrenal gland often secretes far too much cortisol, which then acts to suppress the immune system.[68] When the adrenals manufacture and secrete these corticosteroids, having "no apparent biological brake,"[69] the immune system begins to slow down. University of Iowa psychiatrist Dr. Ziad Kronfol has done a series of studies in which he has subjected depressed people to standard immunity tests. One finding is consistent: The immune systems of depressed people are less responsive than those of normal people—and even those of people with other mental illnesses.[70]

According to allergist William L. Mundy, depression may even cause the immune system to overreact, resulting in autoimmune diseases. "I believe these illnesses in which the immune cells are killing off the normal tissues are simply a

cover way of suicide," he suggests. "It may not have been an overt effort or decision, but I do believe that depression and a wish by the patient 'to just not be
here' is picked up by the body, and destruction from within is begun."[71]

Depression and the Heart

Depression causes irregularities in the nervous system, and when those irregularities become severe enough, heart rate, blood pressure, and coronary artery
function go awry, leading to cardiac problems. A number of impressive studies
have proved just that. In a study of 1300 graduates of Johns Hopkins Medical
School, researchers isolated those for whom depression was a problem. Then they
classified the depressed graduates according to their various symptoms of depression. They found that one particular symptom of depression, early-morning
fatigue, was more often present among graduates who later suffered a myocardial infarction than among those who remained healthy.[72]

In another study, researchers in England examined 2000 patients and an
equal number of matched controls. They questioned the study subjects, and identified which ones were suffering from chronic mild depression. In following the
study subjects, they found that new coronary artery disease was much more
likely to develop in those who suffered from depression than in those who did
not.[73]

The effect of depression on the heart is so profound that researchers have
been able to predict who would have a heart attack based solely on the presence
of depression. In one such prediction, University of Oklahoma Medical School's
Dr. Stewart Wolf examined sixty-five patients who had suffered documented myocardial infarctions, and sixty-five matched control subjects who were healthy
and had not had any sign of heart disease.[74]

To prove his theory, Wolf interviewed all 130 subjects once a month; he also
gave each one a battery of psychological tests to determine how depressed each
one was. After a series of interviews with each subject, Wolf made his predictions
without knowing which ones had previously suffered a heart attack. He chose ten
people who had failed to find meaningful satisfaction in their social and leisure
activities, basically, the ten people who were the most depressed. He predicted
(solely on the basis of depression) that they would be among the first to have a
heart attack and die. All ten of the subjects Wolf pinpointed did, indeed, have a
heart attack and die. In fact, those ten were among the first twenty-three who
died during the four years following the predictions.[75]

Other studies have shown that death due to heart disease is associated with
depression. Robert Anda and his colleagues at the Centers for Disease Control
and Prevention in Atlanta studied 2832 adults ranging in age from forty-five to
seventy-seven who entered the study healthy and free of heart disease. As they
entered the study, volunteers were asked about their feelings of depression, discouragement, and hopelessness. Researchers then followed them for an average
interval of twelve years. They found that those who felt depressed and hopeless
suffered significantly more deaths from heart disease; in fact, death from heart

disease was four times more common among the profoundly hopeless subjects than among those who were not hopeless.[76]

Other researchers studied heart disease in smokers. Findings showed that potentially fatal blood vessel disease progressed more rapidly among the smokers who were mildly to moderately depressed than among those who were not depressed.[77] One reason may be that depression appears to magnify risk factors associated with heart disease; in other words, depression makes risky behaviors even riskier. In a study reported at an American Heart Association meeting, researchers say that depression adds to the danger of all the standard risk factors for heart disease. The negative effects of smoking are 3.4 times greater for people who are depressed; depression doubles the negative impact of low-density lipoproteins ("bad" cholesterol).

Perhaps some of the most profound effects of depression hit persons who already have coronary artery disease or another cardiac problem. A striking example was provided by a study conducted by psychologist Robert M. Carney and his colleagues at the Washington University School of Medicine in St. Louis. The researchers followed fifty-two persons who had been diagnosed with coronary artery disease for one year.[78]

Of the people in the study, 18 percent were seriously depressed before the diagnosis,[79] compared with only 4 percent of all Americans, and fewer than 3 percent of the St. Louis–area population.[80] The researchers used a strict definition for depression, too: To qualify as "depressed," a person had to have suffered extreme sadness or hopelessness, loss of interest or pleasure in most activities, insomnia, loss of energy, or thoughts of suicide for at least two weeks.[81]

Major depression was found to be the best single predictor of serious problems and complications among the heart patients, and it was an even stronger predictor than factors such as age, smoking, severity of artery damage, and levels of cholesterol in the bloodstream.[82] Researchers found that 78 percent of the depressed patients had some cardiac event during the twelve months after the diagnosis, and one died. Only a third of the nondepressed patients had problems.

Recent findings from a Canadian hospital show that, shortly after their heart attack, patients who are seriously depressed have a greater than average chance of dying, whatever their physical condition. In the study, more than 200 patients were given diagnostic interviews a week after entering the hospital and again six months later. All else being equal, say the researchers, depression raised the risk of death 3.4 times and the risk of recurrent coronary events 5.7 times. One reason, they say, is that physiological changes associated with depression affect the nerves leading to the heart and increase the danger of coronary artery thrombosis.[83] (See the discussion of these mechanisms in Chapter 6.)

According to researchers, depression increases activity of the sympathetic nervous system. The result of that activity may be reduced blood flow, arrhythmias, and progression of atherosclerosis, all factors that could increase the risk of heart problems.

A study in New York of 283 myocardial infarction patients found that 45 percent were depressed one week later: 18 percent had major depression; 27 percent, minor depression. Depression was not associated with severity of heart disease, but those who were depressed did have a greater prevalence of other medical problems. Three to four months later, 33 percent were still depressed. Even though their heart impairment was no worse, depressed patients were more disabled after the infarction. Among those who had been working before their heart attack, most who had major depression had not returned to work three months later; only 38 percent eventually returned, as compared with 63 percent of the heart attack victims who were not depressed. Minor depression was not as disabling.

Of interest in this study was the fact that medical problems masked the depression: Only 10 percent of those with major depression and 4 percent of all depressed patients had received treatment for depression. Another impressive finding is that, particularly in women, depression appears to predict death from heart disease more accurately than either hostility or Type A behavior; it may also be more important in accelerating atherosclerosis (see the related discussion in Chapter 6).[84]

Findings of this and other studies show that heart patients who are happier, rather than depressed, are less likely to have heart attacks, bypass surgery, and other heart disease–related problems.[85] With depression established as a major coronary risk factor, and based on preliminary results, longer-term studies are now under way to determine the outcome of actively treating heart disease patients for depression. Researchers suspect such treatment will show substantial benefit, not only for quality of life, but also for less risk of subsequent coronary events.[86, 87]

Focus on Research

Researchers followed more than 6000 men and women as part of a national health survey. People who participated in the study completed standard psychological tests that measured for factors like depression; approximately one-sixth of the people in the survey (just over a thousand) showed some level of depression (measured by factors like crying spells, lack of concentration, loss of appetite, and insomnia). Researchers then followed the subjects for ten years, keeping careful health records and noting the development of any disease. At the end of the ten years, 11 percent of the depressed people had developed cancer. But so did 10 percent of the people who were not depressed at the beginning of the study. Exactly 4 percent in each of the groups had died from cancer at the end of the ten years.

The research, sponsored by the National Institute on Aging, provides what Johns Hopkins researchers call "the most convincing evidence to date disputing the so-called "cancer/attitude connection"—and contradicts a number of older studies suggesting that depression might be a risk factor of cancer." * The researcher who spearheaded the project, National Institute on Aging psychologist Alan Zonderman, said the researchers "found that depressive systems didn't predict who was going to get cancer or who was going to die from cancer ten years later." †

* "Is There a Cancer Personality?" *The Johns Hopkins Medical Letter*, March 1990, p. 1.
† Alan Zonderman, quoted in "Depression Found Not Linked to Cancer," *Executive Health Report*, 26:3 (December 1989), p. 5.

Depression and Cancer

Until recently, scientists were convinced that depression could lead to cancer. While researchers argued about how great the effect was—and how strong the link—most agreed that there was a link between depression and cancer. Top medical researchers were convinced that depression either contributed to the development of cancer or caused it to be more severe once it did develop, and a variety of studies seemed to support that conviction.

In harmony with that belief, Arnold Hutschnecker wrote in *The Will to Live* that "depression is a partial surrender to death, and it seems that cancer is despair experienced at the cellular level."[88]

Then researchers started to waffle. While findings were coming in that suggested depression could possibly cause both the development and the spread of cancer, *Science News* reported that the finding that depression "was associated more strongly with cancer mortality than with cancer incidence suggests that it may promote, rather than initiate, the disease process."[89]

But more recent research wipes out the link between depression and cancer altogether. A study published in the *Journal of the American Medical Association*[90] says that many factors probably raise the risk of cancer, but depression isn't one of them.

Even with Zonderman's conclusive findings, some scientists think depression may at least contribute to cancer. University of Miami researcher Karl Goodkin says that depression might affect different types of cancer in different ways. Pointing out that Zonderman and his colleagues didn't specify which kinds of cancer cropped up among their study subjects, "We don't know whether their results are supportive of depression's effect on the incidence of viral tumors or not." Speaking of the danger of lumping together all types of cancer and drawing a single conclusion, he adds that "there may be two strong, opposite effects hidden by mixing all types of cancers."[91]

Feeling Sad, Feeling Bad

The hopelessness, frustration, sadness, and dissatisfaction that constitute depression can quite literally make you feel bad physically. In many studies, the greater the depression, the higher is the number of physical symptoms associated with any illness.[92] The facts and figures from hosts of studies tell the story.[93] An estimated one-fourth of all patients who see primary care physicians are depressed; more than one-tenth are suffering from what experts call major depression. An estimated three-fourths of all depressed people see physicians because they are physically ill.

People who are depressed tend to magnify their medical problems. They are apt to have multiple chronic medical illnesses. Depressed patients tend to do much more poorly on self-treatment and self-monitoring of chronic illnesses, such as making sure they inject insulin on schedule.

Depressed people tend to have more aches and pains, too, though researchers are unclear as to whether depression causes pain or pain causes depression, but the fact that the pain tends to greatly diminish, or even disappear, when the depression is treated suggests that the depression (and its associated endorphin deficiency) underlies the pain. Studies have shown that depressed people have unusually high rates of headache, back pain, chest pain, and pelvic pain (as shown earlier in Table 10.1).

They may not do as well in surgery, either. According to a study published in the *American Journal of Public Health*, depressed elderly women who had hip fractures did much more poorly following surgery than did the same type of patients who were not depressed.[94]

At least part of feeling better appears to involve getting control over depression. That may not be as difficult as it seems. Experts estimate that 80 to 90 percent of persons who suffer from depression can be helped substantially. Because of the underlying neurochemical (and conditioned) vulnerability, however, depression tends to be a recurrent illness. Eight years after a first episode, three-fourths of the previously depressed patients will have had a recurrence. Treatment studies show that combined medication and counseling–behavioral treatment is best; recent results are confirming that longer-term medication is superior to counseling in preventing recurrence.[95] Treatment is effective, and usually shows striking improvement in most of the medical problems associated with depression. Longer-term outcome studies are needed to determine if treatment of depression substantially prevents many of these associated medical illnesses.

Ongoing research is providing new clues about the malady we call depression, and scientists continue looking for even more effective treatments. One recent landmark study provides new evidence about how pervasive depression can be.

The study, conducted by researchers at the University of Washington in Seattle, studied the infants of women who were classified as clinically depressed. According to research director Geraldine Dawson, the infants of mothers who are depressed showed changes in electrical brain activity that led to unusual responses. Simply stated, the infants were depressed, too.

Dawson has called for further research to determine the exact reasons for the infants' depression. She theorizes that the infants may be reacting to nonresponsive mothers or that the depression may be genetic.[96] The mothers' stress hormones can also affect fetal brain development. What *is* clear, say researchers, is that depression may include a broad circle of influence.

While studies like these indicate that depression may be genetic, at least part of the cause of depression is cultural, says San Diego psychiatrist Dennis Gersten. As a response to years of practice, Gersten likens personalities to crystalline structures, like diamonds, quartz, ice, mica, and so on. "Each fractures under predictable lines when stressed," Gersten says. "When the stress is massive enough, each structure will collapse."[97]

It's important to remember that depression can be caused by physical factors—certain prescription drugs (e.g., heart medications, cortisone, glaucoma medication, and antihistamines), premenstrual syndrome, other female hormone disturbances (including oral contraceptives), diabetes, rapid–weight-loss diets, lack of exercise, sunlight deficiency, inadequate nutrient intake (especially of iron, thiamine, and magnesium), and inadequate carbohydrate consumption. Depression is also a common side effect of thyroid problems; researchers estimate that 10 to 15 percent of all depressed people have thyroid problems.[98]

The depression-prone personality, Gersten concludes, is one that can fracture under multiple stresses. Those stresses—genetic, psychological, chemical, allergic, and toxic—offer not only a clue to the causes of depression but a valuable panorama of ways we may prevent it.

Notes

1. Bernie S. Siegel, *Love, Medicine, and Miracles* (New York: Harper and Row, 1986).

2. Winifred Gallagher, "The Dark Affliction of Mind and Body," *Discover*, May: 1986, 66–76.

3. Gallagher.

4. Depression Guideline Panel, *Depression in Primary Care: Volume 1, Detection and Diagnosis* (Rockville, Maryland: U.S. Department of Health and Human Services, Agency for Healthcare Policy and Research, Publication No. 93–550, 1993), p. 23.

5. Joseph Alper, "Depression at an Early Age," *Science*, May: 1986, 45–50.

6. W. Katon, M. Von Korff, E. Lin, T. Bush, and J. Ormel, "Adequacy and Duration of Antidepressant Treatment in Primary Care," *Medical Care*, 30: 1992, 67–76.

7. J. E. Mezzich, K. J. Evanczuk, R. J. Mathias, and G. A. Coffman, "Admission Decisions and Multiaxial Diagnosis," *Archives of General Psychiatry*, 41: 1989, 1001–1004.

8. Depression Guideline Panel, pp. 47–48.

9. Martin E. P. Seligman, *Learned Optimism* (New York: Alfred A. Knopf, 1991), p. 75.

10. I. Grant, T. L. Patterson, and J. Yager, "Social Supports in Relation to Physical Health and Symptoms of Depression in the Elderly," *American Journal of Psychiatry*, 145(10): 1988, 1254–1258.

11. Anne H. Rosenfeld, "Depression: Dispelling Despair," *Psychology Today*, June: 1985, 28.

12. Rosenfeld.

13. Alper.

14. G. J. Kennedy, H. R. Kelman, C. Thomas, W. Wisniewski, H. Metz, and P. E. Bijur, "Hierarchy of Characteristics Associated with Depressive Symptoms in an Urban Elderly Sample, "*American Journal of Psychiatry*, 146(2): 1989, 220–225.

15. Kenneth B. Wells, Anita Stewart, Ron D. Hays, M. Audrey Burnam, William Rogers, Marcia Daniels, Sandra Berry, Sheldon Greenfield, and John Ware, "The Functioning and Well-being of Depressed Patients," *Journal of the American Medical Association*, 262(7): 1989, 914–919.

16. Depression Guideline Panel, pp. 24–25.

17. P. E. Greenberg, L. E. Stiglin, S. N. Finkelstein, and E. R. Berndt, "The Economic Burden of Depression in 1990," *Journal of Clinical Psychiatry*, 54: 1993, 405–418.

18. W. R. Coryell, R. Noyes, and J. Clancey, "Excess Mortality in Panic Disorder: A Comparison with Primary Unipolar Depression," *Archives of General Psychiatry*, 39: 1982, 701–703.

19. Gallagher.

20. Gallagher.

21. Clive Wood, "Who Gets Depressed?" *Advances*, 4(2): 1987, 61–65.

22. G. W. Brown, A. Bifulco, and T. O. Harris, "Life Events, Vulnerability, and Onset of Depression: Some Refinements," *British Journal of Psychiatry*, 1987.

23. R. M. Post, "Transduction of Psychosocial Stress into the Neurobiology of Recurrent Affective Disorder," *American Journal of Psychiatry*, 149: 1992, 999–1010.

24. Rosenfeld, p. 30.

25. D. L. Rosenhan and M. E. P. Seligman, *Abnormal Psychology* (New York: Norton, 1984), p. 307.

26. Depression Guideline Panel, pp. 18, 49, 50, 64, 80.

27. E. R. Braveman and C. C. Pfeiffer, "Suicide and Biochemistry," *Biological Psychiatry*, 20: 1985, 123–124.

28. Rice, p. 100.

29. Christopher Vaughan, "The Depression-Stress Link," *Science News*, 134: 1988, 155.

30. J. Bancroft, D. Rennie, and P. Warner, "Vulnerability to Perimenstrual Mood Change: The Relevance of a Past History of Depressive Disorder," *Psychosomatic Medicine*, 56: 1994, 225–231.

31. T. Silverstone and C. Thompson, editors, *Seasonal Affective Disorder* (London: Clinical Neuroscience Publishers, 1989).

32. Emrika Padus, *The Complete Guide to Your Emotions and Your Health* (Emmaus, Pennsylvania: Rodale Press, 1986), p. 625.

33. Padus.

34. D. A. Oren and N. E. Rosenthal, "Seasonal Affective Disorders," in E. S. Paykel, editor, *Handbook of Affective Disorders*, 2nd ed. (London: Churchill Livingstone, 1992), pp. 551–567; and M. Terman, "On the Question of Mechanism in Phototherapy for Seasonal Affective Disorder: Considerations of Clinical Efficacy and Epidemiology," *Journal of Biological Rhythms*, 3: 1988, 155–172.

35. M. Terman, et al., "Seasonal Symptom Patterns in New York: Patients and Population," in Silverstone and Thompson, editors, *Seasonal Affective Disorder* (London: Clinical Neuroscience Publishers, 1989), pp. 77–95.

36. Michael Freeman, "Don't Be SAD," *Medical Self-Care*, January/February: 1989, 31.

37. S. Kasper, N. E. Rosenthal, S. Barberi, A. Williams, L. Tamarkin, S. L. B. Rogers, and S. R. Pillemer, "Immunological Correlates of Seasonal Fluctuations in Mood and Behavior and Their Relationship to Phototherapy," *Psychiatry Research*, 36: 1991, 253–264.

38. Frederic Flach, *Resilience* (New York: Fawcett Columbine, 1988).

39. Study results were reported in *Psychopharmacology Bulletin* and summarized in Padus, p. 626.

40. Study results were reported in *American Journal of Psychiatry* and summarized in Padus, p. 625.

41. "Does Emotional State Affect Disease?" *MD*, April: 1986, 30, 41, 43.

42. Vaughan.

43. Flach.

44. Depression Guideline Panel, p. 23.

45. Blair Justice, *Who Gets Sick: Thinking and Health* (Houston, Texas: Peak Press, 1987), pp. 100, 102–103.

46. Depression Guideline Panel, pp. 51–52.

47. J. I. Hudson, M. S. Hudson, L. F. Pliner, D. L. Goldenberg, and H. G. Pope, Jr., "Fibromyalgia and Major Affective Disorder: A Controlled Phenomenology and Family History Study," *American Journal of Psychiatry*, 142: 1985, 441–446.

48. Gregory Manov and William Guy, "Medical Disorders That May Present as Depression," *Physician and Patient*, January: 1985, 46–51.

49. Linda C. Higgins, "Depression May Shorten Survival," *Medical World News*, July 10: 1989, 20.

50. G. I. Keitner, C. E. Ryan, L. W. Miller, R. Kohn, and N. B. Epstein, "12-Month Outcome of Patients with Major Depression and Comorbid Psychiatric or Mental Illness," *American Journal of Psychiatry*, 148: 1991, 345–350; P. J. Lustman, L. S. Griffith, and R. E. Clouse, "Depression in Adults with Diabetes: Results of a Five-Year Follow-Up Study," *Diabetes Care*, 11: 1988, 605–612; and R. M. Carney, M. W. Rich, K. E. Freedland, et al., pp. 627–633.

51. Barry W. Rovner, Pearl S. German, Larry J. Brant, et al., "Depression and Mortality in Nursing Homes," *Journal of the American Medical Association*, 265: 1991, 993–996.

52. Higgins, p. 21.

53. Higgins, p. 21.

54. Janice K. Kiecolt-Glaser and Ronald Glaser, "Psychological Influences on Immunity," *Psychosomatics*, n.d., p. 624.

55. D. W. Black, G. Winokur, and A. Nasrallah, "Mortality in patients with primary unipolar depression, secondary unipolar depression, and bipolar affective disorder: A comparison with general population mortality," *International Journal of Psychiatric Medicine*, 17: 1987, 351–360.

56. Howard S. Friedman, *The Self-Healing Personality* (New York: Henry Holt and Company, 1991), p. 61.

57. Kiecolt-Glaser and Glaser.

58. W. A. Greene, S. Goldstein, and A. J. Moss, "Psychosocial Aspects of Sudden Death," *Archives of Internal Medicine,* 129: 1972, 725–731; R. M. Charney, K. E. Freedland, M. W. Rich, L. J. Smith, and A. S. Jaffe, "Ventricular Tachycardia and Psychiatric Depression in Patients with Coronary Artery Disease," *American Journal of Medicine,* 95: 1993, 23–28; and E. M. Levy, D. J. Borelli, S. M. Mirin, P. Salt, P. H. Knapp, C. Peirce, B. H. Fox, and P. H. Black, "Biological Measures and Cellular Immunological Function in Depressed Psychiatric Inpatients," *Psychiatry Research,* 36: 1991, 157–167.

59. J. B. Imboden, *Archives of Internal Medicine,* 108: 1961, 393.

60. S. E. Locke, M. W. Hurst, J. S. Heisel, L. Kraus, and R. M. Williams, *Life Change Stress and Human Natural Killer Cell Activity* (Research Report) (Boston: Department of Biological Sciences and Psychosomatic Medicine, Division of Psychiatry, Boston University School of Medicine, 1979).

61. "Bereavement: An Immune Reaction," *Mind/Body/Health Digest,* 1(2): 1987, 2.

62. "Bereavement".

63. From *Medical World News* as summarized in Padus, p. 577.

64. Padus, p. 577.

65. Steven Locke and Douglas Colligan, *The Healer Within: The New Medicine of Mind and Body* (New York: E. P. Dutton, 1986), p. 68.

66. "Depression and Immunity," *Harvard Medical School Mental Health Letter,* 1986, p. 8.

67. Margaret Kemeny, "Clinical Psychoneuroimmunology in Genital Herpes Recurrence," paper presented at the Annual Meeting of the Society for Behavior Medicine, 1986; and Justice, p. 157.

68. "Depression and Immunity."

69. Locke and Colligan, p. 66.

70. Locke and Colligan.

71. William L. Mundy, "Curing Allergy with Visual Imagery," *The Psychology of Health, Immunity, and Disease,* vol. A, p. 421, in Proceedings of the Sixth International Conference of the National Institute for the Clinical Application of Behavioral Medicine.

72. Donald E. Girard, Ransom J. Arthur, and James B. Reuler, "Psychosocial Events and Subsequent Illness—A Review," *The Western Journal of Medicine,* 142(3): 1985, 358–363.

73. Girard et al.

74. James J. Lynch, *The Broken Heart: The Medical Consequences of Loneliness* (New York: Basic Books, Inc., Publishers, 1977).

75. Lynch.

76. *Science News,* 144(5): 1993, 79.

77. *Science News.*

78. R. M. Carney, M. W. Rich, K. E. Freedland, J. Saini, A. TeVelde, C. Simeone, and K. Clark, "Major Depressive Disorder Predicts Cardiac Events in Patients With Coronary Artery Disease," *Psychosomatic Medicine,* 50: 1988, 627–633.

79. Mia Adessa, "Sad Hearts," *Psychology Today,* August: 1988, 23.

80. "Hearts and Minds," *Longevity,* April: 1989, 14.

81. "The Heart of Depression," *Science News,* January 7: 1989, 13.

82. R. M. Carney, M. W. Rich, K. E. Freedland, J. Saini, A. TeVelde, C. Simeone, and K. Clark, "Major Depressive Disorder Predicts Cardiac Events in Patients with Coronary Artery Disease," *Psychosomatic Medicine,* 50: 1988, 627–632.

83. Nancy Frasure-Smith, Francois Lesperance, and Mario Talajic, "Depression Following Myocardial Infarction: Impact on Six-Month Survival," *Journal of the American Medical Association,* 270: 1993, 1819–1825. (See also the editorial by Williams and Chesney in the same issue.)

84. Margaret A. Chesney, "Social Isolation, Depression, and Heart Disease: Research on Women Broadens the Agenda," *Psychosomatic Medicine,* 55: 1993, 434–435.

85. Adessa.

86. R. B. Lydiard, "Effects of Sertraline on Quality of Life: A Double Blind Study," Scientific Exhibit at the American Academy of Family Physicians Annual Assembly, 1993.

87. Redford B. Williams and Margaret A. Chesney, "Psychosocial Factors and Prognosis in Established Coronary Artery Disease," *Journal of the American Medical Association,* 270: 1993, 1860–1861.

88. Siegel.

89. B. Bower, "Science News of the Week/ Depression and Cancer: A Fatal Link," *Science News*, 132: 1987, 244.

90. Alan B. Zonderman, Paul T. Costa, and Robert R. McCrae, "Depression as a Risk for Cancer Morbidity and Mortality in a Nationally Representative Sample," *Journal of the American Medical Association*, 262(9): 1989, 1191–1200.

91. Karl Goodkin, quoted in S. Hart, "Depression and Cancer: No Clear Connection," *Science News*, 136: 1989, 150.

92. K. Bolla-Wilson and M. L. Bleecker, "Absence of Depression in Elderly Adults," *Journal of Gerontology*, 44(2)1989, 53–55.

93. Information on medical ailments is from Wayne Katon, "Depression: Somatization and Social Factors," *The Journal of Family Practice*, 27(6): 1988, 579–580.

94. Jana M. Mossey, Elizabeth Mutran, Kathryn Knott, and Rebecca Craik, "Recovery After Hip Fractures: The Importance of Psychosocial Factors," *Advances*, 6(4): 1989, 23–25.

95. Frank et al, *Archives of General Psychiatry*, 47: 1990, 1093ff.

96. "Infant Brains Reflect Moms' Depression," *Science News*, 138: 1990, 28.

97. Dennis Gersten, "Depression: Is It a Product of Our Culture?" *Brain/Mind Bulletin*, 16(6): 1991, 6–7.

98. "Ten Physical Reasons You May Be Depressed," *Prevention*, June: 1992, 69–76.

11

THE DISEASE-RESISTANT PERSONALITY

The mind is its own place,
and in itself
can make a heaven of hell,
a hell of heaven.
—JOHN MILTON

Too often we ask ourselves why someone became ill instead of how someone has managed to stay well. As Pennsylvania State University's Evan G. Pattishall reflected, if we study twenty-five people who are exposed to the influenza virus and five of them get sick, "we tend to study the five who developed influenza, when we should be exerting even more effort studying the twenty who didn't become ill.[1]

Howard S. Friedman echoes that sentiment when he wrote, "Each week the prestigious *New England Journal of Medicine* publishes a 'Case Record of the Massachusetts General Hospital,' detailing the pathology of an unusual or informative patient's case. There is no corresponding 'Case History of a Person Who Remained Well Throughout a Long Life.'"[2]

Researchers have long known that certain groups of people enjoy "remarkable good health and longevity." Among them are "Mormons, nuns, symphony conductors, and women who are listed in *Who's Who*. This suggests that something in the way these people live, possibly even such abstractions as faith, pride of accomplishment, or productivity, plays a role in diminishing the ill effects of stress."[3]

The way we behave influences health. Whether we smoke cigarettes, sip wine before dinner, start the day with a brisk walk, and eat fatty foods all affect our health. But could something other than behavior play a role in our ability to withstand stress and stay healthy? Researchers believe so. And the key may lie in personality, because apparently personality is a major determinant in how well we are able to resist stress.

The Role of Stress in Health

Stress plays a major role in disease. Biologist and neuroscientist Robert M. Sapolsky of Stanford Medical School points out the pervasive influence of stress:

> *As recently as 1900, the leading causes of death in America were tuberculosis, pneumonia, and flu. In just a few generations, we have conquered these and nearly all other infectious diseases, as well as those of poor hygiene and undernutrition. Suddenly, Americans live and die differently from any other humans in history and most other people on Earth. Instead of succumbing to childhood infection, or passing away in one night's malarial fever, we now survive long enough to witness the slow deterioration of our bodies—the steady clogging of arteries, the gradual weakening of the immune system until it finally lets the seed of a tumor take root. One of the most important medical insights of recent decades has been that these diseases of aging—and the pace at which they advance—can be greatly affected by how we lead our lives, in particular, by how much stress we experience.[4]*

Medically speaking, stress is a fairly new concept. Only in the last fifty years or so have researchers been able to pinpoint some of the effects of stress on the human body. And much of what we know about stress today originated with pioneer researcher Hans Selye. Early in this century, physicians believed that each disease was caused by a distinct and separate agent. But Selye, then a medical student in Prague, was puzzled by something he observed in the hospital: Patients with a wide variety of illnesses shared a number of symptoms (especially fatigue, joint pains, and weight loss). If distinct organisms caused each disease, Selye wondered, how could patients with so many different diseases all have the same symptoms?[5]

Unable to solve the mystery, Selye moved on, largely forgetting the puzzling patients in the hospital. Ten years later, a totally unrelated experiment with rats focused Selye's mind sharply back on those hospital patients.

Selye set out to test a chemical extract that he believed contained a new ovarian hormone. The experiment required that the laboratory rats be injected at frequent intervals with the extract; a control group of rats was injected at the same frequency, but with ordinary saline. After days of being jabbed with the needle, the rats who were receiving the chemical extract started developing an unexpected set of symptoms: enlarged and overactive adrenal glands, withered thymuses (a sign of a deteriorating immune system), and gastric ulcers. The rats who were injected with the saline solution developed the same set of symptoms.

Selye thought back to the hospital where he had worked ten years earlier. What occurred to him then became the cornerstone of stress research: He realized that both the patients and the rats were reacting to stress. And he believed that no matter what causes distress (whether it's a terminal illness, an overdrawn checking account, or a fight with a spouse), the body's reaction is the same. Selye called that reaction "the stress response," and it has become well documented during the ensuing decades of medical research (see Chapter 3).

The decades of research that have focused on the human stress response and its associated ills have also posed a fascinating question: Why do some people who undergo chronic stress fall ill while others sail through unscathed? One of the researchers most intrigued by that question was Suzanne Ouellette Kobasa, who teaches psychology in the City University of New York's graduate school. She was familiar with all the state-of-the-art research that drew definite connections between stress and illness—but she believed there had to be a middle ground. It is impossible to avoid stress altogether; some stressful events (such as the death of a loved one) are completely beyond control. And, she concluded, even if it *were* possible to completely avoid stress, that would be "a prescription for staying away from opportunities as well as trouble. Since any change can be stressful, a person who wanted to be completely free of stress would never marry, have a child, take a new job, or move."[6]

Kobasa had other concerns, too. The popular notion regarding stress and illness, she believed, ignored "a lot of what we know about people. It assumes we're all vulnerable and passive in the face of adversity. But what about human resilience, initiative, and creativity? Many come through periods of stress with more physical and mental vigor than they had before."[7]

The more she pondered the stress–illness connection, the more engrossed Kobasa became with the people who *didn't* get sick under stress—and the more intent she became on discovering why. In 1975, she mobilized a group of her colleagues and went to work on a study of what she calls "the walking wounded of the stress war"—a group of high-powered business executives faced with personal and career upheaval.

As Harvard University professor Douglas Powell put it, "There's a story about two sons of an alcoholic. One turned out to be a drunk, the other a tee-totaler. When asked to explain themselves, each gave exactly the same reply: 'With a father like that, what can you expect?' The moral of the story, it seems to me, is that it's not the problems we have in our lives, but how we manage them that makes so much difference."[8]

The Mechanisms of Stress

The American Academy of Family Physicians has estimated that 60 percent of all problems brought to physicians in this country are stress-related, and the problems that aren't directly caused by stress are made worse—or last longer—because of it.[9] Every week, some 95 million Americans suffer a stress-related problem and take medication for their aches and pains. And there's a greater toll than just the personal one; American businesses lose an estimated $150 billion each year to its employees' stress-related problems.[10]

Hosts of experiments have shown that people are susceptible to the ravages of stress. In one particularly interesting study, pediatricians wanted to determine why some children get sick when they are exposed to a certain bacteria while others stay healthy. Pediatricians Roger Meyer and Robert Haggerty chose the streptococcus bacteria, a variety that was usually harmless, not the virulent form that

Focus on Research

The executives that Kobasa chose for her study were 200 middle- and upper-level executives at Illinois Bell. At the time of Kobasa's study, Illinois Bell was undergoing tremendous tumult as a result of the AT&T divestiture; many executives would be experiencing a change in responsibility, and some would likely be dismissed completely. Worst of all, for a long while no one knew for sure how the company would eventually settle, so employees and management were in a state of uncertainty for an extended period.

The initial phase of Kobasa's study encompassed the seven years of change and redefinition experienced by Illinois Bell; she is still following the executives as part of her ongoing study. As part of the study, she learned that half of the executives who were under stress got sick. But the group Kobasa was more interested in was the other half—the ones who were under the same stress but who *didn't* get sick.

Kobasa had narrowed down her group of 200 executives from a larger group of nearly 700 who filled out questionnaires. The questionnaires were designed to detect how much stress each executive was under (with some questions specifically modified to fit Illinois Bell's situation) and included a checklist of ill-

nesses and symptoms. The 200 executives were the ones judged to be under the greatest amount of stress.

Kobasa and her colleagues then conducted in-depth interviews that sought information about the executives' age, educational background, jobs, income, and other lifestyle factors. They also gave each executive a questionnaire designed to detect personality features.

After extensive computer analysis, Kobasa and her colleagues found out that "the healthy executives were not younger, wealthier, higher on the career ladder, or better-educated than their colleagues who became sick under stress." * The executives were a fairly homogeneous bunch; most were male, middle-class, middle-aged, married, and Protestant. The healthy executives shared a unique set of personality traits that determined how they dealt with stress—and that Kobasa came to call "hardiness."

Based on her study of the Illinois Bell executives, Kobasa determined that stress is not the problem; it is our response to stress that largely determines whether we get sick or stay healthy. The key to wellness, she determined, is a different way of looking at and dealing with stressful events. †

* Suzanne Ouellette Kobasa, "How Much Stress Can You Survive?" *American Health*, September 1984, pp. 71–72.
† Blair Justice, "Those Who Stay Healthy," *New Realities*, July/August 1988, pp. 35–39, 69–71.

causes strep throat, ear infections, and scarlet fever, noting that "peaceful coexistence between this organism and its human host is the rule, while disease is the exception."[11] Many children harbor the bacteria—but only a few get sick as a result. The researchers wanted to figure out why.

To get some answers, they watched sixteen families, each with two or more children, for a year. They noted every possible factor: the child's age, sex, family health history, antibody response, size of family, housing conditions (such as type of heating system and number of rooms), type of medical treatment received, whether the child had had a tonsillectomy, weather conditions throughout the study, and special stresses at home. Every three weeks, the two doctors checked on the family's health and took throat cultures from everyone.

After monitoring the rates of infection for a year, the doctors started to look for patterns. One was age: school-aged children got sick the most often, probably because they are continually exposed to a wider range of bacteria. Also, children who shared rooms with infected people had a higher rate of infection. And time of year seemed to have a role: Most outbreaks were in the early spring (March or April).

Throughout the study, family members were asked to keep diaries in which they noted particular stresses. Crises were noted, ranging from a grandmother dying in one family to the house burning in another. As researchers noted increases in stress in the diaries, they saw a corresponding increase in strep illness among affected family members.

The results were specific and astonishing. In one family, a visiting uncle with tonsillitis exposed the entire family to infection at the beginning of a month. Of the family of six (four children and the parents), only one was ill by the end of the month—the oldest daughter, who was under tremendous pressure at the time of her uncle's visit to learn her catechism in time for her confirmation.

The researchers concluded that stress was four times as likely to precede an infection as to follow it. Throughout the year of the study, only about one-fifth of the low-stress families had any infection, whereas half of the high-stress families did. Does stress cause infection? Researchers don't think so. They are convinced, however, that stress compromises the immune system enough for infection to take hold.[12]

Stress has been definitely implicated in an entire checklist of symptoms, involving most of the body's systems. Stress can cause tension headaches, jaw pain, muscle aches and pains, back pain, and grinding of teeth. It's responsible for migraine headaches, dizziness, difficulty in breathing, heartburn, nausea, hives, rapid heartbeat, chest pain, diarrhea, constipation, and sexual problems. It can result in anxiety, moodiness, depression, forgetfulness, frequent crying, fearfulness, nervous habits, sleep problems, inability to concentrate, and a wide range of other behavioral problems.[13]

If stress research has shown one thing, it is that stress alone won't cause illness. How a person reacts to stress does. Your personality, your unique way of viewing things, will determine what impact stress has on you.

Watching general population groups during stress demonstrates this principle well. The Irish are one example. When the Irish were transplanted by the thousands to the eastern seaboards of America during the last century, their standard of living improved dramatically. Conditions were much cleaner, and they had plenty of food to eat (while they faced starvation in Ireland). But the death rate from tuberculosis soared. While the transplanted Dubliners were better housed and better fed, the tuberculosis death rate was 100 percent higher than it was during the same period in Dublin, where the conditions were much worse. Why did the Irish die of tuberculosis despite such dramatically improved conditions? Many did not want to migrate to America—and they were unprepared for the discrimination they faced.[14]

It happened with the American Indians. When they were forced off the plains and onto reservations (often within only a few miles of where they had lived), they had much better sanitation and a higher standard of living. Considering physical conditions alone, they should have enjoyed much better health. But that was not the case. Again, deaths from tuberculosis increased.[15] They were being uprooted from the land of their forefathers. Their traditions were in danger. They felt powerless—and they gave in.

It happened with the Bantu natives in South Africa. They were moved in droves from their native villages into Johannesburg, where sanitation was dramatically better and where food and housing were vastly improved. Thousands became ill with tuberculosis. When hundreds of the dying were permitted to return to their native villages to die, the tuberculosis bacillus was then spread throughout the villages. But the people who had remained in the villages didn't get sick.[16]

Was it the move alone that made these populations sick? Chinese and Hungarian refugees overcame great odds and dangerous political upheaval to immigrate to the United States. Although their new home represented a place vastly different than the one they left, they thrived. They viewed their new lives as an opportunity and a challenge, not as a negative.[17]

The effect is even more pronounced in populations in which one segment has a different outlook than another. Take, for example, a group of Portuguese who immigrated to Canada for employment reasons. The men who immigrated saw the move as a chance for a better job and a new future—and their health actually improved after their move to Canada. Their wives saw the move as a disruption of their valued family ties in Portugal—and they were more likely to get sick.[18]

Stress Buffers

Some things have been identified as "stress buffers," or elements that alleviate the deleterious effects of stress. Controversy surrounds some of these findings, but researchers have generally shown that social support, a sense of control, physical fitness, a sense of humor, self-esteem, optimism, coping styles, and Kobasa's "hardiness" personality all help to buffer stress.[19] Most important may be what's within a person—how a person reacts to and views the situation that has created stress. Dr. N. Lee Smith defines the components of stress resilience as caring love (committed to the fulfillment of the other), responsible free will (able to create your own life experience and influence events), integrity (being true to core values), challenge (enjoying growth), and hope (feeling positive expectation).

In her revolutionary studies on stress and illness, Kobasa and her colleague Salvatore Maddi commented, "We could not believe that the same human imagination responsible for urbanization and industrialization was somehow incapable of coping with the . . . ensuing pressures and disruptions. It seemed obvious that the individual differences in response to stress were important."[20]

With that attitude, Kobasa and her colleagues decided to expand their stress and illness studies beyond the original group of Illinois telephone company executives. Would the same principles hold true in other populations?

Focus on Research

Kobasa and the researchers who worked with her in the Illinois Bell study looked at a group of 157 general practice attorneys. Many of these attorneys experienced severe stresses off the job, and almost all of them went through frequent changes as well as intense pressures at work. The researchers constructed their study as carefully as they did the Illinois Bell study, examining not only the attorneys' health but also every aspect of their professional and personal lives.

They found no correlation between stressful life events and physical illness. They did find a powerful connection between physical health and certain attitudes and beliefs. The attorneys who got ill were angry, withdrawn, and indifferent. Most smoked or drank alcohol. The attorneys who stayed healthy valued what they were doing, had a strong belief in the importance of what they were doing, and showed a strong sense of overall purpose in their lives. They were, as Kobasa put it, "hardy." Kobasa came away from the study with the theory that many of the attorneys developed responses to stress that kept them healthy because they *believe* that lawyers are expected to thrive under pressure.

Next the group studied 100 gynecology outpatients. Again, the group looked at not only health history and status, but at lifestyle, stresses, and other factors that could impact on health. They also studied the women's person-

alities and styles of coping. The patients involved in the study were all white, middle class, and between the ages of twenty-five and thirty-five.

Kobasa and her group learned that all the women had experienced a significant amount of stress. Sixty of the women were ill and forty had stayed well. What made them different? The women who stayed well showed traits common to the "hardy" personality: They had a greater sense of control, showed a stronger sense of challenge, and had more commitment to their work, their families, and themselves.

Finally, the group studied 259 executives for a period of five years. By this point in her research, Kobasa had identified what she believed were the personality traits that helped people stay well, even under stress. Therefore, she and her colleagues approached this study a little differently. At the outset, they identified which executives were strong in the traits that appeared to protect health. Then, over the next five years, they followed medical records to confirm the frequency and severity of illnesses of each executive in the study.

Kobasa's suspicions were confirmed. The executives who were identified at the study's beginning as being "hardy"—as having personality traits that boosted their immunity and helped them buffer stress—had only half the illness of the other executives.

Source: Blair Justice, "Those Who Stay Healthy," *New Realities,* July/August 1988.

Others have done similar studies, and their findings have been remarkably consistent with Kobasa's. Lawrence Hinkle and his associates in the departments of medicine and psychiatry at New York Hospital's Cornell Medical Center conducted a series of studies over a twenty-year period. They found that personality traits had a definite bearing on health. They concluded that those with "a good attitude and an ability to get along with other people" enjoyed the lowest frequency of illness.[21]

In another study, two psychiatrists, an endocrinologist, and a cancer specialist in New York teamed up to determine the stress reactions and hormonal changes that occurred when people were faced with a truly life-threatening situation. To test their theories, they picked a group who did face a life-threatening situation: thirty women who were undergoing biopsies for breast tumors at Montefiore Hospital and Medical Center.

To determine the amount of "distress" each woman was suffering, researchers did tests to measure how much hydrocortisone each woman secreted per day. (Hydrocortisone is a hormone secreted by the adrenal gland in response to stress. The researchers measured it each day for the three days preceding each woman's biopsy.) At the end of the study, the researchers concluded that the crisis of possibly having cancer wasn't what determined how much or how little distress each woman experienced. The determining factor was each woman's "psychological defenses" or coping style—especially her outlooks and beliefs. The lowest amount of adrenal hormone was secreted by a forty-five-year-old woman who consistently used faith and prayer to deal with life's stressful events. The woman who fared the next best was a fifty-four-year-old who had a healthy philosophical acceptance of adversity.

Personality Traits That Keep Us Well

The cumulative results of studies conducted over the past three or four decades—Kobasa's as well as others—show beyond a doubt that certain personality traits keep us well, boost our immunity, and improve our immune systems. Perhaps most convincing was a study of 650 children in Hawaii.

In their book *Vulnerable But Invincible*, researchers Emmy Werner and Ruth Smith report their study of the 650 children, born and reared on the island of Kauai in Hawaii. The children in the study were followed from a few months before their birth until they were in their early twenties. They were assessed at regular intervals with a battery of interviews, questionnaires, and examinations; researchers monitored their health records closely.[22]

By all standards, these children were at high risk. All were born into poor families and lived in chronic poverty. Many were born to single mothers, some of whom were depressed or schizophrenic. The fathers of those who did have fathers in the home were semiskilled or unskilled laborers. The children were born prematurely at higher than average rates; many were victims of severe perinatal stress. The mothers had little formal education (none had graduated from high school). The families themselves were plagued by a multitude of problems.

The stresses didn't end there. As psychologist Robert Ornstein and physician David Sobel put it:

> *They came of age in the years 1955 to 1979—a time of unprecedented social change. They had to deal with the influx of many newcomers from the U.S. mainland during the long war in Southeast Asia and later with the burgeoning of tourism. They witnessed the assassination of one president and the resignation of another. They were the first generation to deal with the invasion of the home by television. They faced unprecedented choices since they had access to contraceptive pills and mind-altering drugs.*[23]

The combination of these biological and social stresses took their toll on some of the children. By the age of ten (the first major interval the researchers used), at least half of the children were in serious trouble. They were in physical ill health, had serious behavioral problems, and had learning disabilities that impacted their ability to progress through the school system.

By the age of eighteen, the next major follow-up period, an additional 25 percent—or three-fourths of all the children in the study—had very serious problems. Those who didn't have profound psychological problems did have learning disabilities, behavioral problems, and poor health.

That didn't surprise anyone. After all, these kids had started out under the most dreadful conditions and had grown up in an environment charged with unrelenting stress. What *did* surprise researchers was the group of kids—approximately one-fourth of the group studied —who, despite all the stress, rallied. They prevailed with strong psychological adjustment, good health, and enviable school records. Ornstein and Sobel describe three of them:

> *Life did not start out well for Michael. His mother was sixteen years old, unwed, and lived with her mother and grandmother. She managed to hide her pregnancy from her own mother until the third trimester when she married a nineteen-year-old boy. The child's biological father was very much against the marriage. The mother did not receive any medical care until the seventh month of pregnancy, and Michael was born prematurely and weighed only four pounds ten ounces. Michael spent the first three weeks of his life in an army hospital. At two, Michael's adoptive father was sent with the army to Korea, where he remained for two years. At age eight, Michael's parents divorced and his mother left, leaving him with his father and three younger siblings.*
>
> *Early life was also not easy for Kay. She was born of seventeen-year-old unmarried parents. They had both been asked to leave school because of the pregnancy, and the father was without a job. Family Court sent Kay's mother to a Salvation Army Home to have her baby; placing her for adoption was considered but rejected, and the parents were eventually married when Kay was six months old despite objections from their parents. Kay's parents later separated.*
>
> *Mary got off to a rough start as well. Her mother's pregnancy occurred after many unsuccessful attempts to conceive and a previous miscarriage. Her mother was very much overweight and had various minor medical problems during pregnancy. She was hospitalized three times for severe false labor and eventually was in labor for more than twenty hours. During Mary's childhood her parents experienced financial difficulties, and her mother found it necessary to work outside the home for short periods. Between Mary's fifth and tenth birthdays, her mother had several major illnesses, surgeries, and two hospitalizations for "unbearable tension," nervousness, annoyance with her children, and fears that she might harm them.*[24]

How did things turn out for the three? Despite everything, they grew up to be healthy, well-adjusted, successful adults. Michael ranked at the top of his class and was awarded a college scholarship. Well-liked by his peers, he was described as confident, persistent, self-assured, dependable, and realistic. Kay did well throughout life. She was an alert, healthy, affectionate, and robust baby; as a child, she had above-normal grades in school and was described as agreeable, relaxed, and mentally normal. As an adult, she was described as poised, sociable, self-assured, respectful and accepting of others, and a person who made good use of the abilities she had. She planned to go into the entertainment field and to marry. Mary was described as having high self-esteem, persistence, concern for others, and an outgoing personality; she was willing to open herself up to new possibilities after only initial hesitancy. She planned to enroll in college, and was keeping her future career goals open. At eighteen, Mary described herself this way:

> *If I say how I am it sounds like bragging—I have a good personality and people like me. . . . I don't like it when people think they can run my own life—I like to be my own judge. I know right from wrong, but I feel I have a lot more to learn and go through. Generally, I hope I can make it—I hope.*[25]

Hope seemed to be a key attitude with the children who prevailed over their difficult circumstances. So did perseverance. They were what Indiana psychiatric social worker Katherine Northcraft calls *transcenders*—people who, "in the worst of times, envision themselves as elsewhere, imagining that they can do great things despite their surroundings."[26] Despite difficult family situations, these resilient children developed strong bonds with a parent, grandparent, sibling, or other caretaker, usually early in life (almost always during the first year). When they felt confused or troubled, they sought help—but they were also children who eagerly accepted challenge. These children had personalities that kept them healthy, and enabled them to overcome adversity. They were, in Kobasa's terms, "hardy."

Where do resilient traits come from? No one knows for sure. Some of them may be inborn. Werner found that most of the resilient children in her study had been alert, sociable, even-tempered, responsive infants. "There seems to be a group of children who temperamentally and probably constitutionally have a better chance of making lemonade out of lemons," she believes. Does that doom the rest—those who are introverted, shy, or difficult? Not necessarily, she says—it's just that "it's easier for those who are more outgoing to find support."[27]

According to psychologist Ann Masten, associate director of the University of Minnesota's Institute of Child Development, the fact that Werner's resilient children had a strong adult figure is important. "When resilient adults talk about how they made it, virtually everyone mentions a key adult," she explains. But that adult doesn't have to be a parent. In fact, in her study of more than two hundred resilient children, many found inner strength through bonds they developed with a neighbor, family friend, teacher, minister, or other respected adult.[28]

A similar study—started by one researcher in the early 1920s and continued by others over a period spanning seven decades—provides what scientists call "the first evidence of its kind" and may give further information about the concept of disease resistance. In the early 1920s, Stanford researcher Lewis Terman recruited

1178 eleven-year-old gifted children who had been recommended for the study by their teachers.

At the outset, Terman had parents and teachers rate the children on more than two dozen psychological and intellectual traits. Terman himself then used a set of scales—called "remarkably modern" by University of California at Riverside researcher Howard Friedman—to rate the children. Terman's scales included sociability, energy level, self-esteem/motivation, conscientiousness/dependability, moodiness, and cheerfulness. Terman began the study, and his successors continued to track the volunteers over the next seventy years.

According to the researchers, two clear patterns emerged. First, conscientious, dependable people who showed permanence and stability of mood lived significantly longer than the others. Second, in a surprise to researchers, cheery optimists lived substantially *shorter* than normal.

Why? One reason might be the tendency of an optimist to underestimate the gravity of certain risks—and the tendency of the conscientious to stay organized, plan ahead, and be prepared for the unexpected.[29]

Hardiness

Hardiness is "a set of beliefs about oneself, the world, and how they interact. It takes shape as a sense of personal commitment to what you are doing, a sense of control over your life, and a feeling of challenge."[30]

Kobasa defines the personality traits of hardiness as "the three Cs": commitment, control, and challenge. Commitment is an attitude of curiosity and involvement in what is happening around you; control is the belief that you can influence events instead of becoming a victim; and challenge is the belief that change brings a chance for growth instead of the fear that change is threatening.[31]

Commitment

Commitment—an attitude of curiosity and involvement in what is happening around you—means a commitment to yourself, your work, your family, and the other important values in your life. This is not a fleeting involvement, but a deep and abiding interest. People who are committed in this way have a deep involvement with their work and their families, a deep sense of meaning, and a pervasive sense of direction in their lives. In one study involving students at Harvard Medical School, students best able to withstand stress were personally committed to a goal of some kind.[32]

A sense of challenge often drives us to a hectic pace filled with plenty of pressures—but it is healthy, because there is a drive to live life to its fullest. The important element, say some researchers, is commitment to an ideal greater than oneself.[33] For some people, that commitment comes in the form of commitment to a religion; for others, it's a commitment to political reform or to a certain philosophy. And some healthy people have a deep sense of commitment to something as simple as a hobby.

A perfect example is Mohandas K. Gandhi, a man who by all standards was a driven workaholic. He went on countless fasts, depriving himself of nourishment, and spent months in prison—one of the most stressful scenarios possible. Yet he was strong and healthy until his assassination at the age of seventy-seven. Many believe it was because of his unwavering commitment to become one of the world's great leaders and to win political freedom for his homeland.

Control

As defined by psychologist S. C. Thompson in 1981, control is "a belief that one has at one's disposal a response that can influence the aversiveness of an event." It's the belief that you can cushion the hurtful impact of a situation by the way you look at it and react to it. The kind of control that keeps you healthy is the opposite of helplessness. It is the firm belief that you can influence how you'll react, and the willingness to act on that basis. It's the refusal to be victimized. It is not the erroneous belief that you can control your environment, your circumstances, or other people; that kind of an attitude leads to illness, not health. The control that keeps you healthy is a belief that you can control yourself and your own reactions to what life hands you.

The healthiest Harvard Medical School students were the ones who approached problem-solving with a sense of control; the least healthy were those who were passive.[34] The healthiest and hardiest people are those who focus on what they can control, ignoring the rest. Through skill, planning, and diligent attention to detail, they believe that every problem has a solution.

We all want to be able to predict what will happen to us. We all crave a sense of mastery. No one wants to feel responsible without being in control.[35] A sense of control—a belief that you can control your own behavior, not necessarily control the people and events around you—promotes health. It endows you with the belief that even if everything around you gets bad, you will still be fine.

Challenge

Challenge means the ability to see change as an opportunity for growth and excitement. Excitement is critical, because boredom puts people at a high risk for disease.[36] People who are constructively challenged are more healthy—and a German philosopher mused that one of the two biggest foes of human happiness is boredom.

A person who is not healthy and hardy views change with helplessness and alienation. A healthy, hardy person can face change with confidence, self-determination, eagerness, and excitement. Change becomes an eagerly sought-after challenge, not a threat. Joan C. Post-Gorden, psychologist at the University of Southern Colorado, says that healthy people don't even *see* the negatives, because they thoroughly *expect* a positive outcome.

That healthy view of challenge is exemplified by Mary Decker Slaney, the world-class runner who has broken four world records.[37] The stress of competition is crushing—yet she has stayed healthy, and keeps competing. When asked why, she responded, "I love it. Running is something I do for myself more than anything else." Those positive emotions and personal triumph demonstrate a great sense of healthy challenge. And since every life is filled with obstacles, it stands to reason that the way we view those obstacles—whether as crushing problems or as challenges to be eagerly met—determines in part how healthy we are.

Research showed that among more than sixty HIV-positive gay men, those who treated their HIV-positive status as a challenge—and then developed strategies to fight it—had improved natural killer cell activity. University of Miami psychiatrist Karl Goodkin, who spearheaded the study, said that an active coping style, along with fewer life burdens and good social support, led to improvement of natural killer cell activity and immunity.[38]

Coherence

Adding to Kobasa's "three C's" is coherence—a "pervasive, enduring though dynamic feeling that one's internal and external environments are predictable and that there is a high probability that all things will work out as well as can be reasonably expected."[39] Other research verifies that stress-resistant personality traits include involvement in work or other tasks that have great meaning, the ability to relate well to others, and the ability to interact in a strong social network. The most vulnerable people are those who are socially isolated. The healthiest Harvard Medical School graduates sought out other people, were actively and empathically engaged with other people, and had strong social networks.[40]

Healthful Choices

People with a disease-resistant personality tend to exercise regularly; 80 percent of the healthiest Harvard Medical School students engaged in regular aerobic exercise, while only 20 percent of the ill students did.[41] They relax for at least fifteen minutes a day.[42] They limit refined sugars in their diet, and limit stimulants (such as nicotine and caffeine).[43] In the Harvard study, healthy students used a minimum of "substances"—things they considered to be drugs or drug-like, including nicotine and caffeine.[44] "Hardy" people also tend to engage in more consistent health behaviors—"and, therefore, when under stress are physically more resistant to disease and illness."[45]

Hardiness or stress-resistant personality traits may combine with healthy behaviors to result in enhanced resistance to disease. "When individuals have high health concern they are more likely to engage in appropriate health behavior if they are at the same time high in hardiness," one researcher concluded. "When hardy people become concerned about their health, they are more likely than nonhardy people to engage in appropriate health-protective behaviors."[46]

The hardy (or disease-resistant) personality is summed up in a profile provided by Ornstein and Sobel:

A small, neat man in his mid-50s, Chuck L. introduced himself as someone who enjoys solving problems. In the company, his specialty is customer relations, even though he was trained as an engineer. His eyes light up as he describes the intricacies of investigating customer needs and complaints, determining the company's service capabilities and obligations, formulating possible solutions that appear fair to all parties, and persuading these parties to agree. He thinks customer relations work is more demanding as the company streamlines and approaches reorganization. Asked in a sympathetic manner whether this is making his job unmanageable, he notes an increase in stress but adds that the work is becoming all the more interesting and challenging as well. He assumes that the role he plays will become even more central as the company's reorganization accelerates. He looks forward to this and has already formulated plans for a more comprehensive approach to customer relations.

Chuck doesn't seem to neglect family life for all his imaginative and energetic involvement at work. He married in college, and the couple has two grown children. His wife has returned to school to finish a college degree long ago interrupted. Although her absence from the home causes Chuck some inconvenience, it is clear that he encouraged her. He is full of plans about how he can preserve a close home life. Should he find too much time to himself, he imagines he will get involved in useful community activities.

In the past, Chuck's family life has hardly been uneventful. His daughter's two-year-old son died; then her husband divorced her, and she returned home for a year. This was a difficult time not only for her but for Chuck and his wife, who felt their daughter's pain and sense of failure in a very personal way. Chuck describes the long talks they had. Although he mentions their crying together, it is also clear that he was always searching for a way, a formula, to relieve mutual pain. He encouraged his daughter to pick up the pieces of her life, learn from what had happened, and begin again. He tried to help his wife see that she had little responsibility in what had happened and that it was not the end of the world. He told himself the same thing. This difficult time, in his view, drew the three of them closer together.[47]

In a comprehensive year-long study of college students, researchers at Boston University School of Medicine concluded that there's a definite series of events that precedes illness. Here's what they believe happens:[48] A person perceives a distressing life situation. For whatever reason, he or she is not able to resolve the distressing situation effectively. As a result, the person feels helpless and anxious; those feelings of helplessness weaken the immune system and the resistance to disease, and the person becomes more vulnerable to disease-causing agents that are always in the environment.

The traits of a disease-resistant personality interrupt this cycle, and therefore help prevent illness. A study of women with breast cancer shows that personality and behavior can help protect against cancer and can help improve survival.[49] There's a real difference between the way healthy people and ill people look at things.[50] Healthy people, for example, tend to maintain reasonable personal control in their lives. If a problem crops up, they look for resources and try out solutions. If one doesn't work, they try another one. People who are frequently ill, on the other hand, leave decisions up to others and try to get other people to solve their problems. Their approach tends to be passive.

Furthermore, those researchers say healthy people are generally committed to a goal of some kind—and they typically spend at least a few hours every week doing something that provides a sense of challenge or enhances their sense of meaningful participation in life. What they do holds personal significance for them. People who are ill, on the other hand, often report being bored; they are not able to find things that interest them. Healthy people generally seek out other people and are actively involved with them. Ill people, on the other hand, tend to be more socially isolated.

In discussing people who were able to overcome disease and heal themselves, *Psychology Today* editor Marc Barasch said that if "there is a thread that stands out, it is that each person, some readily, some reluctantly, wound up doing the opposite of what sick people are supposed to: Rather than only trying to 'get back to normal,' they embarked on a voyage of self-discovery. Like early circumnavigators, they seemed to cling to an instinctive faith that the only way home was forward, into the round but unknown world of the self."[51]

"One reason people can undergo tremendous stress and not get sick," says Yale surgeon Bernie Siegel: ". . . has a lot to do with meeting your own needs, expressing your own feelings, learning to say 'no' without guilt. Now, I'm not suggesting that people blame themselves for an illness. Rather, they should see the illness as a message to redirect their life accordingly—to resolve conflicts with other people, express anger and resentment and other negative emotions they've been bottling up inside, to begin looking out for their own needs. And, in so doing, the immune system becomes stimulated and healing takes place."[52]

In part, Siegel is describing the hardy personality. And hardiness promotes health. Following the initial phase of their landmark study at Illinois Bell, Kobasa and Maddi began training the telephone executives in hardiness—began helping them develop disease-resistant personalities. Specific health benefits came to the people who received the training. They not only enjoyed more job satisfaction, but had reduced anxiety, less depression, fewer physical ills (such as headaches), lower blood pressure, and better sleep.[53]

An entire spectrum of studies verifies the findings: People with the traits of a "disease-resistant" personality do, indeed, enjoy better health. They have fewer episodes of illness, even when people around them have contagious diseases. The results of preliminary studies show that a resilient personality may even help boost recovery from illness. In fact, scientists have identified what they call a "self-healing personality"—and they say it's characterized by enthusiasm, alertness, responsiveness, energy, curiosity, security, and contentment. Scientists say "self-healing" people have a continual sense of growth and resilience; achieve balance in meeting their biological needs, gaining affection, and having self-respect; are good problem-solvers; have a playful sense of humor; and have good relationships with others.[54]

With all the research and the scientific backup, disease resistance emerges as an extremely individual thing. What works for one person might not necessarily work for another, so we must exercise great caution and resist the tendency to create fool-proof universal "formulas." In expressing that thought, Friedman wrote, "Self-healing personalities have an inherent resilience, but they are not identical. They share an emotional equilibrium that comes from doing the right combinations of activities appropriate for the individual."[55]

Siegel sums up the entire personality/wellness picture by advising people to take control over their own lives and to have hope:

> If there's one thing I learned from my years of working with cancer patients, it's that there is no such thing as false hope . . . hope is real and physiological. It's something I feel perfectly comfortable giving people—no matter what their situation. I know people are alive today because I said to them, "You don't have to die."
>
> If statistics say that nine out of ten people die from this disease, many physicians will tell their patients, "The odds are against you. Prepare to die." I tell my patients, "You can be the one who gets well. Let's teach you how."[56]

Is it possible to *develop* hardiness? Researchers believe so. Kobasa herself has two exercises she recommends to people who are trying to develop a more disease-resistant personality.

The first is called *compensating through self-improvement.* What it entails, she says, is an important strategy that helps you overcome stressful situations that you *can't* control by experiencing personal growth in an area you *can* control. Here's how it works: Say the company you work for is purchased by a larger corporation, and your division is abolished as part of the merger. Or say a favorite brother-in-law is killed in a traffic accident. You can't control either of those things—so, says Kobasa, you compensate. How? You might learn to pilot a small-engine plane, write the family history you've been researching for a decade, or learn a difficult foreign language that has always interested you. Simply stated, you focus your energies on a new challenge instead of on the stress you can't control. This strategy, she says, helps you feel confident and in control.

Kobasa's second strategy is what she calls *reconstructing stressful situations.* In essence, it's a clever way of "rewriting" your own history—only this time, you come out the winner. Here's how: Start by mentally recalling a stressful event that happened to you—the more stressful the better, the more recent the better. Rehearse the whole thing in your mind, and concentrate on remembering as many details as you can. Now, write down three ways the event could have been worse. Finally, write down three ways it could have been better—in other words, what could you have done to improve the situation?

This kind of an exercise does three things for you, says Kobasa. First, it helps you realize that things weren't as bad as they could have been (a realization that, in itself, can help change your perspective on stress). Second, it gives you ideas about what to do better next time (ideas that can help relieve stress about the future). Third, and most important, it gives you a sense of control by teaching you that *you* can influence the way things turn out.

Following are some additional suggestions on what you can do to increase your resilience:

- Do whatever you can to develop creativity, to find new ways of looking at things, or to transform confusion into order. The creative expressions you make through writing, playing a musical instrument, dancing, or painting can also help you work through inner strife.
- When confronted with a challenge, rely on keen insight. Ask tough questions; be a careful observer; use brainstorming techniques to come up with as many ways as possible to *look at* the situation. Learn to trust your own interpretation of things instead of relying on what other people tell you.
- If you start to feel stressed, break your problems down into smaller "chunks" that you can face more easily. Take on the easiest challenges first; those help you gain confidence and make the next problem easier to solve.
- Try to change your perspective on problems: Instead of seeing them as negatives, try finding the positives—the exciting challenges that can result. An upcoming professional examination is an undisputed stress; however, look at studying for it as a chance to hone your skills, increase your knowledge, and give yourself an edge over competitors in the job market.
- Do whatever you can to build your network of social support. If a friend has failed you, that's okay—start now to cultivate a circle of even better friends. Develop a sense of humor, a sense of compassion, and empathy. Whatever happens, stay involved with the people around you—start a study group, join a church committee, get involved in a political campaign, volunteer at your child's school.

Developing resilience means developing a sense of control—of recognizing that *you* are ultimately the one in charge of what happens to you. One of the best tips comes from psychiatrist Steven Wolin and developmental psychologist Sybil Wolin: "Get revenge by living well instead of squandering your energy by blaming and faultfinding."[57]

Notes

1. Evan G. Pattishall, "The Development of Behavioral Medicine: Historical Models," *Annals of Behavioral Medicine,* November 1989, pp. 43–48.

2. Howard S. Friedman, *The Self-Healing Personality* (New York: Henry Holt and Company, 1991), p. 99.

3. Claudia Wallis, "Stress: Can We Cope?" *Time,* June 6: 1983, 48–54.

4. Robert M. Sapolsky, "Lessons of the Serengeti," n.s., n.d., p. 38.

5. Sapolsky.

6. Suzanne Ouellette Kobasa, "How Much Stress Can You Survive?" *American Health,* September: 1984, 67.

7. Kobasa, p. 67.

8. Dr. Douglas Powell, speech at the 8th Annual Conference on Health and Wellness, Brigham Young University, 1988.

9. Ronald G. Nathan, Thomas E. Staats, and Paul J. Rosch, *The Doctors' Guide to Instant Stress*

Relief (New York: G.P. Putnam's Sons, 1987), p. 39.

10. Nathan et al.

11. Steven Locke and Douglas Colligan, *The Healer Within: The New Medicine of Mind and Body* (New York: E. P. Dutton, 1986), p. 127.

12. Locke and Colligan, pp. 127–128.

13. Nathan et al., pp. 41–43.

14. W. F. Adams, *Ireland and Irish Emigration to the New World* (New Haven: Yale University Press, 1932); and G. J. Drolet, "Epidemiology of Tuberculosis," in B. Goldberg, editor, *Clinical Tuberculosis* (Philadelphia: F. A. Davis, 1946).

15. L. J. Moorman, "Tuberculosis on the Navajo Reservation," *American Review of Tuberculosis*, 61: 1950, 586.

16. J. B. McDougal, *Tuberculosis—A Global Study in Social Pathology* (Baltimore: Williams & Wilkins, 1949).

17. L. E. Hinkle, "The Effect of Exposure to Culture Change, Social Change, and Changes in Interpersonal Relationships on Health," in B. S. Dohrenwend and B. P. Dohrenwend, editors, *Stressful Life Events: Their Nature and Effects* (New York: Wiley, 1974), pp. 9–44.

18. E. Roskies, M. Iida-Miranda, and M. G. Strobel, "Life Changes as Predictors of Illness in Immigrants," in C. D. Spielberger and I. G. Sarason, editors, *Stress and Anxiety* (Washington, D.C.: Hemisphere, 1977), pp. 3–21.

19. Robert J. Wheeler and Monica A. Frank, "Identification of Stress Buffers," *Behavioral Medicine*, Summer 1988, pp. 78–79.

20. Joshua Fischman, "Getting Tough," *Psychology Today*, December 1987, pp. 26–28.

21. Blair Justice, *Who Gets Sick: Thinking and Health* (Houston, Texas: Peak Press, 1987).

22. Robert Ornstein and David Sobel, *The Healing Brain* (New York: Simon and Schuster, 1987), p. 230.

23. Ornstein and Sobel.

24. Ornstein and Sobel, pp. 228–229.

25. Ornstein and Sobel, p. 229.

26. Kenneth Pelletier, *Sound Mind, Sound Body: A New Model for Lifelong Health* (New York: Simon and Schuster, 1994), p. 57.

27. Susan Chollar, "The Miracle of Resilience," *American Health*, April 1994, p. 74.

28. Chollar, p. 74.

29. *Journal of Personality and Social Psychology*, as reported in *The Meninger Letter*, March 1994, p. 6.

30. Fischman.

31. Joan Borysenko, *Minding the Body, Mending the Mind* (Reading, Massachusetts: Addison-Wesley, 1987), p. 24.

32. Raymond B. Flannery, "The Stress-Resistant Person," *Harvard Medical School Health Letter*, February 1989, pp. 1–3.

33. Friedman, p. 110.

34. Flannery.

35. Friedman, p. 106.

36. Friedman, p. 111.

37. Friedman, p. 114.

38. *Journal of Psychosomatic Research*, pp. 635–650.

39. Paula Tedesco-Carreras, "Maintaining Mental Wellness," *NSNA/ Imprint*, February/ March 1988, p. 38

40. Flannery.

41. Flannery.

42. Flannery.

43. Raymond E. Flannery, Jr., "Towards Stress-Resistant Persons: A Stress Management Approach to the Treatment of Anxiety," *American Journal of Preventive Medicine*, 3(1): 1987, 26.

44. Flannery, "The Stress-Resistant Person."

45. T. Edward Hannah, "Hardiness and Health Behavior: The Role of Health Concern as a Moderator Variable," *Behavioral Medicine*, Summer 1988, pp. 59–62.

46. Hannah.

47. Robert Ornstein and David Sobel, *Healthy Pleasures* (Reading, Massachusetts: Addison-Wesley, 1989), pp. 280–281.

48. M. A. Jacobs, A. Spilken, and M. Norman, "Relationship of Life Change, Maladaptive Aggression, and Upper Respiratory Infection in Male College Students," *Psychosomatic Medicine*, 31(1) 1969: 31–44.

49. Darius Razavi, Christine Farvaques, Nicole Delvaux, Tania Beffort, Marianne Paesmans, Guy Leclercq, Paul Van Houtte, and Robert Paridaens, "Psychosocial Correlates of Estrogen and Progesterone Receptors in Breast Cancer," *The Lancet*, 335: 1990, 931–933.

50. Flannery, pp. 5–6.

51. Marc Ian Barasch, "The Healing Path: A Soul Approach to Illness," in Proceedings of the

Sixth International Conference of the National Institute for the Clinical Application of Behavioral Medicine, *The Psychology of Health, Immunity, and Disease,* Vol. B, p. 9.

52. Bernie Siegel, "Mind Over Cancer," *Prevention*, March 1988, pp. 61–62.

53. Fischman.

54. Howard S. Friedman and Gary R. VandenBos, "Disease-Prone and Self-Healing Personalities," *Hospital and Community Psychiatry,* 23(12): 1992, 1178.

55. Friedman.

56. Siegel, p. 64.

57. Chollar, p. 75.

12

SOCIAL SUPPORT, RELATIONSHIPS, AND HEALTH

Help thy brother's boat across,
and lo!
thine own has reached the shore.
—HINDU PROVERB

A group of researchers went to Alameda County, California, and gathered data on more than 7,000 people over a nine-year period. At the end of the study, they found the common denominator that most often led to good health and long life: the amount of social support a person enjoys.

Researchers who conducted the study concluded that people with social ties—regardless of their source—lived longer than people who were isolated. And people "who have a close-knit network of intimate personal ties with other people seem to be able to avoid disease, maintain higher levels of health, and in general, to deal more successfully with life's difficulties."[1]

The people with many social contacts—a spouse, a close-knit family, a network of friends, church, or other group affiliations—lived longer and had better health. People who were socially isolated had poorer health and died earlier. In fact, those who had few ties with other people died at rates two to five times higher than those with good social ties.[2] The link between social ties and death rate held up regardless of gender, race, ethnic background, or socioeconomic status.[3] "Some well-loved people fall ill and die prematurely," researchers concluded; "some isolates live long and healthy lives. But these occurrences are infrequent. For the most part, people tied closely to others are better able to stay well."[4]

Writing in *The Sciences,* the journal of the New York Academy of Sciences, California physician and epidemiologist Leonard Sagan made a sobering observation of the state of social connectedness in our nation. The United States, he wrote, spends far more per capita on health care—but has far lower life expectancies than Greece, Spain, and Italy. The difference, he believes, "exists because of the decreasing level of natural family support in America. Many of us badly need an activity that boosts our sense of social support and our connections with other people."[5]

Nobel Prize–winning author Saul Bellow agrees. In commenting on life in America today, he says that "something is wrong, something is missing. There is ice in the heart—the ice of self-interest—which has to be thawed out by anyone who really wants anything human from himself or from others."[6]

In talking about the impact of social ties on health, one doctor commented that all diseases are "social diseases"—and that it seems "as though a breakdown in the social support structure precipitates a breakdown in the body's immune system."[7] Another physician echoed the same sentiment when he stated that "there are, of course, no pharmacies available to fill a prescription for 'spouses, confidants, and friends, p.r.n. (as needed),' but the point remains that social isolation is in itself a pathogenic factor in disease production. Mechanisms of social bonding are as ancient as the evolution of our species; their disruption has devastating impact. Good friends are an essential ingredient for good health."[8]

Dr. Kenneth Pelletier of the Stanford Center for Research in Disease Prevention, says that "a sense of belonging and connection to other people appears to be a basic human need—as basic as food and shelter. In fact, social support may be one of the critical elements distinguishing those who remain healthy from those who become ill."[9]

Although researchers aren't sure why, it has become apparent that social support affects physical health—both in terms of mortality and in the onset and progression of disease.[10] According to the research, social support influences behaviors that impact health—such as diet, the amount of exercise you get, whether you smoke cigarettes, and whether you drink alcohol (as well as how much you drink). The amount of social support you enjoy also appears to have an impact on biological processes, such as neuroendocrine responses, immune responses, and changes in blood flow. In their negative influence, these behavioral and biological influences together may directly or indirectly lead to stroke, coronary heart disease, coronary artery disease, cancer, infectious diseases, allergies, autoimmune diseases, and liver disease.

Sidney Cobb, president of the Society of Psychosomatic Medicine, claims that the notion of social support as an element of health is not new. What is new, he says, is the collection of hard evidence that proves the case—proof positive that social support can indeed protect people in crisis from what he calls a "wide variety" of diseases. Adequate social support, Cobb says, has been proven to protect against conditions "from low birth weight to death, from arthritis through tuberculosis to depression, alcoholism, and other psychiatric illness. Furthermore, social support can reduce the amount of medication required, accelerate recovery, and facilitate compliance with prescribed medical regimens."[11]

Social Support Defined

As defined by most researchers, social support is the degree to which a person's basic social needs are met through interaction with other people. It's the resources—both tangible and intangible—that other people provide. It's a person's perception that he or she can count on other people for help with a problem or for help in a time of crisis.

Leading researchers who have studied the effect of social support on heart disease say it involves five components.[12]

- Being cared for and loved, with the opportunity for shared intimacy
- Being esteemed and valued; having a sense of personal worth
- Sharing companionship, communication, and mutual obligations with others; having a sense of belonging
- Having "informational" support—access to information, appraisal, advice, and guidance from others
- Having access to physical or material assistance

The resources that your social network provide may come in the form of tangible, instrumental aid—lending you money, driving you to your doctor's appointment, doing your grocery shopping, or helping assume responsibility for your children while you are sick. But another kind of resource is equally important: It's the emotional, "intangible" kind of help such as affection, understanding, acceptance, and esteem.[13]

According to University of Michigan researchers James S. House and Robert L. Kahn, three factors comprise social resources:[14]

1. *Social network*—the size, density, durability, intensity, and frequency of your social contacts.
2. *Social relationships*—the existence of relationships, number of relationships, and type of relationships
3. *Social support*—the type, source, number, and quality of your resources.

Sources of Social Support

Social support can come from family members, friends, professional associates, members of the church congregation, neighbors, people who belong to the same bowling league or bridge club, and so on. The people who make up one's social support network are the people with whom one associates and to whom one could turn in time of need.

Sources of social support vary, depending on gender, age, and other factors. In one study, 900 people selected at random from six states were interviewed. All were aged sixty-five and older; none were living in an institution. Almost half were married, and more than half—64 percent—were retired.[15]

The main source of social support for married men was their wives—but the same didn't hold true for women. The married women in the study relied more heavily on other family members and friends than they did on their husbands. According to the results of the study and the findings of other researchers, women seem to get their greatest health benefits from contact with other women. Those with the best health had close female friends or relatives. There may be a number of reasons why, and one of them, according to sociologists at the University of Texas/Austin, may be evidence showing that "women are just more effective at providing support" than are men.[16] When it came to "instrumental" support—the rendering of physical help and the sharing of responsibilities—women used family helpers, agency personnel, and paid helpers more than men did.[17]

Research has also exploded some long-held myths about elderly people and social support. For years, the elderly were often regarded as being "takers"—being the ones who gained from a network of social support. Recent research, however, dispels that myth. A national survey involving more than 700 elderly adults demonstrated that their health and vitality have more to do with what they *contribute* to their social support network than what they *receive* from it.[18]

How Does Social Support Protect Health?

No one knows for certain how social support works to protect health, but some theories by prominent researchers who have done the most specialized work in the field of social support seem to be standing up to close scrutiny:[19]

1. Social support enhances health and well-being no matter how much stress a person is under; the enhancement may result from an overall positive feeling and a sense of self-esteem, stability, and control over one's environment.
2. Social support acts as a buffer against stress by protecting a person from the diseases that stress often causes.

Still other researchers believe that a strong social network and healthy social ties gradually lead to a greater, more generalized sense of control. An impressive array of studies has shown that a sense of control improves and protects health, whereas a feeling of little control can have serious health consequences.

Regardless of *how* social support protects health, we know that it does. Psychologist Joan Borysenko writes, "The consequences of emotional abandonment are no less serious than those of physical abandonment. Babies in foundling homes that are fed and changed on schedule but starved emotionally often develop a syndrome called hospitalism or failure to thrive. No one is present to coo when the baby coos, to smile when the baby smiles, to mirror back its existence to the child. As a result of this loneliness, the babies' pituitary glands fail to produce sufficient growth hormone and the children wither away despite adequate nutrition. Many of these children die before reaching toddlerhood, and those who do survive are often severely damaged psychologically."[20]

Early researchers who struggled to determine what sort of patient has disease found striking similarities in the circumstances of people with conditions as diverse as depression, tuberculosis, high blood pressure, multiple accidents, and even complications in pregnancy. The people who were ill usually lacked a strong supportive network or had experienced a recent disruption in their traditional sources of social support.[21]

Unfortunately, the number of people in that category seem to be increasing. In comparing people in the United States today with those of earlier generations, a disturbing trend is evident. People today are more likely to live alone, less likely to be married, and less likely to belong to a social organization.[22] The result is a generation of people with weaker social ties—and poorer health.

Besides buffering the effects of stress and protecting health, strong social ties might give people still another edge in good health. The range of problems people bring to friends and neighbors is much broader than those brought to doctors, says Dr. Eva Salber, professor emeritus of Duke University's School of Medicine. Fewer than 5 percent of all physician visits are for psychological problems, she says, "because we learn that if we want a doctor's attention, we must focus on a physical symptom. A woman might tell her doctor she has a bladder infection," but she'll tell a friend "that she's lost her job, had a fight with her husband, and has a bladder infection." What it boils down to, says Dr. Salber, is that "the great majority of human ills are never seen by a doctor. The real primary care is provided by one's family, close friends, and neighbors."[23] These natural helpers—friends, family, and neighbors—may "very well prove to be our most important untapped resource," she adds.

The act of confiding may be one of the most important health boosts of all. Southern Methodist University psychologist James W. Pennebaker has done some of the most impressive research in the area of confiding.

Apparently all kinds of health benefits are associated with confiding. In his pioneering book, *Opening Up: The Healing Power of Confiding in Others*,[24] Pennebaker sums it up simply by saying, "Not disclosing our thoughts and feelings can be unhealthy. Divulging them can be healthy."

In recounting more than two decades of specialized research into the health benefits of confiding, Pennebaker says his initial interest was piqued by a polygrapher in San Francisco. The polygrapher, who was examining a forty-five-year-old bank vice-president for embezzlement, explained to Pennebaker that the banker's physiological signs—such as heart rate and blood pressure—were very high at first, which is normal for both guilty and innocent people confronted by the threatening dilemma of taking a polygraph test. When quizzed about the details of the embezzlement, however, his vital signs skyrocketed so dramatically that he broke down and confessed to embezzling $74,000 over six months.

That in itself was not dramatic, says Pennebaker. The surprise came later, when the bank official was retested—standard procedure to test the possible deception of a confession. This time the man was completely relaxed. His breathing was slow and relaxed; his heart rate and blood pressure were not only normal, but extraordinarily low; and his palms were dry.

Focus on Research

In one study, Pennebaker and his colleagues recruited Holocaust survivors—people who had experienced a wide spectrum of horrors, from being imprisoned in concentration camps to witnessing the execution of family members. Pennebaker and his colleagues interviewed each of the survivors, noting how freely they were able to discuss their experiences and how well they were able to confront their feelings. The researchers labeled each survivor as either a "high discloser" (someone who was willing to talk and readily showed emotion) or a "low discloser" (someone who may have recounted past traumas, but who held his or her emotions closely in check).

More than a year after the initial interviews, Pennebaker and his colleagues followed up with each of the Holocaust survivors. Those who had been labeled as "high disclosers"— those who had confided their experiences and emotions—had fewer physical symptoms, fewer physician visits, and a more positive outlook in the months since they had confided their experiences. Commenting on previous studies that showed tight-lipped survivors to be the most healthy ones, Pennebaker said, "I'd predict the well-adjusted Israeli survivors talked about their Holocaust experiences with others many years ago and largely resolved the trauma. Thus, it's easier for them not to think about the Holocaust now. They're probably high disclosers."

Source: "Healthy Talk Among Holocaust Survivors," *Science News,* October 21, 1989, p. 271.

"You can appreciate the irony of this situation," Pennebaker writes. "This man had come into the polygrapher's office a free man, safe in the knowledge that polygraph evidence was not allowed in court. Nevertheless, he confessed. Now, his professional, financial, and personal lives were on the brink of ruin. He was virtually assured of a prison term. Despite these realities, he was relaxed and at ease with himself. Indeed, when a policeman came to handcuff and escort him to jail, he warmly shook the polygrapher's hand and thanked him for all he had done. This last December, the polygrapher received a chatty Christmas card written by the former bank vice-president with a federal penitentiary as the return address. "Even when the costs are high," Pennebaker concludes, "the confession of actions that violate our personal values can reduce anxiety and physiological stress. . . . Revealing pent-up thoughts and feelings can be liberating, even if they send you to prison."[25]

The healthful aspects of confiding can also occur when the confession is written, says Pennebaker. In an experiment that demonstrated the power of written confession, Pennebaker and his colleagues at Southern Methodist University asked a group of student volunteers to write about their experiences for fifteen minutes a day over a total of four days.

The students could choose to write either about superficial topics or about a traumatic experience. The students who chose to write about a traumatic experience were instructed to describe their emotions about the event, describe the facts surrounding the event, or write about *both* the facts and their emotions. Researchers then attempted to determine how often the students got sick by noting how often they visited the student health center. Researchers compared the number of visits in the two and a half months before the students wrote with the number of visits in the five and a half months after they wrote.

All of the students who participated in the experiment visited the health center at the same rate before writing. After writing, those who wrote *both* the facts and their feelings about a traumatic experience visited the health center *50 percent less often* than those who simply wrote about a superficial topic—or those who wrote *either* the facts or their feelings.

Interestingly, says Pennebaker, writing about a traumatic experience didn't make the students feel better right away. In fact, just the opposite was true—at first, they were depressed."[26]

In a subsequent study, Pennebaker and Martha E. Francis recruited forty-one university employees to write for twenty minutes once a week for four consecutive weeks. The employees wrote about personal experiences, either traumatic or nontraumatic.

During the month that the employees were writing, those who wrote about traumatic experiences had a 28.6 percent decrease in absentee rates; those who wrote about nontraumatic experiences had a 48.5 percent *increase* in absentee rates. Pennebaker and Francis followed up with blood tests that showed significant health benefits from writing about traumatic experiences.[27]

Although heart rate and blood pressure almost always increase significantly during the act of confiding, they decrease significantly afterward. It's a long-lasting effect, too: People who confide continue to show smaller increases in blood pressure when under stress or when confronted with a challenging task—a benefit that can make big differences in overall health.

There are other health benefits associated with confiding, says Pennebaker, but perhaps the one most associated with good health is immunity. People who confide enjoy better functioning of the immune system. Those who don't face a myriad of immune system disorders; their white blood cell counts are "seriously disturbed." Natural killer cells are weakened and decrease in number; T lymphocytes can't do their job. Almost without exception, Pennebaker says, the people in his studies who began confiding enjoyed enhanced immune function. They showed improvement in physical symptoms; they visited the doctor less often.

Best of all, Pennebaker says, immune system enhancement related to confiding lingers. In one test, students who wrote about troubling experiences they had never before confided experienced significant improvement in immune function as a result—and the improvement from that one session tended to persist for *six weeks* following the confiding experience.[28]

Part of the benefit from writing about feelings is that it doesn't require feedback—in other words, we're not restricted by how others react. "One reason why writing is so potent is that usually when we start to tell somebody about some personal thing," Pennebaker explains, "we're watching their face very closely to see how they react. If we see any sign that the other person is shocked or disapproving, we immediately start to change the story.[29]

Want to try it yourself? To get started, follow Pennebaker's guidelines for effective written confession:

- To get started, write continuously about the most upsetting or traumatic experience of your entire life. Keep writing until you can't think of anything else to say.
- Don't worry about spelling, grammar, or sentence structure; work on a free flow of your feelings and the facts as you remember them.
- Go beyond the surface—discuss your deepest thoughts and feelings about the experience.

"You can write about anything you want," says Pennebaker. "But ideally, it should be about something you have not talked about with others in detail. It is critical, however, that you let yourself go and touch those deepest emotions and thoughts that you have. In other words, write about what happened and how you felt about it, and how you feel about it now."[30]

The Ties That Bind

According to one researcher:

Despite the potential for stress in close personal relationships, it's becoming increasingly clear that healthy, long lives depend on strengthening our bonds with others. A full and rewarding social life can nourish the mind, the emotions, and the spirit, and good physical health depends as much on these aspects of ourselves as it does on a strong and well-functioning body.[31]

Social ties—good friendships, good relationships with family members, the presence of people we know we can lean on—play an important part in our good health. A scientific panel convened by the United States government found that social support not only reduced mortality, but was a key in protecting health as well. According to the panel, there is a close relationship between the number and strength of an individual's social relationships and an individual's health and longevity. Panel experts say that strong social support can be shown to reduce complications in pregnancy, aid in recovery from surgery, reduce the need for medications in some chronic illnesses, combat the symptoms of stress, protect against a variety of emotional and psychological problems, and help to keep patients in needed medical treatment and promote adherence to needed medical treatment regimens.[32]

Dr. James Lynch, a specialist in psychosomatic medicine at the University of Maryland's School of Medicine and a well-known researcher in the field of social support, concludes that "those individuals who lack the comfort of another human being may very well lack one of nature's most powerful antidotes to stress."[33] In summing up the results of his research, Lynch remarked, "The mandate to 'Love your neighbor as you love yourself' is not just a moral mandate. It's a physiological mandate. Caring is biological. One thing you get from caring for others is you're not lonely; and the more connected you are to life, the healthier you are."[34]

Leonard Syme, a professor of epidemiology at the University of California at Berkeley, echoed scientific frustration with the subject as well as realization of its impact on health when he said, "Statistically, this is one of the strongest areas under study. What isn't clear is how it works. How does a relationship get into the body and influence biological processes? All we know at this point is, something very important is happening."[35]

Information continues to pour in as studies are completed that prove that, indeed, something very important is happening. "The ties that bind," as we so often call them, are also apparently the ties that can keep us healthy and help us live a long, happy life.

In a long-term study, almost 3,000 adults in Tecumseh, Michigan, were studied for ten years. At the beginning of the study, each adult was given a thorough physical examination to rule out any existing illness that would force a person to become isolated. Researchers then watched these people closely for the next ten years, making special note of their social relationships and group activities. Those who were socially involved were found to have the best health. When social ties were interrupted or broken, the incidence of disease increased significantly. Researchers particularly noticed that certain conditions seemed related to marginal social ties. Among them were coronary heart disease, cancer, arthritis, strokes, upper respiratory infections, and mental illness. In fact, researchers concluded, interrupted social ties actually seemed to suppress the body's immune system.[36]

Those who conducted the study, called close personal relationships a "safety net." They stated that people without such a safety net fall vulnerable to a wide variety of diseases far more frequently than people who are surrounded by the comfort of good social relationships.

We seem to derive an odd sort of comfort from other people—a comfort that can literally influence us biologically. One researcher observed that the menstrual cycles of close friends and roommates in a college dormitory appeared to be related—but randomly selected girls on the same campus showed no similarities in cycles.[37]

In another experiment, researchers from Walter Reed Army Institute studied a group of three crewmen who worked closely together on a lengthy B–52 flight. The crew members were studied for both physical and emotional symptoms and disorders, and blood tests were taken as part of the study. Researchers found that the levels of seventeen stress-related hormones peaked in all three crewmen at the same time each day.[38]

Dr. Stanley Schachter and his colleagues at Columbia University tested the importance of social relationships with a group of volunteers.[39] Each had agreed to be part of a study in which they would receive a series of electric shocks. Some of the subjects were told that they would receive mild electric shocks, while the others were threatened with receiving painful electric shocks. Dr. Schachter and his colleagues then gave the volunteers the choice of waiting alone or in the presence of other volunteers.

The volunteers who were threatened with only a mild shock chose most often to be alone. Those who were threatened with a painful electric shock most often asked to wait with others—probably, say researchers, because being with other people helped reduce the stress of waiting for an electric shock. "People do serve a direct anxiety-reducing function for one another," Dr. Schachter concluded. "They comfort and support, they reassure one another and attempt to bolster courage. There can be little doubt that the state of anxiety leads," he said, "to the volunteers' desire to be with other people."[40]

Battle Stress

That support factor was demonstrated even more clearly in a comprehensive study conducted by the United States Office of the Surgeon General. In 1973, twenty-eight years after the end of World War II, the office finally completed its thorough analysis of American war casualties.[41] As part of the study, researchers looked at the way troops reacted to the intense stress of battle. Researchers decided that the sustaining influence of other people, the strength imparted by social ties, was what kept troops from crumbling under the stress of battle. Soldiers who benefited from "group identification," "group cohesiveness," or "the buddy system"—those who had strong social support—were able to withstand even intense battle stress. Those in the small combat groups who were sustained by other members suffered the lowest casualties.

Those who did not feel the cohesiveness of a small group, who were not encouraged to come together in "the buddy system," or whose small group was disrupted during combat were the ones who mainly suffered psychiatric breakdown in battle. These soldiers—the lonely, isolated ones—were the ones who suffered the greatest casualties.[42]

Epidemiologist Leonard Syme, who was one of the researchers instrumental in the study of the seven thousand Alameda County residents, confirmed the importance of social support in helping people deal with "battle stress"—not the kind encountered in combat, but the kind real people contend with every day. He remarked that "people who have a close-knit network of intimate personal ties with other people seem to be able to avoid disease, maintain higher levels of health, and in general, to deal more successfully with life's difficulties."[43]

Unemployment

Can social support help ease the problems associated with unemployment? Apparently it can. In one study, researchers looked at 110 men who were forcibly unemployed when a plant closed. The men were given thorough examinations at various times before and after the plant closing. Examiners measured levels of serum cholesterol, symptoms of illness, symptoms of depression, and the degree of social support each man had from his family and his friends.

Focus on Research

One widely acclaimed study conducted by graduate students and faculty members at the University of California at Berkeley School of Public Health demonstrates exactly how important social support is to people who deal with "battle stress" in their lives. Called The Tenderloin Senior Outreach Project, it was a ten-year study that delved into San Francisco's seedy Tenderloin District—a cluster of low-priced, single-room-occupancy hotels crammed with the poverty-stricken elderly. The district was characterized by skyrocketing crime rates, deteriorating housing conditions, poor access to food, and remarkably bad physical and mental health among its residents.

For the study, the Berkeley group organized weekly support groups for the elderly residents of the district. They organized "Safehouse Project," in which more than eighty stores and agencies in the neighborhood became places of refuge where residents could flee in case of emergency. The students acted as leaders in organizing groups of hotel residents; buoyed by each other's strength, the residents themselves soon began working on their problems.

The results were dramatic. Several resident groups formed "mini-markets" in the lobbies of their hotels so that residents could get access to fresh fruit and vegetables. Other groups successfully blocked attempts to increase rents. Others were able to get food service restored to several of the hotels. And still others succeeded in getting the city to enhance public transportation access to the district.

In the eighteen months following initiation of the project, crime dropped by a startling 26 percent. Nutritional status of hotel residents improved dramatically. So did their physical and mental health.

The sense of control and the social networking that came out of the project has been studied and acclaimed for their health-enhancing benefits. Researchers delight in making an example of one elderly resident, who had habitually checked himself into mental institutions every month or so for "reality orientation." After two years of involvement with the program, his monthly visits stopped completely. When researchers asked him about it, he quipped, "I'm a co-leader of my hotel support group, a founder of the anticrime project, and a member of the Mayor's Task Force on Aging. I don't have time for reality!"

Source: Robert Ornstein and Charles Swencionis, editors, *The Healing Brain: A Scientific Reader* (New York: The Guilford Press, 1990).

The result was a firm testimony of social support. The men who had little social support during the study were significantly more likely to get sick, become depressed, and suffer from elevated levels of serum cholesterol. The men who had good social support from their friends and family members and who had plenty of opportunity for social interaction were significantly more healthy, despite the stress of losing their jobs.[44]

Pregnant Women under Stress

Another study looked at pregnant women who were undergoing stressful life events. Researchers studied the 170 women, assessed how stressful the life events were both before and during pregnancy, and also determined how much social support each woman had. (A number of other "psychosocial assets" were also measured.) Researchers then recorded the outcome of each of the pregnancies.

Again, social support seemed to be the key: Only 33 percent of the women under stress had complications during pregnancy *if* they felt they had strong social support. Among the stressed women who perceived that their social support was weak, 91 percent had complications during pregnancy.[45]

Relocation and Disruption

Part of the stress from relocation is connected to unfamiliar geographic territory, but another (and perhaps even more significant) part is related to the loss of familiar friends. It is, in a real sense, a loss of social support.

Experiments in the animal world have demonstrated how important it is to be surrounded by friends. In one experiment, chickens were injected with neoplasms (which would have been expected to cause cancer). The chickens that remained in their familiar pecking order stayed healthy; the chickens that were housed with unfamiliar chickens developed cancer.[46]

In another study, mice were put in a situation where there was intense competition for food. The mice that were kept with their familiar litter mates handled the stress of competing for food well—without getting sick over it. The mice that were placed with unfamiliar mice, however, developed high blood pressure.

In yet another experiment, young goats were repeatedly subjected to harmful stimuli in a laboratory. Those that received the stimuli while they were isolated became neurotic; those that were allowed to remain with their mothers while they were stimulated showed no symptoms.

The same thing holds true for people. When people are uprooted and forced to move away from familiar people or places, they often get sick. People who have moved or who have otherwise experienced great disruption in their situations are sicker more often and absent from work at a higher rate than their coworkers.

Researchers were able to observe the effect of disruption by watching the coal miners and their families who moved from small valleys in Appalachia to the company towns created when coal mines were reopened. By looking at the family names of the workers, it was possible to determine how many had relatives living in the towns to which they had come.

Researchers found that those who moved to towns where they did not have family members had a significantly higher rate of absenteeism due to sickness. The coal miners who moved to towns where they had kinfolk were able to stay significantly healthier. The only real factor that distinguished the two groups was the amount of social support they had.[47]

These findings have particular significance for the elderly, whose disrupted social ties are a common part of daily life associated with bereavement, retirement, or a change in residence. Researchers have noted that these changes tend to cause severe depression among the elderly—but that people are able to maintain good health and avoid depression if they have even one close supportive confidante.[48]

A fascinating study conducted on the Sinai peninsula in Israel sheds light on social support in general, but gives particular insight into the phenomenon of re-location, disrupted ties, friendships, and the presence of kinfolk.[49] In 1972, a civilian community named Ophira (Sharm-el-Sheik in Arabic) was established at the southernmost tip of the Sinai peninsula, primarily by families with a pioneering spirit who had wanted to build a town in the desert. Geographically, Ophira was quite isolated. The closest Israeli town of any size, Eilat, was more than 200 miles away.

Because of its distance from Eilat, the town of Ophira quickly became self-contained and self-sufficient, both physically and psychologically. Not only were residents of the town self-sufficient, but they were unusually similar to each other, partly because the living conditions in the community were so uniform. All the people in town lived in a single housing complex. There was only one shopping center, one school, and one medical center with one doctor and one nurse, so everyone in town also shared the same support services.

Ten years after it was established, Ophira was disbanded as part of the Camp David accords with Egypt that ordered evacuation of the Sinai peninsula. The residents of Ophira, who had lived as such a tightly knit group for ten years, were forced to evacuate—and were relocated over a widely scattered area throughout Israel. Some of the Ophira residents were relocated to rural areas, and others moved to urban areas.

Researchers interested in the effect of the relocation assessed the residents six weeks before the final evacuation and again two years later. A questionnaire and a variety of tests were given to the residents who participated in the study; researchers focused on eighteen husband/wife pairs (a total of thirty-six people) similar in age, ethnic background, educational level, and occupational status.

Several interesting findings emerged:

1. The demoralization and distress that stem from stressful life events (such as relocation) is long-lasting, not temporary. Sophisticated psychological tests given to Ophira residents showed that the stress associated with the relocation was basically as severe after two years as it was six weeks before the actual evacuation. Researchers concluded from their findings that an individual's adjustment to stress at the time it occurs is a good predictor of how adjusted he or she will be two years later.

2. Each individual in the study was asked to list his or her friends, both six weeks before evacuation and two years later. As could be predicted, the first list of friends—the one made six weeks before the relocation—consisted almost entirely of other Ophira residents. The list made two years later, predictably, contained an entirely new group of friends, with only one or two Ophira residents still included.

In almost all cases, the lists were almost exactly the same size at two years as they had been at six weeks! Even though the friends themselves changed, the size of the network remained about the same, which led researchers to conclude that people actively work to shape their own friendship networks. (Previous theories had suggested that the size of one's friendship network is largely dependent on environment and circumstances, not the result of any effort.)

3. A strong social relationship with kinfolk (or family members) seemed to be a better predictor of health and adjustment than a strong relationship with friends. Few of the couples in the study had kinfolk in Ophira. Likewise, few of the couples moved to areas where their kinfolk were. But those who had strong ties with their kinfolk tended to maintain them and gain strength from them regardless of where they lived. Unlike friends, family members seem to be a source of strength even at distances.

Although the example of Ophira provided researchers with a case in which entire family units were relocated, scientists have also been interested in what has happened when children are separated from their parents in a forced evacuation. To determine how such relocation would affect the children, researchers studied children in England during World War II who were separated from their parents and relocated to safer areas.[50]

As expected, children in both situations were under a tremendous amount of stress: The children who remained with their parents lived with the constant stress of physical danger from the war; the children who had been moved to safer areas to escape the danger of physical injury suffered the stress of being separated from their parents.

Which group fared the best? The children who stayed with their parents exhibited the fewest signs of stress—even though they lived with the daily threat of injury from the enemy blitz. The children who exhibited the greatest signs of stress were those who were separated from their parents—those who lost their most meaningful source of social support—even though they were physically safer.

In summing up the general protective nature of social ties, California psychiatrist Robert Taylor said, "When people have close relationships, they feel less threatened, less alone, more confident, and more in control. Knowing you have people you can turn to in times of need can provide some very important feelings of security, optimism, and hope—all of which can be great antidotes to stress."[51]

Love Stronger, Live Longer

Larry Dossey, M.D., co-chair of the newly established Panel on Mind/Body Interventions at the National Institutes of Health, says about one of the most celebrated emotions, "The power of love to change bodies is legendary, built into folklore, common sense, and everyday experience. Love moves the flesh, it pushes matter around—as the blushing and palpitations experienced by lovers attest.

Throughout history, 'tender, loving care' has uniformly been recognized as a valuable element in healing."[52]

The results of a variety of studies prove that if we want to live longer, we surround ourselves with at least a few good people who can act as friends and confidants. That finding has consistently held true across the board, regardless of how studies have been set up or what population was studied. Healthy people with good social support are at consistently lower risk for mortality than are their isolated counterparts.[53] Again, that finding holds true across the board. Some studies show results for both men and women. Others have studied only women and show that women with good social support have much less disease than those who are more isolated.

Social support is such a powerful factor in mortality that it even lowers mortality among those who are *unhealthy* (such as survivors of heart attacks). In one study of more than 2,500 elderly men and women, researchers asked each how many sources of social support they had. The researchers then observed those who were eventually hospitalized for heart attack.

The differences were stark. Only 12 percent of those with two or more sources of social support died in the hospital, but 23 percent of those with only one source of social support died while still in the hospital. And *38 percent* of those who said they had no source of social support died in the hospital. The results applied to both men and women even after taking into account differences in the severity of the heart attack, illness due to other diseases, the presence of traditional risk factors (such as cigarette smoking and high blood pressure), and symptoms of depression.

"It appears that being married or unmarried, living with someone or living alone, are not as critical to surviving a heart attack as just having *someone* to turn to for emotional support," the researchers concluded. "And this support seems to work like a drug—the higher the dose, the greater the protective effect."[54]

In a paper presented by residents from Portland's Kaiser Permanente Center for Health Research at the Society of Behavioral Health Meetings, the strength of social networks was shown to predict mortality at two-, five-, ten-, and fifteen-year follow-up visits.

The Alameda County Study

In the Alameda County, California study discussed at the beginning of this chapter, the residents were initially studied for nine years. First, researchers separated people into two groups: those who lived lonely lives (without many friends or relatives) and those who had rich resources of family and friends. To determine which category a person fit into, researchers looked at marital status, a person's contact with friends and relatives, church membership, organizational affiliations, political activities, and group activities (such as membership in a garden club or bridge club or participation on a bowling league).

Then researchers wanted to make sure they were comparing the right set of statistics, so they accounted for things that might artificially shorten life. They made allowances for factors such as obesity, cigarette smoking, alcohol consumption, lack of exercise, harmful health practices, and poor health at the beginning of the study.

Researchers then painstakingly sifted through all the data, examining the records of the state health department and cross-checking death certificates. As a final check, the researchers checked each name to determine which category the individual had initially been classified in—lonely or friendly.

The results were convincing: The people who had been classified as lonely and isolated were dying at three times the rate of those who had stronger social ties.[55] To put it simply, people with many social contacts had the lowest mortality rates; those with the fewest contacts had the highest rates.[56]

The results of that study, as well as many others, show that people with social ties—no matter what the source—live longer than isolated people. This holds true regardless of cigarette smoking, alcohol consumption, obesity, sleeping and eating habits, and medical care.[57]

As part of the follow-up to the initial Alameda County study, researchers continued to monitor health and death records for the next eight years; as a result, they had access to complete records for a seventeen-year period. When later analyses of the data were made, the same results held true: People with the strongest social ties had the lowest mortality rates. Those rates were lowest for the people with the best social contacts even after allowances were made for age, sex, race, health status at the beginning of the study, depression, health practices, and the way people viewed their own health.[58]

According to the researchers who analyzed the data from the study, the types of social ties seemed to vary in importance to health depending on the person's age. At the beginning of the study, the participants ranged in age from thirty-eight to ninety-four years. For those under sixty, marital status seemed the best way to predict health and mortality. For those over sixty, ties with close friends or relatives, or both, seemed to be more important to health and long life than did marital status.[59]

The Michigan Study

In a study constructed similarly to the Alameda County study, psychologists and other researchers studied 2,754 adults in the small community of Tecumseh, Michigan. Each person in the study underwent a thorough medical examination to rule out any existing illness that might force a person to become isolated. They then participated in elaborate psychological tests and were rated according to their personal relationships. Researchers took special note of each person's number of friends, degree of closeness to relatives, participation in group activities, and choice of activity.[60]

Researchers then carefully watched the adults in the study for ten years (from the early 1970s to the early 1980s). Those who had the strongest social ties and who were the most socially involved had the best health. Those who were the most socially isolated had four times the mortality rate of those who were more socially involved.

The North Carolina Study

In another study involving more than 100 communities in North Carolina, researchers looked at black men of all ages. The highest death rates—regardless of the men's age—occurred among those who were "socially disorganized." Social disorganization in the study was characterized by family instability, separation, divorce, single-parent families, and many illegitimate children.[61]

The Swedish Study

A study of Swedish men who were born in 1914 showed that good social supports and social networks decreased mortality from all causes.[62] In the study, the men who did the worst were those who felt a lack of social and emotional support, those who were dissatisfied with their social activities, and those who lived alone.

The Japanese Studies

Some of the most fascinating evidence regarding social ties and mortality involved a group of studies of Japanese people. A number of studies showed that people in Japan—even though they smoke cigarettes, have high blood pressure, endure crushing stress, and live in polluted and crowded cities—live longer than we do. In fact, despite those normally unhealthy factors, they enjoy the longest life expectancy in the world. And, even though those factors—cigarette smoking, high blood pressure, stress, and crowding—are characteristically considered to be factors leading to heart disease, the Japanese enjoy relative immunity from heart disease. Researchers who strived to figure out why, finally decided that the Japanese are protected from ill health and death by their unusually close ties to friends, family members, and community. University of California/San Francisco School of Medicine researcher Ken Pelletier believes that the longevity of the Japanese is due to the emphasis they place on the community. The social aspect of human companionship, Pelletier believes, is one of the most important factors in health.[63]

Dr. S. Leonard Syme of the Department of Epidemiology and Public Health at Yale University teamed up with researchers from the University of California at Berkeley to study the situation in greater depth. Syme and his colleagues studied 12,000 Japanese men in three different groups: (1) men who still lived in southwestern Japan; (2) men who had immigrated from Japan to Hawaii and who had resisted a Westernized lifestyle; and (3) men who had immigrated from Japan to the San Francisco Bay area.[64]

To their surprise, researchers found the highest life expectancy and the lowest rate of heart disease among the group in which they least expected it: the men who had immigrated to San Francisco. The men who had immigrated to San Francisco had formed the closest social ties, the closest family ties, and the strongest social networks. Researchers found that the Japanese men in the San Francisco area stayed heavily involved with Japanese people, moved into Japanese neighborhoods, formed close friendships with other Japanese people, attended Japanese-language schools in addition to English-language schools, and returned to Japan for further schooling.

Research from a variety of studies shows, in essence, that people who are socially isolated—the unmarried, divorced, widowed, people with few friends, and people who have few church or social contacts—are three times as likely to die of a wide variety of diseases than those who have happy, fulfilling social lives.[65]

Social Connections and the Heart

Researchers who studied the Japanese men found that those who had immigrated to the San Francisco Bay area were the ones with the lowest incidence of heart disease. The unique and intense social ties they formed in San Francisco seemed to offer protection against heart disease. The Japanese men had significantly lower heart disease, even though they had the same high serum cholesterol level as their Western counterparts, often ate Western foods, smoked cigarettes, and had high blood pressure.[66]

Social support—even the most simple social support—appears to affect the heart. One particular study shows how simple that support can be. Researchers at the University of Pennsylvania gave a series of college girls stressful tasks to do. As the students struggled to complete the stressful tasks, researchers measured their blood pressure and heart rates. The girls who brought a friend along had significantly lower blood pressure and heart rates while under stress than the girls who faced doing the stressful task by themselves.[67]

The Roseto Study

A landmark study in Roseto, Pennsylvania, confirms other research and theories that social support and social ties protect the heart. Roseto is a close-knit Italian-American community nestled among other traditional eastern communities. Researchers interested in the lifestyle of the community residents followed their health status and rates of death for years. They found that the residents of Roseto had average incidences of exercise, cigarette smoking, obesity, high blood pressure, and stress. In addition, their diets were higher in fat, cholesterol, and red meat than the average American diet. But the men in Roseto had only about one-sixth the incidence of heart disease and deaths from heart disease as random population groups in the United States. The rates for Roseto's women were even better.

Researchers concluded that the protective factor was the people's strong sense of community and their strong social ties. Stewart Wolf, a professor of medicine at Temple University School of Medicine in Philadelphia and one of the study's researchers, said:

More than any other town we studied, Roseto's social structure reflected old-world values and traditions. There was a remarkable cohesiveness and sense of unconditional support within the community. Family ties were very strong. And what impressed us most was the attitude toward the elderly. In Roseto, the older residents weren't put on a shelf; they were promoted to "supreme court." No one was ever abandoned.[68]

Researchers continued to watch the residents of Roseto, and they found that when the younger generations began changing—moving away, marrying "outsiders," severing the close emotional ties to the "old neighborhood"—the physical health of the Rosetans began to deteriorate. By the mid 1970s, the mortality and heart disease rate of the Rosetans was comparable to that in surrounding Pennsylvania communities.

Community members had tremendously strong social ties, and their hearts were protected. When the social ties started to vanish, so did the protection. "The experience clearly demonstrates that the most important factors in health are the intangibles—things like trust, honesty, loyalty, team spirit," Wolf concluded. "In terms of preventing heart disease, it's just possible that morale is more important than jogging or not eating butter."[69]

Indeed, studies have shown that human interaction itself has a biological value: Human interaction causes changes in blood pressure, heart rate, and blood chemistry. Those changes promote good health for the heart.

Dr. James Lynch, who has become renowned for his research involving social support, says that "nowhere is the power of human contact more readily apparent than in the period of emotional crisis that follows the sudden occurrence of a heart attack. Warm, interpersonal support is a critical element in the recovery process of such a patient."[70] Lynch explains that the therapeutic power of human contact begins immediately after a heart attack with the physician and nurse; strong contact throughout the recovery process can, he says, lead to a fuller and more complete recovery.

Swedish Studies

Supporting research was conducted by Dr. Gunnar Biorck, who studied more than two hundred cardiac patients in the town of Malmo, Sweden. Biorck found that the patients gained physical and psychological strength in the hospital where teams of nurses and physicians were at close hand and where there was plenty of human contact. The most serious medical problems among Biorck's study patients occurred *after* the patients left the hospital—a time when "many patients feel deserted and very lonely." When the social support drops off, the protection is often lost.[71]

In another Swedish study, 150 middle-aged Swedish men were studied for ten years to determine the effects of various factors on ischemic heart disease. The men were divided into three groups: (1) men with clinically manifest ischemic heart disease (men who were already sick); (2) men with risk factors for ischemic heart disease; and (3) healthy men. Each man was given standardized interviews and answered questionnaires; researchers recorded factors such as socioeconomic factors, marital status, educational level, occupational status, social class, cigarette smoking, alcohol consumption, Type A behavior, social activities, and social integration. Each was then given a complete physical examination, which included an electrocardiogram and fasting serum lipids.

During the ten-year follow-up, thirty-seven of the men died—twenty of them from ischemic heart disease. The greatest factor in who lived and who died was not necessarily the presence of disease or the presence of risk factors, but social isolation. The men who had the greatest social isolation also had the poorest survival rates.[72]

Type A Studies

The Swedish study, a Finnish study,[73] and others show that social support may actually help reduce or modify risk factors. One well-known risk factor for heart disease is the Type A personality—a person who is time-oriented, hard-driving, stressed, and competitive. In an attempt to find out what factors might help modify the risk to people with Type A personality, researchers at Duke Medical Center interviewed 113 patients (most of them men) who had come to the hospital for coronary angiography (x-rays of the heart that reveal how much blockage exists in coronary arteries).[74]

All the men in the study were given psychological tests to determine if they were Type A personality or Type B personality (a much more easy-going, relaxed type of personality, much less prone to coronary heart disease). The patients were also given a questionnaire to help determine whether they had strong or weak social support. Finally, patients had a coronary angiography.

When researchers analyzed data from all of the tests and questionnaires, they found that the Type A personalities who had strong social support were on a par with the Type B personalities. The Type A personalities who were isolated or who had weak social support had the most severe coronary artery disease. The study indicates "that social support moderates the long-term health consequences of the Type A behavior pattern."[75]

Other Studies

Even with established heart disease, social support can be a healing and protective factor. The National Heart and Lung Institute did a five-year study of angina pectoris among men at the Sackler School of Medicine at Tel Aviv University. Even when coronary risk factors were present, the men who had loving wives and strong social relationships did significantly better than those who did not have good social relationships.[76]

In another study, researchers at Yale studied men with coronary heart disease; they looked at how much social support the men in the study enjoyed and focused their interest on men who had survived myocardial infarction. Their findings add dramatically to the evidence that strong social support can help prevent heart disease. They found that good social support actually *reversed* the effects of stress and distress on cardiac symptoms. Social support acted not only as a powerful preventive, but as a healer. The effects of social support were greatest in the first six months following myocardial infarction.[77]

Two new studies[78] show the benefits of social support for people with coronary disease. In the first, 1,234 people who survived for the first few days after a heart attack were observed by researchers. Only 5.7 percent of those who lived with other people died during the first year after the heart attack—but more than twice as many (12.4 percent) of those who lived alone died during that first year.

According to researchers, the risk was highest during the first six months. People living alone had a 16 percent probability of dying during that period compared with a 9 percent probability for those who lived with others.

In the second study, researchers at Duke University interviewed 1,368 patients who underwent cardiac catheterization, were found to have coronary disease, and were treated with medication. They tracked the patients for nine years. Those who were married fared better than those who were unmarried. But those who fared the worst were unmarried people who also had no confidant—their five-year survival rate was only 50 percent compared with 82 percent for those with *either* a spouse or a confidant. When researchers accounted for other factors that affect mortality, the unmarried people who had no confidant had more than a three-fold increase in the risk of death within five years.

The Best Health Bet—Good Social Ties

Perhaps one reason that social support is so conducive to good health is that it appears to improve immune function. A review of a number of studies shows that interpersonal relationships reverse the adverse effects of both short-and long-term stress. Well-documented studies show that stress generally decreases the number and function of natural killer cells and lowers the percentage of T lymphocytes. Strong interpersonal relationships, however, protect the functioning of the immune system—even in the face of stress.[79]

In several studies of college students, researchers measured the rate of immunoglobulin A (s-IgA) secreted in the students' saliva; s-IgA is an important immune defense against upper respiratory infections caused by both viruses and bacteria. In one part of the study, researchers found that students under stress secreted significantly less s-IgA than students not under stress. Students under stress were not as able to resist or fight infection. But researchers also found that students who had good social ties and valued warm personal relationships secreted *more* s-IgA at all points than did the other students in the study. The students who were socially connected were always in a better position to fight infection, regardless of whether they were under stress.[80]

Ohio State University psychologist Janice Kiecolt-Glaser tested groups of people with psychological profiles designed to determine how lonely they were. Those who were lonelier—those with the lowest levels of social support—also suffered in other ways: Their immune systems did not function as well as their counterparts who had good social support. The lonelier people in the studies had significantly lower levels of natural killer cells, an important part of the immune system that helps control viruses and cancerous tumor formation. Kiecolt-Glaser reported that the lonelier people in her study were less capable of fighting cancer because of immune system weakness.[81]

Increasing social support and reducing loneliness seem to help strengthen the immune system significantly. In a study of thirty elderly patients in retirement homes, researchers took blood tests at the beginning of the study and continued to measure immune system components throughout the test. Volunteers visited the patients in the retirement home three times a week for one month. There was a significant increase in both antibodies and natural killer cell activity, proving that there had been a real boost in the immune system.[82]

Possibly because of the immune system boost, social support seems to have significant impact on a number of disease conditions. Take cancer, for example. Some studies show no correlation between isolation and cancer, but others show a link between social isolation or disruption and cancer.

Lawrence LeShan studied the personalities and emotional life histories of more than 300 cancer patients. When he compared the life histories and emotional circumstances of cancer patients with those of healthy patients, he noticed a pattern in more than 60 percent of the cancer victims—but in only 10 percent of the healthy people:

> *Early in life, these patients learned to perceive relationships as dangerous, to be invested in only at the risk of much pain and rejection. To protect themselves, they kept relationships with others on a superficial basis. They held back emotionally and felt isolated and different from others, though they appeared to be functioning well.*[83]

Usually in adolescence or early adulthood, "a relationship came along that seemed relatively safe. Slowly this new relationship became the central focus of life. Then, for one reason or another, the loved one was lost. A spouse died, children grew up and moved away, or a divorce occurred. Cancer developed following the loss."[84]

Social support may even help determine the outcome of cancer. One study that supports that theory was conducted at the Stanford University Medical School and was reported to professionals gathered for annual meetings of the American Psychiatric Association; similar studies in Michigan, Georgia, Sweden, and Finland have produced comparable results.

For the Stanford study, professor of psychiatry David Spiegel followed eighty-six breast cancer patients for ten years. During the first year, the women were randomly divided into two groups. The first group of thirty-six received traditional medical treatment. The second group of fifty received weekly ninety-minute group therapy sessions in addition to traditional medical treatment. At the end of ten years, those who had received therapy lived for approximately thirty-seven months following diagnosis, whereas those who did not receive therapy lived an average of only nineteen months.

Spiegel originally designed the research to refute the notion that the mind plays a role in the course of disease. What he *did* find was the powerful effect of social support. Taking care to describe his findings, Spiegel commented that "we did not find that any psychological variables—like mood—were associated with survival time. It was only participation in the groups that seemed to make a difference."[85]

Describing himself as "stunned" at the study results, Spiegel said the magnitude of the effects on the body was "much greater than anything I expected."[86] William Breitbart, assistant professor of psychiatry at Memorial Sloan-Kettering Cancer Center, says the important factor is "an intervention addressing two factors: social support and feelings of hopelessness and isolation."[87]

Spiegel says that social support may influence health because of the "grandmother effect": People who feel that others care about them are more likely to eat well, sleep well, exercise, and avoid harmful habits, thus maximizing the body's ability to cope with illness. It's also possible, he says, that people who interact well with family and friends also have better relationships with their health-care providers.[88]

In commenting on the study, Spiegel expressed concern that some cancer patients might be made to feel "responsible" for their illnesses or be labeled a "failure" because they did not defeat the disease. The effect of the social support, he maintains, "comes not by denying the illness or wishing it away, but by more successfully managing one's life in terms of family relationships, relationships with physicians, and one's own feelings about having a terminal illness, and dealing with these factors as directly as possible."[89]

In fact, Spiegel says, it's important to face the issues head-on. "It doesn't demoralize patients to talk about these things," he says. "The less hidden the problem, the better. Isolation is a symbol of death. The more isolated patients feel, the more helpless and already dead they feel. This is a time to strengthen social networks, not let them wither."[90]

In a similar study headed by UCLA psychiatrist Fawzy A. Fawzy, researchers provided a ninety-minute weekly group therapy session for one group of malignant melanoma patients; the other group received no therapy. The therapy sessions, which continued for six weeks, focused on education about melanoma, stress management, coping and problem-solving skills, and psychological support.

Six years after their initial diagnosis and treatment, the people in the support group had a *60 percent reduction in death rate* as compared with the other patients— and approximately half as many recurrences of the melanoma.[91]

Similar findings emerged from separate studies involving people with breast, lung, and colorectal cancer. Researchers in each of the studies found that social support and a sense of control were important to coping with serious illness.[92]

And an interesting new study shows that social support may impact patients differently depending on the cancer site and the extent of the disease. In the seventeen-year study, socially isolated women were shown to have a significantly higher risk of dying of cancer of all sites and of smoking-related cancers. Cancer *incidence* was not associated with social connections among men, but men with few social connections had significantly poorer survival rates from cancer.[93]

Social support can even affect the unborn. To test what kind of impact social support had on newborns, researchers studied single adolescent Navajo mothers at the University of Arizona. Questionnaires and detailed interviews enabled researchers to categorize the mothers-to-be into three different groups—those who had low social support, medium social support, and high social support. Researchers then followed the women through their pregnancies and deliveries.[94]

The teenagers who had only medium or low social support delivered babies who were significantly more prone to complications. The mothers with medium or low social support also had four times the rate of neonatal complications when compared with the mothers with high levels of social support![95]

Controlled tests by researchers at Baylor College of Medicine showed that the presence of a female companion who provided continuous emotional support throughout labor and delivery was a significant benefit. When such a woman was present, Caesarean section rates dropped from 18 percent to 8 percent. The need for epidural anesthesia dropped from 55 percent to 8 percent, and the average labor was shortened by about two hours. Finally, the need for prolonged hospitalization of the babies after birth was significantly decreased.[96]

In another study, researchers measured the *perceived* availability of emotional and tangible support among expectant mothers—how much support they *believed* they had, whether that support actually did or did not exist. Researchers found that the mothers who perceived that they had good support had fewer premature births and fewer infant complications than those who believed their support to be scant.[97]

The amount of social support given to a mother can even influence the way she bonds to her infant. In one study, researchers evaluated how much social support mothers had from family members and friends; they then rated how well the mothers and infants had become attached to each other. Among the women with good social support, only 10 percent had problems bonding with their infants. But among the women with poor social support, more than half—55 percent—had inadequate or insecure bonding with their infants.[98]

Convinced of the need for good social support? If you need to strengthen your own social connectedness, try the following suggestions:

- Start by making your needs known; let others know that you're interested in strengthening your friendships and your circle of support.
- Look for groups to join. Many corporations offer groups for people who share the same interests (such as stress management); also, you can often find groups through your community or church. Find a group that you feel comfortable in and that deals with a subject you're interested in learning more about.
- Consider enrolling in special classes (such as how to create furniture from willows), special courses (such as how to administer cardiopulmonary resuscitation), or adult education classes offered through your local school district. These classes are usually widely varied in subject—almost everyone can find something of real interest.

- Find a cause you're committed to, and volunteer. You'll find more information about all aspects of volunteer work in Chapter 18.
- Plan now for what you'll be doing a year from now, ten years from now, and during your retirement years. Too often, people restrict their social connections to the workplace; once they retire, they become isolated and lonely. Make active decisions now to help you stay involved.

Touch: A Crucial Aspect of Social Support

As important as social support is to health, perhaps one of its most powerful components is also one of its simplest: People who touch others and are touched themselves seem to enjoy the best health!

Observations made by researchers nearly four decades ago as they watched groups of monkeys provided us with some of the best information we have on the power of touch. University of Wisconsin researchers Harry and Margaret Harlow compared monkeys who were raised together in cages with monkeys whose only social contact came through seeing, hearing, and smelling other monkeys.[99]

The Harlows found that the monkeys who did not have touch, or actual body contact with other monkeys, grew up with a variety of emotional abnormalities. While young, the monkeys seemed especially prone to self-mutilation; as they grew older, their self-aggression turned into aggression against other monkeys. Perhaps most striking was the example of how mothers behaved toward their young: The mothers who grew up without touch showed less warmth and affection toward their offspring. Some even killed their own babies.

The same thing happens with humans. Countless studies have borne out the deleterious effects on people who are deprived of touch. One landmark study of victims of child abuse spanned three generations of families in which child abuse had occurred. The most powerful predictor of child abuse was not necessarily whether the abuser had himself been abused—but, instead, whether the abuser had been deprived of touch and its associated pleasure.[100]

The skin is the earliest sensory organ to develop. Many researchers argue that it is also the most important.[101] According to one health journal,[102] a piece of skin the size of a quarter contains more than 3 million cells, 12 feet of nerves, 100 sweat glands, 50 nerve endings, and 3 feet of blood vessels. Overall, the skin has about 50 receptors per 100 cm^2, or a total of 900,000 sensory receptors. "Viewed from this perspective," reports the journal, "the skin is a giant communication system that, through the sense of touch, brings messages from the external environment to the attention of [the body and the mind]."[103]

Some researchers have shown that touch is stronger than either verbal or emotional contact—and that touch affects nearly everything we do.[104] Cornell University researcher Diane Ackerman points out that "massage therapy"—the act of reaching through the holes in isolettes to stroke and massage premature babies—literally saves their lives. Ackerman cites a previously published article in *Science News* confirming that preemies who are touched are "better able to calm and console themselves." Eight months after being released from the hospital, the preemies who benefited from massage therapy, says Ackerman, are healthier, have better weight gain, and have fewer physical problems than the infants who were not touched regularly.[105]

Although the research linking touch to emotional behavior occurred nearly four decades ago, the first research linking touch to physical health happened—by accident—nearly seventy years ago. Anatomist Frederick Hammett did an experiment in which he removed rats' thyroid and parathyroid glands—and he was astonished when some of the rats survived. Careful research led him to the discovery that the rats who survived the surgery came from colonies where they had been regularly "petted and gentled" by their keepers. They were six times as likely to survive the operation than were rats who had not been touched regularly—and were also much less timid, apprehensive, and high-strung.[106]

According to researchers, touch has both physical and emotional benefits. For example, studies show that touch subdues heart irregularities; people who have a certain type of irregular heartbeat have a more normal heartbeat in the minute after they are touched as their pulse is being taken. And touch can relieve depression; in one study, daily massage improved depression and anxiety scores in children and adolescents who were hospitalized for depression.[107]

What does all of this mean? People who enjoy regular, satisfying touch—a pat on the back, a hug—enjoy health benefits as a result. Their hearts are stronger, their blood pressure is lower, their stress levels are decreased, and their overall tension is reduced. So try these simple ways to add more touch to your life: Acknowledge your children with a hug, kiss, or gentle squeeze of the arm; shake hands when greeting someone; hold a friend's hand while you talk; have a massage; get a manicure; have someone else wash your hair; or volunteer to rock babies at a local hospital.[108]

Having good relationships with other people seems to help us resist infection. It seems to protect us against disease. It helps protect us against stress, and it makes us healthier physically and mentally. It can even help us live longer.

Truly, no man is an island. Only by surrounding ourselves and becoming involved with others can we live the longest, healthiest, happiest life possible.

Notes

1. Emrika Padus, *The Complete Guide to Your Emotions and Your Health* (Emmaus, Pennsylvania: Rodale Press, 1986).

2. Meredith Minkler, "The Social Component of Health," *American Journal of Health Promotion*, Fall: 1986, 33–38.

3. Minkler.

4. Marc Pilisuk and Susan Hillier Parks, *The Healing Web* (Hanover, New Hampshire: The University Press of New England, 1986).

5. Allan Luks and Peggy Payne, *The Healing Power of Doing Good* (New York: Fawcett Columbine, 1992).

6. Susan Bell, "Thawing the Ice in the Heart: An Interview with Saul Bellow," *The Writer*, May 1988, p. 15.

7. Padus.

8. Padus.

9. Kenneth Pelletier, *Sound Mind, Sound Body: A New Model for Lifelong Health* (New York: Simon and Schuster, 1994), pp. 137–138.

10. Sheldon Cohen, "Social Support and

Physical Illness," in *Advances*, 7(1): 1990, 35–48; original source, *Health Psychology*, 7(3): 1988, 269–297.

11. Pilisuk and Parks.

12. Terrence L. Amick and Judith K. Ockene, "The Role of Social Support in the Modification of Risk Factors for Cardiovascular Disease," in Sally A. Shumaker and Susan M. Czajkowski, *Social Support and Cardiovascular Disease* (New York: Plenum Press, 1994), pp. 260–261.

13. Deborah Preston and Jorge Grimes, "A Study of Differences in Social Support," *Journal of Gerontological Nursing*, 13(2), 36–40.

14. Cohen.

15. Preston and Grimes.

16. Editors of *Prevention* Magazine and the Center for Positive Living, *Positive Living and Health: The Complete Guide to Brain/Body Healing and Mental Empowerment* (Emmaus, Pennsylvania: Rodale Press, 1990), p. 165.

17. Preston and Grimes.

18. C. E. Depner and B. Ingersoll-Dayton, "Supportive Relationships in Later Life," *Psychology and Aging*, 3(4): 1988, 348–357.

19. Sheldon Cohen and S. Leonard Syme, editors, *Social Support and Health* (London: Academic Press, Inc., 1985).

20. Joan Borysenko, *Fire in the Soul* (New York: Warner Books, 1993), p. 83.

21. Minkler.

22. "Social Isolation Pessimism: Link to Poor Health," *Medical Abstracts Newsletter*, October 1988, p. 5.

23. Tom Ferguson, "The Invisible Health Care System," n.s., January/February 1988.

24. James W. Pennebaker, *Opening Up: The Healing Power of Confiding in Others* (New York: William Morrow and Company, Inc., 1990).

25. Pennebaker.

26. Martha E. Francis and James W. Pennebaker, "Putting Stress into Words: The Impact of Writing on Physiological, Absentee, and Self-Reported Emotional Well-Being Measures," *American Journal of Health Promotion*, 6(4): 1992, 280–287.

27. Francis and Pennebaker.

28. Pennebaker.

29. "Writing as a Means of Healing," *HealthFacts*, 16(145): 1991, 1.

30. Henry Dreher, "The Healing Power of Confession," *Natural Health,* July/August: 1992, 80.

31. Barbara Powell, *Good Relationships Are Good Medicine* (Emmaus, Pennsylvania: Rodale Press, 1987).

32. Leonard A. Sagan, *The Health of Nations* (New York: Basic Books, Inc., 1987).

33. James J. Lynch, *The Broken Heart: The Medical Consequences of Loneliness* (New York: Basic Books, Inc., 1977).

34. Brent Q. Hafen and Kathryn J. Frandsen, *People Who Need People Are the Healthiest People: The Importance of Relationships* (Provo, Utah: Behavioral Health Associates, n.d.).

35. Jeff Meade, "How to Enrich Your Relationships," *Prevention*, March: 1988, 86–89.

36. Hafen and Frandsen.

37. Lynch.

38. Lynch.

39. Lynch.

40. Lynch.

41. Lynch.

42. Lynch.

43. Padus.

44. Minkler.

45. Minkler.

46. Animals studies from Pilisuk and Parks.

47. Pilisuk and Parks.

48. Pilisuk and Parks.

49. From Peter Steinglass, Eli Weisstub, and Atara Kaplan De-Nour, "Perceived Personal Networks as Mediators of Stress Reactions," *American Journal of Psychiatry*, 145(10): 1988, 1259–1263.

50. Blair Justice, *Who Gets Sick: Thinking and Health* (Houston, Texas: Peak Press, 1987), p. 128.

51. Hafen and Frandsen.

52. Larry Dossey, *Healing Words* (San Francisco: Harper San Francisco, 1993), p. 109.

53. Cohen.

54. "Surviving a Heart Attack: Emotional Support Is Key," *Mental Medicine Update*, Spring: 1993, 2.

55. S. Leonard Syme, "Coronary Artery Disease: A Sociocultural Perspective," *Circulation* 76 (Supplement I), I-112, 1987; and Steven Locke and Douglas Colligan, *The Healer Within* (New York: E. P. Dutton, 1986), p. 89.

56. Padus.

57. Cohen.

58. Seeman, Kaplan, Knudsen, Cohen, and

Guralnik, "Social Network Ties and Mortality Among the Elderly in the Alameda County Study," *American Journal of Epidemiology* 126(4): 1987, 714– 723.

59. Seeman et al.

60. Locke and Colligan, p. 89.

61. Robert Ornstein and David Sobel, *The Healing Brain* (New York: Simon and Schuster, 1987), p. 121.

62. Bertil S. Hanson, Sven-Olaf Isacsson, Lars Janzon, and Sven-Eric Lindell, "Social Network and Social Support Influence on Mortality in Elderly Men," *Advances*, 7(1): 1990, 16–18, in *American Journal of Epidemiology*, 130(1): 1989, 110–111.

63. Editors of *Prevention* Magazine and the Center for Positive Living, p. 163.

64. Hafen and Frandsen.

65. Jeff Meade, "How to Enrich Your Relationships," *Prevention*, March: 1988, 86–89.

66. Hafen and Frandsen.

67. Thomas W. Kamarck, Stephen B. Manuck, and J. Richard Jennings, "Social Support Reduces Cardiovascular Reactivity to Psychological Challenge: A Laboratory Model," *Psychosomatic Medicine*, 52: 1990, 42–58.

68. Hafen and Frandsen.

69. Hafen and Frandsen.

70. Lynch.

71. Lynch.

72. Kristina Orth-Gomer and Anna Lena Unden, "Type A Behavior, Social Support, and Coronary Risk: Interaction and Significance for Mortality in Cardiac Patients," *Psychosomatic Medicine* 52: 1990, 59–72.

73. G. A. Kaplan, J. T. Salonen, R. D. Cohen, R. J. Brand, S. L. Syme, and P. Puska, "Social Connections and Mortality from All Causes and from Cardiovascular Disease: Prospective Evidence from Eastern Finland," *American Journal of Epidemiology*, 128(2): 1988, 370–380.

74. "Friendship: Heart Saver for Type A's," *Men's Health*, November 1987, p. 4.

75. "Friendship."

76. Hafen and Frandsen.

77. Alan F. Fontana, Robert D. Kerns, Roberta L. Rosenberg, and Kathleen L. Colonese, "Support, Stress, and Recovery from CHD: A Longitudinal Causal Model," *Health Psychology*, 8(2): 1989, 175–193.

78. "The Lonely Heart," *Harvard Heart Letter*, 3(4): 1992, reporting on studies in the *Journal of the American Medical Association*, January 1992.

79. S. Kennedy, J. Kiecolt-Glaser, and R. Glaser, "Immunological Consequences of Acute and Chronic Stressors: Mediating Role of Interpersonal Relationships," *British Journal of Medical Psychology*, 61: 1988, 77–85.

80. Hafen and Frandsen.

81. Editors of *Prevention* Magazine and the Center for Positive Living.

82. Justice, p. 134.

83. Powell.

84. Powell.

85. David Spiegel, "A Psychosocial Intervention and Survival Time of Patients with Metastatic Breast Cancer," *Advances*, 7(3): 1991, 10–19.

86. Spiegel.

87. "Can the Right Attitude Cure Cancer?" *Patient Care*, June 15: 1991, 208–209.

88. "A Strong Circle of Friends," *Consumer Reports*, February 1993.

89. Spiegel.

90. "Can the Right Attitude Cure Cancer?"

91. Fawzy I. Fawzy, "Malignant Melanoma: Effects of an Early Structured Psychiatric Intervention, Coping, and Affective State of Recurrence and Survival Six Years Later," *Archives of General Psychiatry*, 50: 1993, 681–689.

92. K. O. Ell, J. E. Mantell, M. B. Hamovitch, and R. H. Nishimoto, "Social Support, Sense of Control, and Coping Among Patients with Breast, Lung, or Colorectal Cancer," n. s., 7(3): 1989, 63–89.

93. Kathleen Ell, Robert Nishimoto, Linda Mediansky, Joanne Mantell, and Maurice Hamovitch, "Social Relations, Social Support and Survival Among Patients with Cancer," *Journal of Psychosomatic Research*, 36(6): 1992, 531–541.

94. W. Thomas Boyce, "Stress and Child Health: An Overview," *Pediatric Annals*, 14(8): 1985, 539–542.

95. Boyce.

96. J. Kennell et al., "Continuous Emotional Support During Labor in a U.S. Hospital: A Randomized Controlled Trial," *Journal of the American Medical Association*, 265: 1991, 2197–2201.

97. Cohen.

98. Boyce.

99. Albert L. Huebner, "The Pleasure Principle," *East / West*, May: 1989, 14–19.

100. Huebner.

101. Huebner.

102. Barbara Montgomery Dossey, Lynn Keegan, Leslie Gooding Kolkmeier, and Cathie E. Guzzetta, *Holistic Health Promotion: A Guide for Practice* (Rockville, Maryland: Aspen, 1989), p. 255.

103. Diane Ackerman, "The Power of Touch," *Parade Magazine*, March 25: 1990, 4–6.

104. Ackerman.

105. Ackerman.

106. Robert Ornstein and David Sobel, *Healthy Pleasures* (Reading, Massachusetts: Addison-Wesley, 1989).

107. *Mayo Clinic Health Letter*, June 1994, p. 7.

108. *Mayo Clinic Health Letter*.

13

LONELINESS AND HEALTH

We are, most of us, very lonely in this world; you who have any who love you, cling to them and thank God.—AUTHOR UNKNOWN

The dayroom on the fourth floor of the nursing home was spanking clean. The television was on. The sun streamed in. There were only two patients in the room, each in a wheelchair. The woman slumped in her chair. Her hair was dull; I could hardly see her face. She rolled her chair toward where I sat on a couch talking with the psychiatrist, stopped, looked us over, turned, and wheeled away.

The man, who, I was told, was over a hundred years old, was dressed in a blue polka-dot shirt and gray pants. Nurses came in to check on him from time to time, touching his shoulder, adjusting his wheelchair. He didn't come near us. From afar, he tapped out a rhythm with his hand on the arm of the chair. Every once in a while, he let out a sound. At first, I thought he was whining.

Did he feel fatherless?

Was his freedom unbearably curtailed?

Not this man. He had been kissed and stroked and fussed over.

"Loneliness," Dr. Cath had said, "has to do with an individual's failure to create an inner, soothing presence." This man, for whatever reasons, had not failed. He was not whining. As I came closer, I heard, distinctly, the rhythm and the pitch.

He was singing.[1]

What Is Loneliness?

Loneliness—a condition that has been shown to affect both health and long life—can be present when we're surrounded by people. As the popular saying goes, a person can be "lonely in a crowd." According to psychologist and cell biologist Joan Borysenko, "To be isolated is the greatest tragedy for a human being and the most generic form of stress."[2] According to research at Kent State University, loneliness is connected less with the number of people in our lives than to satisfaction with those relationships. Loneliness occurs when we believe that current relationships fall short of our ideal.[3]

Feelings of loneliness are worse when the lonely person is surrounded by people who don't seem to be lonely—people who seem to have secure interpersonal attachments—or when the lonely person suffers from a sense of low self-esteem.[4] And, although loneliness can stem from lack of attachment to someone else, loneliness can be just as intense if there is a sense of not belonging within an accepting community.[5] Carin Rubenstein, former associate editor of *Psychology Today*, pointed out that loneliness and being alone aren't necessarily the same thing: "If people feel lonely, it has nothing to do with the number of people around them, but rather with their expectations of life and reactions to their environment. And those are risk factors you can do something about."[6]

Loneliness has been characterized as an "unpleasant experience that occurs when a person's network of social relationships is significantly deficient in either quality or quantity."[7] And loneliness can be more than just unpleasant; it can be profound. One prisoner during the Korean war endured extreme physical torture and starvation with surprising stamina. His worst point came, however, when he was placed in solitary confinement and separated from the friends he had made during his confinement in the prison camp. "I was captured and tortured," he remembers, "and after a while I could stand it. But I couldn't stand even a few days of this," he said, referring to his loneliness.[8]

Rubenstein and University of Denver's Phillip Shaver were curious to find out what factors surrounded loneliness, so they sent out a questionnaire about loneliness—and it was placed in five United States newspapers. More than 22,000 people over the age of eighteen responded. The survey confirmed that feeling lonely is associated with greater health risks. What was a little surprising was that loneliness is not necessarily a consequence of living alone.[9]

In fact, almost one-fourth of the survey respondents who lived alone fell into the "least lonely" category. (Survey results, however, showed that they had more friends on average than people who lived with other people.) The loneliest respondents were people who lived with their parents.

Researchers pointed out that "young people who live with their parents after high school or college graduation tend to be lonelier than older people who live alone. A young person in this situation has different expectations. If there's no boyfriend or girlfriend in the picture, they face a psychological conflict. For young adults, in particular, being alone—especially on a Saturday night—can be a stigma. This makes them feel rejected and lonely."[10]

Loneliness versus Aloneness

According to epidemiologist Leonard A. Sagan, loneliness is quite different from merely being alone. In *The Health of Nations*, Sagan writes that the number of persons with whom we surround ourselves is not what counts—what counts, he says, is the *satisfaction* we get from our relationships and whether we *perceive* that we are isolated.[11] These factors help determine whether someone who is "alone" is also "lonely":

- *General attitude.* People either react to being alone by being sad and passive or by developing "creative solitude": spending time reading, listening to music, working on a hobby, studying, writing, playing a musical instrument, or some other creative endeavor.
- *Boredom.* Researchers concluded from the survey that some loneliness stems from simple boredom.
- *Attitude toward self.* Researchers concluded that a person must feel secure with the self in order to be content when alone.

Associate professor of psychology David A. Chiriboga has this advice: "When you find yourself alone, see it as an opportunity to discover yourself. Take it as a challenge. Find out what you want to be, where you want to go, and what gives you pleasure. Anyone can be an interesting person. All you have to do is look inside yourself." And, he concludes, people who are loving—who completely accept themselves and others—can be happy and content whether they are in a crowd of people or quietly at home by themselves. In a study of more than 9,000 people reported in the *Journal of Community and Applied Social Psychology*, researchers found that living alone can be healthy if those who live alone seek outside contacts (such as friends and extended family members) and limit their alcohol intake.

Anne Morrow Lindbergh wrote in *Gift From the Sea*:

> *I find there is a quality to being alone that is incredibly precious. Life rushes back into the void, richer, more vivid, fuller than before. It is as if in parting one did actually lose an arm. And then, like starfish, one grows it anew; one is whole again, complete and round—more whole, even, than before, when the other people had pieces of one.*

Trends in Being Alone

Although being alone doesn't necessarily mean people are lonely, many people who are alone *are* lonely. And there are more people than ever living alone—more than 20 million in the United States alone. Between 1950 and 1980, the figure rose by 385 percent. And the most radical change has been in the number of men living alone: twice as many now as ten years ago.[12]

In 1985 there were more than 35 million households in the United States headed by singles. Estimates at the time suggested that by the first few years of the 1990s there will be almost as many American households headed by divorced, separated, and widowed people as by married ones.[13] That prediction is now a reality.

A number of trends and factors help explain why so many Americans in such increasing numbers are living alone.

1. The divorce rate is rising.

2. In the United States, there has been a trend away from marriage. People are waiting longer to get married, and many are not marrying at all. Today, almost one-fifth of all women in their early thirties have never married, one-fourth of the women in their later twenties have never married, and more than one-half of those in their early twenties are unmarried. Not too long ago, most women were married by the time they were twenty-two.

The older women get, the less their chance of getting married, says a study conducted by researchers at Yale and Harvard. For women in their late twenties and thirties, the prospects can be dim. Never-married, college-educated Caucasian women have a 50 percent chance of eventually marrying if they are twenty-five. The chance dips to 20 percent by age thirty, 5 percent by age thirty-five, and only 1 percent by age forty. The study is based on averages; obviously, women in these age groups are still getting married, although their chances decrease with each passing year.[14]

3. Household size is getting smaller. The average household size in the United States was 4.1 members in 1930; that figure dropped to 2.8 in 1980.[15] Today, 42 percent of all households are composed of only one person.

4. Mobility is increasing. In the United States, one in five persons changes residence every year; almost half the U.S. population relocates within any five-year period. Young, educated people move—often long distances—in search of employment and more favorable environments. Poor people move—usually short distances—as the economic and ethnic characteristics of their neighborhoods force them out. We are free—free to relocate to another area, free to quit our job, free to quit our family, free to move on. The changing face of America reflects this "freedom"; the individual is in many ways replacing the family as the basic unit of society.[16]

Other trends have led to the alone and lonely trend in the United States. Fewer face-to-face business transactions are completed; computers write letters, make telephone calls, and handle all financial transactions. People sit alone in front of the television set and video machine instead of going out into the community to watch movies, go to the theatre, attend plays, or patronize the arts. Our larger cities, especially, have become impersonal—and the high crime rate in many cities discourages people from leaving home for purely social reasons.[17]

Reasons for Loneliness

There are very personal reasons for being lonely. Researchers have divided these into five separate categories:

1. Being alone (coming home to an empty house);
2. Needing friends (feeling different, being misunderstood);

3. Forced isolation (being housebound, being hospitalized, having no transportation);

4. Being unattached (having no spouse, having no sexual partner); and

5. Dislocation (being far from home, being in a new job or school, moving too often, traveling often).[18]

Whatever the reason, many Americans feel lonely. Estimates reveal that more than 35 million are lonely each month. According to a national survey completed by the United States Department of Health and Human Services, more than one-fourth of all Americans—an estimated 50 million—have been lonely recently.[19] Nearly one-fifth of the U.S. adult population feels lonely at least once a month, and one in ten feels overwhelming loneliness at least once a week.

Recent research also shows that education may play a role in loneliness. In a study involving the effects of loneliness on heart attack, Dr. William Ruberman and his colleagues found that the best-educated people had the least amount of social isolation. On the other hand, poorly educated people had the most job stress and the most social isolation—and the highest risk of dying.

Although Ruberman and his associates considered social isolation to be the most potent factor in the increased death rate among their study subjects, they believe that poor education may also result in less access to good health care and the tendency to neglect self-care practices.[20]

Causes of Loneliness

According to researchers with the Department of Health and Human Services, loneliness has two basic causes: (a) predisposing (general cultural values, the characteristics of the situation, or the characteristics of the individual), and (b) precipitating (what happens following a specific event, such as a move to a new community or the breakup of a love relationship). The following causes are the most common.[21]

Personal Characteristics

Many lonely people have distinctive social characteristics that make it difficult for them to form and maintain relationships. They may be extremely shy, for example, and may find it very difficult to introduce themselves, participate in groups, enjoy parties, make phone calls to initiate social activities, and so on. They may lack self-esteem or may be excruciatingly self-conscious. Many lonely people are unable to be assertive, and some feel they are controlled by others.

Lonely people also tend to have distinct patterns of interaction. When they are conversing with someone else, they respond slowly to the other person's statements, change the subject often, talk more about themselves, and ask few questions of the other person. A researcher who studied these patterns says that lonely people are "self-focused and nonresponsive."

Lonely people often had problems relating to their parents, too. Many lonely people say their parents did not give emotional nurturance, failed to give guidance or support, and did not encourage their children to strive for relationships or popularity. Many lonely people remember their parents as remote, untrustworthy, and disagreeable.

Characteristics of the Situation

Certain situations have everything working against them as far as fostering relationships and becoming involved in meaningful social networks. Some constraints are very basic—time, distance, and money. The student who carries a full course load and a heavy work schedule may have little time for sleep, let alone for making friends. The fire spotter who lives in a remote part of the forest has few opportunities to socialize. The single parent on a tight budget may not be able to afford the babysitter who would allow time for social activities.

Constraints can also limit the number of "eligible" people. For example, a person may not be surrounded by people considered appropriate as friends. An elderly person may live in an apartment building full of young married couples, or a Hispanic family may be the only one of that ethnic group on the block. This kind of "situational" isolation sometimes makes it difficult to initiate relationships.

Cultural Values

American culture encourages us to be independent, individualistic, and eager to travel our own paths. In addition, as mentioned, we have become a highly mobile, urban society; many people who live in condominiums or townhouses in crowded urban areas could not tell you the name of their next-door neighbors.

The Nature of Social Relationships

Lonely people tend to have fewer social contacts and relationships than people who are not lonely. They spend less time with other people, and are likely to spend their time with people they are not close to rather than with good friends. Children who are lonely often have poor relationships with their mothers; adults who are lonely are apt to lack meaningful relationships with other adults.

The quality of relationships is important as well. People who have shallow, withdrawn relationships are much more likely to feel lonely (even when surrounded by throngs of people) than those who have deep, intense, and close friendships with others.

Relationships That Don't Meet Needs

A person might have ten close relationships with others and still be lonely. For most people, relationships have to provide a feeling of personal attachment and social integration; they have to provide nurturance, reassurance of one's worth, a sense of reliable alliance, and guidance. Relationships that meet those needs are more likely to keep a person from feeling lonely.

Precipitating Events

Countless events in life (many of which are beyond our control) can make us feel lonely, rejected, alone, and inadequate. The most frequent precipitators of loneliness are the death of a spouse, divorce, geographical moves, leaving family and friends to begin college or start a new job, the breakup of a romantic relationship, and a fight with a good friend or family member.

Risk Factors for Loneliness

No one is immune from loneliness. Depending on one's needs, relationships, and life circumstances at any given time, anyone may fall prey to loneliness. However, two groups are at higher risk for loneliness overall: teenagers and people over age eighty.

It shouldn't surprise many that people over eighty are at risk. As people mature, they tend to become more satisfied with their relationships, and loneliness is not as common—until people experience the death of friends, loved ones, and spouses. But aren't teenagers the most socially active? They usually have more opportunity for social interaction, but many teenagers also have unrealistic expectations about what friendships should involve. Therefore, their needs aren't met, and they feel lonely.

Also, people who are happily married are less lonely than people who are single. Among single people, those who have never been married are less lonely than those who have been divorced or widowed.

Loneliness tends to be less of a problem for women—although women are more willing to admit they are lonely. Women fare slightly better because they tend to form deep and intimate relationships; they generally remain friends with people, even though time and distance separate them. Their conversations are more personal and intimate; women tend to discuss feelings, whereas men tend to discuss things (such as the structure at the office or the results of last night's football game).

As one researcher put it: "In public, the loneliness of men is more visible than the loneliness of women. Men make friends less easily as they grow older; women seem to continue to replace the friends they have lost. Most older men lack what social scientists call the social skills for making friends with other men and have had little experience in making friends with women."[22]

People with certain kinds of family structure are also more prone to loneliness than others. In doing research on loneliness, psychologists commented on many people who described a family life in which:

The parents clung tightly to one another and shut out both the world and the child. The parents had no friends; there were no models in the home of what it meant to have friends. There was a sense of being stranded, both shut out from the clinging marriage and alone in the rest of the world. Nobody ever came to dinner. Nobody ever called or went to the movies. Nobody confided in anyone. The family seems, to people who talk this way, the most antisocial unit imaginable, less a haven than a dungeon. Some children growing up in families like these become compensatory—filling their lives with other people, looking for other families to "adopt" themselves into, marrying young. Others repeat the patterns they learned at home, isolating themselves, walling themselves off from intimate connections, ignoring the thirst.[23]

People with lower incomes are more likely to be lonely than those at middle- or high-income levels, probably because there are fewer opportunities for socializing due to economic restrictions.

Other groups at higher risk for loneliness are: recent widows, couples who are separating or getting a divorce, students changing schools, people starting new jobs, people who are moving, unemployed people, people who live alone, prison inmates, patients with chronic or terminal illness, children of divorced parents, and women whose children have left home (commonly called the "empty nest syndrome").[24]

The Health Consequences of Loneliness

Loneliness carries with it a big risk for health problems. Psychologist James J. Lynch, scientific director of the Psychophysiological Clinic at the University of Maryland Medical School, says loneliness is "the greatest unrecognized contributor to premature death in the United States."[25]

Loneliness—and the stress that accompanies it—has been connected not only to premature death, but a host of physical and mental disorders as well. Loneliness has been definitely linked to disease; people who are not lonely have a better chance of staying healthy or recovering from disease than people who are lonely. Researcher Louise Bernikow reports:

Loneliness can, indeed, make you sick. Heart disease and hypertension are now generally thought of as loneliness diseases, exacerbated by a person's sense of abandonment by the world, separation from the rest of humanity. Most addictions are also considered loneliness diseases, which the medical profession is beginning to recognize but which recovering alcoholics, drug addicts, even smokers have been long aware of. Most addicts admit that their best friends have been booze, drugs, or tobacco.[26]

Apparently one of the crucial factors in determining whether loneliness will make you sick is what it *means* to you to be lonely. In one study, California Department of Health Services epidemiologists Peggy Reynolds and George A.

Kaplan used data from the Alameda County study, which involved 7,000 healthy adults. What they found was that socially isolated women had a significantly greater chance of developing cancer and dying from it.

But what interested the researchers most was the fact that the determining factor seemed to be the women's *perception* of loneliness—what being lonely meant. Some of the women had many social contacts, but still *felt* isolated; Reynolds and Kaplan found those women had 2.4 times the normal risk of dying from cancers of the ovary, uterus, and breast. Then there were the women who had few social contacts and felt isolated: they were five times as likely to die from the same cancers.[27]

In a comprehensive study that shed light on the health impact of loneliness, Dr. Caroline Thomas and Dr. Karen Duszynski of The Johns Hopkins School of Medicine examined 1,185 Johns Hopkins medical students who had attended medical school between the years 1948 and 1964. While they were still in medical school, all the students were given a questionnaire that probed into their attitudes and behaviors. All of the students were healthy at the time they completed the questionnaires.

The researchers then followed the progress of the medical students who had completed questionnaires. In 1974, they began reporting on the relationship between a variety of attitudes and behaviors and the health problems that students subsequently developed.

Thomas and Duszynski found that the physicians who eventually committed suicide, were hospitalized for mental illness, or developed malignant tumors had initially reported similar feelings: They had significantly greater problems in interpersonal relationships and had suffered significantly more from loneliness.[28]

Interestingly, those who later developed cancer not only reported a lack of closeness to parents in childhood, but were found—based on the Rorschach test—to have the poorest "relationship potential." When researchers recently reviewed personality test findings for 972 of the physicians in the study, they found that those who were "loners" and who suppressed their emotions were sixteen times more likely to develop cancer.[29]

Lynch, who has done intensive research into the Johns Hopkins study, says that much of the loneliness reported by the students stemmed from an absence of "closeness" to parents early in life. In commenting on the parent-child relationship, Thomas and Duszynski remarked:

> *Early in life damage is done to the child's developing ability to relate to others, resulting in marked feelings of isolation, a sense that intense and meaningful relationships bring pain and rejection, and a sense of deep hopelessness and despair. Later, a meaningful relationship is formed in which the individual invests a great deal of energy. For a time, he enjoys a sense of acceptance by others and a meaningful life, although the feeling of loneliness never is completely dispelled. Finally, with the loss of a central relationship, whether the death of a spouse, forced job retirement, or children leaving home, comes a sense of utter despair and a conviction that life holds nothing more for him.*[30]

That early attachment is critical to the health and well-being of infants and children. Infants who fail to develop attachment sometimes do not survive. Those who do survive are believed to be more likely to develop psychopathic personalities (personalities that render them unable to care and be responsible for others).[31] The resulting loneliness leads to a variety of physical and mental health problems, and sometimes premature death. People with strong attachments, on the other hand, suffer far less loneliness—and are less vulnerable, less helpless, more likely to have the confidence to take risks, more likely to have the confidence to move in new directions, and more creative.[32]

Attachment—the social ties it brings, and the loneliness in its absence—appears to be an extremely important health factor. Dr. James House, a sociologist at the Institute of Gerontology at the University of Michigan, has done an in-depth review of a series of studies conducted in the United States, Sweden, and Finland. The studies examined various health issues in relationship to how lonely people were—with loneliness calculated in terms of whether a person was or was not married, had contacts with extended family, had a strong network of friends, was active in a church, or had any other social affiliations. In cooperation with a team of two other researchers who also examined the studies, House concluded that loneliness constitutes a "major risk factor" for health—rivaling the effects of "well-established health risk factors such as cigarette smoking, blood pressure, blood lipids (fats), obesity, and physical activity."[33]

Even research in the laboratory with animals shows the health risks of loneliness and the health benefits of companionship. House and his colleagues point out that "the mere presence of a familiar member of the same species can lessen physiological impact of stress in producing ulcers, hypertension, and neurosis." House says that affectionate petting by humans—or even their mere presence—can reduce stress (as measured by heartbeat and other cardiovascular symptoms) in dogs, cats, horses, and rabbits. Research shows that the opposite may be true, too: Humans may benefit from the companionship of pets (discussed in greater detail later in this chapter).[34]

The effects of loneliness may be even greater than originally thought, as researchers look into a variety of situations. In one fascinating study, researchers decided to find out whether companionship that alleviated loneliness could make a difference in the outcome of labor and delivery. To test their notion, researchers randomly divided first-time mothers into two groups. In the first group, each mother went through labor alone, except for occasional checks by the hospital staff; in the second group, each had the companionship of an untrained woman throughout labor. The mothers in the second group had never met their companions; the support provided during labor varied from mere companionship to holding hands, talking, or rubbing the mother's back during labor.[35]

The results were striking. Among the mothers who underwent labor alone, 75 percent developed complications during labor or birth, including induced labor, fetal distress, stillbirths, or Caesarean section deliveries. Only 12 percent of the mothers with companions developed complications. When researchers looked at just the uncomplicated labors, there was still a marked difference. The unsupported mothers had an average length of labor of 19.3 hours; the mothers who enjoyed support averaged 8.7 hours—less than half as long.[36] The differences continued even after birth. When physicians and researchers observed the mothers for the first hour after the babies were born, the supported mothers were more awake and alert, talked to their babies more, stroked their babies more, and smiled more at their babies.[37]

In a new study that involved 616 women, research director John Kennell of Case Western Reserve University estimated that emotional support during labor could save the health industry $2 billion a year. In his study, Kennell compared women who went through labor and delivery alone to those who were given emotional support and companionship by another woman. Those who were less lonely during labor and delivery required fewer Caesarean sections, less anesthesia, and fewer induced deliveries. Those with companionship delivered their babies faster, and the babies required shorter hospital stays than those born to women who went through the experience alone.[38]

Loneliness and Longevity

University of Maryland psychologist James J. Lynch says that all the available data from hundreds of in-depth studies point to several factors, including lack of human companionship, chronic loneliness, and social isolation, as "among the leading causes of premature death."[39] And, says Lynch, although the effects of human loneliness are related to "virtually every disease," they are particularly strong in heart disease, the leading cause of death in the United States.

Samuel Silverman, associate clinical professor of psychiatry at Harvard University, claims a person can add up to fifteen years to life simply by reducing two "emotional aging factors," one of which is loneliness.[40]

A study by University of Michigan researchers followed 2,754 men and women to determine which behavioral factors influenced health and longevity. Loneliness turned out to be a substantial health risk—and an apparent cause of premature death. According to researchers, women who were lonely and isolated were one-and-a-half times more likely to die prematurely than women with close social ties. For men, the risk was double.[41]

In the study conducted on residents of Alameda County, California (detailed in Chapter 12), researchers followed 7,000 men and women for nine years, looking for clues on what leads to health and long life. Again, loneliness was strongly implicated as being detrimental. In that study the genders seemed to "switch risk": Lonely women had a nearly three times greater risk and lonely men had a doubled risk of illness and premature death than men and women who had close ties with family and friends.

Loneliness and Immune Function

A host of studies have shown that loneliness has a considerable effect on immune system function. In one study, University of Denver psychologist Mark

Laudenslager and his colleagues separated two baby macaque monkeys from their peers and two others from their mothers. At the time of separation, the baby monkeys were about six months old—comparable to two or three years old in a human child. And, even though the separations were brief, the stress they caused was high; the monkeys didn't know that they'd soon be reunited with their loved ones. Later, when the monkeys were three or four—comparable to adolescence in humans—researchers compared their immune systems with those of five monkeys who had never been isolated during childhood. All the lonely monkeys, those who had been separated, showed lower levels of both B-cell and T-cell activity. The monkeys were at a higher risk for disease.[42]

In another measure of loneliness, researchers at Harvard Medical School studied 111 students—78 men and 33 women. All students in the study were physically healthy, and none was taking drugs that would have suppressed the immune system. Students were given the Minnesota Multiphasic Personality Inventory, a questionnaire-form test that rates, among other things, depression, loneliness, social isolation, and maladjustment. They were also given blood tests that measured the activity of natural killer cells, white blood cells that attack tumors and viruses even without being previously exposed to them. There was a definite correlation in the study: Students who showed high levels of loneliness also had significantly low functioning of the immune system. Researchers found that their natural killer cells were not as active and that they were less able to fight off the Epstein-Barr virus.[43]

A closely related study yielded the same results. Researchers administered a blood test and the UCLA Loneliness Scale—a psychological test measuring loneliness—to a group of first-year medical students and a group of psychiatric inpatients. When researchers measured immune system function, they found that the lonelier medical students and the lonelier psychiatric patients both had significantly lower levels of natural killer cell activity than those who were not lonely.[44]

Apparently there's a medical reason for the reduction in immune system functioning: Lonely people secrete an excessive amount of the hormone cortisol, which suppresses the immune system. And when loneliness is coupled with stress—another condition that stimulates cortisol production—the results can be particularly crippling.

A study that measured the effects of loneliness coupled with stress was carried out at Harvard Medical School; researchers measured the levels and activity of natural killer cells in students both before and after they took exams. As expected, the activity of natural killer cells declined under the stress of taking an exam. But the students who were also lonely had the lowest natural killer cell activity.[45]

Researchers at Ohio State University carried the tests a step further by involving a specific disease: herpes. Researchers looked at herpes simplex Type I, which causes common cold sores, and herpes Type II (genital, or venereal, herpes). Those who were lonely were not able to fight against herpes viruses of either type. Their immune systems were compromised.

In a similar study, psychologist Margaret Kemeny and her colleagues at the University of California School of Medicine in San Francisco studied thirty-six people with Type II (genital) herpes. Those who were lonely—whose immune systems were not functioning well—had significantly more recurrences of the disease than those who were not lonely. The critical element in averting loneliness seemed to be at least one frank and confiding relationship—having at least one person with whom to share open and honest thoughts and feelings. At least one person in whom to confide, researchers summed, is better than an entire network of more superficial relationships.[46]

Loneliness and Heart Function

Researchers looked for ways in which the mind had an influence over the heart. One of the brain's perceptions—that a person is lonely—apparently has a significant effect on that individual's heart. In the largest study yet attempted of the impact of loneliness on cardiac health, Dr. Kristina Orth-Gomer of the Karolinska Institute in Sweden and Dr. Jeffrey Johnson of Johns Hopkins School of Public Health studied 17,433 Swedes. Orth-Gomer and Johnson looked at how lonely the Swedes were—as measured by how much they interacted with family, friends, neighbors, and coworkers—and compared the loneliest with those who were not lonely for a period of six years. Then the researchers made allowances for typical heart disease risks, such as age, smoking, physical inactivity, and a family history of heart disease. After making these allowances, they reasoned, they should be able to determine what actual impact loneliness had. They found that those who were lonely had a 40 percent greater risk of dying from cardiovascular disease than the rest of the people in the study.[47]

Orth-Gomer and her colleagues followed up with a second study that zeroed in even more carefully on loneliness and its impact on heart disease. She and her colleagues studied 150 middle-aged men between the ages of 40 and 65, observing them for ten years beginning in 1976. One-third of the men were healthy; one-third had heart disease; and the last third were at high risk for developing heart disease. The researchers tested the men's physical health in a variety of ways and examined a range of psychosocial factors to determine which factors were most strongly associated with those who eventually died of heart disease. After ten years, thirty-seven men had died from heart disease. Of those who died, almost all had been initially categorized as socially isolated and lonely. In fact, loneliness was as strong a factor as the strongest physical factor—having an irregular heartbeat—in determining who would eventually die from heart disease.[48]

Another interesting finding stemmed from the study at Karolinska Institute: Researchers found that there is apparently an actual physiological link between loneliness and heart disease. According to the researchers, loneliness creates neuroendocrine changes that lead to atherosclerosis.[49]

In still another study of more than 1,700 elderly men and women in Odense, Denmark, a feeling of loneliness was found to be associated with death from cardiovascular disease. That association was especially true for the men.[50]

One of the most comprehensive retrospective studies of early predictors of disease and premature death involved 50,000 former students from the University of Pennsylvania and Harvard University who attended college between the years of 1921 and 1950. Dr. Ralph Paffenbarger and his colleagues carefully studied the records of the first 590 men who had died of coronary heart disease and compared them with 1,180 randomly selected classmates of equivalent age who were still alive.[51]

Nine factors distinguished the men who died of heart disease: heavy cigarette smoking, high blood pressure, increased body weight, shortness of body height, early parental death, absence of siblings, nonparticipation in sports, a higher emotional index, and scarlet fever in childhood. Researchers said several of those factors, including early parental death, absence of siblings, and nonparticipation in sports, were clear and accurate indicators of which were the loneliest. And, researchers say, those who were loneliest and most socially isolated were the ones most at risk to die of heart disease.[52]

Paffenbarger and his colleagues then did a second study involving 40,000 students. In the years following graduation, 225 of them had committed suicide. When researchers compared the suicides with a large number of randomly selected students, they found that the students who committed suicide were lonely, socially isolated, and came from homes in which the parents had separated early or in which the father had died early. The students who committed suicide tended to have fathers who had a professional status and parents who were college-trained.[53]

All of these factors worked together to bring about loneliness, researchers say. As Paffenbarger commented, "Lack of participation in extra-curricular activities seems to acquire meaning in loneliness, fear, hostility, or frustration. Wealth or success of the father may have an adverse influence on the son through paternal absence, deprivation of companionship and counsel, overbearing demand for emulation, possible lack of interest or lack of need for individual success or effort in the son."[54]

An opposite scenario is the case study provided by the city of Seattle, Washington, where an unusually high percentage of its population—almost 40 percent—is trained in cardiopulmonary resuscitation (CPR). In Seattle, say observers, it's considered a "civic virtue" to know what to do for possible cardiac arrest; it's considered important to care, to be prepared to save someone else. Seattle has the highest rate in the country for recovery from cardiac arrest, in part because it addresses the question of loneliness.[55]

Loneliness and Cancer

A number of studies have correlated loneliness with unusually high incidences of cancer, and researchers now believe that a great deal of the increased cancer rate among the lonely may have to do with the fact that loneliness cripples the immune system. As years of research have shown, a compromised immune system is not as adept at fighting off cancers.

A significant study that showed the link between loneliness and cancer was conducted by the Johns Hopkins University School of Medicine. Researchers collected psychological data between 1948 and 1964 on nearly 1,000 male medical students who attended Johns Hopkins. The men were divided into five groups based on their personality traits. They then collected medical records each year through 1987 and examined the records carefully. Only 1 percent of the "acting out/emotional" cluster—the group who were anxious, easily upset, and prone to depression—developed cancer during the years of the medical follow-up. Nearly one in five of the "loner" cluster—a group who felt lonely and faced the world with bland, unemotional exteriors—developed cancer.[56]

The Importance of Good Friends

One of the greatest benefits provided by friends is that they avert the distress of loneliness. As Robert Louis Stevenson said, "A friend is a present you give yourself." People without friends are lonelier. Studies involving neurotic people have noted that they have far fewer friends (usually no more than one).[57]

And, even though friends are clearly less important in terms of social support than are spouses, it's also clear that close friendships help buffer stress and help overcome the health effects of loneliness. In the study of 7,000 residents of Alameda County, California, it was concluded that a "larger network size and greater frequency of contact was related to decreased mortality for both men and women at all ages, even when other factors, such as socioeconomic status, initial health status, and health practices" were taken into account.[58]

Researchers stress that although having a few close friends is critical to health, it's also wise to have a large social support network. A larger network gives a greater likelihood of finding someone who can provide the kind of support needed when things get tough.

In some cases, the support of close friends may be even more important than the support of family. One study looked at persons aged fifty-five and older in three North Carolina communities. The researchers first determined who had the greatest satisfaction with life—who were the happiest, healthiest, and generally most satisfied. Then they searched to determine what kinds of social support seemed to contribute most to that satisfaction. For this elderly population, at least, the frequency of contacts with family and the satisfaction with contacts from family weren't what made people happiest in life. It was contact with close friends that made the biggest difference.[59]

In a study conducted at Ohio State University, researchers reviewed how many visitors the patients had and how strong their immune systems were. Researchers measured the immune systems by taking blood samples and measuring both antibodies and natural killer cell activity. The elderly residents who had visitors three times a week or more had significantly stronger immune systems than did the elderly residents who had fewer visitors.

Friends contribute to health by providing all the functions of the family. In some cases, friends may be closer confidants than family members are. And people who are able to build close relationships with friends have greater health protection against stress.[60]

A study of working-class women in London demonstrates the point. Women who were under severe stress were much more likely to be depressed. The women who had close friendships still suffered stress, but the effects of the stress were four times less severe. In summing up the results of the study, researchers said that the difference was due to the "protective effect of confidants," and that those with fewer close friends were more vulnerable to both psychiatric and physical illness.

In one of the Johns Hopkins studies, researchers developed an inkblot test and a method for scoring it. They then showed more than 1,000 graduates the test and evaluated them psychologically based on test results. In the ensuing years, the graduates who developed cancer were the ones who were withdrawn. The ones who remained cancer-free were judged to be congenial, more easily able to interact with others and make friends, and better able to express affection to their friends.[61]

Types of Friends

Judith Viorst has categorized friends by the five different functions they fulfill in our lives:

1. *Convenience friends.* These are the neighbors or the office mates with whom we exchange pleasantries. We engage in "pleasant chitchat," but don't really share our intimate feelings with them. They are important enough to us that we want to keep up a pleasant face with them. We might occasionally ask them for help—such as with a carpool—but don't lean on them for intense support in times of need.

2. *Special-interest friends.* With these friends we share some interest or activity: members of the bowling team, someone we meet on Saturdays for a game of tennis, the people in a ceramics class. We do things with these people, but we don't share our feelings with them.

3. *Historical friends.* These are people with whom we have been close at one time or another, but because of any of a number of reasons, we've drifted apart. We enjoy an occasional telephone call with these friends, perhaps exchange Christmas cards or other infrequent correspondence, and maybe even meet for occasional nostalgic reunions. These friends are important—not because they offer ongoing support, but because they help us maintain a link with the past.

4. *Cross-generational friends.* This type of friendship is between members of different generations. It could be an eighteen-year-old neighbor who used to babysit your children or an elderly man on the corner who brings you bags of tomatoes and onions from his garden. These friendships can be close, and even

intimate, but they don't usually provide intensive support. There's almost always an inequality involved: The older partner usually gives advice, and the younger one is expected to take it.

5.   *Close friends.* These are the gems—the friends we see the most often, the people who are most important to us. They are the ones in whom we confide our deepest feelings, the ones we see and talk with most often, and the ones whose advice and confidence are most important to us. They are the ones who provide the greatest protection from illness and premature death.[62]

Close friendships seem more common among women than among men. Friendship patterns tend to vary a little, too: Women have closer friendships with other women and fewer friendships with men, whereas men tend to have closer friendships with other women. There could be a variety of reasons, but researchers think it might have to do with the confiding nature of women. A variety of studies have shown that conversations with women tend to do more to relieve loneliness for members of both sexes. Women's conversations are generally more pleasant, more intimate, tend to involve more self-disclosure, and are likely to be more meaningful than the conversations of men.[63]

Specific Health Benefits of Friends

One loneliness study found that female students visited their physicians less often if they had close contacts with good friends. If the women had friends who were pleasant, intimate, and encouraged them to confide, they had a considerably lower rate of illness than women students with fewer close friends.[64]

Friends can also help buffer the effects of stress—and it's well established that stress can make people sick. Friends help one to weather stress. From the results of two separate studies, researchers believe the harmful consequences of stress can be "significantly reduced through an active network of friends and relatives."[65] Based on studies, psychologists and other researchers say that people with a number of close friends and confidants, people with a "high capacity for intimacy," and people who can openly discuss their deepest feelings are better able to cope with stress in general. Whereas stress overwhelms and exhausts some, people with friends tend to be challenged and stimulated instead.

Good friends can even help alleviate the stress of something as serious as layoffs and unemployment. When a manufacturing plant shut down, researchers looked at the health effects on 100 married men who no longer had jobs. Those who had few friends and felt that they had little support from their wives became ill. Those who felt support from their wives and relatives and who had a strong network of close friends fared much better: They suffered less depression, had less illness, and had lower levels of cholesterol than their former coworkers.[66]

Lillian B. Rubin, a psychologist who has studied the health benefits of friends, says that "people who have others with whom they can communicate about the tensions in their lives often find relief for those tensions." Other psychologists agree—and some go so far as to say that a good friend who is willing to listen in confidence is as good as professional counseling when facing a problem.[67]

Focus on Research

Probably one of the best examples of the health benefits of close friends is provided by Japanese culture. Dr. Leonard Syme, an epidemiologist with the School of Public Health at the University of California at Berkeley, has spent years studying the health of Japanese immigrants to the United States. What he found puzzled researchers at first—and then served as a brilliant demonstration of the health benefits of close friends.

Japan has both the good and bad features of an advanced, industrialized nation in the twentieth century, and by all accounts, its residents should have more than their share of health problems. According to Syme, air pollution is "horrendous" in and around the large cities. Smoking is widespread. The diet includes highly pickled foods. The pace of life in the great urban centers is as hectic as in any American city—in fact, six-day work weeks are common. All the earmarks of severe stress are present. Yet, the Japanese have among the highest life expectancies in the world.

Researchers were puzzled. At first, they proposed that the Japanese had some sort of genetic superiority. But that notion was quickly abandoned when they studied Japanese who had moved to the United States. Those who arrived on American shores, adopted American lifestyles, and started eating like Americans began dying from heart disease and cancer at the same rate as native-born Americans—and it all happened within a single generation.

Then researchers noticed that some Japanese who immigrated to America were smoking heavily and eating the high-fat foods characteristic in American diets—but they were escaping the diseases and the premature deaths we suffered as a result. After studying 17,000 Japanese—both here and in Japan—researchers concluded that Japan's emphasis on "the group" was the key to health and long life. Traditionally, Japanese are very tied to family and friends; they honor and respect their elderly, and they place a high priority on developing life-long friendships.

It was the Japanese in this country who retained their culture —who used the language, generally resisted Westernization, and kept tightly-knit group ties and friendships—who did so well healthwise. Those who kept close to their life-long friends and their families had significantly lower incidences of heart disease, cancer, and diseases of all kinds. Surprisingly, other factors, such as genetic traits, age, gender, social class, and even health habits, seemed to have little effect, especially when compared with the factor of keeping their Japanese friendships alive.

Source: Steven Locke and Douglas Colligan, *The Healer Within* (New York: E.P. Dutton, 1986), pp. 88–90.

Friendship protects health because it provides a natural outlet for confiding feelings to others. Researchers have found that openly discussing a traumatic event with someone else—such as a friend—can actually improve physical health even when the traumatic event occurred many years previous.[68] In his research, Southern Methodist University psychologist James Pennebaker found that immune system function is boosted by confiding upsetting events. And the health benefits of confiding in a friend are long-lasting: Pennebaker's research shows that immune function improvement lasts as long as six weeks afterward![69]

According to a study conducted by the California Department of Mental Health, close, confiding personal relationships—good friends—have been found to buffer not only the stress from life's major changes (such as death of a loved one), but from life's daily hassles as well. People in crisis—whether from a major life change or from an accumulation of daily hassles—have higher morale, fewer physical symptoms, and less illness if they have support from and contact with close friends.[70]

In addition to the factor of social support, friends may help protect health because they are familiar. They are comforting because we are used to them. What is familiar is often less threatening because it seems more predictable and manageable.

Experiments with animals have proved the point. Those who have the benefit of the familiar are able to withstand the effects of stress; those who don't are crippled by it. In one of a series of animal experiments, researchers induced coronary occlusions—blockages of the heart arteries—in a group of pigs. Researchers then randomly split the group of pigs in half. One group of pigs was housed in a laboratory and tended by staff members with whom the pigs were familiar. These staff members were, in essence, friends. None of the pigs in the group suffered lethal, irregular contractions of the heart muscle—contractions that would have been expected following the inducement of coronary occlusions. The pigs in the other group were housed in a new, unfamiliar laboratory and were tended by strangers—laboratory crew members they had never seen before. Many of those pigs suffered fatal arrhythmias of the heart.[71]

Other experiments proved the same thing. At the UCLA School of Medicine, researchers tried to create high blood pressure in mice by severely overcrowding them in their cages. Only the mice that were surrounded by strange mice—mice with whom they were unfamiliar—developed the high blood pressure the researchers expected. The mice surrounded by litter mates and other familiar mice had little trouble adjusting to the crowded conditions and did not develop high blood pressure.[72]

The Importance of Pets

Research into the health benefits of pet ownership has shown beyond a doubt that comfort does not always have to come only from people.[73] There are an estimated 100 million pets in the United States—pets who are sheltered, groomed, petted, talked to, babied, and showered with toys. More than half of all American homes have one or more pets. Those pets may return a health benefit to the owners who care for them.

According to research,[74] pets fulfill a variety of needs for their human owners. They provide a chance for interaction with another living thing and fulfill the natural craving for emotional relationships. They provide for our need to care and our desire to be loved. As anyone who owns a pet knows, they also give love in return.

The discovery that pets benefit health came quite by accident at first and was due to three landmark events. The first occurred in 1959, when New York child psychiatrist Boris Levinson happened to have his dog Jingles with him when a patient paid an unexpected visit. The young patient had been withdrawn and isolated, and had failed to respond to repeated attempts of help. Jingles suddenly ran up to the boy and licked his face. The child broke out of his usual withdrawal and started to play with the dog. Levinson began using pets as a way to break the ice with his young patients.[75]

The second landmark event also occurred quite by accident. In the mid 1970s, Ohio State University psychologist Samuel A. Corson kept a kennel of dogs on the grounds for use in his research. When mental patients in an adjoining hospital heard the dogs barking, they insisted on seeing the dogs. They began to visit, they developed relationships filled with trust and affection, and as a result were able to trust their physicians and make great progress in their treatment.[76]

The final landmark event in pet studies occurred in 1980 when University of Pennsylvania researchers Aaron Katcher and Erika Friedmann found that people with pets lived longer after experiencing heart attacks than those without pets. Subsequent research has shown that among people who have heart attacks, pet owners have one-fifth the death rate of those who do not have pets.[77]

The benefits of pet ownership even extend to a population that is traditionally the most prone to health problems: the elderly. A study by Judith M. Siegel and her colleagues at UCLA followed 1,000 Medicare enrollees for 1 year. The elderly were interviewed at the beginning of the study and then every two months throughout the year of the study. In addition, they were assessed for psychological distress at six months and twelve months. Siegel found that more than one-third of the people involved in the study owned pets—cats, dogs, birds, and fish.[78]

She found that pet owners enjoyed better health and had fewer visits to the doctor than did those without pets. Even among those under the most stress during the year of the study, the pet owners had 16 percent fewer physician visits.

Of interest was the finding that the greatest benefit seemed to come from dog ownership—perhaps because those who owned dogs "spent more time outdoors with them, spent more time talking to them, felt more attached to them, and, during the course of the study, had fewer physician contacts than other pet owners."[79] Researchers found that even the most highly stressed dog owners in the study had 21 percent fewer physician contacts than people without pets.[80]

People who own pets have better health, recover more quickly from all kinds of illness and surgery, and live longer lives than those who don't have pets. As the title of Shelley Levitt's article says, "Pet Two Poodles and Call Me in the Morning."[81]

Why Pets Benefit Health

Pets, among other things, alleviate loneliness. They provide companionship. They make us feel safe. They help us feel calm. No matter what else may happen around us, they are a constant amid the change. And they can exert an overall good influence. University of California at Davis researchers found that elderly people with pets enjoyed not only an improvement in their well-being, but worked actively to improve their overall living conditions, too.[82]

As mentioned, the first notice of the health benefits of pets on a scientific level was quite by accident. A team of medical researchers from the University of

Maryland and the University of Pennsylvania designed and carried out a study between 1977 and 1979 to determine how social conditions affect heart disease. They delved into the backgrounds and living conditions of people who had been hospitalized with heart disease. They checked out income, marital status, lifestyle, and a number of other "social" factors. A year after the patients were released from the hospital, researchers followed up to see which ones were still alive. They also did detailed computer analyses to figure out which factors had helped keep those patients alive.

People who owned pets had fared much better than people who didn't. In fact, three times as many of the nonowners had died in the year since they had been released from the hospital![83]

The Cardiovascular System

One of the studies almost exactly duplicated the initial, accidental study. At the University of Pennsylvania's Center for Interaction of Animals and Society, researchers studied ninety-two patients who had been hospitalized for coronary disease. Those with pets had one-third the death rate of the people who did not have pets. In that study, researchers discovered one possible reason for the coronary survivals: Patients actually had lower heart rates when they were with their pets. Friedmann maintains that's an important result because "even small reductions in the heart rate repeated thousands of times per week could provide direct health benefits by decreasing the frequency of arterial damage, and thus slowing the arteriosclerotic process. The results of this research may have important implications for middle-aged and elderly individuals with a variety of stress-related chronic diseases."[84] Subsequent research at Brooklyn College showed that pets do, indeed, slow the heart rate—even among high-stressed, high-intensity Type A personalities.

Pets have another important effect on the cardiovascular system: They help reduce blood pressure. In a number of studies, pets of all kinds have been shown to lower blood pressure. Petting a dog decreased blood pressure among healthy college students, hospitalized elderly, and adults with hypertension. The blood pressure of bird owners dropped an average of ten points when they were talking to their birds. Watching fish in an aquarium brought blood pressure to below resting levels.[85]

One of the least sterile and most clinical studies was carried out by researcher James Lynch in the recreation room of his home—and with the help of his three children. For the study, Lynch and his kids invited neighborhood children to come over and read in the recreation room. Each child's blood pressure was measured both while sitting quietly and while reading aloud—and both while alone and while a dog was in the room. The kids had lower blood pressure while the dog was in the room, whether they were sitting quietly or reading aloud. The dog seemed to be what made the difference.[86]

People in hospitals, including mental hospitals, recover more completely and more quickly and are discharged sooner if they have pets waiting for them at home. The patients might feel a responsibility for the pet and want to get home to resume caring for the pet. Some hospitals have started allowing pets to visit patients, a practice that has been found to speed recovery. Swedish-American Hospital in Rockford, Illinois, initiated use of a "pet visiting room," where pets can be brought to visit their hospitalized owners. Researchers in charge of the project have found that visits from pets calm the patient, boost patient morale, and improve and speed post-surgical recovery.[87] Many believe that for the patients the pet represents an important source of companionship and love and an alleviation of loneliness. And study results still point to the effect of reducing blood pressure.

Effects of reducing blood pressure have been most profound among elderly people and children, even though it seems to work regardless of age. In one experiment, children at the University of Pennsylvania School of Veterinary Medicine were brought into a room and interviewed by a stranger. The reaction of the children was predictable: They experienced stress, and their blood pressure increased. When a friendly dog was brought into the room, the children relaxed and their blood pressure dropped.[88]

There is probably a medical reason and explanation, says researcher Aaron Katcher, associate professor of psychiatry at the University of Pennsylvania:

> *Companion animals, in particular, provide an access to intimacy. You talk to your pet more slowly, you smile a great deal, voice tones become gentle, the cadence of speech changes. It's a much more relaxed dialogue, characterized by a combination of touching and talking. Pets exert a calming influence throughout the day, which probably has a lot to do with the blood pressure–lowering effects. In the patients we've studied so far, a 12 to 15 percent drop in blood pressure has been recorded in the presence of pets. In fact, anything that turns your attention outward to the natural environment around you is a powerful way of controlling tension, thereby lowering blood pressure.*[89]

Stress

Pets also help alleviate the effects of stress. To test that notion, researchers at the University of Oklahoma decided to try it against one of life's most stressful situations: the death of a spouse. Researchers compared two groups of recent widows; one group had pets and the other did not. The two groups were studied to see how they responded in terms of physical complaints, lifestyles, interactions with others, and feelings toward self. The widows with pets did "significantly" better than the widows who did not have pets. Those with pets were healthier, had fewer illnesses and physical complaints, and were able to interact with others better. The widows without pets had more persistent fears, headaches, and feelings of panic—and they tended to take more medications than did the pet owners.[90]

In another study, psychologists Karen M. Allen and James J. Blascovich of the State University of New York at Buffalo, gave forty-five women a challenge that's often used in the laboratory to create stress—performing mental arithmetic. The women had to rapidly count backwards by threes from a four-digit number. During the test, the researchers measured the women's pulse rate, blood pressure, and electrical skin conductance—all measures that can indicate how stressed someone is feeling.

What happened? The women who had a human friend at their side during the test had poor performance and a lot of stress. But the women who had their pet dogs at their side during the test did much better on the arithmetic—and they did it with lower blood pressure and fewer other physical responses to stress.[91]

Pet-Facilitated Therapy

Pets have been shown to have such a benefit on both physical and mental health that they are now being used in a whole new field of therapy called pet-facilitated therapy. They are being used with hospitalized patients, with mental patients, with the elderly in convalescent centers, and even in prisons.

In one of the most successful programs of its kind, social worker David Lee of Lima State Hospital for the Criminally Insane in Ohio introduced small animals—fish, parakeets, and so on—to the prisoners as "mascots." Among the prisoners were murderers, rapists, and others who had committed violent crimes. Allowing the criminals to care for the animals almost completely stopped fighting among prisoners and suicide attempts.[92]

Notes

1. Louise Bernikow, *Alone in America* (New York: Harper & Row, Publishers, 1986).

2. Joan Borysenko, *Fire in the Soul* (New York: Warner Books, 1993), p. 83.

3. "Loneliness: A Healthy Approach," *Longevity*, April: 1990, 22.

4. Boris Blai, "Health Consequences of Loneliness: A Review of the Literature," *JACH*, 37: 1989, 162.

5. Blai.

6. Emrika Padus, *The Complete Guide to Your Health and Your Emotions* (Emmaus, Pennsylvania: Rodale Press, 1986).

7. Blai, p. 163.

8. Robert Ornstein and David Sobel, *Healthy Pleasures* (Reading, Massachusetts: Addison-Wesley Publishing Company, Inc., 1989), pp. 222–223.

9. Padus.

10. Padus.

11. Larry Dossey, *Meaning and Medicine: A Doctor's Tales of Breakthrough and Healing* (New York: Bantam Books, 1991), pp. 71–72.

12. Bernikow.

13. Barbara Powell, *Alone, Alive and Well* (Emmaus, Pennsylvania: Rodale Press, 1985).

14. Brent Q. Hafen and Kathryn J. Frandsen, *People Need People: The Importance of Relationships to Health and Wellness* (Evergreen, Colorado: Cordillera Press, Inc., 1987).

15. Marc Pilisuk and Susan Hillier Parks, *The Healing Web* (Hanover, New Hampshire: The University Press of New England, 1986).

16. Pilisuk and Parks.

17. Carin Rubenstein and Phillip Shaver, "Are You Lonely? How to Find Intimacy, Love, and Happiness," *Shape*, August: 1987, 72.

18. Rubenstein and Shaver, p. 75.

19. Hafen and Frandsen, pp. 29–31.

20. Dossey, p. 70.

21. Hafen and Frandsen.

22. Bernikow.

23. Bernikow.

24. Hafen and Frandsen, p. 32.

25. Hafen and Frandsen, p. 33.

26. Bernikow.

27. Dossey, p. 94.

28. James J. Lynch, *The Broken Heart: Medical Consequences of Loneliness* (New York: Basic Books, Inc., Publishers, 1977).

29. Henry Dreher, "The Type C Connection: A Powerful New Tool in the Fight Against Cancer," presented to the National Institute for the Clinical Application of Behavioral Medicine, December 1992.

30. Lynch.

31. Pilisuk and Parks.

32. Pilisuk and Parks.

33. "Lack of Social Relationships Increases Risk of Illness and Death," *The Wellness Newsletter*, November/December: 1988, 4.

34. "Lack of Social Relationships," p. 5.

35. Robert Ornstein and David Sobel, *The Healing Brain* (New York: Simon and Schuster, 1987), pp. 195–196.

36. Ornstein and Sobel.

37. Ornstein and Sobel.

38. Bruce Bower, "Emotional Aid Delivers Labor-Saving Results," *Science News*, 139: 1991, 277.

39. Sharon Faelten, David Diamond, and the Editors of *Prevention* Magazine, *Take Control of Your Life: A Complete Guide to Stress Relief* (Emmaus, Pennsylvania: Rodale Press, 1988), p. 58.

40. Frances Sheridan Goulart, "How to Live a Longer, Healthier Life," n.p., n.d.

41. "Lack of Social Relationships," p. 4.

42. Nan Silver, "Lonely Child, Sick Adult?" *American Health*, April: 1986, 20.

43. Barbara R. Sarason, Irwin G. Sarason, and Gregory R. Pierce, *Social Support: An Interactional View* (New York: John Wiley & Sons, Inc., 1990), p. 256; and J. Stephen Heisel, Steven E. Locke, Linda J. Kraus, and R. Michael Williams, "Natural Killer Cell Activity and MMPI Scores of a Cohort of College Students," *American Journal of Psychiatry* 143: 1986, 1382–1386 .

44. Janice Kiecolt-Glaser and Ronald Glaser, "Q & A," *Medical Aspects of Human Sexuality*, 19(12): 1985, 56–57.

45. "Depression and Immunity," *Harvard Medical School Mental Health Letter*, n.d., p. 8.

46. Blair Justice, "Think Yourself Healthy," *Prevention*, May: 1988, 27–32, 102, 107.

47. Alix Kerr, "Hearts Need Friends," from *Physician's Weekly*, n.d.

48. "Social Isolation Tied to Heart Attack Deaths," *Deseret News*, May 1: 1988, A10.

49. The Editors of *Prevention* Magazine, *Positive Living and Health: The Complete Guide to Brain/Body Healing and Mental Empowerment* (Emmaus, Pennsylvania: Rodale Press, 1990), p. 154.

50. Rolf Bang Olsen, Jorn Olsen, Finn Gunner-Svensson, and Bodil Waldstrom, "Social Networks and Longevity: A 14-Year Follow-up Study Among Elderly in Denmark," *Social Science Medicine*, 33(10): 1189–1195

51. Lynch.

52. Lynch.

53. Lynch.

54. Lynch.

55. Bernikow.

56. Eleanor Smith, "Fighting Cancerous Feelings," *Psychology Today*, May: 1988, 22–23.

57. Michael Argyle, *The Psychology of Happiness* (New York: Methuen and Company, Ltd., 1987).

58. Sheldon Cohen and S. Leonard Syme, *Social Support and Health* (Orlando, Florida: Academic Press, Inc., 1985).

59. Cohen and Syme.

60. Leonard A. Sagan, *The Health of Nations* (New York: Basic Books, Inc., Publishers, 1987).

61. Dan Zevin, "Blotting Out Cancer with a Smile," *Health*, May: 1987, 14.

62. Sagan.

63. Argyle.

64. Argyle, pp. 182–183.

65. Padus, p. 85.

66. Blair Justice, *Who Gets Sick: Thinking and Health* (Houston, Texas: Peak Press, 1987), p. 133.

67. Faelten and Diamond, p. 272.

68. J. W. Pennebaker, et al., *Psychosomatic Medicine*, 51: 1989, 577.

69. Sarah Hoying, "Confess for Your Health?" *Self*, September: 1990, 96.

70. Faelten and Diamond, p. 273.

71. Justice, *Who Gets Sick*, pp. 139–140.

72. Justice, *Who Gets Sick*, p. 140.

73. Robert Ornstein and Charles Swencionis, *The Healing Brain: A Scientific Reader* (New York: The Guilford Press, 1990), p. 93.

74. Andrew G. Goliszek, *Breaking the Stress Habit* (Winston-Salem, North Carolina: Carolina Press, 1987), p. 150.

75. Editors of *Prevention* Magazine, p. 298.

76. Ornstein and Sobel, p. 229.

77. Ornstein and Sobel.

78. *Journal of Personality and Social Psychology,* June 1990.

79. "Pet Ownership Reduces Stress and Physician Visits Among Elderly," *Healthline*, October: 1990, 8, originally cited by the American Psychological Association.

80. *Journal of Personality and Social Psychology.*

81. Title of an article by Shelley Levitt in *50 Plus,* July: 1988, 56–61.

82. Editors of *Prevention* Magazine, p. 157.

83. Lynne Lohmeier, "The Healing Power of Pets," *East / West*, June: 1988, 52.

84. Leavitt, p. 57.

85. Lohmeier, p. 58.

86. Ornstein and Sobel, p. 166.

87. Editors of *Prevention* Magazine, p. 235.

88. Hafen and Frandsen, p. 78.

89. Padus, p. 604.

90. Padus, pp. 660–661.

91. Bruce Bower, "Stress Goes to the Dogs," *Science News*, 140: 1992, 285.

92. Karen M. Allen, "The Human-Animal Bond," *Insights*, n.d., p. 5.

14

MARRIAGE AND HEALTH

To be happy at home is the ultimate result of all ambition
—SAMUEL JOHNSON

Marriage—a good one, that is—can help protect people from illness and disease, help them bounce back more quickly if they do get sick, and even help people live longer! If current research is accurate, divorced people and those who are unhappily married don't fare nearly as well in terms of health and long life.

According to the latest census figures, marriage demographics have changed dramatically over the last decade. Today, 23 million adults live alone, and married couples make up the smallest percentage of the nation's households in two centuries—only 55 percent of the nation's households include married couples. "Nonfamily" households make up 30 percent of the nation's households; 85 percent of them are single, and the rest are roommates, unmarried heterosexual couples, and gay couples.[1]

The Health Hazards of Divorce

Divorce rates have been on a roller coaster in this country since the end of World War I, when family life was pretty stable and the divorce rate was relatively low. Following World War II, when soldiers started coming back from the war, the divorce rate soared—temporarily. For a period of time after WWII, the divorce rates fell back to their prewar level. Since the postwar period, divorce rates have steadily increased—from about 10 percent in the early 1950s to a rate that approaches 50 percent today. In one disturbing trend, increasing numbers of couples are ending longtime marriages. The percentage of divorces among people over the age of sixty-five more than doubled in the past two decades. Research associate professor Marjorie A. Pett of the University of Utah pinpointed five basic reasons for divorce among older couples: They had grown apart and no longer shared dreams; they had personal differences; there was an extramarital relationship; the couples had poor communication; and the marriage was plagued by financial difficulty.

Overall, as a country, the United States has the highest divorce rate in the world.[2]

According to statistics, the parents of more than 1 million children divorce in the United States every year.[3] Those same statistics tell us that 30 percent of America's white children and 40 percent of black children spend at least part of their formative years in postdivorce, single-parent families. More than 90 percent of all postdivorce children live with their mother—and only one in three children see their noncustodial parent as often as once a month.

Increasingly, children are being subjected to a second divorce during their childhood. In fact, statistics from the 1980 census indicate that a child born in 1983 will have a 40 percent chance of experiencing a parent's second divorce by the time he or she is eighteen years old. The custodial parent of more than 70 percent of all white children involved in divorce remarries within five years—and more than half of those divorce a second time.[4] According to researchers, the children of these "twice-divorced parents are often seriously disturbed."[5]

Effects on the Children

The effect of divorce on children is perhaps a good starting point in the discussion of how divorce impacts health because it is often the children who suffer the most profoundly. And the suffering is long-lasting as well as deep, according to a study that followed more than 100 children for fifteen years following their parents' divorce.[6]

Researcher Ann S. Masten points out:

A stressful event rarely occurs in isolation. Divorce is not a single event, but a series of related events embedded in the ongoing lives of people. It often occurs in the context of extreme family conflict and emotional crisis. It can precipitate recurrent financial problems and separations, custodial conflicts, changes of school, home, and daily routine. Above all, divorce can be so devastating to the parents that the children temporarily lose the most important protective factor in their lives, a healthy, well-functioning caregiver.[7]

The numbers of children affected by divorce and the profile of those caregivers have changed steadily over the past few decades. The number of one-parent families has more than doubled since 1978, and the percentage of children living in one-parent families rose from 12.9 to 25.7 percent in just fifteen years. Although the largest category of single-parent families is that headed by a divorced mother, the number of children living with the father alone has more than doubled since 1970.[8] Even children living in two-parent families are not immune from the stresses involved in divorce. Many are living with one parent who is not their natural parent. The often-hostile relationships that exist between stepparents and stepchildren are well known.

And parents of conventional two-parent families can't be too smug about their children being protected from the damaging consequences of divorce. With the increasing frequency and visibility of divorce, even children in stable families are anxious about the possibility of it affecting them.

A ten-year-old in New York saw the movie *Kramer vs. Kramer*, an emotional portrayal of a couple going through a divorce. A few days later her parents had a fight. "My mother walked out of the house," she remembers. "I thought to myself, 'This is it!' and cried and cried. But she had just gone next door to the neighbor's."[9] In the same study, a fifth-grader proudly told researchers that "we're one of those families that aren't divorced." After a pause, he added, ". . . at least, not yet."[10]

For children, divorce is one of the most disruptive life events possible—and it leads to changes in biological health. Children almost universally experience divorce as a profound personal, familial, and social loss.[11] In addition to health problems, most children involved in divorce suffer emotional and behavioral changes that can also impact health. Adding insult to injury, most divorced families end up with less affluence—forcing children along with the rest of the family to adjust to a whole new spectrum of reduced economic advantages.

In terms of financial loss, women suffer the most profoundly following a divorce. Studies show that a woman's standard of living declines an average of 73 percent in the first year after divorce. Income levels after divorce depend on how long a couple was married, too. Among those married less than ten years, women have only 51 percent of their former income, whereas men have 195 percent. Among those married ten to seventeen years, women have only 64 percent of their predivorce income, whereas men have 222 percent.[12]

There is a wide range of social, academic, and health problems associated with the children of divorce. They visit health clinics and physicians more often; some childhood cancer and other alterations in physical health as a result of injury have been strongly associated with divorce.[13] On the emotional side, children are prone to become depressed, aggressive, and to suffer regression in development; some develop psychosomatic disorders. Many adopt delinquent behavior. Boys especially seem to bear the brunt of divorce. Studies have shown that following a divorce, boys, more than girls, suffer from poor self-image, loss of self-concept, bed wetting, a sense of sorrow, below-average academic performance, anger, withdrawal, delinquent-like behavior, aggression, and frequent fighting.[14]

The propensity for school problems following divorce is well-established. Children of divorce are more likely to be lower achievers in school. Among two-parent children, 30 percent were ranked as high achievers and only 2 percent were ranked as low achievers. The figures do a complete turnaround when divorce enters the picture: Among one-parent children, only 1 percent are ranked as high achievers, and a dismal 40 percent are ranked as low achievers.[15]

There are other school problems, too. Children of divorce are more likely to be truant, late, and subject to disciplinary action at school. Absence rates are much higher. Most children involved in divorce attain less education than children of two-parent families, and studies show they are more than twice as likely to give up on school altogether.

Divorce is particularly damaging to a child's emotional and physical health if it involves a move. Moves have been implicated in "a variety of childhood disorders," and, coupled with the stress of a divorce, can be very damaging to a child. "For children especially," researchers say, "stable identification with a place and home seems to represent an important predictor of health."[16]

Effects on the Adults

Children aren't the only ones who face health risks following divorce. Every major study agrees that divorced people—and others who are separated from their spouses—experience more physical and mental illness than those who are married. Divorced people visit physicians significantly more often than do married or single people.[17] Through in-depth studies, divorce has been significantly related to depression,[18] alcoholism, increased traffic accidents, admission to psychiatric facilities, homicides, and death from disease in general.[19] According to research, divorce has the same impact on health as smoking a pack of cigarettes a day.[20] And most therapists agree that divorced people have higher rates of cancer, heart disease, pneumonia, high blood pressure, and accidental death than do married, single, or widowed persons.[21]

Many theories have been extended to explain why. Perhaps it is because a person who has just been through a divorce all too often loses a major source of protecting social support: the family. The family of origin may not approve of the divorce, or may be going through its own crises at the time, unable to spare the considerable emotional strength to be of real support. The difficulty of coping with divorce is considerable. According to one prominent researcher, new evidence suggests that divorce may be even more devastating to many people than losing a spouse to death, "since it's harder to accept that the relationship is really over."[22]

Various studies give insight into the specific health hazards of divorce. In one study, divorced Caucasian men under age seventy who live alone have twice the death rate from heart disease, stomach cancer, and cirrhosis of the liver, and three times the incidence of high blood pressure. James Lynch, who has done extensive research into the phenomenon of divorce and loneliness, says those facts are true for both men and women of all ages.[23]

Statistics from a variety of nations reveal a significantly higher death rate among divorced men and women than among the married. The divorced die much more frequently from suicide, homicide, and accidental death. The death rate among the divorced is also significantly higher for alcoholism, diabetes, tuberculosis, and lung cancer.[24]

Research has shown that divorce can actually compromise the immune system, which helps explain why there is an increase in illness and death among the divorced. Immune system compromise is especially apparent the first year following divorce. A study of divorced or separated women during the first year following divorce or separation showed that they had poor cellular immune function, a lower number of natural killer cells, and a deficit in their ability to fight disease with responsive lymphocytes.[25]

For some reason, divorce seems to have its most deleterious effects on men. Divorced men suffer significantly more disease and die in far greater numbers before the age of sixty-four than do their married counterparts. The statistics are sobering. Ten times as many die of tuberculosis; seven times as many die of pneumonia and are killed in homicides. More than twice as many die of heart disease, and almost three times as many die of lung cancer. More than twice as many die of complications of strokes, of cancer of the digestive system, and of high blood pressure. More than three times as many commit suicide, and almost eight times as many die of cirrhosis of the liver. Almost four times as many are killed in motor vehicle accidents.[26]

Dr. Robert Seagraves of the University of Chicago Medical School, points out:

It is difficult for happily married individuals to appreciate the extent of disruption caused by divorce. The individual has lost a social network as well as a spouse. Typically, close friends of married couples are themselves married, and many of these friendships are lost following divorce. The divorced individual reenters the world of dating, feeling rusty in middle age, and facing the same insecurities experienced as a teenager.[27]

Studies show that in all psychiatric hospitals, divorced people are overrepresented—and married people are underrepresented. Risks of disease in almost every category soar with divorce. And, apparently, divorce even affects longevity—clearly evidenced by the fact that the state of Nevada had the second highest death rate from all causes in the United States during the years when it was the divorce center of the country.[28]

The Divorced versus the Unhappily Married

New evidence shows that unhappily married people may be the worst off in terms of good health and long life! United Press International recently reported on a collection of studies indicating that among those married in the mid-1970s who are still married, only about one-third are still happy with their spouses. Those studies indicate that women are more unhappy than men, and blacks are less happy than whites. "The outlook for the institution of marriage is bleak," reports the University of Texas sociologist who compiled the study results. And, he says, the study results say "something very negative about marriage"—or at least about the state of the nation's marriages.[29]

Research results from a number of cross-sectional studies are all showing that unhappily married people have poorer health than their single counterparts—even the ones who are divorced. Apparently, a major variable in marriage and health is happiness: It isn't just being married that gives you a better chance of being psychologically well-adjusted and physically healthier, but being *happily* married.[30] According to research, unhappily married people are, healthwise, worse off than anyone else.[31]

Studies now offer preliminary evidence that actual physical changes occur during marital conflict. According to researchers at Stanford University, blood pressure is strongly correlated to positive and negative interactions: During positive interactions, blood pressure is lower, but during negative interactions—fights—it can skyrocket.[32] Similar research at the University of Washington and the University of California at Berkeley show that marital conflict affects the heart rate, pulse, and skin resistance.[33]

New studies show that marital fights actually weaken the immune system (especially in women), raise blood pressure, and speed up heart rate. For women, simply *discussing* their angry feelings leads to these stressed-out body reactions. For men, the stress seems to accompany the act of talking louder and faster.

In one study, researchers brought ninety newlywed couples into the laboratory—those you would normally expect to have the least amount of conflict. The researchers gave each couple a role-play and asked them to resolve the disagreement involved. Interestingly, researchers noted a number of hostile behaviors—including criticizing, denying responsibility, interrupting, disagreeing, making excuses, and trying to coerce each other into accepting their point of view—even among what researchers considered to be *mild* disputes.[34]

Scientists monitored the couples' blood continuously for the next twenty-four hours to determine immune response, including measures of natural killer cells, which fight off infection.

"There was a far stronger effect on the immune system than we ever anticipated," said psychologist Janice Kiecolt-Glaser and immunologist Ronald Glaser, both of Ohio State University. "Those couples who expressed the most hostility during the discussions showed a drop of eight measures [of immunity] for the next twenty-four hours."[35]

In reporting on a large study conducted by the Human Population Laboratory of the California Department of Public Health, researchers believe that in terms of health and longevity, it's better to be single than unhappily married. Unhappy marriage has been implicated in a number of specific health problems by teams of researchers who have studied large groups of people. Coronary disease is among the most prevalent among the unhappily married. In one revealing study, researchers screened 10,000 Israeli men before any symptoms of coronary heart disease had appeared. They then observed this population for five years. The men who later had a myocardial infarction reported far more dissatisfaction with their marital life than those men who remained healthy.[36]

Separate studies seem to confirm these findings. Patients with coronary heart disease reported far more frequent dissatisfaction in their marriages than did those without heart disease—and they reported far more marital problems. A series of recent reports has revealed a trend: The occurrence of marital dissatisfaction and a sense of personal rejection stemming from unhappy marriage is the apparent trigger for a surprising number of acute myocardial infarctions.

Psychologist Vicki Helgeson of Carnegie-Mellon University found in a recent study that male cardiac patients were far less prone to follow-up heart attacks if they were able to discuss matters easily with their wives. Married men in the study who reported poor communication with their wives fared even worse than those who were not married. According to Helgeson, "the strong influence of *good* marriages has caused a general misappraisal of marriage's role in preserving health. A poor marriage may be worse than none at all."[37]

Marital problems apparently can also drive up blood pressure. Researchers at the Department of Psychology at the University of Michigan and at the university's School of Public Health studied almost 700 men and women for twelve years.[38] They found that people with unhappy marriages—especially those who can't easily express their anger—are at *twice* the risk of death. One key appears to be the way they deal with anger and conflict. Those who suppress anger suffer the greatest consequence of all among the unhappily married. The risks of high blood pressure are greatest for women between the ages of forty-five and sixty-nine, who are the most likely to suppress their anger, and for unhappily married women between the ages of thirty and forty-four, who are apt to feel guilty about expressing anger toward their husbands.

Those who are unhappily married are at a much higher risk for all kinds of illness. A reason could be reduced functioning in the immune system.[39]

Interestingly, preliminary data from new research shows that women may bear the greatest health brunt of unhappy marriages. Psychologist Robert W. Levenson of the University of California at Berkeley studied married couples to determine the health effects of unhappiness in marriage. In Levenson's study, there was no correlation between unhappiness in marriage and the well-being of the husbands. On the other hand, the wives in those unhappy marriages suffered from anxiety, depression, and other stress-related illnesses.

In commenting on the study, psychologist Lynn Fainsilber Katz said that our culture makes emotional work "more of a woman's job. Women take on more of the responsibility for regulating the marriage, and in a distressed marriage, this takes a toll."[40]

Finally, marital satisfaction has a real bearing on not just physical, but also mental health. Researchers have found a definite relationship between depression and dissatisfaction with one's marriage.[41] In a study on depression conducted by the National Institute of Mental Health, 15,000 adults were given personality surveys and other tests that helped determine their level of depression. Only 2.4 percent of single men and 3.9 percent of single women reported major episodes of depression. But the figures changed drastically when researchers looked at those who were unhappily married: Almost one-fifth of all unhappily married men and nearly half of all unhappily married women had major episodes of depression.[42]

In a survey conducted several years ago by researchers at Vanderbilt University, sociologists quizzed 1,100 people nationwide about their feelings and followed up by giving these people personality tests. Those who said they were "not too happy" or "not at all happy" with their marriages were in poorer mental health than were people who were single, divorced, or widowed.[43]

Results of a separate study were the same: In the more than 5,000 people who were extensively studied, people who were unhappy or dissatisfied with their marriages were in poorer mental health than any of the people who were single—whether they had never married, had divorced, or had been widowed.

The Health Benefits of a Happy Marriage

The greatest benefits regarding health and long life come to those who are happily married. Those who are happily married seem healthier overall than any other group, according to government researchers with the National Center for Health Statistics. The Center, which recently completed a survey of 122,859 people in 47,240 families nationwide, found that married people have fewer health problems than unmarried people.[44] Charlotte Schoenborn, who was instrumental in conducting the study for the government, said that the results "demonstrate that in spite of the recent changes in American marital patterns, there is still a clear association between being well and being married."

Indeed, statistics dating back to the nineteenth century show that married couples have lower death rates from a whole range of diseases. Researchers with the Framingham Heart Study, which tracked the health of more than 5,000 people for more than three decades, reported that getting—and staying—married was a predictor for a long, healthy life.[45] According to one researcher, "studies consistently find that the married are in better mental and physical health than the unmarried. On the whole, married people live longer than the unmarried, and they make fewer demands on health care services."[46]

Why would being married help people be healthier and live longer? There are probably a number of factors at work—social, emotional, and economic, to name a few. One study sponsored by the Department of Health and Human Services showed that part of the reason why women, in particular, have better health when married is due to economic reasons. When married, women generally have access to income in excess of personal income, home ownership, and private health insurance.[47] And as research data come in, people who are studying the health effects of marriage believe it can probably be traced at least in part to the strong social support most people receive in marriage.[48] (That would help explain why unhappy marriages, in which social support would probably be absent, are not good protectors of health.)

That theory was borne from a study that followed up on more than one thousand fifty-five-year-olds in Scotland that explored which factors caused the married to live longer and have better health. The researchers considered four possible factors: the tendency of the married to have less stress, to have better material resources, to indulge in fewer risky behaviors, and to have better social support.

The factors that seemed to make the difference were better material resources and better social support. According to the researchers who conducted the study, "Married people benefit compared with nonmarried people in the availability, amount, and quality of the social support available to them."[49]

Social Support

Married couples are usually better integrated into the community than are single people. Although single people, especially in large cities, struggle to make friends and meet new people, married couples generally have a much easier time developing a strong social network. It may not be only the marriage, then, but the entire spectrum of social networking that is enhanced or made easier by marriage.

One researcher believes that the health benefits of married life might be because married people seem to follow through better—maybe because each partner has someone to remind him or her. Married couples, she says, have a tendency "to eat more balanced, regular meals or to be more willing to see a doctor when they suspect something's wrong. Maybe it's having someone around to nag them, but married couples also seem to follow through more completely on taking medicines than do singles."[50]

The health benefits of marriage also might be due to economic factors, as previously mentioned. Many married couples have the benefit of double incomes, and married couples are less likely than singles or single-parent families to be living at or below poverty levels. And statistics have established that the more money you make and the more educated you are, the more healthy you will generally be.[51]

The health benefits of marriage seem to be even greater for men than for women, as previously discussed. (Some studies, in fact, indicate that single women who have never married may fare almost as well as married women in terms of health and longevity.) One reason may be the nature of the friendships outside the marriage. A man's friendships are traditionally "situational"—men have friends at work, friends they fish with, sports buddies, and so on. Women's friendships, on the other hand, are traditionally much longer and more permanent, serving as a source of great emotional strength. Women, unlike men, tend to main-

---

Focus on Research

One program has been initiated by Dr. Bernard L. Bloom and his colleagues at the University of Colorado. Theirs is a six-month preventive program that involves newly separated men and women. Participants are offered training in competency skills in areas found to be particularly stressful for the newly separated— things such as social support, child rearing, housing and homemaking, employment, and legal and financial issues. In addition to providing a valuable network of social support, the program makes available experts who counsel the participants in their respective areas of specialty. Program representatives contact each participant every two weeks during the program.

In the initial group, follow-up interviews were conducted after six months, eighteen months, thirty months, and four years. In all, 153 separated people were involved in the first study by Bloom; 101 were assigned at random to the intervention group, and 52 were used as controls who received no counseling or training.

At the end of the initial session, after comparing the men and women who were helped with those who were not, Bloom reported, "The people in the intervention group . . . were in better physical health as well as psychological health than the people who were in the control group. There is no question in my mind that the program relieved stress and it relieved stress very early on."

Source: "Separate Lives," *Mind/Body/Health Digest*, 1(2): 1987, 2.

tain close confidants with whom they stay in regular contact after marriage. Friendships are important, even in marriage. Research shows that single people with strong networks of friends run fewer risks healthwise than do married people who are relatively isolated.

Social support and the socialization aspects of marriage may indeed play a strong role in health—and some researchers are trying to duplicate it or create a stronger social network for high-risk people, those who have separated or divorced. Results are lending credence to the belief that the social support of marriage is at least partially what helps keep marrieds healthy.

Injuries and Medical Insurance

According to the earlier-cited National Health Interview Survey, married people report fewer injuries per year than single and divorced people (but, interestingly, more than widowed people). The survey, which studied 122,859 Americans, showed that divorced people had "by far" the highest rate of injuries, with divorced women having more than twice as many as married women.[52]

The same survey showed an interesting trend about insurance: Married people are more likely to be insured than single people, probably—according to a National Center for Health Statistics researcher—because spouses "share each other's employment benefits."[53] According to the Center, about 84.5 percent of married women had private health insurance, compared with 66.9 percent of divorced women, 66.5 percent of widows, and 46.5 percent of those who were separated. According to government statisticians, women who are separated are the most likely to be uninsured—even though about 23 percent have public coverage, almost one-third are completely uninsured.

Marital status of parents also affects the health coverage of children. Approximately 80 percent of children who live with both parents are covered by private health insurance. Contrast that with children in single-parent families: Close to two-thirds of children living with their father only are covered by private health insurance, and fewer than one-half of children living with their mother only are covered. Even with public coverage taken into consideration, approximately 29 percent of the children living with fathers and 19.5 percent of the children living with mothers are completely uninsured.

Coronary Heart Disease/High Blood Pressure

Detailed studies conducted by several researchers have carefully compared deaths from coronary heart disease between people who are married and those who are single, widowed, and divorced. Marriage seems to be a definite protecting factor. Coronary heart disease deaths in the United States per 100,000 population are 176 among the married and 362 among the divorced. Death rates for single, divorced, and widowed individuals are significantly higher than the rates for married individuals; this holds true for coronary heart disease deaths among both men and women and for both whites and nonwhites. Marriage seems to provide an even greater protection for some groups: Divorced white men between the ages of twenty-five and thirty-four have 2.83 times higher death rate from coronary heart disease than do married men of the same age.[54]

One researcher who has specialized in the study of heart disease says that "the magnitudes of some of the increases in death rates in the nonmarried groups are most impressive, sometimes exceeding the married death rates by as much as five times. The differences are greatest at younger ages and tend to diminish somewhat with age. But *never* do the death rates of the unmarried groups *ever* fall below those for married individuals."[55]

And, the researcher adds, differences are sometimes even more pronounced. "The excess risk in the widowed under age thirty-five, compared to the married, was greater than tenfold for at least one of the specific age-sex groups, involving several leading causes of death, including arteriosclerotic heart diseases," a degenerative disease that can begin in childhood and that generally progresses very slowly throughout life. Bereavement and other emotions connected with the breakup of a marriage, the researcher says, can hasten the progress of arteriosclerotic heart disease—a disease that generally develops at an "imperceptibly slow pace" over the course of decades.[56]

Data from the Israel Ischemic Heart Disease Project[57] indicate another benefit of marriage in relationship to heart disease. Among men with angina, a wife's love and support appear to protect against the disease, particularly in men who also suffer from high levels of anxiety. University of Rochester School of Medicine researcher Thomas Campbell, in fact, believes that angina is an "illness behavior" rather than a sign of underlying coronary heart disease— and he says that statistics show it is much more common in unhappy marriages.[58]

As far as high blood pressure goes, married men and women are 20 percent less likely to have high blood pressure than people who are single, separated, divorced, or widowed.[59] Married men and women are also more likely to be aware of high blood pressure and to get help when they *do* develop it, according to researchers who studied a group of more than 4,000 people. In summing up the study, a University of Texas epidemiologist said, "Married people with high blood pressure were 59 percent more likely to be receiving treatment for it, and 78 percent more likely to have it under control."[60]

Cancer

Earlier research has shown that married people statistically have a lower incidence of cancer at many sites. Only recently, however, has careful study shown that marriage itself actually has an influence on survival rates from cancer.

In one energetic study, researchers collected data on 27,779 cases of cancer on file at the New Mexico Tumor Registry, part of the National Cancer Institute's surveillance program. All the cancer victims in the study were older than twenty years. Researchers did not consider cancers that were diagnosed only from a death certificate or autopsy, cancers on which there was incomplete information, or cancer patients with unknown marital status. Researchers wanted to find out how marital status affected the diagnosis, treatment, and survival of people who had been diagnosed with cancer.[61]

Marital status at the time of diagnosis was used in the study. Patients were coded as single (never married), currently married, divorced, separated, or widowed. Follow-up information and updated files were obtained from the patients' private physicians. At the time of the study, more than one-half of the patients had died; almost two-thirds of the patients who were still alive had been diagnosed more than five years earlier.

In analyzing the results, being unmarried was associated with decreased survival for patients diagnosed with cancer. And the percentage of persons surviving at least five years was greater for married persons than for unmarried persons in almost every category of age, gender, and stage of cancer. Being unmarried was associated with poorer survival at all stages of cancer. All three categories of unmarried people—single (never married), divorced/separated, and widowed—were more likely to develop cancers that had spread beyond a local site, were less likely to receive definitive treatment, and had poorer survival after the diagnosis of cancer.

Researchers point out that the improved survival rate of married persons might be because married people might have better health habits—and they are prone to seeking medical help at an earlier stage. As stated earlier, marriage also provides important social support, which is widely accepted as buffering the effects of many diseases. And, finally, researchers note that survival from cancer increases as socioeconomic status increases—probably because cancer victims with more money can seek earlier and better medical care and are not apt to delay treatment. As discussed earlier, married people tend to be in higher socioeconomic classes and are more likely to have health insurance coverage, which would lead to earlier medical care.

The most controversial finding of the study was this: Even when the disease was diagnosed at a more advanced stage, the best odds for survival seemed to lie with those who were married. James Goodwin, director of the study, summed it up by saying that "the protective impact of being married affected every stage of cancer care."[62]

"Treatment for cancer often involves frequent trips to the hospital for chemotherapy or radiation. If you're married, you're twice as likely to have help getting there, and to have support when your motivation is waning," said Dr. Goodwin. "Sometimes health care is complex, and if there's no one there to say, 'Hey, wait a minute—that doesn't make sense,' you may ignore information you don't quite understand."[63]

A separate study that had similar results involved researchers who combed through information at the M.D. Anderson Hospital and Tumor Institute in Houston, Texas. Researchers studied 910 married white women with breast cancer and 351 widowed white women with breast cancer. They considered a number of factors, such as how old the women were, what their socioeconomic status was, what stage the disease was in at the time of diagnosis, and whether the women delayed in seeking medical treatment. Again, marriage came out a winner: Widowed patients were less likely to survive than married patients with similar histories. According to the researchers, marital status was "the strongest predictor" of survival among the breast cancer patients.[64]

In still another study, Medical College of Wisconsin researcher James Goodwin showed that the married have much better cancer survival rates. The difference, he says, is probably due to social support and/or better financial conditions among the married, both of which can enable a married person to seek a higher quality of medical care.[65]

Immune System Function

A number of tests and several careful studies have shown that marriage helps keep the immune system strong—one possible reason why married people enjoy better health than their single, divorced, or widowed counterparts. According to measures of the immune system function—determined by blood tests that measure the level of immune cells in the bloodstream—married people fare the best. Next are singles—those who have never been married. Singles are followed by those who have been widowed. The group of people with the lowest immune system function are those who are divorced or separated.

Researchers at Ohio State University compared the immune function of thirty-eight separated or divorced women with that of thirty-eight married women. Their findings confirm the belief that a happy, stable marriage provides health benefits. Researchers found the following:

- Women within the first year of separation had significantly poorer immune function than very well-matched counterparts in the community who were married.
- Among the married women, those who described their marriage as better had better immune function.
- The longer separated or divorced women had been separated or divorced (the less they were still attached to their ex-husbands), the better their immune systems were working.[66]

A separate group of researchers at Ohio State University's College of Medicine decided to take a look at men with herpes, an infection that tends to directly mirror the strength of the immune system. (When the immune system is compromised, the herpes infection flares up; when the immune system is strong, the infection is kept in check.) All the men in the study had active herpes infection. All were given psychological and immunological tests, and researchers compared the married men with the ones who were separated or divorced.

Again, strong marriages were demonstrated to be the best protection as far as a boost in immune function. The researchers found that:

- The separated or divorced men were more anxious, depressed, and lonely than were their married counterparts—and, not surprisingly, their immune systems were significantly weaker.
- Among the married men, the ones who were happy with their marriages had the strongest immune functioning. Those who had unhappy or unsatisfying

relationships with their wives had higher levels of active herpes antibodies as well as lower ratios of T helper cells to suppressor cells.[67]

In another study, researchers studied women, comparing married women to divorced women. In tests measuring the strength of the immune system, the married women came out on top. Those who had been separated or divorced for less than a year—and were still attached to their ex-husbands—fared the worst.[68]

Mental Health

A growing body of evidence seems to indicate that the married are in better mental health than the unmarried—and that the married are happier, less likely to commit suicide, and less likely to be institutionalized for psychiatric illness.[69] Hosts of studies show that married people are less likely to have all kinds of mental disorders than the never married, separated, divorced, and widowed. Research shows that a man who has never married is 3.13 times more likely to have a mental disorder than is his married counterpart. Those who are widowed are more than twice as likely to have a mental disorder. But the most devastating risk is for a divorced man: He is more than five times as likely to have a mental disorder than is a married man of similar age and circumstance.[70] In this study, as in others, marriage seems to provide even greater protection to men than women: Single and widowed women are only about one and a half times as likely to have mental disorders as married women, and divorced women are nearly three times as likely to have mental disorders.[71]

Interestingly, recent studies show that the protective factor of marriage does not apply equally across ethnic lines. A study conducted by researchers in Hawaii compared four ethnic groups—white Americans, Japanese-Americans, Filipino-Americans, and native Hawaiians—to determine whether single people suffered more psychiatric symptoms than married people.[72]

The researchers concluded that marriage definitely seemed to provide protection from psychiatric symptoms among white Americans and native Hawaiians, but not among Japanese- and Filipino-Americans. Marriage simply did not seem to be as important to mental health among these two groups. There could be many reasons why, said the researchers, but a main, likely reason is that people in those cultures derive a great deal of good social support from sources outside of marriage.

People who are not married are also more likely to have alcoholism, sometimes considered a manifestation of mental illness. In a Swedish study of middle-aged men, researchers compared alcoholism rates between the married men in the study and the divorced men in the study. More than one-fourth of all the divorced men in the study were registered with the Social Services as having alcohol problems; only 5 percent of the married men were so registered.[73]

A great deal of marriage's protection probably has to do with the fact that it provides "instant" social support: People with a supportive spouse are much less likely to become depressed following stressful incidents in their lives. Among women with stress, almost half who get little or no support from their husbands become deeply depressed. When married women have a high level of support from their husbands, only about 10 percent become depressed.[74]

Marriage and Life Expectancy

As study results poured in, researchers reached the same conclusion: Happy marriage dramatically increases life expectancy. In fact, a man who marries can expect to automatically add about nine years and seven months to his life.[75] In one large-scale study of Swedish men, married men had a mortality rate of only 9 percent during the three years of the study; their divorced counterparts had a rate of 20 percent.[76]

One recent study of unmarried middle-aged men and women showed that they faced twice the risk of dying within ten years as did those still living with their spouses.[77] The study—which involved more than 7,600 people nationwide—was conducted by researchers at the University of California at San Francisco. They found a significant gap between the married and the unmarried—and divorce is a key factor in putting people at risk.

Marriage itself, they concluded, seems to be the key factor. "Of particular interest is that both men who live alone and those who live with someone other than a spouse are equally disadvantaged for survival," said epidemiologist Maradee Davis, who led the study. "The critical factor seems to be the presence of a spouse."[78]

Researchers agree: The unmarried have higher death rates from all causes of death. The differences are greatest at younger ages, and the differences are the most apparent among men. U.S. mortality rates for all causes of death are consistently higher for divorced, single, and widowed individuals of both sexes and all races.[79] In fact, according to one researcher who has specialized in the study of heart disease and other causes of death, some of the increased death rates in unmarried individuals are "astounding," rising as high as ten times the rates for married individuals of comparable ages.[80] The researcher sums up:

> *The overall death rate for divorced individuals in the United States is almost double that of married individuals. For every major cause of death, rates for divorced males range anywhere from two to six times higher than those of their married counterparts. Single and widowed males show similarly high death rates when compared to those who were married.*[81]

Notes

1. Mimi Hall, "Percentage of Marrieds Is Smallest in 200 Years," *USA Today,* June 11, 1991.

2. Leonard A. Sagan, *The Health of Nations* (New York: Basic Books, Inc., Publishers, 1987).

3. Neil Kalter, "Effects of Divorce on Boys Versus Girls," *Medical Aspects of Human Sexuality*, November: 1989, 26–34.

4. Kalter.

5. Sagan.

6. Judith Wallerstein and Sandra Blakeslee, "A Family Divided: Time Bombs of Divorce," *American Health*, June: 1989, 49–59.

7. Ann S. Masten, "Stress, Coping, and Children's Health," *Pediatric Annals*, 14(8): 1985, 544–547.

8. Sagan.

9. Sagan.

10. Sagan.

11. Sheldon Cohen and S. Leonard Syme, editors, *Social Support and Health* (London: Academic Press, Inc., 1985).

12. Kalter.

13. Cohen and Syme.

14. Kalter.

15. Sagan.

16. Cohen and Syme.

17. Barbara R. Sarason, Irwin G. Sarason, and Gregory R. Pierce, *Social Support: An Interactional View* (New York: John Wiley and Sons, 1990), p. 257.

18. Sarason et al.

19. Marc Pilisuk and Susan Hillier Parks, *The Healing Web* (Hanover, New Hampshire: The University Press of New England, 1986).

20. H. Morowitz, "Hiding in the Hammond Report," *Hospital Practice*, August: 1975, 35–39.

21. Bernie S. Siegel, *Love, Medicine, and Miracles* (New York: Harper and Row Publishers, 1986).

22. Siegel.

23. Brent Q. Hafen and Kathryn J. Frandsen, *People Need People: The Importance of Relationships to Health and Wellness* (Evergreen, Colorado: Cordillera Press, Inc., 1987), pp. 33–34.

24. R. Taylor Segraves, "Divorce and Health Problems," *Medical Aspects of Human Sexuality*, June: 1989, 106.

25. Sarason et al.

26. Hafen and Frandsen, p. 35.

27. Hafen and Frandsen, p. 85.

28. Barbara Powell, *Alone, Alive, and Well* (Emmaus, Pennsylvania: Rodale Press, 1985).

29. "Just 1 in 3 Married in '70s Is Still Contented," *Deseret News*, January 27, 1989.

30. Sarason et al., p. 258.

31. Powell.

32. Bonnie Burman and Gayla Margolin, "Marriage and Health," *Advances*, 6(4): 1989, 51–58.

33. Burman and Margolin.

34. *Psychosomatic Medicine*, 55: 1993, 395–409.

35. Linda Murray, "Mad Marriages: Arguing Your Way to Better Health," *Longevity*, October: 1993, 30.

36. James J. Lynch, *The Broken Heart: The Medical Consequences of Loneliness* (New York: Basic Books, Inc., Publishers, 1977).

37. "Communication with Spouse Reduces Cardiac Risk," *Brain/Mind and Common Sense*, 17(12): 1992, 1.

38. Sharon Faelten, David Diamond, and the Editors of *Prevention* Magazine, *Take Control of Your Life: A Complete Guide to Stress Relief* (Emmaus, Pennsylvania: Rodale Press, 1988), pp. 143–144.

39. Sarason et al.

40. Linda Murray, "Love and Longevity," *Longevity*, January: 1993, 56.

41. N. S. Jacobsen, A. Holtzworth-Monroe, and K. B. Schmaling, "Marital Therapy and Spouse Involvement in the Treatment of Depression, Agoraphobia, and Alcoholism," *Journal of Consulting/Clinical Psychology*, 1: 1989, 5–10.

42. Catherine Houck, "Uncovering the Secrets of Happiness," *Cosmopolitan*, n.d., pp. 236–240.

43. Powell.

44. "Marriage and Wellness Linked," *Deseret News*, November 15: 1988, 4A.

45. Carol Turkington, "Have You Hugged Your Immune System Today?" *Self*, October: 1988, 184.

46. Powell.

47. Beth A. Hahn, "Marital Status and Women's Health: The Effect of Economic Marital Acquisitions," *Journal of Marriage and the Family*, 55: 1993, 495–504.

48. Burman and Margolin.

49. Sally Wyke and Graeme Rod, "Compe-

ting Explanations for Associations between Marital Status and Health," *Social Science and Medicine,* 34(5): 1992, 523–532.

50. Turkington, p. 184.

51. Turkington.

52. Emily Friedman, "Marriage May Promote Health," *Medical World News,* December 26: 1988, 34.

53. Friedman.

54. Lynch.

55. Lynch.

56. Lynch.

57. J. H. Medalie and U. Goldbourt, "Angina Pectoris Among 10,000: II. Psychosocial and Other Risk Factors as Evidenced by a Multivariate Analysis of a Five-Year Incidence Study," *American Journal of Medicine,* 60: 1976, 10–21.

58. Burman and Margolin.

59. Sally Squires, "Marriage—Good For the Heart," *American Health,* July: 1987, 111.

60. Squires.

61. James S. Goodwin, William C. Hunt, Charles R. Key, and Jonathan M. Samet, "The Effect of Marital Status on Stage, Treatment, and Survival of Cancer Patients," *Journal of the American Medical Association,* 258(21): 1987, 3125–3130.

62. Turkington, p. 184.

63. Turkington.

64. Neale, Tilley, and Vernon, "Marital Status, Delay in Seeking Treatment, and Survival from Breast Cancer," *Social Science and Medicine,* 23(3): 1986, 305–312.

65. The Editors of *Prevention* Magazine and the Center for Positive Living, *Positive Living and Health: The Complete Guide to Brain/Body Healing and Mental Empowerment* (Emmaus, Pennsylvania: Rodale Press, 1990), p. 337.

66. "Is Marriage Good For Your Health? An Interview with Janice Kiecolt-Glaser," *Mind/Body/Health Digest,* 1(2): 1987, 1.

67. Rick Weiss, "Worried Sick: Hassles and Herpes," *Science News,* 132: 1987, 360.

68. J. K. Kiecolt-Glaser, L. A. Fisher, P. Olgrocki, J. C. Stout, C. E. Speicher, and R. Glaser, "Marital Quality, Marital Disruption, and Immune Function," *Psychosomatic Medicine,* 49: 1987, 13–34.

69. Powell.

70. Michael Argyle, *The Psychology of Happiness* (New York: Methuen and Company Ltd., 1987).

71. Argyle.

72. From D. T. Takeuchi and K. N. Speechley, "Ethnic Differences in the Marital Status and Psychosocial Relationship," *Social Psychiatry and Psychiatric Epidemiology,* 24: 1989, 288–294.

73. A. Rosengren, H. Wedel, and L. Wilhelmsen, "Marital Status and Mortality in Middle-Aged Swedish Men," *American Journal of Epidemiology,* 129(1): 1989, 54–64.

74. Argyle, p. 27.

75. Jo Ann Tooley and Lynn Y. Anderson, "Living Is Risky," *U.S. News and World Report,* January 25: 1988, 77.

76. Rosengren et al.

77. Morton Hunt, "Long-Life Insurance: For Men, It's Marriage," *Longevity,* February: 1991, 10.

78. Hunt.

79. Lynch.

80. Lynch.

81. Lynch.

15

FAMILIES AND HEALTH

The happiest moments of my life have been the few which I have passed at home in the bosom of my family.—THOMAS JEFFERSON

In an October 1965 speech delivered at New York's Abbott House, the Reverend Martin Luther King, Jr., summarized the role of the family this way:

Family life not only educates in general, but its quality ultimately determines the individual's capacity to love. The institution of the family is decisive in determining not only if a person has the capacity to love another individual, but, in the larger sense, whether he is capable of loving his fellow men collectively. The whole of society rests on this foundation for stability, understanding, and social peace.[1]

What Is a Family?

The term "family" describes a "unique cluster of people who enjoy a special relationship by reason of love, marriage, procreation, and mutual dependence."[2] During the past three decades, Americans have virtually remade society—and, along with it, the family. The statistics tell at least part of the story: According to a special issue of *Newsweek*, today's American family is likely to be much different than Ozzie and Harriet or the Cleavers were.

The divorce rate has doubled since 1965 . . . and demographers project that half of all first marriages made today will end in divorce. Six out of ten second marriages will probably collapse. One-third of all children born in the past decade will probably live in a stepfamily before they are eighteen. One out of every four children today is being raised by a single parent. About 22 percent of children today were born out of wedlock; of those, about a third were born to a teenage

335

mother. One out of every five children lives in poverty; the rate is twice as high among blacks and Hispanics.[3]

But the image of Ozzie and Harriet is still with us, say researchers who are studying the family, and it still has a great deal of impact on today's family unit, regardless of how many changes take place. According to Yale historian John Demos, "In a time when parents seem to feel a great deal of change in family experience, that image is comfortingly solid and secure, a counterpoint to what we think is threatening for the future."[4]

Whatever the family unit, a family is a group that shares common goals and values, and they work together to achieve those goals. What goes on in a family— the network of relationships between its members—can have a profound influence on the health and longevity of its members. In fact, the health of each member of the family can be influenced by many factors: how big the family is, how many fights the family engages in, whether one or both parents work, whether family members can effectively communicate with each other, and more. A family member's health can even be affected by whether the family holds regular family reunions!

The Early Influence of Parents

Parents have an incredible impact on the health and development of children. The way parents treat their children determines in large part the way the children will feel about themselves—while they are children and when they become adults. Parents can endow them with a healthy self-image or engender feelings of low self-esteem. Children react to parents' emotions, moods, and behavior. If the parents are stressed, they can rear children who are stressed—and, therefore, children who are prone to disease.

Experiments with Monkeys

Other experiments have shown the importance of a parent's presence and touch. Dr. Harry F. Harlow at the University of Wisconsin noticed that baby monkeys that had cloth pads on the floor of their wire cages were stronger and huskier than the baby monkeys with no cloth pad. The babies treated the cloth pad much as a child treats a teddy bear; they cuddled it, caressed it, and played with it. That observation prompted Harlow to construct a kind of surrogate "mother" for the monkeys—a wire monkey covered with terry cloth that had a light bulb inside (to radiate heat) and a rubber nipple (to dispense milk). The baby monkeys were enthusiastic in their acceptance.

His success with the surrogate "mother" prompted him to examine whether the babies really needed a mother that was so touchable. He constructed a second "mother," this time of wire alone. There was no terry cloth and no light bulb to provide warmth. There was a rubber nipple and a supply of milk, but that was

Focus on Research

One study at the University of Massachusetts clearly shows the tremendous influence a parent can have on a child—even a baby as young as three months of age. Researchers Jeffrey Cohn and Edward Tronick wanted to find out how a mother's depression might affect her three-month-old baby. The mothers and babies were divided into three groups. Mothers were told to imagine being deeply depressed—to think of some time in their lives when they were extremely sad, discouraged, or disappointed. The first group of mothers started out acting depressed for three minutes, and then switched to acting normal for a second three-minute period. During the time they were acting depressed, they spoke in a monotone, avoided much contact with their babies, and kept their faces relatively expressionless. The second group of mothers started out normal and became depressed. The third group of mothers—the control group—remained normal during both three-minute intervals.

The babies reacted to their mothers' depression, and they did not like it. During the period in which the mother was depressed, the baby reacted both behaviorally and verbally. Most babies cried, made writhing movements, arched their backs, grimaced, fussed, or made negative facial expressions. Some reacted with extreme soberness and concern. Even if the baby played for a few seconds, he or she would return quickly to a negative countenance. After the mothers started acting "normal," the babies continued to be upset and depressed. The effect was longer lasting on the child; the child had a more difficult time "recovering" from the mother's bout of depression than she did.

all. Of the eight baby monkeys, four were allowed to nurse from the terry cloth mother while the other four were allowed to nurse only from the wire mother. All eight of the monkeys spent most of their time cuddling the terry cloth mother. At feeding time, the four would go to the wire mother for their milk, but they would instantly return to the terrycloth mother as soon as they were finished eating. Whenever they were frightened, all eight would climb onto the terrycloth mother for solace.

In still other experiments, monkeys were placed in cages with nothing but a wire mother. Although they took their nourishment from her, many of them did not survive. Those who did had poor coping mechanisms. When placed under stress, they cowered in a corner, hid their faces under their arms, or screamed. Their deprived development occurred even though they could see, hear, and smell other baby monkeys.

Studies with Babies

The same thing seems to apply to human beings. Twenty-five years ago Dr. Rene Spitz, now at the University of Colorado Medical Center, first described "marasmus"—the physical wasting away of infants who suddenly lost their mothers. Some infants who suddenly lost their mothers refused to eat and, even when force-fed, would eventually die.[5]

In studies conducted by Dr. Spitz and Katherine Wolf, ninety-one infants in foundling homes throughout the United States and Canada were carefully observed. Even though all of the babies were well cared for physically, they didn't grow as rapidly as normal babies; none gained the weight they should have, and some even lost weight. There were effects other than the physical ones, too; the babies seemed depressed and anxious. A little more than one third of the babies in the foundling hospitals—thirty-four of the babies—died despite what researchers said was "good food and meticulous medical care."[6]

In one study of orphaned infants, half of the orphans were placed in foster homes and half were placed in institutions. After one year, researchers studied both sets of babies. The children who had been placed in foster homes did better in every way, both mentally and physically. At that point, when all the children were one year old, the children who had been originally placed in institutions were placed in foster homes. Researchers then took another look when the children were five. Although the institutionalized children had improved in both behavior and performance, they were, *five years later*, still behind in development when compared with the children who had been placed in foster homes at birth. The researchers concluded that the psychic trauma "of the first year of neglect was never overcome."[7]

The Effects of Neglect

Other experiments had similar results. Researchers studied a group of one-year-old children who had been born to mothers with an average IQ of 70 and who were unable to care for their children. Half of the children were routinely placed in institutions. The other half, who had been randomly selected from the group, were placed in a hospital ward of mentally retarded adults where each was assigned a one-to-one relationship with an individual woman who assumed a motherly role. Three years later researchers took a look at the children. Those in the routine institutional care hadn't fared very well: They had deteriorated and were significantly retarded. As a group, they had each lost an average of 26 IQ points. As a group, the children who had been cared for by the retarded women had *gained* an average of 29 IQ points each.[8]

Researchers didn't stop there. Thirty years later, they followed up on each child who had been part of the study. Again, the institutionalized children presented a bleak picture. All were still institutionalized; a number were dead. The most advanced among them had completed the third grade. In sharp contrast, the children who had been cared for by a "mother" in the hospital had made impressive gains. Most had completed high school. A few had even completed a year of college. All were self-supporting. The children in the study clearly illustrated "the debilitating effect of neglect during childhood, and of the benefit to intellectual development of affectionate care even by retarded mothers."[9]

Apparently the importance of a parent's influence is present at the moment of birth. The animal world presents many examples. Researchers at Cornell Animal Behavior Farm noted that when mother sheep were prevented from licking their newborn after birth, the lambs were unable to stand on their legs—and subsequently died. Almost the opposite occurs when mother animals are allowed "gentling" of their young—the baby animals show an increased immune response when they are experimentally exposed to vaccinations later in life. In one experiment, in fact, the enhanced immune response proved true in *every* animal tested![10]

Again, similar results have been obtained with human babies. In one study, mothers who had extra contact with a child during the first hours after birth demonstrated significantly more fondling, soothing, and eye contact with the child one month later. Two years later, these same mothers spoke to their children with more questions, fewer commands, and more words per proposition.[11]

In a separate study, 301 new mothers were randomly assigned to different postpartum nursing schedules: 134 of the infants were roomed with their mothers; the other 143 were roomed in the nursery and given routine visits to their mothers. Researchers kept track of the infants' progress during the next twenty-one months. Of the 143 babies roomed in the nursery, away from their mothers, 9 were hospitalized because of "parenting disturbances"—for abuse, neglect, abandonment, or failure to thrive. Of the 134 babies who had been roomed with their mothers, only 1 required hospitalization during the subsequent twenty-one months. The study should not only have an impact in setting hospital policy, but should also "demonstrate the extreme sensitivity of the infant to the care given in the first hours of life."[12]

Dr. Mary D. Salter Ainsworth, recognized as one of the top researchers in infant-mother attachment, believes that a parent's influence is significant from the moment of birth—and she's conducted studies to prove her point. In one study, she examined groups of babies who had been treated differently during their first year of life. Some had been virtually ignored, having little physical contact with their mothers; these mothers typically felt that by not "coddling" their babies, they were allowing their babies to develop a sense of independence and were avoiding what they felt to be an unhealthy "attachment." The second group of babies had been occasionally cuddled and held by their mothers—but, for the most part, they had been encouraged to be independent. The third group had mothers who consistently responded to their signals—especially their crying—by picking them up and comforting them.

At one year of age, the most secure, well-adjusted babies were the ones in the third group—the ones whose mothers had comforted them consistently. The babies in the second group—the ones whose mothers had occasionally responded to them—had a form of "anxious attachment." They seemed anxious and worried when separated from their mothers, and yet were not able to relate normally to their mothers, either. The worst of the babies were those in the first group—the ones whose mothers gave them little physical contact during the first year and who did not respond to their signals, such as crying. These babies were anxious and resistant. When researchers first separated them from their mothers by placing them in a strange room and then returning them to their mothers, the babies avoided contact with their mothers and resisted being held.

Ainsworth's conclusion speaks strongly about the influence of parents in a child's early life: "Babies under a year need a certain kind of tender, responsive holding when they're upset. If they don't get it, they learn to count on not having their needs met"—a situation that makes them hostile, angry, and rejecting. The influence of parents and the quality of relationship that a child has with the parents apparently continues to be a strong factor in both physical and mental health—even beyond the first few critical years.

Parental Styles

The influence is great, too, for parental style when it comes to disciplining children. University of California psychologist Diana Baumrind reported findings to the American Psychological Association that were surprising even to her after she studied teenagers, their parents, and their health. Baumrind and her colleagues were looking for evidence that would validate one parenting style over another in terms of producing children who were healthy both physically and emotionally. "We expected that at puberty, some imbalance in favor of freedom over control would have become desirable, but that did not happen," she reports.[13] In fact, the healthiest children came from families in which the parents were authoritative, placing restrictions and demands on children but providing good support as well. These children did better academically, used fewer drugs and less alcohol, and showed the most social competence, maturity, and optimism.

In discussing the study results, Baumrind stressed the importance of support. Authoritative parents, she explains, "are not bossy. They make it their business to know their children, how they're doing in school, and who their friends are. Their control reflects a high level of commitment to the child, and they are not afraid to confront the child."[14]

Another long-range study of medical school graduates followed more than 900 of them from 1948 through 1964. At various intervals these graduates were

---

Focus on Research

One of the longest ongoing studies of its kind was started in 1946. Its aggressive goal was to study more than 1,000 graduates of Johns Hopkins University—to record which ones get sick over the years and to try to figure out why.

The study yielded some important information about the way we relate to our parents. Graduates who eventually committed suicide, developed mental illness, or were diagnosed with cancer were often the ones who expressed an unusual lack of closeness to one or both of their parents. The graduates with cancer in particular believed that they were less close to their parents than most people are; this was especially true for people with major cancers, but also held true for people with minor cancers (such as skin cancer), and even those with benign tumors. Many reported that their fathers were not warm or loving or that their mothers seemed "detached." A startlingly high number of these sick graduates were repressed and, in turn, had difficulty expressing emotions to the people they loved.

Most of the healthy graduates reported that their parents were "warm and understanding." They viewed their parents' relationship as relaxed, close, and congenial. Of particular interest were the father-son relationships—described by the healthy graduates as "comfortable and admiring."

Source: John Pekkanen, "Keys to a Longer, Healthier Life," *Reader's Digest*, March: 1983, 25–32.

Focus on Research

A British nutritionist in occupied Germany shortly after World War II was puzzled by her observation that children in two orphanages were growing at astoundingly different rates— even though they were fed exactly the same rations. The nutritionist decided to take a closer look. First she investigated the orphanage where the children were thriving and growing well; it was supervised by a kind matron who had the love and admiration of the children. Next she looked at the orphanage where the children were doing poorly. She found the opposite scenario; the orphanage was supervised by a strict disciplinarian who showed little affection for the children in her care.

What happened next is a testimony to the need for closeness and affection. The kind matron—the one the children loved and responded to at the orphanage where they were doing so well—left her post to accept other employment. The strict disciplinarian was reassigned to the orphanage where the children had been doing so well. Within a short time, the children who had previously been thriving started to fall behind and lose weight—even though their diet was then supplemented with bread, jam, and orange juice!

given personality tests—tests that measured, among other things, how close they felt to their parents. By the middle of 1973, twenty-six of the graduates had developed malignant tumors. Researchers were curious about what those graduates might have had in common, so they pored over the personality tests the graduates had taken when they were healthy. Twenty of the cancer victims had scored extremely low on questions determining closeness to their parents.

Dr. Sidney Cobb, former president of the American Psychosomatic Society and professor emeritus of community health and psychiatry at Brown University, stated that there is "a great need for a family environment that allows us to be ourselves and to express ourselves openly."[15] Researcher Leonard Sagan adds, "Children raised in an affectionate environment grow more rapidly and reach greater size as adults. On the other hand, there is ample evidence that emotional deprivation can have a deleterious effect on growth.[16]

Parental Loss

Even more devastating is the loss of a parent, especially during childhood. Early parental loss is directly related to a wide variety of physical, emotional, and intellectual problems in the child—and children deprived of one parent during childhood have a greatly increased risk of many individual diseases, as well as suicide and alcoholism.

A research group at Rochester Medical School decided to look into the backgrounds of the patients at the hospital—and they found that a significant number of the adult patients hospitalized with physical disease had lost one or both parents when they were children. And data from two prominent heart studies showed that a significant number of coronary patients had lost their father to death, usually between ages five and seventeen.

Traits of Weak or Stressed Families

Health problems can be traced to weak or stressed families—and many of those families share certain characteristics that help us identify them. Many of those families are also a product of the times. America is no longer a nation of extended families. Fifty years ago almost three-fourths of all households in America included at least one grandparent as an active, full-time member of the household. Today, fewer than 2 percent have a grandparent as a resource. Families have lost that important outlet, a person to lean on in times of stress.

In 1930 children spent an estimated four hours a day in close personal contact with members of the extended family: parents, grandparents, aunts, uncles, and cousins who lived nearby. Today, in a mobile society, chances are great that a child's grandparents, aunts, uncles, and cousins are spread across the state, if not across the nation. Few live in the same neighborhood. Extended families are not living under the same roof any more. Americans have been reduced to what is called the "nuclear" family, consisting of parents and children.

Interaction within the nuclear family does not approach the three or four hours of intensive daily interaction in families earlier in this century. Experts estimate that interaction in most nuclear families is limited to a few minutes a day—and those aren't necessarily positive. "Of those few minutes, more than half are used in one-way, negatively toned communications of parents issuing warnings or reproaching children for things done wrong."[17]

Then there's the trend toward two-career families. In 1940, more than 90 percent of all households in America had a full-time homemaker who spent approximately thirty-nine hours a week doing domestic chores. Even with time-saving appliances and methods, it still takes about thirty-seven hours a week to successfully run a household. Today, nearly 88 percent of all children who return home from school in America enter a household where every living member has been gone the best ten hours of the day. The scenario is vastly different: Everyone comes home at the end of an exhausting day, still faced with the routine business of the household. Little wonder that no one has lots of spare time for meaningful family interaction![18]

And team up those trends with the ten top stresses for today's families:

1. Economics, finances, and budgeting.
2. Children's behavior, discipline, and sibling fighting.
3. Insufficient couple time.
4. Lack of shared responsibility in the family.
5. Communicating with children.
6. Insufficient "me" time.
7. Guilt for not accomplishing more.
8. Poor spousal relationships.
9. Insufficient family play time.
10. An overscheduled family calendar.[19]

No wonder families experience breakdown!

A number of traits signify tension and distress in a family:

1. *Physical symptoms.* Children may bite their nails, stutter, or have other nervous habits usually associated with tension. Those over age six may still wet the bed. When children are placed under stress, they may react by throwing violent tantrums. Parents and children alike may have frequent and unexplainable illnesses, often hallmarked by a collection of vague symptoms that persist for months (such as chronic headache, indigestion, or fatigue).

2. *Signs of stress.* In problem families, molehills often do become mountains. Small disagreements or conflicts often escalate into major battlefields. There are far too many quarrels and misunderstandings, not to mention conflicts between husband and wife. Nobody seems able to relax. There never seems to be enough time to accomplish even basic goals. As a consequence, family members try to escape from each other—at the office, in a room with a locked door, anywhere they don't have to deal with the pressures of the family.

3. *Burnout.* Instead of being a joy, family life becomes a burden. Parents get to the point at which they no longer enjoy their children; they feel as though they are standing by helplessly while the children dominate the family. This is the same kind of burnout that renders executives and medical personnel helpless.

4. *Lack of communication.* Children in troubled families don't feel free to approach their parents about difficult subjects, such as drug or alcohol use or premarital sex. Instead of depending on their parents for help, they try to cope with things on their own. These problem families have trouble talking about simple things as well. Too much of the time confusion reigns—and, in the meantime, nobody explores ideas or talks about feelings or reaches solutions. Nobody really listens to anybody else.

5. *"Controlled" arguments.* A few good shouting matches between family members are okay. In fact, this is desirable—if family members use good communication skills to patch things up afterward. That's what happens in healthy families. In troubled families, arguments are quite different. Troubled families often have an unwritten or unspoken rule that all anger must be controlled. Disagreements are buried in silence. Instead of getting things out in the open, these families let disagreements smoulder beneath the surface for weeks. When somebody finally gets around to talking about what's happened, no one seems to care (or hear) what is being said. Instead of negotiating and compromising, family members become absorbed with who is in control and who is right.

6. *Interaction with others.* In healthy families, members have a deep sense of loyalty and concern for members of the family, but they also have rich and rewarding relationships outside the family. No one in the family is threatened by these. Troubled families seem to be at one of two extremes. At one end of the spectrum, family members belong to a tight-knit group; parents insist that children have no outside friends, interests, or activities. All family members are forced into doing things *only* with other members of the family. At the other end of the spectrum are the families that are extremely loosely constructed; each family member has his or her own interests and activities, and very little interaction occurs between family members.

7. *Lack of affection.* Even if family members were able to share affection when children were young, they stop at some point, and in most troubled families, parents stay a "safe" distance from their children. Little, if any, hugging and kissing goes on—which the children come to interpret as a lack of concern.

8. *Infidelity.* Many troubled families are characterized by sexual infidelity—but there is other infidelity, too. Some spouses become "unfaithful" by having an "affair" with their work, a hobby, an outside interest, or another relationship so that no time or effort is invested in the marriage.

Clinical psychologist Harriet B. Braiker defines the seven deadly sins of toxic relationships as anxiety, helplessness, hostility, frustration, depression, cynicism, and low self-worth.[20]

Health Problems in Weak or Stressed Families

Results of studies gathered over many years demonstrate soundly that a healthy family and supportive family members have a great deal to do with the health of individuals in the family unit. On the other side of the coin, marital stress and tension, troubled family life, and other problems in the family unit can contribute to illness and stress in individual family members.

Learned Pain

Something as basic as pain, for example, may be learned from the family you grow up in. Psychologist Patrick Edwards of North Dakota State University believes that pain can be something children learn, something parents help them "rehearse." In a survey of 288 college students, he asked them to catalog the length, intensity, and frequency of their own pain experiences—pain from things like backache, toothache, headache, muscle ache, abdominal pain, and neck soreness. Then he asked the college students to recall how much and what types of pain their families suffered. He found that children who grew up in pain-plagued households were more likely to experience pain themselves. Girls seemed to be more influenced by the way other family members felt than were boys. Some of the college students who grew up in families with lots of physical pain developed an attitude of helplessness; they believed that pain was beyond their control and would happen no matter what.[21]

Edwards followed up with another study, which again showed the profound influence of families on pain. He asked 224 college students to describe their own pains and the pains of their families—and to describe how much time their parents took off from work because of pain. The findings showed that the students who felt the most pain—and whose parents apparently were in the most pain—were also the ones whose parents missed quite a bit of work. Children interpreted pain as a way to gain—and the "gains of pain" became special attention, sympathy, or a way out of difficult tasks. These children had learned to use pain as a way to miss school, a way to get out of doing chores, or a way to escape other things they wanted to get out of. An additional result was that these children tended to focus on pain more than was necessary. In some cases they were conditioned to look for pain when it scarcely existed.[22]

Other researchers agree with Edwards that families can encourage or discourage physical distress and suffering. Some believe a family's response to a family member's complaints will influence how sick he or she feels, the way he or she feels about the symptoms, and, in the end, even how disabled he or she becomes.

A few researchers think family reaction can cause a sick person to "use" an illness to gain power and position in the family. At first glance, a sick person may seem to be "the weakest and most defenseless member of the family," one researcher says. But, in reality, "he is often the most powerful member, because his illness entitles him to special consideration, and his needs now have top priority: A sick family member can cause routine family life to grind to a halt and center on him."[23] Because illness confers this kind of power, it sometimes becomes a solution to family problems. In families that are rigid, enmeshed, and unable to openly acknowledge their difficulties, a family member's suffering may temporarily stabilize the family.

Strep Infections

Aside from the issue of learned pain or illness used to gain power or attention, stress or weakness in the family unit can actually lead to illness. Two Harvard Medical School researchers decided to test that theory by doing extensive examinations of sixteen families—consisting of 100 people—for a year. Every three weeks these two pediatricians performed throat cultures on each family member in addition to other clinical tests to determine whether the family members had any signs of streptococcal illness. Because of their situations, each of the families had about the same chance as the others to pick up a streptococcal infection: They all had a similar number of school-aged children, lived in similar degrees of neighborhood crowding, and had fathers with similar occupations.[24]

A number of the family members did acquire strep infections during the study period—but most of the time the acquisition of strep bacteria did *not* result in illness. Families that had high levels of chronic stress not only got infected more often but their infections developed into illness four times more frequently than in families without chronic stress.[25]

Cancer

At Jefferson Medical College in Philadelphia, many cancer patients described their parents as "aloof, cold people." Their own emotional rigidity, which may lead to cancer, seemed a product of their strict upbringing.[26] When cancer patients were asked about childhood traumas, they tended to gloss over the death of a parent or sibling; some had to be prodded to even remember that a parent had died when they were very young. Perhaps they repressed the death, or perhaps they were not really emotionally attached to the person who died—but the researchers agreed that cancer patients tended to "bottle up" their emotions. In a number of studies, cancer patients described themselves as "emotionally detached" from their parents—and they described their parents as having been disagreeable to each other. In the study involving Johns Hopkins graduates, more negative attitudes about the family prevailed among the cancer patients than among any other group in the study.[27]

Asthma

Problems in the family may contribute to asthma. Studies of people with asthma reveal that many consider their parents to be rejecting or overbearing. In one study, researchers sent the parents of asthmatic children on paid vacations and left trained observers to care for the children. Without any other treatment, about half of the children improved.[28]

A similar experiment also pointed a finger at the family. In research done nearly thirty years ago, a physician studied a group of children who were genuinely allergic to house dust; inhaling the dust in their homes brought on violent asthma attacks. Then the doctor hospitalized each of the children. Next, he secretly took dust from each child's home and sprayed it into each child's hospital room. Only one of the twenty children had an asthma attack. Away from home and family, the remainder of the children were healthy.[29]

Diabetes

Almost twenty years ago, a psychiatrist from Albert Einstein College of Medicine in New York wondered why diabetes strikes certain people at certain times in their lives. He decided to do some investigating at a local clinic where he had been counseling adolescents with diabetes. The clinic had kept detailed records of the age at which each adolescent became ill, as well as personal information about the family: deaths, divorces, family disturbances, and the like.[30]

In carefully studying these records, the doctor found that well over two-thirds of the diabetes patients had experienced the loss of a parent or a disturbed family life (characterized by serious illness of a parent, parental fighting, chaotic atmosphere, and so on). Only about one-fifth of a diabetes-free control group had experienced similar family problems. In about half of the diabetic teens, the parental loss had occurred *before* the onset of diabetes, suggesting a possible connection between the two.[31]

A separate study involved three girls who were members of apparently stable, pleasant, and cooperative families—but each girl frequently lost control of her treatment and ended up in the hospital. Doctors associated with the cases decided to take a closer look at the families. In each case, the girl had become enmeshed in family conflict. In each case, a parent had insisted that the girl ally herself with one of them, mediate, or in some other way become a party to the family feud.[32]

Anorexia Nervosa

The same pattern seems to hold true for victims of anorexia nervosa. Some professionals think the development of anorexia nervosa is closely related to abnormal patterns of interaction between the patient and her family (anorexia nervosa usually occurs in girls), mostly involving overly restrictive or suffocating relationships. A leading family therapist who has worked extensively with anorectic victims claims that "the boundaries that keep family members overinvolved with each other and separated from the world are well defined and strong. The boundaries within the family, however, are diffuse and weak."[33]

In general, a study conducted at Duke University Medical Center indicated that people from weak families also tended to have weak health. The study showed that families weak in structure and support produced people with more symptoms, impaired physical health, and weakened emotional health.[34]

Traits of Strong Families

Just as weak or stressed families can contribute to illness, strong families can contribute to good health and long lives. Children reared in a healthy, happy family have a better-than-average chance of enjoying a healthy, long life.

What are the hallmarks of a healthy family? Different researchers have different answers, and they have different ways of arriving at an opinion. One, for example, sent out questionnaires to more than 500 family professionals; teachers, pastors, pediatricians, social workers, counselors, and leaders of volunteer organizations. In the end the lists look much the same. Number one, according to all the experts, is the family's ability to communicate. The lists have the following traits in common.[35]

Communication and Listening

Strong families gather around the table at mealtime and talk—about what happened during the day and also about feelings. A lot of listening goes on, too. Parents listen in a way that encourages more communication. Instead of jumping to conclusions and reacting based on scanty information, they listen attentively and draw out more information. They know each family member well enough that they can read nonverbal messages. They know when a child feels inadequate, ugly, clumsy, stupid, unloved, or just plain worthless. Family members use positive words and phrases, and they stay away from sensitive subjects (like a brother's carrot-red hair or a sister's orthodontic braces).

There's a proper perspective on television watching. Family members enjoy it, but it doesn't take the place of fun family activities. Parents use what is on television to stimulate family discussions on subjects such as ethics, politics, sportsmanship, fidelity, or sexuality.

When parents communicate, there is clearly an equality. No one communicates in a way that indicates power or submission. Healthy families resist the urge to use silence as a "weapon" or punishment. When arguments take place, as they inevitably do, there's a reconciliation soon afterward. Things are talked out, and feelings are explored.

Affirmation and Support

Everyone hungers after love and support—and members of healthy families give it freely to other family members. In a healthy family, members develop good self-esteem; they feel good about themselves, and they genuinely like the other members of the family. The parents are positive, confident, and secure; they have the esteem and courage to face the world, knowing that a defeat may be disappointing but not devastating. The family's basic outlook is positive, too: Family members help each other, support each other, and forget their own interests temporarily if someone in the family needs a hand. Each family member takes an active interest in every other family member.

Respect

Children in healthy families are taught self-respect—both verbally and by example. Children are taught to respect each other—and, since individuality is valued, the family teaches respect for individual differences (the two children who love to get up early on Saturday morning, for example, have learned to be relatively quiet so they don't disturb the child who likes to sleep in). Respect isn't a "special-occasion-only" quality, either; it's a universal value meant for all people of all persuasions. Children are encouraged to associate with a broad spectrum of people—people of all religions, races, and philosophies. Because a child has learned self-respect, his or her parents need not fear losing their own sense of values.

Parents in healthy families respect a child's individual decisions (a father who always hoped his daughter would attend college gave her his full support when she enrolled instead in a nursing program at a local technical college). Children in healthy families, too, are taught to respect others and the property of others (a seven-year-old who shoplifts a candy bar is accompanied back to the store by his mother, who stands by him while he returns the candy bar and apologizes to the store manager).

Trust

Members of healthy families trust each other because they have earned that trust. Children are gradually given opportunities to earn trust—and if a trust is broken, family members realize that it can be mended. Having trust is so important that members of healthy families constantly work to help all family members develop it. Family confidences are kept confidential. Nobody breaks a trust by betraying another family member. Trust isn't just for the children. In healthy families, the parents demonstrate that they can be trusted, too. They follow through on commitments, keep promises.

Enjoyment

Healthy families enjoy each other—and they work together to get enjoyment out of life. They get away from the problems and pressures of everyday life. You might find them relaxing on the porch, sipping a glass of icy lemonade, and watching the fireflies dance. They work hard, but they know how to play, too. They get together for a Trivial Pursuit tournament, followed up by some home-made ice cream—or they pack a picnic lunch and ride their bicycles to the park.

Members of healthy families recognize their "breaking point"—the point at which stress has become too much. At that point they step back, cancel their scheduled activities, and get together for some good, spirited fun. They diffuse stress with laughter and play, and the members of healthy families share a great sense of humor.

Positive and Equal Interaction

In healthy families, the family is important; it's a priority to each of the members. Family members take time from work and other activities and give it to each other—and if one member of the family has an emergency or deadline pressure, other members rally around in support. They try hard not to bring work home at night or on the weekends, and they plan carefully so there is plenty of time for family activities. Those family times reflect equality and sharing between family members. No one member dominates; there are no cliques or coalitions. Family members perform sometimes-complicated juggling acts to give a fair share to each other.

Leisure Times

Healthy families have a balanced amount of leisure time—spending some of it in pursuit of their own activities and some of it together as a family. Healthy families usually say that the most-enjoyed activities are the ones that are the least structured: playing touch football in the leaves on the front lawn, shopping for a new television set, deciding to sleep outside on a warm summer night. And although it's important to spend leisure time together as a family, members of healthy families usually spend time, too, with just one other family member: A husband and wife get away together for the evening, two sisters go horseback riding together, or a father takes his six-year-old daughter out to lunch. The leisure time families spend together isn't just "leftover" time; it's a priority that is definitely planned.

Shared Responsibility

Parents in healthy families delight in the chance to give their children responsibility—and then they follow through by helping their children fulfill their responsibility. Family members realize that they need each other, and everyone pitches in to make sure the family keeps running smoothly. Everyone shares in the running of the household; one person does not exist to "serve" the others. Members of healthy families share responsibility for more than just chores; they also take responsibility for creating a great home atmosphere, for boosting each other up, for providing support. Children who take responsibility are praised, recognized, and commended for their efforts.

A Sense of Right and Wrong

Although values are a very personal thing and vary from family to family, values in healthy families clearly include the differences between right and wrong. Those differences are taught to all family members. The husband and wife agree on basic values, and give their children clear, specific guidelines about what is right and wrong.

Traditions

Healthy families share traditions. Some involve special occasions (the kids always put out a plate of cookies for Santa Claus, and there's always a big Easter egg hunt the morning before Easter). But some "traditions" are part of the everyday fabric of life, too (every Sunday afternoon Grandma comes over for dinner, and Mom makes the rounds every night to tuck everyone in bed).

Healthy families treasure their stories and the things family members have left behind—a yellowed diary kept by an early farmer, a collection of letters from a young immigrant to his parents in the homeland, a patchwork quilt pieced from a thousand tiny scraps of fabric and stitched by hand in front of a stone fireplace.

Rituals are an important part of healthy families; some are very simple (a child gets to choose the dinner menu on her birthday). Families are eager to accept *all* their members, new babies and elderly grandparents alike, and the door is always open for visits, even when no invitation has been extended.

Religion

Healthy families seem to share a strong religious core that brings them faith, a set of moral values, and a system of beliefs as a guideline. Parents make it a priority to pass religious faith on to their children by example and to help their children understand various tenets of the faith. Even when parents are not of the same religious faith, they tend to take the strong aspects of each religion and use them as strengths in the family. Healthy parents do not force a child to accept a religion, but encourage it by example.

Respect for Privacy

Although healthy families enjoy each other and do plenty of things as a group, they also recognize the need to nurture each person as an individual. In a healthy family, parents recognize that each person is a private being who has the right to be alone—physically or emotionally—sometimes. The right to be private is the right to be different, the right to change gradually over the years, the right to mature, and the right to eventually leave home as a mature, functioning adult.

Respecting privacy means knocking on a child's closed door before entering the room; it also means allowing a child to make some of his or her own decisions and respecting confidences.

Service

Healthy families stress the importance of service to others—not only within the family circle, but outside it as well. Parents encourage their children to participate in volunteer activities, and they set an example by doing it themselves. In addition, family members are hospitable and make others feel comfortable in their home.

Solving Problems

The healthy family is not a problem-free family, but it is a family that works toward solving problems. Members admit problems, face them head-on, and do whatever is needed to solve the problems. If necessary, they seek outside help. They expect problems—because they know that problems are a part of everyday life, so they develop their own problem-solving abilities to work things out.

The Health Benefits of Strong Families

The family is our refuge and springboard; nourished on it, we can advance to new horizons. In every conceivable manner, the family is the link to our past, bridge to our future.—ALEX HALEY

As with all basic relationships, the family determines to a large extent how healthy its members are. Those who belong to a healthy family find that their stress levels are lower, they suffer significantly less illness, and they recover from illness and disease much more rapidly. Their coping mechanisms are better, and they are able to function at a higher level. Those from healthy families, overall, are healthier people.

In a special Gallup Poll commissioned by *American Health* magazine, Americans credit much of their health—and most of their positive health changes—to the influence of the family. In the poll, 87 percent of those surveyed reported making positive health changes during the past few years; they included quitting smoking, drinking less alcohol, controlling job stress, exercising more, losing weight, and eating healthier foods.

The family, not the physician, was responsible for those changes, poll results show. The editor of the magazine reported the poll results with the comment: "Family and loved ones shape our health habits more than doctors do. . . . The computer showed that marriage and family played an even deeper role than we realized."

Social support has been proved to be an important factor in protecting good health and long life. And if you belong to a strong, healthy family, you've got "an unconditional charter membership in an emotional support group wherever you roam."[36] No one is in a better position to help than your family; no one knows you better. Members of your family can be counted on to provide practical and concrete aid in times of crisis. One family counselor summed it up this way: "The person from a really supportive family doesn't have to go it alone. That person is part of something bigger—a family that cares enough to let him or her know he or she is okay."[37]

The strongest social ties we have are our family—our parents, spouse, siblings, and children. And the family unit itself is a source of the joy that brings good health. In a variety of studies, parents have expressed the feelings that children provide love and companionship, give a sense of self-fulfillment, and bring joy and pleasure as parents watch children develop and grow.

If it is true that stress causes disease, which has been proven beyond doubt through years of scientific studies, it is also true that a strong family helps an individual cope better with stress—thus reducing the risk of illness and disease. As one researcher put it, "During periods of crisis, as doubts arise and confidence flags, families offer reassurance and bolster the individual in his resolution. This is particularly important during periods of loss, desertion, or other crises."[38] Studies of people during particularly stressful periods—such as the Depression and World War II—showed that family integration, family adaptability, and marital adjustment were the factors most enabling people to adjust to crisis.

Studies of other stressful situations illustrate the buffering effect of strong families. The American farm crisis provides an example.[39] During the 1970s, farmers faced incredible odds: The cost of production skyrocketed, but they couldn't command a high enough price for farm commodities. Many farmers faced staggering debt; some underwent foreclosure. A number of family farms were destroyed in the process.

As many as half the farmers in some states were bankrupted. Those who weren't teetered on the edge, not knowing from one month to the next whether they would survive financially—or whether it would be their farm on the next auction block. In one small Iowa community of only 8,000, three farmers committed suicide in an eighteen-month period because of the prospect of losing their farms.

Consider the stress created by this kind of scenario. The family faced not only economic distress, but a feeling of personal failure. Some of the farms had been run by families for many generations; the failure or loss of a farm was an embarrassment and disgrace not only for the farmer, but for dozens of members of the extended family. The economic and emotional load for the head of the family would be unbearable—and the children, who had nothing to do with the source of the problem and little control over its solution, undoubtedly stood to pay much of the price in the form of stress.

Some of these farm families undoubtedly suffered tremendously. But many, according to research, rallied. They fought off the effects of stress. They did not fall prey to illness or disease as a result. They were *families*. The strength of the family—its interactions, communication patterns, problem-solving abilities—enabled it to weather the storm.

The unique social support provided by families comes from several different functions in the family. A family endows a person with the feeling that he or she is loved and cared for. It gives a person a sense of being valued and esteemed. And it gives a person a sense of belonging to a group—a group in which he or she has responsibilities and obligations. All of that translates into a buffer for the stress we all experience in daily living—and it helps prevent disease and illness.

Evidence of that buffering effect abounds.[40] Children experience less stress from hospital procedures when parents are present—so many hospitals are now allowing parents to stay in the room with sick infants and children. People with strong families recover more quickly from surgery, tend to follow medical instructions, maintain treatment recommendations, take prescribed medications, and get better more quickly with fewer complications.

People with strong families also tend to manage chronic illness better. Wendy Auslander, a medical social worker at Washington University, studied children with diabetes; she found that the most significant factor influencing children's metabolic stability was family stress. Her findings are important nationally: Diabetes affects more than one million children in the United States. Auslander and her colleagues discovered that children with the healthiest families were best able to control their disease. It's not just diabetes, either, says Auslander. The strength or weakness of the family and the findings of her study can be generalized "to other diseases, like cystic fibrosis, asthma, renal disease, and leukemia."[41]

People with strong families are more likely to survive a heart attack. And people with strong families are less likely to develop heart disease—even when standard risk factors are present.

People with strong families are able to weather the storm of unemployment—and in a situation that often causes illness, they are often buffered from getting sick. People with strong families do better after the death of a loved one. They do better, in fact, in almost any stressful situation.

Finally, people in strong families tend to live longer than people in weak families or people without children. People with strong families are twice as likely to be alive at any given age. Family therapists and researchers Nick Stinnett and John DeFrain summed it up this way:

> *Strong families are pleasant, positive places to live because members have learned some beneficial ways of treating each other. Family members can count on each other for support, love, and loyalty. They can talk to each other, and they enjoy each other.*
>
> *Members of strong families feel good about themselves as a family unit or team; they have a sense of belonging with each other—a sense of "we." At the same*

*time, no individual gets lost or smothered; each family member is encouraged to
develop his or her potential.*

*Finally, strong families can best be defined as places where we enter for com-
fort, development, and regeneration and places from which we go forth renewed
and charged with power for positive living.*[42]

Family Reunions: More Than a Good Time

Family reunions are more than just fun. They apparently provide some health
benefits, too. Researchers were first prompted to study the health benefits of family reunions after watching what happens in the wild: Elephants have a practice
of gathering around a sick beast, offering help and support. Also, the oldest healing form in tribal medicine involved bringing the whole family—the entire clan—
together and working things through for a few days.

Harold Wise, M.D., who has studied family reunions and believes that they
can have tremendous healing power, even for conditions as serious as cancer,
says, "As I began to work more and more in this area, I realized how much we
underestimate the power of the family. For a million years people lived in families, and only in the last hundred or so years have people split up. But the influence of the family is still there, and the patterning is still there."[43]

As a result of the research of Wise and others, some physicians have begun
encouraging "therapeutic" family reunions. Extended families are brought together to rally around a sick member. Family members are encouraged to tune in
to each other. One person is encouraged to speak for the others. Wise says it's "a
very primal feeling, a sense that you have stepped out of time. And once the family is into that level, no one will leave."

Wise says that although he doesn't understand exactly how the reunions
work, he does know that they work. He has experienced only one reunion in
which the family member did not improve in health. "It's a very moving event,"
he says. "And to my astonishment, there have been some remissions of the disease in the dying person."

Wise believes that the reunions—in which family members are urged to bring
up problems, discuss feelings, and forgive each other—help people feel more "connected," which brings tremendous health benefits. According to Wise:

*I have a lot of notions about what's happening, but I don't have a theory that sat-
isfies me. All I know is that the reunions are very healthful for the family. And
as the ill person is a part of the family, it's also critical to that person.*

*You can clear out everything that prevents families from getting together,
the unresolved grief, the unexpressed anger, and get to what lies underneath—a
tremendous amount of love. If people feel supported and loved, they seem to heal
better. The immune system seems to work better. But whether there's a remission of the disease or not, I know that this work is important for the healing of
the family itself.*

Having a family reunion is only one way to boost the strength of your family. Try developing other family traditions or customs, too, that have special meaning for every member of your family. You might come up with certain rituals you always remember on birthdays, anniversaries, or other holidays. Or your customs might be as simple as gathering the family for prayer before everyone leaves in the morning, reading a few pages of a classic novel together at bedtime, or going on a family walk around the block just before dinner. You might try a "penny parade"—each time you reach a corner, flip a penny. Heads, you go left—tails, you go right.

Another good idea is to take on a volunteer effort as a family. Involve the entire family from the beginning—work together to decide on a project, to plan for what each family member will do, and to carry out all your plans. If you're creative, you'll be able to find ways to involve even young children.

Or try working together on a project that benefits everyone in the family. Try a family garden—work together to plan what you'll plant, read up on how to plant, prepare the soil, place the seeds, and stake off the area. Take turns watering and weeding—and work together to harvest. You might even set up a family "assembly line" to preserve your harvest by freezing, canning, or drying it.

Finally, you might consider setting aside a regular, structured block of time for "family night" or family councils. Use a certain night each week or each month to make plans, compare schedules, discuss problems, set goals, or work on a special project. Make sure you add some fun time—a romp in the leaves, a swim at the local pool, or a round of banana splits for everyone!

Notes

1. Leonard A. Sagan, *The Health of Nations* (New York: Basic Books, Inc., Publishers, 1987).

2. Phillip L. Rice, *Stress and Health: Principles and Practice for Coping and Wellness* (Monterey, California: Brooks/Cole Publishing Company, 1987), p. 122.

3. Jerrold K. Footlick, "What Happened to the Family?" *Newsweek* (Special Issue), Winter/Spring: 1990, 16.

4. Footlick, p. 17.

5. James J. Lynch, *The Broken Heart: The Medical Consequences of Loneliness* (New York: Basic Books, Inc., Publishers, 1977).

6. Lynch.

7. Lynch.

8. Lynch.

9. Lynch.

10. Lynch.

11. Lynch.

12. Lynch.

13. B. Bower, "Teenagers Reap Broad Benefits from 'Authoritative' Parents," *Science News,* 136: 1989, 117–118.

14. Bower.

15. John Pekkanen, "Keys to a Longer, Healthier Life," *Reader's Digest,* March: 1983, 25–32.

16. Sagan.

17. H. Stephen Glenn and Jane Nelsen, *Raising Children For Success* (Fair Oaks, California: Sunrise Press, 1987).

18. Glenn and Nelsen.

19. Dolores Curran, *Stress and the Healthy Family* (Minneapolis, Minnesota: Winston Press, 1985).

20. Harriet B. Braiker, *Lethal Lovers and Poisonous People* (New York: Pocket Books, 1992).

21. "Pain: Is It All in Your Family?" *Executive Fitness,* May: 1987, 7.

22. "Pain: Is It All in Your Family?"

23. Arthur J. Barsky, *Worried Sick: Our Troubled Quest For Wellness* (Boston: Little, Brown, and Company, 1988).

24. Blair Justice, *Who Gets Sick: Thinking and Health* (Houston, Texas: Peak Press, 1987), pp. 37–38.

25. Justice.

26. Steven Locke and Douglas Colligan, *The Healer Within: The New Medicine of Mind and Body* (New York: E. P. Dutton, 1986), p. 141.

27. Locke and Colligan, p. 145.

28. S. I. McMillen, *None of These Diseases*, revised, (Old Tappan, New Jersey: Fleming H. Revell Company, 1984).

29. Locke and Colligan, pp. 118–119.

30. Locke and Colligan, p. 103.

31. Locke and Colligan.

32. Sagan.

33. Barbara Powell, *Good Relationships Are Good Medicine* (Emmaus, Pennsylvania: Rodale Press, 1987).

34. G. R. Parkerson, Jr., J. L. Michener, L. R. Wu, et al., "Associations Among Family Support, Family Stress, and Personal Functional Health Status," *Journal of Clinical Epidemiology*, 42(3): 1989, 217–229.

35. From Dolores Curran, *Traits of a Healthy Family* (Minneapolis, Minnesota: Winston Press, 1983).

36. Sharon Faelten, David Diamond, and the Editors of *Prevention* Magazine, *Take Control of Your Life: A Complete Guide to Stress Relief* (Emmaus, Pennsylvania: Rodale Press, 1988), p. 273.

37. Faelten et al.

38. Sagan.

39. Rice, p. 140.

40. Nick Stinnett and John DeFrain, *Secrets of Strong Families* (New York: Berkley Books, 1985).

41. "Cutting Family Stress Aids in Controlling Child's Illness," *Deseret News*, July 16: 1989, 11A.

42. Stinnett and DeFrain.

43. Emrika Padus and the Editors of *Prevention* Magazine, *The Complete Guide to Your Emotions and Your Health: New Dimensions in Mind/Body Healing* (Emmaus, Pennsylvania: Rodale Press, 1986).

16

GRIEF, BEREAVEMENT, AND HEALTH

Every man has his secret sorrows
which the world knows not;
and oftentimes we call a man cold
when he is only sad.
—HENRY WADSWORTH LONGFELLOW

It is wrong to sorrow without ceasing.
—HOMER

For more than 2,000 years, people have recognized that grief—the overwhelming sorrow that follows a loss—can make people sick; even longer ago, philosophers and physicians knew that grief alone could kill. An early epitaph by Sir Henry Wootton crisply summarizes the effect that grief and bereavement can have on those who mourn:

He first deceased; she for a little tried
To live without him; liked it not, and died.[1]

Clearly, we've made considerable advancements in medical technology during the past 2,000 years. But something else is just as clear: Grief, the overwhelming sorrow that follows a loss, still makes people sick. And, unfortunately, it still kills them. Although some come through the experience of loss and the grief that follows it with relative ease, many are not so fortunate. Grief-related disorders can range all the way from mild distress and depression to major illness and death.

The Loss That Leads to Grief

Researchers and physicians have long recognized a specific pattern relating to human loss: Loss is often followed by depression and disease. Early physicians recognized it. Some chronicled that entire kingdoms and villages in England were "daunted" by the death of a national hero.[2]

Today loss is still recognized as a precursor to distress, depression, and disease. Loss has even been implicated as a factor in premature death. Dr. Arthur Schmale studied forty-two consecutive patients admitted to the Rochester Memorial Hospital; their medical problems ranged from cardiovascular problems to respiratory, digestive, and skin diseases. Hoping to find some common thread among them, he interviewed patients and their families regarding the events that led up to the illness. Schmale found a common thread: loss. Thirty-one of the patients—approximately 75 percent—developed their disease within one week of the loss of a loved one. The loss led to feelings of helplessness or hopelessness, and illness followed.[3] Researchers believe that the illness and death that so often follow loss is no coincidence: Researcher Steven Schleifer of New York's Mount Sinai Hospital estimates that 20 percent of all people who die within a year of losing a spouse die as a *direct result* of the loss.[4]

Loss has been shown to be a factor in a variety of illnesses, but it seems to have particular influence in some—notably, cancer. Renowned general and pediatric surgeon Bernie Siegel, who has become well known for his work with cancer patients, said: "One of the most common precursors of cancer is a traumatic loss or a feeling of emptiness in one's life. When a salamander loses a limb, it grows a new one. In an analogous way, when a human being suffers an emotional loss that is not properly dealt with, the body often responds by developing a new growth. It appears that if we can react to loss with personal growth, we can prevent growth gone wrong within us."[5]

In one study, researchers evaluated a large group of women who had received abnormal results on Pap smears. The women had been classified as Class III—abnormal, and with a predisposition to cancer, but not yet considered to be cancerous. Researchers studied the medical and behavioral histories of the women and then observed their medical progress. Women who had suffered a recent loss were significantly more likely to develop cancer than those who had not.[6]

In another study, researchers evaluated the behavior patterns of 160 women who had been admitted to the hospital for breast biopsy. The most common behavior among those diagnosed with cancer was a recent history of loss.[7]

The loss that precedes illness doesn't always have to be the loss of a person or a relationship. Illness might also follow the loss of a job, the loss of self-respect, the loss of feelings of usefulness, the loss of security, the loss of an important possession. In fact, grief and illness do not always necessarily follow a loss that involves death or separation from a loved one. One study yielded the "unexpected finding" that other losses had greater impact on health than did bereavement.[8]

Possessions may be especially important to elderly people, and the loss of a cherished possession may place them at particular risk for illness. According to researchers, possessions for the elderly seem to explain where they fit in and how they are related to the bigger scheme of things. When the elderly "see their possessions as extensions of themselves or as a personal record of their memories and experiences, then depriving older people of objects they care about may be the equivalent of destroying their identity."[9]

Parents who lose children are at particular risk, too. According to a study conducted in Israel and described in greater detail later in this chapter, the circumstances both in the parent's life and in the child's death partly determine how devastating the loss is to health. According to the study, the loss of a child is especially hard on a mother—and the loss is more prone to bring on illness if the child dies in an accident or if the parent is widowed or divorced.[10]

For children, another kind of loss—the loss of a parent—can be particularly devastating. In research performed twenty-five years ago, Dr. Rene Spitz was the first to describe "marasmus," the physical wasting away of infants who suddenly lost their mothers. These infants refused to eat and eventually died, even when they were force-fed.[11] (Marasmus was discussed in Chapter 15).

In an attempt to determine the impact of parental loss on children, Spitz and Katherine Wolf carefully observed ninety-one infants who were reared in foundling homes in the United States and Canada (see the preceding chapter). All of the infants were physically well cared for, but they didn't gain weight or grow as rapidly as other infants. In fact, some of them even lost weight. Despite excellent physical care, the infants seemed anxious and depressed. Of the ninety-one infants in the study, thirty-four—or more than one-third—died despite what researchers say was "good food and meticulous medical care."[12] Even among those who survived, almost all showed varying signs of emotional and physical retardation. The last trimester of an infant's first year of life seems to be of particular significance. Most of the deaths in the study occurred during this period.

Parental loss—the loss of a parent through death, separation, or divorce—has been shown in a wide variety of studies to lead to later health problems. Unfortunately, the likelihood of losing a parent has remained almost constant since 1900. Even though mortality rates have dipped—making it less likely that a parent will die—the divorce rates have increased, making it more likely that divorce or separation will affect the family.[13]

From what researchers can determine, early loss of a parent leads to both physical and psychological illness. In an expansion of his earlier study, Schmale and other members of the Rochester Medical School research group studied adult patients who had been admitted to the hospital with physical complaints. A significant number of the men and women had lost one or both parents early in life. Now, as adults, they had suffered some new loss—or had merely been threatened with such a loss—and they reacted with physical illness, including cardiac disorders.[14]

Philadelphia researchers studied records of cardiac patients obtained through the Middlesex County Heart Study and the Midtown Manhattan Mental Health Study. A significant number of the coronary disease patients had lost their fathers—most of them between the time they were five years old and seventeen years old.[15]

The psychological problems that follow loss of a parent can be devastating, too. Delinquency, accidents, psychosis, and suicide are all more pronounced among children who lost a parent early in life. The risk of suicide is seven times greater among children who have lost both parents than for those raised in an intact family.[16]

Eager to find how much influence parental loss had over thoughts of suicide, researchers decided to study college students. They examined students who had come from intact families; they also studied students who had been separated from at least one parent during childhood. The differences between the two groups of students were vast: Only 10 percent of the students from intact families had ever had serious thoughts about suicide. In sharp contrast, almost half of the students who had lost a parent had seriously contemplated ending their own lives.[17]

Grief: The Natural Effect of Loss

According to psychologist Donald Tubesing: "Grief is the process of healing from the pain of loss. The process is as natural and predictable as the formation of a scab on a cut and the subsequent itching that signals healing."[18] Psychiatrist Paul Pearsall calls grief a completely natural emotion—as natural, in fact, as joy—and, he concludes, his patients who grieve the most intensely are also those who experience the greatest joy.[19]

Because it's a process of healing, grief is necessary. Those who don't grieve, says professor of psychiatry Glen Davidson, become chronically disoriented. An entire array of studies shows that incomplete or abnormal grief can cause serious physical and psychological problems.

For grief to progress "normally," most experts agree, a person needs to pass through the stages of grief made famous by Dr. Elisabeth Kubler-Ross:

1. *Denial*—a disbelief that the loss has actually occurred.
2. *Anger* over the loss.
3. *Bargaining.* A person typically "bargains" with himself or with God, desperately attempting to reverse the loss by offering something in exchange.
4. *Depression*—feeling intense sorrow over the loss.
5. *Acceptance* of the loss.
6. *Hope* for the future.

Even though grief is normal and natural and necessary, it can cause illness because it involves intense emotions—and because it is so inseparably connected to loss. The best health protection against the consequences of grief is to allow enough time to grieve—enough time for the healing process to take place. And, says psychiatrist Glen Davidson, to "fully recover and move forward past the immediate loss, we must affirm and acknowledge our feelings."[20]

Davidson, who is chief of thanatology at Southern Illinois University School of Medicine, emphasizes that a wide range of emotions is apt to accompany grief. In his in-depth work with mourners, he has found that emotions like sorrow, guilt, anger, depression, fear, shame, anxiety, and loneliness are all normal.[21]

As the old saying goes, "Time heals all wounds." Nothing could be more appropriate in describing what's needed to heal grief. Research now shows that trying to stifle grief, trying to "keep a stiff upper lip," is actually more stressful on the body than allowing yourself to grieve. "Formal psychiatry suggests that 'uncomplicated bereavement' should be over and done with in two months. That's ridiculous," says Gerald Koocher, an expert on grief and chief psychologist at Children's Hospital in Boston. "A person can grieve continuously for a loved one for as long as two years, and intermittently for many years after. There is nothing wrong or unhealthy about it."[22]

Other researchers in the area of grief agree with Koocher's assessment. Stephen Goldston, a psychologist who has done comprehensive research on grief, says we have adopted a cultural attitude that:

Focus on Research

According to a recent University of California at San Francisco study, grief might take almost ten years to completely subside. The study involved forty-nine families, each of which had lost a child to cancer. Researchers followed the families for nine years to determine how the grief and mourning process progressed. Researchers noted three distinct "patterns" of grief among the families. The smallest percentage of the families—about 10 percent—had deliberately attempted to overcome the death and "get on with their lives." They were largely successful. In fact, they wiped out the incident so completely in their minds that many of the parents and children in the group had a difficult time even giving accurate details regarding the death.

The second group acknowledged the child's death, but worked very hard to fill the void left by the child's death with substitute activities. Members of this group—which comprised about 20 percent of the mourning families—sought regular reassurance that their feelings were normal. Ida Martinson, chair of the Department of Family Health Care Nursing at UCSF and one of the people involved in conducting the study, said it was important for the families who mourned the loss of a child "to know that they are not alone and that nothing is wrong with them."

Researchers were surprised to find that the vast majority of the people involved in the study—between 60 and 70 percent—still mourned the death on a daily basis, even nine years later. Rather than being an unhealthy situation, however, it was somewhat positive: Researchers say that the experience made family members "acutely aware of how precious life was as a result of their loss."

In confirming that the longer mourning periods seemed to be standard for the majority of families, Martinson confirmed that "it's important that such bereavement not be seen as pathological."

Source: Rex West, "Good Grief," *Health*, March: 1988, 22.

A person who isn't 'back to normal' four to six weeks after a loss is somehow sick or wallowing in self-pity. This places a burden on grieving people, who then think they should 'snap out of it' after a few weeks. But people just can't recover from a major loss that quickly. And when they don't, they are made to feel abnormal or guilty about experiencing normal, understandable emotions. In fact, it takes most people a full year to resume life after bereavement, and it can take as long as three. They find ways to cope with a loss themselves, at their own pace. In fact, that is really the only way to handle grief.[23]

Although Davidson's research shows that the average recovery time from a major loss is between eighteen and twenty-four months, that time can vary greatly—and can even be much longer under some circumstances—without being considered prolonged or abnormal.

A number of things can help ease the grieving process and can reduce the risk of ensuing illness.[24] Among them are regular exercise, a balanced diet, a healthy fluid intake, and plenty of rest. Critical to the eventual healthy outcome is a nurturing social network. Mourners who have good support from family and friends (even if it's just a few close friends) do better than those who don't have such support. And, researchers say, as important as all the other factors is attitude—"the courage to let go, the faith that they will heal, and the willingness to rejoin life fully."[25]

The Health Consequences of Bereavement

Bereavement is a special kind of grief. It's been described by some as the process of "disbonding" from someone who played an important role in one's life—someone who is now gone. The intense and prolonged grief involved in bereavement has been shown to have significant health risks, ranging all the way from immune system disorders to suicides, sudden deaths, and increased death rates from all causes.

According to the National Institute of Mental Health, the likelihood of suffering through bereavement at some time in your life is great. Each year an estimated eight million Americans suffer the death of an immediate family member. There are approximately 800,000 new widows and widowers each year in this country. Suicide occurs in at least 27,000 families each year (and probably in many more, since suicide is heavily underreported). Approximately 400,000 children and young adults under the age of twenty-five die each year in the United States.[26]

In describing the events that are likely to occur as part of bereavement, National Institute of Mental Health researchers say that "the bereaved are very likely to be susceptible to serious illness and even death. At a minimum, bereaved people may report pain; gastrointestinal, sleep, and appetite disturbances; and other vegetative symptoms that may signal the onset of a depression. Especially in the elderly, these symptoms may be misdiagnosed as organic.

However, some studies suggest a link between bereavement and specific diseases such as cancer, heart disease, and ulcers."[27]

A decade ago a prominent psychologist maintained that every death has at least two victims—and that it is the surviving "victim" who hurts the most deeply. The surviving victim, the one who is left behind, is at significantly higher risk for a number of health problems.

A survivor's health is at least partly dependent on how much he or she thinks about or talks about the death. To study that effect, researchers obtained coroner's records of everyone who had died in a large metropolitan area within a single year and singled out the people who had committed suicide or died in a car accident.[28] To further narrow the study, any deaths used as part of the study had to meet three criteria. The deceased person had to have (a) been married, (b) been between the ages of twenty-five and forty-five, and (c) had to have died within twenty-four hours of the suicide attempt or accident.

Researchers then sent questionnaires to the surviving spouses approximately one year after the death; 62 percent of those who received them returned the questionnaires. The questionnaires tried to determine three things: (a) what kind of illnesses the survivors had in the year following the death; (b) how much they had talked to others about their spouses' death; and (c) how much they thought about their spouses' death.

Three interesting findings emerged. First, the more people talked about a spouse's death, the fewer health problems they had during the year following the death. Second, the more they talked about the death, the less they thought about it. Last, the more they thought about the death, the more health problems they had.

The spouses of car accident victims had more health problems than the spouses of suicide victims. Those whose spouses died in car accidents tended to talk about the accident less and think about it more; those whose spouses died in suicides seemed more eager to seek out "a listening ear" and to talk about the death.

Apparently the health effects of widowhood depend in part on how old a person is when he or she is widowed. Although divorce takes a greater toll at older ages, the harmful health effects of widowhood are greater at younger ages. The younger a person is when a spouse dies, the greater the likelihood that health problems or premature death will follow.[29]

The health effects of widowhood also depend on how swiftly the spouse dies—and, even then, there are differences in the ways men and women react. Research conducted at the University of Utah in Salt Lake City and sponsored by the National Institute on Aging led to findings that women fare better than men when a spouse dies suddenly, and that men do better than women after a spouse dies of a chronic illness.[30] According to the research, men whose wives die suddenly are at 52 percent greater risk of dying soon than are men of similar age and background whose wives are still alive. If the wife dies of chronic illness, her husband's risk of premature death drops to 13 percent—still elevated above normal, but one-fourth the risk of those whose wives die suddenly.

The risks appear to be reversed for women. Sociologist Ken R. Smith, who spearheaded the study, says that a woman whose husband dies of a chronic illness faces 49 percent higher risk of premature death than other women her age whose husbands are still alive. If the husband dies suddenly, her risk of premature death plummets to 1 percent.

Smith speculates that the difference between men and women has to do with the woman's role as caregiver. Men whose wives die suddenly aren't prepared for the loss of the one who nurtured them; if the wife dies of a chronic illness, the man has probably had a chance to "prepare" by finding someone to take care of his needs. A woman, on the other hand, faces the burden of giving care to a chronically ill husband and the financial loss that follows his death.[31]

The profound health effects of widowhood and bereavement, however, are no respector of persons: Both men and women are at significantly increased risk for a number of diseases as well as premature death. In speaking about widows and widowers, Florida cardiologist Stanley Bernstein says,

> *These people have legitimate symptoms. The aging process produces medical problems, but they're magnified so much by loneliness. The doctor is seen much more frequently than he should be. And the doctors make them sicker. What bothers me is the inability of people around to help them. We don't know how to treat loneliness. Neither do the psychiatrists. We give them drugs.*[32]

Indeed, the inability of "people around them" to help is one of the reasons the bereaved may have more health problems: There is a breakdown in the social support network shown to protect health. Not only does a widowed person lose the most significant person in his or her life—the spouse—but there is often a loss of supportive friends as well. Because of cultural factors, the loss can be especially debilitating for older women. They:

> *. . . have not been schooled in independence; they were not encouraged to lead lives of their own; they do not know the ways of the world. Faced with loneliness, I have seen many widows revert to the dreams of their adolescence and imagine that the solution to loneliness is popularity, as it was when they were teenagers. They cannot be friends to each other, this generation of widows, because they grew up in a world where women saw each other as competitors, threats, dangers. They did not have the balance of the other side, as my generation has had, the comradeship among women, the sense of a shared enterprise, the common focus of energy on activities.*[33]

Widowhood seems to have a profound effect especially on the well-being of men.[34] It has been theorized that the effects may be greatest on women because "relationships are more important to women" and because "women measure their importance by how well they attract men. Thus, without a man a widow becomes a lesser creature."[35] Research shows, however, that men may be even harder hit than women.

Dr. Anne Peplau, a psychologist at the University of California at Los Angeles, says:

> *One of the myths we have been debunking is that the people you really need to worry about are lonely old ladies, that men somehow do better. The evidence comes out overwhelmingly opposite—women seem to be better able to adjust to old age and widowhood than men do, especially if the men are not married. Through most of men's lives, marriage seems to provide a social buffer for them. If their wives die before they do, men are in trouble in terms of their physical health and their mental health.[36]*

Studies bear out Peplau's contention that men are less able to make full adjustments. In one large-scale study, researchers observed bereaved men and women beginning in the second year after the spouse's death and continued the study through the tenth year. They found a slight but significant increase in illness and death among the men when compared with the rates of illness and premature death among the women—especially among men who did not remarry.[37]

In general, an entire host of symptoms and illnesses strike with greater frequency among the bereaved. One mail survey evaluated the health of a group of widows in the Boston area; all were under the age of sixty, and each had been widowed thirteen months earlier. Researchers then found a group of 199 other women who were used as a matched control group; they were extremely similar to the widows in age, profession, and other circumstances, except that members of the control group were married.[38] Researchers looked at: (a) what kinds of physical symptoms each of the groups had; (b) which group had the most physical symptoms; and (c) which group had the greatest "deterioration in health" during the previous thirteen months.

Findings of the study confirmed the health problems associated with bereavement. Members of the widowed group had a significantly higher number of physical symptoms—ranging from sleeplessness to serious disease conditions, such as asthma. The most common symptoms generally associated with bereavement were headaches, dizziness, fainting spells, skin rashes, excessive sweating, indigestion, difficulty in swallowing, and chest pain.[39]

The second part of the study continued to confirm that the bereaved have more health problems: 28 percent of the bereaved reported that they had experienced a significant deterioration in health, whereas only about 4.5 percent of the control group had experienced such a decline.[40]

A study of the survivors of more than 200 deaths showed a significant correlation between bereavement and morbidity. Those who lose a loved one (through death, divorce, or separation) are much more likely to become ill than those who suffer no such loss. Studies further show that if the death occurs as a result of chronic illness, the survivors will have an increase in minor illnesses, but if the death is sudden, the survivors will have an increased risk for serious illnesses.[41]

As a result of the many studies that have been completed, we know that bereavement—the process of "disbonding" that follows the loss of a spouse or other significant person in our lives—leads to a significant number of problems, including heart disease, immune system dysfunction, suicides, and sudden deaths.

Heart Disease

We've all heard about people who "died of a broken heart." According to research, there may be much more fact than fiction to that notion. As an example, the heart attack rate of widows between the ages of twenty-five and thirty-four is *five times* that of married women in the same age group.[42] In an attempt to determine the rate of premature death among widowed people, researchers studied nearly 4,500 people aged fifty-five years and older. During the first six months after a spouse's death, the rate of premature death was startling: Nearly 40 percent of the survivors died during the first six months. The mortality rates gradually decreased over the next few years until it had become the same as control groups by the end of five years. Almost half of all the deaths during the first six months were due to heart problems. As a result, researchers dubbed it the "broken heart" study—and announced that the bereaved can, indeed, die of a broken heart.[43]

Subsequent studies have confirmed the findings, although the exact percentages vary slightly. One study concluded that widowers are significantly more likely to die than men the same age who have not lost their wives; the increased risk for the men persists for at least six years unless the man remarries. The study results, they say, bear out the notion of "dying from a broken heart."[44]

Data published by the National Office of Vital Statistics show that people widowed under the age of thirty-five are more than ten times as likely to die from several leading causes of death—including arteriosclerotic heart disease. That kind of heart disease is not unusual unless it occurs in a young person. Arteriosclerotic heart disease normally begins in childhood but progresses very slowly throughout life. Researchers have questioned what it is about bereavement "that seems to hasten a process that usually develops at an imperceptibly slow pace over a period of decades."[45]

A handful of critics have eyed bereavement study results with suspicion, saying that marriage and remarriage may not have that great an influence after all. The people involved in these studies, the critics say, were probably too sick to get remarried—and that's not only why they failed to remarry, but it's probably why they died, too. But the results of a number of studies directly refute that line of thinking. The most persuasive was a study in which a high number of surviving spouses died during the first six months of bereavement. The study finding "clearly implies that the increase in mortality in widows and widowers is not due to the fact that these individuals are simply too sick to remarry. Most of the increase in sudden deaths occurs before there would have been sufficient time to remarry in any event."[46] The "broken heart" syndrome might again have influence: Three-fourths of the bereaved people who died fell prey to either arteriosclerosis or coronary thrombosis.

In another study, the "broken heart" notion held true, but those who died had a different kind of bereavement. Dr. William Greene and his colleagues carefully studied the circumstances surrounding twenty-six Eastman Kodak Company employees who died of sudden coronary deaths. To gather their information, they studied medical records and also interviewed the next of kin, usually the wife. Most of the twenty-six men who had died suddenly from coronary heart problems were grieving—not the loss of a spouse, but a child. More than half were depressed over "the departure of the last or only child in the family for college or marriage." Greene and his colleagues also noticed during the course of the study that a large number of patients who had a heart attack but who survived to reach the hospital mentioned that a child had recently left home.[47]

Immune System Function

Researchers say there's a logical reason why the bereaved have greater health problems than usual: The process of bereavement compromises the immune system. Researchers first discovered a link between bereavement and impaired immune system function in 1977. Four Australian researchers decided to study immune system response in twenty-six people who had lost their spouses. The researchers conducted blood tests two weeks after the spouses died and again six weeks later. They then compared the test results with people whose spouses were still living. The results demonstrated for the first time that bereavement has real, physical effects. In both sets of blood tests—the test two weeks after the deaths and the test six weeks later—there were significant drops in both T- and B-cell activity.[48]

Numerous follow-up studies have shown the same result. Physicians from Florida's Veterans Administration Medical Center and the University of Miami School of Medicine studied a group of sixty men; the average age was fifty-four. Each man had experienced serious illness or death of a close family member during the previous six months. In each case, the men had a reduced activity level of lymphocytes, cells vital to the functioning of the immune system.[49]

A team of researchers at Mount Sinai Hospital in New York City headed by psychiatrists Steven Schleifer and Marvin Stein and immunologist Steven Keller studied a group of men whose wives had died from breast cancer. To test how well the widowers' immune systems were functioning, researchers injected the men with a mitogen, a chemical that kicks the immune system into gear and triggers lymphocyte activity. For two months following the wives' deaths, the widowers' immune activity (measured by the response of T cells and B cells) was "significantly suppressed." For a year longer, the men's immune systems didn't completely bounce back; throughout the year, the immune system lymphocytes showed only an "intermediate level" of activity. In assessing the results of the study, Schleifer and his colleagues summarized that the increased death rate among bereaved widowers is due to the changes in the immune system.[50]

Test results are similar when it is women who are bereaved. Dr. Michael Irwin and his colleagues at the University of California at San Diego measured natural killer cell activity in women whose husbands had recently died. The role of natural killer cells is a vital one: They appear to protect the body against viral disease and against tumor growth; natural killer cells become immediately activated against virus and tumor cells, even when they have never been exposed to those cells previously. The researchers compared natural killer cell activity among widows to natural killer cell activity among women whose husbands were healthy.

The results showed that the women whose husbands were healthy had normal levels of natural killer cell activity. Those who were bereaved—whose husbands had died—had "significantly reduced" natural killer cell activity.[51]

Part of the effect of bereavement may have to do with perception and attitude—how we think and, specifically, our thoughts regarding the loss. Some scientists have theorized that it is the brain (the center of thought) that governs how we react to bereavement.

Results of a study involving women who had undergone abortion demonstrates that the theory may have credence. Research scientists from Israel's Weizmann Institute of Science and Jerusalem's Kaplan Hospital studied women who had lost their unborn children.[52] Some of the women had experienced spontaneous abortion (miscarriage); others had requested medically induced abortions. Researchers were interested in finding out what factor influenced the immune system. Was it the type of abortion, or was it how the women perceived the abortions?

To test the women, psychiatrists divided them into two groups. In the first group were those who did not accept the abortion, regardless of the way it happened. In the second group were the women who were more accepting, less anxious, and less upset. Blood samples were then taken and compared with each other as well as with samples from women of similar ages who had not suffered the loss of an unborn child. The women who were having trouble coping and adjusting to the loss of the child suffered "a definite shift" in immune system activity; they had "more feeble T-cell strength" than the women who had adjusted better to the loss. The woman's thinking seemed to be the critical factor; whether the abortion was accidental and unplanned or medically requested didn't seem to make a difference.[53]

As one researcher said, "The heart cannot decide that a loved one's death in a train wreck is too much to bear; the liver does not feel the shame of embarrassment; the immune system does not know whether its client is employed or not, divorced or happily married. It is the brain that knows and feels."[54]

One reason for immune system shifts during bereavement could be due to a simple hormone. During periods of active mourning, separation, depression, and high levels of uncertainty, the levels of the hormones called corticosteroids are vastly increased. In the bloodstream, corticosteroids put a damper on the immune system's antibody response. They prevent the immune system from completely kicking into gear, they lower immune response, and they make the body susceptible to all kinds of illness.[55]

Sudden Deaths

Those who are mourning a loss have a higher-than-expected rate of sudden death. We already discussed the sudden deaths among Eastman Kodak employees in Rochester; at least half of the sudden deaths studied were preceded by "the departure of the last or only child in the family for college or marriage."[56] Throughout most of medical history, physicians have documented cases in which a person died suddenly and unexpectedly following a loss; in fact, "grief" used to be listed as a cause of death on certificates.[57] As medicine became more sophisticated and technology became more advanced, however, physicians began searching instead for signs of disease or illness; the factor of "grief" as a cause of death became mere speculation among friends and family members.

In any event, a number of researchers have shown that loss, grief, mourning, and bereavement can and *do* result in sudden death. One of the most notable researchers in the field, Dr. George Engle, studied 170 sudden deaths in 1971. Engle, who is affiliated with the Rochester University Medical School in New York, studied 170 newspaper reports (many from the Rochester press) of sudden death during a six-year period. Engle used the 170 deaths in his study because he could rule out suicide as a factor and because he could reconstruct the circumstances surrounding the deaths. The following are examples of the cases:

- During a physical examination, a fifty-two-year-old man passed an electrocardiogram with "flying colors"; the test showed no evidence of coronary disease. Six months later, his wife died of lung cancer. The day after her funeral, he died suddenly of a massive myocardial infarction.
- When an eighty-eight-year-old man was told of the sudden death of his daughter, he began wringing his hands and asking, "Why has this happened to me?" Even though he had no known heart disease, he developed acute pulmonary edema while talking on the phone to his son; he died just as a physician reached his house.
- A seventy-one-year-old woman rode in the ambulance with her sixty-one-year-old sister, who was pronounced dead on arrival at the hospital. The instant she received the news that her sister was dead, the older woman "collapsed." Physicians did an electrocardiogram, which showed she had sustained damage to her heart; within a few minutes she developed ventricular fibrillation (disruption of the heart's rhythm) and died.
- A thirty-one-year-old woman had been having headaches, nausea, and eye problems when her close friend and neighbor—also thirty-one—died suddenly of an abdominal hemorrhage. She herself died two days later of a brain tumor.
- A twenty-two-year-old woman had malignant paraganglioma, a cancer of the sympathetic nervous system, but she was still able to go on automobile rides with her mother. On one such ride, the mother was in an accident, thrown from the car, and killed. Even though the daughter was not injured, within a few hours she lapsed into a coma and died. Results of the autopsy revealed widespread cancer but proved that she had not been injured in the accident.
- A fourteen-year-old girl suddenly "dropped dead" when told that her seventeen-year-old brother had died unexpectedly.

- An eighteen-year-old girl died suddenly and unexpectedly when told that her grandfather, who had helped rear her, was dead.[58]

In more than half of the sudden deaths he investigated, Engle was able to document that the death was immediately preceded by some kind of interpersonal loss. In both men and women, most of the deaths occurred after the collapse or death of a loved one, during acute grief (within sixteen days of the loss), or during the threat of loss of a loved one.[59]

As in the last two cases, the kinds of sudden death that occur as a result of grief or bereavement don't just happen to the elderly or to people who are already ill. Engle points out that they often occur in young, apparently healthy people. When they suddenly and unexpectedly lose someone close, they apparently become convinced that life is "unbearable." In many ways, says Engle, they simply "will their own death."

Other researchers have noted the same phenomenon. In Engle's hometown of Rochester, two cousins provided a classic example—although they were not part of Engle's study. The cousins, Pete and "Re-Pete," were the same age, had married sisters, and had lived within two blocks of each other throughout their lives. At the age of sixty-nine, Pete died of liver cancer. Less than twelve hours later, Re-Pete suffered a heart attack and died at the same hospital.[60]

Researchers Ian Wilson and John Reece reported on the case of inseparable twin sisters in North Carolina. Neither married or stayed away from the other for any prolonged period. When they were twenty-one, both of the young women started showing signs of schizophrenia; within ten years, both had to be hospitalized. During the next year, they were in and out of the hospital several times; with each readmission they became worse, until finally they both refused to eat. Hospital authorities theorized that they reinforced each other's behavior and refusal to accept food, so the twins were separated and placed on separate floors of the hospital. Early one morning, one of the twins was found dead. Within minutes her twin sister went to the window, looked up at her sister's room a floor above, and—without even knowing that her sister was dead—slumped to the floor. She, too, was dead.[61]

The phenomenon isn't isolated in people. Based on his years of research, Engle says that animals, too, seem to give up and die suddenly if a lifelong companion dies. Based on his studies, he tells the following story of Charlie and Josephine, who had been inseparable for thirteen years:

In a senseless act of violence, Charlie, in full view of Josephine, was shot and killed in a melee with the police. Josephine first stood motionless, then slowly approached his prostrate form, sank to her knees, and silently rested her head on the dead and bloody body. Concerned persons attempted to help her away, but she refused to move. Hoping she would soon surmount her overwhelming grief, they let her be. But she never rose again; in fifteen minutes she was dead.

The remarkable part of the study is that Charlie and Josephine were llamas in the zoo! They had escaped from their pen during a snowstorm and Charlie, a mean animal to begin with, was shot when he proved unmanageable. I was able to establish from the zoo keeper that to all intents and purposes Josephine had been normally frisky and healthy right up to the moment of the tragic event.[62]

Another phenomenon related to the sudden death among the bereaved has been dubbed the "anniversary" death: A bereaved person may die suddenly and unexpectedly on the anniversary of a loved one's death. Sometimes these deaths occur on actual anniversaries; at other times, they occur as the result of a powerful reminder of the dead person. For example, the widow of Louis "Satchmo" Armstrong suffered a fatal heart attack as she played the final chord of "St. Louis Blues" at a memorial concert for her husband.[63]

Suicides

Suicide rates increase among the bereaved as well. In an early study, researchers examined the incidence of suicide among the widowed in Massachusetts between 1948 and 1952. Consistent with earlier studies, researchers Brian MacMahon and Thomas Pugh found that the bereaved did have a higher incidence of suicide. The rate of suicide among the bereaved was the highest during the first year after a loved one's death. During that first year, the suicide rate was two and a half times higher than expected. During the second through fourth years of bereavement, the suicide rate dropped, but was still higher than normal—about one and a half times higher.[64]

In a review of death records in Finland for the years 1972 to 1976, more than 95,000 widowed persons were studied. The suicide rate was 242 percent higher than expected among men and women who had lost a spouse. The most profound increase was during the first month of bereavement: Suicides rose 17 times among the men who had lost a spouse and 4.5 times among the women who had been widowed. According to the researchers, the rates gradually dropped after the first month, but still remained "substantially" higher than normal.[65]

General Mortality Rates

When all causes of death are considered, the bereaved have a much higher death rate than people of the same age whose spouses are living. Although the exact statistics vary according to the specific study, the results are the same: People who are widowed are more likely to die early.

In the study conducted in Finland, the rate of death from all causes was six and a half percent higher than expected for their age and gender. The increase was sharpest during the first months; during the first week alone, mortality rates doubled for both men and women. Women seemed to recover more rapidly than men to the emotional rigors of being widowed: Their death rates from natural causes returned to average by the end of the first month. In men over sixty-five, the death rates returned to average by the end of six months. Men under the age of sixty-five fared the worst: After being widowed, their death rates were still 50 percent higher than expected after three years.[66]

Studies done in England confirmed that men are affected more gravely. In those studies, 4,486 bereaved men over the age of fifty-four were studied. During the first six months of bereavement, their death rates increased more than 40 percent over what would have been expected for men of their age. After six months, the mortality rates started to gradually decline until they reached the death rates for married men of the same age.[67] Because almost half the deaths in the study involved heart disease, it became known as "the broken heart study."[68] According to one researcher, the death rate from cardiovascular disease was 67 percent higher among the men in the study than would have been expected among the widowers.[69]

Widows are affected as well. They die at rates three to thirteen times as high as married women for every known major cause of death.[70] For both men and women, the effects of bereavement increase the risk of premature death. In fact, men and women who lose their mates are among the highest risk groups for premature death. Studies conducted at New York's Mount Sinai School of Medicine indicate that about 35,000 bereaved partners die each year—and that one in five can be directly attributed to the loss of their mate.[71]

Results of a study by the National Institute on Aging show that death rates are indeed higher during the first two years after death of a mate—but widowed persons who survive the two years resume the likelihood of living a normal life expectancy. The study, which involved 14,000 adults in the United States and West Germany, half of whom were widowed, was conducted from 1970 to 1981. During the first two years after the death of their spouses, the widowed had a "consistently higher death rate" than those of the same age who were married. The newly widowed were more likely to die as a result of disease or accidents and also more likely to commit suicide. But, data reveal, "after the two-year mark, the mortality rate slowed significantly, and the researchers could see no differences in the health and well-being of the long-term widowed and married people of the same age."[72]

Findings of the U.S./West German study may not hold true across the board, say other researchers. The results of other studies show that the risk of premature death stays high for widowers for at least six years after they lose their wife—unless they remarry. For women, the risk is not as great during the first year, but becomes greatly increased during the second year.[73]

Studies conducted in a rural community in Wales showed that the death rate among the bereaved was considerably higher during the first year. Researchers studied 903 close relatives of almost 400 residents who died during a five-year period. Nearly 5 percent of the relatives died within the first year after being bereaved; only 0.7 percent of the nonbereaved people of the same age who lived in the same community died during the year.[74] Study results showed a sevenfold increase in the death rate for surviving close relatives—spouses, children, parents, or siblings. The place of death also was significant: If the person died in the hospital, the relative's risk of death during the first year was two times higher. If the person died elsewhere, the relative's risk jumped to five times higher.

Although death rates are higher overall for bereaved people, studies consistently show that there are unusually high death rates for certain conditions—and that those differ between men and women, and even somewhat with age. According to statistics, bereaved women tend to die more often than expected from cancer, heart disease, tuberculosis, cirrhosis, and alcoholism. Bereaved women over the age of sixty have a higher death risk from accidents, suicide, and diabetes. Bereaved men have a higher risk of dying from heart disease, tuberculosis, influenza, pneumonia, cirrhosis, alcoholism, accidents, and suicide.[75]

Cutting the Risk

The best thing bereaved people can do to protect themselves, researchers say, is to surround themselves with people who are supportive. If they perceive that their social support is strong, they will reap the protective health benefits.

Researchers studied a group of women thirteen months after the death of their husbands. The group was divided into those who perceived their social support to be adequate and those who did not. Only about one in five of those who felt their social support was good had poor health; in stark contrast, almost nine of ten of the women with inadequate social support had poor health.[76]

Researchers then took the women who felt their support was inadequate and put them in a program of supportive counseling; the women were able to gain tremendous social support from the counselors and the group. As a result, the percentage with poor health went from a staggering 86 percent to only 13 percent. In summing up the findings, researchers said that "adverse health effects associated with bereavement are absent or at least reduced when the individual maintains close supportive relationships."[77]

In a similar study, 200 widows were assessed during the first few weeks following the husband's death. Researchers judged that 64 of them were at high risk for developing disease because of weak support from family and friends, ambiguous relationship with the husband, and additional life crises at the time of the study. Researchers took the 64 widows considered to be at high risk and divided the group in half. Half of the group received no support; the other half received social support and counseling. At thirteen months following the bereavement, the group that had received social support and counseling did the best; only about a third showed increased health problems. Both mental and physical symptoms increased in more than half of the unsupported group.[78]

In the final analysis, support may be the most crucial factor. A study led by Itzhak Levav of the University of Hebrew and Hadassah School of Public Health and Community Medicine looked at the effect of support on bereavement. Researchers examined 3,600 Israeli parents who had lost adult sons either in the Yom Kippur War of 1973 or through accidents occurring between 1971 and 1975. The bereaved parents were compared with the general populace, and researchers compared not only illness and disease but death rates as well. The widowed and divorced mothers of the deceased sons did have increased mortality—but the married parents demonstrated "no consistent evidence of an elevated risk of death." Researchers conducting the study concluded that marriage—and the social support it brings—protects against the potential health and mortality dangers of bereavement.[79]

How can you best help the bereaved? According to research, traits that help protect a person in the event of loss include social support, strong religious belief, rituals, and belief that one can control the bereavement.[80] One writer suggests the following:

- Be there.
- Listen.
- Avoid clichés.
- Keep in touch.
- Send a note.
- Be patient.
- Accentuate the positive.

And, the writer says, don't forget to touch—a hug, or a squeeze of the hand.[81]

Notes

1. Wolfgang Stroebe and Margaret S. Stroebe, *Bereavement and Health* (Cambridge, Massachusetts: Cambridge University Press, 1987), p. 1.

2. Stroebe and Stroebe, p. 2.

3. James J. Lynch, *The Broken Heart: The Medical Consequences of Loneliness* (New York: Basic Books, Inc., Publishers, 1977).

4. Larry Dossey, *Meaning and Medicine: A Doctor's Tales of Breakthrough and Healing* (New York: Bantam Books, 1991), p. 90.

5. Bernie S. Siegel, *Love, Medicine, and Miracles* (New York: Harper and Row Publishers, 1986).

6. Donald E. Girard, Ransom J. Arthur, and James B. Reuler, "Psychosocial Events and Subsequent Illness—A Review," *The Western Journal of Medicine*, 142(3): March 1985, 358–363.

7. Girard et al.

8. S. A. Murrell, S. Himmelfarb, and J. F. Phifer, "Effects of Bereavement/Loss and Pre-event Status on Subsequent Physical Health in Older Adults," *International Journal of Aging/ Human Development*, 27(2): 1988, 89–107.

9. Ann McCracken, "Emotional Impact of Possession Loss," *Journal of Gerontological Nursing*, 13(2): 14–19.

10. I. Levav, Y. Friedlander, J. D. Kark, and E. Peritz, "An Epidemiological Study of Mortality Among Bereaved Parents," *New England Journal of Medicine*, 319(8): 1988, 457–461.

11. Lynch.

12. Lynch.

13. Leonard A. Sagan, *The Health of Nations* (New York: Basic Books, Inc., Publishers, 1987).

14. Lynch.

15. Lynch.

16. Sagan.

17. Sagan.

18. Emrika Padus, *The Complete Guide to Your Health and Emotions* (Emmaus, Pennsylvania: Rodale Press, 1986).

19. Paul Pearsall, *Super Joy: Learning to Celebrate Everyday Life* (New York: Doubleday, 1988), p. 255.

20. Padus.

21. Brent Q. Hafen and Kathryn J. Frandsen,

People Need People: The Importance of Relationships to Health and Wellness (Evergreen, Colorado: Cordillera Press, Inc., 1987), p. 37.

22. Sharon Faelten, David Diamond, and the Editors of *Prevention* Magazine, *Take Control of Your Life: A Complete Guide to Stress Relief* (Emmaus, Pennsylvania: Rodale Press, 1988), p. 134.

23. Faelten et al.

24. Padus.

25. Padus.

26. "NIMH Issues Guides to Bereavement," *Behavior Today*, November 7: 1988, 2.

27. "NIMH Issues Guides," p. 3.

28. James W. Pennebaker and Joan R. Susman, "Disclosure of Traumas and Psychosomatic Processes," *Social Science Medicine*, 26(3): 1988, 327–332.

29. Sheldon Cohen and S. Leonard Syme, *Social Support and Health* (Orlando, Florida: Academic Press, Inc., 1985).

30. "Swiftness of Spouse's Death Affects Mate's Mortality Risk," *Medical World News*, September 11: 1989, 27.

31. "When Death Does Us Part: The Difference Between Widows and Widowers," *Psychology Today*, November: 1989, 14.

32. Louise Bernikow, *Alone in America* (New York: Harper and Row Publishers, 1986).

33. Bernikow.

34. Cohen and Syme.

35. Genevieve Davis Ginsburg, "Coping with Widowhood: 'Who Am I Without My Mate'?" *50 Plus*, June: 1987, 44–53.

36. Bernikow.

37. "On the Health Consequences of Bereavement," *The New England Journal of Medicine*, 319(8): 1988, 510–511.

38. Stroebe and Stroebe, p. 143.

39. Stroebe and Stroebe.

40. Stroebe and Stroebe, p. 145.

41. J. Van Eijk, A. Smits, F. Huygen, and H. van der Hoogen, "Effect of Bereavement on the Health of the Remaining Family Members," *Family Practitioner*, 5(4): 1988, 278–282.

42. James J. Lynch, *The Broken Heart: The Medical Consequences of Loneliness* (New York: Basic Books, Inc., Publishers, 1977).

43. Cohen and Syme.

44. "NIMH Issues Guides," p. 3.

45. Lynch.

46. Lynch.

47. Lynch.

48. Blair Justice, *Who Gets Sick: Thinking and Health* (Houston, Texas: Peak Press, 1987), p. 188.

49. Justice, p. 189.

50. Signe Hammer, "The Mind As Healer," *Science Digest*, April: 1984, 47–49, 100.

51. "Bereavement: An Immune Reaction," *Mind/Body/Health Digest*, 1(2): 1987, 2.

52. Steven Locke and Douglas Colligan, *The Healer Within: The New Medicine of Mind and Body* (New York: E. P. Dutton, 1986), p. 72.

53. Locke and Colligan.

54. Robert Ornstein and David Sobel, "The Healing Brain," *Psychology Today*, March: 1987, 48–52.

55. Marc Pilisuk and Susan Hillier Parks, *The Healing Web* (Hanover, New Hampshire: The University of New England Press, 1986).

56. Lynch.

57. Justice, p. 192.

58. Justice, pp. 192–193.

59. Lynch.

60. Justice, p. 194.

61. Justice.

62. Justice, pp. 194–195.

63. Justice, p. 196.

64. Lynch.

65. Jaakko Kaprio, Markku Koskenvuo, and Heli Rita, "Mortality After Bereavement: A Prospective Study of 95, 647 Widowed Persons," *American Journal of Public Health* 77: 1987, 283–287.

66. Kaprio et al.

67. Lynch.

68. Cohen and Syme.

69. Peter Reich, "How Much Does Stress Contribute to Cardiovascular Disease?" *Journal of Cardiological Medicine*, July: 1983, 825–831.

70. Claudia Wallis, "Stress: Can We Cope?" *Time*, June 6: 1983, 48–54.

71. Brent Q. Hafen and Kathryn J. Frandsen, *People Who Need People* (Provo, Utah: Behavioral Health Associates).

72. "If Surviving Spouse Endures 2 Years, Normalcy Returns," *Deseret News* and United Press International.

73. "NIMH Issues Guides," p. 3.

74. Lynch.

75. Hafen and Frandsen, *People Who Need People*.

76. Pilisuk and Parks.

77. Pilisuk and Parks.

78. Robert Ornstein and David Sobel, *The Healing Brain: Breakthrough Discoveries About How the Brain Keeps Us Healthy* (New York: Simon and Schuster, 1987), p. 195.

79. R. Weiss, "Risk of Death From Grief May Be Low," *Science News*, 184, p. 135.

80. Gass, "The Health of Conjugally Bereaved Older Widows: The Role of Appraisal, Coping, and Resources," *Research in Nursing and Health*, 10: 1987, 39–47.

81. Victor M. Parachin, "Eight Ways to Say I Care," *Complete Woman*, April 1991.

17

THE HEALING POWER
OF SPIRITUALITY

*It is difficult to make a man miserable
while he feels he is worthy of himself
and claims kindred to the great God
who made him.—ABRAHAM LINCOLN*

"Everyone who is seriously involved in the pursuit of science becomes convinced
that a Spirit is manifest in the Laws of the Universe," reflected Albert Einstein—"a
Spirit vastly superior to that of man, and one in the face of which we, with our
modest powers, must feel humble."

Just one decade ago, Dr. Bernard S. Siegel—educated at Cornell University
Medical College and trained in surgery at Yale New Haven Hospital and the
Children's Hospital of Pittsburgh—was a husband, a father of five, and a traditional surgeon operating on cancer patients. He pursued a handful of hobbies; he
admits that his home resembled a cross between a family art gallery, zoo, mu-
seum, and automobile repair shop. But Bernie Siegel, according to his own assessment, was miserable. He felt like a failure because he couldn't do what any
good doctor should be able to: cure all his patients.

That sense of failure led Bernie Siegel to a "fundamental rethinking" of his role
as a doctor, of the roles that patients held, and what medicine was really all about.
In the end, Bernie Siegel became "an unusual combination of preacher, teacher,
psychotherapist, author, cheerleader, stand-up comedian—and, oh, yes, doctor."[1]
His wife, Bobbie, describes his practice as more "clergical" than surgical.

Bernie Siegel found out that diseases weren't walking into his office—patients
were. When he asked people who were close to death what they wanted from
him, they didn't say, "I want cures for cancer and liver transplants." They were
saying, "I want care, I want care, I want care." Siegel realized that he was a healer—
and that, as a healer, his role was to "guide people into self-forgiveness, so that

they will no longer feel that they need to atone, to get them to understand that they are not sinners, and to provide a path to self-healing and self-love."[2]

What Siegel discovered was the spiritual dimension of health—a dimension that could "transform" people and the way they thought about themselves and their illness. Siegel tells the story of a woman who had been reared in an alcoholic family where everyone committed suicide. She wrote that she felt she "didn't have a choice" regarding the family she was born into, and that she felt like she was a prisoner. But, she wrote to Siegel, "when I let love into my prison, it healed all the things in my life." She still has her illness, but she is at peace. "We don't have choices about who our parents are and how they treated us," Siegel says, "but we have a choice about whether we forgive our parents and heal ourselves."[3]

In discussing the tremendous freedom spiritual health can bring, Siegel uses the example of people who, through no choice, are in less than desirable conditions (such as ghettos or the poverty-stricken areas of Third World countries):

> *You always have a choice about how you feel. Listen to Jesse Jackson say that you may not have chosen to be down, but you have a choice as to whether you want to try to get up . . . Listen to Mahatma Gandhi, who said, "Let us not kill our enemies but kill their desire to kill." And so you have a choice about how you behave, whether you are in prison, whether you are in a concentration camp, or whether you are sick. You have a choice.*[4]

Siegel's practice and his philosophy are founded on spirituality and spiritual health—the ability to develop our spiritual nature to its fullest potential. Spirituality is not the same as organized religion, although spiritual experience is the cornerstone of religion. And spiritual health is not the same thing as physical health: A person can enjoy optimum spiritual health while battling the ravages of terminal cancer.

Indeed, healing does not always "result in a physical cure," points out *Psychology Today* editor Marc Barasch. "But the quest for wholeness is never in vain, no matter what the outcome. To find it, we may have to forsake, once and for all, that misapprehension that sees Good in what aggrandizes us, Beauty in what is unblemished, Wholeness only in what is intact. For those who can summon the courage to tread a path with heart, illness's dark passage may provide a glimpse not only of what it is like to become whole, but what it means to be fully human."[5]

What Is Spirituality and Spiritual Health?

Before discussing spiritual health, let's look at the term *spirituality.* Siegel strikes an important distinction between the words *religion* and *spiritual:*

> *In our culture, for many of the people I see, religion can be a destructive force. In some cases religion seems to be teaching people that they deserve to suffer,*

they are sinners, and disease is an appropriate punishment. But I cannot accept this. Those are rules made by humans. If one accepts the messages of spirituality and love, grace is available to all.

Religion can support you and in a sense hold you in the palm of its hand, or it can grasp and possess you. Too often, I think, we are possessed by religion. Spirituality is a healing force. With spirituality there are no rules related to God's love and God's ability to sustain us.[6]

And before we assign any definition to spiritual health, consider history: Spirituality and medicine were intertwined from the beginning of time. The earliest doctors of which we have record were the religious figures in tribes and groups—the priests, the medicine men. Cardiologist Bruno Cortis points out that disease was originally considered to be supernatural, and those who dealt with disease were the ones considered to have power over the spirits. Not until Hippocrates, says Cortis, was medicine separated from religion.

"I believe that the power of the mind goes far beyond what I first imagined," wrote renowned radiation oncologist O. Carl Simonton, following years of research on the connection between the mind and the body. "In addition, I believe that, beyond the body and mind, there is another aspect of healing that needs to be addressed: the spiritual aspect. . . . The dictionary defines *spirit* as the life principle, especially in humans, and the feelings and motivating part of our lives. . . . Our work with patients has demonstrated that health involves body, mind, *and* spirit. And while the mind alone can be used to influence the physical state, it is used most effectively when it is aware of spirit."[7]

Dr. N. Lee Smith, internist and associate professor of medicine at the University of Utah School of Medicine and director of the Stress Medicine Clinic at the University of Utah, defines spiritual health as:

- A state of well-being—not just the absence of disease.
- The quality of existence in which one is at peace with himself and in good concord with the environment.
- A sense of empowerment and personal control that includes feeling heard and valued, feeling in control over one's responses (but not necessarily in control over the environment).
- A sense of connectedness to one's deepest self, to other people, and to all regarded as good.
- A sense of meaning and purpose—giving of self for a purpose of value, having a sense of mission, finding meaning and wisdom in here-and-now difficulties, enjoying the process of growth, and having a vision of one's potential.
- Hope—having positive expectations.[8]

One researcher attempted to arrive at a definition by questioning health professionals, health educators, health students, and others who worked within the health and medical fields. Her characterization eventually merged many of the ideas of people involved in health. Her definition of the spiritual dimension involved eight different ideas:

1. Something that gives meaning or purpose to life.
2. A set of principles or ethics to live by.
3. The sense of selflessness and a feeling for others—a willingness to do more for others than for yourself.
4. Commitment to God, and an ultimate concern.
5. Perception of what causes the universe to work the way it does.
6. Something for which there is no rational explanation—recognition of powers beyond the natural and rational.[9]
7. Something perceived as being known or hazily known— something for which there is no easy explanation, and so it becomes a matter of faith.
8. The most pleasure-producing quality of humans.

Combining all of these ideas and others she collected, the researcher identified what she believed to be the four aspects of spiritual health:

1. The spiritual dimension of health acts as a *unifying force* that integrates the other dimensions of health: physical, mental, emotional, social. The spiritual dimension unites the other dimensions of health, bringing them into a whole.

2. The spiritual dimension of health creates or brings into focus a *meaning in life*. The exact components of that meaning vary from one individual to another. For one, it may be centered on family relationships, whereas for another it may be focused on humanitarian efforts or the result of professional effort. Regardless of the source of the meaning, it can serve as a powerful inner drive for personal accomplishment. And regardless of its source, it is vital. Without some meaning in life, the will to live is lost.

3. Because the spiritual dimension of health transcends the individual, it has the capacity to be a *common bond* between individuals. It rises above the individual and goes beyond the limits of the individual. With this common bond, we are enabled to share love, warmth, and compassion with other people—and we are able to do unselfish and compassionate things for others, things that go beyond ourselves. We are able to put someone else's life and safety and security and interest before our own. This common bond also enables us to follow a set of ethical principles—and to make a commitment to God (or some other powerful being).

4. The spiritual dimension of health is *based on individual perceptions and faith*. We acknowledge that there is some power at work, a power other than the natural and the rational. We acknowledge and perceive that such a power is the cause behind the natural workings of the universe. Our perceptions and our faith bring us pleasure and convince us of our ability to survive.[10]

In *The Path of Transformation*, Shakti Gawain writes that "contact with our spiritual self gives us an expanded perspective on our lives, both as individuals and as part of humanity. Rather than just being caught up in the daily frustrations and struggles of our personality, we are able to see things from the perspective of the soul. We're able to look at the bigger picture of life on earth, which helps us to understand a lot more about why we're here and what we're doing. It helps to make our daily problems seem not quite so huge, and makes our lives feel more meaningful."[11]

Indications of spirituality include prayer, a sense of meaning in life, reading and contemplation, a sense of closeness to a higher being, interactions with others, and other experiences that reflect spiritual interaction or awareness.[12] The scope of decisions influenced by spirituality is vast; the wide range of decisions that have spiritual overtones include the degree of sexual intimacy engaged in, the decision to donate organs, the movies seen, the literature read, the music sung or listened to, smoking, drinking alcohol, taking drugs, and many more.[13]

Still another researcher, using many of the same basic components, developed a slightly different definition of spiritual health. Optimum spiritual health, he says, is the ability to develop our spiritual nature to its fullest potential. Part and parcel of that is the ability to discover and articulate our own basic purpose in life. It's the ability to learn how to experience love, joy, peace, and fulfillment. And it's the experience of helping ourselves and others achieve full potential.[14]

One of the keys to spirituality and spiritual health lies in our relationship with others and the experiences we share. Those experiences are of prime importance. According to researchers who spoke at Harvard Medical School's Conference on Advances in Behavioral Medicine, the greatest benefits of spirituality are rooted in experience, not just belief. Apparently, those who "believe" but do not experience miss out on the psychological and physical benefits of spirituality. (Speakers were quick to point out that many people probably have spiritual experiences all the time, but do not recognize them as such.)[15]

The notion of spirituality itself implies that we are able to give as well as to receive[16]—that we can receive love and joy and peace and fulfillment, but that, through our experiences, we can give those things as well. We can give peace to another by offering words of encouragement or forgiveness. We can give joy by giving someone else a deeply desired gift. We can share love by countless acts of sacrifice, by putting others before ourselves, by considering someone else first. Spirituality can be manifested by listening to a friend's heartaches, by walking with a child, by leaving a box of groceries on the porch of a young family whose husband lost his job. Spirituality can be enhanced by sitting at the edge of a meadow studded with wildflowers, befriending someone who is lonely, listening to a symphony.

Through the spiritual dimension we emphasize our "connectedness" to other members of the human family. Because of that connectedness, say some, we have a responsibility to help others experience spiritual growth—to help others find joy, peace, fulfillment, and a purpose in life. When we do so, we find that the experience is reciprocal; as we affect the spirituality of others, we receive help and support as well.[17]

An important distinction has to be made: In this results-oriented society in which we live, we need to realize that spirituality and spiritual health is a process or a journey, not an end point. It is a lifestyle, not a prescribed set of activities to accomplish on a one-time basis. There is no standard recipe to follow to achieve spirituality or spiritual health; spirituality and spiritual health involve intentional choices made over an entire lifetime. They involve living a series of experiences that define and fulfill our purpose in life and lead us to feelings of joy, peace, and love.

According to Joan Borysenko:

> *Wholeness has to do with the acceptance of both darkness and light, so that the work of healing and transformation can begin. Healing is a state of authenticity that allows freedom of creativity and is marked by peace, joy, compassion, and acceptance of the wide range of emotions that carry the information required to continue learning. It is a splendid coincidence that healing is often associated with better physical functioning, but the person who is truly evolving toward healing realizes that illness is a part of a Sacred Mystery that can never be reduced solely to the physical, emotional, behavioral, or spiritual (in the limited perspective we have as human beings). In the words of Stephen Leaven, we must evolve toward becoming responsible to our illness (and all life-crises), rather than getting stuck in feeling responsible for it.[18]*

Influences on Health

Spirituality and the cultivation of spiritual health can have an influence on physical, mental, and emotional health—sometimes in very dramatic ways. Cardiologist Bruno Cortis asks, "How can health be without spirituality? Can the body live without the soul that makes it? The spiritual powers within far surpass any others; transcendent, they lift all of humanity."[19] Experienced clinician and educator Paul Pearsall, who founded and directs the Problems of Daily Living Clinic in the Department of Psychiatry at Sinai Hospital in Detroit, remembers a woman who exemplified spiritual health:

> *I will never forget her. As she laughed, her hand went to her forehead to brush her hair from her eyes. Purple numbers were tattooed on her wrist. She called them her death marks but said that they had strangely protected and renewed her life during her suffering. She had been tortured, seen her own parents and almost all of her relatives killed, and had lived in the agony, squalor, and starvation of a prison camp for most of the young years of her life. She had every reason to be weak, bitter, sick, and depressed. Instead, she was one of the most joyful, hardy women I have ever met.[20]*

Pearsall attributes her health, strength, and resilience to a deep sense of spiritual strength. She was a person whose spirituality enabled her to find meaning and purpose in life—even in the midst of crisis.

Researchers are beginning to view spirituality with new interest, especially as it relates to physical health. One who is pioneering such research is Kenneth Pelletier who, with his colleagues at the Corporate Health Promotion Project at the University of California at San Francisco, is investigating the link between spirituality and health. Pelletier started his research by investigating the lives of top business executives and other prominent people who have achieved what most consider to be "success."

He found, first, that most of the professionally successful men and women participating in the study had strong spiritual values and beliefs. Further, virtually all of them had suffered a major psychological or physical trauma early in life. Despite these traumas—or maybe because of them, Pelletier surmises—these people now have a more effective style of coping with life crises.[21] (As discussed in the Harvard Medical School conference, spiritual people weather crises better—partially because they are able to find purpose and meaning in life despite the crisis.)

Preliminary findings from the study found the correlation between good spiritual health and good physical health to be "striking." People with a deep sense of spirituality reported less use of medical services, less minor illness, and more complete recovery from minor illness than the national average.

Similar findings were reported from a study of 300 terminally ill and nonterminally ill hospitalized adults. Those with the greatest spirituality, even though their illnesses were terminal, showed resilient emotional health. Spirituality was significantly related to "low death fear, low discomfort, decreased loneliness, emotional adjustment, and positive death perspectives among terminal cancer and other seriously ill patients."[22]

In another study of more than one hundred geriatric patients at a clinic, researchers measured each patient's "religious activity" by determining the amount of each one's religious community activity, private devotional activity (such as prayer), and intrinsic religious orientation. They found that those who had little religious activity had much higher rates of cancer, chronic anxiety, depression, cigarette smoking, and alcohol use. On the other hand, patients with high levels of religious activity enjoyed better overall physical and mental health.[23]

Psychiatrist and psychosomatic physician Gerald Epstein has focused almost two decades of research on the spiritual components of health by analyzing what is found in the Ten Commandments.[24] Rather than relate the Ten Commandments to any specific religion or religious belief, Epstein analyzed their content and teachings in the context of spirituality and spiritual health in general. He found that the Ten Commandments are a "prescription for healthful living . . . The first five outline the proper relationship of human beings to God, the last five the proper relationship of human beings to human society; all of them are finely and intricately related to each other."

And the teachings in the Ten Commandments give us information for our own spirituality, he notes. One message is that we should not place our faith in the authority of a doctor as ultimate healer. Pearsall states, "Determination on the part of the patient, not the physician, is what makes healing and joy possible." [25]

Or, as Buddha summarized, "It is you who must make the effort. The masters only point the way." Pearsall remarks that contemporary psychologists call this combination of faith and determination a "sense of trust"—"a trust in the spirit of God within each of us as the source of all joy."[26]

Epstein points out that spirituality "also means that in understanding illness, one should regard agents such as disease-bearing organisms as simply one component of a process involving God and human beings, human beings and ethics, human beings in relationship to each other."[27] Those relationships are an essential part of spirituality and spiritual health—and, Epstein says, this aspect of spirituality emphasizes what is positive about relationships.

Harvard Medical School conference speakers echoed that sentiment by pointing out that people with a deep sense of spirituality are able to stop focusing on themselves and to start focusing on others—an attitude that as research has shown, promotes better health in general:

> *God tells His children that He has made and destroyed many worlds . . . but that it is in their hands to maintain, enhance, or destroy this one. Each of us is therefore free to choose either life or death, sickness or health, in a very real, existential way by taking or not taking action, and by accepting the consequences of that decision. God suggests that we choose life and that life is action.[28]*

That action, Epstein proposes, involves a commitment on our part to be ethical "towards ourselves"—to take care of ourselves, to make decisions that will promote health, to exercise free choice about the things that will keep us well.

Critical to that choice, says Pearsall, is another aspect of spirituality: a good sense of self-acceptance:

> *We seem to be alienated from our own affection for ourselves. We believe that once we lose weight, make more money, or learn some new skill, we will then become more acceptable to ourselves. This sequence is backward. We must begin with a celebration of self, not a diagnosis of our flaws. If you can't say something good about yourself, maybe you shouldn't be saying anything at all until you look a little closer at just how special you really are . . . To love oneself is only possible by first learning to love others and by developing a tolerance, acceptance, and empathy that are necessary if we are ever going to get closer to one another than we have been until now.[29]*

Crisis as a Growth Experience

People with a deep sense of spirituality see life differently. They have a purpose, they enjoy a sense of meaning in life, and they have a broader perspective. Spirituality buffers stress; people with a deep sense of spirituality are not defeated by crisis. They are able to relax their minds, elicit the relaxation response, and heal more quickly and completely.

Spirituality helps people interpret crisis in a growth-producing way—and, as a result, they are able to use illness as a means of spiritual growth. Even when a disease takes a life, spirituality can make the experience one of positive growth. In talking about how spirituality can influence attitude, Bernie Siegel remarks, "I simply try to heal the life. I hate to have somebody die with an unhealed life. I hate to have somebody die who says, 'I have never lived; I have never experienced love; I have always felt worthless.' Through the disease, I try to bring something to their lives, so the disease can be a gift."[30]

In the effort to "heal a life," Siegel says, we need to figure out "what is the self trying to get me as a patient to learn about myself?" . . . "If you turn toward what threatens you and say, 'Why are you here? Why do you want to kill me? What can I learn from you?' then you help heal your life and find out who you are."[31] He further says that when "you take on life's afflictions and challenges, you are a winner." He adds that he hopes people can:

> . . . *understand that there can be a gift in the disease and you can help heal everyone around you. Hemingway said that the world breaks everyone and some of us are strong at the broken places. I am talking about people who are strong at the broken places: the quadriplegics can have healed lives; people who aren't cured of cancer can be incredibly inspiring and teach all of us; people with multiple sclerosis can teach us.*[32]

Not everyone will attain a cure, Siegel points out. At some time or another, everyone will die. But people who are busy living, who are trying to make changes in their lives, experience great growth even in the face of serious illness. People who face disease with that attitude, Siegel says:

> . . . *define their disease as a gift, a challenge, a wake-up call, a new beginning, and a beauty mark. And they are not necessarily saying, "I am cured." The exceptional people accept their mortality. They have heard they're going to die, but they don't take it as a sentence. So they don't go home and die. They take it as an opportunity to live until they die.*[33]

In discussing the entire issue of spirituality and the growth that can come from illness or other adversity, Siegel talks about what he calls "a spiritual flat tire":

> *I simply say that sometimes adversity and affliction direct you into the proper place so that when you have a flat tire that makes you miss a plane that later crashes, you embrace the tire, bronze it, and hang it over your fireplace as the spiritual flat tire that saved your life. But while you are fixing the tire you are screaming and yelling and getting dirty and mad that you are going to miss your plane. There are many things in life that redirect our lives. So I don't judge things as good, bad, right or wrong. Just sit back and say, "We'll see."*[34]

In using illness as an opportunity for spiritual growth, Siegel says that we need to accept the illness (which is far different from becoming *resigned* to it), view it as a source of growth, and view it as a positive redirection in life. Perhaps most important, says Siegel, is to infuse your situation with spirituality and love:

> *The only way you can live forever is to love somebody: then you can really leave a gift behind. And when you live that way, as I have seen happen with people who have physical illnesses, it is even possible to decide when you die. You can say, "Thank you, I've used my body to its limit. I have loved as much as I possibly can, and I'm leaving at two o'clock today." And you go. Then maybe you spend half an hour dying and the rest of your day living. But when these things are not done, you may spend a lot of your life dying, and only a little living.*[35]

The Reverend Michael Harper pointed out the importance of spirituality to health when he said, "We need to see that we cannot escape from either the spiritual or the physical. We cannot be wholly saved by drugs or medical treatment, nor can we detach our bodies from our spiritual lives. Biblical language and understanding makes it obligatory for us to have a healing ministry which relates the spiritual to the physical and the physical to the spiritual. By ignoring the one we are doing a disservice to the other and are ignoring human and divine realities."[36]

The Power of Prayer on Health

A seventy-six-year-old Spanish-speaking man who lives in a small village north of Santa Fe, New Mexico, described the essential rhythms of his life in this way:

> *For us the day begins with a prayer of thanks to God, for giving us another day here. And in the evening, when we go to bed, we stop and say thank you, dear Lord, for the gift of another day with our children and grandchildren. It is only a few moments any of us is here, we know—because life goes on and on and on, and we're but one stalk of corn, and many stalks are planted and grow and are harvested, season after season. But the one who puts us here and then gathers us up—He is the one who should hear from us with a please, a thank you, a wave, a smile. If we cry, He'd like to know why. If we're happy, He'd like to know why. It's not right to think you're the lord and master of this place. He is the one who has His eyes on us and wants the best for us.*
>
> *True, we have to build our lives for ourselves; He has let us do that. But He's not beyond giving us a boost now and then—if we ask! When we get sick, we don't go right down to Santa Fe or Albuquerque right away. No sir, we stop and try to figure out what has happened; and we call the priest; and we get down on our hands and knees and call Him to us, the Lord, and tell Him what's up. When we do that—well, you hear what you've said, and believe me, there are times when just listening to your own prayers makes you feel better!*[37]

The elderly villager is right: Your own prayers *can* make you feel better. Prayer signals a commitment to a set of moral and ethical values. It is a signpost of our spirituality and is at the core of most spiritual experiences. According to a recent Gallup poll, 87 percent of all Americans pray to God. When we pray, we are in a state of relaxed alertness, peace, joy, contentment, and emotional release. During prayer, we empty the mind, yet we receive some inner direction. Part of the magnetism of prayer comes from our own belief, our own faith—the powerful suggestion that prayer will work, that something will happen.[38]

It's the subtle peace and quiet effect of prayer that may be the most effective. In one study of spontaneous remission of cancer conducted at Kyushu University School of Medicine in Japan, researchers found that prayer preceded the cure *in every case*. But, say the researchers, it wasn't "robust, aggressive prayer for specific outcomes, including eradication of the cancer" that did the trick, but "a prayerful, prayerlike attitude of devotion and acceptance."[39]

Dr. Larry Dossey, an internist who has pioneered prayer research, writes, "I would describe prayer as any psychological activity—conscious or unconscious—that places us in closer contact with the transcendent. This can involve words, but it can also be subconscious or unconscious. Prayer can even occur during sleep. The state of mind that I call prayerfulness seems to involve certain fairly specific qualities. In particular, empathy. The most successful prayer experiments have always linked outcome to the empathy, love, and sense of involvement felt by the people doing the praying."[40]

The Relaxation Response

Prayer has powerful physiological effects on the body as well. Of 131 controlled experiments on prayer-based healing, more than half showed statistically significant benefits.[41] Dr. Herbert Benson, associate professor of medicine at the Harvard Medical School and chief of the Section on Behavioral Medicine at the New England Deaconess Hospital, has focused the last two decades of his clinical work on what he has come to call the "relaxation response." The relaxation response is the body's ability to enter a "scientifically definable state" of relaxation. During the relaxation response, changes occur in the body. Metabolism slows down, blood pressure drops, breathing slows, heart rate lowers, and even the brain waves are less active.[42]

According to Benson, the relaxation response, "with all its physiological benefits, has most often and effectively been elicited through forms of prayer."[43] In his own practice, as he has struggled to teach patients the relaxation response, he has watched the great physical results of prayer. He has written extensively of those results; in one woman, crippling angina was resolved. In another, life-threatening high blood pressure was dropped.

The relaxation response gives us a clue as to one reason prayer improves health: It helps us meditate, relieving stress. University of Utah researcher N. Lee Smith says that when patients pray, "they're focusing on their deepest values and

drawing on spiritual power that develops a sense of connectedness and also develops hope. And that has been known to affect medical outcomes. The mind has
the ability to heal in ways that are largely unexplainable."

Apparently, most of the benefits from prayer come from what researchers call
"meditative" prayer—being still, knowing that God is God. According to University of Akron sociologist Margaret Poloma, research suggests that people who
use only active prayer but don't get into meditative prayer "aren't as likely to find
peace and serenity" through their prayers.[44]

Poloma and her colleague, Brian Pendleton, found that different types of
prayers affected people in different ways. Happiness, they say, seems to be predicted not by the frequency of prayer, but by its quality. In a study of 560 Akron-
area residents, Poloma and Pendleton identified four main types of prayer that
are performed away from church:

1. Meditative (feeling or quietly thinking about God);
2. Colloquial (asking for guidance or forgiveness);
3. Petitional (asking for explicit favors); and
4. Ritual (reading specific prayers).[45]

According to Poloma and Pendleton, meditative prayer was closely associated with "existential well-being" and religious satisfaction, whereas colloquial
prayer was related to overall happiness.

When we ourselves pray, we reap tremendous physical, emotional, and spiritual benefits. And if current research is correct, we may also reap the benefits
from the prayers of others on our behalf.

The Effect on Plants

One researcher, anxious to find out whether the benefits of prayer were simply
due to the power of suggestion, decided to involve research subjects who could
not think for themselves: plants. If prayer worked on plants, he reasoned, then
there must surely be some power connected to prayer—something beyond the
simple explanation that a human mind believed, and therefore reported success.

For his experiment, the Reverend Franklin Loehr—who is also a chemist—ran
a series of seven hundred tests in which he asked 156 people to pray for a randomly selected group of seeds and seedlings. In all, the tests involved more than
27,000 plants. The seeds and seedlings that were prayed for reaped a 52.71 percent advantage in growth—even though all other growing conditions were exactly
the same.[46]

In a separate study, researchers wanted to know if the same thing would hold
true if prayers were uttered from a distance—so a group of people prayed for
some randomly selected rye grass in a town 600 miles from where the rye grass
was planted. The rye grass that was prayed for showed "remarkable" growth,
stacked up against the average growth of the rest of the grass.[47]

In Salem, Oregon, an organization called "Spindrift" has scientifically studied the effect of prayer on plants and other simple biological systems. Some of their experiments have involved the metabolism of yeast cultures, others the germination of seeds. Larry Dossey calls their experiments "elegant, quantitative, and repeatable. They suggest that prayer exerts a powerful effect that can be readily measured."[48]

The Effects on Other People

It's not just plants that seem to benefit from prayer. According to research, prayer can have a powerful impact on people, even though they don't know prayers are being offered in their behalf.

Arthur Kennel, assistant professor of medicine at Mayo Medical School in Rochester, Minnesota, says, "I pray for my own patients, and I feel my prayers benefit them." John Merriman, former professor of medicine and now the chief of staff at Tulsa's Doctors Medical Center, reacted to the study without surprise, saying, "I believe that patients who are named in prayer do better."[49]

Those physicians are not alone. In a nationwide poll asking doctors whether they believe patients benefit from prayer and whether they themselves pray for patients, the results favored prayer. Half of the doctors questioned said that they believe prayer helps patients; two-thirds of the doctors responding said that they pray for their patients.[50]

In commenting on the study, Dr. Lawrence Dorman, an internist from Independence, Missouri, said, "Prayer can be a very powerful tool in helping patients. Many get off their medication much earlier than expected because family members have been praying for them." Although some physicians were skeptical of the study, others were firm in their support. "I've seen recoveries that could only have happened as a result of God," says Nebraska family practitioner Dr. Marlin Bauhard. "My brother-in-law was desperately ill and there was very little we could do for him medically. Once we started a prayer chain, he returned to good health."[51]

A number of physicians pointed out that prayer, as an expression of spirituality, can work in concert with medical treatment to bring about physiological changes and recoveries. Francis MacNutt, director of the Christian Healing Ministries, echoed that sentiment: "In no way do I conceive prayer for healing as a negation of the need for doctors, nurses, counselors, psychiatrists, or pharmacists. God works in all these ways to heal the sick; the ideal is a team effort to get the sick well through every possible means."[52]

The Healing Power of Forgiveness

Essential to a spiritual nature is forgiveness—the ability to release from the mind all the past hurts and failures, all sense of guilt and loss. Counselor Suzanne Simon defines forgiveness as a "process of healing." What some have also called

---

Focus on Research

A San Francisco cardiologist arranged for a group of people around the country to pray daily for 192 coronary care unit patients at San Francisco General Hospital. The patients were not told that they were part of a study or that anyone was praying for them. They were chosen at random in a double-blind process from among 393 coronary patients in the hospital's unit. Every day, each person in the group of 192 had from five to seven people praying for him or her; the 201 patients in the control group had no one in the network praying for them.

The people in the two groups were similar in condition, age, and other factors. The people who did the praying were given the name of the patient, the patient's diagnosis, a description of the patient's condition, and other relevant facts. The people who prayed were then asked to pray for "beneficial healing and quick recovery" of each person. The praying continued for ten months.

When the cardiologist who engineered the study, Randy Byrd, analyzed the data, even he was surprised. The patients who were prayed for had significantly fewer complications while in the coronary care unit. Not one who was prayed for required intubation; 12 in the other group needed intubation. Only three of the patients who were prayed for required antibiotics; sixteen of the others did. Six of the patients who were prayed for incurred pulmonary edema; three times that many in the other group developed pulmonary edema.

After studying the results of the experiment, Byrd proclaimed that prayer is "effective and beneficial" in the clinical treatment of patients.

Source: "Does Prayer Help Patients?" *MD*, December: 1986, 35; and Blair Justice, *Who Gets Sick: Thinking and Health* (Houston, Texas: Peak Press, 1987), p. 284.

"the first step on the pathway to healing," forgiveness enables one to banish resentment. It is, as Dr. Joan Borysenko put it, "accepting the core of every human being as the same as yourself and giving them the gift of not judging them."[53]

According to psychotherapist Robin Casarjian, founder and director of the Lionheart Foundation, forgiveness is "a relationship with life that frees the forgiver from the psychological bondage of chronic fear, hostility, anger, and unhealthy guilt."[54] Forgiveness, she says, is an attitude that implies that you are willing to accept responsibility for your perceptions, realizing that *"your perceptions are a choice and not an objective fact."*

We forgive others, and we must forgive ourselves. According to one researcher, forgiveness "removes whatever has blocked your creative mind from operating positively for you and for your good."[55]

Forgiveness isn't easy; in fact, most people who responded to one poll said they had great difficulty in forgiving others. Apparently, when we are called upon to forgive ourselves, forgiveness is the most difficult. Psychologists estimate that at least seven of every ten people carry throughout life a sense of guilt— a feeling of having committed a sin or mistake for which they have never been forgiven.[56]

Forgiveness is *not* condoning negative, inappropriate behavior, your own or someone else's, says Casarjian. It is also not "pretending everything is just fine when you feel it isn't, or assuming an attitude of superiority or self-righteousness." Instead, she says, it is a "decision to see beyond the limits of another's personality; to be willing to accept responsibility for your own perceptions; to shift your perceptions repeatedly; and to gradually transform yourself from being a helpless victim of your circumstances to being a powerful and loving co-creator of your reality."[57]

To determine the physical effects of forgiveness, it's first necessary to determine what happens to us physically when we *don't* forgive. The body manufactures masses of "high-voltage" chemicals, like adrenaline, nonadrenaline, adrenocorticotrophic hormone, and cortisone.[58] When too many of these high-voltage chemicals build up in the bloodstream, a person becomes a rapidly ticking time bomb, a prime candidate for some specific ills such as tension-vascular headaches. The heart pounds like a sledgehammer in the chest; the muscles in the neck and shoulders start to contract; abdominal pains develop. If the situation continues unchecked, gastric ulcers, gastritis, or irritable bowel syndrome can result.[59] With forgiveness, the anger and resentment dissolve. The body stops pouring high-voltage chemicals into the bloodstream. The healing begins.

One of the greatest examples of the healing power of forgiveness can be found in nature. As one author put it:

> *Nature always forgives. Nature is the great giver and the great forgiver. Should you cut your hand with a sharp knife, the forces of nature set about immediately to repair the damage. It was a mistake to cut your hand, but nature does not withhold the repairing of the wound. Nature immediately forgives and starts at once to make repairs. If you eat food that does not agree with you and you have indigestion, nature immediately starts to repair the damage. Although it was a mistake to eat the wrong food, you do not need to go through the rest of your life with indigestion. Nature even repairs the ravages of the battlefield by covering it with grass and flowers. [No one] can go forward if he is tied to the past. No one can think straight and efficiently if his mind is cluttered up with thoughts of hate or memories of hurts and mistakes; hence the necessity of forgiving so that we can love ourselves, our neighbor, and God.[60]*

To bring a greater sense of forgiveness into your own life, try following what Lotus presented as the "tools of forgiveness."

- Begin by letting go of your unforgiving stance.
- Admit that the events and feelings you are struggling with really happened.
- Admit that the past cannot be undone. After all, there is really no hope for a better yesterday.
- Recognize that you no longer need to depend on others, including your parents for approval. When you realize your independence, you assume your rightful power and you learn to validate yourself (or, at least, to seek validation from more sympathetic people).
- Don't expect others to respond to your efforts to forgive.
- Release any unrealistic expectations of yourself.

- Accept others for who they are rather than who you want them to be.
- Set flexible rules of conduct for yourself and others.
- Talk about issues as they come up.[61]

In addition to those suggestions, Robin Casarjian suggests fostering a forgiving attitude by praying, meditating, expressing gratitude (to people or to a higher power), spending time in nature and allowing yourself to experience its wonder, serving others selflessly, and creating through any art form.[62]

Church Affiliation and Health

Religion, basically, is a science in how to know God—and research has shown that people with active religious faith and people who are strongly affiliated with a particular church generally enjoy better health. Religion is "the personal beliefs, values, and activities pertinent to that which is supernatural, mysterious, and awesome, which transcends immediate situations, and which pertains to questions of final causes and ultimate ends of man and the universe."[63]

There are two basic orientations of religion:

1. *Personal.* Religion involves a person's values, beliefs, and attitudes. Spiritual experience is the cornerstone of religion; if spiritual experience is in one's belief system, it becomes the only way to God. The personal orientation of religion can be either intrinsic or extrinsic. Those with an intrinsic sense of religion participate in their chosen religion for spiritual reasons; to them, the religion comes first and is a dominating force in their lives. Those with an extrinsic sense of religion do not share the "zeal" or commitment of those with an intrinsic orientation; religion for them is secondary and does not represent a primary need. They "belong," but they do not "live" their religion.[64]

2. *Institutional.* Individuals adopt a church or religion because of group-related benefits: They enjoy attending church, participating in group activities or rituals, and so on.

Studies indicate that religion may enhance health and well-being in at least four ways:[65] first, through social integration and support; second, through the establishment of a personal relationship with a divine other; third, through the provision of systems of meaning and existential coherence; and fourth, through the promotion of more specific patterns of religious organization and personal lifestyle.

Regardless of *how* it works, evidence exists that religion does enhance health. In one study of 850 male hospital patients, researchers at a North Carolina Veteran's Administration hospital found that religion was an important coping factor for the men. One in five said religion is "the most important thing that keeps me going." Nearly half of the patients rated religion as very helpful to them in coping with the situation of being hospitalized. According to the men in the study, they derived a feeling of peace and comfort from prayer, Bible study, faith in God, and the emotional support of a pastor or other church members. Those who were religious had high levels of social support, low levels of alcohol use, and significantly less clinical depression.

"Many people—especially those with fewer health, social, and financial resources—turn to religion for solace in the face of situations over which they have no control," said the researchers, commenting on the study. "Their religious beliefs and involvement may counteract feelings of helplessness, provide meaning and order to challenging life experiences, and restore a sense of control."[66]

Attendance and Affiliation

According to nationwide surveys, more than 90 percent of all Americans profess to a belief in God;[67] a recent Gallup poll puts that number as high as 95 percent. According to a recent Gallup poll, almost three-fourths of all Americans believe that Jesus is either God or the Son of God; two-thirds believe that the Bible is "either the literal or inspired word of God." More than half believe in life after death.[68] According to the *New York Times,* almost 90 percent of all Americans report some religious affiliation.

Despite their belief in God, Christ, and the Bible, the majority of Americans are not *active* in church affiliations. According to the Gallup survey, 78 million Americans either do not belong to a church or synagogue, or they attend only on infrequent, special occasions. That number was 61 million just one decade ago.[69]

Even churchgoers have a growing dissatisfaction with organized religion. Of those surveyed, 59 percent think churches spend too much time on organization issues; 32 percent believe organized religion is too restrictive in its moral teachings. And almost one in four of the respondents to the Gallup poll say they turned away from their church in search of "deeper spiritual meaning."[70]

Even so, extensive research indicates that active participation in a church or synagogue boosts health,[71] acts as a buffer against stress, and may even prolong life. Researchers at Southern California College found that elderly people who are religiously active tend to be more optimistic and better able to cope with illness than people who are less religious. Research indicates that even people who no longer recognized family members were able to benefit from attending church or from other religious practices. University of Portland sociologist Robert W. Duff said the research is consistent with other studies, including one of his own that showed religiously active older persons had relatively high life satisfaction ratings.

Religious faith and involvement may be even more life-enhancing than was previously believed, according to research by Yale psychologist Stanislav Kasl and Rutgers University psychologist Ellen Idler. The pair studied the health and well-being of almost 3,000 retirement-aged residents of New Haven, Connecticut. They found that religious involvement *did* enhance the well-being of the seniors. According to Idler, "There actually may be a common-sense connection here. It seems reasonable that those people who say they get a great deal of strength and comfort from religion are often those who need it the most—those who are ill."[72]

People who attend church or synagogue on a regular basis have a much lower rate of diseases than those who attend less frequently or do not attend at all. Churchgoers have especially low rates of heart disease, lung disease, cirrhosis of the liver, and some kinds of cancer.[73] For example, men who attend church infrequently or not at all are at almost twice the risk of dying of arteriosclerotic heart disease—and that's even when other risk factors (such as smoking, social status, and water hardness) are taken into consideration. They are more than four times more likely to die of cirrhosis of the liver. And women are more than three times as likely to die of cancer of the cervix if they aren't frequent churchgoers.[74]

One review of two hundred epidemiological studies found that religion improved health in eight different areas: cancer of the uterus and cervix, all other cancers, colitis and enteritis, cardiovascular disease, hypertension and stroke, general health, general longevity, and disease and death among the clergy.[75]

Relationship to Church Teachings

No one knows for certain how religious participation protects health but there are many theories—and many probable reasons for a religion's protective nature. Many churches prescribe behavior that prevents illness or assists in the treatment of illness. Some religions actively promote healthier lifestyles, such as eating less meat, drinking less alcohol, avoiding caffeine-containing foods and drinks, and not smoking.[76] Other examples of religious prescriptions for healthy behavior include encouragement to eat a diet of healthy, nutritious foods; promotion of proper rest, exercise, and knowledge about bodily functions; encouragement of family and social patterns of helping and caring; and proper utilization of available health care systems.

Organized churches also place people in support groups that can assist in times of need, and they cultivate attitudes that may give individuals a helpful perspective with which to face stressful life situations (a belief in life after death, for example, makes it much less stressful to face the terminal illness of a loved one).[77]

Many churches also discourage behavior that is harmful to health or that would hinder the treatment of disease. Religious proscriptions against unhealthy behavior include behaviors such as the nonuse of tobacco, alcohol, and other harmful drugs; discouragement of immoral activities, including promiscuous sex; and avoidance of activities that have a high probability of injuring the body.[78]

Researchers point out, however, that not all religions act to preserve life and promote health. Some religions include use of contaminated substances in rituals, burials, and other practices; placing the dead in rivers; ritual suicide; religious wars; tortures and executions in the name of religion; and endogamous marriage customs that may engender and perpetuate genetic disorders. Some, too, prohibit members from seeking modern medical treatment or from practicing modern health principles—although churches with these policies are in the distinct minority.[79]

Still another way that churches protect health may lie in attitude. According to researcher Ellen Idler at Rutgers University, the religious teachings of many churches help foster a more positive approach to illness, pain, or disability.[80]

A prominent theory regarding how churches protect the health of their members rests with the well-known fact that social support boosts and protects health—and religious participation includes a rich network of social support. In fact, "for some Americans, becoming an active member of a religious congregation can provide the tradition and social support lacking in their community."[81] People who are active in a church are not as likely to be lonely. Members of a church affiliation are much like members of an extended family; they provide comfort, companionship, and even material assistance when needed. Ministers and other church leaders visit the ill, marry couples, provide comfort when a family member dies, speak at the funeral, and give counsel in difficult circumstances. Churches offer tradition and social support that are lacking in many communities.[82]

Leonard Sagan says that lifestyle prescriptions are probably at least partly responsible for the better health of active church members —but he is convinced that "support provided by the social network" may be the more important force in boosting the health of active church members. "For one thing," he points out, "membership in other organizations, such as the military services, is also associated with a reduction in mortality."[83]

It's not only physical health that is benefited, but mental and emotional health as well. Famed psychotherapist Carl Jung commented:

> *During the past thirty years, people from all the civilized countries of the earth have consulted me. I have treated many hundreds of patients . . . . Among all my patients in the second half of life—that is to say, over thirty-five—there has not been one whose problem in the last resort was not that of finding a religious outlook on life . . . It seems to me that, side by side with the decline of religious life, the neuroses grow noticeably more frequent.*[84]

Other researchers and practitioners have noticed a definite benefit to mental and emotional health from religious participation. Participating in church activities, listening to religious programs on the radio, and watching religious programs on television were all found to be associated with fewer symptoms of depression.[85]

Religious commitment has been shown in other studies to enhance overall mental health. Maryland psychologist John Gartner reviewed two hundred studies on religious commitment and mental health. Those studies showed that the religiously faithful have lower suicide rates, lower drug use and abuse, less juvenile delinquency, lower divorce rates, higher marital happiness, better overall well-being, and better recovery from mental illness.

"Religious belief gives life a context and restrains many self-destructive impulses," explains Gartner. "For many people it appears to be a solid floor for mental health."[86]

Religious participation even appears to be beneficial to those who have existing health problems or are institutionalized. Researchers at Rutgers University expanded on studies conducted at Yale University that examined the mental health of the elderly. Those who attend church regularly and who actively or publicly participate in church services were found to be much less likely to "be functionally disabled or to show signs of depression,"[87] regardless of the other circumstances in their lives.

Regardless of *why* religion works to boost health, regular attendance or participation seems to be a key. Those who participate regularly and attend on a regular basis receive the greatest health benefits from religion. Regular participation has even been shown to increase lifespan and decrease mortality. Frequent church attendance has been associated with a decreased overall mortality, a finding that persists even after controlling for age and various other risk factors. Church membership has been very strongly associated with lower mortality in both sexes and for all ages.[88]

A recent study of more than 400 elderly poor in Connecticut observed both general health and religious participation among the study subjects for one year. Researchers found that "religiousness"—attendance at services, self-rated religiousness, and religion as a source of strength—reduced overall mortality among the subjects.[89]

Specific Illnesses

Regular church attendance apparently has an impact on a number of specific diseases as well. One is cardiovascular disease. Researchers have found that the more active a person is in a religion, the less chance he or she has of incurring myocardial infarction. The same holds true with people born of a religiously homogeneous marriage.[90] In addition, people who attend church regularly are at lower risk for myocardial degeneration, chronic endocarditis, arteriosclerotic heart disease, and degenerative heart disease. People who have high conformity with religious beliefs have lower blood pressure, and those who follow high religious conventionalism have lower blood pressure, a slower, more steady heartbeat, and a healthier cardiovascular system.[91]

In addition to benefiting the cardiovascular system, twenty-two out of twenty-seven studies found that the frequency of religious attendance is "significantly associated" with good health. People who go to church frequently, the studies say, have fewer incidences of hypertension, trichomoniasis, positive pap smears, cervical cancer, neonatal mortality, emphysema, cirrhosis of the liver, suicide, colorectal cancer, cancer-related pain, and physical symptoms in general.[92]

In addition to the health benefits gained from religious participation in general, research has found that regular participation in certain religious sects can mean specific benefits in some areas.

The Essence of Spirituality

What is this essence that can provide obvious health benefits? Physician Rachel Naomi Remen, medical director of the Commonweal Cancer Help Program and a member of the Scientific Advisory Board for the Inner Mechanisms of the Healing Response Program for the Institute of Noetic Sciences, says it may be easiest to define the spiritual by defining what it isn't. The spiritual, she says, is not the moral. Nor is it the ethical. The spiritual is also not the psychic, nor is it the religious.

The spiritual, she says, "is inclusive. It is the deepest sense of belonging and participation. We all participate in the spiritual at all times, whether we know it or not. There's no place to go to be separated from the spiritual . . . The most important thing in defining spirit is the recognition that spirit is an essential need of human nature. There is something in all of us that seeks the spiritual. This yearning varies in strength from person to person but it is always there in everyone. And so healing becomes possible."[93]

As Albert Einstein so eloquently put it, "Everyone who is seriously involved in the pursuit of science becomes convinced that a Spirit is manifest in the Laws of the Universe—a Spirit vastly superior to that of man, and one in the face of which we, with our modest powers, must feel humble."

And our relationship to that Spirit, says allergist William L. Mundy, defines our very being:

> *The wonderful organism that we are, comprised of billions of parts, many working together on a similar project within a confine we call an organ, or hundreds of millions of cells all performing a similar function, all working together to make us tick as a human being, can hardly be brought down to a simplistic (or profoundly complicated) system of chemical reactions. We need more than science to explain such divine miracles.*[94]

Notes

1. Florence Graves, "The High Priest of Healing," *New Age Journal*, May/June: 1989, 34.

2. Quote from Bernie Siegel's *Peace, Love, and Healing* as reported in Graves, p. 34.

3. Graves. p. 36.

4. Graves.

5. Marc. I. Barasch, "The Healing Path: A Soul Approach to Illness," *The Psychology of Health, Immunity, and Disease*, vol. B, p. 10, in Proceedings of the Sixth International Conference of the National Institute for the Clinical Application of Behavioral Medicine.

6. Bernie Siegel, *How to Live Between Office Visits* (New York: HarperCollins Publishers, 1993), p. 172.

7. O. Carl Simonton and Reid Henson, *The Healing Journey* (New York: Bantam Books, 1992), p. 13.

8. "Good Health: More Than Absence of Disease," *Church News*, November 13: 1993, 7.

9. R. Banks, "Health and the Spiritual Dimensions: Relationships and Implications for Professional Preparation Programs," *Journal of School Health*, 50: 1980, 195–202.

10. Banks.

11. Shakti Gawain, *The Path of Transforma-*

tion (Mill Valley, California: Nataraj Publishing, 1993), p. 77.

12. Pamela G. Reed, "Spirituality and Well-Being in Terminally Ill Hospitalized Adults," *Research in Nursing and Health*, 10: 1987, 335–344.

13. Glenn E. Richardson and Melody Powers Noland, "Treating the Spiritual Dimension Through Educational Imagery," *Health Values*, 8(6): 1984, 28.

14. Larry S. Chapman, "Developing a Useful Perspective on Spiritual Health: Love, Joy, Peace, and Fulfillment," *American Journal of Health Promotion*, Fall: 1987, 12.

15. Chapman.

16. Chapman, p. 13.

17. Chapman.

18. Joan Borysenko, "Exploring the Heart of Healing: New Findings on Bodymind and Soul," *The Psychology of Health, Immunity, and Disease,* vol. B, p. 33, in Proceedings of the Sixth International Conference of the National Institute for the Clinical Application of Behavioral Medicine.

19. Dr. Bruno Cortis, "Spirituality and Medicine," in Proceedings of the Fourth National Conference on the Psychology of Health, Immunity, and Disease, published by the National Institute for the Clinical Application of Behavioral Medicine.

20. Paul Pearsall, *Super Joy*, (New York: Doubleday, 1988), p. 1.

21. From "The Spirit of Health," *Advances: Journal of the Institute for the Advancement of Health*, 5(4): 1988, 4.

22. Reed.

23. H. G. Koenig, D. O. Moberg, J. N. Kvale, "Religious Activity and Attitudes of Older Adults in a Geriatric Assessment Clinic," *Journal of the American Geriatric Society*, 36(4): 1988, 362–374.

24. Gerald Epstein, "Hebraic Medicine," *Advances: Journal of the Institute of Advancement of Health*, 4(1): 1987, 56–66.

25. Pearsall, p. 215.

26. Pearsall.

27. Epstein, p. 58.

28. Epstein.

29. Pearsall, p. 54.

30. Graves, p. 38.

31. Graves, pp. 38–39.

32. Graves, p. 39.

33. Graves.

34. Graves.

35. Rick Fields, Rex Weyler, Rick Ingrasci, and Peggy Taylor, *Chop Wood, Carry Water* (Los Angeles, California: Jeremy P. Tarcher, Inc., 1984).

36. Michael Harper, "Whole Again," *Journal of Christian Nursing*, Summer 1988, p. 13.

37. Robert Coles, "The Power of Prayer," *50 Plus*, December: 1987, 44.

38. Blair Justice, *Who Gets Sick: Thinking and Health* (Houston, Texas: Peak Press, 1987), p. 275.

39. Larry Dossey, *Healing Words* (San Francisco: Harper San Francisco, 1993), p. 31.

40. Larry Dossey; "Evidence of Prayer's Healing Power," *Brain/Mind*, December: 1993, 4–5.

41. Rupert Sheldrake, "Prayer: A Challenge for Science," *Noetic Sciences Review*, Summer: 1994, 5.

42. Herbert Benson, *Your Maximum Mind* (New York: Times Books/Random House, Inc., 1987), p. 6.

43. Benson, p. 46.

44. Gurney Williams III, "Holy-istic Healing," *Longevity*, March: 1994, 28.

45. *Journal of Psychology and Theology*, 19: 71–73.

46. Dawson Church and Alan Serr, editors, *The Heart of the Healer* (New York: Aslan Publishing, 1987).

47. Church and Sherr.

48. Larry Dossey, *Meaning and Medicine: A Doctor's Tales of Breakthrough and Healing* (New York: Bantam Books, 1991), p. 183.

49. Justice, pp. 284–285.

50. "Does Prayer Help Patients?" p. 35.

51. "Does Prayer Help Patients?"

52. Church and Sherr.

53. Joan Borysenko, *Minding the Body, Mending the Mind* (Reading, Massachusetts: Addison-Wesley Publishing Company, Inc., 1987), p. 176.

54. Robin Casarjian, "Forgiveness: An Essential Component in Health and Healing," in Proceedings of the Fourth National Conference on the Psychology of Health, Immunity, and Disease, published by the National Institute for the Clinical Application of Behavioral Medicine.

55. Dan Custer, *The Miracle of Mind Power*

(Englewood Cliffs, New Jersey: Prentice-Hall, Inc., 1960).

56. Custer.

57. Casarjian.

58. Arnold Fox and Barry Fox, *Wake Up! You're Alive* (Deerfield Beach, Florida: Health Communications, Inc., 1988), p. 102.

59. Fox and Fox.

60. Custer.

61. Dwight Lee Wolter, *Lotus,* Spring:1994, 53.

62. Robin Casarjian, *Forgiveness: A Bold Choice for a Peaceful Heart* (New York: Bantam Books, 1992), pp. 232–233.

63. Harold G. Koenig, James N. Kvale, and Carolyn Ferrel, "Religion and Well-Being in Later Life," *The Gerontologist*, 28(1): 1988, 18–27.

64. Harvard Medical School and New England Deaconess Hospital, Proceedings of "Advances in Behavioral Medicine: Clinical Practices and Research," February 28–March 3, 1989.

65. Christopher G. Ellison, "Religious Involvement and Subjective Well-Being," *Journal of Health and Social Behavior,* 32: 1991, 80–99.

66. "Religion Aids Coping with Illness," *Mental Medicine Update,* Spring: 1993, 2.

67. "Religion as a Variable in Psychiatric Studies," *Behavior Today*, February 27: 1989, 6.

68. "The Empty Church Syndrome," *Psychology Today*, November, 1988.

69. "The Empty Church Syndrome."

70. "The Empty Church Syndrome."

71. Leonard A. Sagan, *The Health of Nations* (New York: Basic Books, Inc., Publishers, 1987), p. 137.

72. "Faith Vital to Seniors' Well-Being," *Brain/Mind and Common Sense, American Journal of Sociology,* 97: 1052–1079.

73. Michael Argyle, *The Psychology of Happiness* (London Methuen and Company, Ltd., 1987), p. 196.

74. Argyle.

75. Laurel Arthur Burton and Jarad D. Kass, "How to Make the Best Use of a Patient's Spirituality," in Proceedings of the Fourth National Conference on the Psychology of Health, Immunity, and Disease, published by the National Institute

for the Clinical Application of a Behavioral Medicine.

76. Mark Bricklin, Mark Golin, Deborah Grandinetti, and Alexis Lieberman, *Positive Living and Health*, (Emmaus, Pennsylvania: Rodale Press, 1990).

77. George K. Jarvis and Herbert C. Northcott, "Religion and Differences in Morbidity and Mortality," *Social Science Medicine*, 25(7): 1987, 813–824.

78. Jarvis and Northcott.

79. Jarvis and Northcott.

80. Bricklin et al.

81. Emrika Padus, *The Complete Guide to Your Emotions and Your Health*, (Emmaus, Pennsylvania: Rodale Press, 1986).

82. Brent Q. Hafen and Kathryn J. Frandsen, *People Need People: The Importance of Relationships to Health and Wellness* (Evergreen, Colorado: Cordillera Press, Inc., 1987) p. 25.

83. Sagan, pp. 137–138.

84. S. I. McMillen, *None of These Diseases* (Old Tappan, New Jersey: Fleming H. Revell Company, 1984), p. 208.

85. Justice, p. 131.

86. John Gartner, Dave Larson, and George Allen, *Journal of Psychology and Theology*, 19: 6–25.

87. Bricklin et al.

88. Jeffrey S. Levin and Preston L. Schiller, "Is There a Religious Factor in Health?" *Journal of Religion and Health*, 26(1): 1987.

89. Jarvis and Northcott.

90. Levin and Schiller.

91. Levin and Schiller.

92. Jeffrey S. Levin and Harold Y. Vanderpool, "Is Frequent Religious Attendance *Really* Conducive to Better Health?: Toward an Epidemiology of Religion," *Social Science Medicine*, 24(7): 1987, 589–600.

93. Rachel Naomi Remen, "On Defining Spirit," *Noetic Sciences Review*, Autumn: 1988, 7.

94. William L. Mundy, "Curing Allergy with Visual Imagery," *The Psychology of Health, Immunity, and Disease,* vol. A, p. 437, in Proceedings of the Sixth International Conference of the National Institute for the Clinical Application of Behavioral Medicine.

18

ALTRUISUM AND HEALTH

*I don't know what your destiny will be, but one thing I know:
the only ones among you who will be truly happy are those who
will have sought and found how to serve.—ALBERT SCHWEITZER*

Physician and philosopher Albert Schweitzer proclaimed during a selfless career
what he believed to be the prescription for happiness. True happiness, he said, is
to be found only by serving others. New clinical research has verified that service
is not only a prescription for happiness but is a prescription for improved health
as well. As German-born physicist and Nobel Prize winner Albert Einstein said,
"Only a life lived for others is worth living."

Altruism—the act of giving of oneself out of a genuine concern for other people—has been called one of the healthiest of human attributes. Albert Einstein
said, "Many times a day I realize how much my own outer and inner life is built
upon the labors of my fellow men, both living and dead, and how earnestly I
must exert myself in order to give in return as much as I have received."

A recent Gallup Poll shows that Americans contribute more than $104 billion
to good causes. The value of our volunteer time equates to an additional $150 bil-
lion each year. According to studies, altruism is one of the biggest sources of revenue for the United States Gross National Product.[1]

The ability to "connect" by regarding another's needs above one's own appears to contribute to a longer and healthier life. Scientists are beginning to conclude that doing good for others is good for a person—especially for the nervous
system and the immune system. The effects of genuine altruism may be so powerful that even *thinking* about altruistic action may give your immune system a
boost.[2]

Harvard psychologists who wanted to find out how altruistic thoughts impact us conducted a precise experiment on a group of volunteers; the accurate
measure was the amount of germ-fighting substance in the saliva of the volunteers. The amount of the substance provides a clear indication of how well the

immune system is working. Psychologists measured the saliva of the volunteers both before and after they watched each of three films. The first was a gentle film on gardening; the second was a Nazi war documentary; the third was a documentary about Mother Teresa, the Nobel Prize–winning nun who has dedicated charitable works to the poor, the lepers, and the orphans in India's most poverty-stricken regions.

Measurements of saliva showed no change during the first two films. After reviewing the third film, the amount of immune agent in the volunteers' saliva rose sharply, even among those who said they dislike Mother Teresa. Volunteers who merely *watched* altruistic service experienced an actual physical change—one that could possibly help them stay healthier.[3]

Altruism may actually be one of our earliest skills. Bowling Green State psychologist Jaak Panksepp believes that helping had an integral part in our biological evolution because it's necessary for reproduction and the survival of certain species. In evolution of the human species, cooperative efforts may have been not only helpful to survival, but, says Panksepp, a key factor in development and expansion of the human brain. "Intrinsic helping tendencies may thus, like dominance urges, be embedded in the human brain structure," he theorizes, or "may even be part of what we think of as human nature itself."[4]

How Altruism Boosts Health

While researchers know that altruism promotes health, they are just beginning to find out how and why. In addition to the direct link to the immune system, it may counteract stress. Canadian physician Hans Selye, one of the world's authorities on the physiological effects of stress, concluded that altruism can help combat the effects of stress by preventing nervous system "overload." By doing good deeds for others, Selye believed, a person wins their affection and gratitude—and the resulting "warmth" helps protect the person from stress.[5]

There may even be a physiological reason for that "warmth": Varied research has shown that altruistic action stimulates the brain to release endorphins, powerful natural painkillers that literally make us feel better. Those endorphins may also be a key to relieving the effects of stress.

Allan Luks, executive director of the Institute for the Advancement of Health in New York City, shares the view that altruistic deeds help relieve stress. He says that "people who help others frequently report better health than people who don't help. They relate an improved sense of well-being, and decreased problems with stress-related health conditions."[6]

We know that the cumulative effects of stress are negative. Kenneth R. Pelletier, associate clinical professor at the University of California School of Medicine, says, "Under conditions of extreme stress, the immune system is depressed. The number and activity of white cells falls. The activity of the natural killer cells is reduced. There are changes in the ratio of helper cells to suppressor cells of the immune system."[7]

New evidence shows that the cumulative effects of altruism, of giving a helping hand, of reaching out to others are positive. Although stress can compromise the immune system, positive emotions related to altruism—emotions like love and compassion—help stabilize the immune system against the normal immunosuppressing effects of stress. That effect may go so far, Pelletier believes, that altruism may even help slow down the inevitable deterioration of the immune system as a person ages.[8] And, because of the social contact and sense of purpose associated with altruism, good deeds may help prevent some stress to begin with.

In his landmark book, *The Broken Heart: The Medical Consequences of Loneliness*, University of Maryland School of Medicine researcher James Lynch says, "The mandate to 'Love your neighbor as you love yourself' is not just a moral mandate. It's a physiological mandate. Caring is biological. One thing you get from caring for others is you're not lonely. And the more connected you are to life, the healthier you are."[9]

Some specialists believe that altruism actually helps to preserve life—and a few believe that it is even part of the survival instinct. University of California at Los Angeles sociologist Linda Nilson studied data from more than a hundred disasters—and she found that those who survived and did the best were those who reached out to help others. The "tribal cohesiveness" that stemmed from the helping process, says Nilson, is what enabled many to survive even tremendous odds.

Epidemiologist James House and his colleagues at the University of Michigan's Survey Research Center carried out a landmark study of 2,700 people in Tecumseh, Michigan. The study period spanned more than a decade as House and his coworkers followed the volunteers carefully to determine what impact their social relationships had on their health. What House discovered was a powerful testimony for altruism. Among the people studied in Michigan, those who did regular volunteer work had better health and longer lives. House concluded that doing volunteer work, more than any other activity, dramatically increased life expectancy—and probably health as well.[10] Among the Michigan residents studied, the men who did no volunteer work were two and a half times as likely to die during the study as men who volunteered at least once a week.

Other studies confirm House's findings. Psychiatrist George Vaillant followed Harvard graduates for four decades. He found that altruism was one of the major qualities that helped the graduates cope with the stresses of life. The absence of altruism apparently has the opposite effect. After an in-depth study, social psychologist Larry Scherwitz of San Francisco's Medical Research Institute concluded that people who are self-centered are more likely to develop coronary heart disease, even when other risk factors are taken into account.

The factor of self-centered thoughts and behavior can in itself contribute to the stress that may lead to disease. Dean Ornish, director of California's Preventive Medicine Research Institute, says, "When a person has a sense of isolation, often what comes with that are feelings of not *having* enough or not *being* enough. The person says, 'if only I had more'—more power, more money, more love, whatever—'then I'd be happy.' Once that view of the world is set up, it's ultimately self-defeating because if people don't get more of it, whatever *it* is, they feel stress. And even when they do, it's never enough."[11]

Altruism and its associated good deeds, says Ornish, helps free us from "the stress cycle" by turning our focus away from self-involvement—and toward those we are helping.[12] Once our involvement is focused on others, we begin to show the qualities consistent with altruism: a high degree of optimism, a strong sense of purpose and spirituality, and a continued involvement with other people.

Even the way we talk reflects how we feel about others—and possibly how healthy we are. In interviews, people with the least evidence of altruism were those who referred to themselves with the pronouns *I*, *me*, and *my* most often—and they were also the ones most likely to develop coronary artery disease.

A group of studies done on altruism found that people who care for others are physically, emotionally, and mentally healthier than those who concentrate more on their own needs. Many researchers believe that altruism is an inborn characteristic intended to help boost health and longevity. One of them, bioethic researcher Willard Gaylin, says: "We are born with a natural caring tendency. I don't think it's so rare. We take care of infants who certainly do nothing to deserve it. They're not attractive. They wake you in the middle of the night. They urinate on you. They vomit on you. And yet we love them and care for them."

People who care for others also tend to have an important health-preserving quality: optimism. Psychologist Martin Seligman, author of *Learned Optimism*, says that altruism is an activity "that presupposes a belief that things can change for the better." Optimists, he maintains, "have better health, better immune systems, and so live longer. Indirect evidence would then indicate that altruists might live longer."[13]

One of the most profound examples of the health and longevity benefits of altruism comes from the life of philanthropist John D. Rockefeller, Sr.[14] Rockefeller entered the business world with gusto and drove himself so hard that by age thirty-three he had earned his first million dollars. Ten years later he owned and controlled the world's largest business. By the time he was fifty-three, he was the world's first billionaire.

Meanwhile, the people he had crushed in this pursuit of wealth hated him; workers in Pennsylvania's oil fields hanged him in effigy, and he was guarded day and night by bodyguards pledged to protect his life. He had developed alopecia, a condition in which hair falls out; his digestion was so poor that all he could eat was crackers and milk. He was plagued by insomnia. The doctors who struggled to help him agreed that he wouldn't live another year.

Then something happened to John D. Rockefeller. He began to think of—and care about—others more than he did himself. He decided to use his billions of dollars for the benefit of others. Hospitals, universities, missions, and private citizens were the beneficiaries of the hundreds of millions of dollars he gave through the Rockefeller Foundation. His generosity aided in the discovery of penicillin. His contributions to medicine enabled researchers to find cures for tuberculosis, malaria, diphtheria, and many other diseases that had robbed so many of life. His contributions helped rid the South of its greatest physical and economic plague, the hookworm.

When Rockefeller began using his riches to help other people, he helped himself. For the first time in years, he was able to eat normally. He felt renewed. He slept soundly. He defied the odds and lived to see his fifty-fourth birthday—and many birthdays after that. He kept on giving and caring for others, in fact, until he died at the age of ninety-eight.

The Altruistic Personality

What makes a person altruistic? Some believe it's instinct, stemming from the time when people lived in small groups of hunters and gatherers. According to Stanford anthropologist John Tooby, those early hunters/gatherers depended highly on each other, not only for food and shelter, but for survival.[15]

In a supporting point of view, New York psychologist Linnda R. Caporall cites a series of experiments conducted over ten years and reported in *Behavioral and Brain Sciences*. The studies show that human nature is basically social, not selfish—and she agrees that altruism probably stems back to hunter/gatherer times.[16]

A growing number of researchers believe that altruism is a capacity shared by everyone to some extent or another. Altruism can be learned, say the researchers, depending on social and cultural background, the stage of moral or self-development, previous opportunities to learn altruism, the sense of responsibility and empathy, and the particular situation in which one is called upon to help.[17]

Other researchers believe in a certain "personality"—that altruistic people seem to have a set of personality traits enabling them to reach out to others. In a classic study of altruism, Samuel P. Oliner and Pearl M. Oliner studied the "rescuers" who provided help to the Jews during Hitler's reign of terror. These rescuers were altruistic—so much so that they often risked their own lives and safety to help others. According to Oliner, altruism is fueled by "empathy, allegiance to their group or institutional norms, or commitment to principle."[18] University of California at Irvine professor Kristen Monroe says that research shows altruists tend to view themselves as one with all of humanity rather than acting only in their own behalf.[19]

The Oliners say altruistic people never regard others as inferiors; they have a firm conviction that all people have universal similarities.[20] One rescuer summarized the attitude by remarking that "Jews were just people. We neither looked down on them nor did we look up to them. We never felt they were any different."

The altruistic people the Oliners studied valued human relationships more than money, and focused on others rather than on themselves. They believed that ethical values were to be applied universally—that people are worthy of tolerance and respect regardless of their race, religion, or class. They emphasized the values of helpfulness, hospitality, concern, and love—and they sensed a universal obligation to be of help to others. Their commitment to caring for others extended well beyond their friends and loved ones.

The "rescuers" believed in the right of innocent people to be free from persecution—and most were moved by the pain of others. They also had a tendency to believe in a victim's innocence, to believe that people are victimized by external circumstances and not by inherent character flaws. With deep empathy for the sadness and helplessness of others, these rescuers felt a personal responsibility for helping to relieve others' pain and sadness.

That empathy may have been one of their most important emotions. Considerable evidence, both anecdotal and that based on scientific experiments, suggests that empathy somehow connects people. It forms a literal bond, acting almost as a "glue" between living things. We know it works between people, and even between people and animals. Now researchers at Princeton University's Engineering Anomalies Research Laboratory have proved that it even works to connect people and machines. According to Larry Dossey, studies show that "the effects of empathic bonding transcend space and time."[21]

These altruistic people had a healthy perspective about themselves. They did not suffer from self-interest or self-preoccupation, both of which reduce the ability to care for others. They did not think too highly of themselves (people with too much self-esteem believe they should be the recipients, not the bestowers, of attention and care). Nor did they think too poorly of themselves (people with too little self-esteem become so absorbed by their own distress that they can't worry about other people's needs). Most were highly independent of the opinions and evaluations of others; they tended to act on their own and did seek or need external reinforcement for their activities. Actually, most were embarrassed by the thanks or appreciation they received.

The altruistic people the Oliners studied were very "connected" to others, especially to diverse people and groups. They enjoyed close family relationships and had a strong sense of belonging to the community. Their attachment to others began early in life, and extended beyond family to embrace friends, acquaintances, and even strangers. The rescuers had a tendency to befriend people who were different from themselves. They perceived their relationships with their family of origin as being very close.

Their commitment to caring was profound—and their internal compulsion was so strong that they often made the decision to help almost instantaneously. They felt a strong sense of inner control, but did not feel the need to control others; although they believed they could control events and shape their own destiny, they were also willing to risk failure. When something didn't go as planned, they spent little time mourning those failures. Most important, they believed they could succeed when others were convinced of failure.

To these rescuers, caring was not a spectator sport—it compelled action. They assumed personal responsibility not because others required it, but because they would have been unhappy if they had failed to act. Although they placed a value on hard work and economic prudence, they never expected monetary reward for their altruistic actions. They performed those deeds without ulterior motives. The Oliners summed up the rescuers in their study as "not saints, but ordinary people who nonetheless were capable of overcoming their human frailties by virtue of their caring capacities."

The personality traits the Oliners observed among the rescuers are not peculiar to that group of people; the traits, researchers believe, are common among most altruistic people. Nor does altruism necessarily stem from a church or a religious belief; repeated research shows that church members are no more altruistic as a group than are other people.[22] University of Massachusetts psychologist Ervin Staub believes that altruistic people share three general traits:

1. They have a positive view of people in general.
2. They are concerned about others' welfare.
3. They take personal responsibility for how other people are doing.[23]

The tendency toward altruism is a trait that is established early in life, according to a number of researchers. Psychologist Alfie Kohn noted that altruism may be as dramatic as donating a kidney, or as "mundane as letting another shopper ahead of you in line. But most of us do it frequently and started doing it very early in life . . . Caring about others is as much a part of human nature as caring about ourselves."[24]

In studying outstanding altruists, researcher Christie Kiefer found that background and family values help determine the altruistic personality. The altruists she studied "came from families that were warm and nurturing. The emotional self-acceptance they developed in that environment liberated them to be generative, creative, playful, and relaxed." In addition, says Kiefer, they learned a sense of social responsibility from their parents or from another prominent person in their early lives—a sense that "committed them to action on behalf of others or their community."[25]

In their book, *The Altruistic Personality*, the Oliners cited the important lesson all of us can learn from the "rescuers":

> *Rescuers point the way. They were and are "ordinary" people. They were farmers and teachers, entrepreneurs and factory workers, rich and poor, parents and single people, Protestants and Catholics. Most had done nothing extraordinary before the war nor have they done much that is extraordinary since. Most were marked neither by exceptional leadership qualities nor by unconventional behavior. They were not heroes cast in larger-than-life molds.* What most distinguished them were their connections with others in relationships of commitment and care. *It is out of such relationships that they became aware of what was occurring around them and mustered their human and material sources to relieve the pain. Their involvements with Jews grew out of the ways in which they ordinarily related to other people . . . .*

They remind us that such courage is not the providence of the independent and the intellectually superior thinkers but that it is available to all through the virtues of connectedness, commitment, and the quality of relationships developed in ordinary human interactions.[26]

The Health Benefits of Volunteerism*

A recent Gallup survey revealed that 52 percent of all American adults and 53 percent of all American teenagers are involved in some kind of volunteer work. Many do it without organizational support. On their own, they figure out ways to help those who need it or those who are less fortunate. When asked why, two-thirds say it is because they want to "help people." That instinct to help occurs early in life; as early as the second year of life a child will respond to someone in distress by reaching out with a comforting touch, offering a favorite toy, or bringing a parent to help.

Volunteering, caring for, and helping others benefits more than the recipients of the help. The act of volunteering, helping, and serving appears to bring important health benefits to the volunteer. Examples abound. Consider the Retired Senior Volunteer Program, which places a quarter of a million elderly people in community volunteer jobs each year. National Director Alfred N. Larson recognizes the health benefits those seniors have, saying, "Doctors tell us that elderly people who engage in volunteer work are a lot better off, visit the doctor less often, and have fewer complaints."[27] A study of 2,700 residents of Tecumseh, Michigan, showed that men who volunteer for community organizations are two and a half times less likely to die from all causes of disease than those who don't get involved in volunteer work.[28]

One elderly volunteer in Baltimore explained, "Involvement makes you keep well so you can keep giving. It makes you take care of your health. It's a blessing to ward off old age."

The health benefits aren't restricted to consciously taking better care of health, however. Yale University professor of public health, Lowell Levin, points out that "when you're a helper, your self-concept improves. You are somebody. You are worthwhile. And there's nothing more exhilarating than that. That can influence your health." Consider these examples:

- Kay Arnold joined SENSE, a group of Connecticut entertainers who perform for the elderly and disabled. Her audiences benefit—and Kay herself says her

---

*Readers who are interested in volunteerism might consider the following: local church congregation or parish projects; fraternal orders, teams, clubs; local phone directory (under Social Services, United Way, or Voluntary Action); national organizations (many communities have chapters of the American Cancer Society, The American Heart Association, the March of Dimes, or the Easter Seal Society, for example); RSVP; Foster Grandparents; Big Brother/Big Sister; Vista; ACTION; Sierra Club; American Red Cross.

volunteer work gives her "a sense of worth I never had before." And when she performs, her arthritis pain disappears.

- Vince Ward is advertising and public relations director for one of the nation's largest telecommunications firms. His job is considered one of the highest stress positions imaginable, yet he does not have high blood pressure. How has he been able to overcome one of the the most common physiological effects of stress? The key could lie in the way he spends his spare time. Vince Ward is busy away from the office, too, raising money for a children's home, working with parolees from Kansas State Penitentiary, and donating blood to the Community Blood Bank of Greater Kansas City.

- In one study, the experiences of more than 1,700 women who regularly volunteered to help others were analyzed at the Institute for the Advancement of Health in New York City. The women who helped experienced relief of actual physical ailments, including headaches, loss of voice, pain due to lupus and multiple sclerosis, and depression. Approximately 90 percent of the women in the survey rated their health as better than or as good as others their age.[29]

Women in two major studies about volunteerism described a "helper's high," similar in nature to the "runner's high" experienced during exercising.[30] Research at Carnegie Mellon University shows that volunteerism helps improve mood and gives a "high." Scientists studying the phenomenon believe the act of volunteering, of serving and helping others, may cause release of endorphins. One researcher who has been studying the effects of altruism in animal studies concludes that it is "just about proven that it is our own natural opiates, the endorphins, that produce the good feelings" associated with reaching out to help others.[31]

Deeper insight about the "high" experienced by volunteers stemmed in part from a study conducted by Allan Luks, then at the Institute for the Advancement of Health, and psychologist Howard Andrews, a senior research scientist with the New York State Psychiatric Institute.

What did they learn?

After collecting surveys from more than three thousand volunteers, they found twofold health benefits from volunteer work. The "healthy-helper syndrome," as they call it, starts with a physical high—a "rush" of good feeling that is characterized by increased energy, sudden warmth, and a sense of euphoria. The physical sensations associated with the "helper's high"—which 95 percent of the people surveyed experienced—suggest that the brain releases endorphins in response to the act of helping.

The second stage of the "healthy-helper syndrome"—which more than half of the volunteers reported—is a longer-lasting sense of calm and heightened emotional well-being. Together, say Luks and Andrews, the "high" associated with volunteering is a powerful antidote to stress, a key to happiness and optimism, and a way to combat feelings of helplessness and depression.[32]

A national survey that led to the definition of the "healthy-helper syndrome" definitely delineated the two distinct phases—one an "immediate physical feel-good sensation," the second a sense of calmness and relaxation. According to Luks, the survey showed that those who volunteer have better perceived health—and that the more often they volunteer, the greater the health benefits. Luks says those who volunteered once a week reported ten times better health and had specific improvements in health that ranged from less pain and fewer colds to overall well-being.[33]

Famed Harvard cardiologist Herbert Benson, well-known for his research on the effects of relaxation, feels that helping others works much the same way as yoga, spirituality, and meditation to help people "forget oneself, to experience decreased metabolic rates and blood pressure, heart rate, and other health benefits."[34] Volunteer service can result in a condition sometimes described as "helper's calm" or "helper's high." Under stress, the heart pumps faster; the adrenal glands release corticosteroids (the "stress hormones"); organ functions are disrupted; breathing speeds up. As a result, the person is more sensitive to pain—and the "stress hormones" that start coursing through the veins raise the level of blood cholesterol, elevate blood sugar, and reduce functioning of the immune system.

Apparently volunteer service works in the opposite way, reducing the effects of stress.[35] It works so well, in fact, that people in various studies have reported "treating" their stress-induced illnesses by engaging in altruistic volunteer work.

According to Luks and Howard, the volunteers who experienced the "healthy-helper syndrome" noticed an improvement in their own physical ills—including fewer arthritis pains, lupus symptoms, asthma attacks, migraine headaches, colds, and bouts of flu. The researchers believe that volunteerism, or altruism, can also alleviate the stress and other physiological conditions that lead to heart attack.

Luks and Howard credit a combination of factors for the improved health of volunteers: "the strengthening of immune system activity; the diminishing of both the intensity and awareness of physical pain; the activation of emotions vital to the maintenance of good health; the reduction of the incidence of attitudes, such as chronic hostility, that negatively arouse and damage the body; and the multiple benefits to the body's systems provided by stress relief.[36]

One-on-One Contact

The benefits of volunteer work depend on several factors. According to Allan Luks and Peggy Payne, the most health benefits from volunteering occur when you make personal contact, do it frequently (two hours a week), help a stranger, find a shared problem, work with an organization, use your skills, and "let go" of results.[37]

Of those, one of the most important is one-on-one contact—that the helper actually *connect with people*. The health benefits of volunteer work don't seem as pronounced when the volunteer simply donates money (no matter how important the cause) or spends volunteer time doing things isolated from close physical contact.[38] The physical contact seems to be a key. It is vital to good health and longevity.

In their book *The Healing Brain,* physician David Sobel and psychologist Robert Ornstein argue that the brain's major function is not logical thought, but protection of the body from illness. And, they say, the brain "cannot do its job of protecting the body without contact with other people. It draws vital nourishment from our friends, lovers, relatives, lodge brothers and sisters, even perhaps our coworkers and the members of our weekly bowling team."[39]

The direct contact involved in volunteer work seems to provide some of its value—but the direct contact apparently doesn't have to be physical, as long as it's one-on-one. In various studies, people who have done one-on-one crisis counseling or intervention by telephone have experienced and reported "helper's high," whereas those doing non-people tasks, such as stuffing envelopes, don't experience the "high."

And "helper's high" results most from helping people we don't know: The greatest chance of experiencing helper's high in several experiments was correlated with giving service to strangers.[40]

Desire to Volunteer

In addition to actual contact with the people one is helping, another important factor in achieving the health benefits of volunteer work seems to hinge on the word *volunteer*: A person has to *want* to do it. Forcing a person to be of help doesn't reap the health benefits of the helping service. In fact, some researchers now believe that one reason altruism benefits health is that it gives one a sense of control—but only by being able to *choose* the circumstances of the altruistic deeds.

That sense of control may even be crucial. A number of studies have shown that a lack of control can undermine health (as discussed elsewhere in this book). One landmark project carried out in a housing project for the elderly in San Francisco underscores the health benefits that follow the sense of control that volunteer work brings.

Meredith Minkler, cofounder of the project and a professor at the University of California's School of Public Health, reports that isolated elderly people living in single-room-occupancy hotels were brought together as volunteers to improve the neighborhoods where they were living. Together, they established minimarkets in the hotels in which they lived, brought down the crime rate, and brought about a number of other improvements. Meanwhile, their health improved. Their sense of well-being increased. Some even recovered from serious illnesses, and one ignored a doctor's "death sentence," living several years longer than had been predicted.[41]

Liking the Work

Another factor in reaping health benefits from volunteer work is to choose work a person *likes* to do—something that is suitable, brings pleasure, and is a joy to do.

If volunteer work does not bring happiness, or even make a person feel slightly exhilarated, he or she should probably consider switching to another project or type of work.

Consistency

Consistency seems important, too. Although an occasional good deed is certainly appreciated by the recipient, it doesn't seem to carry the same health benefits to the bestower as regular altruistic acts or consistent volunteer work. In studies of altruism and volunteerism, the greatest health benefits have been reaped by those who do consistent, regular volunteer work—at least once a week.[42]

Motive

Will you get the good-health benefits of volunteer work if you embark on a project out of selfish motives, to improve your own health? Some say you can. Luks, who has been involved in studying the benefits of altruism, points out that "people help for all sorts of reasons: empathy for the homeless; peer pressure from a neighbor; guilt over some problem; or pressure from church or community. But it doesn't seem to matter. If they continue with the helping, most likely, they'll get the feel-good sensation."[43]

Research shows that people may not fare as well if they expect repayment for their altruism or if they expect something in return. If repayment is expected but withheld, the helper does not gain the emotional benefits from helping, says Carnegie Mellon University researcher Gail Williamson.[44] The "repayment" expected by some volunteers varies tremendously, too; some expect monetary reward, others hope for payment in terms of increased status.[45]

Volunteer work has several unique aspects that could make the health benefits even greater. First, good feelings—and, almost certainly, health benefits—last far beyond the altruistic act itself. People in one study described more than one positive benefit associated with helping; 95 percent felt good while helping, and almost 80 percent said that the good feelings kept recurring long after the helping activity had ended.[46]

Participants in studies say they can recapture the "helper's high," although sometimes not as intensely, by merely *remembering* or thinking about their charitable acts. For those participants, the health benefits of helping—fewer aches and pains, relief of depression, strength, energy, and increased self-worth—kept returning when they remembered the altruistic deeds. In fact, more than 80 percent could recapture the physical benefits just by thinking about their volunteer work.[47]

For the best health benefits from volunteering, researchers advise avoiding "unhelpful helping"—a style of volunteerism that causes the person being helped to actually become progressively more helpless and to eventually lose skills. To avoid that kind of helping, David Sobel offers these suggestions:

- Try to empower the person you're helping; you need to help that person gain as much control over his or her own life as possible.
- Encourage independence.
- As much as you can, allow the other person to make decisions.
- Give the other person clear responsibilities whenever possible—even for things you know you could do better or faster.
- Break down complicated tasks into small, easy steps.
- Allow mistakes and reward efforts, even if the results fall short of what you expected or what you know is possible.
- Limit your availability; the person you are helping should be increasingly independent. If you are always there, you stifle independence instead.
- Don't shield the person from all bad news or all problems; allow the person to appropriately express disappointment, anger or sadness.[48]

And, because volunteering can become very demanding, Sobel advises that you avoid burnout by doing the following:

- First, monitor yourself and watch for the signs of burnout. You're probably getting burned out if you feel overwhelmed, helpless, out of control, resentful, guilty, or stressed.
- Pay attention to your own needs; if your own bucket is empty, you won't have anything to share with someone else.
- Recognize your limits. It would be nice to help at the homeless shelter every night, but that's just not realistic for most people. Or you might have a difficult time volunteering at a center for abused children if you were abused and have not dealt with those issues in your own life.
- Get help if you need it.
- Pace yourself; go only as fast as you comfortably can. Take what you can handle, and pass on what will overwhelm you.
- Don't get discouraged; if things don't work out with a certain situation, find another helping situation that's better for you. You might feel overwhelmed in a situation where you're expected to help a gang member rehabilitate—try helping an elderly person learn to read instead.
- Cancel any guilt trips you're considering.
- Finally, give yourself a pat on the back. You deserve it![49]

Love, the Emotion behind It

In essence, the health benefits of altruism and volunteer service may depend on the driving emotion behind it all—love, a projection of one's own good feelings onto other people. True love for others is a reflection of love of oneself,[50] a willingness to project warmth and affectionate concern. The love that brings health benefits goes beyond romantic love and kinship ties to include feelings of friendship, compassion, respect, admiration, and gratitude for others. True love, too, is a verb—an action word that calls on us to demonstrate and apply our good feelings through specific actions or deeds.

After a careful analysis of thousands of his patients, psychiatrist Alfred Adler wrote, "The most important task imposed by religion has always been, 'Love thy neighbor . . . ' It is the individual who is not interested in his fellow man who has the greatest difficulties in life and provides the greatest injury to others. It is from such individuals that all human failures spring."[51]

According to researchers who have studied the effects of love, a truly loving relationship—one of acceptance and safety—is earmarked by freedom from expectations and demands. And when that kind of relationship exists, they say, love and health go hand in hand.

Some even believe that love is an important key in the healing process. People who become more loving and less fearful, who replace negative thoughts with the emotion of love, are often able to achieve physical healing.

Take the example of people faced with life-threatening illness. What emotion is usually predominant? Fear. In fact, "fear is at the top of their list—fear of death, fear of the future, fear of pain."[52] Fear is a negative emotion that can drain one's ability to heal oneself and can incapacitate a person.

Once love becomes the overriding emotion, great changes can take place. "What we're talking about is love," says one researcher. "That's where the power is. Once you tap into it, you have joined up with a universal energy force. And with that power, nothing is impossible."[53]

Most of us are familiar with the emotional effects of love, the way love makes us feel inside. But it doesn't stop there. True love—a love that is patient, trusting, protecting, optimistic, and kind—has actual physical effects on the body, too.

Bernie S. Siegel, prominent Yale surgeon and oncologist, claims that love and support, whether from an individual or a group, is an important facet of all healing. Its importance is so marked that even outsiders who observe the loving process can see clear evidence of its healing effects. Based on his own observations over the years, Siegel says, support and love from a physician can even result in noticeable improvement in a patient's condition.[54] Reflecting on his own practice, which has spanned more than three decades, Siegel concludes, "Someday we will understand the physiological and psychological workings of love well enough to turn on its full force more reliably. Once it is scientific, it will be accepted."[55]

Although we are not yet at that ideal level of understanding, there is much we *do* know and understand about the physiological effects of love. One of the most important effects of love is a boost of immune system function. Based on his studies, Harvard psychologist David McClelland concludes that love aids lymphocytes and improves immune functions—even though he is not sure *how*.[56]

Tests conducted at the Meninger Clinic in Topeka, Kansas, seem to confirm the effect of love on the immune system. At the clinic it was found that people who were romantically in love had white cells that were significantly more active in fighting infection. As a result, they suffered fewer colds. They also had lower levels of lactic acid in their blood, which means they were less likely to get tired, and they had higher levels of endorphins in their blood, which may contribute to a sense of euphoria and may help reduce pain.[57]

People with personality traits that enable them to love others and to enjoy intimate relationships tend to fare better overall in immune system function. In a group of studies, those who loved and cared most for others had the best immune system balance; a high ratio of helper/suppressor T cells and low levels of the stress hormone norepinephrine.[58] Those who scored highest on the ability to have an intimate relationship also had the highest levels of immunoglobulin A, an important immune agent that enables people to resist disease.[59]

Scores of other studies point out the importance of love to good health.[60] In one, people who were isolated had a twofold to threefold increased risk of death from heart disease and all other causes. In another, people who felt loved and supported developed much less atherosclerosis of the coronary arteries (a major risk factor for heart disease). In another, elderly adults who felt loved and supported had lower cholesterol levels and better immune function.

Writing in the journal *Science*, Dr. James House summed up the notion that it's the "10 to 20 percent of people who say they have nobody with whom they can share their private feelings, or who have close contact with others less than once a week, who are at most risk."[61]

Love and Animals

The power of love has even been profoundly demonstrated in experiments with animals. Love and the handling that goes along with it have been shown to influence a baby animal's weight gain, emotional reactions, ability to respond to stress, and learning behaviors.[62] Studies have shown that animals raised without love (and the handling that goes along with it) have weakened immune systems.

Animals deprived of love also have a greater tendency to develop disease, whereas those exposed to love and handling seem better able to resist disease. In one experiment, two groups of laboratory rabbits were each fed a diet high in fat. One group of rabbits was treated routinely in the laboratory. The other group was shown "love"; these rabbits were talked to, handled gently, and petted often. The rabbits that were shown affection developed significantly less atherosclerosis than the rabbits treated routinely.[63]

Love and Children

Although an absence of love seems to weaken the immune system in animals, it has also been shown to reduce an animal's ability to deal with stress. The same appears to be true of humans. And the earlier people have the benefit of a strong, loving relationship, the better they seem to be able to resist the deleterious effects of stress.

In the book *Vulnerable but Invincible*, the effects of an early loving relationship become apparent. To determine in part what helps us resist stress, researchers studied 650 children reared in poverty on the Island of Kauai in the Hawaiian Islands. Their families had a multitude of problems. Many of the children were reared by single-parent mothers who were themselves troubled by depression and schizophrenia in addition to the rigors of extreme poverty.

Researchers first did an extensive follow-up on the children when they turned ten years old. Half of them were already in serious trouble. Many had serious physical problems and problems in school, among other difficulties. Eight years later, researchers did another follow-up on the children, now eighteen years old. One-fourth of them had developed "very serious" physical and psychological problems. By the time they became adults, more than three-fourths showed the effects of their impoverished environment. Many had profound psychological and behavioral problems; even more were in poor physical health.

Of greatest interest to researchers, however, were the 15 to 20 percent who remained resilient. Despite their impoverished and difficult existence, these children were able to successfully resist the stress of that environment. Study findings give us a powerful insight into the effect of love. The children who remained resilient and well had a warm and loving relationship with another person *during their first year of life.* The children who developed serious psychological and physical problems did not.

Psychotherapist Harmon Bro, a former professor at Syracuse University, emphasizes the importance of early, affirming love. People who have "never developed the capacity for loving find lovelessness reflected in their bodies"—in poor health, muscular tension, shallow breathing, and other physical "ills" that reflect in a very real way an illness of the spirit.

Notes

1. Alfie Kohn, "Do Religious People Help More? Not So You'd Notice," *Psychology Today,* December: 1989, 66.

2. Eileen Rockefeller Growald and Allan Luks, "Beyond Self," *American Health,* March: 1988, 51–53.

3. Growald and Luks.

4. Allan Luks and Peggy Payne, *The Healing Power of Doing Good* (New York: Fawcett Columbine, 1992).

5. Growald and Luks.

6. Sarah Lang, "Extend Your Hand, Extend Your Life," *Longevity,* March: 1989, 18.

7. Lang, p. 19.

8. Lang.

9. James, Lynch, *The Broken Heart: The Medical Consequences of Loneliness* (New York: Basic Books, Inc., Publishers, 1977).

10. Growald and Luks, pp. 51–53.

11. Lang, p. 19.

12. Lang, p. 19.

13. Lang.

14. S. I. McMillen, *None of These Diseases,* revised (Old Tappan, New Jersey: Fleming H. Revell Company, 1984), pp. 188–189.

15. Geoffrey Cowley, "A Disaster Brings Out the Best in People. Why?" *Newsweek,* November 6: 1989, 40, 44.

16. Bruce Bower, "Getting Out From Number One," *Science News,* 137: 1990, 266–267.

17. Tom Hurley, "Another Look at Altruism: Notes on an International Conference," *Noetic Sciences Building,* August/September: 1989, 3.

18. Samuel P. Oliner and Pearl M. Oliner, *The Altruistic Personality: Rescuers of Jews in Nazi Europe,* (New York: Macmillan/The Free Press, 1988).

19. "Dr. Frederick Franck: An Artist, Physi-

cian, and Author Searches for What It Means to Be Human," *Your Personal Best*, November: 1989, 14–15.

20. Oliner and Oliner.

21. Larry Dossey, *Healing Words* (San Francisco: Harper San Francisco, 1993), pp. 110–113.

22. Kohn.

23. Alfie Kohn, "Beyond Selfishness," *Psychology Today*, October: 1988, 38.

24. "Research: Altruism and Transformation," *Noetic Sciences Review*, Autumn: 1990, 33.

25. "Research: Altruism and Transformation."

26. Oliner and Oliner.

27. Allan Luks with Peggy Payne, "Helper's High," *New Age Journal*, September/October: 1991, 49, 121; from Allan Luks with Peggy Payne, *The Healing Power of Doing Good: The Health and Spiritual Benefits of Helping Others* (Ballantine Books, 1991).

28. David Sobel, "R$_x$: Helping Others," *Mental Medicine Update*, Winter: 1993, 6.

29. Allan Luks, "Helper's High," *Psychology Today*, October: 1988, 39–42.

30. Allan Luks, "Helper's High," *Psychology Today*, October: 1988, 39.

31. "The Return of Generosity," *Health*, August: 1989, 13.

32. Luks and Payne.

33. Luks and Payne.

34. Luks, p. 42.

35. Luks.

36. Luks and Payne, p. 121.

37. Luks and Payne.

38. Luks.

39. Growald and Luks, p. 52.

40. Luks and Payne.

41. Lang, p. 19.

42 Lang.

43. Lang.

44. "The Return of Generosity," *Health*, August 1989, p. 13.

45. Cowley.

46. Howard F. Andrews, "Helping and Health: The Relationship Between Volunteer Activity and Health-Related Outcomes," *Advances*, 7(1): 1990, 25–34.

47. Luks, p. 42.

48. Sobel.

49. Sobel.

50. Arnold Fox and Barry Fox, *Wake Up! You're Alive* (Deerfield Beach, Florida: Health Communications, Inc., 1988) p. 75.

51. McMillen, p. 124.

52. Padus.

53. Padus.

54. Mary Carpenter, "Modern-Day Faith Healing: Why Doctors Are Listening, Not Laughing," *Self*, September: 1987, 202–205.

55. Blair Justice, "Think Yourself Healthy," *Prevention*, June: 1988, 31–32, 105–108.

56. Justice.

57. Justice.

58. Blair Justice, *Who Gets Sick: Thinking and Health* (Houston, Texas: Peak Press, 1987), p. 257.

59. Justice.

60. Studies summarized from Dean Ornish, "The Healing Power of Love," *Prevention*, February: 1991, 60–66, 135–141; from Dean Ornish, *Dr. Dean Ornish's Program for Reversing Heart Disease* (New York: Random House, Inc., 1990).

61. Ornish.

62. Fox and Fox, p. 85.

63. Justice, *Who Gets Sick*, p. 258.

19

THE HEALING POWER OF FAITH

We act in faith,
and miracles occur.
—DAG HAMMERSKJOLD

French novelist George Sand penned the sentiment that faith "is an excitement and an enthusiasm: it is a condition of intellectual magnificence to which we must cling as to a treasure, and not squander in the small coin of empty words." If the results of recent scientific studies are correct, faith is, as Sand stated, a treasure—not only in the spiritual sense of the word, but as a potent factor in both good health and healing influence. Jonas Salk claimed that "the mind, in addition to medicine, has powers to turn the immune system around."

American philosopher Ralph Waldo Emerson wrote extensively of faith, and penned in his later years the sentiment that "all he had seen and experienced caused him to have faith in that which he could not see. Whoever reasons only according to what the five bodily senses reveal or believes that the only means of knowing is through seeing, hearing, tasting, smelling, and feeling is controlled by appearances."[1]

Indeed, faith must "rise above what our five senses tell us, for they only report the appearance of the physical world."[2] Or, as one behavioral health scientist put it, "I see miracles as the playing out of natural or divine law with which we were not formerly acquainted. For example, though some considered the fact that Columbus did not fall off the edge of a 'flat' earth to be a miracle, the real miracle was the opening of the layer of consciousness that allowed Columbus to perceive the earth as being round before he set sail.[3]

That scientist, Deirdre Davis Bingham, said she sometimes thinks of us "as being in the center of nesting Russian eggs. Our reality is limited by the wooden shell of the particular egg in which we find ourselves. As we drill conceptual holes in the immediate shell and glimpse a new layer of possibilities, that shell begins to crack and we have a new realm of "reality." It is in the nature of scientific inquiry (and human consciousness) that major advances come from people who look at things in a different way—who break through the shell of their immediate nesting egg.[4]

Medical and scientific research conducted over the past two decades has demonstrated clearly that what exists is not as important as what we *believe* exists. Personal belief gives us an unseen power that enables us to do the impossible, to perform miracles—even to heal ourselves. It has been found that patients who exhibit faith become less concerned about their symptoms, have less-severe symptoms, and have less-frequent symptoms with longer periods of relief between them than patients who lack faith.

That is not to say that faith should replace modern medicine. Instead, it should be used in conjunction with modern medicine—used to enhance the effects of medicine and to strengthen its impact. Even staunch medical practitioners recognize that faith plays a vital part in the healing process. As early as the sixteenth century, the great surgeon Ambrose Pare noted in one surgical report, "I dressed the wound, and God healed it."

The growing appreciation of faith among members of the medical community is characterized in the comments of Dr. Joan Borysenko, a former instructor at Harvard Medical School:

> *Two thousand years ago a woman who had suffered prolonged uterine bleeding approached Jesus of Nazareth. Coming up to him in a crowd, she touched the hem of his garment and was instantly healed. Jesus turned to her and explained that it was her faith that had made her whole. After centuries of slow progress toward rational explanations of the physical world, even scientists can at least begin to appreciate the truth of His assessment. We are entering a new level in the scientific understanding of mechanisms by which faith, belief, and imagination can actually unlock the mysteries of healing.*[5]

The Impact of Faith

An excellent example of the impact of faith—and the detriment of its absence—occurred in the Philippines during World War II.[6] American soldiers who had been bathing in contaminated streams had been infected with schistosomiasis, a parasitic worm infection. The soldiers had been treated with a complete regimen, but remained hospitalized four months after they were first diagnosed. They should have been healed, but they felt vaguely ill; they complained of symptoms ranging from abdominal cramps to headaches to vague weakness and fatigue. Attending physicians were puzzled: The soldiers were well fed. They were being housed in comfortable accommodations. They had benefited from the best available medical care for the condition. Yet none had healed.

Johns Hopkins School of Medicine psychiatrist Jerome D. Frank, then an Army doctor, was asked to investigate the situation and offer some clues as to why the men were not responding to treatment. After exhaustive interviews and examinations, he found that faith had a great deal to do with the soldiers and their prolonged illness.

The soldiers were confused and frightened about their prognosis and about what would happen to them. They were getting a mixed message about their illness. Their doctors were telling them that schistosomiasis was not a serious malady and that they would regain their health. At the same time, radios in the background were broadcasting "scare stories" about the disease in an effort to keep the American soldiers from bathing in the contaminated streams. The soldiers didn't know who to believe—the doctors who tried to soothe them or the radio announcers who detailed a grisly fate. Then there was confusion about what would happen. The Army was incredibly inconsistent about how the soldiers were treated. Some were shipped home. Some were detained in the Army hospital. Still others were sent back into combat.

Making the situation even worse were the doctors and nurses themselves. Carrying overwhelming caseloads, they did not have the time to devote undying attention to the soldiers stricken with schistosomiasis; as time went on, they were faced with the frustration that none of the soldiers was recovering. Before long, doctors and nurses were treating the soldiers with abrupt detachment—a sign to the soldiers that something was seriously wrong. The soldiers lacked faith—not because of some fault of their own, but because the confusing situation did not allow the opportunity to develop faith. The soldiers did not *expect* a cure, so none came.

Another example of faith's healing power was manifest when a group of neurologically diseased veterans were moved from a dismal, depressing Veterans Administration facility to a different area of the institution where a special rehabilitation team had taken great effort to transform the facility into a cheerful, optimistic place. For the first time, patients who had been hospitalized for three to ten years experienced faith and the hope that things would get better. They had been moved from a warehouse for the chronically ill to a place of hope and determination. Within three months, 70 percent had been discharged from the hospital; 40 percent became self-supporting.

The evidence says that faith can heal—or that it can be a very powerful element in the healing process. When combined with conventional treatment and optimism, faith can make the difference.

The Influence of Faith on Health

Cardiologist Herbert Benson makes a convincing case for the power of the mind with the example of the classic film, *Lawrence of Arabia*. While watching this epic, even people in air-conditioned theaters became extremely hot and thirsty; during intermissions, the concession stands were inundated with people demanding ice-cold drinks. It was, as Benson terms it, an "epidemic of thirst." The moral of the story, Benson says, is that "the influential and even life-changing forces we encounter are often not those things that are externally real. In the case of the film, of course, people weren't really deprived of water, but they identified with those waterless conditions so thoroughly that their bodies became 'convinced' they were on the Arabian dunes."[7]

According to Benson, medical and scientific research "is demonstrating ever more clearly that the things we can touch, taste, and measure frequently have to take a back seat to what we *perceive* or *believe* to be real. If the mind is that powerful, then what the mind believes can, in fact, have tremendous influence over the body. Belief or faith, says Benson—whether it's deep in the mind or heart or focused on some outside object, like a physician—can play a key role in generating a response in the body. Apparently, he says, "just having a strong belief is enough to cause things to happen in our physiology, but this is a very ticklish point. It does seem that just the state of belief, which can emanate from a variety of personal, philosophical, or religious orientations, is itself a powerful force.[8]

In his book *Super Immunity*, psychologist Paul Pearsall sums up research conducted at Michigan State University that proves that a single cell can be controlled by how we think. In describing the study results, Pearsall says that "the mind alters every cell in the body."[9]

A dramatic example of that power was provided by a sixteen-year-old boy with congenital ichthyosiform erythrodermia, a serious skin disease that causes a hardening and blackening of the skin. There is no known cure for the disease. The boy's condition had deteriorated to such a degree that his skin was harder than fingernails, and bacterial infection had set in. To demonstrate the power of the mind over the body, a hypnotist challenged the boy to "see" his skin as becoming normal. Within five days of the hypnosis, the boy's hard, damaged skin fell off; it was replaced with reddened, but more normal-looking, skin. Within ten days, the boy's skin had returned to normal—a phenomenon verified by three independent medical researchers.[10]

According to Benson, faith has been shown in countless studies to have a powerful influence over the body. So great is its power, in fact, that faith has been used to successfully relieve headaches, reduce angina pains, control hypertension, overcome insomnia, prevent hyperventilation attacks, help alleviate backaches, enhance cancer treatment, control panic attacks, reduce cholesterol levels, reduce overall stress, and alleviate the symptoms of anxiety—which include nausea, vomiting, diarrhea, constipation, short temper, and inability to get along with others.[11]

A review of studies measuring faith shows some impressive results and helps confirm the power of faith over physiological processes.[12] In one study, people showed a powerful ability to inhibit the growth of fungus cultures by concentrating on them for fifteen minutes from a distance of several feet. In another, people were able to significantly stimulate or inhibit the growth of bacteria. In a study conducted by the Mind Science Foundation, people were able to decrease the destruction of red blood cells. In still other studies, people even exerted influence over plants and animals. In one study conducted at the Mind Science Foundation, volunteers had a potent effect over people several rooms away.

A good example of faith's power over physiological processes is its influence over blood pressure. According to researchers Jeffrey S. Levin of Eastern Virginia Medical School and Hearold Y. Vanderpool of Galveston's University of Texas, devoutly faithful groups of people tend to have lower blood pressure than comparison groups of people.[13] Faith is so powerful, say researchers, that it has been shown to be effective against diseases like cancer, believed incurable in many cases. Harvard's Joan Borysenko studied cancer patients who were considered to be long-term survivors; she found that the attribute they had in common was strong faith.[14]

Faith also apparently increases the ability to resist stress and strengthens the body against the physical changes that can accompany stress. In one study, two psychiatrists, an endocrinologist, and a cancer specialist in New York City teamed up to determine which hormones were released under the stress of a truly life-threatening situation. For their "life-threatening situation," they chose women who were undergoing breast biopsies to determine whether they had cancer. To ascertain how much distress each woman was suffering, the researchers took daily measurements of hydrocortisone (a hormone secreted by the adrenal glands in response to stress) for three days before the women underwent the biopsy.[15]

They found that the amount of distress a woman suffered was not dependent on the crisis of probably having cancer. Instead, researchers determined that

---

Focus on Research

California internist Arnold Fox remembers a patient who taught him the power of faith, even against a disease as ominous as cancer. Fox had to tell the woman, a fifty-four-year-old mother of three, that she had cancer—and that the outlook was grim. Instead of being upset, as would have been expected, she merely smiled and said: "If you have faith, even as small as a tiny mustard seed, nothing is impossible." When Fox questioned her, she told him firmly that as long as she had faith, she could "shake off cancer."

Fox knew for a fact that her cancer was growing larger and more deadly every day, and that it was inoperable. He also knew from his experience with other patients that this patient had only about six months to live. But she stubbornly insisted that faith could conquer the cancer. "Belief would not—could not—cure the cancer," Fox writes in telling about the woman. "But if it made her happy to think about belief, well, I felt that was her privilege."

When Fox asked her about the cancer, she replied that the cancer "exists; it's in me. But I refuse to believe it will hurt me. I believe I'm healthy. And I know the cancer will go away."

"Much to my surprise," Fox writes, "her cancer *did* go away." The woman lived another ten years in good health.

"This woman with her faith was one of many patients who have taught me that there is a whole realm of medicine we physicians know nothing of," Fox writes. "We doctors can quote chapter and verse on anatomy, biochemistry, physiology, pharmacology, and other scientific subjects, but we are sadly unfamiliar with the miraculous healing powers of the human mind."

Source: Arnold Fox and Barry Fox, *Wake Up! You're Alive* (Deerfield Beach, Florida: Health Communications, Inc., 1988), pp. 49–50.

the amount of stress suffered was determined by the woman's psychological defenses—her outlook and her beliefs in general. The woman who suffered the least amount of stress (and whose adrenal hormones were the lowest) reported that she regularly used faith and prayer to cope with life's stressful events.

"People with a strong faith, whether from religious beliefs or just good experience with trust, are the ones who stick it out in the worst circumstances," reports psychologist Shlomo Breznitz, visiting scientist with the National Institute of Mental Health. "The best example is a mining disaster," Breznitz points out. "Miners are taught that if they should become trapped in a cave-in, there are certain things they should do and not do to stay alive. There is only limited oxygen, so they have to conserve their energy. It's futile to spend it trying to dig their way out. It's the miners who are able to maintain hope that they will be rescued, even when there's nothing else they can do, who have the best chances of surviving."[16]

The Healing Power of Faith

The power of faith is probably apparent in the healing process more than any other aspect of medicine. And, according to researchers who have studied the effects of faith, the stronger the faith, the more certain the healing power. As one researcher put it, "the faith that heals, that 'removes mountains,' must be a *certainty* about something which cannot be seen and cannot now be proved."[17]

Researcher Daniel Goleman maintains that belief "is the hidden ingredient in Western medicine and every traditional system of 'healing' I know about. In the West, doctors have long been aware of its curative power. A large number of illnesses can be treated more successfully if the patient believes in a particular cure."[18]

Psychiatrist Jerome Frank ascribes even greater powers to faith. He says faith is the element in even modern medicine that brings about a recovery. "The physician's main function is to use his medical skills to stimulate the patient's mechanisms of repair," Frank explains. "Nonmedical healers, whether African witch doctors or religious faith healers in Western countries, intuitively understand this. Their rituals and laying on of hands are designed to release or strengthen the patient's inner healing powers."[19]

"Faith" is not the property of a certain religion, nor does it owe its effectiveness to a certain shrine or ritual. All religions have members who have experienced seemingly magical, spontaneous cures from life-threatening or incurable diseases. Miracles have occurred at shrines scattered throughout the world, and patients who seemed stripped of any possibility of a cure have responded to a broad spectrum of rituals (such as laying on of hands). The key to these experiences is not the religion or the shrine or the ritual itself, but the faith of the person who is healed.

"There is no denying that religious shrines unleash powerful healing emotions of hope in the pilgrim," maintains Frank. "One cannot attribute this to any particular religious faith or object of worship, since all religions can cite instances of these seemingly magical cures. The more likely explanation is that the cure results from the individual's state of mind—his expectant faith."[20]

Lourdes

One obvious example is that of probably the best-known healing shrine, Lourdes. Since the visions of Marie Bernarde Soubirous and the discovery of the healing spring in the middle of the nineteenth century, there have been countless documented cases of people who went to the spring with faith and who were cured of severe illness. Lame people have left Lourdes with the ability to walk; the deaf have been blessed with the gift of sound; and sight has been restored to the blind. Many of the cures have been dramatic.

Today, more than two million people visit Lourdes each year in hope of being healed; they come from all corners of the world, and many have been told there is no cure for their condition. For most people, Lourdes is a last resort. Many make the pilgrimage only after years of drugs and therapies that have not yielded results.

The reputation of Lourdes as a "healing" shrine is well-deserved. People are healed, sometimes of life-long conditions. Are those healings due to some magical property of the springs themselves? Or to a special healing power possessed by the priests, nurses, and orderlies? Probably the healing is due to the expectant faith of the pilgrim who comes to Lourdes to be healed. As one eyewitness describes the scene at the shrine each afternoon, "The sick line up in two rows. . . . Every few feet, in front of them, kneeling priests with arms outstretched praying earnestly, leading the responses. Nurses and orderlies on their knees, praying too. . . . The Sacred Host is raised above each sick one. The great crowd falls to its knees. All arms are outstretched in one vast cry to Heaven. As far as one can see in any direction, people are on their knees, praying."[21]

The stirring services, the sense of support, and the outpouring of emotion at Lourdes and shrines like it "can only serve to reinforce the expectant faith that pilgrims bring with them," explains Frank. This faith, he adds, explains "the spontaneous remissions of disease and improved bodily functions experienced by some, as well as the increased sense of hope and improved morale that even the uncured take home with them."[22]

Other Examples

Lourdes (and other shrines like it) is only one example of how faith works to heal the sick. There are many other examples—and a number of scientific studies have even been able to document the healing power of faith. In one study, researchers studied a group of patients who were about to undergo surgery for detached retina. The researchers gave each patient a "score" that reflected his or her expectations about the surgery. After the surgery, the surgeon—who did not know the patient's "score"—gauged the speed of recovery and noted any complications. Those who had faith in the surgeon and faith in their own ability to cope with the surgery did the best. The researchers concluded that the body's own healing ability is actually stimulated "by a patient's faith in the healer and his methods, an optimistic outlook toward the treatment, and other psychological variables that, taken together, may be called an attitude of expectant faith."

In one stunning experiment, Harvard psychologist David McClelland took thirteen Harvard undergraduates with common colds to a psychic healer within twenty-four hours of the time their symptoms first appeared. The therapy was simple: The healer said, "You're healed."

But were they?

McClelland had listed thirty-two cold symptoms and had asked the students to rate their symptoms both before and after the visit to the psychic healer. All but five students said their symptoms were better. But here's the best part: The nine students who felt better also had higher levels of immunoglobulin A (IgA) in their saliva. IgA is an immune antibody that battles upper respiratory infections. In other words, their immune systems had been activated.[23]

A separate study provides a graphic description of how powerful faith can be in the healing process—even when the faith is not justified. A hospital-based physician was frustrated with three patients who, despite his best efforts, had not been helped by medical treatment. All three were women in their sixties. One suffered from chronic inflammation of the gall bladder. One was wasting away after failing to recuperate from surgery for pancreatitis. And one had inoperable cancer of the uterus; to complicate matters, she also had tremendous swelling of the legs and anemia.

The doctor called in a faith healer but did not tell any of the women about him. He practiced his rituals on an absentee basis, without any of the three patients knowing anything about it. After twelve healing sessions, there was no change in any of the patients' conditions. The physician dismissed the faith healer.

Then the physician went to the three patients, described the faith healer in enthusiastic and glowing terms, and told the women that they were extremely lucky: The faith healer would be working on their behalf each morning for three days. Of course, this wasn't true; the doctor had dismissed the faith healer. But as far as the women were concerned, they believed that the faith healer was working for them.

What the doctor saw was both dramatic and almost unbelievable: All three patients were relieved of their symptoms. All three were able to leave the hospital within a week. The patient with pancreatitis, who had been literally wasting away, got out of bed after what she believed to be the first "healing session." She rapidly gained thirty pounds—a feat medical science had been unable to help her accomplish. And she remained well, without any relapse of her condition. Most amazing was the cancer patient. The swelling in her legs disappeared. Her red blood cell level rose, reversing her anemia. Five days after the "healing sessions" began, she returned home—where she was able to function normally until her death several months later.

Faith can not only stimulate the body's own healing mechanisms, but it can also apparently influence the way drugs work in the body. Mary Baker Eddy, the founder of Christian Science, pronounced before the turn of the century that "when the sick recover by the use of drugs, it is the law of a general belief, culminating in individual faith, which heals."[24] And cardiologist Herbert Benson makes much the same argument in our day when he maintains that "a new drug given by a doctor who believes in it enthusiastically is far more potent that the same drug given by a skeptical doctor. The doctor marshals his patient's belief and power to help himself. But a patient may be able to get better without a doctor, simply calling on his belief in some outside force."[25]

One of the most striking and profound examples of how faith influences even the course of medication is the well-known story of a patient treated by Dr. Bruno Klopfer in the late 1950's. The patient was suffering from a widespread lymphoma—a serious cancer of the immune system—that was in its late stages. At the time, a drug called Krebiozen was being touted as a cure for cancer. The patient demanded that Klopfer administer Krebiozen, and the doctor agreed. Within two days of receiving the Krebiozen, the patient experienced a remarkable turnaround. As one account described it, the large tumors that covered his body began "melting like snowballs." After ten days of treatment with Krebiozen, the patient was released from the hospital, apparently free of disease. Klopfer believed that a medical miracle had occurred.

A medical miracle *had* occurred—but it was due to the patient's faith in the Krebiozen, not due to the drug itself. As fate would have it, that faith was short-lived. A few months after the patient was released from the hospital, newspapers around the country announced that Krebiozen was worthless. The patient's tumors promptly reappeared.

Klopfer was fascinated by this turn of events. Based on the patient's history, he strongly suspected that it had been the patient's *belief* that had cured him and that the drug had nothing to do with it. Klopfer became convinced that he could once again harness the man's faith if the conditions were right. He called his patient in, reassured him, told him the newspaper accounts were inaccurate, and that an extra-strength, improved, refined form of the drug had just been released to physicians. Klopfer offered this "refined" form of the drug to his eager patient. But Klopfer didn't actually have any improved Krebiozen. What he gave his patient was actually distilled water.

With distilled water coursing through his veins, the patient who believed that he had a new super Krebiozen staged another remarkable recovery. Within days, his tumors again disappeared. He was released from the hospital a second time, again apparently disease-free.

Unfortunately, it didn't last. Three months after his recovery, the patient read a newspaper report published by the American Medical Association. Definitive tests had proven beyond a doubt, the report said, that Krebiozen was worthless. Top-ranking officials in the American Medical Association proclaimed the drug as useless in the fight against cancer. The patient, who had left the hospital three months earlier free of tumors, read the report. His faith was shattered. His tumors ballooned. Two days after he read the newspaper report, he literally laid down and died.

Transfer of Energy Theory

One way in which faith healers have attempted to harness faith and bring about healing is through "laying on of hands," a ritual that dates to ancient times. "Spiritual healing by the laying on of hands has been practiced for as long as recorded history," notes psychiatrist Daniel Benor. "The Bible is replete with tales of unusual cures by the prophets, Christ, and the Apostles. Virtually every known culture has included healers among its health-care professionals."[26]

An eighteenth-century physician who practiced the laying on of hands expressed his hope that a physicist would someday be able to substantiate scientifically what went on during these rituals:

> Why should not the proximity of the human body, which can restore the brilliance of a faded pearl, exert upon a neighboring body, by means of an aura or radiation, an influence which stimulates or tranquilizes the other's nerves? Surely there may be attraction and revulsion, sympathy and antipathy, between individual and individual.[27]

Today's faith healers, says psychiatrist Jerome Frank, explain their power in different ways:

> Some believe they serve as a conduit for supernatural healing energy or that they transmit healing power generated by other members of the group; others believe that the healing force comes from within them. Patients who have undergone healing by laying on of hands often report a sensation of intense heat, although this does not register on a thermometer. Nevertheless, the evidence suggests that laying on of hands often does accelerate wound healing, and there have been cases in which patients who have been in wheelchairs for years suddenly rise and walk during the ritual.[28]

The "transfer of energy" theory has received widespread support among faith healers who practice the laying on of hands. Dolores Kreiger, a professor of nursing at New York University, teaches a version of laying on of hands to her students—and claims that the ritual "redistributes the patient's energy."[29]

Another practitioner who claims to be using the laying on of hands for "some kind of an energy exchange" is University of South Carolina nursing researcher Janet Quinn. The U.S. Department of Health and Human Services has awarded Quinn grant money to prove her hypothesis—and to determine whether the practice might benefit heart surgery patients.[30]

The person who practices laying on of hands has a specific task related to energy fields, according to Toni Tripp-Reimer, associate professor of nursing and adjunct professor of anthropology at the University of Iowa. The practitioner first identifies, then brings back into equilibrium, disrupted energy fields that surround the patient's body. "In theory, the therapist has a balanced energy field," Tripp-Reimer explains. "Being stronger, the therapist's field helps to bring the patient's back into proper balance."[31]

Indeed, a technique called *Kirlian photography* may give some credence to the "energy exchange" theory. Kirlian photography is a special kind of photography that reveals the spectacular color corona that surrounds the body. The corona of a healthy person is sharp and bright; a sick person has a blurry or cloudy corona composed of duller colors. Researchers who have photographed a practitioner's hands before and after "laying on of hands" show that the coronas surrounding the fingers and hands are brighter and more colorful after the ritual than before.

Other interesting research has studied the effects of "therapeutic touch," which doesn't involve physical contact. Instead, the healer's hands are held a short distance away from the skin as the healer performs the technique.

In one landmark study, researcher David P. Wirth used forty-four patients who had full-skin-thickness surgical wounds on their arms. The patients were asked to stick their arms through holes in a wall for five minutes a day; researchers told the patients that physicians were measuring "biopotentials" from the surgical site.

In actuality, however, something else was happening. For twenty-one of the patients, the room on the other side was vacant. For twenty-three of the patients, a therapeutic practitioner did noncontact therapeutic touch each day. Every few days, physicians who had no knowledge at all of the therapeutic touch measured the wounds of all forty-four patients.

What happened? By the eighth day, wounds of the patients who received therapeutic touch were significantly smaller and showed much less variation than those of the other patients. By the sixteenth day, thirteen of the twenty-three patients who had therapeutic touch were completely healed. *None* of the patients who had stuck their arms through holes into a vacant room were healed.

Wirth points out that the therapeutic touch itself was the reason for the healing. Because the patients didn't know they were receiving the touch, they weren't influenced by the placebo effect, suggestion, expectation, or belief.[32]

Faith and the Placebo Effect

One of the most striking demonstrations of faith in action is the placebo effect: the physical change that occurs as a result of what we *think* a pill or a procedure will do. According to Yale oncologist and surgeon Bernie Siegel, "What the placebo suggests to us is that we may be able to change what takes place in our bodies by changing our state of mind."[33]

What Is a Placebo?

A placebo has been defined as "any effect attributable to a pill, potion, or procedure, but not to its pharmacodynamic or specific properties."[34] Another general definition of placebos is "substances or procedures without specific activity against the condition being evaluated."[35] If a person deeply believes that a pill is going to work in a certain way, chances are it will—even if the pill is fashioned of nothing more than table sugar. The healer is actually faith, not pharmacology.

The word *placebo* comes from the Latin word meaning "placate" or the phrase meaning "I will please." In fact, one of the earliest medical definitions of "placebo"—penned in the early 1800s—described it as "an epithet given to any medication adopted more to please than to benefit the patient."[36] Placebos have been used by physicians since the time of Hippocrates.

We know a placebo to be "a pill that is given with the intention of treating a medical disease, but which has no specific biological or chemical activity against the condition."[37] But a placebo doesn't necessarily have to be a pill; it can be a potion, a surgical procedure, or any other medical procedure. A physician can even be a placebo. And, according to researchers, the effects of a placebo are not imaginary but can be physically measured with physiological tests. Experts tell us also that the effects of a placebo are often more potent than those of the actual medication or procedure.[38]

One dramatic example of the placebo effect occurred in a New York hospital in 1950. In the experiment, Dr. Stewart Wolf treated women who were suffering severe nausea and vomiting from pregnancy. Wolf told the women he was going to give them a drug known to alleviate nausea and vomiting. In reality, however, Wolf gave the women syrup of ipecac—a drug used to *induce* vomiting.

What happened? The patients' nausea and vomiting disappeared after taking the syrup of ipecac. According to researchers, the women's *belief* in the drug's powers was so potent that it actually counteracted the pharmacologic actions of the drug.[39]

A more recent example of the placebo effect stemmed from a large, multi-center study called the Beta Blocker Heart Attack Trial. As reported in the British medical journal the *Lancet*, Dr. R. Horowitz and his colleagues gave heart attack patients either a beta blocker or a placebo. The researchers then compared the rates of death among patients who did or did not take their medication.

Even after taking into account factors like family history, cigarette smoking, or psychological characteristics, the researchers found that those who didn't take the beta blocker as prescribed were 2.6 times more likely to die than those who did take the beta blocker. The surprise occurred with the *placebo* group: Those who did not take the placebo also had an increased rate of death when compared with those who *did* take the placebo—even though it contained no medication at all.[40]

Norman Cousins defined a placebo as:

> . . . not so much a pill as a process, beginning with the patient's confidence in the doctor and extending through the full functioning of his own immunological system. The process works not because of any magic in the tablets but because the human body is its own best apothecary and because the most successful prescriptions are those that are filled by the body itself.[41]

Placebos have everything to do with faith: A patient believes that the pill or procedure will work, so it does. The key is the meaning of the experience for the person. Placebos work on a wide range of medical disorders, and they work an astounding percentage of the time—an estimated one-third to one-half of the time. Officials also estimate that almost half of all the prescriptions written today are for placebos—drugs that have no actual effect on the condition for which they are prescribed, but that may bolster a patient's belief (and therefore the patient's own healing mechanisms). A perfect example is when a doctor prescribes antibiotics for the flu. Antibiotics are not effective against viruses, such as the influenza virus. But patients who faithfully take antibiotics in the belief that these will make them better usually recover faster.

According to a review published in the *Journal of the American Medical Association*, placebos can be effective in a variety of disorders—and can affect practically any organ system in the body. A host of studies have shown that placebos are effective against angina pectoris, rheumatoid arthritis, pain, hay fever, headache, cough, peptic ulcer, and high blood pressure. Studies cited in the *Journal of the American Medical Association* article also show that placebos can be effective when used against psychiatric disorders, such as depression, anxiety, and schizophrenia.[42]

Placebos are often actively prescribed by physicians who know they have no actual effect on the condition for which they are being prescribed. Why? Because, according to behavioral scientist Morton Hunt, "patients expect doctors to *do* something. So when there is nothing much to be done—as is often the case, for instance, with chronic pain, which affects 70 million Americans—many doctors will prescribe some therapeutically active preparation (a vitamin, tonic, or even mild tranquilizer) that has no known effect on the ailment in question but can't hurt and may just make the patient feel better. A clue to how common this is: One pharmacology textbook estimates that 35 to 45 percent of present-day prescriptions are unlikely to have specific effects on the diseases for which they are ordered."[43]

How Do Placebos Work?

No one is absolutely certain how placebos work, but there are several theories. A number of studies show that the answer might be endorphins; absolute belief in a pill, a treatment, or even a practitioner seems to stimulate the brain to release endorphins, which relieve pain and may speed healing.[44]

Another theory revolves around research conducted by a Finnish physiologist in which actual physiological changes were triggered by the patient's imagination. According to the study, powerful influences on the placebo effect include the patient's observation of his own physical reactions, the patient's observation of the physician's behavior, and information from other sources that may verify the effects of the placebo.[45]

Another theory is that placebos may be explained by people's differing sensitivity to bodily symptoms. There are two general types:

1. *Reducers.* These people are slow to perceive symptoms consciously. Even when they do perceive symptoms, they tend to deny them or ignore them until they get quite severe. In general, reducers do not get worried or alarmed about bodily symptoms—and are not as vulnerable to the effect of placebos.[46] Being a reducer isn't good in all situations, however. Studies have found that the absence of sensory input and stimulation can be very disturbing. Researchers have even noted that prisoners who are reducers and who are incarcerated get so starved for sensation that they deliberately hurt or mutilate themselves.

2. *Amplifiers.* These people amplify sensations that other people would be unaware of. They are even made uncomfortable by situations that most people would find to be neutral. According to researchers, these people seem "hard-wired" into their brains from the time they are born.

Somewhere in between the reducers and the amplifiers are the rest of us. How vulnerable a person is to the effects of a placebo depends on how aware you are of body symptoms. Researchers have found that seven characteristics determine whether you feel more symptomatic than the average person:

1. *Age.* Generally, the older the person, the more symptoms he or she feels and reports to a physician.

2. *Gender.* Women consistently report more bodily symptoms than do men. In fact, many studies indicate that women are more sensitive to changes in their bodies, feel less healthy, take more medications, and think of themselves as prone to illness more than do men in general.

3. *Social class.* People who have higher incomes and who are better educated generally believe themselves to be in better health. In general, as social class declines, the prevalence of medical symptoms and ill health increases.

4. *Ethnic background.* Studies show that Jews and Italian-Americans exhibit an emotional and expressive response to pain. White Anglo-Saxons, on the other hand, are more stoic and less likely to become as overwrought about illness. At the extreme end of the scale are the Irish-Americans, who tend to completely deny pain.

5. *Marital status.* Single people over the age of thirty are more troubled by symptoms than are their married counterparts.

6. *Degree of self-consciousness.* People who are extremely self-conscious are more aware of bodily symptoms and more likely to report symptoms of illness.

7. *Control.* People who feel dependent on others and who feel less able to control what happens to them in life report more frequent and more severe symptoms.[47]

Myths

To understand how powerful faith is, it's important to understand how powerful the placebo effect can be—and important to debunk the most common myths about placebos:[48]

1. *Any symptoms that respond to placebos must be imaginary.* Nothing could be further from the truth. Research conducted at Harvard Medical School shows that placebos have been effective in relieving the very real symptoms of colds, headaches, seasickness, angina, anxiety, and post-operative pain.[49]

Placebos have been shown to relieve symptoms that can be scientifically monitored. An excellent example of this was a woman who was complaining of severe nausea and vomiting. Nothing her doctors had been able to do for her seemed to help. Laboratory instruments were used to measure her stomach contractions; the pattern of contractions she exhibited was proof that she was indeed suffering from the nausea that she reported. Her symptoms were very real.

Her doctors finally offered her what they called an "extremely powerful" new wonder drug that would, without a doubt, relieve her nausea. Sure enough, within twenty minutes of taking the new drug, the woman's nausea disappeared. Not only did the nausea disappear, but the stomach contractions she was having returned to normal.

The drug the woman had been given was syrup of ipecac, a standard remedy to *induce* vomiting. The woman's faith was so strong—and the placebo effect, as a result, was so powerful—that the drug actually had an opposite effect in relieving her nausea and vomiting.[50]

In other studies, placebos were powerful enough to stop symptoms that could not have been imaginable because they are easy to observe: coughs, nasal discharge, and skin rashes, for example. They have also been effective against symptoms that are easy to measure, such as fever and high blood pressure.

2. *Response to a placebo is a sign of mental illness.* As shown in the previous example of the woman who was nauseated and vomiting, placebos have an actual effect. It's faith, not mental illness, that is at work.

3. *Placebos cannot influence objective physiologic processes.* Just the opposite is true. Placebos have been found to have a profound influence over physiologic processes. One dramatic example was the story cited earlier about the lymphoma patient whose tumors "melted like snowballs" when he was given distilled water that he believed was a wonder drug. Placebos have been shown in scientific studies to affect the rate of stomach secretions, white blood cell counts, fever, blood cholesterol, dilation and constrictions of the pupils of the eye, and the stages of sleep.

In a classic experiment at a medical school, a pharmacology professor lectured to the students about the differences between stimulants and sedative medication. He went into great detail, describing the effects that each has on the body. He also described the side effects that each might have. He then told the students that he wanted them to take the medications and measure each other's responses. Half the class was given a pink pill ("stimulant") and the other half was given a blue pill ("sedative") to take. The students then measured and recorded each other's symptoms, blood pressure, and heart rate. Even though the pills were not real, the students experienced physiological reactions. About half had specific sedative-related physiological reactions that could be measured with laboratory equipment—such as decreased blood pressure, slowed heart rate, or increased pulse and blood pressure. They also experienced characteristic effects of the "stimulants," such as dizziness, watery eyes, and abdominal pain.

The researchers concluded that the color of the pills, coupled with the students' expectant faith, brought on literal physiological changes when they took the placebos.[51]

4. *Placebos can do no harm since they cannot cause any real side effects.* In the case just described, half of the medical students who took the pink or blue pills experienced not only appropriate physiological changes, but also the side effects generally associated with stimulants and sedatives.

In a variety of studies, placebos have been shown to cause very real side effects including nausea, skin irritation, hearing loss, diarrhea, constipation, headache, erratic heartbeat, pain, dizziness, insomnia, and even addiction. One researcher described a total of thirty-eight toxic effects directly attributable to placebos. The most common was drowsiness; others included headaches, nausea, and vomiting. Some of the effects were serious, such as impairment of liver function. Some side effects of placebos are so serious that patients have required hospitalization.[52]

In one study, researchers tested the effects of a drug called mephenesin on anxiety. Half of the patients in the study were given the drug, and half were given a placebo. The drug and the placebo produced almost identical side effects in the patients. Study participants complained of dizziness, nausea, and sleep disturbances as side effects. But these side effects were incurred by the people who took the medication *and* the people who took the placebos.

One of the subjects had a severe reaction that mimicked shock: fainting, reduced blood pressure, and clammy white skin. That patient displayed the exact same reaction whether he took the drug or the placebo.[53]

Physicians' Expectations

Many studies have indicated that a drug—real or placebo—is much more effective when the physician who administers it has strong faith in it. In fact, studies cited by Dr. Alfred Berg of the University of Missouri show that a physician's expectations of a drug's effectiveness can alter the "outcome of therapy by about 25 to 30 percent in either direction."[54] Studies have repeatedly shown, he says, that a drug works best when a physician's hopes for it are at their highest.

Researcher Jerry Solfvin extensively examined the power of the physician's underlying beliefs. Solfvin did three separate double-blind studies of the use of vitamin E in treating angina pectoris, the chest pain caused by coronary artery disease. Two of the studies were conducted by skeptics who did not believe the vitamin E had any effect; sure enough, it didn't have any effect for the patients involved in the study. But the third study was conducted by an enthusiastic doctor who *did* believe that vitamin E would work. And, sure enough, it did.[55]

A similar, but earlier, experiment took place during the 1950s, when controversy surrounded the new drug meprobamate (one of the earliest tranquilizers). The doctors who believed in it consistently found that it worked; the skeptics thought it was no better than a placebo.

Researchers designed a double-blind study and involved two physicians—one who had an "enthusiastic, therapeutic" approach, and the other who had a "skeptical, experimental" approach toward the drug. Here's the catch: The doctors didn't know which pills were the placebos and which were the meprobamate. Neither did the patients. In fact, they didn't even know they were being involved in an experiment.

What happened? The meprobamate proved to be much more powerful than the placebo—but only for the physician who *believed* in it. The patients treated by the skeptical physician enjoyed no drug benefit at all from either pill.[56]

Dr. J. Mostyn Davis, a family practitioner at Pennsylvania's Geisinger Medical Center, remembers the time he prescribed what he believed to be a long-acting appetite suppressant. His patients, he relates, had great success with the drug. When he found out that the drug was, in fact, only a short-term appetite suppressant, he continued to use the drug in the same way, without telling the patients. But, he remembers, "now it worked for only a few hours! Was I unconsciously giving cues to my patients?" The mystery remains to this day.[57]

Focus on Research

A physician gave a patient a new experimental drug; the physician strongly believed that the drug would help relieve the patient's severe asthma. Just as the doctor had expected, the patient enjoyed significant relief from his symptoms—and he did much better on lung function tests, too.

The patient's improvement was so dramatic that the doctor became curious. He wondered whether the experimental drug had really made the difference, or whether the patient's own belief in the drug (the placebo effect) had made his asthma clear up. To test his hunch, the doctor treated the patient with a placebo instead of the experimental drug at his next checkup. Just as the doctor expected, the patient returned to the office and complained that the symptoms of his asthma had returned.

The patient was disappointed that the drug no longer worked.

Satisfied that the patient's original improvement was in fact due to the drug and not the placebo effect, the doctor contacted the pharmaceutical company and requested more of the new experimental drug. Imagine his surprise when the company told him that the "effective" experimental drug was merely a placebo!

"The patient responded in both cases to the *doctor's* differing expectations of the treatment," researchers report. "The doctor communicated to the patient in very subtle ways, perhaps tone of voice, facial expressions, or word choice, whether he thought the treatment would be efficacious or not."

Source: Robert Ornstein and David Sobel, *The Healing Brain* (New York: Simon and Schuster, 1987), pp. 85–86.

The physician, in fact, may be one of the most powerful placebos. One writer commented that the placebo effect "demonstrates that the physician functions as a healer. Because the medical profession relies so heavily on science and thus concentrates on diseases rather than illness, deals with cases rather than patients, and seeks to cure rather than provide care, physicians have lost faith in themselves as therapeutic instruments. Medicine has long been accused of being the silent profession, and it must be recognized that a physician is not merely a conduit of pills and procedures. Throughout history, rhetoric has moved people; and if people can be so moved to march, vote, or go to battle, certain words can have a tremendous effect on how someone feels."[58]

Negative Effects

While the placebo effect can be positive and can bring on relief of symptoms as well as overall cures, the placebo effect can also be negative. People who believe that they are going to get sick actually can—and do. Cardiologist Herbert Benson, who has studied the placebo effect in depth, maintains that there are "dozens of examples throughout history of the scourge of negative placebo effects. Some even mimic terrible contagious diseases and can spread through large populations."[59]

An example of a negative placebo effect from history is the dancing manias that occurred during the Middle Ages. People who believed that they were "possessed" jerked around and danced around uncontrollably in the streets. According to Benson, the sight of one person would arouse others until there were sometimes groups of more than a hundred jamming the streets. After hours of this dancing, Benson says, the victims would fall to the ground, exhausted. Some—who were actually healthy but believed that something was wrong with them—"dashed their brains out by running against walls and corners of buildings or rushed headlong into rapid rivers."[60]

Two examples from our own day show the power of faith and what can happen when it is misdirected. During the morning shift at a midwestern electronics plant, one worker suddenly became faint. Just moments later, a coworker who had helped the first victim also dropped to the floor. Within three hours, twenty of the factory workers had been taken to the hospital by ambulance complaining of the same set of symptoms: dizziness, headache, nausea, and difficulty breathing. Before the "plague" was over, at least ninety-three of the factory workers were afflicted with the strange sickness, which the victims attributed to a sickening odor wafting through the factory. These sicknesses persisted, even though the plant was closed three times while the maintenance engineers conducted detailed inspections and found no possible source for an odor.

In another example, a cargo ship damaged at sea was forced to dock in New Zealand. When it docked, unlabeled containers of an unknown chemical split open, spreading terrible-smelling fumes throughout the entire area. Local officials, alarmed by the fumes, immediately evacuated the area. People's belief that the horrible-smelling fumes were toxic was fueled by the quick reaction of local officials in evacuating the area. Panic spread like wildfire; hundreds of people were rushed to local hospitals, supposedly sick from inhaling the toxic fumes. When calmer heads prevailed and the chemical was finally identified, it was thoroughly tested. Even though it smelled bad, it was totally harmless.

Another powerful example of the placebo stems from Chinese astrology: It teaches that depending on the astrological phase during the year you are born, you are predisposed to certain diseases. Researchers examined the death records of more than 28,000 Chinese Americans. They found that those who developed a disease that was linked to their astrological phase died an average of one to five years earlier than those who developed the *same* disease but were born during a different phase. The stronger the belief in the astrological connection, the sooner the ill-fated person succumbed to the disease. Why? It was the placebo effect: Those who developed a disease associated with their astrological phase simply worried themselves sicker.[61]

The Power of the Placebo

How powerful is the placebo effect? In recent tests, the placebo has "reduced attacks in angina patients by 82 to 93 percent; eased the suffering of almost two-thirds of migraine patients by 50 percent or more; given significant relief to about a third of patients with severe pain (without being addictive or interfering with mental function); led to improvement in up to half of patients with ulcerative colitis; resulted in healing of duodenal ulcers in 50 to 60 percent of patients; and significantly reduced tenderness of the joints in 22 percent of rheumatoid arthritis sufferers."[62]

There are many medical examples of the placebo effect—and examples of how it has worked, whether in medical form or in the form of surgery. In one study, the Coronary Drug Project Research Group compared five-year mortality rates among patients who were given the cholesterol-lowering drug clofibrate (Atromid-S) or a placebo.[63] Researchers observed each patient in the study to determine how faithful each was in taking the prescribed medication. The patients who took the clofibrate every day lived longer than the patients who frequently missed doses. The patients who took placebos every day also lived longer than the patients who frequently missed doses of placebos. There was no difference in mortality between the patients who regularly took clofibrate and the ones who regularly took placebos.

In another study, researchers tested the drug Stellazine on patients with chronic psychiatric illness. Half of the patients in the study received Stellazine, and half received a placebo. Neither the doctors who administered the medications nor the patients knew which were receiving active drugs and which were receiving placebos.[64]

To double-check their results, the researchers ran the test twice, using different sets of patients and different doses of both the drug and the placebo. In the first experiment, the patients who took Stellazine showed an improvement rate of 32 percent. The patients taking the placebo did even better, showing an improvement rate of 35 percent. In the second experiment, researchers doubled the dose of both the drug and the placebo. The patients experienced even greater improvement this time: The ones who took the Stellazine enjoyed an improvement rate of 67 percent. But, again, the ones taking the placebo did even better: Their improvement rate was 72 percent.

In summing up the results of the experiment, researchers say that "in many cases, particularly in those involving a person's state of mind, the effect of medication is influenced by the hope of cure, coupled with a belief in the physician, who in some unknown way conveys his sense of the strength and effectiveness of the drug."[65]

The placebo can even work in cases of "faith healing." New York psychologist Lawrence LeShan, an avid experimenter and authority in faith healing, relates an incident that he calls "the most dramatic single result" in his long experience. According to LeShan, a man he knew asked LeShan to do a long-distance healing for an extremely painful condition that required immediate and intensive therapy.

As LeShan tells it, "I promised to do the healing that night, and the next morning when he awoke a 'miraculous cure' had occurred. The medical specialist was astounded, and offered to send me pre- and post-healing x-rays and to sponsor publication in a scientific journal. It would have been the psychic healing case of the century except for one small detail. In the press of overwork, I had forgotten to do the healing!" The patient who believed that he had meditated in his behalf had been healed anyway.[66]

The power of the placebo also extends to surgery. Alan Roberts, director of medical psychology at Scripps Clinic and Research Foundation, and his colleagues studied almost seven thousand patients who once had one of a number of treatments that were later thoroughly discredited, such as a surgical procedure for intractable asthma or the use of special dyes and fluorescent light on herpes sores. Even though the treatments were later found to be useless, 40 percent had reported "excellent" improvement, and another 30 percent had reported "good" results.

In summing up his findings, Roberts said, "I think physicians have always been embarrassed by the notion that people get better when they're given dummy pills or dummy treatments."[67]

Some of the most convincing evidence regarding the placebo effect stems from surgical procedures in which incisions are made while the patient is under anesthesia, but no operation is performed.[68] One of the most classic examples of this hails from the mid-1950s. At that time, a new surgical procedure was introduced to help relieve the chest pains from coronary heart disease. The surgery, called an "internal mammary artery ligation," involved tying off an artery in the chest, with the result that more blood was available to the heart.

Initial response to the surgery was overwhelming. Almost half of the patients reported an improvement in chest pain—and two-thirds of them said that the improvement was considerable. Surgeons who pioneered the operation said that the patients also did better on an electrocardiogram after the surgery, and their exercise tolerance also improved. Thousands of patients requested the surgery, and the operation gained in popularity.[69]

But all of the surgeons who looked into the operation were not equally enthusiastic about it. In fact, two groups of surgeons were extremely skeptical and decided to test the procedure against a placebo. *(Note: This kind of a test would not be allowed under today's rules of medical ethics.)* For their test, the skeptical surgeons randomly divided patients slotted for surgery into one of two groups. The first group would receive the internal mammary artery ligation, as planned. The second group, without knowing it, would be put under general anesthesia, an incision would be made in the chest, the incision would be closed, yet no surgical procedure would have been performed on any artery.

The results were almost identical, whether the patients had arteries tied or not. Many of the patients in both groups experienced less anginal pain, increased tolerance for exercise, improvements on the electrocardiogram, and a reduced need for nitroglycerin. The studies demonstrated that "ligation of the internal mammary artery was no better than a skin incision, and that such an incision could lead to a dramatic, sustained placebo effect."[70]

After more than 10,000 patients underwent surgery, the surgery was abandoned. It was replaced by coronary artery bypass surgery, an operation that is still performed today. In coronary artery bypass surgery, diseased sections of the arteries that feed the heart are replaced by a new vein created from sections of veins removed from the patient's legs. At first glance, the surgery seems to be a resounding success: More than 90 percent of the patients who receive it report that their symptoms are relieved. Three-fourths of the patients who undergo surgery also perform better on an exercise stress test than they did before undergoing surgery.

But the placebo is at work again. All the patients actually receive the surgery, but of those who say they feel better, only about one in five—20 percent—show actual improvement of heart function when they are tested. Approximately 60 percent show no improvement at all; they are the same as they were before the surgery. And the other 20 percent are actually *worse* than they were before the surgery.[71] The percentages bear strong testimony to the power of faith: Patients who receive bypass surgery believe it will help them. And it does "help" more than 90 percent of them to feel better, even though only a small fraction actually improve.

The placebo effect has been shown to influence even the immune system. A number of animal studies have shown that the immune system can literally be "conditioned" by placebos—and a human study conducted at the University of Arkansas proved that expectations can determine the outcome of immune function.[72]

The researchers in the study told nine people who were positive for the tuberculosis skin test that they would be given a skin test on each arm once a month for the next six months to determine if they were still positive for the bacteria. Each month the subjects were tested. For the first five months, the right arm of each person was injected with a tuberculin solution. The left arm of each person, without the patient's knowledge, was injected with a simple saline solution. Naturally, the skin reaction appeared on the right arm of each person, but not the left arm. For the test during the sixth month, the researchers reversed the procedure:

Saline was injected into the right arm, and the tuberculin solution was injected into the left arm. Nobody expected a reaction to occur on the left arm, so it did not. Only traces of a reaction occurred on any of the volunteers, even though all were still positive for the bacteria.[73]

Medically speaking, faith can move mountains. What we believe and what we expect are often more powerful than even the most potent pill or the most skilled surgeon's knife. Our task, then, is to unleash that powerful faith in a positive way, a way that will enhance our own healing.

One of the most diligent physicians of all time recognized the power and value of our faith and our beliefs. When he was asked to explain the secret of African witch doctors, humanitarian Albert Schweitzer replied with a simplicity that carries a message for all of us:

> The witch doctor succeeds for the same reason all the rest of us succeed. Each patient carries his own doctor inside him. We are at our best when we give the doctor within each patient a chance to go to work.

Notes

1. Dan Custer, *The Miracle of Mind Power* (Englewood Cliffs, New Jersey: Prentice-Hall, Inc., 1960).

2. Custer.

3. Deirdre Davis Brigham, "Shifting Consciousness, Creating Epiphanies, and Enabling Miracles," *The Psychology of Health, Immunity, and Disease*, vol. B, p. 49, in Proceedings of the Sixth International Conference of the National Institute for the Clinical Application of Behavioral Medicine.

4. Brigham.

5. Joan Borysenko, *Minding the Body, Mending the Mind* (Reading, Massuchusetts: Addison-Wesley Publishing Company, Inc., 1987), p. 10.

6. Examples of Servicemen are from Jerome D. Frank, "Emotional Reactions of American Soldiers to an Unfamiliar Disease," *American Journal of Psychiatry*, 102: 1946, 631–640, as reported in "The Medical Power of Faith," *Human Nature*, August: 1978, 40–47.

7. Herbert Benson, *Beyond the Relaxation Response* (New York: Times Books, 1984).

8. Benson.

9. Paul Pearsall, *Super Immunity* (New York: McGraw-Hill Book Company, 1987).

10. Pearsall.

11. Benson.

12. Studies summarized from "Review Confirms 'Healing' Effects," *New Sense Bulletin*, 16(8): 1991, 1.

13. Christina V. Miller, "Mental Powers: Divine Power Over Blood Pressure," *Longevity*, September: 1989, 78.

14. Borysenko.

15. Blair Justice, "Those Who Stay Healthy," *New Realities*, July/August: 1988, 35–39, 69–71.

16. Daniel Goleman, "Denial and Hope," *American Health*, December: 1984, 54–61.

17. Custer.

18. Daniel Goleman, "The Faith Factor," *American Health*, May: 1984, 48–53.

19. Frank.

20. Frank.

21. Frank.

22. The study descriptions are from Frank.

23. Larry Dossey, *Meaning and Medicine: A Doctor's Tales of Breakthrough and Healing* (New York: Bantam Books, 1991), pp. 158–159.

24. Mary Baker Eddy, *Science and Health* (New York: Harper and Row, 1875).

25. Goleman, "The Faith Factor."

26. "Review Confirms 'Healing Effects.'"

27. Leonard A. Sagan, *The Health of Nations* (New York: Basic Books, Inc., Publishers, 1987).

28. Frank.

29. "Healing or Hoping?" *American Health,* January/February: 1987, 55.

30. "Healing or Hoping?"

31. Bernhardt J. Hurwood, "Healing and Believing," *Health,* June: 1984, 15–21.

32. Larry Dossey, *Healing Words,* p. 48.

33. Bernie Siegel, *Peace, Love, and Healing* (New York: Harper and Row, 1989), p. 21.

34. Stewart Wolf, "The Pharmacology of Placebos," *Pharmacological Reviews,* II: 1959, 689–704.

35. "Success of Placebos May Be Connected to Imagery," *Brain/Mind Bulletin,* 14(10): 1989, 1, 8.

36. O.H.P. Pepper, "A Note on the Placebo," *American Journal of Pharmacy,* 117: 1945, 409–412.

37. Arthur J. Barsky, *Worried Sick: Our Troubled Quest for Wellness* (Boston: Little, Brown, and Company, 1988).

38. Stewart Wolf, "Effects of Suggestion and Conditioning on the Action of Chemical Agents in Human Subjects: The Pharmacology of Placebos," *Journal of Clinical Investigation,* 29: 1950, 100–109.

39. Herbert Benson and Eileen M. Stuart, *The Wellness Book* (New York: Birch Lane Press, 1992), p. 9.

40. Benson and Stuart.

41. Robert Ornstein and David Sobel, *The Healing Brain* (New York: Simon and Schuster, 1987), p. 87.

42. Herbert Benson and Mark D. Epstein, "The Placebo Effect: A Neglected Asset in the Care of Patients," *Journal of the American Association,* 232: 1975, 1225–1226.

43. Morton Hunt, "Faith, Hope, and Placebos," *Longevity,* May: 1991, 70.

44. Hunt, p. 74.

45. "Success of Placebos May Be Connected to Imagery."

46. Information on "reducers" and "amplifiers" is from Barsky.

47. Barsky.

48. Howard Brody, "The Placebo Response," *Drug Therapy,* July: 1986, 106, 115–131.

49. Hurwood.

50. Robert Ornstein and David Sobel, *Healthy Pleasures* (Reading, Massachusetts: Addison-Wesley Publishing Company, Inc., 1989), p. 29.

51. Ornstein and Sobel, *The Healing Brain,* pp. 79–80.

52. J. Mostyn Davis, "Don't Let Placebos Fool You," *Postgraduate Medicine,* 88(4): 1990, 22.

53. Wolf, "The Pharmacology of Placebos."

54. "Success of Placebos."

55. Dossey, *Healing Words,* p. 135.

56. Dossey, *Healing Words,* pp. 135–136.

57. Davis.

58. Howard M. Spiro, "Are Placebos Legitimate Therapy?" *Patient Care,* May 15: 1991, 69.

59. Benson.

60. The three examples are from Benson.

61. *Consumer Reports on Health,* June 1994, p. 66.

62. Hunt, p. 68.

63. Brody.

64. Frank.

65. Frank.

66. Larry Dossey, *Healing Words* (San Francisco: Harper San Francisco, 1993), p. 78.

67. Rita Rubin, "Placebos' Healing Power," *U.S. News and World Report,* November 22, 1993, p. 78.

68. Herbert Benson and D. P. McCallie, "Angina Pectoris and the Placebo Effect," *The New England Journal of Medicine,* 300(25): 1979, 1424–1429.

69. E. G. Diamond, C. F. Kittle, and J. E. Crockett, "Evaluation of Internal Mammary Artery Ligation and Sham Procedure in Angina Pectoris," *Circulation,* 18: 1958, 712–713; L. A. Cobb, G. I. Thomas, D. H. Dillard, K. A. Merendino, and R. A. Bruce, "An Evaluation of Internal-Mammary-Artery Ligation by a Double-Blind Technic," *The New England Journal of Medicine,* 260(2): 1959, 1115–1118.

70. Benson and McCallie.

71. Ornstein and Sobel, *The Healing Brain,* p. 81.

72. G. R. Smith and S. M. McDaniel, "Psychologically Mediated Effect on the Delayed Hypersensitivity Reaction to Tuberculin in Humans," *Psychosomatic Medicine,* 45(1): 1983, 65–70.

73. Smith and McDaniel.

20

THE HEALING POWER
OF HOPE

He who has health has hope;
and he who has hope has everything.
—*ARABIAN PROVERB*

"People tell me not to offer hope unless I know hope to be real, but I don't have the power not to respond to an outstretched hand," explains former *Saturday Review* editor Norman Cousins.[1] "I don't know enough to say that hope can't be real. I'm not sure anyone knows enough to deny hope. I have seen too many cases these past ten years when death predictions were delivered from high professional station only to be gloriously refuted by patients for reasons having less to do with tangible biology than with the human spirit, admittedly a vague term but one that may well be the greatest force of all within the human arsenal."

What Is Hope?

Hope—defined as "a wealth of optimism, a want of fear"—is apparently one of the strongest influences on health and the human body. David SteindlRast defined it aptly when he said, "Hope looks at all things the way a mother looks at her child—with a passion for the possible." As Cousins so eloquently points out, medical lore is replete with examples of "terminal" patients who, awash with hope, defied all medical odds. Some lived months or years longer than predicted. Some were able to remain symptom-free and enjoyed comfort for the last period of their lives. Some defied the odds in a total way: They lived and they were healed.

University of Kansas psychologist C. Rick Snyder claims that hope is more than—indeed, quite different from—a vague feeling of optimism. As he defines it, hope is a pragmatic, goal-oriented attitude, a stance a person assumes in the face of difficulty. It combines, he says, a goal-directed determination with the ability to generate the means of reaching the goals.[2]

As one writer defined them, the characteristics of hope include the following:

- Hope is a crucial antidote to fear.
- Hope is commonly found in a life situation that has an element of captivity or uncertainty.
- Hope is always set in the context of time.
- Hope is as likely to be experienced in the symbolic, unconscious realm as in the cognitive, rational realm.
- Hope is experienced in relationship to someone or something.
- The experience of hope runs through all dimensions of life.
- Hope is basically a shared experience.[3]

More and more, physicians are finding that hope is a powerful tool in their work with patients. Cousins relates the experience of physician William M. Buschholz, as reported in *The Western Journal of Medicine*.[4] As Buschholz was eating breakfast one morning, he overheard two oncologists discussing papers they were going to present that day at the national meeting of the American Society of Clinical Oncology. One of the physicians complained bitterly, "You know, Bob, I just don't understand it. We used the same drugs, the same dosage, the same schedule, and the same entry criteria. Yet I got a 22 percent response rate and you got a 74 percent. That's unheard-of for metastatic lung cancer. How do you do it?"

The other responded, "We're both using Etoposide, Platinol, Oncovin, and hydroxyurea. You call yours EPOH. I tell my patients I'm giving them HOPE. Sure, I tell them this is experimental, and we go over the long list of side effects together. But I emphasize that we have a chance. As dismal as the statistics are for non-small cell, there are always a few percent who do really well."

Psychologist Robert Ornstein and physician David Sobel define hope as "a special type of positive expectation. Unlike denial, which involves a negation of reality, hope is an active way of coping with threatening situations by focusing on the positive. No matter how dark or grim a situation may appear, certain people seem to be able to extract the positive aspects and concentrate on them. They fill their mind with hopeful scenarios, stories with happy endings, or lucky outcomes."[5]

Psychologist Shlomo Breznitz, director of the Center for the Study of Psychological Stress at the University of Haifa and visiting scientist with the National Institute of Mental Health, says that the "major difference between hope and denial is that in denial you try not to pay attention—not to see, not to hear, not to think about negatives. But in hoping you look at the situation, no matter how negative, to seek out the few remaining positive elements and build on them.[6] Breznitz points out that the "healthiest attitude is a hope that is based on a realistic evaluation of the situation. Mature hope dwells on what is positive about life, but also what's realistic."

The Influence of Hope

Hope has a powerful influence on the physical health and well-being of all of us— and, as a quality of positive personality, it can bring not only enhanced health, but improved longevity. In fact, genuine hope—hope that is more than mere lip service—is one of the most dynamic elements of a healthy personality. Hope is an active, not a passive, emotion; when we have real hope, we work to make things happen.

Dr. Elisabeth Kubler-Ross, whose work with dying patients revolutionized the medical profession, stressed the importance of hope, saying that dying patients insist on holding on to some hope. Although they can't hope for a cure, she says, "they can hope for a few more days or hours of life, for contact with loved ones, for freedom from pain, or for peaceful death with dignity. . . . Hope is a satisfaction unto itself and need not be fulfilled to be appreciated."

Physicians themselves have begun to realize the importance of hope. Counsel printed in the *Journal of the American Medical Association* periodically stresses that no part of a diagnosis should ever be hidden—but that no patient should be stripped of hope, either. Even in the last hours, many physicians feel, patients should be given some shred of hope to cling to.

Physicians and patients themselves are speaking out more frequently about the importance of hope. Dr. M. G. Jacoby of Brookhaven Memorial Hospital wrote in "A Father's Letter to a New Intern," published in the *Journal of the American Medical Association*, "Why do some excellent, scientifically oriented doctors fail in practice whereas others, whom both you and I know give inferior care, achieve enormous success? You know the answer as well as I do. They give their patients what they really need, hope, the shot of psychopenicillin that should be injected at every visit."[7]

Washington, D.C., journalist Natalie Davis Spingarn, who has lived with cancer for ten years, claims that "hope is the essential ingredient. Without it, patients find no reason for struggling to survive; without it, we find it easy to give up and stay in bed."[8]

Hope sets in motion an entirely new set of expectations—it boosts belief about what can be achieved, and it makes possible the setting of new goals. Hope is the belief that something is obtainable. As one writer stated, "Social movements are not caused by failure and frustration but spring from rising strength and what T. George Harris, *Psychology Today*'s editor-in-chief, calls 'the snake of hope'; prison riots, he says, start when the food is getting better, not worse."[9]

Hopelessness versus Hope

If hope can profoundly influence health for the better, then its opposite—hopelessness—can have the opposite effect. According to a definition in the *Journal of Psychosocial Nursing*,[10] hopelessness is marked by negative future expectations and the belief that the future holds nothing good or positive. It is also characterized by the inability to reach a desired goal, futility when it comes to planning for goals, and a lack of motivation for using constructive action to gain control of life. People who feel hopeless also usually feel despondent, desperate, and despairing; they feel that they have lost control and feel helpless about what the future holds.

In an editorial published in the *Western Journal of Medicine*,[11] Los Angeles physician Alexandra M. Levine gives a poignant example of what happens when hope is lost. She remembers a fifty-five-year-old woman who was admitted to the hospital with a lesion in the upper lobe of her lung. Levine describes her as "a real dynamo, vigorous and friendly. She became the extra pair of hands on the ward, helping to pass the meal trays, running minor errands. We all came to love her."

When the woman underwent biopsy, it revealed a deadly cancer that had already invaded the nodes; the surgeons could not remove it, so they closed the incision. The next day a group of residents and interns surrounded her bed. One of them looked down and said, "Well, it's cancer, and we couldn't really resect it, so we just opened and closed."

The patient kept repeating the question, "Opened and closed?" As the intern nodded and repeatedly confirmed the procedure, she finally asked, "You mean you left the cancer there?" "Yes," he replied. She closed her eyes and told the interns she was tired. They left the room.

As Levine relates it, the woman died that night. When she was taken to autopsy, there was no specific cause of death—just the cancer, but it had been there for months. Levine wrote, "I have never been able to get her words out of my mind . . . I don't really know why she died, but to be honest, I will always believe that she died because all hope had been taken away from her . . . The resident's words took away her hope, and I honestly believe, as crazy as it may seem, that those words took away some of her potential lifetime."

Researchers stress, however, that helplessness and hopelessness are not the same thing. Hope can exist, in fact, in the face of utter helplessness. According to one researcher, "Helplessness is what you feel in the situation where you can do absolutely nothing, like the heart attack patient in intensive care. But hope can be especially important in times like that, when there is nothing to do. It's a passive sort of coping."[12]

The same researcher points out that a loss of control does not necessarily mean a loss of hope. In "American culture, there is a very powerful equation that says to lose control is to lose everything," he says. "But it often happens that the most serious problems—a terrible accident, a major disease—are those in which we are objectively helpless. Then the best way to cope is to find out how to live with it rather than try to fight it, because there is nothing to fight."[13]

According to researcher Leonard Sagan, who authored a comprehensive look at the world's health patterns in *The Health of Nations*,[14] an attitude of hopelessness can develop early in life—and it's an attitude that can stem from a variety of childhood experiences. Hopelessness can develop in a child who is parented by people who are conformist and authoritarian. Children who are not subjected to challenge are prone to develop a hopeless outlook when, later in life, difficult or challenging situations arise. (Never having met and overcome a challenge before, they feel hopeless at the prospect now.)

Children who lose their mother or caregiver during the early developmental years, when they are most vulnerable to separation or loss, are also more likely to develop a hopeless attitude. Research has shown that suicide, delinquency, accidents, and psychosis all increase among those who have had early parental loss. Risk of suicide is seven times higher than in the general population for children who lose both parents. According to one study, half of all college students who had lost a parent early in life had seriously considered suicide.

Finally, death in the family can inspire feelings of hopelessness—as can traumatic experiences other than death. Sagan uses as an example the June 1976 commandeering of a school bus filled with children. The twenty-six children, who were on their way to school, were driven at gunpoint by the kidnappers for eleven hours and were then buried alive in a truck trailer. Two of the kidnapped boys eventually dug their way out of the bus and released the rest of the children. A psychiatrist examining the children four years later found that *every child* involved in the incident felt hopelessness and had what researchers term "post-traumatic syndrome," marked by fear, pessimism about the future, belief in omens, nightmares, shame, and dreams about death.

Psychologist Lawrence LeShan confirms that hopelessness can be detrimental to health—and he has found hopelessness to be a common pattern among the cancer patients he has examined. LeShan maintains that "damage was done to the ability of the child to relate to others, resulting in marked feelings of isolation, a sense that intense and meaningful relationships bring pain and rejection, and a sense of deep hopelessness and despair. Later, a strong relationship is formed in which the individual invests a great deal of energy. For a time, he enjoys a sense of acceptance by others and a meaningful life, although the feelings of loneliness never completely disappear. Finally, with the loss of the central relationship, whether the death of a spouse, forced job retirement, or children leaving home, comes a sense of utter despair and a conviction that life holds nothing more for him."[15]

A study of Israeli solders clearly demonstrates how hope and hopelessness can make a tremendous difference in physical stress and perseverance. Researchers forced the solders to march a long distance —almost twenty-five miles— at a rapid clip. During the march researchers measured the levels of cortisol, a hormone secreted in response to stress, which is generally suppressed by a strong attitude of hope.

Researchers divided the men into three groups before the march began. The men in the first group were told exactly how far they had to march; in addition, they were provided with distance markers along the way to show them how much farther they had to go. The men in the second group were told they had to march almost twenty miles; at the last minute, they were told they had to march five more miles. The men in the third group were told they had to march almost thirty miles—and they were stopped when they reached the twenty-five-mile mark.

The soldiers who had realistic information and who were kept fully informed of how far they had to go were in the best shape. They maintained the highest levels of hope, secreted the fewest stress hormones, and weathered the march in the best condition. The soldiers who were told they had to go twenty miles and who were then told they had an additional five miles to march didn't do nearly as well. They had no markers and did not know how far they traveled at any one time—and their cortisol levels were consistent with their own *estimates* of the distance they had marched, not by the actual distance traveled. Those in the roughest shape were the ones who were initially told they had to march thirty miles. Researchers believe it is because the initial mileage estimate seemed too difficult and dashed their hopes. "By the time they heard the good news—that they only had to go twenty-five miles—they were so exhausted and hopeless it didn't matter much," researchers summarized. "Some of them actually dropped out after they had marched a little more than six miles, a distance they marched almost every day before breakfast."

False Hope

Just as hope is distinctly different from hopelessness, it is also distinctly different from false hope. False hope

> . . . *is built on pathological denial. Take someone who has just learned he has a serious medical condition, but denies what he's been told, and on top of that has all kinds of hopes for what he'll do in the future. His hopes are built on shifting sands; they are fragile. Such hopes collapse the moment reality intrudes with some undeniable, bitter truth—when the symptoms get so bad he can no longer ignore them, say. Then the person is left with no hope, which is the worst attitude of all."*[16]

Cousins points out that real hope, unlike false hope, "is not a Pollyanna concoction aimed at deception. It is not a verbal tranquilizer for creating a mood of synthetic calm." It is, he says, "a way of putting the human spirit to work; a way of respecting the desire of a patient to confront a new challenge; a way of summoning all one's strength and resources in the most important fight of one's life. No one would argue against the logic and necessity for a patient to reach out for the best medical help available. Why, then, argue against reaching within oneself for the best that the human apothecary has to offer?"[17]

The Impact of Hope on Health

Researchers in the field of psychoneuroimmunology have found that what happens in the brain—the thoughts and emotions we experience, the attitudes with which we face the world—can have a definite effect on the body. An attitude like hope is not just a mental state; it causes specific electrochemical changes in the body that influence not only the strength of the immune system but can even influence the workings of individual organs in the body.

Medical literature is filled with "remarkable" stories of remissions, healings, and patients who lived much longer than expected—and these stories are tales of hope. A growing body of evidence shows that the attitude of hope boosts the immune system, improving health in general. The stories told by patients and physicians alike also demonstrate that hope is a powerful healer and sustainer that can help patients overcome the effects of even terminal illness.

Expectations

The late Norman Cousins is perhaps best known for his work with what he called "the biology of hope." As he explains it, hope is tremendous expectation—and expectation can have powerful influence over the human body.

Expectations are important, and one of the purest forms of expectation is hope. One of Cousin's favorite examples about expectation and hope demonstrates the powerful effect hope can have on the physiology of the human body.[18] Cousins saw an ambulance drive up to the Rancho Golf Course near his home, and he walked up to investigate what was happening. Lying on a stretcher outside the ambulance was a man who had suffered a heart attack.

"He was ashen," Cousins recalls. "He was trembling. The paramedics worked systematically and methodically. They gave oxygen; they hooked him up to the cardiograph; they inserted a heparin lock. No one was talking to the poor fellow." Cousins watched the cardiograph monitor on the stretcher at the man's feet. He noted that the man was experiencing rapid heartbeat—and, although he could not be certain, it looked like he was having premature contractions of the heart.

While the paramedics said nothing, Cousins leaned over and

> . . . *lied to the man. I put my hand on his shoulder and I said, "Sir, you've got a great heart." He opened his eyes and he looked at me and asked, "Why do you say that?" I said, "Well, I can see on the cardiograph that you've got a wonderful heart. What happened is that it's been very hot out here today. You've probably dehydrated on the golf course and that upset the balance of sodium and potassium that provides the electricity your heart needs for the next flip. But you're in good hands now. In a few minutes you'll be in one of the best hospitals in the world. You'll be just fine."*

Cousins kept his eye on the cardiograph monitor. Within *thirty seconds* the cardiogram began to change. In just two minutes the man's heartbeat had slowed, and his pulse was under a hundred beats per minute.

Because of countless experiences like these, physicians are realizing how critical hope is to the maintenance of the human body. Writing in the *New York State Journal of Medicine*, Dr. Stephen Nordlicht told fellow physicians, "How we speak to the patient, the vocabulary we use, the time we select to do this can all serve

Focus on Research

One of Norman Cousin's favorite stories about the power of expectations involves the chain of events that happened at a high school football game in Monterey Park, California. Apparently, a few people left their seats in the stadium because they felt nauseated. The physician in attendance examined the football fans, questioned them about their activities during the previous few hours, and concluded that all had become queasy after drinking the cola that was being served at the game. The physician then asked that a public announcement be made informing people of the possible cola contamination and asking that no one drink any cola beverage.

Astoundingly, almost 200 people in the stadium became instantly ill, *and had to be hospitalized.* These were people who had been fine, who had felt no symptoms, until the warning sounded over the public announcement system. The severity of symptoms and the

suddenness with which they struck amazed everyone, especially the physicians at the area hospital.

A sample of cola beverage was immediately obtained and, in the next few hours, was analyzed for possible contamination. Based on the results of sophisticated tests, health officials proclaimed that the cola was completely free of contamination and couldn't have caused any illness.

The 200 desperately ill people in the local hospital suddenly and miraculously recovered as soon as they heard that nothing was wrong with the cola. Those who had been writhing in agony only minutes before walked out of the hospital, symptom-free. Cousins proclaims that the connection between attitudes and illness or recovery is "a potent factor" in overall health, as was demonstrated on that afternoon of the football game.

Source: Norman Cousins, *Head First: The Biology of Hope* (New York: E. P. Dutton, 1989).

to either strengthen the patient or weaken him." Nordlicht, a clinical associate professor of psychiatry at Cornell University Medical College and consulting psychiatrist at Memorial Sloan-Kettering Cancer Center, maintains that "hope, which is inherent in every human being, will have to be utilized as a medical instrument to a much greater degree than in the past."[19]

One of the most stirring examples of hope is the story of William Calderon, the first documented case of recovery from Acquired Immune Deficiency Syndrome (AIDS).[20] Calderon, whose case is discussed in detail in *New Realities*, was diagnosed in December 1982, and told by physicians he had only six months to live. Hopeless and depressed, he was ravaged by Kaposi's sarcoma, the rare form of skin cancer characteristic of AIDS.

Through a chain of events, however, Calderon began to believe in his ability to beat the disease. He developed hope for his survival. He concentrated on caring for his body with good nutrition, vitamin and mineral supplements, and exercise. His immune system began to strengthen. Then he began using imaging to combat his disease. He worked at repairing strained relationships and concentrated on forgiving those who had hurt him. He achieved peace of mind.

His tumors began to shrink. His immune system continued to strengthen. As he enjoyed support from those around him and renewed hope in his own ability to fight the disease, he became stronger and stronger. Two years later, he was free of AIDS.

Hope is so powerful and so real, say an increasing number of physicians, that it can even influence the outcome of supposedly terminal and irreversible diseases, such as cancer. Yale oncologist Bernie Siegel says, "If there's one thing I learned from my years of working with cancer patients, it's that there is no such thing as false hope. Hope is real and physiological. It's something I feel perfectly comfortable giving people—no matter what their situation. I know people are alive today because I said to them, 'You don't have to die.' "[21]

Siegel says his style differs from that of most physicians, who concentrate on the bleak side of statistics. "If statistics say that nine out of ten people die from this disease, many physicians will tell their patients, 'The odds are against you. Prepare to die,'" Siegel says. "I tell my patients, 'You can be the one who gets well. Let's teach you how.' I'm not guaranteeing immortality. I'm asking them if they want to learn how to live."[22]

There are countless examples of cancer patients who suddenly improve when they find something new to live for—and just as many examples of cancer patients who suddenly take a turn for the worse when they lose hope. Researchers recently studied more than four hundred reports of "spontaneous" cancer recoveries; the treatments these patients had ranged all the way from grape juice cures to visits to Lourdes. There was only one common element that connected all the cases: a shift to a more positive and hopeful attitude before remission.[23]

Studies show that people who have a spontaneous remission have certain qualities in common—many of them characteristic of a hopeful outlook. Those with spontaneous remissions, for example, confront the disease and make an active decision about it; express a sense of healing from within instead of a dependence on others to effect the healing; and improve their attitude toward life and quality of interpersonal relationships.[24]

Hope has even been shown in a number of studies to be a protective factor against the development of cancer, just as hopelessness has been shown to be a risk factor in the development of cancer. Psychologist Lawrence LeShan, whose pioneering research three decades ago contributed tremendously to our knowledge of cancer, described many cancer patients as "helpless and hopeless people" who had suffered serious losses that contributed to their sense of hopelessness.[25]

Hope as a Predictor of Disease or Health

Although hope is a difficult trait to measure, Dr. Louis A. Gottschalk—a University of California/Irvine professor of psychiatry and human behavior—developed a "hope scale" designed to help scientists and researchers discern how hopeful a patient is. In essence, Gottschalk's "hope scale" involved listening for key words in a patient's conversation that researchers believe denote either hopefulness or hopelessness. As a result of his work in developing a measurement of hope, Gottschalk found that hope correlates closely with health. In one study, Gottschalk "measured" for hopefulness twenty-seven patients who were about to receive radiotherapy for advanced cancer at Cincinnati General Hospital. He found that those who exhibited the highest levels of hope were also the ones who survived the longest.

In a variety of studies, hope has been shown to be a surprisingly accurate predictor of cancer. New Jersey's Carrier Foundation physicians R. L. Horne and R. S. Picard concluded after experimental studies that hope was as great a factor in lung cancer as cigarette smoking was; those who felt hopeless were dramatically more likely to develop lung cancer.

Dr. Arthur Schmale and Dr. Howard Iker conducted a number of experiments that demonstrated the impact of hope on the development of cancer. In one, they interviewed and evaluated for levels of hope a group of women coming to the hospital for a cervical biopsy following an abnormal Pap smear. According to the results of the study, the attitude of hopelessness was a potent factor. The women were interviewed before they knew the results of the biopsy, so their hopelessness stemmed from other factors, not from the diagnosis of cancer. Of those who lacked hope, eleven of eighteen had cancer. Of those brimming with hope, only seven in thirty-three developed the disease.[26]

In another similar study, Schmale and Iker wanted to see if they could accurately predict which women would have a diagnosis of cancer—and they determined to make their predictions based on the attitude of hope or hopelessness each woman exhibited. The two researchers interviewed sixty-eight women who had had abnormal Pap smears and who had reported to the hospital for cervical biopsies. Before anyone knew the results of the biopsies, Schmale and Iker made their predictions about which women would be diagnosed with cancer —and they made their predictions based on which women seemed hopeless. They were able to predict with 68 percent accuracy the women who had cancer, based on attitudes of hopelessness. And they were able to predict accurately 77 percent of the cancer-free women based on their hopeful attitudes.[27]

In a similar study, researcher Donald Spence and his colleagues interviewed women who were slated for cervical biopsies. They were able to accurately predict which women would have cancer diagnosed based on evidences of hopelessness in their interviews; the researchers looked for words like *dark, disgusting, difficulty, conflict, cancer,* and *tense.* They were also able to predict the healthy women based on attitudes of hope—evidenced by words like *desire, eager, expect, longing, wish,* and *yearn.*[28]

Hope as a Healing Factor

Studies have even shown that an attitude of hope contributes significantly to the healing process. One program put into effect in a Veterans Administration hospital demonstrated the power of hope for patients with chronic neurological diseases.[29] The hospital was, as one writer described it, "a dreary warehouse where patients were stored for years." The researchers worked to make it "a place of hope where they expected to be healed and eventually discharged from care."

As part of the program, the physicians, social workers, and other health professionals worked together to effect the changes. The treatment plan for each patient was examined and reevaluated; appropriate changes were made. Efforts were made to reestablish each patient's ties with family members and others in the community. Group activities were sponsored to boost morale and reduce the feelings of isolation among the patients.

Researchers call results of the program "impressive." Most of the patients had been hospitalized from three to ten years; within three months, the discharge rate rose to 70 percent. Researchers add that "the rate of discharge continued over the next two and a half years. Even more impressive is the fact that 40 percent of those who were released became self-supporting, which means that they were not only physically healthier, but also psychologically better adjusted."[30]

The importance of hope as a healing factor was stressed by Dr. Isaac Djerassi, director of research oncology at Mercy Catholic Medical Center in Philadelphia and one of the world's foremost authorities on cancer. Djerassi, who discovered the cures for both childhood leukemia and bone cancer, maintains that hope is essential—and that it has to encompass not only the patient but the physician as well:

> *I can say from my own experience that patients who have given up, who have come to me feeling defeated and desperate, feeling that nothing can possibly help them, have often made their own prediction come true. The fighter-type patients who are willing to try anything that has a chance to help them, who have real faith in their survival, always do better. The same thing holds true of doctors. Some of the doctors get discouraged too early and give up on patients who could still be helped. When you pick a doctor, make certain he's a fighter, someone who will stand by you and fight for you.*[31]

The same sentiment was echoed by Robert S. Mendelsohn, associate professor of preventive medicine at the University of Illinois School of Medicine. In his revealing work, *Confessions of a Medical Heretic*, Mendelsohn penned, "A doctor who tells a patient that there's no hope . . . is making an enormous assumption in presuming his power is the only one that can restore . . . health. Telling a patient he or she is going to die is tantamount to a curse. The patient believes it, so it comes true."[32]

Siegel, renowned for his work with cancer patients, agrees:

> *People aren't statistics. They are individuals. And they should be treated as individuals. If a doctor told me that everybody with my illness dies in six months, I would say to myself, 'That's impossible. No two cases are alike. What he's talking about is the average. Maybe one person lived for five years and someone else dropped dead in three days. To me, the worst thing a doctor can do is tell a person he's going to die. For one thing, it's a deception. There's no way anyone can predict with any certainty the course a disease will take in an individual. Secondly, it's the quickest way to make that patient another statistic.*[33]

Hope as a Survival Factor

In a report published in *Medical World News*, writers proclaimed that "hope can play an important role in vulnerability to disease, the course of illness, and possibly in determining whether a patient lives or dies."[34] University of Arkansas psychiatrist Fred O. Henker stated in the same report that "whether we acknowledge the influence of hope or not, it's real, and it may even determine the life or death outcome of a patient."

Hope has a particular bearing on cardiac health, claims Dr. Thomas B. Graboys, cardiologist and assistant professor of medicine at Harvard Medical School and Brigham and Women's Hospital—and the loss of hope can lead to cardiac death. One of the most famous examples, says Graboys, is college football coach Paul "Bear" Bryant. Thirty-seven days after his retirement from college sports, he died of myocardial infarction. "Just a day or two before his death," Graboys relates, "Bryant was quoted as saying there were 'no more Saturdays'. . . He really had nothing to look forward to."[35]

In an experiment demonstrating that very principle, Dr. Curt Richter and his colleagues at Johns Hopkins University restrained rats in plastic bags and dropped them into a tank of water. Shortly afterward, the researchers rescued some of the animals, but not others. Within minutes of the rescue of some of the animals, the rats that were left in the water—the ones that had not been rescued—stopped trying to swim. They simply gave up hope. They quickly died. But they didn't drown. Autopsies showed that their lungs were dry; instead, they died of cardiac arrest. They lost hope, and their hearts stopped beating. The rats that had been rescued were dumped into a tank of water a second time. They began swimming with all their strength. They had learned that their situation was not hopeless. They had hope, and they made the effort to survive.

One of the most convincing examples of hope stems from one of the bleakest and most hopeless situations in human history; the Nazi concentration camps in World War II. Psychiatrist Joel Dimsdale of Massachusetts General Hospital tracked down and interviewed some of the survivors of the Nazi death camps in an attempt to learn what had given them the edge in survival.

The prisoners learned to cope in a number of different ways. Some became childlike, eliciting sympathy from the guards and from the other inmates. Some appeared to totally accept the Nazis' attitude toward them. Others became completely passive. Some even became psychologically numbed, mentally separating themselves from the situation. But the overriding expression among all the survivors was this: They survived because of *blind, naked hope*. They set goals for themselves. They imagined life after the camps. They dreamed of reunions with their families. They never gave up—and they survived.

A chilling story of the power of hope was told by medical Army officer Major F. Harold Kushner, whose story was recorded by Martin Seligman in his book, *Helplessness: On Depression, Development and Death.*[36] Kushner was shot down in a helicopter in North Vietnam in November 1967; seriously wounded, he was captured by the Viet Cong. He spent the first three years in First Camp, where twenty-seven Americans were eventually imprisoned. Five were released by the Viet Cong; ten died in the camp; and twelve survived to be released from Hanoi in 1973.

Kushner described the conditions at the camp as beyond belief. "At any one time there were about eleven men who lived in a bamboo hut, sleeping on one crowded bamboo bed about sixteen feet across. The basic diet was three small cups of red, rotten, vermin-infested rice a day. Within the first year the average prisoner lost 40 to 50 percent of his body weight, and acquired running sores and atrophied muscles. There were two prominent killers: malnutrition and helplessness."

Kushner arrived at First Camp in January 1968; by then, twenty-four-year-old parachutist Robert had already been captive at the camp for two years. As Seligman described Robert, "he was a rugged and intelligent corporal from a crack Marine unit, austere, stoic, and oblivious to pain and suffering . . . Like the rest of the men, he was down to a weight of ninety pounds and was forced to make long, shoeless treks daily with ninety pounds of manioc root on his back. He never griped. 'Grit your teeth and tighten your belt,' he used to repeat. Despite malnutrition and a terrible skin disease, he remained in very good physical and mental health. The cause of his relatively fine shape was clear to Kushner. Robert was convinced that he would soon be released. The Viet Cong had made it a practice to release, as examples, a few men who had cooperated with them and adopted the correct attitudes. Robert had done so, and the camp commander had indicated that he was next in line for release, to come in six months."

Sure enough, six months later things started falling into place. The prisoners recognized that the same event was occurring that had occurred before all the previous token releases. A high-ranking Viet Cong official came to give the group a political course—and it was understood that the top pupil would be released. Robert was chosen to head the thought-reform group, made the statements as required, and was told to expect release within a month.

The month came and went, and Robert gradually began to sense a change in the way the guards treated him. Finally he realized that he had been deceived—that he had already served his captors' purpose and was not going to be released. Kushner saw a transformation before his eyes as Robert went from a prisoner who was filled with hope—and whose physical condition remained relatively strong despite overwhelming odds—to a prisoner who gave up hope.

As Seligman records it, Robert "stopped working and showed signs of severe depression; he refused food and lay on his bed in a fetal position, sucking his thumb. His fellow prisoners tried to bring him around. They hugged him, babied him, and when this didn't work, tried to bring him out of his stupor with their fists. He defecated and urinated in the bed. After a few weeks, it was apparent to Kushner that Robert was moribund; although otherwise his gross physical shape was still better than most of the others, he was dusky and cyanotic. In the early hours of a November morning he lay dying in Kushner's arms. For the first time in days his eyes focused and he spoke: 'Doc, Post Office Box 161, Texarkana, Texas. Mom, Dad, I love you very much. Barbara, I forgive you.' Within seconds, he was dead."

Why did Robert die? Kushner, although a medical officer, could not perform an autopsy; he was allowed no surgical tools. Kushner stated that an immediate cause of death was probably electrolyte imbalance. But, because Robert had been in relatively good physical condition, Kushner believed that the more specific cause of death was psychological, not physical. "Hope of release sustained Robert," he summed. "When he gave up hope, when he believed all his efforts had failed and would continue to fail, he died."[37]

Denial: Making Room for Hope

At first thought, denial may seem to be a negative emotion—and, as we have learned through the work of countless researchers, negative emotions tend to have a negative impact on health. But denial can be positive, especially for health. Denial makes room for hope. As Norman Cousins remarked in regard to serious illness, "Don't deny the diagnosis. Try to defy the verdict."[38]

One of the most revealing studies on the benefits of denial was a study of World War I fighter pilots, conducted by Dr. Thomas Hackett, chief of psychiatry at Massachusetts General Hospital.[39] The pilots Hackett studied were heroes—men who ventured forth in the infant days of aviation, when the airplane was exciting but extremely dangerous. These men became known for their bravery and ability. Some of the pilots during World War I never even made it off the ground; one-fourth of them were killed during training in unreliable aircraft; and many of them were killed in combat.

Those who survived, though, went on to survive many other calamities—among them the stock market crash, the Depression, World War II (in which many of them enlisted), the loss of loved ones, and divorce. Hackett sat down with forty of these amazing survivors many years after their initial World War I flying days and interviewed them in detail. What made them survivors? What was the common thread?

The pilots had hope. They had optimism. And they were able to nurture that hope and optimism because of a special kind of denial. They saw themselves as indestructible, even when confronted with tremendous odds. Even when they could see that many of their buddies were being shot down, they never believed that they themselves would be shot down. They maintained that great sense of hope *and* denial after the war—and it led them through serious crises with the unfailing ability to adapt. Hackett calls them *deniers*; they deny the seriousness of their own situations. Instead, they call on optimism, hope, and humor. And they survived.

Hackett noticed the same mechanism at work among the patients in Massachusetts General Hospital's Coronary Care Unit. According to Hackett, "patients who denied being frightened, who minimized the seriousness of their illnesses, and gave the appearance of being unruffled tended to survive in larger numbers than did those who worried constantly." One explanation, say researchers, is that denial makes room for hope—or at least a positive outlook. Hackett explains that "deniers see the machines they're hooked up to as helping them to get well, not as a sign of a badly functioning heart. Those who feel most positive about their ability to get well tend to do better than those who fear and worry more."[40]

Informed Denial

Shlomo Breznitz, director of the Center for the Study of Psychological Stress at the University of Haifa and a survivor of the Nazi regime in Czechoslovakia, makes the important distinction between total and "informed" denial. "A person who completely denies a disease condition doesn't leave room for hope. Why hope, when you don't admit you are sick? People who accept the fact that they are sick but who deny the possibility of complications, hazards, and death are the ones who come out the winners."

Total denial—the kind that does not leave room for hope—may appear to be healthy at first, but can have major health consequences later on. In one study, Yale University psychologist Jacob Levine and his colleagues followed forty-five men who had suffered a heart attack, coronary bypass surgery, or both. The researchers saw each man within days of his transfer from intensive care to a regular hospital ward, and the researchers assessed each man's level of denial. They then tracked the men for one year after they left the hospital and recorded how well they followed their physicians' instructions.

The "deniers" did better at first. They spent less time in the hospital, and they had fewer complications while they were there. But deniers didn't do as well once they left the hospital. Researchers think it's because their denial kept them from taking steps to improve their chances of recovery. They denied that they were ill, so why follow a bunch of instructions from their physician? The deniers during the year that followed surgery had less positive recovery and were readmitted to the hospital more times than those who did not practice denial.[41]

Total deniers also have problems when it comes to cancer, indicates Bernie Siegel. Some cancer patients

> . . . seem to disbelieve the diagnosis, going on with their lives as though nothing is wrong. Usually they are simply denying their emotions: internally they are coming apart, but they refuse to reveal their feelings, perhaps because of early parental messages, such as 'Don't tell the neighbors your troubles.' That is a sure way to self-destruct. Performing for the sake of others destroys you.
> A small number may act almost psychotic, really believing that nothing has happened to them. If a person can maintain that kind of abnormal denial, then cancer is not an emotional stress. But the majority cannot.[42]

"Informed" denial, on the other hand—the kind that allows for hope, the kind that actually inspires hope—can promote health and healing. Dr. Thomas Hackett and his colleague, Dr. Edwin Cassem of the department of psychiatry at Harvard University, developed what they called a "denial scale" to measure the kinds of denial patients experienced. Hackett explains that "those patients classified as major deniers in our studies and others—that is, individuals who thought the least about the possibility of dying and felt the most positively about the ability to get well—tended to go back to work sooner, resumed sexual activity earlier, and their lives after the heart attacks were generally better than those who feared and worried more.[43]

In a similar study, psychiatrist David G. Folks and his colleagues at the University of Alabama School of Medicine questioned patients scheduled for coronary bypass surgery. The patients were interviewed before surgery and again at four days, six months, and one year after surgery. "Informed," hopeful deniers generally had better health after surgery; they were also less anxious and depressed following surgery.

Researchers in the study concluded that "deniers minimize their symptoms and move more rapidly toward recovery." They believe that denial may also trigger other adaptive mechanisms in the body. For example, most deaths after coronary surgery are due to arrythmias; deniers have much lower levels of adrenalin, which is the main culprit in triggering arrhythmia.[44]

Avoiders versus Vigilants

In one study, psychologist Richard S. Lazarus of the University of California at Berkeley and Francis Cohen interviewed patients the day before they were to undergo relatively common surgical procedures, such as hernia repair and gall bladder surgery.[45] Lazarus and Cohen classified each patient into one of two groups; each was labeled as either an "avoider" or a "vigilant."

The "vigilants" were alert to every detail of their upcoming surgical procedure. They wanted to know all about the surgery, the risks, the potential complications, and the likelihood that their condition might recur even after surgery. These people actively sought out articles, brochures, and other information and asked for detailed explanations of the surgical procedure.

The "avoiders" were completely different. They showed what researchers called "remarkably little interest" in what was about to happen to them. They did not really want to know anything about the surgery, and had not discussed it with anyone in detail. They didn't think the surgery was anything to really worry about.

When Lazarus and Cohen compared the two groups following surgery, they found that the avoiders fared much better. They had a much lower incidence of common surgical complications (such as fever, infection, headache, and nausea), and they were discharged from the hospital sooner. They didn't know much—so there was plenty of room for hope. The vigilants basically knew *too much*—and, in light of all those details, it was too difficult to foster hope.

According to Lazarus and Cohen, surgery "is one of those stressful occurrences that can be more effectively dealt with by denial than by vigilance. The reason is that although many threats exist in the surgical context, few actually materialize."[46]

Dr. Thomas Hackett of Massachusetts General Hospital conducted a series of studies on the cardiac patients on the Coronary Care Unit of his hospital—including the one discussed earlier in this chapter. Although he stresses that some medical conditions (such as diabetes and asthma) require great vigilance to prevent life-threatening complications, he believes that avoidance—denial—is better in most cases because it leaves room for hope. The cardiac patients "who denied being frightened, who minimized the seriousness of the their illnesses, displaying a calm, fatalistic attitude and gave the appearance of being unruffled, tended to survive . . . in larger numbers than did those who worried constantly and seemed unable to reduce their distress."[47]

In *It All Begins with Hope,* we are invited to take on "The challenge of every helper—family, friend, or professional—is to encourage hope that is helpful. The challenge of every patient is to use whoever and whatever enhances a sense of hope. The problem arises when helpers and patients differ on what they believe to be helpful."[48]

Lazarus observed:

Illusion can sometimes allow hope, which is healthy. The critical determinant is whether you're denying facts or the implications. Implications are ambiguous. Let's say I get a biopsy that says I have a malignant tumor. I can face the facts, decide this is a terrible illness, that I'm in trouble, will die very soon, and so give up hope. Or I can face the fact that this is a serious illness, but acknowledge the ambiguity; people sometimes recover; it's curable. I've got to be treated, but I don't have to give up.[49]

Is it possible to acquire hope? Researchers think so—and they give these suggestions:

- When you fail, learn to believe your failure occurred because you simply used the wrong strategy—not because of some character flaw.
- Break down each long-term goal into short-term goals.
- Remember that people who succeed are not necessarily brighter or better educated than others—they just have better coping abilities.
- Use your friends not only for companionship, but as sources of ideas and advice.[50]

What does all this tell us? It impresses us with the importance of hope. It confirms that researchers are now proving what writers and poets through the ages have penned about the life-giving emotions that fill us with hope. As Thomas Campbell wrote, "Cease, every joy, to glimmer on my mind. But leave, oh leave, the light of hope behind."

In his book *Human Options,* Norman Cousins observes that we "must never underestimate the capacity of the human mind and body to regenerate—even when the prospects seem most wretched." And, he says, whereas medical treatment is essential, it "will be far more effective if people put their creative hopes, their faith, and their confidence fully to work in behalf of their recovery."[51]

In summing up the importance of hope, Cousins leaves us with this thought:

Hope, faith, love, and a strong will to live offer no promise of immortality, only proof of our uniqueness as human beings and the opportunity to experience full growth even under the grimmest circumstances. The clock provides only a technical measurement of how long we live. Far more real than the ticking of time is the way we open up the minutes and invest them with meaning. Death is not the ultimate tragedy in life. The ultimate tragedy is to die without discovering the possibilities of full growth.[52]

Notes

1. Norman Cousins, *Head First: The Biology of Hope* (New York: E. P. Dutton, 1989), pp. 65–66.

2. "Where There's Hope, There's Life," *Berkeley Wellness Letter,* March: 1992, pp. 2–3.

3. Ronna Fay Jevne, *It All Begins with Hope* (San Diego: LuraMedia, 1991), pp. 149–152.

4. Cousins, p. 99.

5. Robert Ornstein and David Sobel, *The Healing Brain* (New York: Simon and Schuster, 1987), p. 243.

6. Daniel Goleman, "Denial and Hope," *American Health*, December: 1984, 54–61.

7. "Hope: That Sustainer of Man," *Executive Health*, Section II, 20(3): 1983, 1–4.

8. "Hope: That Sustainer of Man."

9. Gilbert Brim, "Losing and Winning," *Psychology Today*, September: 1988, 48–52.

10. *Journal of Psychosocial Nursing*, 25(2): 1987, 21.

11. Alexandra M. Levine, "The Importance of Hope," *Western Journal of Medicine*, 150: 1989, 609.

12. Goleman.

13. Goleman.

14. Leonard A. Sagan, *The Health of Nations* (New York: Basic Books, Inc., Publishers, 1987).

15. Sagan.

16. Goleman.

17. Cousins, p. 66.

18. "Hope: That Sustainer of Man."

19. "Mind Over Cancer: An Exclusive Interview with Yale Surgeon Dr. Bernie Siegel," *Prevention*, March: 1988, 59–64.

20. "Mind Over Cancer."

21. "Mind Over Cancer."

22. "Mind Over Cancer."

23. A. David Feinstein, "Psychotherapy with Cancer Patients," in Proceedings of the Fourth National Conference on the Psychology of Health, Immunity, and Disease, published by the National Institute for the Clinical Application of Behavioral Medicine.

24. Deirdre Davis Brigham, "Shifting Consciousness, Creating Epiphanies, and Enabling Miracles," *The Psychology of Health, Immunity, and Disease*, vol. B, p. 46, in Proceedings of the Sixth International Conference of the National Institute for the Clinical Application of Behavioral Medicine.

25. Madelon Visintainer and Martin Seligman, "The Hope Factor," *American Health*, July/August: 1983, 58–61.

26. Ornstein and Sobel, p. 245.

27. Ornstein and Sobel, p. 245.

28. Ornstein and Sobel.

29. Jerome Frank, "The Medical Power of Faith," *Human Nature*, August: 1978, 40–47.

30. Frank.

31. "Hope: That Sustainer of Man."

32. R. S. Mendelsohn, *Confessions of a Medical Heretic* (New York: Warner Books, 1979), pp. 192–193.

33. Emrika Padus, *The Complete Guide to Your Emotions and Your Health* (Emmaus, Pennsylvania: Rodale Press, 1986), p. 540.

34. "Studies Show Hope Can Play Role in a Patient's Risk, Illness, Death," *Medical World News*, June 11: 1984, 101–102.

35. "Studies Show Hope Can Play Role."

36. From M. E. P. Seligman, *Helplessness: On*

Depression, Development and Death (W. H. Freeman and Company, 1975).

37. Seligman.

38. Cousins.

39. "Hope: That Sustainer of Man."

40. "Hope: That Sustainer of Man."

41. Beryl Lieff Benderly, "Ill-Fated Denial," *Psychology Today*.

42. Bernie S. Siegel, *Love, Medicine, and Miracles* (New York: Harper and Row Publishers, 1986).

43. "Hope: That Sustainer of Man."

44. Lynn Crawford, "Healthy Denial," *Psychology Today*, October: 1987, 24.

45. Ornstein and Sobel, pp. 241–242.

46. Ornstein and Sobel, pp. 241–242.

47. Goleman.

48. Jevne, p. 147.

49. Ornstein and Sobel, p. 242.

50. "Where There's Hope, There's Life."

51. Norman Cousins, *Human Options* (New York: W. W. Norton, 1981).

52. Cousins, *Head First: The Biology of Hope*, p. 25.

21

EXPLANATORY STYLE
AND HEALTH

*An optimist may see a light
where there is none,
but why must the pessimist
always run to blow it out?*
—MICHEL DE SAINT-PIERRE

It's the first baseball game of the summer, but the sultry afternoon is unusually hot for June. The sun hangs lazily above the western horizon and you absent-mindedly wipe the moisture from your forehead with the back of your hand. In an effort to get some relief from the heat, you lift your frosty soft drink to your lips. Take a look at it. Is it half empty? Or is it half full? Your answer reveals what researchers call your *explanatory style*—and it can help determine your physical and mental health.

What Is Explanatory Style?

Explanatory style is the way in which people perceive the events in their lives. It's the habitual way in which people explain the bad things that happen to them. In reality, it's a habit; it's a way of thinking that people use when all other factors are equal and when there are no clear-cut right and wrong answers.

According to Martin E. P. Seligman, "Explanatory style is much more specific and scientifically testable than mood. It focuses on three dimensions of our accounting for the good and bad events in our lives. Pessimists attribute bad events, such as the loss of a job, the breakup of a marriage, or a falling-out with a friend, to causes that are long-lasting or permanent, that are pervasive and affect everything they do, and that are their own fault. Optimists see the causes of such events

463

as temporary, limited to the present case and the result of circumstances, bad luck, or other people's actions. A pessimist sees success at work, in love, or in friendship as due to luck; an optimist, as due to his or her own efforts and skill.[1]

Imagine that a driver skids into a school bus on a snowy day. The person with the pessimistic explanatory style moans: "I'm such a poor driver. I'll never learn to drive safely. Every time I try something new, I screw it up." The person with the optimistic explanatory style thinks "I'm just a beginner, and beginners have to expect a banged fender once in a while. I'll have to be extra careful until I'm a little more practiced. Besides, these roads sure are slick! And the snow made it so it was difficult to see exactly where I was and how far I had to stop."[2]

The person with the pessimistic explanatory style interprets one negative event as an "omen," a sign as to how the rest of his life will turn out. The person with the optimistic explanatory style sees an isolated bad event as just that: isolated.

People with a pessimistic explanatory style can be identified by three thought patterns that give clues about what they're thinking in their conversation.

1.   Pessimists assume the problem is stable, or *never-ending*. They are sure "it will never go away" instead of "it's a one-time thing." The pessimistic snowy-day driver, for example, believes "I'll *never* learn to drive safely" in the snow.

2.   Pessimists believe the problem is *global*, that it affects a broad spectrum of activities instead of an isolated incident.[3] The snowy-day driver opines, "Every time I try something new, I screw it up." A pessimist believes that a bad event "is going to ruin my whole life" instead of seeing a bad event as something with a specific cause that "has no bearing on the rest of my life."

3.   People with a pessimistic explanatory style *internalize* everything. They believe everything is "my fault." The snowy-day driver is convinced that the accident happened because "I'm a bad driver." In contrast, the person with an optimistic explanatory style ascribes the accident to slick roads, poor visibility, some other adverse weather conditions, or merely a spot of bad luck—being in the wrong place at the wrong time.

To sum it up, pessimists tend to attribute their problems to permanent personal inadequacies that undermine everything they do. Optimists usually view a setback as a one-time thing attributable to bad luck, some external factor, or at least to a specific cause that can be remedied.[4]

University of Pennsylvania psychologist Martin Seligman describes it neatly: "Explanatory style is a theory about your past, your future, and your place in the world."[5] Once you've formulated your theory, he adds, you tend to find evidence for it in any situation that comes along.

Paul Rosch, president of the American Institute of Stress, used the example of a roller-coaster ride to illustrate the difference between someone with an optimistic and a pessimistic explanatory style: "Look at how two people might experience a roller-coaster ride. One has his back stiffened, his knuckles are

Focus on Research

University of Pennsylvania psychologist Melanie Burns compared the teenage diaries of people who are now in their seventies with current writing samples. Researchers combed through the diaries and rated them according to explanatory style. They then asked each elderly volunteer to write a long essay on the current status of his or her life—family, work, and status of health. The same researchers then rated the current essay for explanatory style.

In most cases, the explanatory style remained the same through five decades of life.[*]

But researchers found a big difference between the explanatory style about *good* and bad events. They found that the explanatory style for good events was completely changeable across the fifty-year stretch.[†] A person might at one point attribute good events to sheer fate, but at another time ascribe them to his own skill. But the explanatory style regarding bad events was almost always exactly the same for the entire fifty-year period.

[*] Nan Silver, "Do Optimists Live Longer?" *American Health*, November: 1986, 50 53.
[†] Martin E. P. Seligman, *Learned Optimism* (New York: Alfred A. Knopf, 1991), p. 178.

white, his eyes shut, jaws clenched, just waiting for it to be over. The wide-eyed thrill seeker relishes every plunge, can't wait to do it again."[6]

How Permanent Is Explanatory Style?

Once you've developed an explanatory style, are you stuck with it forever? This question evokes considerable controversy among the nation's leading researchers. Many believe that we stick to one explanatory style throughout our lives. Some evidence does exist to support that notion.

Burns's colleague at the University of Pennsylvania, psychologist Martin Seligman, doesn't think that explanatory style—of even bad events—has to stay the same. Seligman, a pioneer in psychoneuroimmunology research, is convinced that explanatory style—which is basically a belief system—can be changed. Results of his work demonstrate that people can be trained to change their outlook.[7]

What Are the Effects of Explanatory Style?

Regardless of whether researchers believe that a basic explanatory style can be changed, they do agree on one thing: Explanatory style has an extremely powerful influence on health and wellness. According to research found in *Health and Optimism*, certain kinds of thoughts are more powerful in predicting health and wellness:

- Manifest thoughts and beliefs
- Explanations for setbacks and disappointments

- What someone thinks about the real world—its events, their causes, and their aftermath
- Thoughts that are responsive to other people
- Beliefs that lead to action[8]

Explanatory style, says Seligman, works like a self-fulfilling prophecy. The way a person "explains events in his life can predict and determine his future," Seligman explains. "Those who believe they are the masters of their fate are more likely to succeed than those who attribute events to forces beyond their control."[9]

Yale oncologist and surgeon Dr. Bernie Siegel agrees, and points out that a negative explanatory style can halt the healing process and put a damper on the immune system. From his work with cancer patients, he points out, "If I said to patients, you have two choices if you want to get well—you can change your lifestyle or have an operation—the majority would say, 'Operate. It hurts less.'"[10] Siegel says that patients who get well when they're not supposed to are "not having accidents or miracles or spontaneous remissions. They're experiencing self-induced healing."[11]

Siegel, who works with patients to help them change their explanatory style and to resolve stress and conflict in their lives, tells of remarkable changes in the course of disease as a result. "As I saw people learning to live with their illnesses, I saw them gaining incredible control over their wellness," he says. "I saw people dealing with conflict in their lives and then, suddenly, having their cancer shrink or disappear. These were things I had never seen before. I was astonished. And as a physician, I felt uncomfortable with it. They were getting better and I hadn't lifted a finger."[12]

A woman named Roz had cancer so advanced that her physicians sent her to a nursing home to die. But Roz hated the nursing home—and she had the kind of explanatory style that enabled her to take hold of the situation. Instead of "passively accepting her situation," Siegel says, "she stood up and led a revolution in the nursing home. She returned home and her cancer went away."[13]

In referring to explanatory style, William Wilbanks, professor of criminal justice at Florida International University, refers to "the New Obscenity. It's not a four-letter word, but an oft-repeated statement that strikes at the very core of our humanity. The four words are: 'I can't help myself.'"[14] This kind of explanatory style, says Wilbanks, "sees man as an organism being acted upon by biological and social forces, rather than as an agent with a free will. It views offenders not as sinful or criminal but as 'sick.' By ignoring the idea that people face temptations that can—and should—be resisted, it denies the very quality that separates us from the animals."

The Influence of Explanatory Style on Health

Siegel maintains that a negative explanatory style is harmful to the body. On the other hand, he says, an optimistic explanatory style and the positive emotions it embraces—such as love, acceptance, and forgiveness—stimulate the immune system and kick the body's own healing systems into gear. An optimistic explanatory style sends "live" messages to your body and helps promote the healing process.[15]

Although it's essential to have an optimistic explanatory style, says Siegel, it's also crucial to use that explanatory style to deal with the realities in life:

> *Learning to let go of negative emotions is the key. The person who smiles on the outside and is hurting on the inside is not dealing with himself or his life. All his "live" mechanisms are told to stop working. Doctors see examples of this every day. You are making rounds at the hospital and you ask a patient how she's doing and she says "Fine." But you know she's not doing fine. Her husband ran off with another woman. Her son is on drugs. And she has cancer. But still she says, "Fine." When I find a person who answers, "Lousy," I say, "That's wonderful! You want to get better so you're dealing with the truth. If your mind and body are feeling lousy and you're relating to that, you'll ask for help."[16]*

Impact on Mental Health

According to the most recent research, explanatory style can have a tremendous impact on mental health—and the explanatory style that is considered "normal" is probably much more optimistic than what researchers once believed it was. According to researchers writing in the *Psychological Bulletin*, it was once considered "normal" for people to have accurate perceptions of themselves, the world, and their future; this was a quality considered essential for good mental health. Recent research, however, indicates that "overly positive" evaluations of self, "exaggerated" perceptions of control, and "unrealistic optimism" are characteristic of normal human thought.[17]

The kind of optimistic explanatory style that researchers describe helps promote other aspects of mental health—the ability to care about others, the ability to be happy or contented, the ability to engage in productive or creative work—because it "distorts" incoming information in a positive direction and dilutes negative input until it is no longer threatening. All in all, say researchers, an optimistic explanatory style helps people adapt in a healthy way when something negative or stressful happens.

A pessimistic explanatory style, on the other hand, can lead to depression. Princeton University psychologists Susan Nolen-Hoeksema and Joan Girgus showed in their study that explanatory style was a much more important factor in depression than was mood—and that explanatory style is much more permanent than mood. In their study, Nolen-Hoeksema and Girgus repeatedly tested third-, fourth-, and fifth-graders on both mood and explanatory style. The kids who started out in a momentarily happy mood but who had a pessimistic explanatory style were depressed within three months of the time the study began. The ones who had an optimistic explanatory style but who were depressed for some reason in the month the study began tended to bounce back and feel upbeat and happy three months later.[18]

According to researchers, a pessimistic explanatory style can lead to anxiety, eating disorders, and a number of emotional problems. It also leads to what researchers call "dysphoria"—a variety of negative emotional states that cause you to "just feel bad." That dysphoria can take the form of depression, anxiety, guilt, anger, or hostility.[19]

Impact on Physical Health

A growing body of evidence suggests that explanatory style can be a potent predictor of physical health. According to research, a pessimistic explanatory style can depress immunity. Scientists from the University of Pennsylvania, Yale University, and Sydney's Prince of Wales Hospital involved elderly men and women in a study designed to determine the effect of explanatory style on immunity. According to researchers, those with a pessimistic explanatory style had a lower ratio of T-helper cells to T-suppressor cells and had a poorer T-lymphocyte response when their immune system was challenged.[20]

Explanatory style can even affect the way the body reacts to surgery. After years of medical practice, one surgeon vowed that he would never operate on a patient who believed he would die—because that's what always happened.

In one study designed to measure the impact of explanatory style on surgical outcomes, researchers asked patients six to twelve months before their surgery was to take place to rate their expectations of surgery and the problems associated with surgery.[21] Researchers then gave the patients questionnaires just

---

Focus on Research

In a study showing the definite predictive nature of the explanatory style, researchers Christopher Peterson, George Vaillant, and Martin Seligman randomly chose a group of mentally and physically healthy and successful members of Harvard University's classes of 1942, 1943, and 1944. These men enjoyed academic success, were nominated as being the most independent and healthy students by their deans, and were judged to be healthy on the basis of comprehensive physical and psychological testing. The men were interviewed in 1946 and were asked open-ended questions about difficult wartime experiences. Based on their answers, they were classified as to explanatory style.

The men were given repeat physical and psychological examinations every five years—beginning at age twenty-five—until they were sixty. Researchers noted the presence of any physical problems, rated their severity, and also noted which participants appeared to be in good health.

Overall, the men with optimistic explanatory styles at age twenty-five were enjoying good health twenty years later. The ones with pessimistic explanatory styles at age twenty-five were much less healthy at age forty-five. The ability of explanatory style to predict health held true even considering the fact that all the participants were healthy at the beginning of the study.

Source: Christopher Peterson and Lisa M. Bossio, *Health and Optimism* (New York: The Free Press [A division of Macmillan, Inc.], 1991), pp. 23–27.

before surgery and four more times over the next two years. The patients' attitudes and expectations about the surgery (their explanatory style) turned out to be powerful predictors. The patients who expected fewer problems had better outcomes. The ones who expected more problems got exactly that. Two years later they had physical problems, dissatisfaction with the surgery, and mood disturbances.

Apparently, how people feel about their own health can actually *determine* how good their health is. Yale Medical School researchers Stanislav Kasl and Rutgers University sociologist Ellen Idler studied more than 2,800 men and women aged sixty-five years and older. What they discovered is that our own opinion about the state of our health is an even better predictor of health than objective factors—such as what a physician can determine through laboratory tests. It's even a better predictor than behaviors, such as cigarette smoking. For example, people in the study who smoked cigarettes were twice as likely to die during the next twelve years as people who didn't smoke. But people who thought they were in "poor" health were *seven times* as likely to die as those who thought they were in "excellent" health.[22]

People with pessimistic explanatory styles have a tendency to blame themselves for anything bad that happens to them. That tendency can interfere with health, recovery, and healing. In one study, researchers analyzed the hospital reports of people who were hospitalized for the treatment of acute burns. People with pessimistic explanatory styles tended to blame themselves for the burn—and also had more pain, greater depression, and less compliance with the instructions of nurses and physical therapists.[23]

Researchers who have studied explanatory style and its impact on health have found that it can influence healing time and the course of the illness in several major diseases, such as cancer and coronary disease. In one pilot study of cancer patients who had advanced melanoma, University of Rochester researcher Sandra Levy reported that "an optimistic explanatory style was the number one psychological predictor of who would live the longest."[24]

One study conducted by Martin Seligman and his colleagues at the University of Pennsylvania involved thirteen patients with malignant melanoma. They found that the best predictor of a patient's survival time was the "absence of a helpless explanatory style." The absence of a helpless style, in fact, was even a more potent predictor than the activity of the patient's natural killer cells.[25]

In another study—this one of women who had recurring breast cancer—Levy and her colleagues studied the common links among women who had the longest cancer-free period between episodes of the disease. The most common denominator among women whose cancer was slow to return was an optimistic explanatory style.[26]

Siegel maintains that one of the most important keys to cancer survival is attitude—and, based on his work with cancer patients, explanatory style contributes a great deal to the ability of people to fight their cancer. He says the majority of cancer patients are willing to take on the role of "observer," sitting back and letting a physician direct the treatment. About one in five are happy to die because "their lives are in shambles." The rest—about 15 to 20 percent—have explanatory styles that make them "truly exceptional survivors."[27]

University of Georgia researcher James Dabbs studied a group of male college students to determine the effects of explanatory style on health. He found that the optimists in the group had a higher level of the male hormone testosterone—which, he says, provides evidence that optimism and explanatory style influences our secretion of hormones.[28]

Attitude and explanatory style can even impact the circulatory system and the outlook for people with coronary heart disease. Sophisticated instruments and testing procedures have enabled researchers to watch the brain in action. Blood flow in the brain literally changes as thoughts, feelings, and attitudes change. The results of a variety of studies show that people with pessimistic explanatory styles are at increased risk of atherosclerosis, blockage of coronary arteries, and heart attack.

Study results reported to the Society of Behavioral Medicine by Dr. Daniel Mark, a Duke University heart specialist, followed up on 1,719 men and women who had undergone heart catheterization—a common procedure to check for clogging of the arteries. All of the people in the study had heart disease. Those with pessimistic explanatory style—the ones who doubted they would recover—fared much more poorly than those with an optimistic style. Of the pessimists, 12 percent were dead within a year—more than twice as many as the 5 percent of the optimists. In summing up the study, Mark emphasized that "the mind is a tremendous tool or weapon, depending on your point of view."

In another study, researchers found those with an optimistic explanatory style also had much better results following coronary bypass surgery. One of the most dangerous complications following coronary bypass surgery is high blood pressure. In this study, people with optimistic explanatory styles had better attitudes about the surgery, had more favorable pulse rates after surgery, and had less hypertension after surgery. High blood pressure following surgery was reduced from 75 percent to less than 45 percent among those with healthy attitudes. An optimistic explanatory style also strongly affects the pace of recuperation, the incidence of complications, and the overall outcome of the surgery.[29]

Explanatory style may even enable researchers to *predict* which people will get sick. In one study, Martin Seligman and his colleagues at the University of Pennsylvania rated 172 undergraduate students on what kind of explanatory style they had. The researchers then predicted which ones would get sick. After a month, they found their predictions were right on. A year later, their predictions still held true.[30]

People with an optimistic explanatory style have better health for reasons that are described in more detail in the chapters that follow. Some of those factors include stronger immunity, good social support, and a willingness to continue better health habits.[31] Another reason, say researchers, is that people with a pessimistic explanatory style generally react to illness with helplessness and a lack of fighting spirit—factors that have in themselves been linked to poor health.[32]

A Healthy Style, A Healthy Immune System

One of the reasons an optimistic explanatory style leads to better health may be that an optimistic style tends to increase the strength of the immune system. Robert Good, former president and director of the Memorial Sloan-Kettering Cancer Hospital in New York, maintains that an optimistic explanatory style and the positive attitude it fosters can actually alter our ability to resist "infections, allergies, autoimmunities, or even cancer."[33]

According to researchers, the hypothalamus control center of the brain—the part that is involved in attitudes and outlook—is directly "wired" to the immune system. If a portion of the hypothalamus is electrically stimulated, antibodies increase; if it is cut, immune activity is depressed. The same thing happens in response to thoughts, beliefs, and imaginations—things that are "not ephemeral abstractions, but electrochemical events with physiological consequences."[34] Siegel mirrors that belief and points out that positive emotions and attitudes actually stimulate the immune system.

Michael A. Lerner, the founder of Commonweal and a MacArthur Foundation Genius Award winner, says the attitudes linked to an optimistic explanatory style can even boost the immune system enough to defeat cancer: "Attitudes themselves have a very potent effect on the immune system. You become different than the person who developed the cancer. Becoming a different personality may change the environment the cancer grew in; it may become so inhospitable that the cancer shrinks."[35]

Explanatory style may have enough influence over the immune system to affect even infectious disease resistance. In one study, psychologist Stanislav Kasl and his colleagues at Yale University followed the development of infectious mononucleosis among a group of West Point cadets.[36] During a four-year period, all cadets entering West Point were given blood tests that screened for the presence of antibodies to the Epstein-Barr virus, the agent that causes mononucleosis. The cadets were also given interviews that included questions about their outlook, their expectations, and their family backgrounds.

About one in five of the susceptible cadets was infected—but only about one-fourth of those actually got sick. The ones who did get sick had a number of threads in common—including a pessimistic explanatory style, high expectations (usually centered in pressure from parents), and poor academic performance.

In a separate set of studies, researchers conducting studies at Yale University and the University of Pennsylvania compared immune function and explanatory style among a group of elderly people. According to the researchers, people with a pessimistic explanatory style had suppressed immune function.[37]

Specifically, said the researchers, the ratio of T-helper cells and T-suppressor cells was low, as was the number of lymphocytes, which arm the body for waging war against infection or disease.

To sum up the research, scientists have found direct evidence that a pessimistic style and a sense of helplessness may depress the immune system and decrease resistance. An optimistic style that allows for a sense of control boosts immunity. The end result does indeed depend on whether you see the glass as half full or half empty.

Notes

1. Morton Hunt, "Don't Worry, Be Happy," *Longevity,* December:1991, 80.

2. Example is from Joan Borysenko, *Minding the Body, Mending the Mind* (Reading, Massachusetts: Addison-Wesley Publishing Company, Inc., 1987), p. 120.

3. Christopher Peterson, George E. Vaillant, and Martin E. P. Seligman, "Pessimistic Explanatory Style Is a Risk Factor for Physical Illness: A Thirty-Five-Year Longitudinal Study," *Journal of Personality and Social Psychology,* 55(1): 1988, 23.

4. Carolyn Jabs, "New Reasons to be an Optimist," *Self,* September: 1987, 170–173.

5. Jabs.

6. "Good Stress: Why You Need It to Stay Young," *Prevention,* April: 1986, 28–32.

7. Martin E. P. Seligman, *Learned Optimism* (New York: Alfred A. Knopf, 1991), p. 178.

8. Christopher Peterson and Lisa M. Bossio, *Health and Optimism* (New York: The Free Press, a Division of Macmillan, Inc., 1991), p. 60.

9. Seligman.

10. "Mind Over Cancer: An Exclusive Interview with Yale Surgeon Dr. Bernie Siegel," *Prevention,* March: 1988, 59–64.

11. "Mind Over Cancer."

12. "Mind Over Cancer."

13. "Mind Over Cancer."

14. William Lee Wilbanks, "The New Obscenity," *Reader's Digest,* December: 1988, 23.

15. "Mind Over Cancer."

16. "Mind Over Cancer."

17. S. E. Taylor and J. D. Brown, "Illusion and Well-Being: A Social Psychological Perspective on Mental Health," *Psychological Bulletin,* 103(2): 1988, 193–210.

18. Nan Silver, "Do Optimists Live Longer?" *American Health,* November 1986, pp. 50–53.

19. Christopher Peterson and Lisa M. Bossio, *Health and Optimism* (New York: The Free Press [A division of Macmillan, Inc.], 1991), p. 106.

20. Leslie Kamen-Siegel, Judith Rodin, Martin E. P. Seligman, and John Dwyer, "Explanatory Style and Cell-Mediated Immunity in Elderly Men and Women," *Health Psychology,* 10(4): 1991, 229–235.

21. H. Asuman Kiyak, Peter P. Vitaliano, and Jeffrey Crinean, "Patients' Expectations as Predictors of Orthognathic Surgery Outcomes," *Health Psychology,* 7(3): 1988, 251–268.

22. Larry Dossey, *Meaning and Medicine: A Doctor's Tales of Breakthrough and Healing* (New York: Bantam Books, 1991), p. 16.

23. Janice K. Kiecolt-Glaser and D. A. Williams, "Self-Blame, Compliance, and Distress Among Burn Patients," *Journal of Personality and Social Psychology,* 53(1): 1987, 187–193.

24. Silver.

25. Dossey, p. 33.

26. Silver.

27. "Mind Over Cancer."

28. Peterson and Bossio, p. 99.

29. Joseph Lederer, "Surgery: A Mind-Body Event," *Mind/Body/ Health Digest,* 1(4): 1–4.

30. Dossey.

31. Seligman, pp. 173–174.

32. Emily H. Lin and Christopher Peterson, "Pessimistic Explanatory Style and Response to Illness," *Behavioral Research Therapy,* 28(3): 1990, 243–248.

33. Blair Justice, "Think Yourself Healthy," *Prevention,* May: 1988, 27–32, 102, 107.

34. Justice.

35. Daniel Goleman, "The Mind Over the Body," *New Realities,* March/April: 1988, 14–19.

36. Robert Ornstein and David Sobel, "The Healing Brain," *Psychology Today,* March: 1987, 48–52.

37. Leslie Kamen-Siegel, Judith Rodin, Martin E. P. Seligman, and John Dwyer, "Explanatory Style and Cell-Mediated Immunity in Elderly Men and Women," *Health Psychology,* 10(4): 1991, 229–235.

22

LOCUS OF CONTROL
AND HEALTH

How shall I be able to rule over others
when I have not full power
and command over myself?
—FRANCOIS RABELAIS

Noted psychologist Martin Seligman paints for us what he calls the infant's "dance of development." In it, the good mother mirrors and responds to the actions of her infant son or daughter. The baby smiles, and the mother smiles. The baby coos or gurgles with delight, and the mother does the same. The baby cries with hunger, and the mother responds with the warm sweetness of milk. Through this "dance of development," Seligman says, infants learn that they have control. And through the sense of control that results, the infant learns that they can ensure their own survival.[1]

What Does Locus of Control Mean?

What, exactly, is a sense of control—and why is it so important to health? The concept of a locus of control originated several decades ago with the work of Julian Rotter; it involves the belief that our own actions will be effective enough to control or master the environment.[2] Control does not mean that we need to control everything around us—such as other people, the environment, or our circumstances, whether good or bad. Control does entail a deep-seated belief that we can impact a situation by how we look at the problem.[3] We can choose how we react and how we respond. If we regard a loss with gloom and doom, we allow it to hurt us; if we view it as a chance for growth and opportunity, we minimize its ability to hurt us.

Suzanne O. Kobasa and Salvatore Maddi, renowned for their research into what makes us "hardy" and able to resist disease, theorize that a sense of control is crucial to health. They say that those "high in control believe and act as if they can influence the events of their experience, rather than being powerless in the face of outside forces." That kind of attitude allows people to take responsibility and act effectively on their own.[4]

Researchers working in the field of psychoneuroimmunology theorize that a person lies somewhere along a continuum as far as a sense of control is concerned. At one end of the continuum is the "external locus of control"; at the opposite end is the "internal locus of control." Where a person is along the continuum relates to his or her health.

People with an external locus of control believe that the things that happen to them are unrelated to their own behavior—and, subsequently, beyond their control.[5] Likening the victim of external locus of control to a boxer in the ring, physician S. I. McMillen explains:

> When the stresses of life buffet them, they lay against the ropes of despair and wish that things would get better. They erroneously decide that their opponent, stress, is much too strong for them, so they don't even try to fight back. [They feel that] everything that happens to them is controlled by external forces and that their actions do not influence what happens to them. Like pawns in a chess game, externals believe that they are randomly moved about by the players of "luck, chance, fate, or predestination."[6]

At the opposite end of the spectrum are the people with an "internal locus of control." These people believe that negative events are a consequence of personal actions, and can thus be potentially controlled.[7] As McMillen defines them, "Internals believe that their own actions have a large influence on what happens to them. If they get fired from a job, internals believe that when they go out to look for a job they will be able to find one. They do not give up; rather, they hope for a brighter future."[8] As researcher Phillip Rice so aptly put it, "If the theme song of the external is *Cast Your Fate to the Winds*, the theme song of the internal is *I Did It My Way*."[9]

A Brief History

Philosopher and researcher Leonard Sagan believes that an external locus of control dominated many cultures throughout a significant period of the world's history. As he states:

> Almost universally, the social adjustment to poverty and helplessness has been the adoption of a fatalistic, authoritarian world view: "These events are out of our hands, they are in the hands of God." Children are taught that bad outcomes are

the result of forces beyond their control, that life must be lived in the present, since, in an incalculable world, individual effort counts for naught.

"[This] pervading sense of helplessness dominated the human condition throughout history—until the Enlightenment. The Enlightenment encouraged the attitude that all natural phenomena operate in conformance with universal physical-chemical properties and are predictable, not the result of whimsical divine forces. If men could understand those principles, they could control their environment and their destiny. These were heady and revolutionary thoughts, unique in human history.[10]

Sagan—an epidemiologist at Stanford University—points out that these perspectives are more than merely revolutionary; they have tremendous impact on the health and life expectancy of all of us. Sagan maintains that life expectancy has leapt by thirty years during this century because we have more control over our lives. The control that acts as a buffer against disaster in this century, he says, includes things like police and fire departments, insurance against loss, and a steady and reliable food supply. Because "we can foresee, avoid, and mitigate problems," he points out, "we have more resources to adapt and cope with them."[11] We have a greater sense of control over our environments.

What Is the Source of Control?

A sense of increased control can come from a variety of sources:

1. Gaining information. People who are informed about a situation feel an increased sense of control because the situation becomes predictable and manageable.
2. Adopting a less pessimistic outlook.
3. Placing faith in someone or something we deeply trust.
4. Learning new coping skills.
5. Building a stronger support system.
6. Being prepared. When people feel prepared for something, they perceive a much greater ability to control even a difficult situation.[12]

The latter point is illustrated beautifully by a study conducted on a Special Forces unit in Vietnam that was expecting an enemy attack.[13] Then an Army psychiatrist, researcher Peter Bourne lived in the camp with the men and took blood samples daily. He measured the amount of an adrenal hormone present when a person is under extreme stress.

It's difficult to imagine any situation much more stressful than anticipating an enemy attack in a war zone—but, to Bourne's surprise, the hormone levels of the men indicated that they were not experiencing any elevated stress. Other tests showed that the men had lower levels of anxiety and depression than even the basic recruits who were entering training.

What enabled these soldiers to rally so valiantly in such difficult circumstances? Bourne believes it was their sense of control. They gained that sense of control, he believes, by being prepared. The soldiers coped with the threat of impending battle by engaging in "a furor of activity," maintaining their equipment and building their defenses.

Only three men in the unit showed elevated stress hormones. They were the two officers and the radio operator who had to receive—and respond to—orders from a distant command post over which they had no control.

Hardiness and Control

Psychologists Suzanne Kobasa and Salvatore Maddi first developed the now-well-accepted theory that people who are able to stay healthy even while under stress have behaviors and personalities marked by "hardiness." One of the key components of hardiness, say the pair, is a sense of control. Dr. Arthur Schmale, a University of Rochester researcher, was one of the first to identify the importance of control—his research, paired with the work of Kobasa and Maddi, demonstrates the importance of control as a factor in health and well-being.

As a classic example, Schmale cites the case of a woman who was diagnosed with leukemia.[14] Her diagnosis came shortly before her husband's death from tuberculosis. She told her physician that she hoped to live until her son—then aged ten—was grown up and settled.

The course of leukemia can be charted by measuring red blood cell count, an indication of how well the body is battling the disease. As her physician measured her red blood count over the years, he was interested to note a trend. At times when she felt in control, her disease lapsed into remission. At other times, when she felt that she was losing control, her disease intensified.

The leukemia soared, for example, as she entered menopause. It intensified, too, when she finally admitted that her second marriage was failing. It even came and went during various times of the year. For example, her disease became much worse every year about the time her physician was scheduled to take his annual summer vacation. Possibly she felt a dangerous loss of control in contemplating his absence.

The worst period of her disease occurred when her son left home to join the Army. Her condition became so critical that, for the first time since becoming ill, she required blood transfusions to stay alive.

The four years while her son was in the military were extremely difficult for her. According to her physician, she required almost constant medical treatment and various hospitalizations just to keep the disease under control. When her son was released from the military, he announced that he was engaged to be married. Shortly afterward, she died. As her physician related, she would now have almost no control in relationship to him.

Another example of the importance of control and the problems that arise in its absence was demonstrated by an executive whom Kobasa studied while she was doing her original research.[15] The patient showed strong alienation, a disconnectedness from people, and a lack of commitment to his job. For a man in his mid-thirties, he had a particularly dismal medical history, peppered with problems such as high blood pressure, peptic ulcer, and migraine headaches.

When he visited Kobasa's office, the executive gained great insight into the cause of his problems. As she describes it, the visit to her office was "a catastrophe. The executive rushed into the office forty-five minutes late, commandeered her secretary's phone, and began making business calls to alert his cronies to where he would be. Kobasa recalls preparing to approach the sensitive subject of his apparent lack of connection to people, but she barely finished a sentence because each time her phone rang, the executive jumped up, convinced that the call was for him." As Kobasa put it, he was obviously not a man in control; his telephones ruled him, and he could not shut them out of his life for a moment.

According to Kobasa and Maddi and the other researchers who have since studied hardiness, it is earmarked by a sense of control. The control that characterizes hardiness is a belief that we can influence events coupled with a willingness to act on that belief rather than just be a victim of circumstances. It is not a desire or a need to be in control of situations or to control other people.

The Influence of Control on Health

The results of a host of studies show the importance of control. As a whole, people with a greater sense of control are at less risk of illness. As new research is completed, scientists are realizing that an internal locus of control has an even more profound role in protecting health than we once thought.

Former *Saturday Review* editor Norman Cousins, renowned for his work linking attitudes and health, maintains that, in general:

> *Anything that restores a sense of control to a patient can be a profound aid to a physician in treating serious illness. That sense of control is more than a mere mood or attitude, and may well be a vital pathway between the brain, the endocrine system, and the immune system. The assumed possibility is that it may serve as the basis for what may well be a profound advancement in the knowledge of how to confront the challenge of serious illness.[16]*

Cousins cites as an example the case of a well-known actor referred to him with cancer of the larynx. The actor spoke in a hoarse whisper. "It was a particularly poignant case because his voice was his prime asset," Cousins remembers. The disease had understandably caused the actor to sink into a deep depression. Cousins worked with the actor to help him understand that his depression was defeating him physically—and together they worked on figuring out ways to control the depression. Once the patient regained a sense of control over what was happening to him, his physician was better able to work at his best. Three months later, the cancer was in remission and the actor's voice was being restored.[17]

A sense of control can affect health and well-being in a number of ways. Studies show that people with little sense of control—those who see their lives and futures controlled by luck or fate—suffer much greater psychological distress. These people, who believe that nothing they do will significantly change their circumstances or their reliance on "luck," have higher levels of depression and anxiety and are much less effective in dealing with chronic pain.[18]

A pilot study of long-term AIDS survivors conducted by Dr. George Solomon and his associates found that the survivors had a number of psychosocial characteristics in common—many of which pointed to an increased sense of control over their situation. The survivors were assertive, able to nurture themselves, actively involved with others who had the disease, and able to communicate openly about their needs, according to Caryle Hirshberg. In addition, says Hirshberg, the long-term AIDS survivors in the study took personal responsibility for the disease, but did not perceive it as a death sentence; felt they could influence the outcome of the disease; had a sense of purpose; and took control by altering their lifestyles. Finally, many of the long-term AIDS survivors had successfully overcome a previous life-threatening illness—something that would certainly impart a sense of control.[19]

Studies with Animals

A number of animal studies have shown the devastating effects on health and life when a sense of control is lost. In one of them, Johns Hopkins psychologist Curt Richter found that rats put in a situation over which they had no control would quickly die.[20] After immersion in a jar full of water, the rats died, but not from drowning: Their lungs were dry. Instead, they died because their hearts literally stopped beating. In summing up the study, Richter theorized that their situation was one characterized by total lack of control: "The rats are in a situation against which they have no defense. . . . They seem literally to 'give up.'"

In another study, discussed by Rice University psychologist Blair Justice, squirrel monkeys were confined in pairs to chairs for eight hours a day. One of the monkeys in each pair had to turn off a light once a minute to prevent a shock from being delivered to the tails of both monkeys.[21] At the end of the experiment, researchers studied both sets of monkeys—the ones who had not been able to control the shocks, and those who had. The task of turning off a light every minute for eight hours was obviously stressful—and, as expected, researchers found that the monkeys who had to control the light had elevated blood pressure. But of the six monkeys who had no control over the light or the electric shock, five collapsed from excessively slow heart action; four of them died from irregular cardiac rhythm.

Studies with Humans

Carried to the extreme, a loss of control can have the same physiological reaction in humans. Authorities on heart disease gathered in a forum on coronary-prone behavior; they concluded that slowing of the heart causes death, even though there are no apparently fatal physiological changes in the heart itself.[22]

Source: Robert Ornstein and Charles Swencionis, editors, *The Healing Brain: A Scientific Reader* (New York: The Guilford Press, 1990).

Focus on Research

The positive effects of control on health have been observed in some of the most difficult situations in which people find themselves, such as nursing homes. Judith Rodin, a professor of psychiatry and medicine at Yale University, studied nursing home patients who had both failing mental and physical health. These patients were in a classic "no-control" situation: They were told which room to live in; their meals were prepared for them and served at a predetermined time every day; they were provided with certain furnishings; and so on. As in most nursing homes, none of the patients had a say in what happened—or when it happened.

The patients were then given some control over some of the major and minor aspects of their lives. They were given a choice of which room they wanted to live in—and how that room would be furnished and decorated. They had control over when they moved to the room. They were given control over which movies they watched and when the phone would ring in their room.

According to Rodin, the results were "profound." The physical health of the patients improved dramatically. The levels of stress-related hormones dipped. Even memory and alertness were improved. Longevity increased by 50 percent.

Taking control, on the other hand, can have the opposite effect on health. According to a study reported in *Clinical Psychiatry News*,[23] researchers at the University of Connecticut School of Medicine observed a group of more than 200 heart-attack survivors for eight years. The researchers noted that the patients who accepted the responsibility for their attacks had fewer second attacks than patients who blamed their genes, their spouse, or other factors. According to study leader Glenn Affleck, "The value in accepting responsibility for a heart attack could stem from its being a sign of taking control. Passing the buck, on the other hand, could be indicative of the very sort of thinking that may contribute to heart attacks in the first place—namely, feeling a lack of control. This, in turn, could lead to a feeling of helplessness in making adaptive lifestyle changes."

Biochemical Imbalances

One reason control has such a profound influence over health is that a lack of control disturbs the biochemical balance in the brain and body. An internal locus of control has a significant influence over the body's release of hormones, which has been found to be a powerful determinant of health. Three of these hormones that are influenced by a lack of control are:

- *Serotonin*, which regulates moods, relieves pain, and helps control release of the powerful pain-killing brain chemicals, the endorphins.
- *Dopamine*, which is largely responsible for a sense of reward or pleasure.
- *Norepinephrine*, which causes depression when depleted.

Both norepinephrine and dopamine are critical to relaying nerve impulses from one neuron to another; they are essential to the nervous system's ability to "communicate" among its many cells. All three of these hormones are essential to activity, appetite, moods, sleep, sex, reinforcement, reward, and pleasure, and they play an important role in healthy mental functioning.[24]

When we feel little sense of control, the levels of norepinephrine, dopamine, and serotonin drop.[25] As a result, a disturbance in our sense of control can also seriously disturb our mental functioning, appetite, mood, sleep, sex drive, and senses of reinforcement, reward, and pleasure.

Furthermore, when we have little internal locus of control, the level of corticosteroids in our bloodstream soars. The corticosteroids, released by the body during stress, cause a variety of physical damage. They lower our resistance to disease, and suppress the body's manufacture of norepinephrine, dopamine, and serotonin—making lack of control a two-edged sword.

Lack of Control versus Stress

A lack of control may have an even stronger influence over health than do high levels of stress. Turning to a situation where people often have little control—the workplace—researchers have found that those with little control suffer more severe health problems than do those with high levels of stress.

Researcher Rena Pasick, with the University of California School of Public Health, studied almost 800 working adults in Alameda County, California. She found a "significant association" between the amount of control on the job and health status.[26]

The study bore out some seeming contradictions, until researchers considered the issue of control. For example, upper-level management and other white-collar employees have been considered at highest risk because of the amount of stress and responsibility they have. But Pasick's study showed that they actually enjoy better health than those they supervise or than blue-collar workers in general. They have more control.[27]

Various studies among work populations have shown that lack of control can be deleterious to health. People with little control but high demands have more than three times the risk of heart disease and chronically escalated blood pressure than people with few demands but a high level of control. Robert Karasek, an industrial engineering professor at Columbia University, has found that people who have little control over their jobs have higher rates of heart disease than people who can dictate the style and pace of their work. Worst off are those whose work makes substantial psychological demands but offers little opportunity for independent decision-making—occupations such as telephone operators, waiters, cashiers, cooks, garment stitchers, and assembly-line workers. According to Karasek, the combination of high demands and low control appears to raise the risk of heart disease as much as "smoking or having a high cholesterol level."[28]

According to researchers with the Framingham Heart Study, women clerical workers and others with little control have twice as much heart disease as

Focus on Research

A group of students from the University of Texas were given a series of arithmetic problems to complete. At the same time, they were subjected to random bursts of loud noise (measuring more than 100 decibels), which researchers believed would have a distracting and disturbing effect on the students as they attempted to complete the arithmetic problems.

The researchers told half of the students that they could stop the noise by pressing a button on the side of the table. In reality, the button would do nothing, but the students believed because it gave them the control to stop the noise. The other half of the students were told that they could not control the noise.

The students with the buttons never tried to push them. Apparently, it was enough just to know that they could push the buttons if they wanted to. Even though the students with the buttons never pushed them, their perceived sense of control had a significant effect: They showed far fewer physiological signs of stress than the students without the buttons. The students who were not given a button to push exhibited many more common stress symptoms, such as headache, ringing in the ears, perspiring palms, and pounding of the heart.

Source: J. W. Pennebaker, M. A. Burnam, M. A. Schaeffer, and D. C. Harper, "Lack of Control as a Determinant of Perceived Physical Symptoms," *Journal of Personality and Social Psychology*, 35(3): 1977, 167–174.

women in occupations with higher levels of control.[29] The Framingham researchers suggest that the clerical workers and others with a low sense of control "experience severe occupational stress, including a lack of autonomy and control over the work environment, under-utilization of skills, and lack of recognition of accomplishments."[30]

In another study of the link between control and heart disease, researchers found that heart disease is greater among waiters and assembly-line workers than among managers who are faced with equally high stress and demands but who have more control and decision-making ability.[31]

The Stress-Buffering Power of Control

A person in a stressful situation who believes that he or she has some control over the situation suffers far less physiological damage normally associated with stress. And control acts as a buffer against stress when we believe we have control even if we really don't.

In a similar study,[32] individuals were placed in booths and asked to perform arithmetic problems in their head. To make the situation even more stressful, researchers piped noise into the booths. Half of the people in the study were able to control the noise level by turning a knob in the booth; the other half were dependent on the first half for volume control. Both groups were exposed to an identical level of noise; the only difference between the two was the ability to control the volume of noise. At the end of the experiment, researchers took blood samples and studied the level of stress hormones in the blood. The people who did not have a knob to turn had much higher levels of cortisol, a major stress hormone. According to the research authors, "the ability to control external stress has a large influence on how much internal stress we experience."

The stress-buffering effects of control have been observed in a wide variety of situations—and have even been seen in the most stressful conditions, such as those endured by hostages and prisoners of war. Those who have been able to maintain hardiness and survive their ordeals, according to researchers, are those who have somehow been able to achieve some sense of control, even in "prison." National Institute of Mental Health psychologist Julius Segal found that one of the hostages in Iran "achieved this by saving a bit of food from his meals and then offering it to anyone who came into his cell. That simple coping strategy had the effect of turning the cell into a living room, the hostage into a host welcoming visitors."[33]

Finally, control has been known to work in the less-severe, everyday problems of big-city noise and crowding. According to Rice University psychologist Blair Justice, city dwellers combat the intrusion of unwanted noise by masking it with music from their own radios or tape players—something they can do to put the situation in their own control. Similarly, they combat the sense of crowding by "filtering" out the crowd—paying little attention to the people, sounds, and stimuli that surround them. Thus, they maintain a sense of control in a situation they otherwise can't control.[34]

The Influence of Control on Immunity and Healing

One reason a lack of control may lead to poor health lies within the immune system. According to research, control may have a significant effect on the function of the body's immune defenses. People who feel powerless, helpless, and out of control generally have compromised immunity, whereas those who feel a sense of control have healthier immune systems.

Physicians tested women with early-stage breast cancer. Those who felt some control over their lives and their disease were compared with women who felt a distressing lack of control. The women with control had a far greater level of natural killer cell activity—a much stronger immune system.[35]

In a related study, researchers did a thirty-year follow-up study of children who had received psychological counseling during a period of juvenile delinquency. The researchers were surprised to find that the children who had received help for their problems had far more health problems than those who had not received help. When they probed into the situation, the researchers found that the issue, again, was one of control:

The untreated group may have perceived the world as more under their control than the group that was given assistance. One of the effects of outside intervention may be to lessen patients' sense of control of life's events. It is as if they have adopted the idea that the counselor is taking care of their troubles, not they themselves. They are like the animals locked in the cage that cannot control the delivery of shocks. This attitude may in turn affect the immune system, with troublesome consequences for the patients' health.[36]

A sense of control also appears to trigger the body's internal healing mechanisms. Several different studies with patients about to undergo surgery demonstrate that a sense of control can have significant effect on the healing process. In one, psychologist Ellen Langer took a randomly selected group of surgical patients at Yale–New Haven Hospital and divided the patients into three groups. Members of the first group were simply asked questions about what they expected to happen. Members of the second group were given some basic information about the surgery, including probable after-effects and discomfort. Members of the third group were given what Langer called a "coping device," consisting of detailed information, help in placing the experience in an optimistic light, and instructions detailing how patients could exercise control over their bodies.

When the surgeries were completed and Langer compared the three groups, the first two weren't much different from each other. But the people in the third group—the ones who were given the coping primer—used half as many painkillers and sedatives and stayed in the hospital an average of two days less than the people who received just basic information. The difference in recovery, suggests Langer, "was due to the patients' learning that they could diminish postsurgical discomfort and in so doing feel that they were in control."[37]

A similar experiment conducted by psychologists at the University of Iowa School of Medicine involved patients about to undergo coronary bypass surgery. The researchers structured their study much like Langer's, using three separate groups of patients. The patients in the group that had received enough information to give a sense of control "fared significantly better on all counts. There was less hypertension, anxiety, and pain." A greater sense of control "proved to be the most powerful predictor of recovery without complication."[38]

Other studies at other hospitals have had the same result: Patients with a sense of control heal more quickly with fewer complications. All of the studies together show us the power of an internal locus of control. With it, we may have improved immune function, have the ability to fight disease, and recover more quickly when illness does strike. Control may possibly be the weapon researchers were referring to when they told us, "You carry with you the most powerful medicine that exists. Each of us has it if we choose to use it, if we learn to use it."[39]

Notes

1. Joan Borysenko, *Minding the Body, Mending the Mind* (Reading, Massachusetts: Addison-Wesley Publishing Company, Inc., 1987), p. 22.

2. Phillip L. Rice, *Stress and Health* (Monterey, California: Brooks/Cole Publishing Company, 1987), p. 109.

3. Blair Justice, *Who Gets Sick: Thinking and Health* (Houston, Texas: Peak Press, 1987), pp. 61–62.

4. Aaron Antonovsky, *Unraveling the Mystery of Health: How People Manage Stress and Stay Well* (San Francisco, CA: Jossey-Bass Publishers, 1987), pp. 36–37.

5. H. M. Lefcourt, *Locus of Control: Current*

Trends in Theory and Research (Hillsdale, New Jersey: Erlbaum, 1976), p. 29.

6. S. I. McMillen, *None of These Diseases*, revised (Old Tappan, New Jersey: Fleming H. Revell Company, 1984), p. 177.

7. Lefcourt.

8. McMillen, pp. 177–178.

9. Rice, p. 109.

10. Leonard A. Sagan, *The Health of Nations* (New York: Basic Books, Inc., Publishers, 1987).

11. Tony Eprile, "Longevity Tied to Self-Mastery," *Omni Longevity* 2(10): 1988, 109–111.

12. Justice, p. 145.

13. P. G. Bourne, R. M. Rose, and J. W. Mason, "17-0HCS Levels in Combat: Special Forces 'A' Team Under Threat of Attack," *Archives of General Psychiatry*, 19: 1968, 135–140.

14. Case cited in Steven Locke and Douglas Colligan, *The Healer Within* (New York: E. P. Dutton, 1986), p. 96.

15. Locke and Colligan, pp. 96–97.

16. Norman Cousins, *Head First: The Biology of Hope* (New York: E. P. Dutton, 1989), p. 120.

17. Cousins, pp. 119–120.

18. J. E. Crisson and F. J. Keefe, "The Relationship of Locus of Control to Pain Coping Strategies and Psychological Distress in Chronic Pain Patients," *Behavioral Medicine*, 35(2): 1988, 147–154.

19. Caryle Hirshberg, "Spontaneous Remission: The Spectrum of Self-Repair," *The Psychology of Health, Immunity, and Disease*, vol. B, p. 186, in Proceedings of the Sixth International Conference of the National Institute for the Clinical Application of Behavioral Medicine.

20. Carl Richter, "On the Phenomenon of Sudden Death in Animals and Man," *Psychosomatic Medicine*, 19(3): 1957, 191–198.

21. K. C. Corley, H. P. Mauck, and F. O'M. Shiel, "Cardiac Responses Associated with 'Yoked Chair' Shock Avoidance in Squirrel Monkeys," *Psychophysiology*, 12: 1975, 439–444.

22. National Institutes of Health, *Proceedings of the Forum on Coronary Prone Behavior* (Bethesda, Maryland: National Institutes of Health, Department of Health, Education, and Welfare Publication No. 78-1451), p. 162.

23. *Clinical Psychiatry News*, as reported in "Health Briefs," *Executive Fitness*, November: 1987, 8.

24. H. S. Akiskal and W. T. McKinney, "Overview of Recent Research in Depression," *Archives of General Psychiatry*, 32: 1975, 285–305.

25. P. Ahluwalia, R. M. Zacharko, and H. Anisman, *Dopamine Variations Associated with Acute and Chronic Stressors*, Presentation at the Annual Meeting of the Society of Neuroscience, Dallas, Texas.

26. W. Vale, J. Spiess, C. Rivier, and J. Rivier, "Characterization of a 41-Residue Ovine Hypothalamic Peptide That Stimulates Secretion of Corticotropin and Beta-Endorphin," *Science*, 213: 1981, 1394–1397.

27. Vale et al.

28. Claudia Wallis, "Stress: Can We Cope?" *Time*, June 6: 1983, 48–54.

29. S. G. Haynes, "Type A Behavior, Employment Status, and Coronary Heart Disease in Women," *Behavioral Medicine Update*, 6(4): 1984, 11–15.

30. Haynes, p. 13.

31. R. A. Karasek, T. G. T. Theorell, J. Schwartz, C. Pieper, and L. Alfredson, "Job, Psychological Factors, and Coronary Heart Disease," *Advances in Cardiology*, 29: 1982, 62–67.

32. U. Lundberg and M. Frankenhaeser, "Psychophysiological Reactions to Noise as Modified by Personal Control Over Stimulus Intensity," *Biological Psychology*, 6: 1978, 51–58.

33. Wallis.

34. Justice, pp. 148–149.

35. Sandra M. Levy, *Emotional Expression and Survival in Breast Cancer Patients: Immunological Correlates*, Paper Presented at the Meetings of the American Psychological Association, August 1983, Anaheim, California.

36. Michael S. Gazzaniga, *Mind Matters* (Boston: Houghton Mifflin Company, 1988).

37. Locke and Colligan, pp. 210–211.

38. Justice, pp. 310–311.

39. R. S. Eliot, *Cognitive and Behavioral Stress Management Considerations*, Presentation at a Conference on Stress and the Heart of the American College of Cardiology, July 1986, Jackson Hole, Wyoming.

23

SELF-ESTEEM AND HEALTH

We can secure other people's approval, if we do right and try hard; but our own is worth a hundred of it.—MARK TWAIN

American humorist and author Samuel Clemens—the legendary Mark Twain—believed that it's a hundred times more valuable to approve of ourselves than to have the approval of others. A century after he penned that advice, it is proving to be true.

In his book on *Honoring the Self*, psychologist Nathaniel Branden calls self-esteem the reputation we have with ourselves; when we believe that we are bad or unworthy, the reputation is poor, and low self-esteem is the result.

We stand in the midst of an almost infinite network of relationships: to other people, to things, to the universe. And yet, at three o'clock in the morning, when we are alone with ourselves, we are aware that the most intimate and powerful of all relationships and the one we can never escape is the relationship to ourselves. No significant aspect of our thinking, motivation, feelings, or behavior is unaffected by our self-evaluation.[1]

According to a growing body of evidence, a healthy self-esteem is one of the best things a person can do for overall health, both mental and physical. And a good, strong sense of self can boost the immune system, improve heart function, protect against disease, and aid in healing.

What Is Self-Esteem?

Self-esteem is a sense of positive self-regard. It's a way of viewing oneself as a good person who is well in all aspects. It's a sense of feeling good about one's capabilities, physical limitations, goals, place in the world, and relationship to others. Self-esteem is a powerful element. The perceptions about oneself are what set the boundaries for what we can and cannot do. Self-esteem can be called the blueprint for behavior.

Self-esteem should not be confused with *self-concept*. Self-concept is a broad term used to encompass all the ways we compare and evaluate ourselves to those around us. It refers to the way we compare ourselves physically, mentally, and socially. Self-esteem contributes to, but is not the same as, self-concept.[2] Instead, self-esteem is characterized by a powerful source of inner strength—the willingness to cope with the basic challenges of life, knowing you are more than your problems, learning to discriminate, having self-acceptance and self-responsibility.[3]

Self-esteem, the value we assign to ourselves, is generally based on five factors—two physical and three psychological. The physical factors that determine our self-esteem are (1) our appearance (the way we look) and (2) our physical abilities. The psychological determinants of self-esteem are (1) how well we do in school (our perceived intelligence), (2) how confident we are in social situations, and (3) how we regard ourselves.[4] Recent research by Finnish scientist Mirja Kalliopuska suggests that empathy—the ability to put oneself in the place of other people and appreciate their feelings—may also be linked to self-esteem.[5]

Esteem toward "self" necessarily encompasses more than one "person" because none of us is one unified person. We all are collections of multiple selves that have different minds, different intelligences, and different sets of emotions. Psychologist Robert Ornstein and physician David Sobel explain:

> *You can see this when you remember a face but not a name, or when your intellect tells you that something is a good idea but your emotions disagree. Each of us acts differently and is genuinely a different person to lovers than to coworkers, to children and to the police, different to old, close friends and to new business acquaintances. We have a great range of abilities and talents within ourselves, and the more we use them, the healthier we are.*[6]

Ornstein and Sobel continue, "An innovative study of 'self-complexity' finds that men and women who are complex and diverse, whose selves reach out in different directions, suffer fewer signs of life's stresses. They report less depression and fewer foul moods, colds, coughs, stomach pains, headaches, and muscle aches than their less complex counterparts."[7]

Researchers have been able to identify what constitutes a healthy self-esteem. One of the most focused definitions was presented by Leonard Sagan in his examination of the factors that influence health and wellness in the world's various nations. In his comprehensive work, *The Health of Nations*, Sagan writes that those with a high level of self-esteem also have an inner locus of control:

> *They are confident of their ability to make competent decisions. They do not rely solely on traditional authority for guidance, but are able to acquire and evaluate information and make decisions independently. In contrast with traditional people who believe that outcomes are determined by gods, chance, or*

persons of influence, healthy people believe that their decisions can be effica-
cious in determining outcomes—that is, they believe that what they think and
do will matter.⁸

In his definition of healthy people, Sagan pointed out a vital characteristic
among those with high self-esteem. Although healthy people have high regard
for themselves, he said:

> *They are not self-indulgent or preoccupied with their personal identity or wel-*
> *fare. Rather they are committed to goals other than their own personal welfare.*
> *Goals may be global in scope or quite modest; most important, however, they are*
> *not egotistical in nature but will benefit others. Healthy people are compassion-*
> *ate, they have a strong sense of community. I believe that these qualities are in*
> *a state of decline in the United States—and it may not be a coincidence that evi-*
> *dence of worsening health is appearing at the same time that Americans are pre-*
> *occupied with "self-realization."⁹*

In summary, he says, those with a healthy self-esteem have confidence in
themselves and their ability to control their own lives; those who have low self-
esteem tend to view themselves as passive victims—and are much more prone to
illness and the stress of difficult life situations.

When you have a strong sense of self-esteem, "You are somebody. You are
worthwhile," says Lowell Levin, professor of public health at Yale University and
a leading researcher in his field. "There's nothing more exhilarating than that.
That can influence your health."¹⁰

Self-esteem has a positive influence on health, indeed—and a variety of studies have shown a strong correlation between the two. When the California Department of Mental Health surveyed 1,000 Californians, they found that the
healthiest ones cared most for others—and for themselves. One reason for the
finding, suggests researcher James Lynch, is that people with high self-esteem
take better care of themselves: "Really caring for yourself includes caring for your
body."¹¹

People with positive self-esteem view themselves as good people who are
well in all aspects of life. They have a physical, mental, social, emotional, and
spiritual balance that enables them to achieve an equilibrium that acts as a buffer
against stress and difficult life situations.

Where Does Self-Esteem Come From?

The formation of self-esteem begins early in life. Some of the first ingredients that
make up self-esteem are the messages we receive during childhood from our parents, our other relatives, our teachers, and our friends. It depends partly on physical limitations—whether we are overweight, hard of hearing, or incapable of
speaking without stuttering. It is influenced by social class and by cultural re-

strictions. And it depends to a great extent on how much love we feel from those around us—how much acceptance, how much compassion, how much we are able to identify and feel identified with.

So far, the factors that influence self-esteem seem to be largely beyond our control. We can't determine how our third-grade teacher deals with us, for example, nor can we change the fact that a mother's problem pregnancy left us severely visually impaired. But each of us can control one large factor in self-esteem. It's the way we communicate with our self-esteem, the words we say about ourselves, which may have a powerful effect not only on our minds but also on our bodies.

Psychologist Susan Jeffers likes to use a demonstration to impress people with the importance of what they're communicating to their self-esteem.[12] Whenever she gives a talk, she invites a volunteer from the audience to come up to the front. She has the volunteer make a fist and extend his or her right arm in front of the body, angled down to the left for strength. She then asks the volunteer to resist as powerfully as possible while she tries to push down on the arm. She relates that she's never "won" this initial trial.

She then asks the volunteer to stand at ease, close his or her eyes, and repeat ten times aloud, "I am a weak and unworthy person." She encourages the volunteer to really *feel* the words while speaking them. She then asks the volunteer to open his or her eyes, assume the original posture, and resist her efforts to push the same arm down.

"I wish I had a camera to record the expression on my volunteer's face as I press his arm and it gives way," Jeffers exclaims. "A few object, 'I wasn't ready!' So I do it again."

Once again, Jeffers has the volunteer close the eyes, stand at ease, and repeat aloud a different set of words: "I am a strong and worthy person." Jeffers says that, to everyone's surprise, she once again cannot budge the arm.

She concludes that she can run this experiment backward and forward almost any number of times, and "it makes no difference if I leave the room while he speaks and I don't know what he has said: Weak words mean a weak arm; strong words mean a strong arm."

Jeffers explains this phenomenon by stating:

> It is as though the inner self doesn't know what is true and false, and believes the words it is told without judging them. . . . We can control our self-esteem by speaking to it. I think the conclusion is obvious: Stop feeding yourself negative words, and start building yourself up with positive ones.[13]

The Impact of Self-Esteem on the Body

Whether people do or do not get sick—and how long they stay that way—may depend in part on how strong their self-esteem is. A growing body of evidence indicates that low self-esteem often is a factor in chronic pain, for example. And several studies show that recovery from infectious mononucleosis is related to "ego strength"; the higher the self-esteem, the more rapid the recovery.[14]

The level of self-esteem one has appears to be a crucial factor in how people respond to stress, regardless of their personality type. Low self-esteem is a common denominator in stress-prone personalities, such as Type A and helpless-hopeless types.[15] Self-esteem may also be an important factor in the risk of heart disease. As discussed previously, scientists for years ascribed the highest risk of heart disease to the classic "Type A" personality. More recent in-depth research, however, has isolated two factors—anger and hostility—as the real culprits in the Type A personality pattern. A person can be a Type A personality and not have an increased risk of heart disease as long as he or she is not angry and hostile.

Self-esteem is so powerful an influence on health that it even impacts the way we react to life events. Some sources of stress can be categorized as "life events"— situations in life that researchers have determined cause stress. Many are negatives, such as the death of a loved one, divorce, a jail term, or assuming a new debt. But researchers have found that positive life events—such as getting married, getting a new job, or giving birth—are also sources of stress. Whether these stressors cause a person to become ill depends on many factors, including one's ability to cope with the stress.

In their research in life events, scientists have found that self-esteem has significant influence on how positive life events impact our health. If we've got strong self-esteem, the outlook is good: The more positive life events, the better

---

Focus on Research

Research conducted by Laura Hubbs-Tait and Christopher J. Blodgett, psychologists at Washburn University in Kansas and at New York's Buffalo State College, respectively, show that self-esteem may in part influence the degree of hostility that Type A personalities experience. In their study, Hubbs-Tait and Blodgett asked both Type A and Type B men to solve ten matrix problems; part of the men in the study solved the problems under low stress, and part of them solved the problems in an atmosphere of high stress. Before solving the problems, the men were also identified as having either high or low self-esteem.

Those who had low self-esteem *perceived* that they were much more hurried and under much more stress. They also made more errors. Even more significant was that they also became much more hostile, signaling an increased risk for cardiovascular disease. In summarizing the results of the study, the researchers noted that there was very little difference in the ability of the two groups to solve the problems—but there was a great deal of difference in the hostility shown by the men with low self-esteem.

"In particular, the difference in hostility between the two groups must be emphasized," wrote the researchers. "Recent research suggests that hostility plays a major role in the etiology of coronary heart disease. The significantly higher level of hostility reported by the Type A subjects with low self-esteem under high stress suggests that low self-esteem Type A's may be more at risk for developing coronary heart disease than high self-esteem Type A's.

Source: "Self-Esteem Linked to Type-A Risk," *Brain/Mind Bulletin*, 15(10): 1990, 1, 6; and Laura Hubbs-Tait and Christopher J. Blodgett, "The Mediating Effects of Self-Esteem and Coronary-Prone Behavior on Problem Solving and Affect Under Low and High Stress," *Behavioral Medicine*, Fall: 1989, 101–110.

our health. But if our self-esteem is poor, our health can decline in direct proportion as our life becomes peppered with more positive life events.[16]

Results of various studies show that positive self-esteem helps protect health. One reason behind its protective nature may be its effect on the immune system. One study that gives a glimpse of the self-esteem/immunity link was conducted by psychiatrist J. Stephen Heisel and his colleagues at McLean Hospital. They studied 111 college students who had completed the Minnesota Multiphasic Personality Inventory (MMPI), a 566-item questionnaire that describes personality and other measures of mental health, such as level of depression. In analyzing the students' scores, he found that those with the highest self-esteem were also the ones with the strongest natural killer cell activity. High self-esteem seemed to provide a boost to the immune system and give students stronger immunity against disease.[17]

Harvard Medical School psychiatrist Steven Locke cites the work of psychoneuroimmunology pioneer Dr. George Solomon in making a further case for self-esteem as an influence on immunity.[18] According to Locke, Solomon gave the example of two homosexual men, both of whom had been diagnosed with AIDS. One was "a conservative, cultured college professor whose sex life was relatively monogamous," explains Solomon, but his self-esteem was battered because he had difficulty accepting his homosexuality and expressing negative emotions. The other man was a highly promiscuous individual who was heavily involved in sadomasochistic sex, drinking, smoking, drug abuse, and the frequenting of bars that catered to his whims. But "his self-esteem was excellent," Solomon notes. "He has a number of close friends and with a number of other sadomasochists he has formed a sadomasochist support group that meets every week to talk about their problems. He feels that his self-esteem in the past years is the highest it has ever been in his life."

When Solomon took blood tests and compared the immune systems of the two, the sadomasochist—the one who, by all rights, should have been in the poorest condition because of his deleterious health habits—had the strongest immune system. Solomon theorizes that his strong sense of self-esteem had kept his immune system in better shape.[19]

Researchers have also found a possible connection between poor self-esteem and premature death from coronary heart disease. Researchers from McGill University in Montreal gave thorough psychological questionnaires to two hundred men recovering from heart attack. Over the next five years, the men who reported feeling "useless" or unable to "do things well" were nearly four times as likely to die from coronary disease as men with higher self-esteem. That association remained strong even after researchers adjusted for other factors.[20]

Self-Efficacy: Believing in Yourself

An important part of self-esteem is what psychologists call self-efficacy, one of the components of self-esteem that apparently leads to both psychological and physical well-being. Self-efficacy is your perception of your own ability to do a specific task. It's your belief in yourself, your conviction that you can manage the adverse events that come along in your life.

Just as with self-esteem, various factors combine to determine how strong your self-efficacy is:

1. *Past performance.* If you've handled things well in the past, your faith in yourself is bolstered, and you are more likely to feel confident about facing any new situations.

2. *Vicarious experience.* This means keeping your eyes open and watching what goes on around you. You see how a friend deals with the death of her spouse. You watch what happens to a coworker when he loses several big accounts and then gets fired. You watch a television documentary about a midwestern farm family that faces seemingly insurmountable odds—but emerges with spirit and courage after losing farm, home, and source of income. You read a magazine article about a young mother who faces with great courage the task of caring for her severely handicapped baby. You take all of that in, and the message comes through: If they can do it, so can I. You gain strength from their strength, courage from their courage. You make the unspoken commitment that when your time comes, you'll rally, too.

3. *The encouragement of others.* It's much easier to believe in yourself when the people around you are cheering you on.

Self-efficacy is an important component of self-esteem, because it can in a very real way predict your behavior. It determines your level of effort: If you really believe you can succeed, you're apt to keep on trying. It endows you with perseverance in the face of failure: If you really believe in yourself, you're less likely to give up. Your level of self-efficacy determines whether you will help yourself or hinder yourself. It determines, too, how well you will react to stress: If you are low in self-efficacy, you may become overwhelmed by stress because you become convinced that your life—or a particular situation—is unmanageable.

To sum it up, people with solid self-efficacy believe they'll come out on top—so they usually do. Dr. Albert Bandura of Stanford University has identified three landmark characteristics of people with high self-efficacy:

1. They believe the intended outcome of a given behavior is of value to themselves.
2. They believe that performing the behavior will lead to that outcome.
3. They believe that they can successfully perform the behavior.[21]

As Bandura says, "When beset with difficulties, people who entertain serious doubts about their capabilities slacken their efforts or give up altogether, whereas those who have a strong sense of efficacy exert great effort to master the challenges."[22]

Psychologist Blair Justice gives an example of the difference that self-efficacy can make in one of the most stressful situations; the relocation of an elderly person from one place to another or from one institution to another. A marked increase in death rate often occurs, he says, usually within the first three months after relocation. When a home for the elderly in Chicago was closed, Justice writes, "the mortality rate was substantially lower for those who accepted the news of relocation philosophically but not with a sense of defeat or helplessness."[23] Those who became angry about the move fared almost as well—possibly because their anger mobilized them "to take care of themselves by eating, keeping as active as possible, and not giving up."

Self-efficacy can actually cause physiological changes in the body. When under stress of any kind, the brain releases chemicals called catecholamines, which trigger a complex set of physiological reactions enabling a person to meet the challenge of the stress—the classic fight or flight syndrome. By measuring the levels of catecholamines in the blood, researchers can determine the degree of stress.

Bandura and his colleagues selected twelve women who had arachnaphobia and measured the level of catecholamine secretion when the women were faced with situations that frightened them—looking at a spider, putting a hand in a bowl with a spider, or allowing a spider to crawl on a hand. When women felt that they could handle a situation, catecholamine levels were low; when they felt that a sit-

---

Focus on Research

A series of experiments was conducted at the Stanford Arthritis Center by Ann O'Leary, Kate Lorig, and their colleagues. They designed a self-management course to help arthritis sufferers improve by learning more about the causes of arthritis, the treatments available, the exercises that could impart strength and endurance, relaxation techniques, nutrition, joint protection, and the interrelationship of stress, pain, and depression.

One group was accepted immediately into a self-management course; the second group had to wait four months while the first group finished its course. At the end of the first course, the researchers compared the patients who had been through the instruction with those who had not. No one was surprised that the patients who had finished the class were doing much better. The pain from their arthritis had decreased dramatically. O'Leary, Lorig, and their colleagues assumed that the patients had less pain because they had more knowledge, were using relaxation techniques,

and were doing the therapeutic exercises described in the self-management course. But that wasn't the case. They had attended the class and had heard all kinds of information about how to manage arthritis. They came to believe that arthritis was a manageable disease. Even more important, they began to trust in their own ability to make a difference in how they felt. Their self-efficacy soared, and their pain diminished.

"The people who improved were not necessarily the ones who knew more about arthritis or engaged in therapeutic exercise," wrote Ornstein and Sobel. . . . Careful interviews with class participants suggested that those who improved had a positive outlook and felt a sense of control regarding their arthritis. Those who failed to improve, even if they exercised, felt 'there was nothing they could do about their arthritis.' The key difference appeared to be the person's perception of his or her own ability to control or change the arthritis symptoms." It depended on self-efficacy.

Source: Robert Ornstein and David Sobel, *The Healing Brain* (New York: Simon and Schuster, 1987), p. 249.

uation was more than they could handle (in other words, when their self-efficacy was low), catecholamine levels shot up.

Bandura and his colleagues at Stanford worked with the women to bolster their level of self-efficacy regarding spiders. The women gained confidence, and some began to believe that they could manage an encounter with a spider. When that happened, says Bandura, catecholamine levels stayed low. Stress was eased, and the women did not suffer the physiological reactions as before.[24]

The real power of self-efficacy on health is demonstrated quite simply. If you want to get a fairly accurate prediction of how healthy someone is or will be, ask people how healthy they *think* they are. Researchers have found that "self-rated" health—much the same as self-efficacy—determines to a large extent how healthy a person will actually be. Some studies have even shown that asking that simple question will tell you more about a person's health than an entire battery of sophisticated laboratory tests.

Ornstein and Sobel report on a seven-year study carried out in Manitoba, Canada. More than 3,500 elderly people were asked, "For your age would you say, in general, your health is excellent, good, fair, poor, or bad?" Researchers conducting the study also sought health reports from physicians that gave detailed records on illnesses, surgeries, hospitalizations, and other medical problems. When researchers correlated actual health at the end of the study with self-ratings and medical observations seven years earlier, they found the self-ratings to be more accurate and predictive than the health measures from the physicians. Even more surprisingly, "those who were in objectively poor health by physician report survived at a higher rate as long as they believed their own health to be good."[25] The only thing more powerful than self-rated health, in fact, was increasing age.

Belief in oneself is one of the most powerful weapons we have in protecting our health and living longer. It has a startling impact on wellness. And we are able to harness it to our advantage. As Madeline Gershwin said, "What wise people and grandmothers have always known is that the way you feel about yourself, your attitudes, beliefs, values, have a great deal to do with your health and well-being."[26]

Notes

1. Joan Borysenko, *Guilt Is the Teacher, Love is the Lesson* (New York: Warner Books, 1990), p. 45.

2. Phillip L. Rice, *Stress and Health. Principles and Practice for Coping and Wellness* (Monterey, California: Brooks/Cole Publishing Company, 1987), p. 111.

3. National Branden, "Living with Self-Esteem," *Lotus*, Fall: 1992.

4. Rice.

5. *Psychological Reports* 70: 1119–1122.

6. Robert Ornstein and David Sobel, *Healthy Pleasures* (Reading, Massachusetts: Addison-Wesley Publishing Company, Inc., 1989), p. 189.

7. Ornstein and Sobel, p. 190.

8. Leonard A. Sagan, *The Health of Nations* (New York: Basic Books, Inc., Publishers, 1987), p. 187.

9. Sagan.

10. Emrika Padus, *The Complete Guide to Your Emotions and Your Health* (Emmaus, Pennsylvania: Rodale Press, 1986), p. 125.

11. Padus.

12. Described in Susan Jeffers, "Building Your Self-Esteem: Your Positive Words Will Make You Strong," *Success*, October: 1987, 72.

13. Jeffers.

14. S. Michael Plaut and Stanford B. Friedman, "Biological Mechanisms in the Relationship of Stress to Illness," *Pediatric Annals*, 14(8): 1985, 563–567.

15. Brian Luke Seaward, *Managing Stress* (Boston: Jones and Bartlett Publishers, 1994), p. 104.

16. Barbara R. Sarason, Irwin G. Sarason, and Gregory R. Pierce, *Social Support: An Interactional View* (New York: John Wiley & Sons, Inc., 1990), p. 164.

17. "Research Strengthens Link Between Poor Mental and Physical Health," *Sexuality Today Newsletter*, November 24: 1986, 4.

18. Steven Locke and Douglas Colligan, *The Healer Within* (New York: E. P. Dutton, 1986), pp. 131–132.

19. Locke and Colligan.

20. "Danger From Depression," *Consumer Reports on Health,* August: 1992, 63.

21. Aaron Antonovsky, *Unraveling the Mystery of Health How People Manage Stress and Stay Well* (San Francisco, CA: Jossey-Bass Publishers, 1988), p. 59.

22. "Self-Efficacy," *University of California Berkeley Wellness Letter*, 3(8): 1987, 1–2.

23. Blair Justice, *Who Gets Sick: Thinking and Health* (Houston, Texas: Peak Press, 1987), pp. 144–145.

24. Robert Ornstein and David Sobel, *The Healing Brain* (New York: Simon and Schuster, 1987), p. 249.

25. Cited in Ornstein and Sobel, *The Healing Brain*, pp. 246–248.

26. Ornstein and Sobel, *The Healing Brain*, pp. 249–250.

24

PESSIMISM, NEGATIVISM, AND HEALTH

Whatever the situation, and however disheartening it may be, it is a great hour when a man ceases adopting difficulties as an excuse for despondency and tackles himself as the real problem.—HARRY EMERSON FOSDICK

A mother brought her twin boys to a psychologist.

"They're the same in every way, right down to the last freckle," the mother told him. "But there's one big problem. Roy is the eternal pessimist. Everything is rotten to him no matter what we do or say. His twin brother Tom is just the opposite. He's the eternal optimist. Help me, Doctor, to balance them up. Make Roy more optimistic and Tom a little more pessimistic."

"That's easy," said the doctor. "For Roy's birthday next week, give the little pessimist a roomful of the best toys in the world. On their shared birthday, give Tom the optimist a pile of horse manure. I know it sounds strange, but toys for the pessimist and manure for the optimist will help balance them out."

The mother reluctantly complied. She and her husband prepared the boys' bedrooms as instructed. On the boys' birthday the parents quietly looked in on Roy the pessimist. There he sat with all the magnificent toys. "What junk!" he said. "There are too many things here to play with. My parents must have something up their sleeve. I hate this stuff. They can't buy me off."

The disappointed parents moved to Tom the optimist's room. There sat Tom, happily digging through the manure. "You can't fool me," said Tom, looking up at his parents. "Where there's manure, there must be a pony!"[1]

Characteristics of Pessimists

When pessimists are confronted by a problem, they don't even try. They figure that any effort to change themselves or the situation would be futile. In moderation, that's good. A little bit of denial can be positive, says University of

Miami's Dr. Charles S. Carver, because it can keep us from overreacting.[2] But the denial shouldn't carry on too long. The longer you put off dealing with the problem at hand, the worse it often gets.

Another characteristic of pessimists is that, instead of focusing on the problem or the source of the stress, they focus on their own feelings. They zero in on the hurt, anger, frustration, or other emotional distress that stems from the problem. Eventually they get upset and give up altogether.

Again, that's okay—in moderation. It's healthy to acknowledge and express your feelings, to a point. But, says Dr. Carver, "the more you lie around feeling sorry for yourself, the more you reinforce those negative feelings, until your negative expectations are eventually fulfilled."[3]

Are pessimists born that way? Researchers are convinced not. In fact, they say, pessimism—like optimism—appears to be a learned behavior, something developed based on past experiences. Many researchers believe that pessimism is learned early in life, and is reinforced by circumstances; according to Michael F. Scheier, professor of psychology at Carnegie-Mellon University, pessimists "are the way they are because they've experienced trouble in the past and expect more of the same."[4]

As some of their most characteristic cognitive disorders:

- *Pessimists practice all-or-nothing thinking.* Situations are evaluated as extreme; any mistake is considered a complete inadequacy.
- *Pessimists have a mental filter.* They pick out a single negative detail in a situation that is positive in every other way, and they concentrate on the negative—unable to see the good.
- *Pessimists magnify.* They exaggerate the significance of a negative event or mistake.
- *Pessimists label.* There's always a label for themselves or someone else; if they make a single mistake, they decide, "I'm so stupid. I'm a jerk."
- *Pessimists exaggerate*—in both directions. They wildly overestimate the size of their problems, and they grossly underestimate their ability to cope with or solve their problems.
- *Pessimists ignore the positive.* In common situations, they are impressed by and remember only the negative events or aspects. If a situation is completely positive, they will perceive it or view it in a negative way.
- *Pessimists personalize.* They tend to think that everything revolves around them. A friend doesn't return a phone call because she's bogged down with a project at work—but the pessimist is convinced that the friend doesn't call because she's offended by or angry at the pessimist.
- *Pessimists practice either/or thinking.* For the pessimist, there's no in-between or gray area. It's either positive or negative.
- *Pessimists overgeneralize.* They are convinced that they can *never* do anything right, that *everyone* hates them, *nothing* will ever turn out right for them.
- *Pessimists jump to conclusions.* They usually do it in two ways: First, they try to read people's minds ("That woman is staring at me because she thinks I'm ugly"). Closely related, they dabble in what researchers call "fortune telling";

they decide what's going to happen based on a few sketchy details ("The doctor hasn't called me back yet; I must be very sick").[5]

Author Cheri Carter-Scott coined a new phrase for this type of thinking, in her book, *Negaholics: How to Recover From Your Addiction to Negativity and Turn Your Life Around*. According to Carter-Scott, there are four separate categories of "negaholics":

1. *Attitudinal negaholics* look perfect on the outside, but are tormented and falling apart on the inside. These people are often perfectionists who drive themselves without mercy in an attempt to be "the perfect" this or that.
2. *Behavioral negaholics* never seem to measure up—but it's not because they are incapable. Instead, they procrastinate. They have a difficult time grappling with deadlines and details. They frustrate the people around them. They set themselves up for failure.
3. *Verbal negaholics* complain profusely and protest loudly. They tell anyone who listens that they can't perform the task, can't measure up to the expectations, can't possibly win the prize.
4. *Mental negaholics* constantly rehearse their negative attitudes in their mind, thinking about the past, present, and future in negative terms. They regret what they've said—or wish they had said nothing at all. They believe that their decisions are all faulty. They are their worst enemies, their biggest critics, and their finest fault-finders.[6]

And, according to psychologist John P. Kildahl and psychiatrist Joseph T. Martorano, there are six basic "cognitive" styles that are negative in nature:

1. *Anxious thinkers* are convinced the world is dangerous and they will be unable to handle it.
2. *Depressed thinkers* believe they lack the essentials for a happy life.
3. *Obsessive thinkers* trap themselves in circular reasoning that never resolves itself.
4. *Narcissistic thinkers* are preoccupied with themselves.
5. *Masochistic thinkers* get sweet pleasure from suffering.
6. *Detached thinkers* believe that staying to themselves and being self-sufficient is the greatest virtue.[7]

Two Styles of Pessimism

Defensive Pessimism

Although pessimism is almost always overwhelmingly negative for us, it can occasionally be positive. A style of thinking called "defensive pessimism"[8] apparently works like a strategy. It involves preparing for the worst even though you know that success is much more likely.[9] Defensive pessimism involves setting unrealistically low expectations to prepare yourself for possible failure. That can be positive in situations that involve a great deal of risk. It can also be positive, if it motivates a person to work hard to avoid potential failure.[10]

Unfortunately, defensive pessimism can backfire. Too many use defensive pessimism as an excuse to "throw in the towel." To see who fared best over the long run, University of Michigan researchers Nancy Cantor and Julie Norem studied defensive pessimists who were among a group of honors students at the university. During the first year of study, there wasn't much difference between the two groups; both the optimists and the defensive pessimists earned good grades and were equally satisfied with their academic performance. After the first year, however, differences started to emerge. By the end of their college career, the differences were pronounced. The defensive pessimists had earned lower grades and felt more stress and less pleasure while studying or in class. They had more depressed moods and "rocky" emotional terrain. The effects extended outside the academic realm as well: Defensive pessimists felt less challenged and more tired while socializing.[11]

Awfulizing or Catastrophizing

Another form of pessimism, "awfulizing" or "catastrophizing," is the tendency to escalate every situation into the worst possible scenario.

> [It] is characterized by anticipating and dwelling on the most negative and painful of possible outcomes. . . . It is a way of looking at the future in the worst possible light. Catastrophizing can also be defined as frequently becoming intensely absorbed in an unpleasant event and talking to oneself about it in ways that help realize its aversive properties. For example, panic during a myocardial infarction ("My God, I am dying") can make the event worse by inducing a constriction of the blood vessels that thereby increases the cardiac load.[12]

In addition to the thought patterns characteristic of pessimism, awfulizing is characterized by the following three modes of irrational thinking:

1. Awfulizers tend to have a narrowed perspective that causes them to dwell on disaster. Instead of rationally looking at the safety record of the airline industry, an awfulizer thinks, "With all the plane crashes we've had recently, I should really cancel my trip."
2. Awfulizers refuse to deviate from their mindset, becoming trapped in one-track thinking. No amount of evidence or information to the contrary can dissuade awfulizers from their way of thinking. The awfulizer bemoans, "Maybe other people think flying is as safe as driving on the freeway, but, if you ask me, it's just a lie the airlines perpetuate to get more customers."
3. Awfulizers drag out old and often inappropriate coping mechanisms to deal with the problem at hand. The awfulizer who is about to board the plane, for example, thinks, "Since I have to fly, I might as well stock up on tranquilizers. It's the only way I'll have the courage to step on the plane."[13]

Several large-scale studies have shown that awfulizing wreaks tremendous havoc on the body. What starts out as a negative thought tends to keep the individual's attention focused on the negative event. Hormones start to surge, and the sympathetic nervous system is activated. Muscular aches and pains develop; a wide range of negative physical and psychosocial consequences result. A variety of studies have linked awfulizing and catastrophizing to headache, low back pain, dental pain, chronic pain, and higher levels of pain and distress generally.[14]

Not only does awfulizing have a particularly devastating effect on the body, but awfulizers tend to have higher levels of pain and higher overall pain ratings. In one study, only 12 percent of the control group required antidepressants for help in coping with pain; a staggering 86 percent of the catastrophizers needed the extra help of antidepressants.[15]

Almost all researchers now agree that pessimism and negative thinking are harmful to health. What researchers *don't* agree on is duration: Does pessimism have to be long-lasting and pervasive in order to harm the body? Some believe that it does. Others believe that pessimism can result in physical harm even if it "crops up in just one situation—say, when you're battling cancer."[16] Whether a person has been negative about an isolated situation or generally pessimistic for years, there are some good reasons to change his or her way of thinking.

Effects of Pessimism on the Body

Everyone has a way of thinking, an "explanatory style" (the topic of Chapter 21). It's the way we ascribe the cause when something bad happens to us. Optimists generally have a good, healthy explanatory style; pessimists generally have a bad one. When something bad happens to optimists, they take into account all kinds of possible reasons, most of them external—other people, outside circumstances, or outside conditions. They also realize that one negative thing is not going to mean that all future events are going to turn out the same way.

Contrast that with pessimists' explanatory style. When something bad happens to pessimists, they automatically assume "it's me," there's some inherent deficit as the source of the problem. Further, they figure things will never change for them ("It's always going to be this way"). And they believe that one bad experience will have a "ripple" effect in discoloring everything else that happens throughout life ("This is going to ruin everything I do").[17]

As you might imagine, explanatory style has a major impact on most aspects of life. Researchers have found that it affects performance on the job, performance in sports, personal relationships, and the general ability to cope. Pessimism leads to indecision, anxiety, depression, inertia, and a general feeling of unhappiness.[18] Most significantly, perhaps, it affects health and longevity. Based on numerous studies, researchers have found an impressive correlation between "bad style and bad health."[19] In study after study, the pessimists have consistently had the poorest health.

The way we look at things has such an influence over our health that researchers have even been able to *predict* which people would get sick based on their outlook in life. In one well-known example, University of Pennsylvania's Martin Seligman and his colleagues interviewed and gave questionnaires to 172 undergraduate students. Based on the students' explanatory styles, the researchers rated each student as an optimist or a pessimist. Then they predicted which of the students were going to be sick most often both one month and one year later. Seligman and his colleagues were on target. They were able to accurately predict which students would be sick the most often—and it was the pessimists.[20]

Seligman and his associates tried their experiment again and again, always with the same result. A large-scale study of Harvard graduates is ongoing. Almost five decades ago, researchers carefully interviewed a group of graduates, and detailed records have been kept for more than forty-five years on both their physical and mental health. Seligman and his colleagues were given the transcripts of twenty of the interviews, which were staged in 1946. Without seeing any of the medical records, Seligman and his colleagues went to work, examining each graduate's explanatory style and classifying each as an optimist or pessimist. With those ratings in hand, they predicted which of the graduates would have the poorest health. Again, they were accurate: The ones with the bad style had the bad health.[21]

In still another experiment, Seligman studied thirteen patients who had malignant melanomas, a particularly devastating and rapidly spreading form of cancer. He found that a patient's tendency toward pessimistic thinking and a bad explanatory style was a more powerful predictor of survival than even the patient's immune system strength.[22]

In an expanded study of the Harvard graduates, Seligman and his colleagues looked at a group of ninety-nine men who were first interviewed as undergraduates in the early 1940s. Each of the men in the study was close to the age of twenty at the time of the first interview. Each of the men was again interviewed in 1946, when most were twenty-five years of age. In addition to an in-depth interview, each man answered a questionnaire about his wartime experiences. The optimists had many external explanations for what happened to them during the war. The pessimists, on the other hand, tended to blame unfortunate wartime events on themselves and to attach the blame to other causes that were very vague. The optimists figured that unpleasant wartime experiences were limited and temporary; the pessimists determined that they were permanent and would discolor every future aspect of their lives.

Based partly on the interviews and partly on the men's observations about the war, Seligman and his colleagues rated each according to his explanatory style. For purposes of the study, Seligman separated the optimists from the pessimists as he collected health-related data. The ninety-nine men were then interviewed and examined again at five-year intervals until they were sixty years of age. In his first major comparison, Seligman compared the health of the men at the age of forty-five with their explanatory styles at the age of twenty. He made statistical adjustments that allowed for early physical and emotional health.

Even with the allowances he made, he found that the men who were pessimistic in their early twenties were the ones who were most likely to be in poor health at the age of forty-five. The pessimists in the group were most likely to have many minor complaints as well as serious chronic illnesses.[23]

In one study, 262 undergraduate students at a large university completed the Life Orientation Test and, later, a questionnaire on flu episodes and expectations. Interestingly, the optimists and pessimists did not differ in the number of flu incidents. But in the pessimists, the flu lasted longer and caused more symptoms—and the pessimists reported a higher expectancy of flu in the future. The optimists, on the other hand, were more likely to take measures to prevent the flu.[24]

Pessimism was shown in another study to shorten the lives of cancer patients. In research reported to the American Psychosomatic Society, University of Pittsburgh psychologist Richard Schulz studied 231 cancer patients. First he gave them personality tests, then tracked their progress. All had been given life expectancies of at least one year by their physicians—but men and women under the age of sixty who had highly pessimistic attitudes were most likely to die within the first eight months.

According to a report published in *USA Today,* Schulz said that "the power of pessimism to predict shorter survival among younger people was significant," even when researchers took into account the severity of the illness and the type of cancer.

Pessimists may actually view themselves as being unhealthy or sick far more often—and it's a viewpoint that can strongly influence health. British researcher Dr. Stephen D. Harding surveyed mental and physical health among nearly 1,000 respondents. He found that the pessimists—those with a strong tendency to get upset and view things in a negative way—were also the ones who were most likely to report themselves as "feeling generally run down."[25]

Unfortunately, even the attitudes of people close to us can influence our health—and researchers have found that pessimistic physicians can have a negative influence on the health of their patients. In studying physicians who treat patients with cancer, for example, pessimistic physicians often believe "that the

---

Focus on Research

Christopher Peterson, an associate professor of psychology at the University of Michigan, one of Seligman's colleagues, rated a group of students as either optimistic or pessimistic, and then watched the students for four weeks. He found that the pessimists were sick twice as many days as the optimists were during the four-week period.

He then monitored the students over the course of the next year. The pessimistic students still fared the worst: During the year,

they visited a doctor four times as often as the optimistic students. A staggering 95 percent of the pessimistic students had colds, sore throats, or the flu during the year. Some of them also had ear infections, pneumonia, and mononucleosis.

The surprising thing about the study, says Peterson, is that all the pessimists' illnesses were infectious—suggesting that "how we view things may directly affect our immune system."

Source: Carolyn Jabs, "New Reasons to Be An Optimist," *Self*, September: 1987, 170–173.

disease comes from without, that it's synonymous with death, that the treatment is bad, and that the patient has little or nothing he can do to fight the disease."[26] The pessimistic views of a physician can be devastating to a patient, say researchers—and can even heavily influence the outcome of the disease.

Although physicians have an obligation to give an honest diagnosis, the way in which they do it is critical, says Norman Cousins. He reviewed the cases of 300 people who had malignancies and was struck by how the disease often accelerated right after the patients received their diagnoses from the doctor. "Is it possible," he asked, "that the diagnosis has the effect of a pronouncement of doom?"[27]

Robert Mendelsohn of the University of Illinois School of Medicine, who describes himself as a "medical heretic," put it this way: "It's one thing to inform a patient that he or she suffers from a deadly disease and that the magic of the doctor doesn't go far enough to do any good. But it's another thing entirely to tell a patient that the end is inevitable."[28]

Negative comments can even impact a patient who is under anesthesia. The negative words of a pessimistic surgeon or other operating room technician can have devastating influence over a patient for days after the surgery. Psychologist Henry Bennett of the department of anesthesiology at the University of California at Davis has done research that shows that a patient's autonomic nervous system—which is already aroused in surgery—is particularly sensitive to negative words spoken by medical personnel in the operating room. "Clinical cases make clear that massive autonomic effects can follow pessimistic or insulting remarks made around the adequately anesthetized patient," Bennett claims. "These effects often are not apparent until the second or third postoperative day."[29]

A pessimistic attitude, whether evidenced by the physician or the patient, apparently has tremendous influence on the outcome of the disease. According to Dr. Gerald Jampolsky, who has done extensive research in the area:

> [There's] no question that negativity can be incapacitating. If you spend your whole life determining what is impossible, it limits you as to what is possible. If you spend your whole life worrying and feeling guilty, you will never know what it feels like to be truly happy and at peace. And that makes it pretty tough to tap in on our healing energies.[30]

Why Does Pessimism Affect Health?

A pessimistic attitude obviously has a big impact on health, but do we know why? We have some pretty good ideas. In the first place, negative programming has an incredible influence over the mind. Bernie Siegel, a renowned surgeon who has done extensive research on attitude and disease, says that "negative programming is one reason why a fourth of all chemotherapy patients start throwing up *before* they get to their next treatment. In England a group of men were given saline and told it was chemotherapy; 30 percent had their hair fall out."[31]

Another factor may be that pessimists give up control and assign control to outside factors. In a very real way, they simply give up. In reference to the effect of pessimism on the heart, one researcher stated:

> *It is not Type A behavior that kills, but the type of thought the brain insists upon that leads the supersystem to fail us. . . . We reject the heart by clogging all the arteries around it. The result may be a more gradual cutting than is removal by scalpel, but the effect is the same. The heart has been cheated of the positive chemistry that comes with the thoughts and feelings of joy, celebration, love, faith, and laughter. It is cheated of the will to lead life. Instead, life leads us.[32]*

There may be other, more functional reasons why a pessimistic attitude can lead to poor health. According to Seligman, people who develop an "I surrender" attitude are, simply, less likely to take good care of themselves.[33] They may neglect health care basics in the first place because they don't believe that taking preventive measures will make a difference.[34] In line with their negative thinking, they may become completely passive about prevention and treatment overall.[35]

Pessimists are less likely to eat a well-balanced, healthy diet. They are less likely to get regular exercise. They are less likely to do other things that have been proven to protect health. They are less likely to visit the doctor for regular checkups. In addition, pessimists are less likely to seek—and less likely to enjoy—support from family and friends. As has been shown elsewhere in this book, strong social support has been shown to be a critical link in health maintenance.

Pessimism and negative thinking work just like stress on the body: Every time a person thinks the worst, the body reacts as though it were actually in the throes of a tension-filled situation. Pessimists often suffer from stress-related physical problems such as headaches, high blood pressure, and gastrointestinal problems. If they dwell on their negative thoughts, their bodies become exhausted. Pessimism apparently compromises the immune system, which can lead to illness and disease. In studies involving elderly people, optimists displayed better helper-to-suppressor T cell ratios and mitogen responses. The optimists who were studied had stronger immune systems than did the pessimists—and better ability to fight infection and disease.[36]

In one detailed study of 280 men and women, researchers identified those who reacted to problems with a pessimistic explanatory style. They then tested the immune systems of all the participants in the study. The optimists had the strongest immune systems, by far. The pessimists had significantly lower immune system function in both T lymphocytes and natural killer cells. According to researchers who conducted the study, the differences in the immune system of the pessimists "might contribute to premature death as well as illness."[37]

According to the results of research, pessimism can actually "turn off" the immune system by causing the depletion of a set of chemicals in the body called catecholamines. When the catecholamine level drops, the level of endorphins goes up. And when the endorphin level increases, the immune system turns itself down.[38] The inevitable result of a compromised immune system is that pessimists don't live as long as optimists. To prove the point, Martin Seligman and his colleagues studied the sports page quotes of thirty-four Baseball Hall of Famers who played between 1900 and 1950. They were able to label each as either a pessimist or an optimist by their statements about the games. The pessimists, for example, attributed their ballpark victories to "luck"—and expressed the belief that their victories were short-lived. The pessimistic players lived significantly shorter lives than the ball players who had optimistic outlooks and explanatory styles.[39]

The Gastrointestinal Tract

More than any other disorder, gastric ulcers seem to be a hazard of pessimistic thinking and explanatory style. In an attempt to determine what causes ulcers—defects or holes in the lining of the stomach or the upper small intestine—two gastroenterologists, professors of internal medicine at the University of Texas Health Science Center in Dallas, conducted a series of studies.[40] Originally, ulcers were thought to be caused by too much hydrochloric acid and pepsin, which eat away at the mucosal lining of the stomach. Charles Richardson and Mark Feldman wanted to find out what caused the increase in gastric acidity in the first place. They conducted a series of studies both separately and together with the Veterans Administration Medical Center in Dallas. They studied groups of normal control patients as well as ulcer patients; both groups were under the same number and types of stress. They found that even though both groups were under the same kinds and intensity of stress, people who developed ulcers perceived the stressful events as "having a far more negative impact on their lives." They were pessimists.

As a result of their studies, Richardson and Feldman constructed what they believe to be an "ulcer personality." At the top of the list of personality characteristics was pessimism. People prone to ulcers also tend to be excessively dependent, have less social support, have emotional distress, battle depression, and suffer from anxiety.[41]

We are, quite literally, what we think. Pessimists, who think the worst will happen, are, unfortunately, usually right.

Notes

1. From Paul Pearsall, *Super Joy: Learning to Celebrate Everyday Life* (New York: Doubleday, 1988), p. 80.

2. Sharon Faelten, David Diamond, and the Editors of *Prevention* Magazine, *Take Control of Your Life: A Complete Guide to Stress Relief* (Emmaus, Pennsylvania: Rodale Press, 1988), p. 308.

3. Faelten et al., pp. 308–309.

4. Ruth Dailey Grainger, "The Use—and Abuse—of Negative Thinking," *American Journal of Nursing*, August: 1991, 13; and Faelten et al.

5. Emrika Padus, *The Complete Guide to Your Emotions and Your Health* (Emmaus, Pennsylvania: Rodale Press, 1986); and Herbert Benson and Eileen M. Stuart, *The Wellness Book* (New York: Birch Lane Press, 1992), p. 198.

6. Cheri Carter-Scott, in "Good News for Negaholics!" *Your Personal BEST*, June: 1990, 10–12.

7. Steve McKee, "Beyond Negative Think-

ing: Been Down So Long It Looks Like Up To You?" *American Health*, June: 1990, 32.

8. Christopher Peterson and Lisa M. Bossio, *Health and Optimism* (New York: The Free Press, 1991), p. 107.

9. Cheryl Simon, "Pessimism's Price," *Psychology Today*, April: 1988, 15.

10. Carolyn Jabs, "New Reasons to Be An Optimist," *Self*, September: 1987, 170–173.

11. Simon.

12. Ian Wickramasekera, "Risk Factors Leading to Chronic Stress-Related Symptoms," *Advances*, 4(1): 1987, 9–35.

13. Joan Borysenko, "How to Put Your Mind on Your Side," *Shape*, August: 1988, 78–84.

14. Wickramasekera.

15. Wickramasekera.

16. Nan Silver, "Do Optimists Live Longer?" *American Health*, November: 1986, 50–53.

17. Blair Justice, *Who Gets Sick: Thinking and Health* (Houston, Texas: Peak Press, 1987), p. 229.

18. Grainger.

19. Justice, p. 231.

20. Justice, p. 230.

21. Justice, p. 231.

22. Justice, p. 230.

23. Christopher Peterson, Martin E. P. Seligman, and George E. Vaillant, "Pessimistic Explanatory Style Is a Risk Factor for Physical Illness: A Thirty-Five-Year Longitudinal Study," *Journal of Personality and Social Psychology*, 55: 1988, 23–27.

24. P. Nicholas Hamid, "Optimism and the Reporting of Flu Episodes," *Social Behavior and Personality* 18(2): 1990, 225–234.

25. Clive Wood, "Tired All the Time: A Mind-Body Approach to Fatigue," *Advances*, 4(3): 56–59.

26. Justice, p. 293.

27. Justice.

28. Justice.

29. Justice, p. 294.

30. Padus, pp. 519–520.

31. Bernie S. Siegel, *Love, Medicine, and Miracles* (New York: Harper and Row Publishers, 1986).

32. Paul Pearsall, *Super Immunity* (New York: McGraw-Hill Book Company, 1987).

33. Silver.

34. Jabs.

35. Peterson et al.

36. "Longevity: Men Are Catching Up," *Medical World News*, October 12: 1987.

37. Justice, p. 231.

38. Martin E.P. Seligman, *Learned Optimism* (New York: Alfred A. Knopf, 1991), pp. 176–178.

39. Silver.

40. "Is There an Ulcer Personality?" *The Wellness Newsletter*, July: 1987, 2.

41. "Is There an Ulcer Personality?"

25

OPTIMISM AND HEALTH

*Every good thought you think
is contributing its share
to the ultimate result of your life.*
—GRENVILLE KLEISER

According to Webster's dictionary, optimism is "an inclination to anticipate the best possible outcome." To redefine it psychologically, according to Ornstein and Sobel, optimism is "the tendency to seek out, remember, and expect pleasurable experiences. It is an active priority of the person, not merely a reflex that prompts us to 'look on the sunny side.'"[1]

A growing body of evidence indicates that optimists live longer and they probably enjoy better health along the way as well. Scientific evidence suggests that optimism, the habit of positive thinking, has a specific effect on the physiological functioning of the body. In a real, physical sense, optimists are healthier. Their immune systems are stronger. And as a group, they do live longer.

Who Are Optimists?

Optimists are people who generally believe that good, rather than bad, things will happen to them. They believe that the future will work out well; they approach the world in an active, productive way. They take reality into account, but they do everything possible with the reality they find. Optimism has a lot to do with other positive qualities as well, such as happiness, self-efficacy, and hardiness.

The readers of *Psychology Today* were asked what happiness means to them. More than 52,000 responded. Compiling their answers, the authors of the survey concluded that happiness "comes from tending one's own garden instead of coveting one's neighbor's. . . . Happiness, in short, turns out to be more a matter of how you regard your circumstances than of what the circumstances are."[2]

Research shows that an optimistic bias is far more common than was once considered. The community of psychotherapy is realizing that normal, healthy individuals do downplay their faults and the negative things that happen to them—and that the people who lean toward optimism are the most healthy, both physically and mentally.

Psychologists Shelley Taylor of UCLA and Jonathon Brown of Southern Methodist University in Dallas say that research shows that most people view themselves in an optimistic light. "They judge themselves to be nicer, smarter, more charming, and prettier than even their closest admirers judge them to be," the psychologists assert. "Normal, healthy people see themselves more kindly than does the cold eye of the camera or even the caring eyes of family and friends. They think they're more talented and able than they are."[3]

Even aside from improving health, optimism is a positive force. "Optimism galvanizes people," says University of Michigan psychologist Christopher Peterson. "It sets you in motion. To be optimistic in the true sense is not to wear a smile button, but to be a problem-solver."[4]

The "experts" used to believe that it was important to have a cold, hard perception of reality. Psychologist Robert Ornstein and physician David Sobel point out that psychologist Sidney Jourard once wrote, "The ability to perceive reality as it 'really is' is fundamental to effective functioning. It is considered one of the two preconditions to the development of health." Ornstein and Sobel continue that modern psychologist and clinical research contradicts this—and that healthy people are not accurate perceivers of reality. "Expecting to be pleased, healthy people cultivate a set of illusions. They inflate their own importance and have an exaggerated belief in their ability to control their destiny."[5]

Characteristics of Optimists

Seven-year-old Kealan Jewell is positive about everything. She unabashedly declares she's one of the most popular girls in her class. When asked what she wants to be when she grows up, she doesn't think twice. "I'm going to be an artist," she says. "I'd like to write a book, but I can't find the time."[6]

Kealan is an optimist—as are most other children her age. So was American philosopher Henry Thoreau, who used to lie in bed for a few minutes every morning to think positive thoughts. He would remind himself that he was healthy, that his mind was alert, that his work was interesting, that the future looked bright, and that many people trusted him. When he got out of bed, he entered a world filled with the kind of positive, good people and opportunities that he expected—a kind of "self-fulfilling prophecy."

It usually is easy to tell the difference between an optimist and a pessimist. The optimist has an entirely different explanation for things. The optimistic driver acknowledges (or "blames") the reduced visibility, the slick and snow-packed streets, and other adverse conditions for his accident. Then he realizes he hasn't had much experience on snowy roads and tells himself that he'll have to be more careful until he gets more experience. The pessimistic driver, on the other hand, blames himself. His internal reasoning goes something like this: "I'm such a poor driver. I'll never learn to drive safely. Every time I try something new, I screw it up."[7]

Optimists have a number of qualities in common. Probably the most common is that they see the good in situations and they truly expect things to go their way. According to Michael Scheier, professor of psychology at Pittsburgh's Carnegie-Mellon University, researchers are finding that "anticipating a favorable outcome leads an optimist to do things that actually determine the final outcome. Optimists expect things to turn out well, but they also do things that can change the course of events."[8]

In addition, optimists see events in their lives as controllable—an apt attitude because, says Scheier, optimism comes from the Latin word *ops*, meaning power. When something bad does happen, optimists are not defeated. Instead, they make a plan of action, follow it, and work quickly before the situation gets out of hand. They expect that they will be able to handle anything that comes along (and they are usually right).

Optimists don't give up; they are known for their perseverance. Optimists have a knack for staying focused on the positive and are able to keep going when others might quit.

When something bad happens, optimists view it as an isolated occurrence—not as part of a general trend or life pattern. In day-to-day events, in fact, optimists dismiss the bad and instead internalize the good. They interpret events and circumstances in their favor, a trait that helps them stay positive even when confronted by situations they truly cannot control (such as the death of a loved one).

Optimists tend to see the future through "rose-colored glasses." They believe that they will have a happy life filled with adventure and good health. When they marry, they believe that the marriage will succeed and be fulfilling; they don't consider or dwell on the possibility of divorce. When they have children, they believe that their children will be happy and healthy and well-behaved. In essence, they don't think about the bad things that could happen. But underlying their attitude is a firm belief that if something bad does somehow occur, they'll be able to "fix it" with no problem.

All this cheerfulness is not to say that optimists can't face reality or see when they're "in over their heads"; optimists express acceptance or resignation when needed. University of Miami psychologist Charles Carver says that researchers "don't want to imply that people should put on a happy face and go around being mindlessly cheerful all the time. Even optimists have occasional doubts or fail sometimes. By resignation, we mean the ability to say, 'I'm not going to pretend this isn't happening, but if I have to put up with it, I will.'"[9] Scheier maintains that they have the instinct to know when to charge forward or when to back off—and their optimistic attitude helps them cope far more effectively when situations come up.

In his book *You Can't Afford the Luxury of a Negative Thought*, popular author Peter McWilliams and his co-author John-Roger summarize optimism with this challenge:

> *It's as though there were two attorneys in your mind, one gathering evidence for "Life is Awful" and the other gathering evidence for "Life is Wonderful." You're the judge and can rule out any evidence you want. Your decision is final. Which judicial ruling do you suppose would lead to more joy, happiness, peace, and ease?*[10]

How Optimism Influences Health

When diagnosed with ankylosing spondylitis, a devastating degenerative disease, former *Saturday Review* editor Norman Cousins refused to give up. He fought back, using a number of factors (such as enhanced nutrition, optimism, and laughter) to overcome his disease. When news of his amazing recovery surfaced, much of the attention focused on the factor of laughter—which, although it was important, was not the only thing that Cousins believes led to his recovery.

"I didn't say that I was cured through laughter, but it made for interesting and catchy newspaper treatment," Cousins says, referring to the accounts of his fight against the illness. "Laughter played a part, of course, but laughter was a metaphor for the full range of positive emotions—hope, faith, love, determination, confidence—all the things that are part of the ability of the human mind to get the most out of whatever is possible."[11]

A growing body of evidence gives increasing credibility to the idea that optimism and positive emotions promote health. Even positive denial can be health-promoting. Psychologist Richard Lazarus believes that a sense of "positive denial"—a refusal to believe in something negative, as long as it is not carried to the extreme—helps keep hopes up, sustains morale, improves health, and reduces anxiety.[12] But researchers who have conducted studies on attitude and beliefs agree with one basic principle: A positive attitude and belief in the body's own healing abilities can certainly supplement medical treatment, but should never replace it. Cousins, Yale oncologist and surgeon Bernie Siegel, and others who are at the "battle front" stress the idea that the best possible outcome results when optimism and positive thinking work hand-in-hand with the medical treatment offered by competent physicians.

Exactly what role can optimism play, then?

For one thing, it appears that an optimistic attitude can actually protect a person from getting sick in the first place. In the study conducted by Petersen and Vaillant on a group of armed services veterans who had graduated from Harvard University, Seligman and his colleagues recently reviewed the original comments, questionnaires, health records, and other data for ninety-nine of the Harvard graduates who participated in the study. The researchers found that the men who were the most optimistic in their original writings had the best health forty years later. Their own perception of their experiences was significantly associated with later physical and mental illness; those with an optimistic outlook were healthy, and those with a gloomy outlook were ill (or dead).[13]

In writing down their experiences during the war, the pessimists, who were in worse health at the end of the study, penned remarks like, "Giving orders was sometimes very hard, if not impossible, because I always had this problem of dealing with men under me, even later in the war when I had the appropriate rank."

The healthy optimists, on the other hand, recorded sentiments such as, "During the war I was occasionally bored, because anyone who's ever been on a ship is bored to tears." The optimist, even though he had a bad experience, didn't blame it on his own shortcomings. He was bored, but isn't everyone bored on a ship?

In summing up the study, Seligman and his colleagues wrote: "If you always go around thinking, 'It's my fault, it's going to last forever, and it's going to undermine everything I do,' then when you do run into further bad events, you become at risk for poor health."[14]

Optimism and pessimism can even play a role in maladies as simple as the common cold. Carnegie-Mellon University psychologist Sheldon Cohen worked with other researchers at the Common Cold Unit in England to determine what factors were at play in susceptibility to colds. Their findings point the finger at optimism and pessimism, and "suggest the possibility that there is a relationship between psychological factors and susceptibility to colds."[15]

In three separate studies constructed in much the same way, researchers tested undergraduate college students to see which had optimistic outlooks and which had pessimistic outlooks; they then tracked the students for various periods to see which got sick, had adverse symptoms, or had to visit the doctor.

Psychologist Christopher Peterson studied students at Virginia Tech in Blacksburg, Virginia. He reported that pessimistic students were ill twice as many days and had four times as many doctor visits over the course of a year compared with optimistic students. Peterson expressed particular interest in the fact that 95 percent of all the ill students had infectious diseases—the common cold, sore throats, flu, pneumonia, ear infections, venereal diseases, and mononucleosis. Apparently the pessimistic students were less able to fight infection. "This suggests that how we view things may directly affect our immune system," he says.[16] The pessimists, he points out, may have been more likely to get colds and other illnesses in part because they were less apt to seek medical advice or take simple medical precautions.

Peterson was able to confirm his theories with results from several other studies. In one study,[17] he and his colleagues studied summer school students at the University of Michigan. Again, he assessed general style to determine whether each student was pessimistic or optimistic. Then researchers carefully followed the health of each student, asking for an assessment on a daily basis. Again, the pessimists were the most ill— and 95 percent of the reported symptoms were from colds or the flu, suggesting a breakdown in the ability to resist infectious diseases.

In a similar study, in which Carnegie-Mellon researchers found that optimistic students reported fewer ills, researchers wrote, "Pessimists, as a rule, care less about their health. In addition, pessimists blame themselves for their failures but then do little to further improve their lot. Optimists, on the other hand, view failures as problems that can be fixed. They meet their problems head on, form a plan of action, and achieve results."[18]

Optimism and Healing

Not only can optimism help keep a person healthy, but it can also boost the body's own mechanisms to speed the healing process. Anxious to see exactly how much power the mind has over the body, researchers decided to look at the example of warts. Warts are caused by a virus, and they are controlled by the immune system. When the immune system does not work to control the virus, warts appear. Researchers at Boston's Massachusetts General Hospital hypnotized patients with intractable warts and told them, under hypnosis, that the body would heal itself. In almost all the cases the body did just that; the warts disappeared.

Psychologist and avid skier Lonnie Barbach pulled the ligaments in her left knee and spent a painful six weeks on crutches. Two years later, she injured her right knee in the same way—skiing—and to the same extent. This time she pulled all her optimism to the fore and used mental training to imagine that her ligaments were tightening and that the pain, soreness, and swelling were diminishing. Without using crutches, she was completely healed in fewer than three weeks.[19]

Optimism can make a big difference in surgical outcomes, too. In a study conducted by Dr. Charles S. Carver of the University of Miami and Dr. Michael F. Scheier of Carnegie-Mellon University, coronary bypass surgery patients were questioned the day before surgery and again one week after surgery. Based on the results of the first interview, researchers categorized each patient as being an optimist or a pessimist. While their mental attitudes were different, their physical conditions were similar and the outlook for their recovery was the same.[20]

Not everyone had the same results after surgery, however. The optimists were busy making plans for the time when they would be released from the hospital; after surgery, they sought information about what they could do to improve their recovery. The pessimists, on the other hand, took an "observer" stance and were much less involved in helping themselves. Although the outlook was the same for all patients, the optimists had a much speedier recovery, marred by fewer complications. In summing up the study, Carver concluded that "optimists may experience more success because they deal with their problems earlier than pessimists do, and in a more direct, goal-oriented way. . . . They use a strategy for coping that is most adaptive and least dysfunctional."[21]

Optimism may make such a difference to recovery that some hospitals have begun using aids to boost it—such as an "artificial window" that provides a peaceful scene as well as simulating the change between day and night. Stanford was the first medical facility in the country to use the window, a four-by five-foot computer-controlled light box behind a blowup of a slide shot by California nature photographer Joey Fischer. Fischer saw the need for the "window" when his own father had a heart attack and spent many hours counting holes in the hospital ceiling tiles because there was nothing else to look at. In the window is a peaceful pasture topped by billowing clouds; an electronic digital timer produces 650 separate light changes every twenty-four hours, mimicking dawn to twilight.[22]

Optimism can even make a difference in illnesses as grave as cancer. A University of California at Los Angeles research team launched a national survey of cancer specialists in an attempt to find out which psychosocial factors were most important in helping patients overcome the disease. A total of 649 oncologists responded to the survey, and reported on their experiences in treating more than 100,000 cancer patients. More than 90 percent of the physicians who responded to the survey said that the most significant factor in effective treatment was the attitude of hope and optimism.[23]

A number of studies confirm that point of view. In one, Sandra Levy and her colleagues at the University of Pittsburgh School of Medicine studied middle-aged women who had breast cancer. They put special emphasis on the psychological factors that seemed related to survival, especially the differences between optimism and pessimism. They carefully interviewed each of the thirty-six women at the beginning of the study and then observed them for four years. Although optimism was not the strongest predictor (the number of initial cancer sites was the strongest predictor), Levy was able to fairly accurately predict who would still be alive at the end of four years based on their outlook. The optimists won out.[24]

Dr. G. Frank Lawlis and Jeanne Achterberg, a husband-wife team at the University of Texas Health Science Center in Dallas, conducted a series of studies that showed that people become and stay healthy in response to optimism and positive attitude—and that optimism has an impact even on cancer. In their studies, Lawlis and Achterberg studied the personalities of 200 terminal cancer patients; they found that certain personality traits were common to those who lived much longer than they had been expected to live: The survivors utterly refused to give up. They were open to new ideas. They rejected their role as invalids. They refused to accept the limits of their illness. And, most important, they were optimistic. They believed in themselves, in their ability to beat the cancer.

Thirty years of cancer research by Dr. Lawrence LeShan has shown that those who do best are those who remain optimistic. Norman Cousins, a long believer in the impact of emotions, says that "emotions play a profound part in bringing on disease and in helping to combat it. What you think, what you believe, and how you react to experiences can impair or aid the workings of the body's immune system."

Indeed, a positive attitude and a belief that you can overcome illness go a long way in boosting immunity and conquering disease, according to significant evidence obtained from clinical practice and carefully controlled studies. Many examples have been reported of patients whose positive attitudes helped them conquer their supposedly terminal conditions—especially cancer.

One study in England helps substantiate that philosophy. Dr. Steven Greer and his colleagues followed the progress of women who underwent mastectomies for early-stage breast cancer; he evaluated the psychological condition of each patient and her attitude toward her disease. Five years later he noticed a common thread among those who had overcome the disease: They reacted with either strong denial or a fighting spirit, buoyed by the optimism that the cancer would not defeat them.[25]

Imaging

A positive personality and mindset can do even more. Researchers now believe that a positive practice called "imaging" may mobilize the body's physical resources. *Positive imaging*—the ability to concentrate on images that represent the body's fight against disease—is a newly recognized and little-understood phenomenon that has begun to attract considerable attention in the medical profession. It was first used as a therapy to treat illness by Dr. O. Carl Simonton, with the Cancer Counseling and Research Center in Fort Worth, Texas. Although scientists and researchers don't understand its effects on the immune system, one thing is obvious: It can sometimes help, even when the odds for recovery seem bleak. As we understand it, positive imaging seems to be an example of the power of the mind over the body.

Impressed by Simonton's results and curious about the effect of imaging on the immune systems of cancer victims, George Washington University biochemist Nicholas Hall began teaching the system of positive imaging to his patients. One of Hall's patients was a man with prostate cancer that had metastasized to the bone marrow. Hall taught his patient imaging, and the patient was tested one to two times a week while he was practicing it. While the patient was practicing imaging, his white blood cell count was up and his body produced greater amounts of thymosin, a thymic hormone that might help regulate the immune response. When instructed to stop imaging, the patient's white blood cell count dropped severely and thymosin was almost undetectable in his body. Research has found that imagery can help reduce pain and stress, alter the course of disease, and improve patients' outlook on their illness.[26]

Psychologist Patricia Norris, clinical director of the Biofeedback and Psychophysiology Center at the Meninger Foundation, relates a remarkable story about positive imaging. Anna, who had a malignant tumor growing rapidly at the back of her neck, had been given only three months to live. The cancer had virtually crippled her: She was hunched over, her head was forced painfully to one side, and her right arm was paralyzed and contracted. Her doctor had instructed her to do the sensible thing: Go home and make the necessary arrangements for the futures of her young children.

Norris instructed Anna in positive imaging. Anna began to visualize her tumor as a dragon on her back; she imagined her white blood cells to be knights that were attacking the tumor with swords.

A year later, Norris saw Anna again. A remarkable change had taken place: Her arm was fully mobile, and the tumor had shrunk. The next time the two met, Anna was in total remission. (Note: Although imaging may be helpful in some circumstances, it should never replace appropriate and proven medical treatment.)

Other Measures

One oncologist in Houston utilizes optimism to its fullest: Before he ever treats a patient for cancer, he introduces the patient to another patient who has survived and conquered the same condition. This method has met with some success.

Another factor that can't be ignored is the simple fact that optimists tend to do more toward prevention and respond more actively if they do become ill.[27] They tend to exercise better health behaviors. And if they get sick, they respond in a more positive way by getting more sleep, decreasing work loads, visiting the physician, and following the physician's orders.

Optimism: A Boost to Immunity

Experts in the field of psychoneuroimmunology have learned that there is a complex relationship between the brain and the immune system. Tucked beneath the breastbone in the chest is the thymus gland, the organ that produces T cells (immune blood cells). Psychologists Karen Bulloch, Denis Darko, and Michael Irwin found that an intricate network of nerve fibers connects the thymus gland with other parts of the immune system—the spleen, lymph nodes, and bone marrow—as well as to the cells of the body and the brain itself.

Research also indicates that there are hormonal and chemical links between the brain and the immune system.[28] According to experiments by immunologist Ed Blalock at the University of Alabama at Birmingham, "The immune cells communicate with the brain in the same way the brain and glands talk to them—through hormones." Blalock found that "the immune cells can produce hormones, such as growth hormone, thyroid-stimulating hormone, and reproductive hormones."[29]

While at the National Institute of Mental Health, Candace Pert and her colleague, Michael Ruff, announced that monocytes—the immune cells that help heal wounds, ingest bacteria, and repair tissue—are sensitive to chemicals produced in the brain. These chemicals, called neuropeptides, are concentrated in the brain's limbic system—the center that controls emotions.[30]

Emotions, then, can have impact on the immune system—and optimism is one of the emotions that seems to have the strongest ties. In his work over several decades, psychologist Seligman found real physiological differences between pessimists and optimists. In one study, he and his colleagues measured the disease-fighting cells in the blood of 300 people whose average age was seventy-one. The optimists had the healthier immune systems.[31]

In another study measuring optimism and the immune system, Leslie Kamen and her colleagues at the University of Pennsylvania studied mostly healthy middle-aged and elderly adults. Each was interviewed, and blood samples taken from each were measured to determine robustness of the immune system. Adults who were optimistic were found to have the strongest immune response; those who were pessimistic had the weakest.[32]

Other studies have yielded similar results. At the Medical Illness Counseling Center in suburban Maryland, ten cancer patients added guided imagery to their conventional chemotherapy treatment in an attempt to mobilize their own defenses against their cancers. After a year, all ten were still alive. And blood tests showed that their white blood cells had multiplied to fight the cancer cells.[33]

In a study at Michigan State University, patients used a combination of imagery and relaxation coupled with the optimistic belief that their treatment would work. Among those in the study, patients were able to cause an average of 60 percent of their white blood cells to leave the bloodstream and enter the surrounding tissue.[34]

In a study at Harvard, a group of people imagined that their T cells were attacking cold and flu viruses. That imagery—boosted by optimism—caused both T-cell counts and immunoglobulin A counts to increase, multiplying the strength of the immune system.[35]

The ability of optimism to boost the immune system may hold benefits for victims of acquired immune deficiency syndrome (AIDS), which ordinarily knocks out the body's immune system. New York psychologist Lewis Katoff maintains that positive thinking plays "an important role" in helping AIDS victims survive longer. Katoff, reporting on the first-ever study of the attitudes of AIDS victims who have survived three years or longer, said of the victims that they "are not depressed. They refuse to give up."[36]

Optimism's Impact on Mental Health and Performance

In addition to better physical health, optimists score better on performance and mental health—especially in resisting the effects of stress. Writing about some of the greatest entrepreneurs of our day, *Success* editor Scott DeGarmo penned the sentiment that "learning how to rebound with optimism is part of adapting to a world of constant change." Optimism, he says, is one of the key characteristics of the men and women who change the shape of the nation through their entrepreneurial ventures. He quotes Ralph Waldo Emerson in saying that these optimists display "a wild courage, a stoicism not of the schools but of the blood."[37]

Seligman, who has studied optimism extensively, says that the "link between optimism and performance is basically persistence. Optimists keep at it; pessimists give up and fail, even if they have equal talent. And because optimists are always hopeful about the outcome, they tend to take more risks and try more new things."[38]

Seligman has shown that optimists are more successful and perform better than pessimists in almost all fields—including education, business, sports, and politics. He successfully predicted that Bush would face Dukakis in the 1988 presidential campaign long before the crowded field of contenders was narrowed—

and he made his prediction based solely on optimistic characteristics. "Forget about the deficit and prayer in schools," one researcher summed. "A leading determinant for political wins is the level of optimism candidates convey. Dukakis and Bush came out on top, based on careful analysis of their stump speeches. Alexander Haig, on the other hand, was at the bottom of Seligman's list of optimistic traits (as was Gary Hart), and the first to withdraw."[39]

Seligman has long been convinced that optimists perform so much better than pessimists in almost every way that optimism should be taken into account when hiring personnel. He was able to convince insurance giant Metropolitan Life that his theory was right—and he developed a twenty-minute written examination to screen applicants for the trait of optimism. Metropolitan Life then administered the test to 15,000 recruits, many of whom had failed the industry examination the first time. The examination separated the optimists from the rest of the pack, and Metropolitan Life hired a new sales force based on optimism.

The new hiring strategy was an unfailing success. By the end of the first year, the optimists were outselling the others by 20 percent. By the end of the following year, they were outselling the others by 50 percent.[40]

Optimism is also one of the best known buffers against the deleterious effects of stress. Studies have shown that people who meet stress head-on with a sense of optimism and control don't get ill as often as those who meet stress with pessimism. Or, as one writer so aptly put it, "winners are healthier than whiners."[41]

Optimists do better under stress because they're less likely to believe that the source of stress is all-encompassing or overwhelming. They're less likely to turn to drugs or alcohol in an attempt to escape from stress. They're more likely to make recommended changes when ill—and more likely to follow prescriptions by a physician. They're more likely to take better care of themselves—a boon no matter what the source of stress.

Another reason optimists fare better under stress than pessimists is the trait called "dispositional optimism." According to researchers from Carnegie-Mellon University, optimists view the world more positively:

> . . . for the simple reason that they take more positive actions to improve it. They were found to deal with stressful situations by focusing directly on the problem at hand. They tended to "positively reinterpret" a difficult situation, focusing on what they could learn from it or the discovery of some new truth about life. Pessimists, by contrast, tended to deal with stress by attempting either to disengage from it, to deny it, or simply to complain about it—techniques poorly suited for achieving positive results.[42]

Optimists and Longevity

There's a real physiological reason why optimists live longer—and researchers believe that it lies in a complex set of "messages" that the mind sends to the body. As a result of his work with thousands of critically ill patients, Yale surgeon Bernie Siegel believes that:

The body responds to the mind's messages, whether conscious or unconscious. In general, these may be either "live" or "die" messages. I am convinced we not only have survival mechanisms, such as the fight or flight response, but also a "die" mechanism that actively stops our defenses, slowing our body's functions and bringing us toward death when we feel our life is not worth living.[43]

Optimists, it seems, give consistent "live" messages to the body—and, as a result, live longer. Results of a number of studies have confirmed the theory that people with a cheerful outlook on life generally get to enjoy life longer.

In one study, researchers pored through the pages of *The New York Times* and *The Philadelphia Inquirer* analyzing the quotes of all the Baseball Hall of Fame players who played major-league baseball between the years 1900 and 1950. Based on the players' comments about the game, researchers were able to tag which were optimists and which were pessimists. The pessimists—those who ascribed their success as being short-lived or due to luck—lived significantly shorter lives than the optimists.[44]

How you *perceive* your health to be—whether your perception is or is not accurate—also seems to have a significant bearing on how long you will live. People who believe that they are in bad health—even if they are, in reality, in good or excellent health—have an increased mortality risk. And those who believe that their health is good are literally at a reduced risk of dying, even if "objective" measures (such as medical examinations and laboratory tests) show that they are actually in poor health.

Focus on Research

Researchers in Manitoba, Canada, asked more than 3,500 senior citizens the question, "For your age, would you say, in general, that your health is excellent, good, fair, poor, or bad?" After researchers had each person's self-rating, they obtained medical records, hospital reports, surgical records, and opinions from physicians on how each person's health stacked up. Researchers then tracked the seniors for the next seven years.

Those people who rated their health as poor were almost three times more likely to die during the seven years of the study than those who perceived their health to be excellent. Surprisingly, subjective self-reported health was more accurate in predicting who would die than the objective health measures

from physicians. Those who were in objectively poor health by physician report survived at a higher rate as long as *they believed their own health to be good.*

According to researchers, the predictive power of self-rated health was incredibly powerful. The way that people in the study viewed their own health—even when that viewpoint was not accurate—predicted how long they would live whether they were men or women, older or younger, lived in urban or rural areas, or were in fact sick or well. According to the researchers who conducted the study, only increasing age appeared to have a more powerful influence on death rates than self-rated health.

Source: Robert Ornstein and David Sobel, *The Healing Brain* (New York: Simon and Schuster, 1987), p. 250.

Researchers in one study tracked 6,298 adults in Alameda County, California, for nine years. Men who were "health pessimists" (believed they were in poor health) had two times the mortality risk of men who were "health optimists." The mortality risk among women was a striking five times higher for those pessimistic about their health.[45]

Optimism, then, can be a powerful factor in life. It can, according to results flooding in from the vast number of studies being conducted, be a potent determinant in how healthy we are and how long we live. An increasing number of physicians who are "in the trenches" with patients every day continue to express the firm belief that optimism, more than almost any other attitude, can open the way to health and healing.

Interested in becoming more optimistic? Researchers suggest the following ways to boost your optimism:

- Realize you may need to make a lifestyle change.
- Start small by choosing one area of your life in which to become more optimistic, then become aware of the way you think in relation to that area.
- Take a good, hard, critical look at your beliefs about yourself and about that area of your life: How realistic are they?
- Set goals that are small enough to achieve quickly, then reward yourself when you meet those goals. It's important to reward yourself when you reach even the most *modest* goal.
- Seek out optimistic people; seek a good friend.
- "Play" at being optimistic; stay flexible.[46]

In the book *Mind/Body Medicine: How to Use Your Mind for Better Health,* editors Daniel Goleman and Joel Gurin suggest the following ways to raise an optimistic child:

- Be consistent, positive, and responsive.
- To the extent that you can, "program" the child's world to be consistent, positive, and responsive.
- Give the child responsibility; encourage independence and involve the child in a variety of age-appropriate activities.
- Set realistic goals and encourage problem solving.
- Teach the child not to generalize from specific failures; instead, help the child see failure as a challenge to do better next time.
- Encourage humor as a way of coping.
- If the child expresses pessimistic views, challenge them.
- As best you can, screen the child's peers and teachers for pessimistic tendencies.
- And, finally, be a role model yourself of realistic optimism.[47]

Norman Cousins, whose own experiences formed the foundation for his remarkable work with others, says:

Yes, I know that my optimism can be carried too far—but I also know that no one is smart enough to fix its limits; and that it is far better to pursue a remote and even unlikely goal than to deprive oneself of the forward motion that goals provide. My life has been an education in these essentials, and I could no more turn away from them than I could deny my own existence. . . . Some people may interpret the effort as overwrought do-goodism; but the risk is worth taking nonetheless, for every once in a while it happens that hope can rekindle one's spirits, create remarkable new energies, and set a stage for genuine growth. At least nothing I have learned is less theoretical than the way the entire world seems to open up when courage and determination are connected to truly important aims.[48]

Notes

1. Robert Ornstein and David Sobel, *Healthy Pleasures* (Reading, Massachusetts: Addison-Wesley Publishing Company, Inc., 1989), p. 149.

2. P. Shaver and J. Freedman, "Your Pursuit of Happiness," *Psychology Today*, August 26: 1976, 29.

3. Ann Ranard, "The World Through Rose-Colored Glasses," *Health*, August: 1989, 58.

4. Carolyn Jabs, "New Reasons to Be an Optimist," *Self*, September: 1987, 170–173.

5. Ornstein and Sobel, p. 169.

6. Example is from Ranard, p. 58.

7. Joan Borysenko, *Minding the Body, Mending the Mind* (Reading, Massachusetts: Addison-Wesley Publishing Company, Inc., 1987), p. 120.

8. Sharon Faelten, David Diamond, and the Editors of *Prevention* Magazine, *Take Control of Your Life: A Complete Guide to Stress Relief* (Emmaus, Pennsylvania: Rodale Press, 1988), p. 306.

9. Faelten et al., p. 308.

10. Peter McWilliams and John-Roger, *You Can't Afford the Luxury of a Negative Thought* (Los Angeles, California: Prelude Press, Inc., 1989), p. 133.

11. "Hope: That Sustainer of Man," *Executive Health*, Section II, 20(30): 1983, 1–4.

12. T. P. Hackett and N. H. Cassem, "Development of a Quantitative Rating Scale to Assess Denial," *Journal of Psychosomatic Research*, 18: 1974, 93–100.

13. Bruce Bower, *Science News*, July 23: 1988.

14. From Ornstein and Sobel, p. 167.

15. Daniel Goleman, *New York Times*, April 20:1989.

16. Jabs, p. 171.

17. Christopher Peterson and Lisa M. Bossio, *Health and Optimism* (New York: The Free Press), 1991, p. 34.

18. Devera Pine, "Cruising Attitude," *Health*, August: 1987, 20.

19. Bernie Zilbergeld and Arnold A. Lazarus, "Use Your Head," *Shape*, June: 1988, 115, 146–152.

20. Clive Wood, "Optimism and Health: Expecting the Best," *Mind/Body/Health Digest*, 1(3):3.

21. Wood.

22. Jean Seligman and Linda Buckley, "A Sickroom with a View," *Newsweek*, March 26: 1990, 61.

23. Norman Cousins, *Head First: The Biology of Hope* (New York: E. P. Dutton, 1989), p. 217.

24. Peterson and Bossio, pp. 35–36.

25. Henry Dreher, "Cancer and the Mind: Current Concepts in Psycho-Oncology," *Advances*, Institute for Advancement of Health, 4(3): 27–43.

26. Rebecca Stephens, "Imagery: A Strategic Intervention to Empower Clients," *Clinical Nurse Specialist*, 7(4): 1993, 170–171.

27. Peterson and Bossio, pp. 124–126.

28. Steven Locke and Douglas Colligan, *The Healer Within* (New York: E. P. Dutton, 1986).

29. Armand Tanny, "The Healthy Optimist," *Men's Fitness*, February: 1989, 112.

30. Daniel Goleman, *New York Times Magazine*, September 27: 1987.

31. Ranard, p. 59.

32. Peterson and Bossio, pp. 36–37.

33. Will Stapp, "Imagine Yourself Well," *Medical Self-Care*, January/February: 1988, 27–30.

34. Stapp.

35. Stapp.

36. "Expert Hopeful About AIDS Therapy," *Deseret News,* June 20: 1991, A8.

37. Scott DeGarmo, "Optimism: The Secret Weapon," *Success*, July/August: 1987, 4.

38. Eric Olsen, "Why Optimists Win," *Success*, December: 1988, 32.

39. Olsen.

40. Jill Neimark, "The Power of Positive Thinking," *Success*, September: 1987, 38–47.

41. Faelten et al., p. 309.

42. "Squelching Stress with Optimism," *Men's Health*, September 1987: 3, summarizing information from the *Journal of Personality and Psychology*, 51(6): 1987.

43. Editors of *Prevention* Magazine Health Books, *The Complete Book of Cancer Prevention* (Emmaus, Pennsylvania: Rodale Press), p. 495.

44. Ornstein and Sobel, p. 168.

45. Blair Justice, "Think Yourself Healthy," *Prevention*, June: 1988, 31–32, 105–108.

46. David Burns, *Feeling Good.*

47. Daniel Goleman and Joel Gurin, editors, *Mind/Body Medicine: How to Use Your Mind For Better Health* (New York: Consumer Reports Books, 1993), p. 364.

48. Cousins, pp. 68–69.

26

PROTECTING HEALTH WITH A FIGHTING SPIRIT

You gain strength, courage, and confidence by every experience
in which you really stop to look fear in the face. You are able to say
to yourself, "I lived through this horror. I can take the next thing
that comes along." You must do the thing you think you cannot do.
—ELEANOR ROOSEVELT

The prognosis was in: Robert's physician told him he had only three months to live.[1] In his twenties, Robert had developed cancer in his testicles; it had spread to his lymph nodes, chest, and lungs. A tumor on his neck had become so large that it forced him to tilt his head almost until his ear was resting on his shoulder. Robert was given cobalt radiation treatments—not as a possible cure, but merely to keep his pain under control by limiting the size of the tumors. But although his physicians had nothing more than a grim outlook for Robert, he saw things differently.

"They told me I had essentially a zero chance of survival," Robert remembers. But he faced that prognosis with a fighting spirit, saying "I wasn't going to curl up my toes and die."

He took the bull by the horns. He had a good relationship with a woman, but he'd never really decided what to do about it. He had also completed his seminary studies that prepared him to become an Episcopal priest, but he had felt ambivalent about entering the priesthood. Within a month of his "death sentence," he was married and was ordained a priest.

"I argued and fought with my nurses and doctors," he says, "insisting on explanations for everything they wanted to do, not accepting the lord-and-master routine. And I collaborated with the cobalt machine, rooting it on, not being passive."

Within a month of Robert's decision to "do things more appropriate to living than dying," his doctor had one of the biggest shocks of his medical career: X-ray examinations revealed no trace of cancer in Robert's body. Almost thirty years later, he is still cancer-free.

"Everyone wanted to lay claim to being the healer," recalls Robert, now a New York City psychologist. "My psychologist said it was the therapy. My radiologist, who admitted that even with treatment I had no chance, still said it was the cobalt. My bishop said it was divine grace."

An increasing amount of convincing evidence indicates that the healing influence was probably Robert's fighting spirit—his refusal to give up, his aversion to becoming helpless.

Dr. Keith Peterson, the chief of gastroenterology at LDS Hospital in Salt Lake City, maintains that a "patient with a fighting spirit has a much greater chance of recovering from cancer and other life-threatening diseases than people who capitulate to their illness. It can be the difference between life and death."

Peterson tells of a patient of his, a seventy-five-year-old man with severe pancreatitis. Gravely ill, he had been fed intravenously for eight months and had undergone two massive surgeries—difficult for anyone under any circumstances, but particularly devastating for an elderly man already ravaged by weakness and disease. He was cadaverously thin and drawn with pain. No one held out any hope for any kind of recovery; physicians merely shook their heads at the question of any kind of a normal life for the man.

But, according to Peterson, "he put up a terrific fight." He refused to give up. Today, he's at home, doing fine. He simply has to be careful about the foods he eats.

Dr. Isaac Djerassi, one of the world's leading cancer researchers and the director of oncology at Philadelphia's Mercy Catholic Medical Center, says that from his own experience "older cancer patients who have quit, who have come to me feeling defeated, feeling that nothing can possibly help them, have very often made their own predictions come true. The patients who have faith in their survival always make out better."

One of Djerassi's patients who "made out better" was a brilliant Washington lobbyist who developed a devastating case of lung cancer. One of her lungs had already been surgically removed. The cancer had recurred in the other lung, which was riddled with tumors. By the time she and Djerassi met, cancerous tumors were also blocking her windpipe; every breath was an agonizing ordeal, and she could scarcely speak. Djerassi figured that she only had a few weeks left to live.

"I absolutely refuse to die," she told Djerassi. "I've got too much to do."

"If you're willing to fight," Djerassi told her, "then so am I."

The woman whose life was so perilously close to ending waged her biggest battle ever as she joined forces with the physician who also refused to give up on her. He administered massive doses of an anticancer drug so toxic that it brought her to the edge of death several times; her hair fell out, and she felt weak and almost defeated. But she never gave up. Through it all, she kept on fighting.

That was sixteen years ago. Today, the Washington lobbyist is still alive and very well, living in New York state. And her long white hair, which fell victim to the chemotherapy, grew back in a glossy raven black.

Dr. Wayne Eisom, head of the division of cardiothoracic surgery at New York Hospital–Cornell Medical Center, remembers a man in his fifties who fought a tremendous battle. His heart stopped fifteen different times after surgery, but he never gave up. After each episode, he'd manage a smile and tell Eisom, "Doc, I'm not dead yet."

Then he developed a fungal infection in his sternum; all the experts examined him and declared that the infection would be fatal. Not only was it supposedly fatal, but it was, according to Eisom, "brutally painful. I know. I had to cut out the infected tissue."

After each gut-wrenching session, the man would grin at Eisom and say, "Don't worry, Doc, I'll make it."

And he did make it—Eisom gets a Christmas card from him every year.

"It's hard to put numbers on it," Eisom explains. "You can't put a blood count on it; you can't put a temperature curve on it. But it makes a tremendous difference when a patient comes in feeling that he's going to get well, that everything is going to be all right."

Eisom adds that "it can hurt like hell on the day after an operation when a nurse asks the patient to take a deep breath and cough, but it's urgent that the patient do it. It opens up the collapsed air sacs. A patient who is a fighter will cough hard and often. The other kind of patient won't, and very often dies of pneumonia."

What makes a patient with a fighting spirit so much more likely to get better? There are probably many factors—and they stem from the patient's determination itself. For starters, patients who have a fighting spirit will do a lot more for themselves in terms of following orders, taking prescriptions, and making prescribed changes in lifestyle.

"A cancer patient who is a fighter will eat and build up his strength regardless of how much nausea he feels," says Dr. Vincent DeVita, Jr., the director of the National Cancer Institute. "Furthermore, a cancer patient who gets up from bed and struts down the hall can tolerate much more chemotherapy than a patient who is bedridden."

A fighting spirit also makes a person just that: a fighter. Dr. Willibald Nagler, chief psychiatrist at New York Hospital-Cornell Medical Center, points out that "when an older patient says to you, 'Damn it all, I'm going to walk again no matter what', he probably will. He'll get up out of his wheelchair and try to walk. Maybe he'll fall down, but he'll pick himself up and try again. The patient who keeps moaning, 'I'm never going to walk again' won't even try."

There's probably another important factor at work in favor of patients with a fighting spirit: When a physician sees that a patient is a fighter, he or she is much more likely to join in the fight.

"Doctors will go the extra mile for a patient who is a fighter," says Dr. Phillip Casson of New York University Medical Center, one of the nation's most distinguished surgeons. "They'll operate when the odds against success are overwhelming. They'll come to the hospital at two A.M. to see how the patient is getting along. You've got a much better chance for a long, healthy, and happy life if you're willing to fight for it."

Dr. Djerassi echoes that opinion, and adds the sentiment that a fighting spirit is as important for a physician as it is for a patient. "The same thing holds true of doctors," he says, referring to the fighting-spirit patients who have faith in their own recovery. "Some of the doctors get discouraged too early and give up on patients who could still be helped. When you pick a doctor, make certain that he's a fighter, someone who will stand by you and fight for you."[2]

Psychology Today editor Marc Barasch quoted one survivor as saying, "When I refused to play the Good Little Patient, it pissed off just about everyone." According to Barasch, survivors "do not tend to be *good little patients*. Numerous studies have noted, in fact, that stubbornness, fighting spirit, willingness to express negative feelings are all traits associated with enhanced immune profile."[3]

The quality needs to be part of the personality from the beginning, however. As one psychologist told Barasch, "If you don't already know how to fight, learning how when you're scared, sick, and in pain may be next to impossible."[4]

What Is a Fighting Spirit?

A fighting spirit has been defined as the open expression of emotions, whether they are negative or positive.[5] A lapse into hopelessness, on the other hand, represents a surrender to—rather than an open expression of—despair.

The news media are filled with heroic stories of people who exhibit a fighting spirit.[6] Take, for example, Miami couple William and Simone Butler, who had sailed 3,000 miles and two months into their around-the-world voyage. Somewhere off the coast of Panama, a hundred whales attacked their vessel at four in the morning; they sank into the Pacific Ocean in less than half an hour. They stayed adrift for sixty-six days on a tiny raft, erecting a canopy to shelter themselves from the sun and devising a system to convert seawater to fresh water. William, who caught tiny white fish with his hands, lost fifty pounds and developed a huge open sore on his back. Hammerhead sharks battered the raft ceaselessly until the couple was finally rescued by the Costa Rican Coast Guard.

"I should have been more worried," William reflects, "but I had the feeling we'd do what we had to do to survive. I always figured we'd get out of it." Theirs were attitudes of survivors; they had a fighting spirit.

And consider the Central Park jogger, who was severely beaten, raped, and left for dead; despite extensive brain damage, she emerged from her coma and recovered sufficiently to resume her job as an investment banker. Consider Nelson Mandela, who survived for twenty-seven years in a South African prison. Consider Frank Reed, who survived forty-four months of captivity in Lebanon.

The Role of a Fighting Spirit in Recovery from Disease

Physicians have found that a fighting spirit can play a major role in recovery from disease. In one study, attitudes of patients faced with serious illness fell into one of four categories:

1. A fighting spirit.
2. Denial.
3. Stoic acceptance.
4. Helplessness/hopelessness.

People with a fighting spirit fully accept the diagnosis, adopt an optimistic attitude filled with faith, seek information about how to help themselves, and are determined to fight the disease. Their attitude is, "I won't let cancer beat me! I'm trying everything to get better." In a study at Kings College Hospital in London, researchers followed women with breast cancer that had not yet spread beyond the breast; all were given a simple mastectomy. Five years after surgery, those with a fighting spirit were most likely to be alive and free of recurrences.[7]

British psychologist Steven Greer used scientifically rigorous studies to show that breast cancer patients who had a "fighting spirit" were twice as likely to be alive fifteen years after diagnosis than patients who were stoic or helpless in their response to diagnosis.[8] In another study of breast cancer patients, researchers observed fifty-seven women from the time of diagnosis for ten years. The ones who did the best were those who reacted with denial or a fighting spirit: After a decade, 70 percent of the fighters were still alive, whether or not the cancer had spread, and 50 percent of the deniers were still alive. However, only 25 percent of those who reacted with stoic acceptance were still alive after ten years—and a mere 20 percent of those who felt helpless or hopeless at diagnosis made it for ten years.[9]

Patients with denial either reject the diagnosis of serious illness completely, or they minimize its importance. A mastectomy patient who is a denier, for example, might voice the belief that "the doctors just took off my breast as a precaution." In the Kings College Hospital study, the deniers were the second most likely to be alive and free of recurrence at the end of the five-year study period.

Patients with what researchers call "stoic acceptance" accept the diagnosis, but it stops there. They do not seek further information, do not take steps to participate in their own recovery, and merely adopt a fatalistic attitude. Their attitude becomes one of, "I know what it is; I know it's cancer, but I've got to carry on as normal. There's nothing I can do." Those who express stoic acceptance have a much more grim outlook for survival, according to the researchers in the Kings College Hospital study.

The group of patients who express helplessness or hopelessness have the poorest prognosis, say the researchers. Unlike deniers, they accept the diagnosis and realize its seriousness; if anything, they exaggerate it. Unlike the stoics, they don't vow to carry on as normal—they feel engulfed by their diagnosis and allow their entire life to become disrupted by it. And unlike those with a fighting spirit, they don't make a determination to fight back. Their attitude is one of resignation and defeat: "There's nothing they can do for me. I'm finished."

A growing number of researchers believe that a fighting spirit may be the underlying factor in what is called "spontaneous remission"—the inexplicable recovery from incurable illness.[10] Physicians and researchers on both sides of the line are embroiled in bitter controversy over the issue of possible spontaneous remission. Doubters attribute it to errors in diagnosis (the disease really wasn't incurable) or to some unrecognized mode of treatment (there was a specific reason for this disease to be cured, but we haven't figured out what part of the treatment was responsible yet). Still other skeptics figure that the disease may be in "remission," but it has not been "cured"—and that it's only a matter of time before it recurs.

But more and more physicians and researchers believe that the patient himself or herself is the key in spontaneous remission—and that the phenomenon is real. These researchers believe that the patient's attitude, especially the presence of a fighting spirit, is responsible for the victory over disease.

"The forces exist in the body to arouse its natural disease-fighting abilities," says Dr. Lloyd Old of Memorial Sloan-Kettering Cancer Center in New York City. "The task ahead is to find ways to unleash them."[11]

Neurochemist Brendan O'Regan, vice-president of research for a firm that does research on mind-body interactions, has compiled the world's largest data base on spontaneous remissions. His files hold information on more than 3,500 cases culled from 800 medical journals in twenty languages. According to O'Regan, they are very real—and science's task now is to document them. Spontaneous remission, according to O'Regan, "is a legitimate area of research, a gold mine. Nature is conducting a successful experiment with these people. They represent, in an evolutionary sense, the survival of the fittest. We want to track how it happens in the body and learn how to imitate that in medicine."[12] The spontaneous remissions, he adds, "point to extraordinary self-repair capacities in these people, and they plead for an answer to the question: How can you turn them on?"

The answers that keep surfacing involve attitudes and emotion—and the belief by many that a "fighting spirit" mobilizes the immune system and thus effects the outcome of the disease. An attitude of helplessness or one of giving up, on the other hand, can immobilize the immune system and impair the body's ability to fight the disease.

Researchers believe that denial can actually *help* a fighting spirit. According to physician Larry Dossey, denial is the most *effective* psychological coping strategy in the acute phase of a heart attack. Genuine denial, he says, is highly irrational and flies in the face of obvious facts; a physician may tell a patient he's had a heart attack, but the patient may insist it's just indigestion.

"Even though this response is irrational," says Dossey, "studies have shown that people who use it survive in greater numbers than those who confront the facts squarely and honestly. In fact, no other psychological coping style is correlated with such a high survival rate in the acute phase of myocardial infarction." Why does denial work so well for heart attack victims? Dossey believes it may allay anxiety, which in turn leads to lower levels of adrenalin, calmer blood pressure, a slower heart rate, and a decreased chance of heart irregularies. "Thus the unconscious seems to set in motion through denial a pattern of physical responses tailor-made for survival," he adds.[13]

The Devastating Effect of Helplessness

University of Rochester psychologist Dr. Arthur Schmale, one of the first researchers to recognize the importance of a sense of control, defines helplessness as a giving-up attitude, "a feeling of being deprived, let down, or left out" and a sense of complete "powerlessness."[14]

Dr. Joan Borysenko, psychoneuroimmunology researcher, defines helplessness as "an attitude of powerlessness, of victimization . . . . It's hiding feelings, believing that you have no right to experience them, and therefore feeling helpless that leads to a more dangerous emotional state and, at least in some cases, to a worse medical outcome."[15]

Closely related, says Borysenko, is shame—an emotion that "feels like a sudden severing of our connection with the world. It leaves us feeling emotionally . . . naked . . . Shame is shocking and painful and isolating. [It] is the absolute picture of helplessness. We are beaten, and we know it."[16]

Martin Seligman, a research psychologist at the University of Pennsylvania, believes that it is not so much situations, but *thoughts* that generate helplessness. If you consistently respond to situations with pessimism, says Seligman, "that negative style can actually amplify your feelings of helplessness and spread to other areas of your life."[17] Schmale points out that "feelings of helplessness may appear not only as a response to stress or threatened loss, but may constitute the pervasive or learned response to the common tribulations and frustrations of everyday living."[18] Once people "learn" the response of helplessness, it governs the way they respond to even ordinary frustrations. It no longer requires an overwhelming situation to make them feel helpless.

How is helplessness learned? Sometimes it stems from past experience. If people are repeatedly put in situations over which they have no control, they may begin to feel helpless. Helplessness can also be learned at home; particularly at risk are children of authoritarian families in which parents repeatedly say, "Do what I tell you to do, and don't ask why." When children in these families fail to comply, they are punished—but they still are not given explanations.

"Such children never learn how to cope effectively or how to control stressors," explains researcher Leonard A. Sagan. "They learn passive acquiescence, and with that comes helplessness and resignation: It is the will of God. This explains, in part, why natural disasters take such a high toll . . . ."[19]

According to Seligman, people who are repeatedly placed in situations over which they have no control "are permeated by a sense of helplessness that often extends beyond any specific event. They begin to believe they have no power to change their world."[20] Seligman believes that the signatures of learned helplessness are poor self-motivation, with no attempt at self-improvement; cognitive distortion, in which perceptions of failure repeatedly eclipse prospects of success; and emotional dysfunction, in which repeated failures result in chronic depression.[21]

What causes a feeling of helplessness for me would not necessarily cause you to feel helpless—and a situation that might not seem serious to one person might have profound impact on another person, chiefly because of background and experiences. Schmale uses the example of a young man who graduated from college, left home, and moved to a distant city (an eight-hour drive from home) to seek employment.[22] He felt homesick and lonely, and relied heavily on his mother for solace (in the first five months he was away, he and his mother exchanged four visits, despite the long commute).

In an attempt to ease his loneliness, he arranged with a friend to go bowling. The friend was an hour late. As the young man waited impatiently for his friend, he had to cope with a rising sense of panic. His mind and his emotions were carried back to the time when he was eight years old: His father died, his mother had to go to work, and he was left alone and on his own. As he stood at the bowling alley waiting for his friend, he began thinking, "Isn't this the way it always works out?"

Unable to wait any longer, he began bowling by himself. After gently rolling the ball down the alley a few times, he suddenly developed excruciating pains in his lower back. The pains were so debilitating that he had to return to his mother's home, where he was hospitalized. Having to wait for a friend who's an hour late would not be a crisis for most of us—but for this young man it brought a flood of helplessness that led to lower back pain. Researchers believe helplessness can cause physical problems. People who feel hopeless about their situation or helpless to do anything about it traditionally have higher disease rates, are unable to fight infection and disease as well as their counterparts, and succumb to disease at a much higher rate. Says Sagan, "All physicians know that the will to live is crucial in overcoming serious illness or in recovering from surgery. The opposite is also true: patients who are pessimistic about outcomes will often not survive."[23]

The Type C Personality

Helplessness is a key trait in what researchers have dubbed the "Type C" personality—the collection of personality traits that make a person more at risk for cancer. Helpless people are, according to psychiatrist Paul Pearsall, "still, apparently contemplative, but, in fact, ruminating and persevering with despair. They sense loss of control. Less threatened than defeated, they are in the vigilance stance. As spectators helplessly watching their houses burn, wall after wall crumbles for them, and they are vigilant only for more destruction."[24]

Pearsall says that helpless people share certain personality traits.[25] Rather than fight or flee in the face of stress, they merely flow helplessly. They are observers instead of actors; whereas most people are actively involved in life, helpless people "sit by" and wait for things to happen. They receive little positive information from their environments; as a result, they are difficult to compliment because they disqualify any positive things that do occur. They capitalize on and exaggerate the negative, while minimizing the positive; in a very real way, says Pearsall, they "look through the binoculars of life from the wrong end." When they see a negative that reinforces their sense of helplessness, they "tend to take one small bit of information from the pallet of life and paint the whole world a different color."

Helpless people feel totally alone and withdrawn; they long for attention and concern. A trait that emphasizes that feeling of aloneness is their tendency to take the burdens of the entire family—if not the entire world—on their shoulders and their psyche. As a result, they feel burdened, overwhelmed, ineffective, and hopeless. A growing sense of helplessness weakens these people in the event of stress. They have difficulty acknowledging problems they experience. Instead of coping in a healthy way, they are able to only temporarily hold things back—and then they crumble quickly.

Physiological Effects

A sense of helplessness has real physiological effects on the body. According to research done by George Engel and his colleagues at the University of Rochester School of Medicine, people who feel helpless withdraw into a state of immobility and inactivity they call the "conservation-withdrawal response."[26] The conservation-withdrawal response is characterized by specific physiological reactions in the body—and they are the same physiological reactions found in helpless people.

The heart slows down, the blood pressure drops, and the heart is prone to arrhythmia (disruptions in its normal electrical rhythm). The stomach pumps out less gastric secretion, and there's a decrease in the urinary water and sodium. The body secretes the stress hormone cortisol, which causes an entire range of damage itself. But the most powerful physiological feature of helplessness involves the nervous system. When the body is functioning smoothly, the two branches of the nervous system work in a reciprocal way to balance each other; one speeds up the vital organs and systems, while the other slows it down. When helplessness sets in, the nervous system reacts in a predictable way: Activity is slowed, muscle tone is decreased, and the entire system becomes less responsive to the environment. In a very real sense, the body "gives up." Immunity is depressed, and the body becomes more vulnerable to an entire range of illnesses and diseases.

Impacts on Health

A team at the University of Rochester School of Medicine—including researchers George Engel, Arthur Schmale, William Greene, and Franz Reichsman, among others—spent twenty years studying what they call the "giving-up complex." As part of their work, they sought to identify the conditions under which illness occurs and to isolate the most pervasive factors. They concluded at the end of their comprehensive studies that no one condition or agent is sufficient for illness to occur, but that a combination of factors work together to impact vulnerability and susceptibility.

Dr. George L. Engel and his colleagues at the University of Rochester School of Medicine spent six years studying reports of sudden death. They found that most deaths happened within an hour of an emotional event—and one of the most common settings is a sense of helplessness, where people believe they can neither fight nor escape. Harvard Medical School's Joel E. Dimsdale believes that it's not just the stress of the incident, but how the person interprets the stress, that is so devastating.[27]

For their study, the research team investigated patients with many different diseases, disorders, and symptoms. People who were studied represented all the various disorders to be found in a random sampling of patients at a large hospital—and researchers homed in on people with conditions such as leukemia, multiple sclerosis, cancer, colitis, and psychiatric disturbances.

The research group determined that a common thread in the tapestry of ills was the "giving-up complex." They noted, essentially, that "people who are at high risk of illness not only seem to believe that they themselves can do nothing about their problem, but no one else can, either."[28] As the researchers put it, they had given up on themselves and believed that others had also given up on them; they had usually experienced a loss, and did not believe that anything could be done to regain what was lost.[29] The "giving-up complex," or helplessness, became the window through which these people interpreted all their life events and rendered them incapable of coping successfully with stress and other adverse situations.

Control versus Helplessness

The importance of control versus helplessness can be readily seen by watching infants. Psychologist Seligman says the ability to develop control develops in infancy. A good, attentive mother mirrors and responds to the actions of the baby. "Baby smiles, mother smiles. Baby coos, mother coos. Baby cries with hunger, and mother responds with milk." Through this "dance of development,"[30] "infants learn that they have control, that they can ensure their own survival."

What happens when an infant doesn't have that kind of experience? Watching infants who are institutionalized provides the answer. These babies are deprived of the important "dance of development." They don't have any control: They are fed on schedule. They are changed on schedule. Caregivers provide custodial care, but little else. As Borysenko penned, "Previously happy infants become weepy. After a few months they stop crying and become withdrawn, staring at the wall. At first they ignore people who approach them; later they begin to shriek. They lose weight, often develop insomnia, and are very prone to infections. Many die before they are three years old."[31] The infants have become helpless. When no control is possible and helplessness sets in, health and life itself are impacted.

Borysenko, the former codirector of the Mind/Body Clinic at New England Deaconess Hospital, gives an excellent example of the effect of helplessness in her book, *Minding the Body, Mending the Mind*. She draws her example from the movies, comparing the ever-controlled James Bond to the insecure Woody Allen characters.

James Bond, as she points out, "is nothing if not stress hardy. Bombs explode around him as he parachutes into the supervillain's diabolical nuclear reactor, but he calmly combs his hair and picks lint off his navy blazer." On the other hand, she writes, are the insecure characters in Woody Allen's films, who "are prone to develop ulcers when faced with what to order for dessert. The potential hazards of helplessness and emotional repression didn't escape Marshall Brinkman and Woody Allen in their script of *Manhattan*. In it, Allen plays one of his typical retiring males. Diane Keaton, playing his girlfriend, announces that she is leaving Allen for his best friend. When the Allen character looks unperturbed, Keaton becomes agitated, demanding to know why he doesn't react. He sighs and tells her that he can't express anger. 'I grow a tumor instead,' he says."[32]

In studies of patients with cancer, those who triumph over the disease are much more likely to be fighters who feel in control. Only about one-third of those who feel helpless are able to triumph over their disease after five years; among the fighters, 88 to 90 percent are able to come out on top. According to physician Herbert Benson, "short survivors" who are least successful in fighting cancer are typically those who are described as "despairing and helpless."[33]

Several animal studies demonstrate with clarity the devastating effect of helplessness. In one, Seligman suspended dogs in a cloth hammock that allowed for the dogs to be restrained as safely and as gently as possible. Then the dogs were conditioned to associate the sound of a certain tone with an electric shock. After a few sessions in the hammock, it became obvious to the dogs that when the tone sounded, a painful electric shock would soon follow. Seligman separated the dogs into three groups. The first group heard the tone but did not receive any shock. The second group was trained to turn off the shock by pressing a panel with their noses. The third group received shocks at the sound of the tone but was not given any means by which to control the shocks.[34]

The dogs were then put into a shuttle box—a small chamber divided in half by a low barrier; half of the floor in the shuttle box was electrified. When the dogs from the first group—those that had not received a shock while in the hammock—were put into the shuttle box and the shock was turned on, the animals usually ran around frantically until they accidentally jumped over the low barrier to the shock-free side. After a few times, the dogs were skilled at avoiding shock. According to researchers, they "sat close to the divider and at the first tingle of electricity nonchalantly hopped over the barrier to safety."

The same thing happened when Seligman tested the dogs that had learned to turn off the shock by pressing a panel with their noses while in the hammock. These dogs quickly discovered that they could hop over the barrier and avoid the electrical shock, and they did so without seeming anxious.

The reaction of the dogs that had been shocked in the hammock but that had been given no means of controlling the shock was "bizarre." At first the dogs ran around frantically for about thirty seconds, just as the other two groups had. But then they stopped moving; they lay down and whined. After one minute of this, the shock was turned off; the dogs had failed to cross the barrier and had not escaped from the shock. On the next trial, the dogs did it again: At first they struggled a bit, and then, after a few seconds, seemed to give up and accept the shock passively. On all succeeding trials, the dogs failed to escape.[35]

Seligman even tried to help out the dogs by putting long leashes on them, dragging them over the barrier, and forcing them to escape. Revealing how powerful helplessness is, some of the dogs did not initiate their own response and try to escape themselves until they had been dragged over the barrier up to two hundred times. Seligman concluded from his study that it wasn't the shock itself, but the dogs' inability to control it that caused the sense of helplessness.

How a Fighting Spirit Makes a Difference

Fighters aren't stronger or better or more capable than the rest of the people. But they don't give up easily. And, in study after study, they have been shown to enjoy better health and live longer—even when physicians and laboratory tests say they shouldn't.

According to author Steve Fishman, specific factors bolster a fighting spirit and help promote survival.[36] One is the desire to bear witness, to want to survive badly enough to tell others the story of what happened; that deep-seated desire is what kept many prisoners of war and concentration camp victims alive. Another is the desire to survive for some purpose above and beyond self—to rescue someone else, to return to family, to resume critical medical research. Still others have an uncanny ability to keep an attitude of faith, to maintain an attitude of cheer in the face of gloom, or to deny the seriousness of the situation.

Perhaps one of the greatest examples of such an attitude is former New York City Opera director Beverly Sills, who has faced incredible personal tragedy in her life. Both her children were born deaf; one was also mentally handicapped. She survived cancer. An arsonist destroyed her new home. All the while, she says, she "became a much more rational person despite all the irrationality of the events. I had lived through the worst day of my life. I felt that, from that time on, everything else had to be up."[37]

In summing up her life's philosophy, she remarks that "everything does not happen for the best. But I do think there's a reason for everything. We poor mortals just aren't clever enough to know what that reason is. I must say that I still love life. There are an awful lot of good things ahead of us, and there are some wonderful things behind us. Every crisis is a challenge. You just have to shake your fist and meet it."[38]

A fighting spirit itself makes a person stand up and take charge. When illness or disease is present, that makes a big difference. As heart surgeon Dr. Wayne Eisom of New York Hospital–Cornell Medical Center points out, "A fighter gets

---

Focus on Research

When researchers at Johns Hopkins University Medical School learned that an influenza epidemic was about to strike a military base nearby, they seized the opportunity to find out just how much difference there was between fighters and people who give up. They administered personality tests to the personnel and rated them; each was then classified into one of the two categories.

When the flu struck, the researchers followed it with interest. The illness struck all its victims with about the same intensity, but the fighters recovered within about eight days. The "morale-loss" group, the people who tend to give up, continued to have flu symptoms for about three weeks.

Source: Jerome Frank, "The Medical Power of Faith," *Human Nature,* August: 1978, 40–47.

out of bed earlier and walks, even with painful incisions. A non-fighter doesn't, and gets an infection in his lungs."[39] Fighters are intrinsically different from people who give up, and their health reflects those differences.

A Fighting Spirit against AIDS

A fighting spirit can apparently make a difference even in disease situations as serious as AIDS. The message that AIDS patients usually get is one of giving up; as one researcher put it, "all that is emphasized to AIDS patients is that it's 100 percent fatal. Death, death, death."[40]

When someone with a powerful fighting spirit gets infected, the prognosis may be different. One patient is offered as an example. The course of his illness has been difficult: So far, he has survived two bouts of pneumocystis carinii pneumonia, one bout of cryptococcus, and lymphoma—the worst of the opportunistic infections in AIDS patients, which claims most of its victims within nine months. But this man is still alive.

"He is feisty as hell," his physician says of him. "He seeks out treatments. He takes charge of his own care. He doesn't put up with anything. He has the fiercest determination to live that I have ever seen. He has projects; he is involved. He has a marvelous support system. He is now teaching in a college, and his helper cell count is twenty-eight. Normal count is between five hundred and fifteen hundred. This shows that with twenty-eight helper cells, which 'ain't too good,' you can still live, which shows you can't just go by the lab workup."[41]

A Fighting Spirit against Cancer

Probably the most remarkable studies involving the effect of a fighting spirit have dealt with cancer—a disease that, by its very name, inspires medical terror in many people. The spirit with which a patient accepts the diagnosis is apparently a major determinant in how the disease will progress—and, according to some researchers, an overall fighting spirit in general may even help stave off cancer.

"Cancer is often an indication of problems elsewhere in an individual's life, problems aggravated and compounded by a series of stresses six to eighteen months prior to the onset of cancer," explains Dr. O. Carl Simonton, an oncologist who pioneered a revolutionary and controversial approach to cancer treatment. "The cancer patient has typically responded to these problems and stresses with a deep sense of hopelessness, or 'giving up.' This emotional response, we believe, in turn triggers a set of physiological responses that suppress the body's natural defenses and make it susceptible to producing abnormal cells."[42] In summing up his argument, Simonton points out that "stresses and conflicts do not *cause* cancer, but they lead to feelings of helplessness or hopelessness that permit cancer to develop."

The "giving up" style compared with the active, fighting style has been repeatedly shown to significantly affect prognosis in cancer cases. In one interesting study, Michael H. Antoni of the University of Miami and Karl Goodkin of the University of Texas Southwestern Medical Center in Dallas conducted psychological studies on seventy-five women who had returned for further diagnosis after "abnormal" Pap tests. (An "abnormal" result can signal that changes are occurring that can cause cervical cancer in some people.) Also tested were women with papillomavirus infection, a disease that is benign but that can lead to cancer of the cervix in women who are susceptible.[43]

When Antoni and Goodkin determined which of the women did indeed have cervical cancer, they pored over the psychological test results. They found that the women who had cancer displayed a marked personality type characterized by helplessness and giving up. The cancer victims, say the researchers, were found to deal with stress in a passive manner (with helplessness or an attitude of giving up) rather than actively coping (by fighting back) or coping neutrally (through methods such as relaxation).

In general, the women displayed what researchers have come to term the "Type C" personality: They were conforming, cooperative, respectful, and likely to repress emotions. They were also more pessimistic about their futures even before they learned they had cancer.

Psychologist Lydia Temoshok, an assistant professor of medical psychology in the Department of Psychiatry at the University of California at San Francisco, maintains that the Type C–coping style—characterized by giving up rather than by fighting—signals a poorer prognosis when it comes to cancer.

In one study, she evaluated videotapes of patients with malignant melanoma. All had been given identical prognoses and diagnoses by their physicians. When Temoshok watched the videotapes and identified the patients she classified as Type C, she found they had thicker tumors that were dividing at a higher rate; they also had weaker immune responses and were doing the most poorly at fighting off the cancer. Two years later, Temoshok checked up on the original group of patients she had evaluated. The ones who had died were the ones who had a tendency to give up. The fighters were still alive.[44]

Yale surgeon and oncologist Bernie Siegel is a firm believer in the potency of a fighting spirit in overcoming cancer—and he knows that the opposite attitude, one of giving up, has the opposite effect. In telling about one patient with liver cancer, he explains that the man was a financial advisor who invested people's life savings according to statistics. "His oncologist told him what statistics said about his chances, and from then on he refused to fight for his life," Siegel explains. "He said, 'I've spent my life making predictions based on statistics. Statistics tell me I'm supposed to die. If I don't die, my whole life doesn't make sense.' And he went home and died."[45]

Likewise, Boston University School of Medicine psychiatrist Bernard Fox believes that a fighting spirit is essential in combating cancer. "Recent studies have suggested that a hopeless, helpless attitude in cancer patients forecasts a shorter survival time than a fighting spirit," he says.[46]

Role of the Immune System

The immune system may bear some of the greatest impact of a fighting spirit—and it may be the reason why fighters do better in all kinds of disease situations. "Convincing evidence" from a host of studies indicates "that the right mental attitude can help your immune system function more effectively," says Dr. Isaac Djerassi.

A fighting spirit can boost the immune system for genuine physiological reasons. The immune system responds to both the brain's and the nervous system's chemical "messengers." More than fifty identified neuropeptides stimulate and mobilize the immune system. A fighting spirit has been shown to stimulate production of these important chemical messengers.

Norman Cousins tells the story of a woman who was diagnosed with breast cancer but who refused to be operated on for the disease.[47] Her surgeon called Cousins and asked if he could help. The woman's surgeon told Cousins, "The tumor is not an ordinary one. It is like a hand grenade under a thin sheathing of skin. The breast is badly corrugated. It's a life-threatening situation. But she is resisting the surgery out of fear of mutilation, loss of femininity, etcetera. I'd be grateful if you could turn her around on this."

Cousins talked to the woman, and in his conversation he told her that "what happens in surgery is not just the result of the surgeon's skill but how you yourself think about the surgery and the confidence you yourself bring into the operating room. You have the power to program yourself for a good result." Cousins then worked with the woman to instill in her a fighting spirit, helping her to realize that she was not a helpless victim but had the power to be a controlling fighter.

The woman returned to her physician and prepared for surgery. A week later, however, the surgeon called Cousins to say that the surgery had been canceled. When the surgical team took radiographs just before the scheduled surgery, the tumor had totally disappeared.

"I could hardly take in what he was saying," remembers Cousins. The surgeon, who "couldn't believe it himself," offered to send the clean x-ray films—and added that the breast was soft and supple in every way. The surgeon termed the recovery "extraordinary."

What had happened, Cousins says, is that the woman's "own cancer-fighting ability had risen to the occasion. Because she had been taking no medication at the time, the only rational explanation is that the full array of immune cells, cells that produce the body's own chemotherapy and infuse it into the cancer cells, had been able to do the job."

Cousins adds another example of how a fighting spirit can make the difference by mobilizing a failing immune system. After a lecture, he was approached by a physician who had been in the audience. The physician had been devastated by a widespread cancer that had spread to his lungs, lymph nodes, and liver.

"My oncologist friend came right out with it and said I had perhaps three to four months to live," the physician told Cousins. "I decided I was not going to accept the prediction. I was going to fight it. I was going to put all my mental and physical energies into the fight. I caressed and cajoled every one of my immune cells into doing its job. For a month or two I went downhill, lost weight, but not confidence. Then, little by little, the tide began to turn. I began to regain weight and strength. When I got through the sixth month, I knew that the cancer didn't have a chance. How long ago was that? About eight years."

A final example comes from Dr. George Solomon, a pioneer in psychoneuroimmunology. He told Cousins of a professor at Harvard who had been stricken with cancer; he had lesions in his head, lungs, and liver. Nonetheless, the professor continued teaching his classes, reassuring his friends and students.

Solomon says of the professor that "it was thrilling to see how powerful the fighting spirit can be. For most of a year, he battled that cancer. And he won. The most important thing he had to teach us came not out of his medical lectures, but out of his own experience and example. He won against all the odds—against the predictions of the specialists and against the reports based on sophisticated technology. This sort of thing doesn't happen very often, but the fact that it happens at all is the most important thing any medical student can learn." It is, perhaps, one of the most important things any of us can learn: If we are willing to fight, we *can* win.

Notes

1. The examples and physician quotes that follow are taken from Gregg Levoy, "Inexplicable Recoveries from Incurable Diseases," *Longevity*, October: 1989, 36–42; and Donald Robinson, "Medical Report: Can a Fighting Spirit Defeat Disease?" *50 Plus*, January: 1988, 23–25.

2. "Hope: That Sustainer of Man," *Executive Health*, Section II, 20(3): 1983, 1–4.

3. Marc I. Barasch, "The Healing Path: A Soul Approach to Illness," *The Psychology of Health, Immunity, and Disease*, vol. B, p. 10, in Proceedings of the Sixth International Conference of the National Institute for the Clinical Application of Behavioral Medicine.

4. Barasch.

5. Henry Dreher, "Psychosocial Factors and Breast Cancer Survival: Recent Developments," *Mind/Body/Health Digest*, 4(1): 1987, 1–2.

6. Steve Fishman, "Absolutely, Positively, Refusing to Die," *Longevity*, September: 1990, 69.

7. Joan Borysenko, and Myrin Borysenko, "On Psychoneuroimmunology: How the Mind Influences Health and Disease . . . and How to Make the Influence Beneficial," *Executive Health*, 19(10): 1983.

8. Henry Dreher, "The Type C Connection: A Powerful New Tool in the Fight Against Cancer," presented to the National Institute for the Clinical Application of Behavioral Medicine, December 1992.

9. Bernie Siegel, *Peace, Love, and Healing* (New York: Harper and Row, 1989), p. 27.

10. Levoy, p. 38.

11. Levoy.

12. Levoy.

13. Larry Dossey, *Healing Words* (San Francisco: Harper San Francisco, 1993), pp. 61–62.

14. Steven Locke and Douglas Colligan, *The Healer Within* (New York: E. P. Dutton, 1986), p. 95.

15. Joan Borysenko, *Minding the Body, Mending the Mind* (Reading, Massachusetts: Addison-Wesley Publishing Company, Inc., 1987), p. 163.

16. Larry Dossey, *Meaning and Medicine: A Doctor's Tales of Breakthrough and Healing* (New York: Bantam Books, 1991), p. 31.

17. Nan Silver, "Do Optimists Live Longer?" *American Health*, November: 1986, 50–53.

18. Leonard A. Sagan, *The Health of Nations* (New York: Basic Books, Inc., Publishers, 1987).

19. Sagan.

20. Borysenko, pp. 119–120.

21. Brian Luke Seaward, *Managing Stress* (Boston: Jones and Bartlett Publishers, 1994), p. 100.

22. Arthur H. Schmale, "Relationships of Separation and Depression to Disease," *Psychosomatic Medicine*, 20(4): n.d., 259–277.

23. Sagan.

24. Paul Pearsall, *Super Immunity* (New York: McGraw-Hill Book Company, 1987).

25. Pearsall.

26. George Engel and Arthur Schmale, "Conservation-Withdrawal: A Primary Regulatory Process for Organismic Homeostasis," in *Physiology, Emotion, and Psychosomatic Illness* (Amsterdam, Netherlands: Associated Scientific Publishers, 1972).

27. Dossey, *Meaning and Medicine,* pp. 52–54.

28. Arthur H. Schmale, "Giving Up as a Final Common Pathway to Changes in Health," *Advances in Psychosomatic Medicine*, 8: 1972, 20–40.

29. Schmale.

30. Borysenko, p. 22.

31. Borysenko, p. 23.

32. Borysenko, p. 22.

33. Herbert Benson, *Beyond the Relaxation Response* (New York: Times Books, 1984).

34. Study described in Locke and Colligan, pp. 68–69; and Robert Ornstein and David Sobel, *The Healing Brain* (New York: Simon and Schuster, 1987), pp. 244–245.

35. Locke and Colligan, p. 69.

36. Fishman.

37. Beverly Sills with Katrine Ames, "Facing Down Disaster," *Longevity*, September: 1990, 69.

38. Sills.

39. Donald Robinson, "Mind Over Disease: Your Attitude Can Make You Well," *Reader's Digest*, April: 1987, 73–78.

40. George F. Solomon, "The Healthy Elderly and Long-Term Survivors of AIDS: Psychoimmune Connections," *Advances*, 5(1) 6–14.

41. Solomon.

42. Barbara Powell, *Good Relationships are Good Medicine* (Emmaus, Pennsylvania: Rodale Press, 1987).

43. Christina V. Miller, "Fighting Spirits vs. Passive Stoics," *Longevity*, April: 1989, 14.

44. Study described in Robinson, "Mind Over Disease"; and Editors of *Prevention* Magazine Health Books, *The Complete Book of Cancer Prevention* (Emmaus, Pennsylvania: Rodale Press).

45. Editors of *Prevention* Magazine, *The Complete Book of Cancer Prevention*.

46. Editors of *Prevention* Magazine, *The Complete Book of Cancer Prevention*.

47. These three stories are told in Norman Cousins, *Head First: The Biology of Hope* (New York: E. P. Dutton, 1989).

27

THE HEALING POWER
OF HUMOR AND LAUGHTER

*With the fearful strain
that is on me night and day,
if I did not laugh I should die.*
—*ABRAHAM LINCOLN*

Mark Twain once penned the sentiment that "against the assault of laughter nothing can stand." What the great American humorist and author believed more than a hundred years ago is being proven true today by some of our most gifted scientists: A sense of humor, and the laughter that accompanies it, can actually banish pain and keep us well.

Laughter as medicine is probably as old as humankind. One of the earliest written accounts recognizing the healing power of humor is found in the Bible, in which King Solomon remarked that "a merry heart doeth good like a medicine" (*Proverbs* 17:22). Members of royal courts around the world and throughout the ages have valued the court jester—the colorful clown who provided the humor that made governing a palatable job.

Henri de Mondeville, a thirteenth-century surgeon, told jokes to his patients as they emerged from operations. Sixteenth-century English educator Richard Mulcater prescribed laughter for those afflicted with head colds and melancholy; a favorite "cure" was being tickled in the armpits. Humor was even used by ancient Americans: Ojibway Indian doctor-clowns, the Windigokan, used laughter to heal the sick.[1]

They may not have had the scientific proof to back up their suppositions, but even early physicians recognized the healing power of humor. The famous seventeenth-century physician Thomas Sydenham said that "the arrival of a good clown exercises more beneficial influence upon the health of a town than twenty asses laden with drugs."[2]

Webster's dictionary defines humor as the quality that appeals to a sense of the comical or absurdly incongruous. According to Loretta LaRoche of Boston's Deaconess Hospital, good humor is "the ability to feel inner joy, peace, and harmony within yourself and your surroundings—to discover that we are all part of a divine comedy."[3] Humor is a way of looking at things that helps to dissipate stress and accentuate the positive. "When we become too serious," says LaRoche, "we help create the components for stress, rigid thinking, helplessness, cynicism, and hardening of the attitude."[4]

Humor has been used across the span of cultures to make people feel better. A number of American Indian tribes—the Zunis, Crees, Pueblos, and Hopis among them—had ceremonial clowns whose sole purpose was to provide humor for their tribesmen. According to accounts, they were called in "to entertain and heal the sick with their hilarity, frightening away the demons of ill health."[5]

One of the most renowned uses of laughter in our own day occurred when former *Saturday Review* editor Norman Cousins incorporated it in a program to treat ankylosing spondylitis, a debilitating connective tissue disease. Cousins employed funny movies and books to relieve the pain of the disease.

"Ten minutes of genuine belly laughter had an anesthetic effect and would give me at least two hours of pain-free sleep," Cousins relates. "When the pain-killing effect of the laughter wore off, we would switch on the motion picture projector again and, not infrequently, it would lead to another pain-free sleep interval."[6] Indeed, claims Cousins, of "all the gifts bestowed by nature on human beings, hearty laughter must be close to the top. The response to incongruities is one of the highest manifestations of the cerebral process."

C. W. Metcalf, an international consultant who helps people use humor to cope with stress, says that "Humor, then, is a set of survival skills that relieve tension, keeping us fluid and flexible instead of allowing us to become rigid and breakable, in the face of relentless change."[7]

The renowned novelist Dostoevski wrote, "If you wish to glimpse inside a human soul and get to know a man, don't bother analyzing his ways of being silent, of talking, of weeping, or seeing how much he is moved by noble ideas; you'll get better results if you just watch him laugh. If he laughs well, he's a good man. . . . All I claim to know is that laughter is the most reliable gauge of human nature."[8]

Professional Trends toward Humor

Researchers are now providing scientific proof that laughter (along with a sense of humor) can literally make a person feel better. Based on the most recent batch of scientific evidence proving laughter's health benefits, hospitals and medical clinics have started to utilize laughter in unique ways to promote the health of patients.[9]

One of the prototypes for "humor centers" in the nation's hospitals is the Living Room of the William Stehlin Foundation for Cancer Research at Houston's St. Joseph's Hospital. The room is filled with greenery and furnished with comfortable, overstuffed pieces. Patients are free to go to the room as often as needed for "comic relief" from the severity of their illness.

The "humor room" at Schenectady's Sunnyview Hospital and Rehabilitation Center boasts a poster reminding patients to take a "humor break" from illness. In the room, patients can check out funny movies, humorous tapes, and funny books. They are also given access to proven "mirth makers," such as balloons, clown noses, and bottles of bubble soap. At DeKalb General Hospital in Decatur, Georgia, patients can spend part of their recovery time in a brightly painted "Lively Room" stocked with funny games, tapes, and movies. Laurel and Hardy movies are shown in the "Living Room" of Orlando's Humana Hospital Lucerne.

An increasing number of hospitals are making humorous films and television programs (such as "Candid Camera" reruns) available to their patients. Two separate Los Angeles hospitals have instituted hospitalwide "humor stations" that enable patients throughout the hospital to tune in funny programs on the television sets in their rooms twenty-four hours a day. And a California-based project is providing "laugh wagons" to hospitals throughout the country. The "laugh wagons"—seen in the halls as frequently as the medication carts in some hospitals—are stocked with humorous videotapes, audiotapes, books, magazines, and games. Patients are encouraged to borrow materials freely, to laugh their way to better health.

Leslie Gibson, creator of the Comedy Cart Connection at Morton Plant Hospital in Clearwater, Florida, points out that being hospitalized puts people at the highest level of stress—and that humor is a natural remedy. "The loss of control often places patients in fearful, compromising situations. Besides promoting healing, humor is an excellent diversionary tool for keeping their minds off their pain."[10]

The trend toward humor as a way of boosting both physical and mental health has spread to private practice. Increasing numbers of physicians throughout the nation have begun using humor and laughter as a way of easing tension, promoting healing, and even boosting immunity among their patients. Nurses, too, have caught the vision: More than one thousand nurses joined forces several years ago to organize Nurses for Laughter (NFL). The members, who try to make humor a part of their bedside manner, boast the motto, "Caution: Humor may be hazardous to your illness." The nurses work to help patients see some humor in their situations, and to bring some life and laughter to the hospital setting, which can too often be sterile and solemn.

The benefits of laughter on physical and mental health are being noted even in the corporate world. According to a report published in *Newsweek*,[11] some of the nation's largest corporations have instituted humor programs to help develop a sense of humor in employees—and the results include an increased employee capacity to deal with stress and an overall improvement in job performance. Management for Safeway Stores, in fact, reports a sharp decrease in the number of debilitating accidents since the stores began holding humor clinics in

1984. Other major entities that hold humor clinics or programs for employees include Manville Corporation, Southwestern Bell, IBM, Hewlett-Packard, the United States Air Force, Monsanto, the Internal Revenue Service, General Foods, and the Hartford Insurance Group.

The Health Impact of Humor

The physiological changes that occur from laughter are so effective that one expert likes to call laughing "internal jogging." And the outlook characterized by a good sense of humor is beneficial to both physical and mental wellness, according to the most recent evidence.

Educator and author John-Roger was traveling with some friends on the lecture circuit. When they arrived at one destination, the plane was late. To make matters worse, everyone else's luggage arrived first. When their luggage finally appeared, one piece of luggage was obviously damaged. Another suitcase had sprung open, and clothing and personal items were spread all over the conveyor belt. The people traveling with John-Roger were becoming increasingly upset.

Finally he turned to the group and said, "Relax, this is funny. In a few weeks we'll be telling stories about tonight and laughing about it. If it'll be funny then, it's funny now."

According to John-Roger, the focus changed. They started looking at the situation, "as if it were a Woody Allen movie. When some of the luggage didn't arrive, we smiled. When the car rental agency didn't have our reservation (or cars), we laughed. When we heard there was a taxi strike, we howled."[12]

American actress Ethel Barrymore echoed the experience of the stranded travelers: "You grow up the day you have the first real laugh—at yourself." Some of the biggest crises we experience turn into some of our funniest moments. The mere passage of time transforms them. Top stand-up comic Judy Carter maintains that "there's a little bit of stand-up comic in everyone; the performance comes not when you're having a fight, but in telling a friend afterward."[13]

Antioch University professor Harvey Mindess, an expert in humor, points out: "Humor at its best encourages a broad perspective on life. It provides a view of the ironies that abound, of the fact that nobody and nothing is as it seems. And recognizing life's zaniness encourages flexibility and adaptability, rather than rigidity and brittleness."[14]

One of the most healing things about humor, say some, is that it acts as a bond between people. Comedy writer Emily Levine suggests:

> *Humor is extraordinary for making connections with people. Everyone has such a separate reality, and it's alienating to feel you'll never really be understood because nobody sees the world the same way you do. But when you make a joke and someone else gets it, it means for that moment, your mind worked exactly the same, you were totally in sync. That's divine grace.*[15]

The Physical Benefits of Humor

The results of recent research show that a sense of humor—a point of view that sees the comical in things, an attitude of merriment—can actually promote good health by strengthening the immune system. Studies have shown that people who tend to have a humorous outlook have greater immunity against a variety of diseases as well as increased ability to fight off infection.

In one study, researchers first tested volunteers and determined how they scored as far as having a sense of humor.[16] Researchers rated each volunteer as to how strong his or her sense of humor was. Then researchers set about finding out how each volunteer's immune system responded.

Under normal conditions, we secrete a substance called secretory immunoglobulin A (s-IgA) in the saliva; it's a sign that the immune system is functioning as it should. Certain situations, such as stress, suppress the immune system. When that happens, the amount of s-IgA in the saliva drops—a sign that the immune system is not functioning up to par.

Researchers subjected each volunteer to a set of "hassles," situations known to invoke stress and reduce the amount of s-IgA in the saliva. The researchers found that people with a low sense of humor reacted strongly to the hassles; the amount of s-IgA in the saliva dropped sharply. Immune function among people with little sense of humor was significantly impacted by stress. But those who rated high on the humor scale showed very little change in immune function, even when subjected to hassles and stressors.

The Psychological Benefits of Humor

A sense of humor has tremendous psychological benefits as well. Researchers have found that a humorous outlook on life can have far-reaching benefits including enhancing self-esteem, promoting creativity, improving negotiating and decision-making skills, maintaining a sense of balance, improving performance, bestowing a sense of power, relieving stress, and improving coping abilities.

Enhancing Self-Esteem

The ability to laugh at yourself denotes a healthy sense of self-esteem. But there's an important caveat: You need to *laugh* at yourself, not ridicule yourself.

Psychotherapist Frank Prerost delineates three stages of humor:

1. You ridicule your own inadequacies, often weeping as well as laughing.
2. You direct your hostile angers at others.
3. You are able to laugh at your own shortcomings in a confident, nonthreatened way.[17]

In the third stage, says Prerost, "you can look at your own failings in a humorous fashion and no longer blame other people for your problems. It works two ways. Laughing at yourself means taking responsibility for your own life, and when you feel in control of your life, you are able to laugh at yourself more."[18]

When you develop the ability to laugh at yourself in a healthy way, Prerost says, "you start to develop a different attitude. You stop believing that life owes you certain things. You know that you have to work for what you get. You become more effective in life. It's a kind of paradox. Until you can really accept your shortcomings, you can't go out and do what you are capable of doing."[19]

Promoting Creativity

People with a good sense of humor are generally more creative—and tend to have much more creativity in the way they approach life's problems. Edward de Bono, the world's leading authority on creativity, says that humor and the creative process are actually one and the same thing. With both, he says, the brain recognizes the value of the absurd or the creative idea only in hindsight—because, before that, both seem "crazy." The hallmarks of creative thinkers, then, are the willingness to play with ideas and to risk foolishness without fear.[20]

Improving Negotiating and Decision-Making Skills

A good sense of humor apparently improves the ability to negotiate and to make decisions. Researchers who wanted to measure the impact of humor on negotiating situations set up a role-playing situation in which paired volunteers played the roles of buyers and sellers of appliances.[21] The volunteers were given a range of alternatives and were told to achieve the highest profit (the sellers) or the best deal (the buyers).

The pairs who read funny cartoons—of the B.C. and *New Yorker* variety—did best. During the face-to-face negotiation involved in the role playing, they were less anxious, had fewer contentions, and were better able to reach a solution that pleased both the "buyer" and the "seller."

Focus on Research

In a study by University of Maryland psychologist Alice Isen, she split volunteers into two groups. One either watched a math film or did a monotonous exercise; the other group watched a clip of funny television "bloopers" or received candy.

Isen then gave all the volunteers a box of tacks, a candle and a book of matches. She challenged the volunteers to use their "equipment" to attach the candle to the wall so it could be lit without dripping any wax.

The comedy audience and the gift recipients—those Isen calls the "feel good" groups—attacked the problem with much greater efficiency and creativity. One volunteer emptied the box of tacks, tacked the box to the corkboard wall, and used it as a candleholder.

Source: Susan Lang, "Laughing Matters—At Work," *American Health,* September: 1988, 46.

Maintaining a Sense of Balance

Renowned American clergyman Henry Ward Beecher wrote that a person without a sense of humor "is like a wagon without springs—jolted by every pebble in the road." Indeed, a sense of humor helps us achieve and maintain that delicate balance that puts life in perspective. We all suffer stress; we all endure heartache; we all struggle with situations that are less than perfect. Viewed through a sense of humor, it all seems okay. We don't take things too seriously, and we are able to coast through situations that would otherwise tip us precariously off-balance.[22]

Improving Performance

Humor helps to improve both group and individual performance. The greatest benefits occur, says University of Tennessee psychologist Howard Pollio, when the humor is directly related to the task at hand.[23]

Bestowing a Sense of Power

A sense of humor can give us a sense of power. According to "jollyologist" Allen Klein, laughter helps us to transcend our predicaments.[24] He gives the example of Anatoly Sharansky, the Russian human rights advocate who was confined for nine years in Soviet prisons. His prison sentence included sixteen months of solitary confinement and the constant threat of the death penalty.

Klein relates that Soviet police constantly threatened Sharansky with the *rastrel* (the "firing squad"), knowing that Sharansky's greatest battle was against fear. Sharansky managed to win the war against fear through humor. He started actually joking about the firing squad and talking about it on a daily basis. "You make jokes fifteen to twenty times," Sharansky remembers, "and the word becomes like any other word. The ear gets accustomed to it, and it no longer prompts fear."

Klein relates a second example involving eighteenth-century philosopher Moses Mendelssohn. While walking down the streets of Berlin one day, he accidentally collided with a plump Prussian officer. "Swine!" the officer bellowed. Mendelssohn, knowing that a reprisal would invite punishment from the officer, decided on a different approach—one laced with humor. He smiled, tipped his hat, and replied, "Mendelssohn." As Klein points out, humor can turn any situation around—and can give us a feeling of power over our circumstances.

Relieving Stress

Numerous studies have shown that people who withstand even tremendous stress without becoming brittle, bitter, and broken have several traits in common—they are altruistic (they actively care about the welfare of others), they get plenty of support from friends and the community, and they gain control over difficult situations with humor.[25]

Humor has been demonstrated in a wide variety of studies to help alleviate the effects of stress. In one, researchers showed that people with a good sense of humor don't get as stressed to begin with. They placed an old tennis shoe, a drinking glass, and an aspirin bottle on a table and asked volunteers to make up a three-minute comedy routine using the objects on the table. Results of the study showed that the volunteers who wrote the funniest routines were those who were least likely to become tense, depressed, angry, fatigued, or confused when stress occurred in their lives.[26]

Other studies produce the same results. In one, researchers obtained measures of stress, anxiety, coping, and appreciation on 101 volunteers. The scores revealed that the ones with the greatest appreciation of humor were also the ones who were most effective in coping with stress. The ones who were least effective in coping with stress were also the ones who had a very dismal outlook when it came to humor.[27] In a similar study involving 56 volunteers, researchers showed that a good sense of humor relieved stress and moderated the volunteers' physical responses to stressors.[28]

In one study, researchers split a group of volunteers in half. One group watched an hour-long humorous video; the other group participated in a neutral activity. All members of both groups knew ahead of time which group they were being assigned to.

As researchers had expected, several stress hormones were significantly lower in the group that watched the humorous video. But here's where the surprise came in: Those who *anticipated* watching a humorous video had lower levels of stress hormones even before they actually started watching the video. Those who anticipated the neutral activity didn't.[29]

Humor has been shown repeatedly to be a tool that helps relieve the stress of illness, terminal disease, and hospitalization. Lenore Reinhard, coordinator of the humor program at Schenectady's Sunnyview Rehabilitation Hospital, says she has seen repeated evidence that humorous books and tapes really help relieve the stress of being confined to a hospital. She remembers one patient in his forties who was under significant stress and who was not helped by relaxation tapes.

"I suggested that he check out some of our humor tapes—we have Woody Allen, Bill Cosby, 'Father' Guido Sarducci, George Burns, Rodney Dangerfield, Mel Brooks, and others," she relates. "Several weeks later, after he left, I checked the sign-out book—he'd borrowed *nine* tapes. They really helped him relax and get his mind off the very difficult situation he was in."[30]

Norman Cousins points out that humor neutralizes emotionally charged stress and is especially helpful for people who are facing serious or terminal illness. He says that humor "accomplishes one very essential purpose. It tends to block deep feelings of apprehension and even panic that all too frequently accompany serious illness." In addition, he says, it frees concentration on the body and enables healing to begin.[31]

Improving Coping Abilities

Lawrence Mintz, a professor of American Studies at the University of Maryland, believes that "humor is the way we cope with living in an imperfect world with imperfect selves. When we can't win, the best thing to do is to laugh about it."

Antioch University professor Harvey Mindess agrees that humor is "a great coping mechanism. When a client of mine is very anxious about something, I try to get him to break out of his anger or fear by laughing at himself."

As early as the turn of this century, eminent psychoanalyst Sigmund Freud touted humor as one of the only socially acceptable ways to release pent-up frustration and anger, and he hailed it as a way to preserve the emotional energy that would normally be required to cope with a stressful situation. "The essence of humor is that one spares oneself the effects to which the situation would naturally give rise," he explained, "and overrides with a jest the possibility of such an emotional display."

Humor increases coping capacity in a number of ways. Deborah Burton Leiber, founder of the nationally organized Nurses for Laughter, says study results verify that humor helps us avoid feelings that are too frightening to face; this kind of humor, known as "gallows humor," was first noted among prisoners in Nazi concentration camps who were about to face death. Leiber points out that humor also has a "normalizing" effect, helps reduce the severity of tense situations, and can actually reduce nervous tension to help us cope.[32]

Alison Crane, a registered nurse who founded the American Association for Therapeutic Humor, maintains that humor can help people cope even in the most harrowing situations. She remembers a thirty-one-year-old man who had been admitted to the hospital with a serious heart condition. One morning he began experiencing severe chest pains, and the cardiologist decided that the patient needed immediate surgery. The patient was frightened and panicked, and the cardiologist felt that he would do better in surgery if his wife and child—who lived an hour away—could visit with him before he went into surgery.

Crane says that the patient's condition rapidly deteriorated, and there was no way the team of surgeons could wait for the patient's family any longer. She and the others who attended the patient had to find a way to allay his fear and panic (and to keep a lid on their own sense of rising panic). Crane says that her coping mechanism is humor —and that she had a gut instinct that it would work for the patient, too.

"I tried to joke around—not as in gales of laughter, but just a little lightness to break the tension," she remembers. "For example, when hanging his IVs I put a baseball cap on his IV pole and said, 'This will be your friend for awhile.'" The humor was a success in breaking up the panic and tension of the situation. Surgery was successful; the patient's family attributed his survival to the staff's ability to squelch his sense of panic.[33]

A study among patients waiting for medical treatment showed that a good sense of humor could, indeed, relieve tension and reduce anxiety, helping the patients to better cope. Researchers chose 75 patients who were waiting for medical procedures at a hospital; one-third saw a nonhumorous film, one-third saw a funny film, and the other third did not see a film. When researchers measured each group's level of anxiety, those who saw the funny film were the least anxious and the best able to cope with the upcoming medical treatment.[34]

Allen Klein cites the examples given by psychologist Samuel Janus and scientists Seymour and Rhoda Fisher of famous "funny people" who used humor to cope with deep psychological pain. In Klein's book, *The Healing Power of Humor*, he points out that Totie Field's mother died when she was five, David Steinberg's brother was killed in Vietnam, Jackie Gleason's father deserted him, W. C. Fields ran away from home because his father was going to kill him, Dudley Moore was born with a clubfoot, Art Buchwald's mother died when he was very young, and Carol Burnett's parents were both alcoholics who fought constantly.

"Charlie Chaplin, too found solace in humor," Klein writes. "Raised in one of the poorest sections of London, he was five years old when his father died of alcoholism; after that his mother went mad. Chaplin used these gloomy memories in his films and turned them into comedic gems. Who could forget the scene in *Gold Rush*, for example, where he eats a boiled leather shoe for dinner because no other food is available?"[35]

Laughter: The Best Medicine

Psychologist Robert Ornstein and physician David Sobel recite the scientific definition of a laugh as "a psychophysiological reflex, a successive, rhythmic, spasmodic expiration with open glottis and vibration of the vocal cords, often accompanied by a baring of the teeth and facial grimaces."[36]

The Physiology of Laughter

Laughter may seem simple, but it's actually a complex physical process. According to studies reported in the *Journal of the American Medical Association*, laughter does the following:

- *Breathing:* increases the breathing rate, increases the amount of oxygen circulated through the blood, and clears mucus from the lungs.
- *Muscles:* provides limited muscle conditioning, provides muscle relaxation, and breaks the pain/spasm cycle common to some muscle disorders.
- *Cardiovascular system:* temporarily increases the heart rate and blood pressure, increases circulation, and increases the amount of oxygen delivered to all body cells.[37]

Stanford Medical School psychiatrist William Fry, Jr., says that laughter is valuable for strengthening the heart muscle—and, he says, just *twenty seconds* of laughter is the cardiovascular equivalent of *three minutes* of strenuous rowing.[38]

Consider this description, published in a scientific journal around the turn of the century:

> *There occur in laughter and more or less in smiling, clonic spasms of the diaphragm in number ordinarily about eighteen perhaps, and contraction of most*

of the muscles of the face. The upper side of the mouth and its corners are drawn upward. The upper eyelid is elevated, as are also, to some extent, the brows, the skin over the glabella, and the upper lip, while the skin at the outer canthi of the eye is characteristically puckered. The nostrils are moderately dilated and drawn upward, the tongue slightly extended, and the cheeks distended and drawn somewhat upward; in persons with the pinnal muscles largely developed, the pinnae tend to incline forwards. The lower jaw vibrates or is somewhat withdrawn (doubtless to afford all possible air to the distending lungs), and the head, in extreme laughter, is thrown backward, until (and this usually happens soon) fatigue-pain in the diaphragm and accessory abdominal muscles causes a marked proper flexion of the trunk for its relief. The whole arterial vascular system is dilated, with consequent blushing from the effort on the dermal capillaries of the face and neck, and at times of the scalp and hands. From this same cause in the main the eyes often slightly bulge forwards and the lachrymal gland becomes active, ordinarily to a degree only to cause a 'brightening' of the eyes, but often to such an extent that the tears overflow entirely their proper channels.

Laughter as Exercise

Laughter is one of the best exercises around. And one of the nicest things about it is its simplicity. It requires no special training. It requires no special equipment. You don't have to do it at the gym or on the track or on a Nautilus machine. All you need, in fact, is a sense of humor.

Stanford Medical School's William Fry likens laughter to a form of physical exercise—it causes huffing and puffing, speeds up the heart rate, raises blood pressure, accelerates breathing, increases oxygen consumption, gives the muscles of the stomach and face a workout, and relaxes the muscles that aren't used in laughing. Twenty seconds of laughing can double the heart rates for three to five minutes, he adds.[39]

Laughter provides what some experts have called "a total inner body workout"—and more and more researchers are finding out exactly what it is about a laugh that is so good for us.

In brief, he says that something you see or hear or think of sets off "a massive brain reaction." Nerve fibers in the involuntary nervous system trigger a snowballing cycle of discharges in the brain stem. "Your neural circuits reverberate with the news: something is funny."

Your humor is then converted into electrical and chemical impulses that wash through the frontal lobes of the brain, over the motor centers of the brain, and land smack in the center of the cerebral cortex. The cortex then hands out an order to the body: Laugh!

"A laugh," Brody writes, "can run anywhere from a half-second giggle or guffaw to a sixty-second belly burster, a memorable earthquake down in your abdomen, with many variations in between." Fry, who has studied laughter extensively, estimates that people in good spirits let loose with as many as 100 to 400 laughs a day.

Once you're ready to laugh, the muscles in your face that control expressions start to contort, says Brody. Muscles throughout your body contract like fists. Your vocal cord muscles, designed for intelligible sound, cannot coordinate. Your glottis and larynx open, relaxed and ready to vibrate. Your diaphragm tenses up in anticipation of respiratory spasms. According to Brody, "Air in your body billows until you feel pressure building in your lungs. Trying to hold in a laugh is no less than a violation against nature—rarely successful."

Once the laugh gets into full gear, writes Brody, "your breathing is interrupted for a station break. Your lower jaw vibrates. A blast of air gusts into your trachea, flinging mucus against the walls of your windpipe. Pandemonium! Out comes your laugh, in some cases clocked at 170 miles an hour. You issue a strange machine-gun sound, almost a violent bark."

Once in the throes of a full-bodied laugh, your body bucks. Your torso is flexed. Your arms flail, your hands slap your thighs. "Your lacrimal glands squeeze out tears, giving your eyes a mirthful sheen. You puff and rasp with symphonic regularity. You can hardly stand so much glee coursing through you. You're wobbly in the knees, wheezing like an asthmatic. Pleading for mercy, you collapse on the nearest sofa. Sounds like fun, no?"

The complicated combination of physiological reactions makes laughing what some researchers have called "inner jogging." Your metabolism steps up, and calories are burned off. Your body temperature increases. And your entire system is showered with adrenaline, making you feel good all over. Best of all, the physical effects of laughter endure for up to two hours after you stop laughing.

Laughter is essentially an act of respiration—and the lungs immediately fill with air. Air volume is dramatically increased, and your breathing rate goes up. Because of increased air volume and breathing rate, much more oxygen is delivered to the body than with normal breathing. You also breathe out more carbon monoxide and water vapor, which can encourage bacterial growth if it stays in the lungs. Once you finish laughing, you usually cough—a reaction that finishes clearing out the lungs.

Second, your heart rate increases during laughter, and the increase is in direct proportion to how long and hard you laugh. The entire cardiovascular system is stepped up, and the circulation increases; as a result, the entire cardiovascular system is toned. Fresh nutrients and oxygen go coursing through your arteries. Your blood pressure goes up. When you finish laughing, your heart rate and blood pressure drop to levels below those when you started laughing.

Laughter improves your digestion and may even stimulate enzymes that act as natural laxatives. It stimulates your central nervous system. And it first contracts, and then relaxes, almost all the muscles in your body. When you begin to laugh, at least five major muscle groups begin a rhythmic movement; when you finish laughing, your muscles—especially those of the abdomen, diaphragm, shoulders, neck, and face—are more relaxed than when you started laughing. Laughter not only improves muscle tone, but enables total relaxation of all major muscle groups in your body.

The Health Benefits of Laughter

In describing the health benefits of laughter, Norman Cousins—who laughed his way back to health from a painful and debilitating disease—likes to relate the story of an encounter he had in a veterans' hospital. Concerned about the glum spirits of the men on the cancer ward at the hospital in Sepulveda, California, physicians asked Cousins to impress the men with how optimism and good cheer could actually help them feel better and maybe even help them heal. Cousins met with fifty or sixty of the veterans and discussed the role of humor and cheer. Then he told them he hoped they would work together to create an atmosphere conducive to the best medical treatment available.

When Cousins returned to the hospital a few weeks later, he noted that the men had accepted the challenge. He could see the changes immediately. In their meeting that morning, each veteran was asked to tell about something good that had happened to him since the previous meeting. Each one in turn told about something good, with intermittent cheers bursting forth from the others. When each had taken a turn, they all turned to face Cousins. Obviously, they expected him to relate a story as well.

In his book *Head First*,* Cousins relates the following experience, which he feels demonstrates the power of laughter:[40]

> "What I have to report is better than good," I said, "It's wonderful. Actually, it's better than wonderful. It's unbelievable. And as long as I live, I don't expect that anything as magnificent as this can possibly happen to me again."
>
> The veterans sat forward in their seats.
>
> "What happened is that when I arrived at the Los Angeles airport last Wednesday my bag was the first off the carousel."
>
> An eruption of applause and acclaim greeted this announcement.
>
> "I had never even met anyone whose bag was first off the carousel," I continued.
>
> Again, loud expressions of delight.
>
> "Flushed with success, I went to the nearest telephone to report my arrival to my office. That was when I lost my coin. I pondered this melancholy event for a moment or two, then decided to report it to the operator.
>
> "'Operator,' I said, 'I put a quarter in and didn't get my number. The machine collected my coin.'
>
> "'Sir,' she said, 'if you give me your name and address, we'll mail the coin to you.'
>
> "I was appalled.
>
> "'Operator,' I said, 'I think I can understand the reason behind the difficulties of AT&T. You're going to take the time and trouble to write down my

*From: *Head First, The Biology of Hope,* Copyright © 1989 by Norman Cousins. Used by permission of publisher, Dutton, an imprint of New American Library, a division of Penguin Books USA Inc.

name on a card and then you are probably going to give it to the person in charge of such matters. He will go the cash register, punch it open and take out a quarter, at the same time recording the reason for the cash withdrawal. Then he will take a cardboard with a recessed slot to hold the coin so it won't flop around in the envelope. Then he, or someone else, will fit the cardboard with the coin into an envelope, first taking the time to write my address on the envelope. Then the envelope will be sealed. Someone will then affix a twenty-cent stamp on the envelope. All that time and expense just to return a quarter. Now, operator, why don't you just return my coin and let's be friends.'

"'Sir,' she repeated in a flat voice, 'if you give me your name and address, we will mail you the refund.'

"Then, almost by way of afterthought, she said, 'Sir, did you remember to press the coin return plunger?'

"Truth to tell, I had overlooked this nicety. I pressed the plunger. To my great surprise, it worked. It was apparent that the machine had been badly constipated and I happened to have the plunger. All at once, the vitals of the machine opened up and proceeded to spew out coins of almost every denomination. The profusion was so great that I had to use my empty hand to contain the overflow.

"While all this was happening, the noise was registering in the telephone and was not lost on the operator.

"'Sir,' she said, 'what is happening?'

"I reported that the machine had just given up all its earnings for the past few months, at least. At a rough estimate, I said there must be close to four dollars in quarters, dimes, and nickels that had just erupted from the box.

"'Sir,' she said, 'will you please put the coins back in the box.'

"'Operator,' I said, 'if you give me your name and address I will be glad to mail you the coins.'"

According to Cousins, the veterans "exploded with cheers. David triumphs over Goliath. At the bottom of the ninth inning, with the home team behind by three runs, the weakest hitter in the lineup hits the ball out of the park. A mammoth business corporation is brought to its knees. Every person who has been exasperated by the loss of a coin in a public telephone booth could identify with my experience and share both in the triumph of justice and the humiliation of the mammoth and the impersonal oppressor."

One of the doctors in the room, noticing how relaxed and mobile the men were, asked how many had been experiencing their usual amount of pain when they arrived at the meeting. More than half of the veterans in the room raised their hands. The doctor then asked how many noticed that their pain had receded or completely disappeared. The same hands went up.

The example given by Cousins is just one of the many that doctors and researchers studying laughter are hearing. Because of the physiological changes that take place during laughter, it packs a punch in terms of physical benefits, pain relief, boosts in immunity, and psychological benefits.

Physical Benefits of Laughter

Stanford University researcher William Fry concluded after a series of experiments that laughter increases respiratory activity, oxygen exchange, and heart rate, improving and toning the cardiovascular system. According to Fry, laughter stimulates the sympathetic nervous system, the pituitary gland, the cardiovascular system, and the hormones that relieve pain and inflammation—making it a possible benefit in conditions like arthritis and gout.

Psychologist Jeffrey Goldstein of Temple University credits laughter with contributing to longevity, and says that results of his research show that laughter works physiologically to reduce stress, hypertension, depression, heart attacks, and stroke. Laughing, says Goldstein, is much like jogging as a physical exercise—and its benefits are just as great.

Researchers have even found that the tears you shed during a good laugh have the same chemical composition as the tears you shed during a good cry. Both have been scientifically proven to carry away toxins and the hormones manufactured during stress.

Pain Relief Benefits of Laughter

The most well-known example of laughter as an anesthetic is provided by former *Saturday Review* editor Norman Cousins. When his symptoms of achiness, fatigue, and fever worsened instead of getting better, he sought medical help. The diagnosis was devastating: a potentially life-threatening collagen disease that affected all the connective tissues of the body. Involvement was already so extreme that he was having difficulty merely moving his joints. His physician told him that recovery was not probable.

Instead of merely accepting the prognosis that would have sentenced him to pain and then death, Cousins decided to take things into his own hands. He designed a program of positive thinking, nutritious food—and, as a painkiller, laughter.

Cousins found that laughter was the most effective painkiller he could find. Ten minutes of hearty laughter (usually prompted by old "Candid Camera" reruns) provided two hours of pain-free sleep. Even more remarkably, he found that inflammation in the tissues was reduced after each laughter session.

A decade later—fully recovered and functioning as a vital, vigorous man—he wrote of his experience. He gave laughter part of the credit for his miraculous recovery. Following his claims, a number of scientists set out to test his theory that laughter could act as an analgesic.

According to the most recent research, laughter probably relieves pain for several different reasons. Renowned author Raymond Moody, Jr., says one of those reasons has to do with muscle relaxation. Pain often involves muscle tension—the same kind of muscle gripping and spasm you would experience if you tried to stand on one leg for a long time. When you laugh, the tension dissipates—the spasms relax.

Laughter also stimulates the brain to release endorphins. These potent natural chemicals have pain-killing power estimated to be 200 times that of morphine; they also reduce inflammation and can stimulate the immune system. These are the chemicals responsible for the famed "runner's high"—and researchers believe there may be a very real and similar "laugher's high"—that results when these chemicals leave laughers feeling relaxed and good all over.

Laughter and humor can relieve not only physical pain, but emotional pain, too. By providing a new perspective and lightening the emotional tension of a situation, laughing can relieve emotional stress and ease psychological pain.

A number of studies are under way throughout Europe and the United States in an effort to duplicate the experience of Norman Cousins. The results of one study, published in the *Journal of American Medical Association*, involved only a small group of patients but shows great promise for the role of "humor therapy" in relieving pain.

Dr. Lars Ljungdahl and his colleagues at Sweden's Lyckorna Primary Health-Care Centre chose six women who were incapacitated with an extremely painful muscle-bone disorder. The physicians administered psychological tests to the women before beginning the experiment to determine general psychological well-being.

The women were then given "humor therapy" for thirteen weeks. The patients used humorous books, records, and videotapes daily; they also met once a week with nurses who gave lectures on humor and helped the women understand how to better use humor in their everyday lives. The patients were asked to regularly record on separate scales how amused they were and how much pain relief they had.

Ljungdahl said that the women who participated in the study enjoyed "significant relief" from their painful symptoms—and those with the greatest degrees of amusement were also the ones who had the greatest pain relief. Tests administered at the end of the thirteen-week period also showed that the women had a greater overall sense of well-being.

"Their self-confidence also seemed to increase, they coped more ably with their symptoms, and allowed themselves to be happy and enjoy life regardless of their medical problems," he said. Ljungdahl noted that pain relief was greater during the last seven weeks than during the first six weeks, indicating that laughter had the greatest benefits.

Immunity-Enhancing Benefits of Laughter

All of the research on laughter has revealed what may be one of laughter's most important benefits: It apparently enhances the immune system. Researchers believe that the immune-enhancing powers of laughter are due to two separate aspects of laughter: (a) It boosts the production of immune enhancers, and (b) it suppresses the production of stress hormones that weaken immunity. Dr. Lee Berk, an immunologist at California's Loma Linda University Medical Center, has conducted studies involving both of these effects of laughter on the immune system. In experiments with students, those who watched humorous videotapes compared with those who didn't had the highest concentrations of lymphocytes, greater natural killer cell activity, and significantly better measure of overall immune system activity. "The changes in the white cell counts and hormones," he says, "have been more surprising than we ever realized."[41]

The other way laughter may improve immunity is by reducing the stress hormones secreted in the body, which generally suppress the immune system. According to psychologist Robert Ornstein and physician David Sobel, "when confronted with a threatening situation, animals have essentially two choices: to flee or fight. Humans have a third alternative: to laugh."[42]

One series of studies measuring the effects of laughter on stress hormones was carried out by Berk and his Loma Linda University Medical Center colleagues. Berk had five men watch an hour-long comedy video of the comedian Gallagher; he then took blood tests and compared them to test results from five men who did not watch the video.[43]

The five who watched the funny film had lower levels of the stress hormone epinephrine. They also had significantly lower levels of DOPAC (which indicates dopamine activity) and the stress hormone cortisol, which can shut down the body's production of the immune substance interleukin 2. Berk and his colleagues concluded from the studies (and others they conducted on laughter) that

---

Focus on Research

In an attempt to measure how laughter could boost the production of immune enhancers, Dr. Kathleen Dillon of Western New England College measured the salivary immunoglobulin A concentrations in ten student volunteers. Salivary immunoglobulin A (s-IgA) is believed to protect against some viruses, including those that cause upper respiratory infections.

For her experiment, Dillon showed half the students a thirty-minute nonhumorous videotape. The other half of the students watched the thirty-minute film, "Richard Pryor Live." At the end of the thirty minutes of film viewing, Dillon again measured the s-IgA in each of the students.

The s-IgA levels in the students who followed the Richard Pryor film shot up. The s-IgA levels among the students who watched the nonhumorous educational video remained unchanged. Dillon was convinced that laughter made the difference.

She also noticed another phenomenon: In questioning the students, she found those who habitually turned to humor as a way of coping with problems had the highest s-IgA concentrations to begin with. She concluded that a consistently cheerful approach to life can bolster the body's defense and boost the ability to ward off disease.

Source: Norman Cousins, *Head First* (New York: E. P. Dutton, 1989), pp. 143–145.

laughing definitely has beneficial effects on the immune system—and may even help combat certain diseases.

The message for us is clear. As psychologist Gordon Allport suggested, "I venture to say that no person is in good health unless he can laugh at himself, quietly and privately. . . . "

Psychological Benefits of Laughter

Among the psychological benefits of laughter are its ability to diminish fear, calm anger, and relieve depression. But perhaps the most pronounced psychological benefits of laughter are its ability to relieve stress and its tendency to improve our perspective—on everything from pain to life itself.

Laughter as Stress Relief
Steve Allen, Jr.—the physician son of comedian Steve Allen—believes that "laughter is not only as good a method of stress relief as a massage, a hot bath, or exercise, it's *essential* to stress relief." Some of the reasons are tied to the physical outcomes: The body doesn't produce stress hormones as efficiently during laughter and laughter itself physically breaks up tension.

Lawrence Peter, author of *The Laughter Prescription*, considers laughter to be an important safety valve. When you laugh, Peters maintains, you get rid of stress-related tension that can otherwise accumulate and damage health.

The stress-relieving effect of laughter doesn't last just while you're chuckling, either. Experts agree that the ability of laughter to dispel stress lasts long after the laugh—and can even help the person who laughs to build an actual immunity to stress. That's the opinion of *Laughing Matters* magazine editor Joel Goodman, who believes that laughter can "provide immediate relief from life's daily pressures" as well as "build up an immunity to stress for the long haul."

Laughter as New Perspective
According to Yale surgeon Bernie Siegel, renowned for his work in helping patients heal themselves,

> Humor's most important psychological function is to jolt us out of our habitual frame of mind and promote new perspectives. Psychologists have long noted that one of the best measures of mental health is the ability to laugh at oneself in a gently mocking way—like the dear old schoolteacher, a colostomy patient of mine several years ago, who named her stomas Harry and Larry.[44]

Apparently laughter can give us new perspective on almost anything—even something as real and so distressing as pain. Psychologists Rosemary and Dennis Cogan of Texas Tech University in Lubbock designed an experiment to see whether laughter would help change the perspective of pain. They randomly assigned students into one of four groups: one listened to a humorous audiotape, one listened to a relaxation tape, one listened to an informative narrative, and the fourth group did not hear a tape.

The Cogans then fastened automatically inflating blood pressure cuffs around the students' arms and subjected the students to the highest level of discomfort that the cuffs could produce.

The students who were able to withstand even the highest pressure without becoming distressed were those who had listened to the humorous tape. Laughter, the Cogans theorize, changes our perspective of discomfort or distress and enables us to withstand many times what we normally could.

Harvard University psychologist Gordon Allport maintained four decades ago that laughter provides new perspective on our place in society—much as climbing a mountain or activity in a religion does. Dozens of researchers following up on Allport's theory have proved the same thing—and millions of people who laugh merrily at life's circumstances can confirm the truth of it, too.

Ornstein and Sobel tell us:

> *Most of us don't take laughter seriously enough. Too often, laughter is regarded as child's play. To be adult is to be hardworking, responsible, and serious. We need to revive our natural sense of humor. If laughter is as contagious as it is said to be, then let's start an epidemic. Or perhaps we need doctors by the thousands to prescribe regular doses of humor. Though this Great Laughter Cure may not be a panacea, it is reassuring to learn, in these days of painful and expensive medical therapies, that laughter is medicinal and the only side effects are pleasurable.[45]*

If you want to have more fun in your life, try following these suggestions of Leigh Anne Jasheway, coordinator of health promotion at the University of Texas Health Science Center at Houston:

- Make a pledge to laugh out loud or to make someone else laugh at least ten times every day.
- Once a week, set aside time to call someone who always adds fun to your day.
- Read your favorite comics in the newspaper every day.
- Make regular dates with a friend or your spouse to do any recreation that you both enjoy.
- Do something silly at least once a week.
- Start a humor collection—go for jokes, clippings, cartoons, cards, mugs, books, or videos.
- Share funny items with others, and use stick-on notes that have humorous messages.
- Rent funny movies.
- Try to find the humor in every predicament.
- Keep a "fun first-aid kit"—cram it full of things like modeling clay, bubbles, puzzles, brain teasers, and other things you love to do.
- Finally, recall all the fun you had as a child!

Perhaps one of the best suggestions is to create what Loretta LaRoche calls a "humor survival kit"—and one of her best tools, she says, always gets a laugh:

Buy something silly you can put on (a pair of Groucho Marx glasses are my favorite). Put them on in situations where you tend to awfulize. I wear mine driving through Boston, especially when I have to merge. People always let me in. Food shopping is another favorite. Among others, going to the dentist, the doctor, staff meetings, talking to your mate, the children, a coworker. When things have really reached the limits of your endurance, go into a bathroom, look into the mirror, put on your glasses, and ask yourself this question: "How serious is this?"[46]

Notes

1. Loretta LaRoche, "Fully Human, Fully Alive with Humor, Compassion, and Love," *The Psychology of Health, Immunity, and Disease*, vol. A, p. 326, in Proceedings of the Sixth International Conference of the National Institute for the Clinical Application of Behavioral Medicine.

2. Barbara Powell, *Good Relationships Are Good Medicine* (Emmaus, Pennsylvania: Rodale Press, 1987).

3. LaRoche.

4. LaRoche.

5. Powell.

6. Norman Cousins, "The Laughter Connection," *East/West*, February: 1990, 58.

7. C. W. Metcalf and Roma Felible, *Lighten Up: Survival Skills for People Under Pressure* (Reading, Massachusetts: Addison-Wesley Publishing Company, Inc.), p. 9.

8. Fedor Mikhailovich Dostoevski, *The Adolescent*.

9. Nick Gallo, "Lighten Up: Laugh Your Way to Good Health," *Better Homes and Gardens*, August: 1989, 31.

10. Barbara Graham, "The Healing Power of Humor," *Mind/Body/ Health Digest*, 4(2): 1990, 2.

11. Penelope Wang, Karen Springen, Tom Schmitz, and Mary Bruno, "A Cure for Stress?" *Newsweek*, October 12: 1987, 84–85.

12. Peter McWilliams and John-Roger, *You Can't Afford the Luxury of a Negative Thought*, (Los Angeles, California: Prelude Press, Inc., 1989), p. 277.

13. Caryl S. Avery, "Lighten Up," *Self*, September: 1988, 150–157.

14. Avery.

15. Avery.

16. R. A. Martin and J. P. Dobbin, "Sense of Humor, Hassles, and Immunoglobulin A: Evidence for a Stress-Moderating Effect of Humor," *International Journal of Psychiatric Medicine*, 18: 1988, 93–105.

17. Emrika Padus, *The Complete Guide to Your Emotions and Your Health*, (Emmaus, Pennsylvania: Rodale Press, 1986).

18. Padus.

19. Padus.

20. Metcalf and Felible, pp. 9–10.

21. Susan Lang, "Laughing Matters—At Work," *American Health*, September: 1988, 46.

22. Allen Klein, *The Healing Power of Humor*, (Los Angeles, California: Jeremy P. Tarcher, Inc., 1989), pp. 16–17.

23. Lang.

24. Klein, p. 4.

25. Metcalf and Felible, p. 26.

26. Robert Ornstein and David Sobel, *Healthy Pleasures* (Reading, Massachusetts: Addison-Wesley Publishing Company, Inc., 1989), p. 218.

27. R. Fay, "The Defensive Role of Humor in the Management of Stress," *Dissertation Abstracts International*, 44: 1983, 1219B.

28. R. A. Martin and H. M. Lefcourt, "Sense of Humor as a Moderator of the Relation Between Stressors and Moods," *Journal of Personality and Social Psychology*, 45: 1983, 1313–1324.

29. Loretta LaRoche, "Laughter and Healing," presented to the Fourth National Conference on the Psychology of Health, Immunity, and Disease, and published by the National Institute for the Clinical Application of Behavioral Medicine.

30. Cathy Perlmutter, "Comic Relief," *Prevention*, March: 1988, 107.

31. Norman Cousins, *The Healing Heart* (New York: W. W. Norton and Company, 1983).

32. Deborah Burton Leiber, "Laughter and Humor in Critical Care," *Dimensions of Critical Care Nursing* 5(3): 1986, 163.

33. Perlmutter, pp. 106–107.

34. Jolene M. Simon, "Therapeutic Humor: Who's Following Who?" *Journal of Psychological Nursing*, 26(4): 1988, 11.

35. Klein, pp. 5–6.

36. Ornstein and Sobel, p. 216.

37. "Laughter—Can It Help Keep You Healthy?" *Mayo Clinic Health Letter*, March: 1993, 6.

38. Metcalf and Felible, pp. 11–12.

39. LaRoche.

40. From Norman Cousins, *Head First* (New York: E. P. Dutton, 1989), pp. 143–145.

41. Rita Robinson, "He Who Laughs . . . Lasts," *Vibrant Life*, September/October: 1989, 5.

42. Ornstein and Sobel, p. 218.

43. "Laughter and Immunity," *Advances*, 6(2): 5.

44. Bernie S. Siegel, *Love, Medicine and Miracles* (New York: Harper and Row Publishers, 1986).

45. Ornstein and Sobel, p. 219.

46. LaRoche, p. 331.

28

BEHAVIORAL MEDICINE TREATMENT: EFFECTS ON MEDICAL OUTCOMES AND COSTS

> *To a great extent, the very term* psychosomatic *has lost meaning. No longer can we talk about "psychosomatic illnesses," but we must acknowledge that most, if not all, disease is potentially influenced by psychosocial factors. Even dividing the body into systems—such as the immune system or the nervous system—has lost meaning as we observe the overlap and communication among systems.*
> *—STANFORD B. FRIEDMAN*
> *1988 PRESIDENTIAL ADDRESS TO THE AMERICAN PSYCHOSOMATIC SOCIETY*

Outcome research is a hot item these days. A top medical research priority is the proof of whether a treatment or preventive measure actually *changes* the ultimate outcome instead of merely changing some of the steps along the way. If you improve the outcome, you reduce the occurrence, cost, morbidity, or mortality of a disease—or, for that matter, you improve health in general.

In the past, mortality rates were the main focus of research. Today, researchers who seek to change the morbidity of a disease seek not only to reduce the symptoms and disability it causes, but also to improve the patient's quality of life. In other words, we're less likely to seek a powerful treatment that prolongs life, but that creates even more misery and disability for the patient at an even higher cost. A patient may opt for a treatment program that improves the quality of life over one that simply prolongs life. Ideally, of course, we seek an approach that does both.

Another past focus of medical research was on more easily measured intermediate effects that we presumed would be beneficial in the long run. For example, we knew high blood pressure was a coronary risk factor. Our goal, then, was to reduce blood pressure because we figured that would cut down the number of cardiac deaths. How could we accomplish the goal? Simple: higher doses of diuretics. After all, everyone knew higher doses of diuretics helped reduce blood pressure. And as long as we stayed focused on the intermediate effect—lowering blood pressure—everyone was happy.

Not for long. Once actual outcome studies started being performed, we realized that high-dose diuretics actually *cause more cardiac deaths* than untreated hypertension. Why? Probably because they cause blood chemistry problems that subsequently lead to irregular heart rhythm.

Outcome studies like the one cited above are sometimes real eye-openers. They readjust our focus from the intermediate goals to what *really* counts, and they dispel mistaken myths that seem like "common sense." At least that's the case with several behavioral medicine treatments that integrate the way a person thinks and feels with the way a person's body functions. These treatment plans are done as an adjunct to—not *in place of*—proven medical treatments and are directed primarily at two things:

- Creating mental skills that will lessen symptoms and disease processes.
- Melding the behaviors and attitudes that foster optimal health with the patient's own deepest values.

Saying that mental stress causes disease is a great oversimplification. However, if mental factors really play a role in the evolution of an illness, then interventions to remedy those factors should improve the outcome. Documenting whether a factor such as mental distress contributes to a disease process usually requires (1) showing that the disease is worse when the factor is present; (2) demonstrating that the factor worsens the pathophysiological processes that lead to the disease; and (3) proving that treatments (interventions) that reduce the factor also improve the disease outcome—resulting in less incidence, reduced mortality, and improved quality of life.

Of these factors, the last one—which shows that actively reducing the risk factor actually changes the outcome—is usually the most convincing and important.

To see how it works, let's use the example of coronary artery disease. Researchers suspected that a high-cholesterol diet contributed to coronary artery disease. Following the three steps listed above, here's what happened:

1. *Early studies showed that people eating a high-fat diet had a higher incidence of heart attacks and strokes.* That wasn't the only cause, however because people who eat high-fat diets may also have other undetected causes. One tongue-in-cheek researcher, in fact, responded by showing a correlation between wearing a pocket watch (as many of the elderly did at that time) and increased heart attacks.

2. *A high-fat diet was then shown to increase the process of cholesterol forming plaques on the walls of arteries. Those plaques narrowed both the coronary arteries and the arteries supplying blood to the brain, leading to the occlusions that caused myocardial and brain infarcts.* No—the dietary skeptics still persisted. Why? There were other pathological processes (such as blood vessel spasms and blood clotting) that didn't at first seem affected by fat intake.

3. *Active programs to lower dietary fat intake, which subsequently reduced blood cholesterol levels, were shown to reduce the incidence of cardiovascular events by about 12 percent (over 30 percent if cholesterol-lowering medications were added).* The outcome was modest, but it was finally the proof of the pudding—and it triggered major public education efforts to reduce blood cholesterol.

The history of demonstrating the role of mental states and attitudes in disease has followed a similar pattern—with even more profound results. First came the studies correlating mental distress (or loneliness or hopelessness) with higher incidences of various illnesses (as illustrated throughout this book). For example:

- Half or more of general medical outpatients have physical ailments related significantly to psychosocial factors; one in four have major psychiatric diagnoses, such as major depression or anxiety disorder, and almost that many have less severe psychiatric problems. Many additional patients feel excessively distressed or have high-risk behaviors.[1,2]
- Sixty percent of all medical visits are primarily for stress-related symptoms.[3]
- This percentage increases substantially for high users of health care (those who visit the physician often).
- One-third to one-half of hospitalized medical patients also have a psychiatric diagnosis.

Many bothersome medical symptoms, particularly if otherwise unexplained, are likely to be accompanied by underlying medical anxiety or depression:[4]

- Persisting fatigue (55 to 58 percent),[5]
- Insomnia (87 percent),
- Headaches (44 percent),
- Chest pain (28 percent),
- Shortness of breath (33 percent),
- Palpitations (40 percent),
- Constipation (46 percent),
- Diarrhea (29 percent),
- Fainting (47 percent),
- Numbness (28 percent),
- Menstrual problems (56 percent),
- Multiple allergies (62 percent),[6]
- Prolonged convalescence from viral infections, such as influenza,[7]
- Irritable bowel syndrome,[8]
- Premenstrual syndrome.[9]

Patients with combinations of such symptoms that cross over boundaries of different body systems are highly likely to have underlying anxiety, depression, or other mental distress.

These correlations still weren't proof that mental distress causes physical illness, however. Why? Because there were so many "fellow-traveler" risk factors involved. For example, anxious and depressed people often smoke more, eat a richer diet, drink more alcohol, and use illicit drugs. That's not all: Because most of the studies were "retrospective," they analyzed the patient after the illness appeared. Some argued, then, that the distress was caused by the illness—not the other way around. And because the field of mind-body connections was new, skeptics were abundant.

Next came many studies that correlated mental distress, or mental conditioning, to the pathophysiological processes that lead to disease. The three systems most affected by mental factors—the hormone, immune, and nervous systems—form the communicative networks that provide that "homeostatic" balance which in turn maintains good health. Ideally, when health is challenged, these systems allow just enough of a response to keep the challenge under control and to maintain well-being. But if emotional responses are too much (as with anxiety) or too little (as with some depression), the same thing happens with the body's responses—they're either too much or too little. Even the processes of vascular damage that cause heart attacks can partly be traced to disruptions in these three systems that are caused by emotional factors, such as hostility or depression (see Chapters 6 and 10).

Once again, the truly convincing evidence will come with outcome studies. For example, does a treatment program that reduces hostility or depression also reduce heart attacks, cardiac death, or the costs and disability associated with them?

Much effort is now being directed at these mental intervention issues, with interesting and often impressive results. Researchers have tried treatments that are behavioral, psychological, psychoeducational, and even psychopharmacological in nature, and then have measured medical and health outcomes. An example would be a program to create stress resilience; how are subsequent health outcomes and costs affected by participating in such a program? How does treating depression impact the physical diseases shown to be associated with it—and the pathophysiological processes that cause those diseases? Or what changes occur in the activity and prognosis of rheumatoid arthritis, as well as the patient's quality of life, following a psychoeducational program designed to help the patient manage the full impact of the disease?

Although behavioral medicine is still in its childhood, and such intervention studies are really just beginning, some highly interesting results are beginning to emerge. One fact that's becoming clear is that using traditional treatment for people with stress-related medical illness is costly, ineffective, and frustrating for everyone involved.

Behavioral medicine as a "specialty" probably began formally with the 1978 Yale conference called to form the Academy of Behavioral Medicine Research. *Specialty* is a tentative term because, by its very nature, behavioral medicine is just the opposite of specialties. Specialization in medicine has been of great value in creating greater expertise—by delving deeper and deeper into the function of a specific organ system. Behavioral medicine, on the other hand, reaches higher and higher to integrate all systems in an interdisciplinary way—bringing together the physical systems, the mind, and the spiritual issues that make up the whole person.

As you can see from the data provided in this book, those beginnings have been followed by a flood of research—some very solid, some too uncontrolled or involving too few patients to justify broad conclusions. Behavioral medicine attempts to determine what among that research is reliable enough to create new clinical methods for diagnosing, treating, and preventing many problems that, until now, have been somewhat perplexing. Although the field is still new, some very real possibilities are surfacing for changing our approach to patient care and disease prevention. One bottom line that may speak the loudest—and that may reflect overall benefits the most—is the effect on medical costs and the need to use health care services.

High-Volume Users of Medical Care and Resources

Overall, people who use more medical care and who have "multiple medical maladies" tend to have much more stress-related medical illness. They are also much more likely to have depression and anxiety disorders. Certain groups of medical problems are more likely to cluster in patients with mental or stress disorders, such as gastrointestinal problems, atypical chest pain, chronic pain, or fibromyalgia. For example, of all patients entering a gastroenterology clinic, one-third were depressed, one-third had panic disorder, and one-third had anxiety-related somatization disorder (obviously, some overlapped). Of those with irritable bowel syndrome, more than 90 percent will have a diagnosed anxiety or depression disorder at some time in their lives.

Another example is the high rate of multiple-system symptoms seen in patients with low back pain. Among those, anxious somatization is four to six times the usual rate in the population.[10]

Despite the fact that huge numbers of medical patients have stress and mental disorder problems, a large percentage go unrecognized and untreated. Only about one-fifth of those with diagnosable depression and anxiety disorders get help from mental health professionals. And despite considerable recent improvement, medical physicians—even those in primary care—usually only make such diagnoses about half the time.[11,12] The missed mental diagnosis is more understandable when you consider that most patients (and physicians) focus largely on the associated physical problems—and that most patients are reluctant to bring up mental issues, even if they are causing the most suffering. Even when accurately diagnosed, most patients are reluctant to "see a shrink"—and few physicians are taught the needed skills to deal well with "psychosomatic" problems. The result is a huge hole in our total health delivery system—leaving many patients untreated for the real underlying causes. They are likely to return repeatedly and chronically with more stress-related medical problems.

Medical Outpatients

With the above in mind, researchers in the Harvard Community Health Plan (a large Boston-area HMO-managed care program) decided to see if stress-reduc-

tion programs, which patients *do* tend to accept, would benefit high users and reduce health care needs and costs.[13] Patients who used health services more than
twice the average number of times were randomly assigned to one of three different stress-reduction programs available in the Harvard system:

1. An informational, "talk-only" group discussing the role of stress in illness and
   methods for managing stress (much like many of the older stress management classes).
2. An intervention centered around "mindfulness meditation"—experiencing
   deep relaxation and focused attention in the present moment, with daily
   practice.
3. An intervention combining cognitive and language restructuring (new ways
   of thinking about the stressor) with both relaxation and the mental experience of responding more effectively in areas of recurrent struggle.

The second and third programs were "experiential," using mental practice;
the first *talked* about such methods, but allowed no practice. The programs were
reasonably brief; patients attended a ninety-minute session each week for six
weeks.

Outcomes were measured by noting changes in physical and mental symptoms and by recording how often patients used health care over the subsequent
six months. The result? The "talk-only" group showed no change in any of the outcomes. The other two programs, on the other hand, significantly reduced both
symptoms and use. The combined intervention (number 3, above) doubled the
benefits of primary medication (number 2, above).

But does such an intervention just add more cost? Most behavioral medical
intervention programs are very low in cost, especially when done in groups. And,
interestingly, for the majority without severe mental issues, group participation
is usually even *more* effective than individual approaches. (Some of the reasons
why are addressed in Chapter 29.) People are usually much more ready to "learn
how to become stress resilient," for example, than they are to start individual psychotherapy—as valuable as that would likely be for them. For the Harvard treatment programs, health and quality of life benefits were only the beginning—overall cost savings were evident as well. The third intervention, above, reduced
medical utilization by four visits in six months. The estimated net cost savings for
the patients attending the two experiential programs averaged $6,900 per year
(after including the costs of the programs themselves). With ten such programs
offered each year, the Harvard Health Care Plan saw potential first-year savings
of $69,000; if the beneficial effects hold during subsequent years, there will be
compounded savings.

In another experiment, the Department of Behavioral Medicine at Hohf Clinic
and Hospital in Victoria, Texas, studied 235 hospitalized patients referred for
stress-related disorders.[14] Using a more intensive intervention that averaged
eleven full inpatient days, they analyzed the subsequent need for hospitalization
compared with that needed before the intervention. The intervention was some-

what tailored to individual patient needs and used techniques such as biofeedback training, self-management activities, and outpatient psychotherapy.

Researchers then compared the two years following the intervention to the five years before. Hospitalization dropped dramatically—from 22.8 days per year to only 7.3 days per year (a 68 percent reduction). And the 7.3-day average over two years *included* the eleven days of inpatient behavioral treatment program. The total calculated savings were more than $3 for each $1 invested in the intervention—as well as the improved well-being and reduced health risk of participants.

The Implications

The kinds of behavioral medicine interventions illustrated by the Harvard and Texas teams represent an effective but nontraditional approach to some of our most common and perplexing medical problems. Rather than simply trying to control physical symptoms with medications, patients are taught to quiet their over-arousal and to become aware of their thinking and bodily responses to typical stressful situations. They are then taught how to consciously recreate new, more healthy automatic responses that are in line with their reflective values about how they would most like to be in such situations.

The processes involved in such treatments empower patients, giving them a sense of personal control that allows them to react to stress as they would most want to respond. When the relationships between thoughts, values, and behaviors are thus experientially addressed, the physical health and economic benefits follow naturally.

Outcomes for Specific Medical Illnesses

Coronary Artery Disease

To prevent recurrences or cardiac death after a heart attack, patients and their physicians take many approaches to reducing risk factors. Some of the more common include reducing fats in the diet, treating high blood pressure, starting an exercise program, stopping smoking, using aspirin to reduce clotting, and taking various other medications. Each has shown benefit—but it now appears that none, with the possible exception of aspirin, matches the benefits of group behavioral programs designed to reduce stress and transform hostile and socially isolated behaviors into protective behaviors described earlier (see Chapter 6).

Among heart attack survivors, eight well-controlled studies have compared patients who received behavior modification as one of the prevention approaches with patients who did not. When behavior modification is added to the list of preventive approaches described above, there is a 39 percent decrease in recurrent heart attacks and a one-third reduction in cardiac death. Adding treatment of depression when appropriate improves the odds even more. (Standard preventive measures that *don't* include behavior modification result in an 8 to 20 percent

TABLE 28.1   **Secondary Coronary Prevention: Studies of Behavioral Medicine Interventions**

Study	N	Years of Follow-up	% Risk Reduction, Nonfatal MIs	% Risk Reduction, Cardiac Death
Friedman (1986–1987)	862	4.5	− 46	− 28
Frasure-Smith (1985)	453	1.0		− 50
Frasure-Smith (1989)	355	7.0	− 33	− 15
Ibrahim (1974)	105	1.5		− 3
Rahe (1979)	44	3.5	−100	−100
Patel (1985)	169	4.0	− 54	−100
Fielding (1979)	45	1.0	−100	
Horlick	116	0.5		+ 60
Stern (1983)	64	1.0	+149	
Weighted Risk Reduction			−39%	−33%

Source: M. W. Ketterer, "Secondary Prevention of Ischemic Heart Disease" *Psychosomatics* (1993) *34:* 478–484.

reduction range, except in certain cases, such as beta blocker and cholesterol-lowering medication.)

On the other hand, for people with high-risk psychobehavioral styles (such as cynical hostility and social alienation), a similar behavioral program might even effectively prevent the *first* heart attack. One controlled European study suggests exactly that. Of a group of middle-aged people with a high-risk personality profile, half were treated with a behavior modification program for several weeks, and the other half were not. Thirteen years later, *twice* as many of the people treated with behavior modification were still alive.[15]

There is some evidence as well that such behavioral interventions may also be the best we have for changing other risk factors, such as smoking or overeating. Is it possible that these kinds of behavioral interventions, coupled with the usual measures, could become our most important cardiac prevention?

Hypertension

Earlier chapters documented the association of mental stress and lack of social support with chronically elevated hormones that cause high blood pressure (catecholamines, aldosterone, vasopressin, and cortisol); with elevated blood pressure in anxious people who were being examined; and with development of hypertension. These associations have logically led many to try treating hypertension with stress management methods—including mostly biofeedback and relaxation techniques.

A review of twenty-five controlled trials including more than fourteen hundred total patients showed significant benefit in twelve of the studies—but not in the others.[16] That's not all: The benefits tended to be lost over time, with patients showing lower blood pressure three months after the intervention than a year later. A meta-analysis that also included some cognitive methods (to change thinking) also showed no benefit.[17]

Currently, stress management methods can't be fully endorsed for the treatment of high blood pressure per se. At the same time, the reason for treating high blood pressure is to prevent heart attacks, strokes, and kidney failure. So if cardiac outcomes are considered instead of simply blood pressure reduction, and if hostility reduction and improved social connectedness are added to the relaxation methods, the resulting prevention of heart attack may show stress management to be a wise treatment for hypertension patients anyway.

Noncardiac Chest Pain

Patients who have chest pain but normal coronary arteries on arteriograms have high rates of associated depression, anxiety disorders, and stress (as much as seven to nine times the normal incidence of depression and panic disorder). Spasm of the esophagus, coronary arteries, or chest wall muscles may be involved in creating the pain, but it is usually best managed when seen as a complex interaction between mind and body. More than half of new patients referred to cardiac clinics for chest pain fall in this group; many are simply reassured and discharged. Follow-up studies show that most patients continue to have the pain, have considerable anxiety about it, limit their activities because of it, and continue to use medical resources to reevaluate it.[18]

In a controlled study of thirty-one patients with resistant atypical chest pain, clinical psychologists at Oxford used a seven-session program that sensitively explained how "real" chest pain can be caused by stress factors. The program then used progressive muscle relaxation, breathing control, distraction, thought checking, and skills for responding differently to triggering cues.

The results were striking: Significant reductions were achieved not only for chest pain (down 49 percent, with one-third free of pain), but also other physical symptoms—reductions in dizziness (81 percent), breathlessness (56 percent), nausea (70 percent), and palpitations. Psychological benefits included reductions in diagnosable depression (69 percent), anxiety, and functional limitations (51 percent).[19]

The improvements continued to be fully maintained four to six months later. The treatment program was effective for patients both with and without diagnosable anxiety disorders. Pain medication was eliminated by all but one patient. Cost savings were not calculated, but with these degrees of improvements in patients who traditionally used high amounts of medical resources, the savings were probably substantial.

Arthritis

Kate Lorig at Stanford studied arthritis patients who were taught self-management skills by a trained lay person who also had arthritis,[20] a program that cost very little. Four hundred patients with both osteoarthritis and rheumatoid arthritis participated in the controlled study, holding six two-hour sessions to learn how to have more self-efficacy—that is, increase their sense of control and capability despite the arthritis.

The study showed that improved self-efficacy could indeed be learned. Among the patients:

- Quality of life improved substantially.
- Pain was reduced by 20 percent.
- There was an actual decrease in disease activity—there was less inflammation and fewer swollen joints.
- Medical office visits were reduced by 43 percent.
- Costs over a four-year period were reduced an average of $648 for each rheumatoid arthritis patient and $189 for each osteoarthritis patient.

Chronic Obstructive Pulmonary Disease

People with asthma, chronic bronchitis, emphysema, and trouble breathing are frequently anxious—understandably so—and the anxiety compounds the airway spasm, making symptoms worse. In one study, only 39 percent of medical outpatients complaining of shortness of breath were able to get relief with medications.[21] And medications that relax the bronchial passages are often dangerous in the face of serious lung disease. It would seem, then, that learning mentally to relax—especially to relax the airways, which it now appears possible to learn— could potentially provide great relief and possibly improved breathing.

Well-controlled treatment studies in this area have been few and have usually involved only small numbers of patients, despite active, national breathing-education programs. In one very economical approach, patients learned progressive muscle relaxation from a recorded audiotape in four weekly sessions; they then practiced at home daily with the tape. Relaxation effectiveness was measured by Bensen's criteria.[22]

Compared with controls who just sat quietly for twenty minutes, this simple intervention achieved significant reductions in anxiety (29 percent), subjective feelings of shortness of breath (62 percent), and a mildly improved peak expiratory flow rate, one way of measuring the ease of air flow (it was improved by 6 percent in those who listened to the tape, worsened by 7 percent in the controls).[23] There was no long-term follow-up, but the taped intervention could presumably be continued at home indefinitely. Patients with asthma would likely have better improvements in measurable airway flow from relaxation than would those with emphysema.[24]

Menopausal Symptoms

The discomforts of going through menopause are almost universal—and, although not always dangerous (unless depression sets in), can be very uncomfortable and disruptive. Estrogen replacement therapy is often helpful, but what about women who can't take estrogen?

One study described a program of simple relaxation methods using deep, quieting breathing and mindfulness during eight one-hour training sessions. The relaxation significantly relieved hot flashes, night sweats, disturbed sleep, and distressed emotions.[25]

This simple approach illustrates an interesting characteristic about behavioral medicine approaches that are different (and perhaps easier for physicians to understand) from many other psychological therapies. They involve specific techniques that can, if desired, be directed at changing:

- Unwanted symptoms, such as insomnia
- Unwanted, observable behaviors, such as outbursts of anger or cigarette smoking in response to stress
- Physiological reactions, such as hot flashes, in much the way medication might be used

Results are often observable and measurable. In these regards, behavioral medicine is much closer to traditional medical approaches than are most other psychological interventions. These techniques can also often create a relaxed, disengaged state in which the patient is able to more clearly see the real solution to underlying distress and to more effectively "reprogram" habit responses.

Chronic Insomnia

One-third of the population has sleep problems. Sleep deprivation causes:

- A significant increase in accidents;
- Loss of social and performance function;
- Significant health problems;
- Worsened pain;
- Decreased immune function;
- Reduced autonomic nervous system regulation;
- Heightened depression or anxiety (people with chronic insomnia have forty times the normal risk for developing depression, suggesting a neurochemical link between the two); and
- Reduced longevity.

If treatable depression, anxiety, or medical disorders are absent as a cause of the insomnia, treatment with medication alone has not been optimal because medication has the tendency to lose effectiveness after a month or so. Older sleeping pills can also adversely affect the parts of sleep that are most restorative for the body, often causing some fatigue the next day. And most persisting sleeplessness has a strong conditioned component to it: The brain learns that going to bed is associated with struggling to try to sleep, getting frustrated and anxious about the next day's consequences, and being aroused by "trying" to go to sleep. After that happens for a while, just approaching the bed elicits that aroused response. Simply, it's a self-fulfilling prophecy.

A number of behavioral treatment approaches have been developed specifically to address the particular components of sleep that are disturbed. For example, progressive relaxation before bedtime improves deep sleep, whereas stimulus control can be more useful for initially getting to sleep. Short-term medication—particularly the kind that doesn't interfere with deep or dreaming sleep—can help recondition the expectation of what happens when a person climbs into bed; over the long term, behavioral treatments are superior to medication. When both are combined, the health improvement can be substantial.[26]

Cancer

Few areas of medicine have been met with as much emotion and controversy as that of considering behavioral interventions for cancer patients. Although few would argue that people diagnosed with cancer need psychological support, numerous claims that support improved medical prognosis have been met with skepticism.

Stanford's David Spiegel was such a skeptic, but he *did* believe that a group program that created an opportunity for personal expression, comfort, and loving support and that helped women find meaning and healing in their lives would be of value to women with metastatic breast cancer—regardless of the effects on the cancer itself. He set out a well-designed and controlled study to determine the outcome of such a humanistic program. The results surprised him: The women who received the support lived almost twice as long as those without the program.[27]

Part of the reason why such improved outcome could happen among the support group might be explained by improved immunity. Improved immune effects were observed in a similar study involving malignant melanoma patients: After only six weeks of participation in the program, patients showed increases in lymphocytes and natural killer cell activity, which aid in suppressing cancer.[28] The program—which included stress management, relaxation techniques, enhancement of problem-solving skills, and psychological support—created significantly lower levels of distress and greater use of positive coping skills among group members that were even more pronounced six months later.

Cost and Medical Care Utilization Issues

Surgical Patients

Having surgery can be frightening. Much research has developed around how to best deal with that—and what happens to surgical outcomes when you do.

One meta-analysis combined the findings of 191 controlled studies regarding interventions for surgery patients.[29] The interventions included giving patients information, teaching postoperative skills, and providing psychological support—all aimed at giving the patient some sense of control and reassurance for a positive expectation. The average training took only thirty minutes and was usually provided by a registered nurse who used audiovisual aids.

The result? Although the move to outpatient, same-day surgery has limited the practicality of providing these kinds of preparations, they apparently provide significant benefit. In the analysis, 80 percent of the patients had:

- Faster recovery;
- Shorter hospital stay (an average of 1.5 days less time in the hospital);
- Fewer surgical or medical complications;
- Better breathing function;
- Significantly reduced pain, requiring less pain and sedative medication; and
- Relieved psychological distress.

Other studies looked at semihypnotic suggestions during the time anesthesia was administered—a time when the unconscious mind is more receptive. Practitioners suggested to patients, for example, that pain would be minimal, that bowel function would return fairly quickly, or that healing would proceed well. These studies showed beneficial results similar to those listed above.[30] Some of the studies appear to confirm that such suggestion can be subconsciously incorporated even during deep anesthesia, leading to a conditioned automatic response after surgery. Likewise, inadvertent negative remarks made in passing while a patient is anesthetized may also be internalized.

Even the asthetics of the setting—such as color, light, and scenery—after surgery can play an important role in outcome and recovery rates. One study compared surgery patients who recover in a room with a nature view to matched patients who recover in a room with a view of a brick wall. The average patient with a nature view required less pain medication, had less postoperative distress, and left the hospital one day earlier than those who gazed at the brick wall.[31] If that sounds strange, try staring at a dull brick wall for a while then compare that with the feelings you have when you look at trees or meadows. Maybe the "healing" influence isn't so strange after all.

Labor and Delivery

Like surgery, childbirth can be bewildering and frightening. In Latin American countries, anxiety is often effectively handled through help of a *doula*—a gentle woman experienced in childbirth who informs the mother-to-be about what to expect, holds her hand, and provides caring reassurance.

When Latin American physicians and patients anecdotally observed that mothers with a doula seemed to have better birth outcomes, a group in Texas decided to run a controlled study.[32] They randomly assigned 600 first-time mothers in labor to one of three groups: one with a doula, one with an uninvolved observer in the room, and one with usual care (a nurse who periodically came into the room to check monitoring and respond to questions). The cost of having a doula in the room was less than $200. The results, shown in Table 28.2,

TABLE 28.2   Doula Support Compared with Usual Care (Control) among First-Time Mothers

	Control	Support
Caesarean section rates (reduced 56%)	18%	8%
Duration of labor (reduced 25%)	9.4 hours	7.4 hours
Epidural anesthesia (reduced 85%)	55%	8%
Oxytocin to increase labor (reduced 61%)	44%	17%
Forceps delivery (reduced 70%)	26%	8%
Baby hospitalized more than 48 hours (reduced 58%)	24%	10%

were striking. (The group simply observed by a person in the room showed about half the improvement as the group with active support.)

Dr. David Sobel, an internist who analyzes such outcome studies for the Kaiser-Permanente health plans in California, has observed that if we had a perfectly safe pill or device that would result in such reduced obstetrical complications, every woman delivering a baby would likely be using it. Reduced complications weren't the only benefit, either—large overall savings were projected from reductions in operating room time, hospital time, medications, and nursing staff time.

Hip Fracture in the Elderly

Hip fracture can have surprisingly devastating effects on an elderly person's life, and the costs of surgical repair are substantial. James J. Strain and his colleagues wondered what effect psychological consultation might have, not only on disability, but on treatment outcomes and costs. They studied 452 patients admitted for surgical repair of fractured hips at two different hospitals in New York and Chicago. The patients were screened for psychological needs; if clearly indicated, they were referred for psychological care.[33]

Sixty percent of the patients in the study had a significant psychological diagnosis. Psychological consultations increased from 5 percent before the screening to 70 percent after the screening, suggesting that psychological needs may have been significantly overlooked during usual care.

Medical costs were affected by the referral in the following ways:

- Hospital stays were reduced by 1.7 to 2.2 days.
- The interventions cost $40,000, and costs were cut by $270,000.
- There was little difference in hip healing characteristics or location of placement after discharge.

These results confirm the findings of Levitan and Kornfield, who studied general orthopedic patients. They found that introduction of psychiatric care reduced the length of hospital stay by 29 percent, saving five times the cost of the psychological interventions.[34]

Overall Medical Cost Reduction

When added to medical care, psychologic and behavioral interventions generally improve the patient's quality of life and often result in measurable medical benefits. But that's not all: The cost of such interventions is usually low compared with the often-substantial savings in medical costs and resources. A number of other examples confirm that finding. In one, for example, a Harvard study of 109 chronic pain patients—often a costly and frustrating group—found that adding behavioral medicine approaches produced savings of $35,000 over two years, including the cost of the intervention.[35]

Emily Mumford and her colleagues provided a much more global summary of the cost issues in two large-scale analyses. In the first, Mumford and her colleagues analyzed fifty-eight controlled studies of medical and surgical patients that compared results when mental issues were addressed with results when they were not. In the second, the insurance files of 32,450 federal employees' families were studied; researchers looked for changes in medical costs among patients who received outpatient (but not inpatient) mental health services.[36]

The savings were quite remarkable, and the major savings came with reduced hospitalization. Analysis of the fifty-eight studies showed that attention to mental health resulted in a 73.4 percent reduction in inpatient costs and a 22.6 percent reduction in outpatient costs—especially impressive when it's noted that only one of the fifty-eight studies was an exception to that pattern. Researchers also noted that despite a higher need for psychological support among the elderly, they were not psychologically treated as often as were younger people.

In studying insurance files for federal employee families, researchers calculated the change in medical utilization before mental health treatment to the costs after treatment and compared the same trends in patients who did not receive mental interventions. Before mental treatment, those needing it had medical costs substantially higher (50 percent) than those not needing mental treatment. After mental treatment, the costs fell substantially *below* the inflation rate for the four-year period of the study. The costs for those not treated rose well above the inflation rate.

At the end of the four years, the costs for the two groups nearly equalized. That is, the high utilizers who were given mental treatment were no longer high utilizers. Again, the major savings came with less hospitalization, implying less-severe medical illness after mental treatment. The medical savings roughly equaled the cost of twenty mental health visits,[37] though seldom are that many used today. Older people showed greater savings after mental health treatment than did younger people.

When considering costs, group behavioral medicine programs are usually considerably lower than those of individual therapy. Costs may not be the only benefit, either: Groups generally provide more interactive time and feeling of support. And because of their experiential nature, groups can be even faster in changing behavioral responses for people who are stressed but who do not have severe psychological issues.

Another area with great potential—but beyond the scope of this book—is the use of antidepressant medications in the treatment of stress-related medical illnesses that do not meet full criteria for depression. As shown in Table 28.3, studies have shown such a treatment to be of demonstrated benefit.

Much of the psychological dysregulation we have explored in this book is caused by changes in the midbrain chemistry that also underlies depression and anxiety disorders. Consider the analogy of a computer: Behavioral and psychotherapy approaches are like reprogramming computer software to elicit a new response. But if the computer hardware isn't working well, the software changes don't work well, either—and, in some cases, are impossible to create. Antidepressants aren't just symptom-relieving pills that cover up learned responses; instead, they work by correcting the underlying brain dysfunction (the "hardware"), which then allows for much more effective "software reprogramming." Once the brain has done well for a period of time, often with temporary medication, nonpharmacological approaches work to keep it that way much better than they do to get it functioning well in the first place.

Curiously, when treatment is discussed—even among many who are interested in mind and body integration—there still tends to be the old division between the "mind people" (who favor treatments like psychotherapy) and the "body people" (who favor treatments like medication). Rather than having to choose *either* mind or body approaches, it's likely that the best solutions will come from well-timed integration of both.

The "bottom line" suggested by most of the studies is that some of our best possibilities for reducing health care costs, while substantially improving quality at the same time, may lie in conscious and organized attention to the mental aspects of medical illness.[72]

Filling the Hole in the Health Delivery System

Earlier in this chapter we noted the large number of general medical patients— more than half—who have documentable stress-related medical problems. We also noted the small percentages of those patients who are actually being accurately diagnosed and treated. That leaves a big hole in the health care delivery system: A lot of people don't feel well, and they don't know how to get help.

One solution may lie in providing low-cost group behavioral medicine and psychoeducational intervention programs—a solution that is patient-friendly, well-received, and usually even enjoyable. Perhaps more practical in day-to-day clinical life, these methods can also be learned individually. And perhaps the approaches that integrate mind and body will be even more effective—especially in the long run—than some of the traditional ways we have approached these perplexing problems.

TABLE 28.3 The Use of Antidepressant Medications for Medical Disorders Other Than Pure Depression

Of Demonstrated Benefit	Of Probable Benefit
Chronic pain disorders[38]	Medical illnesses to which stress contributes substantially[68]
• Myofascial pain disorder[39]	• Some asthma
• Fibromyalgia[40]	• Multiple allergies[69]
• Migraine and tension headaches[41]	
• Some types of arthritis[42]	
• Trigeminal neuralgia	
• Diabetic neuropathy[43]	
• Herpes zoster neuralgia[44]	
• Idiopathic pelvic pain[45]	
• Temporomandibular joint syndrome[46]	
• Chronic facial pain[47]	
• Back pain[48]	
Other psychiatric disorders[49]	Other endorphin deficiency states
• Panic disorder[50]	
• Anorexia nervosa and bulimia[51]	
• Obsessive compulsive disorder[52]	
• Addiction and alcoholism control[53]	
• Pseudodementia of the elderly[54]	
• Appetite/weight loss of the elderly[55]	
• Hypochondriasis[56]	
• Post-traumatic stress disorder[57]	
• Attention deficit disorder[58]	
• Personality disorders[59]	
Dementia[60]	Somatization disorder (particularly in the elderly)[70]
Chronic fatigue syndrome[61]	HIV dementia[71]
Premenstrual syndrome[62]	
Irritable bowel syndrome[63]	
Sleep disorders (including apnea)[64]	
Urinary incontinence[65]	
Peptic ulcer[66]	
Recurrent hives, dermatitis, eczema, pruritis[67]	

Notes

1. J. D. Stoeckle, I. K. Zola, and G. Davidson, "The Quantity and Significance of Psychological Distress in Medical Outpatients," *Journal of Chronic Disease,* 1964, 959–970; and R. A. Crum, L. Cooper-Patrick, and D. E. Ford, "Depressive Symptoms Among General Medical Patients: Prevalence and One-Year Outcome," *Psychosomatic Medicine* 56: 1994, 109–117.

2. H. C. Shulberg and B. J. Burns, "Mental Disorders in Primary Care: Epidemiologic, Diagnostic, and Treatment Research Directions," *General Hospital Psychiatry,* 10: 1985, 79–87.

3. N. A. Cummings and G. R. VandenBos, "The Twenty-year Kaiser-Permanente Experience with Psychotherapy and Medical Utilization: Implications for National Health Policy and National Health Insurance," *Health Policy Quarterly,* 1: 1981, 159–175.

4. K. Kroenke and R. K. Price, "Symptoms in the Community: Prevalence, Classification, and Psychiatric Comorbidity," *Archives of Internal Medicine,* 153: 1993, 2474–2480.

5. D. W. Bates, et al., "Prevalence of Fatigue and Chronic Fatigue Syndrome in a Primary Care Practice," *Archives of Internal Medicine,* 153: 1993, 2759–2765.

6. Terr, *Archives of Internal Medicine,* 146: 1986, 145–149.

7. J. B. Imboden, *Archives of Internal Medicine,* 108: 1961, 393ff.

8. R. B. Lydiard, M. D. Fossey, W. Marsh, and J. C. Ballenger, "Prevalence of Psychiatric Disorders in Patients with Irritable Bowel Syndrome," *Psychosomatics,* 34: 1993, 229–234.

9. J. Bancroft, D. Rennie, and P. Warner, "Vulnerability to Perimenstrual Mood Change: The Relevance of a Past History of Depressive Disorder," *Psychosomatic Medicine,* 56: 1994, 225–231.

10. M. K. Bacon, S. F. Bacon, J. H. Atkinson, et al., "Somatization Symptoms in Chronic Low Back Pain Patients," *Psychosomatic Medicine,* 56: 1994, 118–127.

11. P. Freeling, B. M. Rao, E. S. Paykel, L. I. Sireling, and R. H. Burton, "Unrecognized Depression in General Practice," *British Medical Journal,* 290: 1985, 1880–1883.

12. S. J. Anderson and B. H. Harthorn, "The Recognition, Diagnosis, and Treatment of Mental Disorders by Primary Care Physicians," *Medical Care,* 27: 1989, 869–886.

13. C. J. C. Hellman, M. Budd, J. Borysenko, D. C. McClelland, and H. Benson, "A Study of the Effectiveness of Two Group Behavioral Medicine Interventions for Patients with Psychosomatic Complaints," *Behavioral Medicine,* 16: 1990, 165–173.

14. U. L. Gonik, et al., "Cost Effectiveness of Behavioral Medicine Procedures in the Treatment of Stress-Related Disorders," *Journal of Clinical Biofeedback,* 4: 1981, 16–24.

15. H. J. Eysenck, "Health's Character," *Psychology Today,* December: 1988, 28–32.

16. D. W. Johnson, "The Behavioral Control of High Blood Pressure," *Current Psychological Research Review,* 6: 1987, 99–114.

17. D. M. Eisenberg, T. L. Delbanco, C. S. Berkeley, et al., "Cognitive Behavioral Techniques for Hypertension: Are They Effective?" *Annals of Internal Medicine,* 118: 1993, 964–972.

18. L. J. Lantinga, R. P. Sprafkin, J. H. McCroskery, et al., "One-Year Psychosocial Follow-up of Patients with Chest Pain and Angiographically Normal Coronary Arteries," *American Journal of Cardiology,* 62: 1988, 209–213; R. A. Mayou, "Invited Review: Atypical Chest Pain," *Journal of Psychosomatic Research,* 33: 1989, 393–406; and R. C. Pasrenak, G. E. Thibault, et al., "Chest Pain with Angiographically Insignificant Coronary Arterial Obstruction," *American Journal of Medicine,* 68: 1980, 813–817.

19. I. Klimes, R. A. Mayou, M. J. Pearce, L. Coles, and J. R. Fagg, "Psychological Treatment for Atypical Non-Cardiac Chest Pain: A Controlled Evaluation," *Psychological Medicine,* 20: 1990, 605–611.

20. K. Lorig, et al., "Outcomes of Self-Help Education for Patients with Arthritis," *Arthritis and Rheumatism,* 28: 1985, 680–685.

21. K. Kroenke, M. E. Arrington, and A. D. Manglesdorf, "The Prevalence of Symptoms in Medical Outpatients and the Adequacy of Treatment," *Archives of Internal Medicine,* 150: 1990, 1685–1689.

22. Criteria for obtaining relaxation include: ≠ skin temperature 2 degrees F; ∅ heart rate 3 beats/minute; ∅ respiratory rate 3/minute. H. Benson, J. F. Beary, and M. P. Carol, "The Relaxation Response," *Psychiatry*, 37: 1974, 37–45.

23. A. G. Gift, T. Moore, and K. Soeken, "Relaxation to Reduce Dyspnea and Anxiety in COPD Patients," *Nursing Research*, 41: 1992, 242–246.

24. P. D. Freedberg, L. A. Hoffman, W. C. Light, and M. K. Kreps, "Effect of Progressive Muscle Relaxation on the Objective Symptoms and Subjective Responses Associated with Asthma," *Heart and Lung*, 16: 1987, 24–30.

25. R. R. Freedman, *American Journal of Obstetrics and Gynecology*, 167: 1992, 436–439.

26. C. Morin, *Sleep Research*, 22: 1993, Abstract 21.

27. D. Spiegel, H. C. Kraemer, J. R. Bloom, and E. Gottheil, "Effect of Psychosocial Treatment on Survival of Patients with Metastatic Breast Cancer," *Lancet*, 2: 1989, 888–891.

28. I. F. Fawzy, "A Structured Psychiatric Intervention for Cancer Patients: Changes Over Time with Methods of Coping and Affective Disturbance and in Immunological Parameters," *General Hospital Psychiatry*, 13: 1991, 361–362.

29. E. C. Devine, "Effects of Psychoeducational Care for Adult Surgical Patients: A Meta-analysis of 191 Studies," *Patient Education and Counseling*, 19: 1992, 129–142.

30. R. P. Blankfield, "Suggestion, Relaxation, and Hypnosis as Adjuncts in the Care of Surgery Patients: A Review of the Literature," *American Journal of Hypnosis*, 33: 1991, 172–186.

31. R. Ulrich, "View Through a Window May Influence Recovery from Surgery," *Science*, 224: 1984, 420–421.

32. J. Kennell, et al., "Continuous Emotional Support During Labor in a U. S. Hospital: A Randomized Controlled Trial," *Journal of the American Medical Association*, 265: 1991, 2197–2201.

33. James J. Strain, J. S. Lyons, et al., "Cost Offset from a Psychiatric Consultation Liaison Intervention with Elderly Hip Fracture Patients," *American Journal of Psychiatry*, 148: 1991, 1044–1049.

34. S. J. Levitan and D. S. Kornfield, "Clinical and Cost Benefits From Liaison Psychiatry," *American Journal of Psychiatry*, 138: 1981, 790–793.

35. M. Caudill, R. Schnable, P. Zuttermeister, H. Benson, and R. Friedman, "Decreased Clinic Use by Chronic Pain Patients: Response to a Behavioral Medicine Intervention," *The Clinical Journal of Pain*, 7: 1991, 305–310.

36. E. Mumford, H. J. Schlesinger, G. V. Glass, C. Patrick, and T. Cuerdon, "A New Look at Evidence About Reduced Cost of Medical Utilization Following Mental Health Treatment," *American Journal of Psychiatry*, 141: 1984, 1145–1158.

37. H. J. Schlesinger et al., "Mental Health Treatment and Medical Care Utilization in a Fee-For-Service System: Outpatient Mental Health Treatment Following the Onset of a Chronic Disease," *American Journal of Public Health*, 73: 1983, 422–429.

38. I. G. Egbunike and B. J. Chaffee, "Antidepressants in the Management of Chronic Pain Syndromes." *Pharmacotherapy*, 10(4): 1990, 262–270; K. R. Krishman and R. D. France, "Antidepressants in Chronic Pain Syndromes." *American Family Physician*, 39(4): 1989, 233–237; M. Valdes et al., "Psychogenic Pain and Depressive Disorders: An Empirical Study." *Journal of Affective Disorders*, 16(1): 1989, 21–25; R. D. France, "The Future for Antidepressants: Treatment of Pain," *Psychopathology*, 20(suppl 1): 1987, 99–113; Z. S. Herman, "Enkephalins and the Action of Psychotropic Drugs," *Pol. Journal of Pharmacol. Pharm.*, 39(5): 1987, 633–639.

39. D. L. Goldenberg, "Diagnostic and Therapeutic Challenges of Fibromyalgia," *Hospital Practice*, 24(9 A): 1989, 39–52.

40. D. H. Finestone and S. K. Ober, "Fluoxetine and Fibromyalgia," *JAMA* 264(22): 1990, 2869–2870.

41. A. Bonazzi, "Fluoxetine versus Amitriptyline in the Prophylaxis of Tension Type Headache," *Cephalgia*, 11(suppl. 11): 1991, 341–342; S. Diamond and F. G. Freitag, "The Use of Fluoxetine in the Treatment of Headache." *Clinical Journal of Pain*, 5(2): 1989, 200–201; H. G. Markley et al., "Fluoxetine in Prophylaxis of Headache. Clinical Experience." *Cephalgia*, 11(suppl. 11): 1991, 164–165; G. Sandrini et al: Antalgic and antidepressant activities of fluoxetine in daily chronic headache. *Cephalgia* 11 (suppl. 11): 1991, 280–281; P. J. Orsulak and D. Waller, "Antidepressant Drugs: Additional Clinical Uses." *Journal of Family Practice*, 28(2), 1989, 209–216.

42. M. Gringas, *Journal of Internal Medical Research*, 4 (Suppl 2): 41; M. Scott, *Practitioner* 202: 802; K. R. Krishman and R. D. France, "Antidepressants in Chronic Pain Syndromes." *American Family Physician*, 39(4): 1989, 233–237; R. D. France, "The Future for Antidepressants: Treatment of Pain," *Psychopathology* 20(suppl 1): 1987, 99–113.

43. M. B. Max, R. Kishore-Kumar, et al., "Efficacy of Desipramine in Painful Diabetic Neuropathy: A Placebo-Controlled Trial," *Pain*, 45(1): 1991, 69, Discussion 1–3; K. A. Theesen and W. R. Marsh, "Relief of Diabetic Neuropathy with Fluoxetine," *DICP*, 23(7–8): 1989, 572–574; K. R. Krishman and R. D. France, "Antidepressants in Chronic Pain Syndromes," *American Family Physician*, 39(4): 1989, 233–237; R. D. France, "The Future for Antidepressants: Treatment of Pain," *Psychopathology*, 20(suppl 1): 1987, 99–113.

44. F. A. Bucci Jr. and R. A. Schwartz, "Neurologic Complications at Herpes Zoster." *American Family Physician*, 37(3): 1988, 185–192.

45. M. B. Hahn et al., "Idiopathic Pelvic Pain," *Postgraduate Medicine*, 85(4): 1989, 263–266, 268, 270.

46. M. Harris, "Medical versus Surgical Treatment of Temperomandibular Joint Pain and Dysfunction," *British Journal of Oral Maxillofac. Surgery*, 25(2): 1987, 113–120.

47. K. R. Krishman and R. D. France, "Antidepressants in Chronic Pain Syndromes," *American Family Physician*, 39(4): 1989, 233–237.

48. R. D. France, "The Future for Antidepressants: Treatment of Pain," *Psychopathology*, 20(suppl 1): 1987, 99–113.

49. R. J. Baldasserini, "Current Status of Antidepressants: Clinical Pharmacology," *Journal of Clinical Psychiatry*, 50(4): 1989, 117–126.

50. J. M. Gorman, M. R. Liebowitz, A. J. Fyer, et al., "An Open Trial of Fluoxetine in the Treatment of Panic Attacks," *Journal of Clinical Psychopharmacology*, 7(5): 1987, 329–332.; K. Brady, M. Zarzar, R. B. Lydiard, "Fluoxetine in Panic Disorder Patients with Imipramine-Associated Weight Gain." *Psychopharmacology*, 9(1): 1989, 66–67; F. R. Scheiner, M. R. Liebowitz, S. O. Davies, et al., "Fluoxetine in Panic Disorder," *Journal of Clinical Psychopharmacology*, 10(2): 1990, 119–121; P. J. Orsulak and D. Waller, "Antidepressant Drugs: Additional Clinical Uses," *Journal Family Practice*, 28(2): 1989, 209–216; L.

Solyom, C. Solyom, B. Ledwidge, "Fluoxetine in Panic Disorder," *Can. Journal Psychiatry*, 36(5): 1991, 378–380.

51. H. G. Pope, Jr. et al., "Bulimia Treated with Imipramine," *American Journal of Psychiatry*, 140: 1983, 554–558; R. G. Granet, "Fluoxetine Treatment of Obsessive Compulsive Disorder," *Journal of Clinical Psychiatry*, 50(11): 1989, 436; H. E. Gwirtsman, B. H. Guze, J. Yager, B. Gainsley, "Fluoxetine Treatment of Anorexia Nervosa: An Open Clinical Trial," *Journal of Clinical Psychiatry*, 51(9): 1990, 378–382; D. B. Herzog, A. W. Brotman, I. S. Bradburn, "Treating Eating Disorders with Antidepressants," *Australian Pediatric Journal*, 24(3): 1988, 169–170; S. H. Kennedy, D. S. Goldbloom, "Current Perspectives on Drug Therapies for Anorexia Nervosa and Bulimia Nervosa," *Drugs*, 41(3): 1991, 367–377; M. R. Trimble, "Worldwide Use of Clomipramine," *Journal of Clinical Psychiatry*, 51(suppl. 8): 1990, 51–54; P. L. Hughs et al., "Treating bulimia with desipramine," *Archives of General Psychiatry*, 43: 1986, 182–186; C. P. L. Freeman and M. Hampson, "Fluoxetine as a Treatment for Bulimia Nervosa," *Internal Journal of Obstetrics*, 11(suppl 3): 1987, 171–177; M. Fava, D. B. Herzog, P. Hamburg, et al., "Long-Term Use of Fluoxetine in Bulimia Nervosa: A Retrospective Study," *Annuals of Clinical Psychiatry*, 2(1): 1990, 53–56; L. Solyom, C. Solyom, B. Ledwidge, "The Fluoxetine Treatment of Low-Weight, Chronic Bulimia Nervosa," *Journal of Psychopharmacology.*, 10: 1990, 421–425.

52. P. J. Orsulak and D. Waller, "Antidepressant Drugs: Additional Clinical Uses," *Journal of Family Practice*, 28(2): 1989, 209–216.

53. C. A. Naranjo, K. E. Kadlec, P. Sanhueza, D. Woodley-Remus, E. M. Sellers, (Clinical Pharmacology Program, Addiction Research Foundation Clinical Institute, 33 Tussel St., Toronto, Ont. M5S 2S1 Canada), "Fluoxetine Differentially Alters Alcohol Intake and Other Consummatory Behaviors in Problem Drinkers," *Clinical Pharmacology Therapy*, 47(4): 1990, 490–498; D. A. Gorelick, "Serotonin Up Take Blockers and the Treatment of Alcoholism," *Recent Developments in Alcoholism*, 7: 1989, 267–281; J. Rosecan, *World Congress of Psychiatry, 1983*.

54. J. T. Moore, "The New Antidepressants," in R. Ham, (Ed), *Geriatric Medicine Annual 1986*, pp. 3–23

55. J. Talley, "Geriatric Depression: Avoiding the Pitfalls of Primary Care," *Geriatrics,* 42(4): 1987, 53–60, 65–66.

56. D. V. Sheehan, J. Ballenger, G. Jacobsen, "Treatment of Endogenous Anxiety with Phobic, Hysterical and Hypochondriacal Symptoms," *Archives of General Psychiatry,* 37: 1980, 51–59; N. Fernando, "Monosymptomatic Hypochondriasis Treated with a Tricyclic Antidepressant," *British Journal of Psychiatry,* 152: 1988, 851–852.

57. C. J. McDougle, S. M. Southwick, D. S. Charney, R. L. St. James, "An Open Trial of Fluoxetine in the Treatment of Posttraumatic Stress Disorder," *Journal of Clinical Psychopharmacology,* 11(5): 1991, 325–327; J. Davidson, S. Roth, E. Newman, "Fluoxetine in Post-Traumatic Stress Disorder." *Journal of Traumatic Stress,* 4(3): 1991, 419–423.

58. P. J. Orsulak and D. Waller, "Antidepressant Drugs: Additional Clinical Uses." *Journal of Family Practice,* 28(2): 1989, 209–216.

59. M. J. Norden, "Fluoxetine in Borderline Personality Disorder," *Progress in Neuro–Psychopharmacology & Biological Psychiatry,* 13(6): 1989, 885–893; J. R. Cornelius, P. H. Soloff, J. M. Prel, R. F. Ulrich, "A Preliminary Trial of Fluoxetine in Refractory Borderline Patients," *Journal of Clinical Psychopharmacolgy,* 11(2): 1991, 116–120.

60. W. M. McDonald et al., "Pharmacological Management of the Symptoms of Dementia," *American Family Physician,* 42(1): 1990, 123–132.

61. M. Sharpe, (Department of Psychiatry, Oxford University, Oxford United Kingdom), "Psychiatric Management of Post Viral Fatigue Syndrome," *British Medical Bulletin,* 47(4): 1991, 989–1005; D. A. Matthews, P. Manu, T. J. Lane, (Division of General Medicine, University of Connecticut Health Center, Farmington, CT 06030), "Evaluation and Management of Patients with Chronic Fatigue." *American Journal of Medical Science,* 302(5): 1991, 269–277; P. J. Goodnick, "Bupropion in Chronic Fatigue Syndrome," *American Journal of Psychiatry,* 147(8): 1990, 1091.

62. R. Rickles, E. W. Freeman, S. Sondheimer, et al., "Fluoxetine in the Treatment of Premenstrual Syndrome," *Current Theory Research,* 48(1): 1990, 161–166; A. B. Stone, T. B. Pearlstein, W. A. Brown, "Fluoxetine in the Treatment of Late Luteal Phase Dysphoric Disorder," *Journal of Clinical Psychiatry,* 52(7): 1991, 290–293.

63. D. S. Greenbaum, J. E. Mayle, et al., "Effects of Desipramine on Irritable Bowel Syndrome Compared with Atropine and Placebo," *Digest of Disease Sciences,* 32(3): 1987, 257–266; J. I. Hudson and H. G. Pope, Jr., "Affective Spectrum Disorder: Does Antidepressant Response Identify a Family of Disorders with a Common Pathophysiology?" *American Journal of Psychiatry,* 148(2): 1991, 280; also 148(4): 1991, 548–549.

64. J. C. Ware and J. T. Pittard, "Increased Deep Sleep After Trazodone Use: A Double Blind, Placebo Controlled Study in Healthy Young Adults," *Journal of Clinical Psychiatry,* 51 Suppl: 1990, 18–20; *Semin. Neurology,* 7(3): 1987, 286–295.

65. P. J. Orsulak and D. Waller, "Antidepressant Drugs: Additional Clinical Uses," *Journal of Family Practice,* 28(2): 1989, 209–216.

66. P. J. Orsulak, D. Waller, D. S. Singh, S. Sunder, K. K. Tripathi, "Tricyclic Antidepressant Therapy in Duodenal Ulcer," *Journal of the Indian Medical Association,* 85(9): 1987, 265–267.

67. M. A. Gupta, A. K. Gupta, C. N. Ellis, "Antidepressant Drugs in Dermatology. An Update," *Archives of Dermatology,* 133(5): 1987, 647–652; B. A. Harris, E. F. Sheretz, F. P. Flowers, "Improvement in Neurotic Excoriations with Oral Doxepin Therapy," *Int. Journal of Dermatology,* 26(8): 1987, 541–543.

68. J. I. Hudson and H. G. Pope, Jr., "Affective Spectrum Disorder: Does Antidepressant Response Identify a Family of Disorders with a Common Pathophysiology?" *American Journal of Psychiatry,* 148(2): 1991, 280; also 148(4): 1991, 548–549.

69. J. S. Seggey and R. C. Eckert, "Psychopathology Masquerading as Food Allergy," *Journal of Family Practice,* 26(2): 1988, 161–164.

70. R. G. Ruegg, S. Zisook, N. R. Swerdlow, "Depression in the Aged. An Overview," *Psychiatry Clin. North America,* 11(1): 1988, 83–99; R. H. Gerner, "Geriatric Depression and Treatment with Trazodone." *Psychopathology,* 20(Suppl 1): 1987, 82–91.

71. J. K. Levy and F. Fernandez, "Neuropsychiatric Care for Critically Ill AIDS Patients." *Journal Critical Illness,* 4(3): 1989, 33–42.

72. We are indebted to David S. Sobel, M.D., MPH, Editor of *Mental Medicine Update,* (Special Report, 1993) for bringing several of these studies to our attention.

29

METHODS OF INTERVENTION AND THE PRINCIPLES OF STRESS RESILIENCE

He who cannot change the very fabric of his thought will never be able to change reality.—ANWAR SADAT

Life *is* stress . . . in fact, it's one stressor after another. Finding life meaningful involves finding the stress meaningful. Having fun with life requires having some "fun" with the challenge of solving problems—or at least seeing the personal opportunity that comes along with them. That holds true even for depression; noting that all episodes of depression are not bad, Scott Peck speaks of the "healthiness of depression."[1]

Much of the effect of stress depends on how you respond to it. One response is, "I want to get back to where I was before." Quite another is a response of humility: "I need to change. I think I'm wiser now."

Times of great stress or crisis provide a catalyst for change—and, at times, quantum leaps in growth. We joke about smaller trials being for our growth, but the fact is that problems *do* indeed provide the opportunity to become wiser. For millennia the Chinese have recognized that fact in their language: The character for *crisis* combines those for *danger* and *opportunity.*

Three simple factors define whether stress is productive or destructive:

- The way you see and regard stress—is it an opportunity or an intolerable burden?
- Whether you can see both the pros and the cons—and whether you can create solutions (whether, simply stated, you have a healthy brain).
- Whether you have mental or behavioral tools and principles that enable you to deal well with the stress.

The first of these factors—the way you choose to regard the stressful situation—is the basis of cognitive therapy. It may be the most rapidly effective of the traditional psychotherapy approaches we have.

The second—a healthy brain—requires normally functioning tissues and neurochemistry. Reversible neurochemical abnormalities, such as depression and anxiety disorders, are actually more common barriers than is organic brain tissue disease. Both the pleasure and pain centers in the midbrain need to be adequately functioning if you're to deal well with stress; for that reason, medication may have a role, at least temporarily.

The third requirement—the tools and principles—form the central focus of this final chapter. We hope to bring together the principles of stress resilience, the central core of what defines well-being (mental, physical, and spiritual), and a synthesis of the research described in previous chapters. With this perspective, we'll describe some tools for transforming thought, behavior, and physiology into a condition congruent with the principles of total health.

Lessons from Cancer Studies

As mentioned in the previous chapter, few areas of behavioral medicine have been as emotionally charged and controversial as the treatment of cancer patients. In *The Type C Connection: The Mind-Body Links to Cancer and Your Health*, Lydia Temoshok and Henry Dreher perhaps best summarize the studies in this field. An enormous paradigm shift is required to see behavioral and mental interventions as a form of "adjuvant" cancer therapy that improves prognosis; such new concepts are bound to be met with resistance. Less controversial is the attempt to use behavioral interventions as "supportive measures" to help a person emotionally deal optimally with the immense stress of confronting cancer and all its specters.

As discussed in a number of previous chapters, the following associations exist between mental factors and cancer risk, morbidity, and mortality:

Good Prognosis:
Feeling a sense of personal control
Hope of survival
Trust in one's ability to deal with crisis
Determination to live, sense of purpose
Connectedness
Good coping ability
Ability to express distressed feelings

Worse Prognosis:
Helplessness/hopelessness
Lack of assertiveness
Lack of meaning in life; apathy
Unsatisfactory personal relationships

Ineffective at solving problems
Clinical depression or anxiety
Stoicism; inability to discuss problems

Temoshok and Dreher concluded that the most important of the mental risk factors listed above—and the pathological core of their risky "Type C behavior"—were the suppression of anger and other negative feelings in an attempt to be "nice." This suppression involves passively giving up important parts of your own values so you'll be acceptable to others—a violation of integrity. Such a behavior pattern may be more associated with the progression and mortality of some existing cancers than it is with getting cancer in the first place. It should also be noted that certain factors have been associated with certain *kinds* of cancers, such as melanoma, lymphoma, or breast cancer—and it's not certain whether they apply to cancer in general.

Even with these caveats in mind, would clinical programs that help cancer patients develop "better-prognosis" mental states also improve outcomes—at least in those cancer types we know to be associated with such psychological factors? We believe that the immune factors of protective cancer surveillance (such as natural killer cell activity) may be involved because those immune responses are influenced beneficially by some of the same mental factors that benefit cancer patients (see Chapter 2).

Dr. Sandra Levy at the Pittsburgh Cancer Institute has shown that prognosis in breast cancer can be improved with an optimistic rather than a pessimistic expectational style; she extended that knowledge to a therapeutic program designed to boost optimism in colon cancer patients. It worked—and it helps confirm hope as one of the principles we are looking for.

This same principle was confirmed by Greer's fifteen-year follow-up on British breast cancer patients. Those with a sense of hope and personal control had four times the survival rate of those who felt hopeless and helpless (80 percent versus 20 percent).[2] Derogatis similarly documented what physicians have sensed for hundreds of years: that an increased will to live, and having a purpose for that living, increased breast cancer survival.[3]

You must, however, tread lightly when creating hope therapeutically. Why? Although large numbers with positive expectation may survive longer, a particular individual with a great deal of hope may die early. To have a sense of control, you need to accept responsibility—but it can be devastating to imply that a person is to *blame* for either developing cancer or for failing to survive longer. What are we "responsible" for? The answer is simple: We're not so much responsible for the *cancer* as for how we choose to respond to the cancer. David Spiegel's support intervention that doubled life expectancy in breast cancer patients (see Chapter 28) was based not so much on expectations, but rather on providing a sense of personal control in dealing with caregivers, a sense of meaning and purpose, a sense of connectedness to others struggling with the same crisis, the ability to deal wisely with the stress, and an opportunity to express and explore distressed feelings. (It also involved a longer period of time—a full year—than the usual psychobehavioral group intervention.)

Caroline Bedell Thomas's landmark study of physicians over a period of twenty-five years confirmed the importance of close, meaningful relationships as a protection from cancer. She found a four times greater incidence of cancer in those who lacked that connectedness.[4] She also found optimistic expectations to be important to overall health.

The same lessons about healing and protective principles we learned from cancer apply as well to other diseases; note the discussions on hostility, anger, depression, and lack of close relationships in the chapters about coronary risk and immune dysfunction.

Four Core Principles Underlying Stress Resilience and Well-Being

If we pull together the healing principles outlined in the previous chapters, we might construct the following "stress-resilient" qualities around which behavioral interventions might best be directed:

- A sense of empowerment and personal control (Chapters 3, 4, and 22)

    —Control over one's responses, not necessarily over the environment
    —The ability to live by one's deepest values (integrity)
    —Feeling heard and valued

- A sense of connectedness and acceptance (Chapters 6 and 8 and Part III)

    —To one's deepest self
    —To other people
    —To the earth and the cosmos
    —To all regarded as good, an to the sources of one's spiritual strength

- A sense of meaning and purpose (Chapters 17, 18, and 19)

    —Giving of self for a purpose of value; a caring sense of mission
    —Finding meaning and wisdom in here-and-now difficulties
    —Enjoying the process of growth
    —Having a vision of one's potential

- Hope (Chapters 19, 20, 24, 25, and 26)

    —Positive expectation
    —The ability to envision what one wants before it happens

This group of core principles arises not only from the multitude of medical and health studies reviewed in this book, but also from careful studies of highly healthy and effective people. The key characteristics of such people include:

- The seventeen common characteristics of Maslow's self-actualizers (see Appendix A)[5]

- The three components of Kobasa's and Maddi's "stress-hardy" people (see Chapter 11)
- The seven habits of Covey's highly effective people (see Appendix B)[6]
- The characteristics of Garfield's peak performers (see Chapter 6)
- The characteristics of Friedman's "cardio-protected" Type Bs (see Chapter 6)

If you synthesize the underlying "ways of being in the world" by which these people function, you find that the four core principles listed above tie all of them together. And the studies discussed throughout this book show that they underlie optimal physical health as well.

Also common to all these groups of healthy people are the values that lead them to the above ends. When people in a relaxed, introspective state in a clinical setting are asked to reflect on who they really are—on the values they most deeply cherish—a small set of what appears to be nearly universal core values keeps appearing. Interestingly, they're the same core values by which well-functioning, healthy people actually operate—the core values that motivate them to do what they do.

What are those deeper, more universal values?

- *Caring love*; the kind that lifts and empowers the loved one
- *Responsible free will*; a feeling in charge of what happens in life and our responses to what happens
- *Integrity*; being true to our clearly defined free will; feeling in charge of our response to what happens in life
- *Growth*; enjoyment of a challenge, the love of continually getting wiser and more capable

Nearly all of what we've discovered about well-functioning people are variants of these four core values. Interestingly, even the most "healthy" *companies* (those whose success lasts longest) tend to operate through these same principles.[7] These principles seem to be basic qualities of well-being; there is a remarkable universality about them, and they seem to be the deeper longings of most people who find them absent.

Professionals who do the hands-on work with patients struggling over mind-body issues often comment that stress finally resolves when "the spiritual issues resolve." They sense, in other words, that spiritual well-being underlies much of both mental and physical well-being. The World Health Organization defines health as "a state of complete well-being in all the aspects of one's life: physical, mental, social, and spiritual—not just the absence of disease."

What is meant by "spiritual well-being"? The answers are varied, and the condition is difficult to measure in a study. We can measure with considerable precision optimal physical health and function. We can even measure with fair accuracy what mental well-being is. But, even though spiritual well-being escapes the precise measurement of these, practitioners claim that it may be possible to demonstrate the *essence* of spiritual well-being. How? In essence, the four core principles listed above make up overall wellness. They are also the ends toward which many spiritual traditions are working: empowerment, deep integrity, connectedness, a sense of purpose and meaning, and hope. It is no coincidence that these principles are also what many in the world are hungering for.

It's important to note that "spirituality" that undermines these principles is likely to be a misconception. For example, being angrily judgmental of "imperfect" people doesn't empower; it puts down. It doesn't foster connectedness; instead, it causes alienation. It doesn't promote hope—instead, it promotes discouragement. With this in mind, are such misguided attempts to be spiritual more likely to advance physical health or to cause physical illness?

How, then, do these stress-resilient principles work? Following are a handful of examples:

Major Issues Causing Distress	*Core Values and Principles That Can Resolve the Distress*
Issues of personal worth: low self-esteem, aloneness, uncertain identity, perfectionism	Integrity to unconditional love, acceptance, connectedness, a sense of purpose, and continued growth
Blaming—feeling "forced"	Responsible free will, bringing a sense of control
Demanding that things be different than they are	Acceptance of self and others; understanding cause and effect, and working with it (wisdom)
Threat, worry, and negative expectation	Hope, caring love, and positive expectation

A person may also need treatment of the neurochemical abnormalities that cause much of the depression and anxiety—even, at times, in the absence of significant situational stress. It can be almost impossible to make the kind of mental change required with these four principles if the mental instrument needed to do it isn't working properly. When that's the case, medication—even on a temporary basis—can be of immense benefit. Medication is usually required for major clinical depression or anxiety accompanied by symptoms of midbrain dysfunction (see Chapters 10 and 28).

A Sense of Empowerment and Personal Control

Creating a personal sense of control in the face of stress is no trivial matter. But it appears to lie at the heart of stress resilience, because the bottom line about feeling *distressed* is that the stressful situation feels beyond control. In fact, all four core principles of stress resilience contribute to a natural sense of control. And all of them create the mental structure that fosters a sense of personal control—of how to be in the world. Some further observations about a sense of personal control will help demonstrate why some of the behavioral treatment approaches work.

Stressed Animals and Control

A mental state of being "out of control" is accompanied by physiology that's "out of control"—a dysregulation of autonomic, hormonal, and immunological balance that protects from disease. An example comes from the work of Martin Seligman and his colleagues.

In Seligman's studies, animals were placed in a classical stress setup: They were confined in a box, and an electrode was attached to their tails that delivered intermittent shocks. Each shock was preceded by a warning bell. Each animal was assigned to one of three groups:

1. The first group was given a wheel that, when turned, aborted the shock, as the animals quickly learned. The bell rang, the animals spun the wheel, and no shock occurred. They were captains of their destiny. They were in control.
2. The second group had no wheel. They were truly victims, cowering at the bell that signalled the imminent misery.
3. The third group acted as controls; they were not given shocks.

The animals were then injected with cancer cells to see which were most likely to develop cancer and which were best able to immunologically reject the cancer and stay healthy. Those in the group who had control over the stress were able to reject sarcoma cells 63 percent of the time compared with only 28 percent of the victims. Interestingly, the group who had control over stress did even better than the group that had no stress at all: Only 60 percent of the unstressed animals rejected the cancer cells. When researchers measured the immune responses in the different groups, those with control over stress had the best immune response; the victims had the worst.

The same pattern holds up across many types of studies dealing with stress: It's not the stressor that matters as much as the ability to control the response to stress. Those who are stressed but who have a sense of control, in fact, are often even more healthy than those who are not stressed at all. Out of control, stress becomes *distress*; under control, it becomes *eustress*. And, as noted in Chapter 3, the neurochemical and physiological responses differ between the two.

It should be noted that a fascinating paradox exists about how to achieve a sense of control. The more you attempt to control the external situation (such as what others do), the more out of control things feel—because, simply, the external world can seldom be reliably controlled. On the other hand, the more you let go—the less you try to control the external world and the more you respond with wisdom and maturity—the greater the sense of personal control. When you accept that things exist as they are for a reason (whether good or bad), you can respond with creative, persuasive wisdom to draw others in a different direction.

Brain Neurochemistry and the Sense of Control

Finding a sense of control also seems to improve the neurochemical abnormalities associated with extreme stress, depression, and anxiety. UCLA's Michael McGuire studied how gaining and losing social control affects serotonin levels.[8]

(Serotonin is a key player not only in depression, but also in keeping physical and emotional responses "in balance.") McGuire studied the different serotonin levels in dominant versus submissive males in three groups: vervet monkeys, fraternity men, and football players.

The results were fascinating. Serotonin levels were twice as high in the dominant monkeys as in the nondominant. Then researchers "dethroned" the dominant monkey by placing him behind a one-way mirror where he could watch the submissive males cozying up to his harem of females. He ranted and raved, as he always did to maintain power, but—unheard and unseen—to no avail. As he began to give up, helpless, his serotonin levels dropped. Some dropped to the level of the submissive males; some dropped even lower. Interestingly, as the previously *submissive* monkeys started to gain some control, their serotonin levels rose to those of the previously dominant male. Similar patterns were found among the fraternity men and the football players.

In the second part of the study, McGuire used drugs to change the serotonin levels, then watched the resulting behaviors. When drugs were given to raise serotonin levels in passive males, they acted dominant. When drugs were given to inhibit serotonin in dominant males, they acted subordinate—and were anxious over tests they had previously done with confidence. Another fascinating observation was that researchers could predict which monkey would soon dominate by watching which monkey the females were cozying up to—regardless of which monkey was winning all the battles. The brain serotonin levels in the male being sought by the females increased, and within two weeks, he dominated.

Social dominance also affects the immunity of animals. In response to stress, dominant animals show a more optimal antibody response; that of submissive animals is decreased.[9] Dominance increases not only brain serotonin levels, but also natural painkillers (opioids), such as endorphins. These opioids, in turn, affect immunity; animals with high endorphin levels have increased resistance to cancer. On the other hand, higher cortisol levels—seen with chronic submission and "helplessness"—are correlated with decreased immune competence. It all plays into why people who feel depressed or helpless have more difficulty clearing infections and a worse prognosis for certain treated cancers (see Chapters 2 and 10).

Boston University researcher David McClelland showed that when frustrated, students with a need to exercise power over others had significantly increased blood epinephrine levels and decreased salivary IgA antibody levels. The effect? More upper respiratory infections when under academic stress.[10] Students under the same stress but *not* under the same need for control didn't have the same rate of infections or the same drop in antibodies.

McClelland's study illustrates another paradox about a sense of control: Those people lower in brain serotonin function are often *driven* to seek control—maybe in an attempt to get levels back up. Examples are seen in people with compulsive behaviors, perfectionism, or hostility toward competitors. Seeking power and control is often a symptom of the underlying insecurity that accompanies diminished serotonin function (as may be seen in some Type A behavior).

Cognitive Structuring and Therapy

Many intervention approaches are built around giving a greater sense of integrity and personal control. One of the most rapidly effective forms of psychotherapy for converting distressed responses into those more healthy is cognitive (thinking) therapy. Cognitive (thinking) restructuring underlies both cognitive therapy and some of its spinoffs (such as rational behavioral therapy or rational emotive therapy).[11] These therapies are based on the realization that stressful situations do not *cause* our feelings and physiological responses as much as the way we choose to think about those situations.

The situation leads to the way we think about the situation—how we regard the situation and its meaning for us. The way we think about the situation leads to our response: feelings, physiological responses, and behavioral responses. Each time this process occurs, it becomes more automatic.

Note that feelings and behavioral response are not caused directly by the situation at all, but rather by the way we think about the situation. The situation is only the event around which the thinking forms. It is the thinking, rather than the event, that creates the reality for that person. That's why one person feels "blown away" by the same situation that another person sees as a creative challenge. When you blame the situation for your feelings and behaviors, you become a victim—you give up your sense of control. On the other hand, if you recognize that most situations aren't as distressing as the way you've chosen to think about them, you open up many possibilities for regarding the situation in more mature and wise ways, for creating a more productive response, and for bringing back a sense of control.

The following is an example. If a father felt upset and angry when his teenager rebelled with provocative remarks, he could regain personal control by refusing to blame the teen's behavior (the situation) for "making" him feel bad or for "causing" him to react in certain ways toward his daughter. By realizing that he himself created the thinking about his daughter that in turn caused the disturbing reaction, he can—in a more reflective, disengaged moment—create new ways of thinking and dealing with a struggling teenager. Then he could mentally practice his new skills, helping his new reaction become more automatic. Instead of being extremely distressful and alienating, his new reaction could be creatively empowering—and even bonding.

At first, the way you think about a situation may seem like the only way to regard it. At that point, it's easy to be misled about what the most rational thoughts are. But there's a key guideline as to whether thinking is maturely rational: Look at the feelings and behavior it engenders. *If the feelings or behavior are destructive, then the thinking that caused it has two characteristics:* It is in some way irrational (that is, it's not totally reliable) and it in some way violates your deepest values.

Let's look again at the example of the father who was struggling with his teenaged daughter. What's so irrational about getting angry over his daughter's rude remarks? It's irrational to think that the father *has* to be angry and upset. Instead, the father may try to understand his daughter's struggle with identity and independence—which is what is really causing her behavior—and may respond with gentle wisdom that encourages his daughter instead of trying to put her down. In the long run, that kind of reaction is probably more in harmony with his deepest values, anyway: He wants to lift and encourage his daughter rather than put her down. There's an important caveat here, too: The father isn't *suppressing* his anger. Instead, his anger *dissipates* when he thinks about his daughter differently.

Remember: If feelings are destructive, there is *always* a wiser, more rational way of thinking that is more in harmony with your deeper values—and that will result in a very different response to the same situation. The first step to gaining control of your responses is giving up blame—fully realizing that you create your own thinking and responses. Accepting that responsible free will is the first step to control.

Typical ways of thinking about distressful situations have to do with:

- The *shoulds* (How does the situation fit with what "should" be true?)
- Issues of worth (What does this situation mean about my worth and value?)
- Threat (Am I likely to lose something of value because of this situation?)
- Force (Am I feeling forced to do something I don't want to do?)[12]

Then what is the most effective way of dealing with a distressful situation? First, re-examine your way of thinking. Second, discover a more rational way of regarding the situation (something more in line with your deeper values). And, finally, use visualization or some other technique to help your new way of thinking and responding become automatic. The result? A sense of personal control—in harmony with your values. And your new response will become as automatic as the way you tie your shoes: You've done it so many times that you do it without any *conscious* thought.

Basic Elements of Behavior Change

To change distressed behaviors, whether emotional or physiological,

1. Clarify the present state.
2. Clearly determine *in explicit, specific terms* what you desire the outcome to be.
3. Change your behavioral response.

Research has shown that it's very difficult to mentally "reprogram" yourself if you're aroused—which is likely if you're also distressed. The key is to become deeply relaxed and receptive through "meditative methods"—behaviors that help you relax, become calm, disengage from destructive thinking, and create and practice new mental models.

There are some meditative methods that elicit the relaxation response—that help you become calm and mentally disengage from old ways of thinking. Other meditative methods help you change to a new, better behavior. You'll need to use both.

Methods of Eliciting the Relaxation Response

Progressive Muscle Relaxation

With this method, you tense specific muscles as you inhale, become aware of the feeling of tension, then totally "let go" to relax those same muscles as you exhale, noticing the difference. You usually involve all the muscles in the body in a systematic way—starting with your foot and leg, for example, and then moving up the body to the buttocks, trunk, chest, shoulders, arms, and hands. Once you know the difference between feeling tense and relaxed, you can recognize situations ("cues") that make you feel tense. You can then practice relaxing, using an "anchor"—a certain kind of breath, body position, or touch—to trigger the relaxation response. The anchor then becomes your cue for deep relaxation.

Mindfulness Meditation[13]

This method involves living fully in the present moment, giving complete, caring attention to whatever you choose. You focus attention on one thing at a time, allowing intruding or distracting thoughts to pass; as a result, you feel a quiet sense of control instead of the frazzled attempt to concentrate on several thoughts at once. To practice, you can devote complete concentration and attention to simple things like breathing or eating, noticing how those things make you feel. The frequent self-monitoring that helps you know what's going on from one moment to the next has been used very effectively in a number of stress reduction programs, including those at the University of Massachusetts, Harvard, and the University of Utah.

Imagery

Imagery involves mentally going to a safe, beautiful place—then you totally experience it with all your senses. With practice, you can take a "mental trip" every day to the mountains or the seashore—and not only experience the sensual sounds, smells, sights, textures, and feelings, but experience the mental detachment and focus that comes from actually traveling to a similar place for a few days.

"Body Work"

Techniques like yoga usually involve "relaxed stretching"—putting the body under stress while you relax your mind. Like progressive muscle relaxation, body work can act as a kind of gauge that helps you get quiet and relaxed—and can help you relax while under stress or in pain.

Methods of Changing Behavior

Several meditative methods stir up your core values and solutions—and, as a result, help you change your behavior.

Quiet Contemplation

In a peaceful, quiet environment free of distraction, you think about what has deepest meaning in your life. It's a key way of clarifying your values.

Guided Imagery[14]

There are two kinds of guided imagery that help you reprogram your thoughts and change your behavior. The first, *imagery to the "inner child,"*[15] helps you mentally visit yourself as a child who is going through a disturbing event. You then reprogram the meaning of that event through mature eyes—you nurture and heal by giving the child new ways of dealing well with the event.

In the second kind of guided imagery, *imagery to the "inner advisor,"*[16] you personify your inner wisdom and values into an "inner advisor." That advisor then provides you rapid access to solutions congruent with your own values.

Visualization[17]

Through visualization, you actually practice "seeing" yourself performing or functioning the way you want to. It's a highly effective way of rapidly changing your behavior, and hinges on four techniques:

- You need to define your desired goal or outcome *in clear detail*. The brain doesn't process "don'ts" very well; to be effective, you need to define the outcome only in terms of what you *do* want. Your outcome, of course, needs to be compatible with your deepest values—and all parts of you must intensely want that outcome.
- You must be totally relaxed.
- You must see and feel yourself achieving the desired result *in great detail*. In essence, you need to "experience" it completely—including the place, cues, who's there, your style of behavior, and your physical sensations. This goes beyond fantasizing; instead, you see yourself with enough feeling and trust that you generate the energy to actually carry out the vision.
- You need to practice regularly.

Other Ways to Change Behavior

There are other keys to changing behavior—ways of achieving a personal sense of control. Although they've been discussed in greater detail earlier in this book, they deserve to be mentioned here.

Increasing the Internal Locus of Control

Training in self-assertion helps you become aware of your own needs and values and then use the combined principles of honesty and kindness to express them. An internal locus of control engenders a proactive spirit—you refuse to choose helplessness and hopeless as a response.

Practicing Forgiveness

Entire treatment approaches have been built around the practice of forgiveness.[18] To some, forgiving someone who has been offensive or caused pain is like giving a gift to someone who doesn't deserve it. In reality, genuine forgiveness involves regaining personal control—refusing to blame someone else's actions for your feelings and behavior. Forgiveness involves choosing to act in ways that are wise and mature—regardless of how someone else has acted. Experiencing real forgiveness is at the heart of gaining personal control.

Keeping a Journal

When you write about your feelings, you become aware of how you think and behave in response to stressful situations. When you capture the experience on paper, you "get a handle on it"—get some sense of how to deal with it. Keeping a journal has the added benefit of creating a sense of who you really are and the values for which you stand.

Building Social Support

Social support not only increases your quality of life, but also increases longevity and reduces your risk of coronary disease.[19] For detailed information on the benefits of social support, see Chapters 6 and 28.

Mind-Body Treatment: Can It Change the Course of Disease?

With all our knowledge about behavioral techniques, we come to a sobering question: If someone starts practicing the techniques described in this chapter at an early age, will it actually prevent or alter the course of disease?

The answer lies in results of pioneering studies in the field of mind-body treatment. For example, Jon Kabat-Zinn at the University of Massachusetts Medical Center Stress Reduction Clinic takes on patients with difficult medical problems that other physicians have given up on. In turn, he uses methods based on mindfulness meditation. Among more than 4,000 patients he has treated over ten years, that simple technique has reduced medical illness in these difficult cases by 35 percent.[20] Even diseases as specific and resistant as psoriasis have responded.[21] Among the elderly, other forms of meditation have had even greater health benefits.[22]

As noted in Chapter 2, distressed thinking can adversely affect the immune system—with an obvious link to disease. Behavioral interventions that have been shown to boost immune response include:

- Clinical biofeedback,
- Meditation,
- Autogenic training,

- Progressive relaxation,
- Visualization,
- Hypnosis, and
- Behavior modification.[23]

Although the results of such studies have been encouraging, they have also been somewhat inconsistent; the field of achieving stress resilience is filled with paradox. A good example is the controversial use of imagery for "healing" cancer. Many years ago, Ainsley Mears used two different types of imagery with cancer patients. The first created a state of relaxed peacefulness and acceptance; patients used the crisis to focus on their deepest values and heal their lives. The result? Cancer progression slowed; more patients actually went into remission.

For the second part of his study, Mears instructed patients to use imagery to imagine active destruction of the cancer cells by white blood cells and macrophages. His aim was rejection of the tumor by the immune system. That didn't happen, though; for a majority of the patients, tumor recurrences began to increase. What went wrong? Maybe it was just a function of time—because the second part of the study took longer, there was time for recurrences to happen. But a greater issue involves whether creating an aroused, hostile state aimed at destroying the tumor may actually be counterproductive; instead of creating a sense of inner peace, it involves a threat to one's sense of control.

The first approach—creating a state of relaxed peacefulness—allowed patients to accept things as they are, to respond with wisdom, maturity, and love to the situation. It let patients use the crisis to get focused on healing the parts of their lives that had been neglected or had gone unresolved. That kind of approach, argue researchers, creates a greater sense of personal control even if the tumor goes uncured.

Other methods of mental control, such as biofeedback that changes body temperature, have been beneficial in the treatment of autoimmune diseases, such as rheumatoid arthritis.[24] Treatments that have included social support, guided imagery, and progressive relaxation have also helped rheumatoid arthritis patients; the psychological interventions have been more effective than social support alone.[25] In one study, 81 percent said that relaxation training was a major factor in reducing pain, reducing inflammation, and decreasing levels of serum rheumatoid factor. In another study,[26] patients were given a cognitive-behavioral treatment designed to boost self-efficacy in managing the disease; patients were taught self-relaxation, cognitive pain management, and goal setting. The more the patients enhanced self-efficacy (a measure of their sense of control), the more their pain and inflammation were reduced.

Ohio State University researcher Janice Kiecolt-Glaser has extensively studied the effects of mental distress on immune function. One such study involved forty-five nursing home residents who were taught progressive relaxation and guided imagery as a way to gain control over their world. This simple step resulted in significantly less mental distress—as well as better prognosis and greater longevity. And that's not all: Those who used progressive relaxation and guided imagery had *significantly* improved cellular immune response, including an increase in natural killer cell activity.

We know that mental conditioning can affect immune response. In Chapter 2, we noted that University of Rochester researcher Robert Ader mentally conditioned a group of mice to suppress their immune response. Here's how he did it: He gave the mice a mixture of the drug Cytoxan—which suppresses the immune response—and saccharine. Later, he gave the mice saccharine but no Cytoxan. What happened? The taste of the saccharine triggered the memory of the Cytoxan, causing immune suppression and the immune response of the mice was suppressed by that memory alone *without* the drug.

Ader then extended his experiment to a group of New Zealand mice that genetically get lupus erythematosus, an autoimmune disease in which an overactive immune system destroys the kidneys and causes death at a predictable age. The drug Cytoxan diminishes the extra immune function—and, as a result, delays kidney failure and prolongs life. Ader gave the mice saccharine with the first few doses of Cytoxan; their immune suppression was linked to the saccharine taste, so giving them saccharine alone later suppressed the immune response. The result? Saccharine alone delayed kidney failure and prolonged life.

Perhaps as we learn more precisely to understand the fascinating interactions between the mind and the body and how to effectively work with them, we can embark on new and safe therapies in the future that we can't even consider today.

The Spiritual Connection

A Harris Poll of 1,254 adults asked respondents about aches and pains, including headaches, backaches, stomachaches, muscle pain, and menstrual pain. When they analyzed the results, pollsters had a number of surprises.

The first surprise was the age group that suffered the most aches and pains. Was it the elderly? No—with the exception of joint pain, they had the *least* amount of pain. The age group with the highest pain prevalence were the young adults: those aged eighteen to twenty-four. Why? There was a high correlation between pain and the kinds of things young adults face—feeling "hassled," being lonely, having money worries, and coping with lack of time.

The other surprise was in who provided the best relief. Physicians were sought by 58 percent of the patients and provided relief 73 percent of the time. Chiropractors and nutritionists provided relief 65 to 70 percent of the time. Acupuncturists provided relief 35 percent of the time. The person providing the greatest relief of pain was a spiritual counselor—effective 85 percent of the time.

Why does spiritual counseling work so well? It is designed to:

- Give meaning and structure to life;
- Empower people to live in accordance with that structure;
- Help people identify and live by their deepest values; and
- Provide social support and caring.

Simply stated, it provides the sense of control, connectedness, meaning, and hope proven to bring about healing.

An interesting point is that the behavioral interventions described in this book are going in the opposite direction of the growing medical trend toward specialization. That specialization—reaching now to the molecular level—has reaped great benefits, but has also tended to separate the parts of a person and his or her care. The studies cited in this book call for a focused and concerted effort to treat the whole person. Integrating both approaches will provide the most optimal outcome.

That integration requires the targeted use of not only behavioral and psychological interventions, but strong educational efforts as well—all preferably in both the medical and health prevention settings. Perhaps the most potent mind-body intervention of all is a deeply trusting and caring relationship with the medical caregiver who is sensitive to these issues and who truly understands how these interventions work.

As we move into that future, we discover the truth of what mathematician Charles Muses proclaimed when he said, "The potentials of consciousness remain well nigh the last reachable domain for man not yet explored—the Undiscovered Country." We anticipate a realm in which we will, as French neurologist Frederic Tilney challenged us, "by conscious command evolve cerebral centers which will permit us to use powers that we now are not even capable of imagining."

Notes

1. Scott Peck, *The Road Less Traveled*, p. 69.
2. S. Greer et al., "Psychological Response to Breast Cancer and 15-Year Outcome," *Lancet*, 1: 1990, 49–50.
3. L. R. Derogatis, *Science*, 200: 1363ff.
4. C. B. Thomas et al., *Johns Hopkins Medical Journal*, 151: 1982, 193ff.
5. Abraham Maslow, *Personality and Motivation*, Chapter 11.
6. Stephen R. Covey, *The Seven Habits of Highly Effective People* (New York: Fireside-Simon and Schuster, 1989).
7. Thomas J. Peters and Robert H. Waterman, Jr., *In Search of Excellence: Lessons from America's Best-Run Companies* (New York: Harper and Row, 1982).
8. Michael McGuire, *The Biology of Power*.
9. Bessel A. van der Kolk, *Psychological Trauma* (Washington, D.C.: American Psychiatric Press, 1987), p. 47.
10. John Jemmott, 1982.

11. Some useful guides to cognitive therapy principles include: Maxie C. Maultsby, *Rational Behavior Therapy* (Englewood Cliffs, New Jersey: Prentice-Hall, 1984); Donald Meichenbaum, *Cognitive Behavior Modification: An Integrative Approach* (New York: Plenum Publishing, 1977); and Donald Meichenbaum, *Stress Inoculation Training: A Clinical Guidebook* (1985).
12. Maultsby.
13. Early books describing the clinical use of mindfulness meditation include: Jon Kabat-Zinn, *Full Catastrophe Living* (New York: Delacorte Press, 1990); Joan Borysenko, *Minding the Body, Mending the Mind* (New York: Bantam Books, 1988); Herbert Benson, *The Relaxation Response* (New York: Morrow, 1975); Thich Nhat Hanh, *The Miracle of Mindfulness: A Manual of Meditation* (Boston: Beacon Press, 1976); and H. Benson and E. Stuart, *The Wellness Book* (New York: Carol Publishing Group, 1993).
14. William Fezler, *Creative Imagery: How to*

Visualize in All Senses (New York: Fireside-Simon and Schuster, 1989).

15. Joan Borysenko, *Guilt is the Teacher, Love is the Lesson* (New York: Warner Books, 1990), Chapters 3 and 4.

16. Martin L. Rossman, *Healing Yourself* (New York: Pocket Books, 1989).

17. Adelaide Bry, *Visualization: Directing the Movies of Your Mind* (New York: Harper and Row, 1978).

18. Robin Casarjian, *Forgiveness: A Bold Choice for a Peaceful Heart* (New York: Bantam Books, 1992).

19. W. Ruberman, "Psychosocial Influences on Mortality of Patients with Coronary Artery Disease," *Journal of the American Medical Association*, 267: 1992, 559–560.

20. Kabat-Zinn.

21. J. Bernhard, J. Kirsteller, and J. Kabat-Zinn, "Effectiveness of Relaxation and Visualization Techniques as an Adjunct to Phototherapy and Photochemotherapy of Psoriasis," *Journal of the American Academy of Dermatology*, 19: 1988, 572–573.

22. *Journal of Personality and Social Psychology*, 57: 950–964.

23. K. R. Pelletier and D. L. Herzing, *Advances*, 5(1): 1988, 27–56.

24. J. Achterberg, P. McGraw, and G. F. Lawis, "Rheumatoid Arthritis: A Study of Relaxation and Temperature Biofeedback as an Adjunctive Therapy," *Biofeedback and Self-Regulation*, 6: 1981, 207–223; and K. A. Applebaum, E. B. Blanchard, and E. J. Hickling, "Psychological and Functional Measurement in Severe Rheumatoid Arthritis Before and After Psychological Intervention: A Controlled Evaluation [Summary]," in Proceedings of the 17th Annual Meeting of the Biofeedback Society of America, 1986, pp. 5–7.

25. L. A. Bradley, L. Young, K. O. Anderson, L. K. McDaniel, R. A. Turner, C. Agudelo, E. J. Pisko, E. L. Semble, and T. M. Morgan, "Effects of Psychological Therapy on Pain Behavior of Rheumatoid Arthritis Patients," *Arthritis and Rheumatism*, 30: 1987, 1105–1114.

26. A. O'Leary, S. Shoor, K. Lorig, and H. R. Holman, "A Cognitive-Behavioral Treatment for Rheumatoid Arthritis," *Health Psychology*, 7: 1988, 527–544.

EPILOGUE

Everything can be taken from a man but one thing: the last of the human freedoms—to choose one's attitude in any given set of circumstances, to choose one's own way.—VIKTOR FRANKL

Sophisticated executives who run this nation's largest cities as well as quiet folks tucked into the hills of America's heartland want to know how to stay well, how to live longer. Interest in behavioral health—in knowing how behavior and emotions affect our well-being—is burgeoning. Researchers have begun answering the call. The frenetic research—and the nation's interest in it—is a hopeful sign that one day we as a people will begin to conquer the diseases that now claim too many of us.

Everyone who leafs through the pages of this book will someday die. The Iowa farmer who wipes sweat from his brow with the back of his hand as he leans against his stilled combine will die. The Louisiana mother who hauls a basket of fresh laundry to the kitchen table while she keeps an anxious eye on her toddler, swinging under the magnolias, will die. The Fifth Avenue advertising executive who agonizes over a new corporate identity scattered on a pile of art boards will die. And the weathered fisherman who catches a sharp breath of salty air off the coast of Alaska as he pulls in a thrashing salmon will die.

The key is not in the dying; we are powerless against its inevitable approach. Norman Cousins tells us that "death is not the ultimate tragedy in life. The ultimate tragedy is to die without discovering the possibilities of full growth."

Realization of death can bring us to the greatest appreciation for the life that still lies ahead. "Good-by world," writes Thornton Wilder. "Good-by to clocks ticking . . . and Mama's sunflowers. And food and coffee. And new-ironed dresses and hot baths . . . and sleeping and waking up. Oh, earth, you're too wonderful for anybody to realize you."

The key is in the living, because in that we exercise tremendous power. "Life is the ultimate prize, and it takes on ultimate value when suddenly we discover how tentative and fragile it can be," Cousins warns us. We need, at this moment, to realize how wonderful it is.

We can't annihilate the world's population of disease microorganisms—but we can cut down our own chances of being felled by them. We may not see a triumphant technician hail the cure for cancer during this decade, but we can do plenty of things—today, tomorrow, and the day after that—to reduce our own chances of becoming a grim statistic.

There is no single factor in disease. If there were, cures would be simple. Instead, there are puzzles. Scientists unraveling the mysteries of the amazingly complex human immune system know that the presence of microorganisms doesn't always lead to infection. Researchers know that only *some* of the executives who lose their jobs during a hostile takeover will be crippled by ulcers or low back pain. And, while one child rising from the squalor of poverty and despair in a ghetto's broken home is tethered by physical and emotional illness, his brother shines with resilience.

We call that resilience "hardiness," and it makes of us a healthier people. University of Chicago psychologist Salvatore Maddi, who helped establish the concept of hardiness, sums it up nicely as a feeling of self-confidence:

> *The world is rather benign. You have commitment, or the knack of finding something important about whatever it is you are doing. You also have control, or the belief that you can influence what is going on around you. Further, you think your life is best led in pursuit of development. Pressures and disruptions, however painful, appear to be something you can learn from and grow from.*

"The world breaks everyone," Ernest Hemingway penned in *A Farewell to Arms*, "and, afterward, many are strong at the broken places."

What determines who is strong at the broken places? Much of it may lie in the way we think and the way we behave. The power of thought—the literal power of the brain—is key to physical well-being. When those thoughts are negative, when depression and doubt and pessimism reign, "illness messages" are sent to every cell in the body. It doesn't take a Nobel scientist to figure out the result. But when those thoughts are positive, "wellness messages" emanate to the body— and literal chemical and physical changes take place that guarantee health and wellness.

The brain is the key. It houses chemical factories that can energize the immune system against bacteria, viruses, even cancer. What goes on in the brain literally determines health or illness—healing and resistance to disease.

The phenomenal power of the brain over the body is illustrated by imagery, the clarion mental visualization that enables a middle-aged secretary in the front office to mobilize her immune system against cancer. A man who visualized his white blood cells as killer white sharks devouring the floating shards of cancer tissue nearly doubled the number of active white blood cells—in just one week. Convincing research shows you can enhance your immune system with just ten minutes a day of imagery—and doing it just three times a week can multiply your natural killer cells. People trained in imagery have even been able to control their response to the chicken pox virus.

There's reason to believe that you can *decide* to fight a disease. Even cancer patients have used imagery to get the greatest benefit from treatment (imagining the radiation as healing rays of sun) and to defeat what was packaged as a terminal disease (imagining immune cells as soldiers destroying the enemy cancer).

With current scientific interest in behavioral health and the power of the brain, volumes could be written. Libraries could be filled. If you're like most people, you don't have time to explore the rows of crowded shelves in even one of them. So we have tried between the covers of this book to give you enough of a glimpse to make a difference in your life.

In a nutshell, then, how can you achieve wellness? Before we start, consider what you mean by *wellness*. Can a chemotherapy patient in her last month of life be considered *well*? Can an AIDS patient languishing between bouts of savage pneumonia be considered *well*? Can a wheelchair-bound grandmother twisted by rheumatoid arthritis be considered *well*? Sometimes they can achieve a higher level of wellness than the muscled competitive swimmer who eats salads sprinkled with wheat germ.

Physical health is only one aspect of *wellness*. Wellness goes far beyond blood cholesterol levels and bone density. Wellness includes mental acuity, a zest for learning, a tolerance of different ideas. Wellness brings with it empathy, compassion, a sense of cohesiveness with the rest of humanity. Wellness encompasses a fighting spirit, an optimistic outlook, an attitude of hope.

When the mental, emotional, and spiritual aspects of wellness are manifested, the physical aspects follow naturally. Renowned surgeon Bernie Siegel predicts that the chemicals we produce in our own brains—the chemicals stimulated in part by our feelings and attitudes—will become the basis of future medical treatment. If you are spiritually or emotionally healthy, you are likely to be physically healthy for your current circumstances, because as you have read on the pages of this book, our attitudes influence our bodies. Stepping outside your own realm of concern to help another person reduces blood pressure—but waving your fist in an explosive burst of rage as you sit in a traffic tie-up clogs your arteries. Charity builds immunity. Revenge literally eats you alive. Guilt enslaves. Forgiveness frees. "Among the prime assets of the human mind," writes Cousins, "is the ability to cut loose from vengeful or burdensome memories."

Essential, too, is the ability to keep things in perspective. Robert Ornstein and David Sobel write in *Healthy Pleasures*, "We need to restore some sensibility to the pursuit of health. Many of us increasingly view ourselves as fragile and vulnerable, ready to develop cancer, heart disease, or some other dreaded disease at the slightest provocation. In the name of health we give up many of our enjoyments. The important point is that worrying too much about anything—be

it calories, salt, cancer, or cholesterol—is bad for you, and that living optimisti-
cally, with pleasure, zest, and commitment, is good. Medical terrorism shouldn't
attack life's pleasures."

Thanks to the battalions of scientists who have designed careful studies, these
are no longer mere theories of a religious zealot or an isolated visionary. They are
scientifically proven prescriptions for better health and longer life. Best of all,
they are here for the taking.

What, then, can you do?

Pay attention to the basics. Attitudes can literally change the pressure of the
blood coursing through your veins, but they can't do it all. Start with a good
foundation. Use your common sense.

Exercise regularly. You don't have to run a marathon or swim the English
Channel. In fact, exercise physiologists agree that regular moderate exercise, such
as walking, packs greater benefits in the long run. Famed British poet William
Wordsworth logged an estimated 180,000 miles during his lifetime, and claimed
that walking along the forested lanes of his homeland inspired his poetic pen.

Wordsworth may have been right: Walking not only improves circulation but
literally stimulates the brain. It increases cerebral metabolism—the brain's ability
to use oxygen. And many of the brain neurotransmitters—the critical circuitry that
links the delicate wiring of the nervous system—depend on oxygen to function.

Get enough sleep.

Eat well—as much as you can, choose fresh foods that are low in fat, low in
sugar, and high in dietary fiber. You don't need to concentrate on food charts—
but do try to eat a wide variety of health-promoting foods every day. Avoid the
things you know will hurt you such as tobacco, alcohol, and too much caffeine.

Work hard, but not too hard. If you can still make choices, opt for work you'll
really enjoy; you spend too many hours at it to be miserable. Choose work that
doesn't sacrifice the other important things in your life and consider the impact
your job has on those things. When you are mulling possibilities, remember that
in the long run satisfaction and reward outweigh a hefty bank balance. Hubbard
reminds us that "We work to become, not acquire."

In your work and in your play, avoid boredom. The old adage that boredom is
deadly may be hauntingly accurate. Some of the nation's leading researchers
have shown that a brain that is bored will do almost anything to spark some interest—even create pain and illness, if that's what it takes. Boredom can even
change the actual physiology of the brain—laboratory experiments with mice
show that the number of neurons decreases among those who are stagnant.

Vary your routine; break out of the rut. Take educated risks. Boredom can exist
even in the face of pressing responsibilities. Make room in your life for exploration
and creativity. Develop new interests. Invite surprise. Relish the unexpected.

Never stop learning. Neurosurgeons tell us that new learning and information actually create new connections between the brain cells. Renew your library
card. Enroll in a community or adult education class. Dust off the leather-bound
collection of Civil War books you inherited from your grandmother; become an

expert on little-known battles. Start a friendly office competition to see who can be the first to order a meal in French.

Savor leisure time. The chant of a nursery rhyme reminds us that "all work and no play makes Jack a dull boy." Learn to play as hard as you work—it can make a staggering difference in your life. Finishing a first-class client presentation complete with color overlays on crisply designed graphs can be euphoric, but so can the first trills of a distant bluejay, singing across the expanse of mountain lake where you and the kids pitched your old Boy Scout tent last night. It's great to win a corporate game; it's even greater to help your grandson win his first horseshoe game.

Do something creative. Capture the first autumn leaves in a swirl of watercolors; tackle a Beethoven sonata on the old piano; or express your thrill at your child's first steps in a free-verse poem. Don't aim for perfection; instead, concentrate on expressing yourself and having fun.

While you're playing—and even when you're not—laugh. Laugh a lot. As Will Rogers advised, "We are here for a spell—get all the good laughs you can." Settle into a chair with a good humorous book. Rent a side-splitting video. It's been proven that laughter raises the level of immune cells that fight viruses. And it's also a great form of "internal jogging." Your whole body gets a workout—your heart, your lungs, your brain, the vast network of lymph and blood vessels that lace through even the most delicate internal organs. Cousins, who healed himself of a crippling and fatal disease in part with laughter, claimed that "of all the gifts bestowed by nature on human beings, hearty laughter must be close to the top."

While you're at it, don't forget to cry when you need to. Science tells us that human tears contain healing chemicals that are carried through the bloodstream to all parts of the body. If you think you feel better after a good cry, you're probably right. Sophisticated tests in laboratories even show that crying actually speeds the healing of skin wounds.

With all your laughing and crying, take the time to build self-confidence. Serve up a hefty dose of belief in yourself. Those who feel good about themselves are less likely to give up; they stay in the battle until the final scene. Your sense of self is strongly tied to your ability to cope—which is, in turn, linked without question to your body's immune response. Break big tasks into small ones—then pat yourself on the back when you accomplish it. Concentrate on the things you do well instead of flogging yourself for the things you haven't mastered. And, above all, treat yourself with patience and kindness.

Get rid of all the stress you can. There are almost surely splatterings of stress in your life that can be totally eliminated with a little strategy. Get up fifteen minutes earlier every day. Leave for appointments ten minutes earlier. Keep your gas tank at least a quarter full. Leave your car keys in the same place every time you come through the door. Unplug the phone if you need a warm bath, a nap, or a half hour of meditation.

Moderate the stress you can't eliminate. Try relaxation—moderate exercise, deep breathing, progressive muscle relaxation, or a warm bath. Another stress-buster is meditation; many believe that the deep breathing used in meditation and yoga not only relieves stress, but also has a powerful effect on the brain. Meditation can range from simple, quiet reflection under the spreading branches of a favorite tree to the full-fledged practice of an art that has gained increasing respect among medical practitioners.

Get a pet. One of the best strategies for dealing with stress doesn't spring from the printed pages of a book, but walks on four legs straight into your heart. It's called "pet therapy," and it does much more than relieve stress. Scientists know that the act of merely stroking a pet stabilizes the heart rate and reduces blood pressure. Pet owners live longer, too—and their survival rates after heart attacks or surgery have made headlines in medical journals.

Change the way you look at stress. If you can't eliminate or moderate it, reshape it. It was Carl Jung who said that "it all depends on how we look at things, and not on how they are in themselves." We know that the most resilient people, the people who just don't seem to buckle under stress, are the ones who confront it head-on. Instead of seeing it as the enemy, they greet it as a friend. They see it as a challenge—one they're eager to meet.

Attend church. People who regularly worship at the church of their choice have less stress, better health, and longer lives.

Get rid of anger and hostility. And while you're at it, work on envy and hatred. Former U.S. President George Bush attracted kudos and criticism alike as he took office with the call to become a kinder, gentler nation. George Bush's call to his countrymen may, in fact, be one of the most powerful keys to good health and long life. Why? We now know that hostility drives up blood pressure, clogs up arteries, batters the heart, chokes the system with menacing hormones. And it kills. So does anger. In fact, anger and hostility are as lethal a combination as science could ever concoct in the laboratory.

Love. Romanticists claim that it makes the world go 'round. And one humorist revised that sentiment to say that "love doesn't make the world go 'round—love is what makes the ride worthwhile." Love is a powerful healer—a determinant of good health. Love is, according to Karl Menninger, "an element which binds and heals, which comforts and restores, which works what we have to call—for now—miracles." Bernie Siegel says it best: if you love, you can never be a failure.

Get involved in service to others. Escape from your own orbit. Charity, or altruism, or whatever you call it, works—not nearly as much for the recipient as for the giver. The act of helping someone else is wired directly to your brain, and it boosts your health and immunity. A powerful example is shown by World War II's concentration camp survivors. There, in the midst of the world's greatest atrocity, the ones who survived were the ones who reached out. Even in the meanest of circumstances that defeated millions, they swept the filth out of a corner, offered a covertly saved morsel of food, and invited friends to "visit."

The poignancy of their story is matched only by that of the brave Dutchmen who risked life itself to help their hunted countrymen. In narrow attic rooms they hid the frightened Jews—whole families—desperate to escape the madman. They gave their own meat and bread, these simple Dutchmen who valued human life above the comforts of compliance. Years later, their health and longevity stood as testament to their charity.

Other examples come to the forefront in every disaster that faces humankind—in tornadoes, floods, and furious storms that tear the roofs from houses and scoop children from their mothers' arms. In every case, newspaper reporters zero in on those who, despite their own loss, busy themselves to soothe the hurt of another.

Involve yourself. The philosopher warned that no man is an island. We weren't designed to be alone. We need each other. And being involved with each other is one of the best ways to protect health.

Find social support. Researchers the world over have analyzed it and dissected it and quantitatively studied it. All you have to do is practice it. People who have good friends have better health. So do people who have even one trusted friend in whom they can confide. So do people who belong to churches and professional organizations and clubs. So do people who are married. So do people who make their families the top priorities in their lives.

Find a confidant. Find one person with whom you can truly communicate your innermost hopes, goals, dreams, fears, sorrows, and disappointments. And be a confidant for someone else.

Keep a journal. Record your emotions and attitudes toward events that happen in your life. If you need to, stretch back into the dank expanses of memory and pull out that one, difficult thing you've never been able to talk about to anyone. Let your pen do the talking, dancing across the lined pages. You'll be amazed at how much better you feel after the secret's out.

Face this world, with all its uncertainties and heartaches, with hope. Hope can be more powerful than anything that confronts it.

Learn to laugh at yourself. Cultivate a sense of humor; find joy in the things around you—even the hard things.

Face this world with a fighting spirit. Confront whatever you will—but never, never give up.

Pray. Your spirit feels a prayer's healing balm . . . and even science has proven that it works.

Finally, have faith.

Norman Cousins summed it all up when he told us that "Hope, faith, love, and a strong will to live offer no promise of immortality, only proof of our uniqueness as human beings and the opportunity to experience full growth even under the grimmest circumstances."

Appendix A

THE ELEMENTS OF HUMAN FULFILLMENT

According to famed researcher Abraham Maslow,* human fulfillment is based on the following characteristics, which describe his studies of self-actualized people:

Growth-motivated rather than deficiency-motivated. As Maslow stated, "The motivation of ordinary men is a striving for the basic need gratifications they lack. But for self-actualizing people, motivation is just character growth, character expression, and maturation." Simply stated, fulfillment rests in the ability to distinguish between living and preparing to live.

Good sense of reality. Self-actualized people, says Maslow, have "an unusual ability to detect the spurious, the fake, and the dishonest in personality. . . . They are far more apt to perceive what is there rather than their own wishes, hopes, fears, anxieties, their own theories (prejudices) and beliefs or those of their cultural group . . . unfrightened by the unknown. . . . Doubt, tentativeness, and uncertainty, which are for most a torture, can be for some a pleasantly stimulating challenge, a high spot in life rather than a low."

Acceptance of self and others. Human fulfillment is characterized by a relative lack of *crippling* guilt, though self-actualized people *do* feel bad about the discrepancy between what is and what ought to be; the ability to see through *unnecessary* guilt and anxiety; the ability to accept the frailties and imperfections of human beings (in other words, the ability to see human nature as it is instead of as they would prefer it to be); a relative lack of disgust and aversion toward average people; a lack of defensiveness, protective coloration or post, and distaste for such artificiality in others; and an unusual lack of hypocrisy, game-playing, and attempts to impress others.

Honest authenticity and naturalness. Self-actualized people have a tendency toward unconventional thinking, though not necessarily unconventional behavior;

*Abraham Maslow, *Personality and Motivation.*

an internalized code of high ethics (not necessarily the same as those around them); and a superior awareness of what they are, what they want, and what they believe.

Commitment and problem centering. Self-actualized people have a strong sense of purpose *outside themselves*—a "task they must do." They are concerned with the good of mankind, and work for that which they love; they have a great sense of care for others. They see problems as a stimulating challenge rather than an intolerable dilemma.

Autonomy. The self-actualized have a greater sense of "free will"; they are less dependent on or determined by their circumstances or other people. Self-movers, they are self-disciplined, and have a sense of determining their own destiny through their personal choices.

Independence and resistance to enculturalization. Human fulfillment is characterized by relative independence from the need for approval, respect, and even love; the tendency to act conventionally in affairs regarded as important or unchangeable; and patient entrepreneurialism in wanting to change the status quo for the better.

An element of detachment and privacy. Self-actualized people practice objectivity; they are able to withstand personal misfortunes without reacting as violently as most would.

Continued freshness of appreciation. The self-actualized have, as Maslow states it, "the wonderful capacity to appreciate again and again (with *newness*), freshly and naively, the basic goods of life, with awe, pleasure, wonder, even ecstasy, however stale these experiences have become to others." They avoid taking things for granted; instead, they "retain a constant sense of good fortune and gratitude for it."

High energy levels, peak experiences. "Their energy is not supernatural," Maslow says of the self-actualized; "it is simply the result of loving life and all the activities in it. They don't know how to be bored. . . . They are aggressively curious. They never know enough. They search for more and want to learn each and every present moment of their lives. . . . They are mystic, with peak experiences of transcendence of self; they have a sense of limitless horizons opening up to vision, coupled with ecstasy and a transforming feeling of strength."

Deep interpersonal relations. Human fulfillment is characterized by the capability of more fusion, intimacy, and obliteration of ego boundaries than seen in most people. The self-actualized tend to be kind to—or at least patient with—almost everyone, particularly children, yet they often have few profoundly close relationships because of the time required to maintain them. When they express hostility, it is not toward someone's character, but to achieve some good end.

Democratic character structure. The self-actualized are oblivious to barriers of class, education, politics, or race; they possess a certain sense of humility that allows them to learn from anyone and to be aware of how little they know when compared with what *could* be known.

Discrimination between ends and means. Ethically, the self-actualized believe that means are subordinated to ends, but means are usually enjoyed as ends in themselves. Simply, the self-actualized appreciate the *process* of doing for its own sake.

Philosophical, unhostile sense of humor. Humor for the self-actualized is usually directed at self or at people who are trying to be big when they are small; humor extends to work—which, though taken seriously, is approached with a sense of play. They find that humor often has an educational function beyond the simple value of laughter.

Creativity. The self-actualized are often not creative in the usual artistic forms; their creativity is more a *process* and *attitude* than a product. Their creativity extends to a way of approaching all of life; they find fresh, direct solutions with naive newness.

Guiltless acceptance of sexuality. For the self-actualized, sex is fused with love and full underlying intimacy; they do not usually seek sex for its own sake. Theirs is a paradox: They seem to enjoy their sexuality far more than average, yet consider it much less important.

Resolution of complementary opposites. Finally, the self-actualized seem to enjoy—even thrive on—differences rather than fear them. They creatively seek overarching principles that make seeming opposites synergic (complementary) rather than antagonistic; peak experiences often occur during the resolution.

Appendix B

THE SEVEN HABITS OF HIGHLY EFFECTIVE PEOPLE

According to Steven R. Covey,* the seven habits of highly effective people are to:

1. Be proactive. Use the responsible free will to act as you desire, with integrity.

2. Begin with the end in mind. Have clearly defined values; cultivate a sense of purpose and mission; and visualize the results ahead of time.

3. Put first things first. Be able to distinguish core values from lesser values and act with integrity toward the deeper ones (with discipline and sacrifice as necessary).

4. Think win/win. Aim for mutual acceptance and empowerment; strive for connectedness; and build on integrity, maturity, and an abundance mentality.

5. Seek first to understand, then to be understood. Use caring love and acceptance and a sense of connectedness when dealing with others.

6. Synergize. Accept, and even appreciate, differences; try creative cooperation and connectedness; work from a common sense of mission and purpose; and have a positive expectation.

7. Renew yourself. Experience a sense of purpose and mission (commitment); continued growth; and meditative reflection and visualization.

*Stephen R. Covey, *The Seven Habits of Highly Effective People* (New York: Fireside—Simon and Schuster, 1989).

NAME INDEX

SUBJECT INDEX

Situations: characteristics of, loneliness and, 296; symptoms related to, 3

Skin, stress response and, 47

Sleep disturbances: behavioral medicine intervention for, 573–574; depression and, 220; emotions and, 15

Small intestine, 64

Social interaction. *See* Interpersonal relationships; Social support

Social support, 261–286; Alameda County study of, 275–276; battle stress and, 270; building, 595; cardiovascular system and, 278–281; definition of, 263; grief and, 373–374; Japanese studies of, 277–278; lack of, 196–197; marriage and, 324–326; Michigan study of, 276; North Carolina study of, 277; physiological effects of, 274–278, 281–285; pregnant women and, 271–272; protection of health by, 264–268; relocation and disruption and, 272–274; Roseto study if, 278–279; sources of, 263–264; strengthening, 284–285; strong families and, 348, 352; Swedish studies of, 277, 279–280; touching and, 285–286; type A studies of, 280; unemployment and, 270–271. *See also* Friends; Interpersonal relationships; Loneliness

Soldiers, social support and, 270

Somaticizing, 206–207

Special-interest friends, 306

Spiritual counseling, 599–600

Spiritual health, 589–590

Spirituality, 377–397; church affiliation and health and, 392–396; crisis as growth experience and, 384–386; definition of, 378–379, 397; healing power of forgiveness and, 389–392; health influences of, 382–384; prayer and health and, 386–389; religion contrasted with, 378; spiritual health and, 379–382. *See also* Faith; Healing power of faith

Spontaneous remissions, fighting spirit and, 528

Stem cells, 31–32

Stomach, 64. *See also* Peptic ulcers

Stress, 41–77; age and, 54–59; altruism and, 403–405, 406; battle, 270; brain and, 61–62, 62–63; buffers and, 246–248, 481–482, 517; cancer and, 74–75, 111–112; cardiovascular system and, 65–70; costs of, 47–48; cultural influences on reactions to, 245–246; definition of, 41–43; effects on body, 43–44; endocrine system and, 62–63; friends and,

307–309; gastrointestinal system and, 64–65; humor and, 547–548; immune system and, 70–74; lack of control versus, 480–481; laughter and, 558; mechanisms of, 243–246; nutrition and, 70; outcomes of, 47–49; perception of, 42–43; pets and, 312–313; physiological reactions to, 59–61; productive versus destructive, 585–586; protecting against, 75–77; resilience against, 588–590; response to, 44–47; role in health, 242–243; self-perceptions of, 75; types of, 44. *See also* Coping with stress; Job stress; Life events

Stressed families. *See* Weak/stressed families

Stress response, 44–47

Strong families, 347–354; affirmation and support in, 348; altruism and, 351; communication and listening in, 347; enjoyment in, 348–349; health benefits of, 351–354; interactions in, 349; leisure times and, 349; problem solving in, 351; religion in, 350; respect for privacy in, 350–351; respect in, 348; shared responsibility in, 349–350; traditions in, 350, 355; trust in, 348; values in, 350

Suicide, 217; grief and, 371; loneliness and, 304

Suppressor T cells, 33. *See also* Immune system

Surgical outcomes: explanatory style and, 468–469, 470; optimism and, 512

Surgical patients, behavioral medicine intervention for, 574–575

Survival: hope and, 454–456. *See also* Fighting spirit; Longevity

Suspiciousness, type A personality and, 146

Symptoms, life situations related to, 3

T cells, 32, 33. *See also* Immune system

Thymus gland, 37

Touching, 285–286

Traditions, in strong families, 350, 355

Transcenders, 250

Treatment: faith in, 425–428, 437–438. *See also* Behavioral medicine intervention

Trust, in strong families, 348

Type A personality, 102, 125–164; in children, 129–130; controversy over, 132–133; definition of, 126–127; diseases other than heart disease and, 160–164; emotional effects of, 154–156; environmental factors and, 130–131; Friedman and Rosenman's research on, 134–136; gender and, 128–129; genetic factors and, 131–132; harmless

Type A personality, *continued*
   behaviors of, 138–142; heart disease risk
   and, 156–160; historical background of,
   133–134; lack of self-esteem and, 489; modifying, 159, 163– 164; MRFIT study of,
   136–137; physiological effects of, 150– 154;
   prevalence of, 127–128; second-generation
   studies of, 137; social support and, 280; toxic
   behaviors of, 142–148; in women, 128–129,
   160; workaholics and, 148–150
Type B personality: developing, 163–164; workaholics and, 148–150
Type C personality. *See* Cancer-prone personality

Ulcers. *See* Peptic ulcers
Uncertainty, 209–210
Unemployment: coping with, 94; job stress and,
   91–92; social support and, 270–271
Urgency, type A personality and, 140–141
Uric acid, stress and, 90

Vaccines, 34
Values: loneliness and, 296; in strong families,
   350
Vascular disease. *See* Cardiovascular system;
   Coronary artery disease
Vigilance reaction, 47
Vigilant(s), avoiders versus, 458–460
Vigilant observation, 151
Vision problems, type A personality and, 162
Visualization, as behavior change method, 596

Volunteerism, 408–413; avoiding burnout and,
   413; consistency of, 412; desire to volunteer
   and, 411; liking of the work and, 411–412;
   motivation for, 412–413; one-on-one contact
   and, 410–411
Voodoo death, 42

Weak/stressed families, 341–347; anorexia nervosa and, 346–347; asthma and, 346; cancer
   and, 345–346; diabetes and, 346; infections
   and, 345; learned pain and, 344–345; traits
   of, 341–344
Western Collaborative Group Study, 157, 178,
   193
White blood cells. *See* Immune system
Widowhood, 363–365; gender and, 364–365, 366,
   371–372
Women: depression in, 221–222; divorce and,
   319; friendships of, 307; job stress and,
   92–93; marriage and, 325–326; maternal depression and, 337; menopausal symptoms
   in, 572; premenstrual syndrome and,
   221–222; type A personality and, 155–156,
   160. *See also* Gender; Pregnancy; Widowhood
Workaholics, 92, 148–150
Worry, 205–210; asthma and, 208–209; circulatory system and, 207–208; definition of,
   205–207; generalized anxiety disorder and,
   206; somaticizing and, 206–207; uncertainty
   and, 209–210. *See also* Anxiety; Fear